Understanding
Abnormal Psychology

Understanding Abnormal Psychology

Clinical and Biological Perspectives

Pamilla Ramsden

Los Angeles | London | New Delhi
Singapore | Washington DC

Los Angeles | London | New Delhi
Singapore | Washington DC

SAGE Publications Ltd
1 Oliver's Yard
55 City Road
London EC1Y 1SP

SAGE Publications Inc.
2455 Teller Road
Thousand Oaks, California 91320

SAGE Publications India Pvt Ltd
B 1/I 1 Mohan Cooperative Industrial Area
Mathura Road
New Delhi 110 044

SAGE Publications Asia-Pacific Pte Ltd
3 Church Street
#10-04 Samsung Hub
Singapore 049483

Editor: Michael Carmichael
Editorial assistant: Alana Clogan
Production editor: Imogen Roome
Copyeditor: Mary Dalton
Proofreader: Rosemary Morlin
Marketing manager: Alison Borg
Cover design: Lisa Harper
Typeset by: C&M Digitals (P) Ltd, Chennai, India
Printed in Great Britain by CPI Group (UK) Ltd

MIX
Paper from
responsible sources
FSC® C013604
www.fsc.org

Library of Congress Control Number: 2012939517

British Library Cataloguing in Publication data

A catalogue record for this book is available from the British
Library

ISBN 978-1-84860-875-7
ISBN 978-1-84860-876-4 (pbk)

Contents

Defining Abnormal Behaviour

Learning aims

At the end of this chapter you should:

- Understand the complexity in distinguishing between abnormal and normal behaviour
- Understand the various definitions of abnormal behaviour
- Be familiar with the differences between deviance and dysfunction
- Comprehend the complexities of legal definitions and insanity.

INTRODUCTION

CASE STUDY

Matt is a 42-year-old construction worker. He has been married for 20 years, has two nearly grown children, served four years in the military and has been employed at the same construction company since he left military service. He is described as steady and reliable. Yet, there is one thing that doesn't seem quite right; he carries small brass bells with him wherever he goes. He has carried these bells since he was a child and will tell people that they are for luck. The reality is that Matt carries them to keep evil spirits away. He stopped telling people his real reason for carrying bells because people were less understanding than if he just said he carried them for luck. Matt's beliefs do not interfere in his life, he has never been treated for a mental illness, and he doesn't appear to use them to control anything else in his life. His behaviour has made him the butt of jokes. He has been called harsh names; he has been physically and mentally abused by others and yet he continues to carry his bells. Time has taught him to hide them in his clothing and he has taken to sewing them in the seams of his shirts and trousers. How would you describe Matt's behaviour? Is Matt mentally ill?

WHAT IS ABNORMAL BEHAVIOUR?

What is abnormal behaviour? How do we define what is abnormal? We can identify behaviour that is 'weird' when we see it but how do we 'define' it. The majority of us avoid what we define for ourselves as 'odd' behaviour, for example we would probably choose not to sit next to someone acting in an odd fashion or dressed in odd clothing on a bus or train. We don't like individuals who smell unclean and whenever possible stay away from them.

On the whole, we would define abnormality as being outside the parameters of what is accepted in our society. But how is this defined and what does 'normal parameters' really mean? Who decides what is abnormal vs. normal? If normal behaviour is defined by a society, what is a society?

A society is a collective of individuals who are defined by the language that is spoken, religious practices and ethnic diversity. Societies are fluid and constantly changing. What was the norm for a society one hundred years ago may not be the norm of the same society today. How an individual behaves within a group is defined by the constraints of the society. Rules and norms govern what are deemed to be normal parameters. If you lived a solitary existence, how you behaved would not be dictated by others as you would be free to do as you chose. Your behaviour would not impinge on anyone else. When an individual lives within a group, the definition of normal behaviour is usually classified by a consensus of what is considered to be normal for that group. Occasionally, certain groups of people can push the boundaries but even this has limitations. For example, many normal behaviours are classified by age ranges. A 16-year-old who chooses to dye their hair a bright lime green colour would probably not be classified as abnormal; perhaps unusual, but not extreme. We would probably agree that this behaviour is pushing the boundaries, but we would also define it as youthful behaviour and therefore acceptable. However, if a 70-year-old engages in the same behaviour, our evaluation of this individual would be outside of normal boundaries. The norms that govern behaviour at different age categories have unwritten rules that guide behaviour. Although it is certainly not illegal to dye hair any colour, at any age, certain colours would be governed by rules of what is considered age-appropriate behaviour and anyone acting outside these boundaries would probably be classified as behaving in an abnormal way. This is also complicated by the number of inappropriate behaviours. If the only behaviour that is outside of the norm, i.e. lime green hair, and

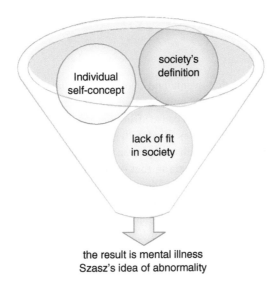

the result is mental illness
Szasz's idea of abnormality

Figure 1.1

all other behaviours are age appropriate and considered normal, the unusual element may be classified as odd or eccentric. The single behaviour displayed with all else being normal may not be defined as abnormal, although it would probably never be considered normal. The consequence of having 'odd' hair would probably result in those individuals within the same age range ostracizing the individual until they changed their hair back to an age-appropriate colour. So, what is abnormal psychology and how do we determine that people are behaving in abnormal ways? Do we define abnormality by the number of extreme behaviours?

Efforts to define psychological abnormality typically raise as many questions as they answer. Ultimately, a society selects general criteria for defining abnormality and then utilizes that criterion to judge particular cases. Szasz (1960) believed that the entire idea of abnormality and mental illness was invalid and what society defines as abnormal are simply problems in living or finding a niche, not that something was wrong with the individual. Other researchers have believed that the concept of mental illness is used to control or change people whose unusual patterns of functioning upset or threaten the social order (Sarbin & Mancuso, 1980; Scheff, 1966).

These viewpoints may seem extreme and hardly anyone would argue that the pressures of being successful and attaining one's goals in society do not contribute to stress and dysfunctional behaviour, but how do we define this contribution and more importantly, what can we do to change the pattern?

Perhaps it is important to look at how the past has defined abnormal behaviour. History has provided us with examples of behaviour that has been defined as abnormal for that society and that time and place. It may be important in our search for meaning to begin with earlier examples of what was defined as abnormal to help us understand how we classify abnormal behaviour today.

HISTORICAL PERSPECTIVES OF ABNORMAL BEHAVIOUR

Ancient societies believed that events and people were controlled by the supernatural and when individuals in the community acted outside of what was considered 'normal' they were then placed at the mercy of evil spirits that could cause affliction, inhabit their bodies or cause terrible events to happen to family members. History is filled with stories of individuals who intentionally exchanged their souls in order to obtain wealth and power. Therefore, ancient societies looked for physical evidence of evil and found it in anything that deviated from the norm (Millon, 2004). Physically and mentally abnormalities were proof of demonic possession. Individuals were generally held to be responsible for their own ailments or had committed some act to place family members in danger.

The treatments used by many early societies in order to purge the person from evil generally involved extreme physical measures in order to make the corporeal manifestation of the demon unpleasant and allow the evil spirit to leave the body. Unfortunately the extreme physical 'treatment' often proved fatal but nevertheless was considered a success as it kept the rest of the community safe from harm (Porter, 2002).

The idea that evil spirits were responsible continued for thousands of years, until Hippocrates, a Greek physician, began to change the way illness was perceived. Hippocrates believed that imbalances and disorders were not the result of evil spirits and instead were problems within the brain and body. He relied on observations and explanations which would be the beginning of the scientific method. Hippocrates greatly influenced medicine by shifting the ideology from corporeal to tangible. He correctly assumed that the most important area of the body was the brain and that it was central to intellectual activity and abnormal behaviour was as a direct result of disease. Hippocrates introduced the theory of heredity and environmental factors into the concept of mental illness and developed more compassionate treatments which subjected individuals to less cruel and violent methods (Porter, 2002).

Hippocrates was also the first to classify abnormal behaviour into three distinct categories; mania, melancholia and phrenitis, giving each detailed clinical descriptions. Others would follow the direction that Hippocrates proposed. Plato continued the belief that abnormal behaviours occurred as a result of brain and body dysfunction and would insist that these individuals should be cared for by their families and not punished for their behaviour. Galen made major contributions with his scientific examination of the central nervous system and how this contributed to abnormal behaviour (Porter, 2002).

Just as mankind appeared to be striding forward, they took a gigantic step backward with the rise of Christianity. Religious dogma reinstated the ancient ideas that abnormal behaviour was the result of supernatural contact; however instead of random, unnamed evil spirits the culprit was the devil. Scientific attempts to understand, classify and explain became less important than accepting disease and dysfunction as a manifestation of God's will.

The influence of Christianity did not promote science and instead actively discouraged it. Physicians were no longer allowed to conduct scientific experiments to determine the cause of death. Anyone who challenged Christian doctrine was denounced as a heretic and condemned. Initially, those who continued the teachings of Hippocrates and Plato were denounced and when

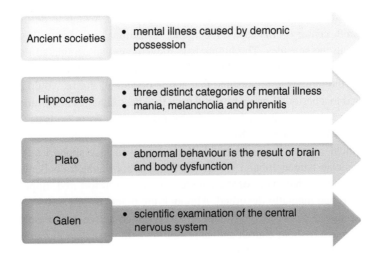

Figure 1.2

this proved an ineffective deterrent they were executed by the church and all their papers and books were seized and burned. Scientific thought was in conflict with church doctrine and religious leaders found it abhorrent to mutilate the dead when clearly the death was at God's will (Porter, 2002).

Illness, whether physical or mental, was now seen as punishment for sin. The sick person was guilty by the hand of God for wrongdoing and relief could only come from repentance. The treatment of individuals at this time was imbalanced; some individuals were treated with compassion while others were subjected to cruel punishments designed to elicit confessions. The downward decline of positive treatment continued and individuals displaying abnormal behaviour, mental and physical illnesses were subject to prayers, curses, flogging, starvation and immersion in hot water. Church leaders deemed what was abnormal behaviour and corrected the inconsistencies (Foucault, 2006).

During the fifteenth and sixteenth centuries religious leaders were constantly battling social and religious reforms. In an effort to quash protests which threatened the Church's power, the Church claimed that these insurrections were the acts of the devil and began to actively endorse demonic possession and witches (Eghigian, 2010).

In 1484 Pope Innocent VIII issued a decree calling on the clergy to identify and exterminate anyone thought to be in league with the devil. This resulted in the publication of the *malleus maleficarum* (the witches' hammer). The document acted to confirm the existence of witches and also outlined various ways of detecting them (Alexander & Selesnick, 1966).

An individual displaying any behaviour that was deemed to be abnormal in any way was suspected of witchcraft. It is probable that anyone with any type of mental illness would certainly have been condemned as being a witch. Individuals behaving outside of traditional norms were seen by the Church as being undesirable or uncooperative and were tortured in order to obtain confessions, with thousands of individuals being burned alive and mutilated in the name of the Church (Alexander & Selesnick, 1966).

A change in attitudes came with the Renaissance period, which is defined as the fourteenth through sixteenth century. This saw a resurgence of rational and scientific inquiry which led to great advances in the sciences. The humanistic movement also originated during this time frame and emphasized human welfare and the worth and uniqueness of the individual. The Renaissance period allowed individuals to understand that acting outside of norms would not lead to total anarchy, rather it led to a period of prosperity and growth. These changes in attitude of allowing individuals the freedom to express themselves slightly outside of the norm leads us to the next element of defining abnormality (Bewley, 2008).

Previously held explanations of mental illness began to lose support and favour and in 1563 a German physician named Johann Weyer published a book which challenged the foundation of witchcraft and alleged that many of the people who had been tortured, imprisoned and burned as witches were instead mentally disturbed. Although the practices of cruelty toward the mentally ill had somewhat subsided, the ideology was still very much active and present. Weyer's book was immediately banned by both church and state and the author was emotionally and physically punished for speaking out against the long held belief of witchcraft and demonology (Bewley, 2008).

However, instead of stifling the information, many began to believe and eventually the beliefs stated by Weyer became the forerunner of the humanitarian perspective towards the mentally ill. The care of people with mental illnesses began to improve and instead of the inhuman treatment of punishment, abandonment and death, people were kept at home and cared for by family members with the help of their friends and neighbours and the financial support of the local parish. During this period, all across Europe religious shrines were devoted to the humane treatment of people with mental disorders (Van Walsum, 2004; Airing, 1975).

The mid-sixteenth century continued to bring positive changes to the care of the mentally ill. Private homes and small communities could only help a small number of mentally ill individuals. Large cities had difficulty housing all the individuals who needed this type of care. The idea of the state providing accommodation and care began with converting hospitals and monasteries into asylums where the insane were to be sheltered from a hostile world, kept from harming themselves or others and given help and treatment. As these began to fill, the government began to build special hospitals specifically designated for the care of the mentally disturbed, many of which were built in secluded areas and surrounded by high walls with locked gates. These hospitals, now called asylums, quickly became overcrowded and what began with good intentions for treatment and care became filthy conditions where the patients began to be physically restrained rather than receiving treatment. Patients became inmates and they were locked in boxes or crates, chained to walls and floors, given bare sustenance, beaten and mistreated, with many dying of starvation and physical illness. The Bethlem Royal Hospital in London (also called Bedlam) became one of these infamous places and was well known for its inhumane treatment of patients. It housed people in such deplorable states and was in such a state of chaos that it became a public spectacle and members of the general public would pay to stare at the various patients chained and locked in their cells, and laugh at their antics. It became so well known that the name entered the English language and is used to describe chaos and confusion. Gradually the general public began to see the mentally ill as a menace and security became more important than treatment (Arnold, 2009).

The reform movement of the eighteenth and nineteenth centuries came about with the influence of two men, Philippe Pinel and William Tuke. Pinel was a physician in France and had been placed

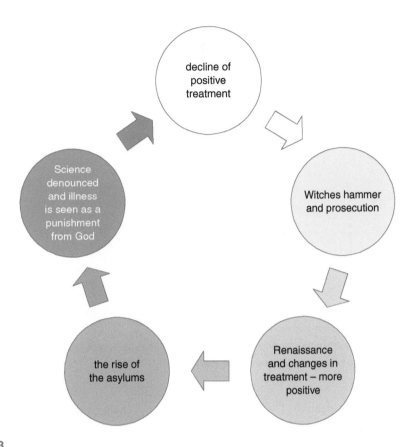

Figure 1.3

in charge of a hospital for insane men. He changed the hospital practices to include humane treatment, moral guidance and respectful techniques which were termed the 'moral treatment movement'. Pinel ordered that patients be released from chains and confinement and encouraged to exercise outdoors. Patients were treated with kindness and respect, which appeared to foster their recovery and improve behaviour. Tuke also changed the way individuals were treated; he abhorred the inhumane practices of confining individuals in crowded, cramped cells, often chained to walls or the floor. He established a retreat at York where patients worked, prayed and talked about their problems (Arnold, 2009; Borthwick et al., 2001).

While physical treatment was improving for many individuals, the mental factors that were believed to be at the heart of mental illness were being investigated. Two distinct schools of thought emerged: the biological viewpoint and the psychological viewpoint. The biological viewpoint was headed by Emil Kraepelin who believed that mental illness was a result of biological factors. Kraepelin would later be considered to be the father of the classification system otherwise known as the Diagnostic and Statistical Manual of Mental Disorders (DSM). The second school of thought was led by Josef Breuer and Sigmund Freud and became the

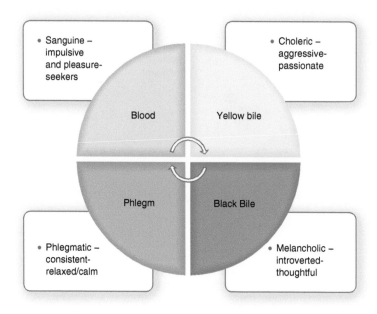

Figure 1.4   The four humours and associated temperaments – kept in balance, allowed the person to be physically as well as mentally healthy

psychological perspective. This ideology held that psychological processes were the reason for mental illness (Kent, 2003).

The early 1900s saw a reversal of the moral treatment movement. Several factors were responsible; severe money and staffing shortages, decline in recovery rates, and a new wave of prejudice and fear from the public (Bockoven, 1963). Quickly public mental hospitals were back to providing custodial care and became filled to over-capacity. With the overcrowding came poor treatment and abuse of the patients. Although many mental health reforms had been passed and hospitals attempted to put humane practices into place, the sheer numbers of individuals with mental illness often made these practices unrealistic. Additionally the humane practices were not sufficient for all cases (those that were dangerous or endangered others) and clearly something more was needed. Psychological treatment was available but was generally only accessible to individuals who had the means to pay for this type of intervention. Individuals who could not afford psychological therapies and private care were relegated to the public mental hospitals (Kent, 2003).

In 1949 the Australian psychiatrist John Cade reported on the success of giving lithium to long-term hospitalized manic patients that calmed them enough for them to be released. In 1950 the drug thorazine was synthesized, which was extremely effective in the treatment of psychotic patients. It has been claimed that this drug alone has been responsible for the single greatest advances in the twentieth century (Andreasen, 1984; Lickey & Gordon, 1991). Suddenly long-term hospitalized patients were able to be released. A new class of drug, the psychotropic medications came in three basic classes. The first category were antipsychotic drugs, to correct disordered thinking and hallucinations, the second were antidepressant drugs to lift the moods of those individuals who were depressed and the third class were anti-anxiety drugs to reduce tension and worry (Sweet, Rozensky & Tovian, 1991).

Many of the patients who were provided with these drugs dramatically improved and were able to be discharged from hospital care. The new drugs created a different system of caring for the mentally ill and a phase of deinstitutionalization occurred. Patients were now being discharged into community care and outpatient care, which solved many of the overcrowding problems at mental institutions. They in turn were able to begin implementing many of the principles that had begun with Pinel and his moral treatment movement, as well as provide psychological therapies that had only once been accessible to the wealthy (Barham, 1997).

In spite of the new drug therapies and deinstitutionalization, many believed that the inhumane physical practices of the past that consisted of chaining individuals who were suffering from mental illnesses to beds, walls and chairs have only been replaced by chaining their minds. Although the new drug therapies appeared to be a significant improvement, the side effects that accompany the drug therapy are considerable (Breggin, 2001). It is not uncommon for individuals to exchange damaged minds for damaged bodies in the form of lowered life expectancy, extrapyramidal effects on motor control, lowered white blood cell count, tardive dyskinesia, sexual dysfunction and tardive psychosis. These have a potential for permanent chemical dependence leading to psychosis that can be even more debilitating than before the drug was administered (Keshavan, 2004).

EVALUATION IN CONTEXT

Abnormal behaviour must be evaluated in its context. All behaviour must be evaluated in terms of its time frame, social norms and rules that govern behaviour. We have expectations of how people should behave at public places. For example our expectation at a train station is that people should be orderly, fairly well dressed, clean and to wait patiently for the departure or arrival of their train. Anyone whose behaviour is outside of these norms becomes suspect. We would avoid dirty, unkempt individuals who push and shove and yell, in loud obnoxious tones.

However at a three-day outdoor music festival someone in a three piece suit would be totally out of place; the norm for this venue is grimy, dirty and dishevelled. In fact many people at these festivals wear mud caked all over their bodies as if they are badges of honour. Generally, the more outrageous the behaviour, the more the surrounding people find this to be entertaining. Individuals who push and shove and yell in loud obnoxious tones are welcomed and cheered. However, even this venue has limits; it is considered outside the norm to attack other people or to cause bodily harm to others. At what point does amusing behaviour become abnormal? It is difficult to describe in detail where the line is drawn – but generally those of us living in a society can readily identify when the behaviour becomes extreme and unwanted. Abnormal behaviour must always be evaluated with regard to a specific time frame, social norms and expectations of behaviour for that venue/place and it must be judged against what is 'normal behaviour' and normal expectations.

GENDER

Our gender plays a major role in our perceptions and how we define ourselves. Being male or female affects the way our parents raise us, our role in life, the way other people respond to us and the way we are treated by society. It has historically also been used to determine normal and abnormal behaviour. Gender defines the range of behaviour that is considered appropriate and permissible and generally the range is narrower for women than for males. Women who do not conform to the current defined roles of femininity are more likely to be labelled as mentally ill (Scheff, 1966). Until relatively recently it was widely accepted that the only desirable roles for a woman were those of wife and mother and that a woman's entire life should revolve around these roles. Even today in the UK archaic remnants of masculine/feminine social definitions continue to exist, e.g. if a woman hasn't married before the age of 25 she is deemed a spinster by the UK Registrar's Office. In comparison, there are no offensive terms for an unmarried man of any age.

Traditional roles form the basis for social behaviour. If we as a society determine that there are certain traditional roles for a group of people, anyone acting outside of these roles would be behaving in abnormal ways. We continue to be influenced by traditional roles that determine that certain types of jobs and careers are preferable to others. A female wanting to work in non-traditional roles is no longer considered abnormal but she is still far from the norm. For example, a female plumber may have a difficult time securing jobs independently as many would feel that only a male plumber would provide good service.

In the past 30 years women were denied opportunities to many different types of professions such as: accountancy, engineering, politics, medical and legal careers although this is slowly changing and women are being trained and securing jobs in these professions. Unfortunately these changes did not occur without a great deal of discord and women were forced to fight for their rights. Many became pioneers and had to break down barriers in order to overcome gender discrimination.

Various studies have documented how boys and girls are socialized into traditional sex roles. Witt (1997) found that children learn at a very young age what the difference in gender means and through a variety of activities, opportunities and positive and negative reinforcement, experience the process of gender role socialization. Sandtrock (1994) found that as children develop they internalize the process of gender roles and these become firmly entrenched and part of a child's self-concept. Rubin, Provenzano and Luria (1974) found that parents have different expectations of sons and daughters as early as 24 hours after birth. Further studies have documented that a child internalizes the parental messages regarding gender at a very early age and their defined self-identity and self-concepts of gender come from parents (Lauer & Lauer, 1994; Santrock & Warshak, 1979; Kaplan, 1991). Hoffman (1977) found that reasons given by women for preferring a son over a daughter were to please their husbands, carry on the family name and to be a companion for their husband. Reasons for wanting a daughter included having a companion for themselves and to have fun dressing a girl and doing her hair.

Stereotyping is defined as attaching an usually unfavourable and inaccurate perception to a group of people. Stereotypes often make it easier to justify unequal treatment of the stereotyped person or group. Among the traditional stereotypes of women is the belief that they are naturally passive, domestic and weak. However unrealistic and inaccurate these stereotypes may be, many individuals in society believe them to be true. One of the unfortunate effects of stereotyping is that even people who are victimized by these labels tend to believe that they are true. They become self-fulfilling prophecies, i.e., if a woman believes that being a car mechanic is an occupation that women are incapable of doing because they are not strong enough, she will not take her car to a female car mechanic, believing her to be incapable, nor will she consider the idea of becoming a car mechanic herself or encourage female children to consider that occupation. Goldberg (1972) found that women value professional work that they think was done by a man more highly than the same work if they think it was done by a woman. Horner (1970) found that many women were motivated to avoid success, fearing that the more ambitious and successful they became, the less feminine they would be.

The norms of a society are an important source of prejudice and discrimination. Anyone outside of these norms will subject themselves to a variety of conforming social pressures and when these do not work, can be labelled as abnormal and even insane. If an entire society believes that women are less valuable, more mentally unstable, emotional and weak, these definitions will be accepted by most members as being accurate.

In early civilization women were equal partners and revered as the bringers of life and fertility (Eisler, 1988). This ideology began to change with the origin of the patriarchal structure most associated with warfare (Brown & Harris, 1978). With warfare, invasions and destruction became the norm and male dominance and enslavement of women became common. Engels (1983) further stated that the changing status of women also came with the beginning of private ownership of land that coincided with warfare. Society moved from a transient state to a static phase where land ownership, social class and patrilineal inheritance became important. As a result of these changes, women have been dominated by men in every aspect of their lives including reproductive rights and sexual freedom.

Chastity and fidelity became important societal virtues and in order for men to ensure that women remained 'pure' and that they retained control they designed chastity belts. These devices first appeared in Europe in the fifteenth century and were used until the late 1800s, first by fathers and then by husbands. They enabled men to have complete sexual and reproductive control which included the prevention of masturbation. The most important role for a woman to have was as wife and mother. Any woman who chose a life outside of these roles was considered abnormal. Working-class women were expected to work until they had children. These women tended to have more children than upper- and middle-class wives. In the middle of the nineteenth century, the average married woman gave birth to six children. Over 35 percent of all married women had eight or more children. It wasn't until the early 1900s that women began advocating for changes in reproductive rights.

Marie Stopes in 1918 wrote a guide for women concerning contraception which caused turmoil with the leaders of the Church of England and the Pope, who believed that the use of birth control was wrong and condemned all forms of contraception. Again, the idea that a woman should be allowed to choose outside of the traditional roles and deny her husband children was considered abnormal behaviour and anyone participating in this behaviour was reprimanded by society as well as the religious organization they were associated with.

The first pharmaceutical form of birth control became available in 1957 and for the first time in history women gained control of their reproductive rights as they no longer were required to have the cooperation of men to prevent pregnancy. They could privately engage in safe and relatively effective methods of birth control without the express permission of a man. Women could now engage in sexual freedom that had previously only been the right of males.

Although women had gained access to their reproductive rights and sexual liberty, the expectations of what is allowed concerning chastity and fidelity continue to be firmly held and what is allowed continues to be a factor in defining abnormal behaviour. Boys are allowed to be sexually active while girls are socialized away from sexual behaviour. When girls behave outside of socialized norms they are often considered to be abnormal and their behaviour is negatively labelled.

Women and men are still considered different and treated differently by social institutions, including the government and its legal system. The range of social norms and values reflects different standards of behaviour for men and women. Women and men are also shaped by the culture in which they are raised, so that most adults are socialized for the roles their culture has prescribed for them. Change threatens individual identity and the society that governs behaviour and norms.

The ideology of male superiority has been perpetuated in religious documents, school textbooks, the media and science. Great men of science such as Aristotle asserted that males were by nature superior and in charge of ruling, whereas women were inferior and required domination. Freud described man as the prototype of humanity and regarded females as incomplete and having a weakened superego (Doherty, 1973). In fact the majority of Freud's patients were women. Men have dominated every component of society and defined women's roles and although this is slowly changing there are elements that continue, as it is difficult to overcome a long history of traditions.

How do these differences in gender relate to psychopathology? The history of abnormal psychology and women has been a picture of mistreatment, cruelty, and at times violence. Women have been subject to long-term institutionalization at the hands of male family members and husbands as a method of control and retribution when they refused to conform to traditional roles (Roth & Lerner, 1974). Women were lobotomized in higher numbers than their male counterparts, again at the behest of male family members and husbands who felt that their nonconformity with social roles was mental illness (Jasper, 1995).

Psychologists and psychiatrists who have been predominantly male have also held stereotypical beliefs about women. In the nineteenth century women were viewed by these professions as prone, by their biological nature, to hysteria and insanity; often just being female was a proof of a disease (Bleier, 1984). Early psychological theories have been written by mostly Euro-American men and have not addressed any of the issues that pertain to women. Research conducted in psychotherapy has found that many therapists continue to foster traditional sex roles and can be biased in their evaluations of their women patients (Hare-Mustin, 1983).

The net effect of these biases is to reinforce traditional roles in women patients and to identify women who do not fit the traditional principles as maladjusted or ill. Brown and Harris 1978 found that the psychiatric influence has been such that any problem is seen as individually based rather than socially determined. As a result many women who have felt miserable and unhappy as housewives have defined themselves as being responsible or inadequate rather than recognizing that in many cases they are victims of social situations which have been the cause of their problems.

In spite of the changes that have occurred in providing women with access to health and better employment practices, the mental health establishments are slow to change. Diagnoses and treatments have continued to be used to control and victimize women. Issues include the sexist use of psychoanalytic concepts and psychiatric diagnoses, the misuse of medication, and sexual misconduct in therapy (Geller, 1995).

Differences in gender have been noted in the literature concerning depression and anxiety (Culbertson, 1997). What accounts for the higher rates of depression and anxiety in comparison to their male counterparts? Many believe that the higher levels of depression and anxiety are a direct result of women being subject to the impact of social forces that they have to endure; the sale of young girls for marriage or prostitution, restriction of liberty and education for women and the considerable control that males exercise on the lives of women in many patriarchal societies around the world (Locke, 1992; McGoldrick, Pearce & Giordano, 1982).

Women's individual differences in the field of abnormal psychology have gone relatively unaddressed. Many researchers believe there is a need to provide a meaningful context for sociocultural understanding, attending to women's individual differences within and across cultural groups, and to the forces of gender socialization and the impact on identity and self-esteem (Jordan, 1991; Steele, 1997).

MULTICULTURAL PERSPECTIVES

Early research supported the idea of a cultural universality that defined abnormal behaviour. In other words, there was a well defined idea of what were normal patterns of behaviour that existed in spite of the differences in culture and these patterns were world wide. For example, if schizophrenia was a universal disorder that appeared in all cultures and societies the processes would be more similar than dissimilar and the disorder would be similar in origin, process and manifestation. Additional research in this area found that the idea of cultural universality in patterns of abnormal behaviour did not exist (Draguns, 1997). If lifestyles, culture and world views affect how we behave overall it would logically follow that it affects the expression and determination of abnormal behaviour. Therefore the importance of culture and diversity cannot be denied in the manifestation of abnormal behaviour which may or may not lead to a mental disorder. Statistics indicate that mental illness appears in greater numbers in cultures that place emphasis on monetary success. How does this factor into third-world nations? Does mental illness exist in smaller numbers because it goes undiagnosed or is it a factor of culture? We return to the discussion of what is normal. What can be outside of the realm of normal behaviour without being judged abnormal? What specifically is the relationship between cultural norms, values and attitudes and the manifestations of abnormal behaviour? How does an individual move from being abnormal to being mentally ill?

All behaviours, whether normal or abnormal, begin from a cultural context. Culture plays a major role in our understanding of human behaviour. But what is culture? Culture is defined as 'shared learned behaviour which is transmitted from one generation to another for purposes of individual and societal growth, adjustment and adaptation' (Marsella & Kameoka, 1989). Culture is not synonymous with a race or ethnic group. Race and/or ethnic groups are surrounded by their own cultural context within the greater society as a whole. The cultural context may be similar or completely different. Individuals may completely embrace their cultural heritage or disregard it completely. Culture can be a powerful determinant of world views and it can affect how we define normal and abnormal behaviours as well as how we treat mental disorders within a defined culture.

Table 1.1   Examples of culture-bound syndromes as defined by the DSM

Amok	Malaysia	Mad uncontrollable rage
Brain fag	West Africa	Mental exhaustion – vague somatic symptoms, depression
Dhat syndrome	India	Anxiety and hypochondriacal concerns associated with semen
Ghost sickness	Native Americans/ North America	Sickness attributed to contact with the dead or dying
Latah	Indonesia	Trance-like reflex where the victim engages in repetitive speech or movements
Shenkui	Chinese	Unresolved anger which disturbs the balance of the five bodily elements
hwabyeong	Korean	
Evil eye	Mediterranean	A look that brings ill health and general bad luck that is cast from a person with unnatural powers
Susto	Central America	Lifelong damage resulting from a severe or frightful experience
Taijin kyofusho	Japan	A form of social anxiety and fear of interpersonal relations
zaar	Ethiopia	Possession of an individual by a spirit

(Adapted from the American Psychiatric Association, 2012)

The concept of cultural relativism originates from an anthropological tradition and emphasizes the belief that lifestyles, cultural values and world views affect the expression and determination of abnormal behaviour. What is universal in human behaviour that is also relevant to understanding abnormal behaviour? Can it be outside the realm of normal behaviour without being abnormal? Our definition is still problematic. If behaviour is common and is embraced by a community of people, can it still be defined as abnormal? For example, binge drinking, defined by an excessive use of alcohol within a short time frame, is a common theme among 16–30-year-olds in the UK. Often this type of behaviour clashes with outside cultures when British youth decide to go abroad and continue with this behaviour in other countries. Evidence shows that this type of behaviour is having serious effects on the health and welfare of an entire generation of people (Crabbe, Harris & Koob, 2011). Although the individuals taking part do not recognize it as deviant, distressing, dysfunctional and even dangerous, a large number are becoming alcohol dependent, which will eventually interfere with their personal life as well as cause lifelong health problems. Would we consider this abnormal behaviour? Would we consider this a mental disorder?

ABNORMAL AS DEFINED AS DEVIATION FROM IDEAL MENTAL HEALTH

The concept of ideal mental health was proposed as a criterion of normality by humanistic psychologists Carl Rogers and Abraham Maslow in the 1950s. Deviations from the ideal are taken to indicate varying degrees of abnormality. Maslow (1946) believed that an individual's life goal was self-actualization, which he described as a desire for self-fulfilment. Many psychoanalytically oriented psychologists have used the concept of consciousness and balance as criteria for abnormality. Humanistic and personal-centred psychologists have proposed aspects of maturity, competence, autonomy and resistance to stress. Utilizing these constructs as the only criterion for defining normality/abnormality leads to a number of problems. The first is which goal or idea should be used and who determines what this will be? The answer to this question depends on the particular frame of reference or values embraced, but again this causes problems in defining abnormal behaviour because there is a large degree of variability. Second, most of these goals/ideas are vague and lack clarity and precision. If resistance to stress is the goal, are the only mentally healthy individuals those who can either resist or adapt to stress? What types of stress? What about environments that produce stress. A war zone would easily be classified as a stressful environment as the people living in the area would be afraid for their lives. What about an individual who lives on a farm in Yorkshire? Are these environments comparable? Would we categorize the person living in a war zone as abnormal because they have an inability to cope with the stresses associated with their environment?

Another well accepted definition of abnormal behaviour is an individual who has lost or distorts their reality. This definition is not comprehensive and does not even cover the above example of stress. Albee (1959) defined a mental disorder as an unusually persistent pattern of behaviour over which the individual has little or no voluntary control; it differentiates them from others; it incapacitates them and interferes with normal participation in life.

Efficiency has also been used as a definition of abnormal behaviour. Decreased efficiency is associated with the more serious aspect of abnormal behaviour, i.e. mental illness. But again efficiency is too broad a concept. Efficiency would discriminate among sensory-perceptual anomalies, motor anomalies and thought disorders but not other, lesser types of mental illnesses.

CRITERIA OF NORMALITY AND MENTAL HEALTH

Consensus regarding positive mental health is far from unanimous. Some identify the mentally ill as anyone who seeks psychological care; at the other end of the spectrum are those who view the mentally ill as those who hallucinate, lose or distort contact with reality, or have suicidal ideation (Bentall, 2003).

The criterion for positive mental health is the absence of mental illness. Evaluation of actions as sick, or normal, or extraordinary in a positive sense often depends on accepted social conventions. When normality is used as a criterion for mental health then it is usually defined either as statistical frequency or normality in terms of the way a person ought to behave (Bartlett, 2011).

Mental health or normality is virtually impossible to define. We generally think of normal people as average or those individuals who do not deviate from what is considered normal in their social living groups. Rosenhan (1973) conducted an experiment in normality and mental health. He had five men and three women disguise the fact that they were normal and claim that they were hallucinating so that they could be admitted as mental patients. Once they were admitted, they behaved as their usual normal selves. Rather than the authorities seeing these pseudo patients as the healthy people they were, they continued to perceive them in terms of their diagnosis at the

Table 1.2   An operational point of view in defining mental illness

1 Exposure to psychiatric treatment
2 Labelled mentally ill by psychiatric diagnosis
3 The individual sensing abnormality seeking assistance
4 Identified as mentally ill by psychological testing
5 Dysfunctional behaviour
6 Dangerous to self or others
7 The absence of positive mental health

time of admission. The only individuals who could identify them as normals were the in-patients. This experiment was somewhat embarrassing, as individuals who were in charge of mental health facilities believed that they had the training and experience to recognize mental illness, when in fact this experiment cast a shadow of doubt upon the way we classify mental illness and the fact that trained professionals could not distinguish mentally ill individuals from the mentally well.

MEDICAL DEFINITION

A medical classification of abnormal behaviour describes the characterization by the presence of specific symptoms that define abnormality. Certain symptoms are the basis of determining whether an individual is experiencing an underlying disorder. There are two basic variations of the medical definition that can be distinguished as either organically based or psychologically based. The organic based definition characterizes a group of disorders that have a biological foundation. Many abnormal behaviours are known to have a biological foundation and the medical classifications are sufficient to clearly identify these disorders. The second variation of the medical definition of abnormal behaviours is more difficult to define in terms of parameters. The psychological element to mental disorders without the presence of a biological determinant can be difficult to classify. These disorders are referred to as functional disorders. Examples of psychological symptoms that can be underlying a mental illness are mood, attitudes and traits. Symptoms such as delusions, hallucinations and depression would be signs of a mental disease (Kutchins & Kirk, 2003).

The medical classification of defining abnormal behaviour is that it departs from the norm and harms the affected individual. This definition does allow for the various criteria and perspectives concerning mental illness as well as implying that there is no specific designation from normal to abnormal but is based soley on harm. A mental disorder under this classification implies recognizable pattern behaviour (Kutchins & Kirk, 2003).

One of the major problems with the medical definition of abnormal behaviour is that mental illness differs from physical disease and the medical approach is difficult to apply. Many mental illnesses cannot be detected in the early stages and often appear difficult to distinguish from normal behaviour. Often the precipiting cause is difficult to identify and the identification and etiology are often debated. In addition, the classification is defined by the presence of symptoms as the sole basis for identifying abnormality. Physiological disorders can be easily detected; fever, swelling, skin rashes are symptomatic of many physical disorders and can be measured and evaluated. A change in mood cannot be evaluated so easily. Another significant difference in the two types of medical classification is that the psychological categorization is also related to the reactions of others and is relative to social norms and desired behaviours (Kutchins & Kirk, 2003). Many social factors can contribute to abnormal behaviour with the individual struggling to cope before they are diagnosed with a mental illness. It is only when the individual becomes harmful to themselves or others that the abnormal behaviours shift to mental illness.

A further complexity in the medical definition of functional disorders is the designation of what symptoms are related to which disorders. Currently, there is a commonly used system of psychiatric classification describing a wide range of psychological disorders that is often utilized to overcome the complexity of determining psychological dysfunction. This system is published as a manual by the American Psychiatric Association and is referred to as the Diagnostic and Statistical Manual (Kutchins & Kirk, 2003).

Guidelines based on research and clinical practice have been collected and documented to provide a basis for what constitutes mental disorders, normal and abnormal psychological development and psychological dysfunction. Although this classification system appears to be a reliable way to classify mental disorders, the reality is much more complicated. If we were to take one of the cultural based disorders such as Ghost sickness, the classification system would quickly evaluate the individual as having some type of psychotic disorder. When culture is taken into consideration this classification would be inadequate; clearly the classification has some significant drawbacks.

CLASSIFICATION OF ABNORMAL BEHAVIOURS

Why is it important to classify abnormal behaviour? Without a systematic structure each abnormal behaviour would have to be evaluated as a separate and distinct element, a decision would have to be reached whether or not the behaviour is abnormal and then whether it is problematic. Without a classification system patterns could not be established, treatment could not be standardized and researchers would not understand each other's categories. Classification systems allow decisions to be made in terms of the treatment and progression of the illness.

DSM-IV-R

The first classification system was developed in the nineteenth century by Emil Kraepelin. He developed a comprehensive model of classifications based on his clinical observations and focused his system on distinctive features, or symptoms associated with abnormal behaviour patterns. His classification systems established the groundwork for future systems that are in

Table 1.3   Purpose of diagnosis

1   To organize clinical information that is concise, coherent and retrievable
2   Communication among professions
3   Prediction of clinical course
4   Selection of appropriate treatment

use today. The diagnostic and statistical manual of mental disorders published by the American Psychiatric Association (DSM) is descriptive, not explanatory, and describes diagnostic features of abnormal behaviours. Utilizing the DSM classification system, the clinician arrives at a diagnosis by matching the individual's behaviour with the criteria that define particular patterns of abnormal behaviour. Abnormal patterns of behaviours are classified as mental disorders and involve emotional distress, impaired functioning or behaviour that places people at risk of personal suffering, pain, disability or death. The DSM system helps to sort out various categories of disorders, to identify the disorder most suitable to describe the condition of the individual (Reigier, Narrow & Kupfler, 2010).

Statistical definition of abnormal behaviour

A statistical definition of abnormal behaviour is based upon the concept of the relative frequency of behaviours in a population. Abnormality could be defined as those behaviours that are relatively infrequent or are atypical of the population. A statistical definition would provide a definition based on behaviours that are numerically rare. Utilizing a statistical definition of abnormality we can classify most behaviours within a distribution. The majority of the 'normal' population would fall into the middle ranges of a bell-shaped curve. As one moves away from the middle range in either direction they could be classified as being statistically more extreme and therefore abnormal (Helzer & Hudziak, 2002). There are several problems with defining abnormality in this way. If we go back to our previous example of binge drinking, just because more people are engaging in a behaviour that might be dangerous or dysfunctional does not make it normal. However, under this definition, the behaviour would be classified as normal because a large number of individuals participate, therefore individuals in the specified age ranges who do not binge drink would be classified as abnormal.

Within the statistical definition there are many examples where extremes are useful. Unusual abilities or talents would be classified as abnormal under this definition but we would not consider a gifted musician as abnormal. If a specific dimension were agreed upon as relevant in determining abnormal behaviour, there might be a problem in deciding whether extremely high or low scores, or both, were to be included in the notion of abnormality. Also for social behaviours only one side of the extreme may be relevant for abnormality, i.e. depressed mood. Further, this definition does not provide a useful category in deciding whether an individual is impaired or mentally ill. The statistical definition oversimplifies the nature of abnormal behaviour. Abnormal behaviour is not a matter of one dimension. There may be several dimensions that need to be included such as: how the individual functions socially, the manner in which the problem is manifested and how an individual meets obligations and expectations of others. As a final problem, the statistical definition implies that being average is desirable or healthy and while society functions on the basis of normality and social conformity, it also restricts the freedom and individualism of people living in a community. There is also the issue of defining standards.

Standards for acceptable performance vary markedly as a function of socioeconomic standing, cultural and ethnic relationships, race, sex, age and various other demographic variables. One problem is that they fail to take into account differences in place, community standards and cultural values. If deviations from the majority are considered abnormal, then many ethnic and racial minorities that show strong subcultural differences from the majority will be classified as abnormal. When we use a statistical definition, the dominant or most powerful group generally determines what constitutes normality and abnormality. How does one evaluate such personality traits as assertiveness and dependence in terms of statistical criteria? People who strike out in new directions − artistically, politically or intellectually − may be seen as candidates for psychotherapy simply because they do not conform to normative behaviour. Our example of lime green hair would fall into this definition of 'least frequently' as there does not appear to be a huge number of people who choose this colour. So under our definition we would classify this behaviour as abnormal – but would you consider someone with this hair colour to be dysfunctional? Definitions based on statistical deviation may at first seem sufficient, but they actually present many problems.

Social definition

A social definition defines abnormal behaviour within the view of conformity. Individuals in society follow norms and widely accepted standards of behaviour. Conformity to these standards defines normal behaviour whereas deviation from these standards defines abnormal behaviour. Behaviours that violate social norms are likely to be those labelled as abnormal. The social definition recognizes that behaviours viewed outside of social parameters as dangerous, disruptive or merely beyond comprehension are likely to be singled out as deviant. Individuals who violate role expectations are

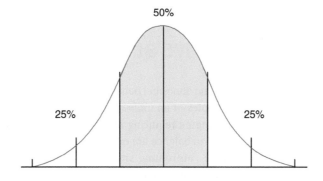

Figure 1.5

likely to be labelled as deviant or mentally ill. The social definition acknowledges the importance of the community that defines when a member is behaving in a socially unacceptable way (Bowers, 2000). Those who identify an individual as behaving abnormally play a major role in defining and detecting deviant behaviour. The social definition of abnormality generally begins with someone being bothered by the behaviour as violating the standard rules of conformity. Abnormal behaviour is not described as disturbed but disturbing to someone other than the individual participating in the behaviour. The identification of deviant behaviour and mental illness involves others who interact with the individual whose behaviour is considered deviant. The behaviour is then socially defined in terms of the particular relative standards for behaviours and expectations of those with whom the individual interacts. These standards are not absolute, but vary according to the social reference group to which the individual belongs. A social definition of abnormal behaviour is whatever society says is a mental illness or psychological impairment. Unacceptable behaviours are defined by people in everyday life who decide what is sufficiently deviant to single out as mental illness (Horwitz, 2004).

There are a few problems with the social definition of abnormality. First, it does not meet the characteristics of many mental health professionals who believe that mental illness is more than a violation of social norms. The social definition does describe an important element of abnormality as there is a social component present in many individuals with disturbed behaviour. For example individuals who are actively hallucinating can be frightening to others, as they interact with people and objects that only they can see, even though the interactions may be harmless. If this person lived outside of a community, there would be no one to define the disturbance.

Thomas Szasz (2004), a noted psychiatrist and social critic of the scientific foundations of modern psychopathology, believes that mental illness is a myth and is a creation by society to use, control and change behaviour. According to Szasz, people may suffer from problems in adjusting to the complicated struggle with living in society and not from mental illness. His argument stems from three beliefs: behaviour is labelled abnormal because it is different not wrong; abnormal behaviour is a reflection of something wrong in society and not the individual; and individuals are labelled mentally ill because their behaviours violate the social order. Szasz further asserted that the concept of mental illness is dangerous and is used as a form of social control by those in power. His critics have dismissed his ideology and state that mental illness is not simply a factor of social definition with the new scientific methodologies and techniques as confirmation.

ADAPTIVE AND MALADAPTIVE BEHAVIOUR

Another element of social definition and abnormal behaviour is adaptation. Adaptation is defined as a dynamic process between the attributes of an individual and their environment (Horwitz, 2004). Our environments are constantly changing requiring individuals to modify how they respond and react. Two elements that must be kept in balance are our personal characteristics (skills, education, attitudes, physical condition) and the confronting situations (divorce, physical illness, failures). Maladaptive behaviour implies that the individual is not coping with the changes that they are required to make. For some individuals the stress causes abnormal behaviour. For example an individual who is made redundant will have to make many changes: they may have to significantly cut their expenditures; their relationships may suffer; they may have to make alternative living arrangements. The stress of all these changes may cause the individual to participate in abnormal behaviour such as a reliance on alcohol as a maladaptive coping strategy.

DEVIANCE VS. DYSFUNCTION

Another way of evaluating abnormal behaviour is to look at the element of deviancy. Deviancy is a sociological term for individuals who violate the norms of society (Dijker & Koomen, 2007). The violation can be informal like dress and appearance or formal, like the rules that govern motoring. An individual can be deviant but not necessarily dysfunctional. So how do we distinguish deviant behaviour from dysfunctional behaviour? Both are considered undesirable and both are abnormal.

In an attempt to distinguish abnormal behaviour and functional/dysfunctional behaviour, psychologists often categorize abnormal behaviour into four groups: deviance, distress, dysfunction and danger (Blackburn, 1995). Patterns of psychological abnormality can then be examined to determine whether the behaviour is functional or dysfunctional. Individuals can have one or more of the categories. Deviant is defined as different, extreme, unusual, perhaps even bizarre; distressing as unpleasant and upsetting to the person; dysfunctional as interfering with the person's ability to conduct daily activities in a constructive way; and dangerous as causing physical or mental harm to themselves or others.

The criterion of deviance is subjective and depends on an individual being judged by society as acting outside of standard rules and norms. Certain sexual behaviours, delinquency and homicide are examples of acts that our society considers deviant and abnormal. But social norms are far from static and behavioural standards cannot be considered absolute, so other types of behaviours that may be considered deviant today may not be considered deviant in the future. Changes in our attitudes towards tattooing and body piercing provide an example of modifications in our society towards this type of previously deviant behaviour. In the 1940s and 1950s, outside of ethnic groups, the military and deviant biker clubs, very few males were tattooed and women were almost never tattooed. To have a tattoo for a female generally branded that person as deviant, undesirable and a woman of disrepute. Today tattooing and piercing are commonplace among men and women of all ages. Body art has become so widespread and ordinary that a tattoo no longer carries any stigma or indicates membership in any type of group.

DISTRESS

Unusual functioning does not necessarily qualify as abnormal. According to many clinical theorists, behaviour, ideas, or emotions usually have to cause distress before they can be labelled abnormal (Blackburn,1996). Individuals who suffer mental distress often seek help to alleviate their discomfort. Many physical reactions stem from a strong psychological component; fatigue, nausea, pain and heart palpitations can all be indications of psychological distress. Discomfort can also be manifested in extreme or prolonged emotional reactions, of which anxiety and depression are the most prevalent and common. It can be normal for an individual to feel depressed after suffering a loss or a disappointment, but if the reaction is so intense, exaggerated and prolonged that it interferes with the person's capacity to function adequately, it is likely to be considered abnormal (Busfield, 2011).

DYSFUNCTION

Abnormal behaviour tends to be dysfunctional; that is, it interferes with daily functioning. It so distracts or confuses people that they cannot care for themselves properly, take part in ordinary social interactions, or work productively. Dysfunction in an individual's biological, mental and emotional states is often manifested in role performance. One way to assess dysfunction is to compare an individual's performance with the requirements of a role. In everyday life, people are expected to fulfil various roles and responsibilities. Emotional problems sometimes interfere with the performance of these roles, and the resulting role dysfunction may be used as an indicator of abnormality (Busfield, 2011).

Another related way to assess dysfunction is to compare the individual's performance with his or her potential. Psychological testing is one way of measuring an individual's capability and then making a comparision with current functioning.

DANGER

The critical element in determining abnormal behaviour is the factor of dangerousness. When an individual becomes dangerous to themselves or others and their behaviour is consistently careless, hostile and hazardous, abnormal behaviour is generally quickly brought to the attention of professionals. As a result of violating social norms and endangering the general public an individual will be promptly upgraded from abnormal to mentally ill (Blackburn, 1997). Mental health professionals are often called on to determine whether an individual is dangerous, and more than likely will be part of a legal proceeding to assess whether the individual should be incarcerated in order to protect the public as well as the individual. Predicting violent behaviour is very difficult and often professionals will err on the side of caution rather than take a risk of misjudging the situation and causing harm to the individual or members of society. Past violent behaviour is generally a predictor of future violence. However, not all past violent behaviour may be reported or known at the time an assessment is conducted. All these elements must be equally considered as the consequences for incorrectly predicting extreme violence are severe. It is often easier to piece together the facts after the individual has committed an act of violence. The majority of individuals displaying aggressive abnormal behaviour never act on them. Another issue is the lack of agreement over what types of behaviour are violent or dangerous. Acts of violence such as murder, rape and assault are easy to identify but other types of violence are less ominous such as destroying property, verbal abuse and receiving ASBOS. It is also thought that less violent behaviours can lead to more serious types of offences. So pushing and shoving at a pub could lead to a violent, possibly lethal physical assault. In addition, violence tends to be situation-specific; a person in a structured environment may be less likely to commit a violent act in a structured environment than in their own home. Another component that must be considered with the determination of abnormal behaviour and dangerousness is substance abuse. The potential for violence and dangerousness is increased when a person is under the influence of drugs and/or alcohol.

LEGAL DEFINITIONS

A legal definition of abnormal behaviour is used by the courts as a basis for their verdicts and is generally of limited use outside of the judicial system. The definition of abnormal behaviour develops out of a need to determine mental disease and whether an individual should be held responsible for an illegal act. The definition of abnormal behaviour will vary depending on the purpose of the decision and whether there is evidence of psychological impairment. This definition is different from the other types we have discussed because it is used for the sole purpose of giving a judgment after an individual has committed an offence against society. Often the issue of guilt or innocence is in little doubt; instead the court system must make a decision whether the person is to be held accountable for their actions. A legal definition of abnormal behaviour is not based on understanding or clarification, rather it seeks to define the boundaries of justice and society (Blackburn, 1997).

Legal definitions do not help to define abnormal behaviour or mental illness and instead reflect the norms and rules of a society on a case-by-case basis. Legal definitions are used in making practical decisions and their sole purpose is to determine whether an individual is responsible for their behaviour and how long they should be incarcerated either in prison or a mental institution. Legal definitions of abnormal behaviour are concerned with whether the judgment is appropriate given the mental stability or instability in direct relation to the crime committed. Legal definitions do not change the way a community or society define mental illness or abnormal behaviour and instead often reinforce the idea that individuals who behave outside the norm are dangerous to society. Legal definitions are directional; they first determine whether the abnormal behaviour is symptomatic of a mental illness and then determine personal responsibility. Ultimately the court system will decide the fate of the individual who has committed a crime, how that individual will be treated with respect to their mental status and what is best for the protection of society (Kapardis, 2002). For example, the crown prosecution will decide whether an individual is able to stand trial, whether they are capable of participating in their defence and if found guilty, whether they should be incarcerated in prison or go to a mental institution for treatment.

Legal decisions in the determination of mental illness and personal responsibility are very complex. Relatives and friends may be called to court to provide evidence of the person's behaviour and mental status previous to the offence. Individuals in contact with the person in question may also provide evidence of what they witnessed, before, during and after the offence in an attempt to determine the presence or absence of mental illness. Professional judgements are solicited for the defence of the individual as well as the prosecution. Expert testimony can be influential when there is a subjective evaluation of the individual's competence and behaviour patterns. However, professional judgement can be inconsistent and often brings the ideology of abnormal behaviour and mental illness into question. It is not unusual for experts within a given discipline to make opposing claims. The differences in opinions that arise in legal situations often reveal that clarity in behaviour and mental illness are difficult to decide (Kapardis, 2002).

Where does the boundary lie between abnormal behaviour and mental illness? If the legal definition is only concerned with individual responsibility the presence of abnormal behaviour may be all that is necessary to determine that the individual is not competent and responsible. Abnormal behaviour is judged in terms of degrees and is constantly changing dependent upon the many elements and phases of the judicial system. Decisions are generally made by a small group of individuals and not the society as a whole.

The legal definition in the UK for mental incompetence is arrested or incomplete development of mind, psychopathic disorder and any other disorder or disability of the mind. The judicial system does not have a specific definition of abnormal behaviour or mental illness. Instead the court system advocates that the criteria should be what an ordinary sensitive person would decide on a case-by-case basis and the decisive factor should be personal responsibility.

The Mental Health Act in the UK does define three forms of mental disorder:

1 Severe mental impairment, a state of arrested or incomplete development of mind which includes severe impairment of intelligence and social functioning and is associated with abnormally aggressive or seriously irresponsible conduct on the part of the person concerned.
2 Mental impairment, a state of arrested or incomplete development of mind (not amounting to a severe mental impairment) which includes significant impairment of intelligence and social functioning and is associated with abnormally aggressive or seriously irresponsible conduct on the part of the person concerned.
3 Psychopathic disorders: a persistent disorder or disability of mind (whether or not including significant impairment of intelligence) which results in abnormally aggressive or seriously irresponsible conduct on the part of the person concerned (Mental Health Act, 1983).

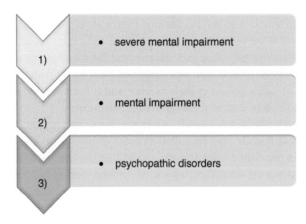

Figure 1.6   Abnormal behaviour and insanity

ABNORMAL BEHAVIOUR AND INSANITY

The major definition of criminal responsibility in the UK was developed from the 1843 trial of Daniel M'Naghten, who shot and killed Edward Drummond in the belief that Drummond was the prime minister of England. M'Nagten was acquitted by a reason of insanity and committed to a mental institution where he spent the rest of his life. His acquittal on the murder charge caused great concern throughout the UK as it was felt that the insanity plea was a way of escaping punishment. This case eventually led to the creation of the M'Nagten rule that states that in order for an individual to be judged insane and not held personally responsible they must be (a) mentally impaired to such a degree that they are incapable of understanding the wrongfulness of their behaviour and (b) unable to conform their behaviour to the law. Before 1843 there was no generally accepted legal definition of insanity and the M'Nagten rule provided guidelines.

The guidelines specify that mental disease may not be defined solely in terms of repeated criminal behaviour and they combine two themes in defining criminal responsibility (Mental Health Act, 1983). These guidelines still leave the judicial system with a highly complex structure in deciding whether or not an individual was truly unable to resist an impulse or merely choose not to do so.

INTEGRATED DEFINITIONS

Various definitions of abnormal behaviour serve different functions and convey different implications. All the definitions that have been discussed have significant limitations. It is imperative that the definition of abnormal behaviour include many factors such as value systems, culture, gender, age, context and societal norms. It is clear that a single perspective may not be appropriate for an accurate definition of abnormal behaviour.

Strupp and Hadley (1977) proposed a three-part method for defining normality and abnormality. They identified three aspects that are useful in the evaluation of an individual's mental health: (1) the individual in question, (2) the society of the individual, and (3) the mental health professional. Each element operates from a different perspective, using different criteria and when combined could provide a three-dimensional evaluation of behaviour that would encompass a multidimensional view.

CONCLUSION

If we returned to our case study and applied the various definitions, the statistical definition would certainly place Matt's behaviour in the abnormal range − it would be fairly uncommon for many middle-aged men to carry around brass bells to ward off evil spirits. In terms of making an evaluation from a medical definition Matt would not fit the criteria; his past indicates that he has never had any type of breakdown, and although he is using the bells to ward off evil spirits he seems to be able to cope and be very successful, so a health professional might feel that the behaviour is 'odd' but it is not dysfunctional. If we evaluated Matt's behaviour from a sociological perspective we would probably judge him to be abnormal, as the rules of behaviour for a middle-aged man would probably not include 'bell behaviour' – although if we added an element of culture, Matt's behaviour might not be as odd as we originally thought. In conclusion if we looked at Matt's behaviour from an integrated perspective we would probably conclude that although it is a bit odd, we would judge Matt to be normal.

Summary

This chapter focused on defining abnormal behaviour from a variety of perspectives. The discussion involved various elements such as deviance, dangerousness, dysfunction and maladaptive patterns of behaviour. The norms and rules of society were also discussed in terms of evaluating abnormal behaviour. A broad framework based on the various theoretical principles for evaluating normal and abnormal functioning was examined.

Key terms

Bell-shaped curve – in probability theory, is a continuous distribution where random variables tend to cluster around a single mean value

Conformity – the act of matching attitudes, beliefs and behaviours to a society

Cultural relativism – the belief that lifestyles, cultural values and world views affect the expression and determination of abnormal behaviour

Culture – shared learned behaviour which is transmitted from one generation to another for purposes of individual and societal growth, adjustment and adaptation

Self-actualization – the final level of psychological development when all basic and mental needs are fulfilled

Social norm – the rules that a group and/or community use for values, believes attitudes and behaviours

Society – a collective of individuals defined by the language that is spoken, religious practices and ethnic diversity

Study guide

1 Evaluate the differences between the legal definition of mental illness and the social element of abnormal behaviour.
2 Research the DSM classification system and the historical changes that have occurred as the norms of society have changed.
3 Investigate the Mental Health Act (1983) and how this applies to psychologists
4 Explore the role of the mental health professional in the determination of violent behaviour.

Case study in focus

Discuss the various ways we would classify our case study of Matt. How would this be defined statistically? Could we define Matt's behaviour in social terms? How could Matt's behaviour be adaptive and therefore functional? What about the elements of deviance vs. dysfunction?

Personal development

Investigate how society has used the term 'abnormal' to label and ostracize groups of individuals throughout history and how this term has been used to the detriment of individuals and our groups.

Suggested reading

Adams, H.E. & Sutker, P.B. (2001) *Comprehensive handbook of psychopathology* (3rd edn), Springer.

Kendler, K.S., Munoz, R.A. & Murphy, G. (2010) The development of the Feighner Criteria: A historical perspective. *American Journal of Psychiatry*, February 1, 167(2): 134–42.

Veit, I. (1969) Historical reflections on the changing concepts of disease. *Calif Med.*, June 110(6): 501–6.

Strauss, D.H., Spitzer, R.L. & Muskin, P.R. (1990) Maladaptive denial of physical illness: A proposal for DSM-IV. *American Journal of Psychiatry*, 147: 1168–72.

Carson, R.C., Butcher, J.N. & Mineka, S. (2009) *Abnormal psychology and modern life* (14th edn). Allyn & Bacon.

Models of Abnormal Behaviour

2

Learning aims

At the end of this chapter you should:

- Understand the different models
- Know why models are used to conceptualize abnormal behaviour
- Understand how a model influences assessment and treatment
- Know how models influence our understanding of abnormal behaviour.

INTRODUCTION

CASE STUDY

Gemma is a 19-year-old who had initially gone to her family GP with her mother because of ill health. Her mother reported to the GP that she felt that Gemma was unwell because she had recently put on a lot of weight. Gemma had dropped out of university and was now nearly 22 stone at 5'3".

Her doctor initially decided that Gemma's ill health was a direct cause of being obese. She was significantly overweight and was suffering from high blood pressure. It soon became apparent that although her weight was important, she was also suffering from extreme depression. Her doctor then referred her to a clinical psychologist. Gemma reported that she felt sad and lonely all the time, she wasn't getting out of bed, never got dressed and stayed in her bed clothes all day. She spent most of her time watching television and eating and her mother was complaining about her personal hygiene.

Gemma's mother (Michelle) reported that Gemma was an intelligent child who had achieved moderate A levels but had never been described as an achiever by any of her teachers. Michelle always qualified Gemma's behaviour by stating that she was exactly the same as Gemma.

Gemma's parents were also short and obese. Her father owned a small mechanic's shop that required long working days so he rarely spent time with Gemma or his wife and often it was only the two of them. Because Gemma's father was self-employed he had little time for holidays or days off, but he was happy to pay for expensive holidays for Michelle and Gemma. When Mark (Gemma's father) came home in time for dinner, the family ate their meals in front of the TV, where they spent the rest of the evening watching a variety of programmes and snacking on high-fat foods until bedtime. Gemma had a few friends in school but as everyone went separate ways after A levels and college, Gemma rarely saw them any more. She had attempted to go to university but felt very isolated; she didn't make any friends, didn't really speak to anyone and after one semester didn't go back. Gemma's mother was nurturant, indulging and over protective and her answer to all the problems in Gemma's life was food. Whenever Gemma felt sad or lonely they would eat cakes and sugary foods together. Gemma's mother felt she was the perfect daughter, she was always home, didn't engage in any bad behaviour and loved to stay at home with her, where they watched their favourite television shows. Gemma's father made a comfortable income so Gemma's mother had never had to work outside the home. Michelle preferred staying at home, didn't have many friends and after the morning cleaning would spend the day watching TV until it was time to begin preparing the evening meal. She admitted that she enjoyed Gemma being at home and that the two of them would often watch television together until the mid-afternoon.

Gemma had been a desperately wanted child. Her parents had tried for years to have a baby naturally and eventually went to a fertility clinic. Michelle did not qualify for the IVF programmes through the NHS because she was overweight and over the age limit. Michelle and Mark had gone private and after five attempts and £20,000, Michelle had become pregnant. The pregnancy was difficult because of Michelle's health issues, and Gemma was born prematurely and kept in the hospital for three weeks. Michelle spent all of her time at the hospital until she could take her baby home. After Michelle brought Gemma home, Michelle never left Gemma's side and her baby appeared to thrive; she gained weight rapidly, slept well and appeared to be a healthy and happy infant. Gemma did have separation issues when it was time for her to begin school and it was a difficult time for both mother and daughter. In spite of Gemma's underdevelopment at birth her motor and language development were within normal limits, she had no further serious illnesses, no accidents, and no further medical intervention.

INTRODUCTION

Gemma's behaviours can be understood in a wide variety of ways, depending on our frame of reference and how we conceptualize her various difficulties. She could be suffering from a disease, the product of heredity or her environment or the combined result of internal and external factors. No single frame of reference has demonstrated validity in accounting for the full range of abnormal conditions. Because each concept contains different directions and consequences we need to elaborate on our conceptualization of what causes abnormality. We have defined abnormality in the first chapter but what explains the variety of causes. Although the models we are about to discuss are not completely independent of each other, they have been grouped into categories to facilitate understanding.

MODELS

Models in abnormal behaviour are patterns or prototypes that provide us with a way of understanding complex relationships. Conceptual models are frames of reference that provide a broad but organized way of understanding and explaining abnormal behaviours in various ways (Tyrer & Steinberg, 2005). We use models because they describe a process that we cannot directly observe. We might be able to account for some elements but generally not all of them. Models make a basic aetiological assumption or hypothesis about a phenomenon. The assumptions then gives rise to differential interpretations of the available data and lead to other assumptions and inferences as the model is elaborated and developed. Usually, models generate their own vocabularies and technical terms which reflect their practical orientation and emphasize their uniqueness (Tyrer & Steinberg, 2005), although when applying to a specific term, they tend to overlap in varying degrees that sometimes blur specific models' boundaries as distinct frames of reference. Models relate to all types of processes − scientific, theoretical and mathematical to name a few. For our purposes we are going to use models to explain how abnormal behaviour occurs.

IMPLICATIONS AND CONSEQUENCES

Psychology uses models to help conceptualize the causes of abnormal behaviour (Tyrer & Steinberg, 2005). We can sometimes see elements but more often than not the aetiology involves processes that we do not directly observe and can only speculate on. A model of abnormal behaviour helps us synthesize the information in a coherent approach. Models help to determine relevant information and direct analytical questions. Conceptual models generate useful research hypotheses and initially can encourage studies designed to either support or refute the proposed model. We generally do not develop a model for a single person or single occurrence. Rather, models develop when there is a consistency in types of behaviours whose causes therefore require an explanation. The adoption of a model not only increases resistance to other views, but it also has a number of important consequences. These include: who is identified as abnormal, criteria used, treatment, types of institutions providing treatment and public attitude toward those labelled abnormal (Tyrer & Steinberg, 2005). Once a model achieves widespread acceptance alternative positions become more peripheral and less influential, regardless of their validity. Models or explanations may persist because of their plausibility and because their advocates maintain a belief in the model's premise. Once a model is accepted by a large population as being fact it becomes very difficult to propose alternatives. For example early explanations or 'models' proposed that supernatural factors were involved in the cause of abnormal behaviour. The belief in witchcraft and demons was reflected in the belief system and a model was designed to explain how groups of people displayed abnormal behaviour. This viewpoint continues even in modern society in spite of contrary scientific evidence and information.

The following provides an example to help explain the advantages and disadvantages of adopting a specific model to explain abnormal behaviour and mental illness.

In the past the adoption of supernatural forces was used to explain why individuals began acting in ways that were abnormal. Individuals would display characteristics that were inexplicable. They came from normal families in normal communities. So why did they behave in such abnormal ways? The belief in the supernatural, demons and witches provided a 'rational' explanation. Individuals were possessed, which explained their radical departures from normal behaviour. The supernatural was the prevalent view, supported by the ideas of religious beliefs, i.e. if there was a god and good and evil were dichotomized, the individuals must be part of the evil side and everyone behaving normally according to the societal rules must be on the 'good' side. The model of abnormal behaviour during these early societies became easily defined. In order to combat mental illness according to this model, religious principles were applied, in the form of removing the evil. Society could also be protected by the application of religious principles to keep the evil away, thereby curing individuals of the abnormal behaviour.

This model achieved widespread acceptance and would determine a number of important events regardless of the validity of its premise. The model assumed that demons were responsible for abnormal behaviour. The assumption set in motion a number of important actions because of its belief system and entire communities allowed individuals to be tortured and/or killed in order to keep them safe from further possession and influence. When augmented by public fear and anxiety, the premise became increasingly difficult to challenge and individuals who attempted to make changes or proposed alternative explanations were also included into the 'possession model'. Therefore further tests or challenges did not occur, scientific advances were discouraged and no improvements were made for hundreds of years. In this case the model that was applied held back the development of alternative conceptual models. Once the model began to lose favour, power and authority it allowed for alternative models to be proposed and explored.

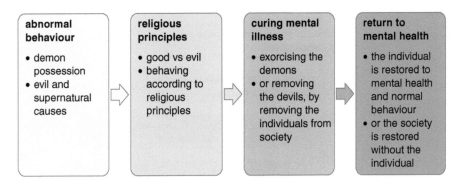

Figure 2.1

MEDICAL DISEASE MODELS

Currently the most prevalent model of abnormal behaviour in our society is the medical model (Stout, 2004). As a result of being created from an already well defined model of disease it incorporated an explanation of abnormal behaviour that came complete with its own language, institutions, professional personnel and types of remediation that reflects disease as its basic assumption. Experts and non-experts widely use and accept words such as mental illness, mental disease and mental health to describe psychopathology. Institutionalized programmes and places have been created to diagnose and treat the disorders. Individuals defined as being mentally ill receive care in hospitals or special treatment facilities. They receive care from a specialized group of individuals trained in mental illness and generally led by a physician or psychiatrist who is a medical doctor trained specifically in diseases of the mind (Stout, 2004). The British government continues to organize and launch programmes to reduce the number of people with mental illness. Funds are allotted to communities to build institutions, train personnel and support research within the medical-disease model. In our society, we hospitalize the mentally ill because we consider them sick and incapable of caring for themselves, in spite of the fact that often no tangible disease has been demonstrated. We follow a disease model, just as if an individual has contracted malaria; they are diagnosed, they are hospitalized, they are provided with the proper medication and treatment until they are cured and released.

The disease model of psychopathology was adopted from physical medicine, where there is abundant evidence for the aetiological link between organic pathology and physical symptoms. The medical model of psychopathology does make a leap of faith as often it assumes the connection between physical and mental disease when there are no perceptible symptoms, but there is a belief that the causes will eventually be connected to biophysical origins. This model assumes that the pathological process occurs within the organism be it genetic, biophysical or psychogenic in nature. However, is this medical model always appropriate? Do all mental illnesses fall into easily diagnosable categories? The reality is that they do not, and often assumptions are made that all the categories will be met, but this is not usually the case. Another element is when an individual has more than one mental illness. How does this fit the medical model? The simple answer is that it usually doesn't, therefore the model is deficient in many important ways.

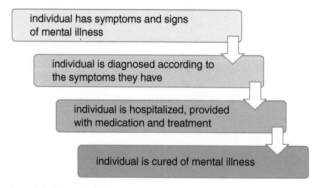

Figure 2.2   Medical model of mental illness

GENETIC MODEL

Since Darwin's publications, heredity has been acknowledged as an important determinant of both the biological and psychological make-up of people. The nature–nurture controversy is as much a part of contemporary psychology as it was at the beginning when psychology was a relatively new science and when our understanding of human genetics was less than it is today.

In terms of a genetic model of abnormal behaviour two positions have been posited:

- the view that genetic factors are primary and sometimes exclusive determinants and that they are only minimally and superficially influenced by environmental forces: and
- that heredity disposes the person to act in certain ways but that these predispositions can be modified by learning and one's life experiences (Eaves et al., 1997).

However, in order to better understand these models, we need to consider some of the basic elements of genetics and the research methods used to study the role of genetics in psychopathology. These will be studied further in depth in later chapters. For the benefit of understanding the genetic model, they will be covered in a general way.

For many human characteristics, genes do not act on the basis of the simple dominant–recessive principles, but rather in a number of complicated ways. One gene of a pair may show only partial dominance over another gene, in which case the manifest characteristic will be similar to the dominant version but less prominent or extreme than that produced by two dominate gene members of that pair. In addition, there are instances when a dominant gene fails to produce a trait 100 percent of the time for unknown reasons. What about the factors of environment? We know that although the genes may be present, environmental factors can play a role in increasing or decreasing the probability that the disorder is triggered. Many human traits are determined by complex combinations of gene pairs rather than by one pair. This is called polygenic inheritance and it is responsible for producing wide variations in a trait such as those often noted in the hair colour or height of offspring from the same set of parents (DeFries, McClearn & Plomin, 1989).

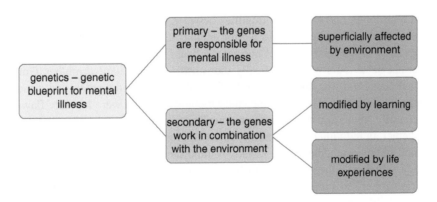

Figure 2.3   Genetic model – a two-tier system

Certainly, it would be easier to study the role of inheritance in determining abnormal behaviour if human characteristics were as simple in their genetic features as those found by Mendel in his studies of the garden pea. However, heredity does not directly produce psychopathology in the sense that specific genes correspond to specific behavioural abnormalities. Instead genetic contribution should be thought of as providing the conditions that could allow psychopathology to occur if all other elements fall into place. Therefore based on this model, it is possible for one child out of the family to develop psychopathology while the other children do not, even if they are raised in the same environments with similar genetic backgrounds. The slight differences in their genetic make-up and experience of their environment may be responsible for the development of abnormal behaviour.

RESEARCH METHODS USED IN GENETIC MODELS

Much of the early thinking about the role of heredity in abnormal behaviour was stimulated by Darwin's theory of natural selection and by the work of Francis Galton, who observed strong hereditary ties between the lineages of certain distinguished British families (Sturtevant, 2001). One of the most influential although inexcusably flawed studies in genetics and mental illness was Goddard's study of the Kallikak family in America, which documented evidence of heredity in abnormal behaviours (Joseph, 2004). Henry Goddard was an American psychologist who was working in a home for the education and care of mentally retarded children in the early 1900s. He became interested in a patient by the name of Deborah who was a resident in the home. He traced her genealogy back to her great-great-great-grandfather, a Revolutionary War hero who apparently had an affair with a mentally retarded barmaid who gave birth to a son who was also mentally retarded. The mentally retarded son went on to father more intellectually deficient children. After his affair Martin Kallikak went back home to his wife in New England and became the father of a large family, who did show signs of mental difficulties (Goddard, 1913).

What is interesting is that Goddard had stumbled upon what was thought at the time to be the perfect scientific experiment in genetics and mental illness. Kallikak was the common denominator while the two women provided the variation in genetic information. Goddard studied the descendants of Martin Kallikak from the two different women and observed the incidence rates of mental retardation and other abnormalities between the two families. He found a large number of descendents from the barmaid having mental retardation and other abnormalities while the descendants of his wife were all normal. Goddard used the data to support the conclusion that abnormal behaviours were genetically transmitted by the retarded mother. Goddard's study is important because it was influential in the field of genetics and mental illness and began other investigations in the area. However, the study methods he used were horribly flawed. His study lacked scientific rigour and relied on the memories of family members as well as photographs to decide whether an individual was mentally retarded or not. Aside from the inadequacies in scientific method and research, the Kallikak study is important because of the direction in which it took psychology, which was the genetic contribution to mental disorders. Prior to the Goddard study, no other researcher had attempted to scientifically establish a link from mental disorders to family pedigrees and although it was hypothesized it had not been explored. The Goddard study began a new line of research into mental disorders (Fancher, 1987).

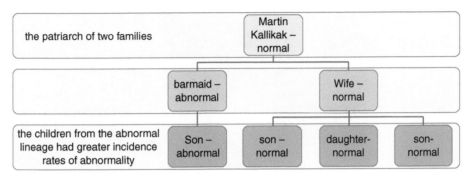

Figure 2.4

GENETIC STUDIES

The pedigree method consists of tracing the incidence of traits or phenotypes in family members over several generations in order to make inferences about the genotype and genetic principle involved (Joseph, 2004). It is a naturalistic method in which data are dependent on selected and infrequent accidents of nature that are too under-representative of the general population to warrant firm conclusions. While pedigree studies are of limited value, they have the potential of uncovering tentative relationships that can be further explored by more rigorous and statistically adequate methods.

The family-risk method of genetic studies represents an improvement over pedigree studies because it uses large samples of relatives of index cases or probands (known carriers of the trait under investigation) to assess the degree to which the trait is related to blood ties, and to compare the incidence of the trait found in the experimental group with that noted in a sample drawn from the normal population (Hall, 1996). The greater the relationship between the trait and the closeness of blood ties (parents, siblings, and children as contrasted to uncles, nieces and cousins), and the higher the incidence of the trait in the family group as compared to normal controls, the more convincing is the evidence for genetic transmission.

However, caution must be exercised in drawing causal inferences from family-risk studies, because correlational data (the relationship between the incidence of a trait and heredity closeness) merely reflects a relationship between two variables and not cause and effect. It is quite possible that other unaccounted variables, such as the environmental impact of being reared in a psychopathological home, may contribute significantly to the positive correlation obtained. Without proper control for environmental factors, the data from contingency studies cannot be regarded as unequivocal with respect to the influence of heredity on abnormal behaviour (Hall, 1996).

The twin study method of genetic research provides more precise genetic control (Hall, 1996). This approach uses monozygotic (identical) twins who originate from the same fertilized egg and have the same genotypes of genetic structure, and dizygotic (fraternal) twins who only have half of their genetic structure in common (much like ordinary siblings). A concordance rate is established by computing the percentage of cases in which both members of a twin pair manifest the trait in question. When identical twins show a higher rate for the trait than fraternal twins, we

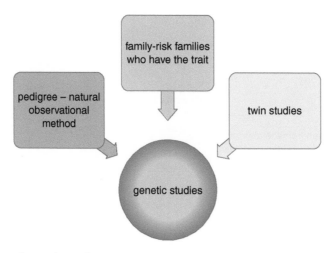

Figure 2.5   Types of genetic studies

have probable cause to believe that genetic influence is evident. However, this is based on the assumption that identical twins and fraternal twins are exposed to the same environmental conditions. This premise has been seriously questioned and weakened with the observation that environmental influences are more similar for identical twins than fraternal twins (Joseph, 2004). It is not unusual for twins to dress alike, share intimate living spaces and be treated alike by individuals outside of the family because of their similarity in appearance, however this is not generally the case for fraternal twins, especially those of the opposite gender.

Although twin studies have been widely used and offer numerous advantages, the method is not without limitations. Differences in identical twins that are assumed to be the result of environmental factors may be produced by gene mutations or chromosomal errors that occur during mitosis, or late in gestation. Finally, twin studies do not provide information about genetic transmission, but rather genetic influence that is inferred from concordance rates (Bentall, 2004).

ADOPTION STUDIES

Adoption studies have been used as a control for the effect of environmental factors (Hall, 1996). One type of adoption study compares the incidence of a disorder in two groups of children who have been placed in presumably normal foster homes but who differ in family genetics with regard to the disorder under study. One group of children, who are called the index cases, are the product of one biological parent having the disorder that is under study, while the other group is the control and comes from two biologically normal parents. If the incident rate of the disorder is more common among the index cases than among the controls then genetic transmission can be inferred. If the incidence rates are equal in the index group and the control group then the disorder can be attributed to factors other than genetics (Andreasen, 2001).

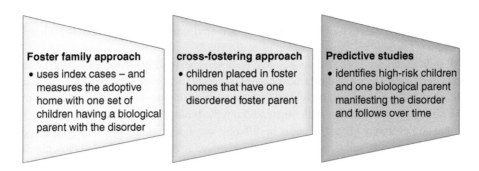

Figure 2.6   Adoption methods

This method recognizes and attempts to control for environmental influences, but it does not provide any certainty that the foster environment is normal or that one or more members of the foster family is not affected by the disorder being studied or some other type of psychological disorder.

Another type of adoption method is the cross-fostering approach. A group of children from biologically normal parents are placed in foster homes in which one or both of the adopted parents are affected by the disorder being studied. They are then compared with a group of children placed in normal foster homes who had at least one biological parent with the disorder. The incidence rates of the disorder found in the adoptees for each group are then used to reflect the relative potency of hereditary and environmental factors. This approach reduces the confounding environmental factors found in other methods (Bentall, 2003).

Predictive studies are not adoptive studies; instead they involve the early identification of high-risk children who have one biological parent manifesting the disorder but who have not themselves shown signs of the disturbance at the time of the initial study, and extreme-risk children with both biological parents affected by the disorder. This research strategy has been instrumental in studying schizophrenia and includes the longitudinal assessment of the impact of environmental factors on children who are at risk for that disorder (Johnstone et al., 2005). This approach prospectively examines populations considered to be either high-risk or extreme risk to identify vulnerable persons at an early age in order to determine the characteristics that are associated with the development of the disorder and to establish preventive intervention.

ASSUMPTIONS OF THE GENETIC MODEL

The genetic model contains two primary propositions: (a) genetic factors are primary and exclusive determinants of abnormal behaviour, and (b) heredity predisposes the person to a disorder but this is modified by learning and one's life experiences. Environmental influence is important but ultimately the individual's genetic structure will determine whether normal or abnormal behaviours will appear and this can happen through genetic transmission, enzymatic control, or mutative effects. Within the majority of genetic disorders, the hereditary component is necessary but not sufficient. It is the interaction of both hereditary and environmental factors that is both necessary and sufficient for producing a disorder (Eaves et al., 1997).

All individuals are born with anatomical distinctiveness, a distinctive endocrine system, nervous system and brain. The same uniqueness carries over into the sensory and biochemical realms and into their individual psyche. Each individual as they reach adulthood will exhibit a unique pattern of likes and dislikes. People are born with innate and unique biological characteristics that are modified by learning and everyday life experiences in different ways depending upon their genetic potentialities. All of these elements will manipulate how the genetic factors will be affected (Joseph, 2004).

A similar proposal is the view of genetic vulnerability in which abnormal behaviour is manifested when innate biological characteristics interact with noxious environmental variables. Vulnerability is a predisposition that increases the risk of breakdown but doesn't assure its occurrence, unless the person lives in an unpleasant environment that prompts the learning of certain maladaptive behaviours. To a great extent, the idea of genetic vulnerability as well as psychological and sociological vulnerability has been bolstered by risk research, which encompasses both the predisposing factors that establish the person's adaptation threshold and the stress factors of life's experiences that combine with these inherited characteristics to produce abnormal behaviour patterns (Hall, 1996).

Table 2.1   Types of genetic studies

Type	Definition	Positive	Negative
Pedigree method	Tracks genetic traits or phenotypes in a family over several generations	Can uncover genotypes and potential relationships for less cost than other methods	Cannot make firm conclusions about a genetic trait – no controls for environmental factors
Contingency of family risk method	Uses large samples of known carriers to assess the degree that the trait is related to relatives	Can reflect a relationship between the incidence of a trait and heredity closeness	No cause and effect conclusions can be made Doesn't control for environmental factors
Twin studies	Comparing identical twins to fraternal twins on a specific trait	Provides more precise genetic control	No information about genetic transmission
Adoption studies	Compares the rates of a disorder in two groups of children who have been placed in normal foster homes	Controls for environmental factors	No environmental controls – doesn't control for environmental factors.
Cross-fostering adoption approach	A group of children from biologically normal parents placed in foster homes in which one or both of the adoptive parents are affected by the disorder being studied	This approach reduces the confounding environmental factors found in other methods	The ethical considerations in this type of approach are difficult – these types of studies are extremely difficult to construct

THE BIOCHEMICAL MODEL

The biochemical model to some extent overlaps with the genetic model. Genetics provides the blueprint for functioning and genetic vulnerability provides the basis for biochemical changes underlying abnormal behaviours, whether they come in the form of an excess or deficiency of certain enzymes needed for mental functioning or inherited errors in metabolism (Hall, 1996).

The search for biochemical agents as the aetiological basis of mental illness, especially with the disorder of schizophrenia, has had a long and elusive history. If virulent germs and toxins can cause physical disease it seems only reasonable to suppose that similar factors can cause a disease of the mind. In fact much of the biochemical research on abnormal behaviour and psychopathology can be characterized as a quest for a toxic agent that is both necessary and sufficient to produce mental illness (Bentall, 2003). Research that studies the causes of mental illness and abnormal behaviour with the biochemical model has followed various medical directions. For example, when bacteria were discovered to be the cause of some diseases, researchers suggested that bacteria in the person's intestinal flora produced a toxin that disrupted the central nervous system. When medical attention shifted to viruses, researchers sought a viral cause of mental illness. The discovery of hereditary metabolic disease prompted the search for some deficiency or aberration in biochemical pathways as the cause of abnormal behaviours. Recent advances in the fields of biochemistry and pharmacology have led to a number of hypotheses concerning the possible alterations in the metabolism of certain brain chemicals (Andreasen, 2001). Current research in genetics is focusing on neurotransmitters in the brain, specifically the monoamines (Leonard, 2007). How does neurotransmitter functioning affect abnormal behaviour and how does genetics factor into this?

The role of neurotransmitters in the central nervous system is one of communication and mediation. In the central nervous system, the basic functional unit is the neuron. Information is transferred in the brain through the interaction of neurons across specialized structures termed synapse spaces between neurons by chemical neurotransmitters such as dopamine and serotonin. Any increase or decrease of these substances will affect neural communication and ultimately behaviour (Ritsner, 2009). It is a possibility that genetics may be responsible for aberrant structures or changes in the neurochemistry that result in changes in the neurotransmitters.

Recent advances in research techniques have made it possible to map pathways of neurons in the brain that are mediated by specific neurotransmitters and have therefore changed the perspective regarding brain and behaviour relations. Formerly, the focus was on the isolation of particular areas in the brain controlling specific functions. The current emphasis is on identifying deficiencies in neurochemistry (Ritsner, 2009).

THE BIOCHEMISTRY OF SCHIZOPHRENIA

The biochemical model suggests that this disorder is a result of an imbalance of monoamines, particularly norepinephrine and dopamine (Smythies, 1963). This hypothesis has received substantial support from a variety of research findings which initially observed a clinical resemblance between amphetamine psychosis and paranoid schizophrenia (Bell, 1965; Snyder, 1973; Janowsky & Risch, 1979). Amphetamine is a central nervous system stimulant drug; when taken at high doses for long periods of time it produces a behavioural syndrome that mimics schizophrenia and includes compulsive grooming, heightened fear and anxiety, suspiciousness, delusions and hallucinations. When amphetamines were administered to schizophrenics in low doses that would not produce psychotic symptoms in normals, it exacerbated their symptoms (Snyder, 1973). The category of amphetamine drugs acts at the biochemical level by enhancing the release and preventing the re-uptake of dopamine and norepinephrine at the central nerve terminals. These actions serve to increase the amounts of dopamine and norepinephrine in the synapse and ultimately raise the activity of these neurotransmitters in the brain. Antipsychotic drugs used to treat schizophrenics act as dopamine and norepinephrine blockers, which reduce the effects of these neuro-transmitters in the central nervous system (Kokkinidis & Anisman, 1980). The last element of research that supports the biochemical model for schizophrenia is that elevated levels of dopamine and norepi-nephrine metabolites have been found in the brains of schizophrenic patients during periods of severe symptomatology (Post, Fink, Carpenter & Goodwin, 1975). The evidence presented of the biochemical model of amphetamine psychosis along with the pharmacological data persuasively suggests that a disor-dered monoamine metabolism provides a strong link between biochemistry and behaviour.

Another area of evidence for the biochemical model has been the strong links of hyperactivity and childhood psychosis and altered monoamine levels (Gillberg, Svennerholm & Hamilton-Hellberg, 1983; Castellanos et al., 1994). Methylphenidate (which is a psychostimulant) is often prescribed to control hyperactive children, suggesting neurochemical action similar to schizophrenia in adults.

The biochemistry of psychopathology is a highly complex and technical area of research that includes methodological issues which are difficult to resolve. It often rests on the questionable assumption that descriptive differences in peripheral measures (such as blood levels of monoamines) have aetiologi-cal implications for underlying biochemical brain mechanisms (Goodwin & Post, 1975). Studies have attempted to correlate specific symptoms with biological and/or physiological results (Whitfield et al., 2000). However, ethical considerations have prevented more direct experimental approaches with humans. In addition, research in this area has also been hindered by poor diagnostic agreement about what constitutes the various disorders under investigation. Subject variables are problematic as they can be contami-nated by the consequences of mental illness, diet, prior treatment, long-term hospitalization, stress, and a large number of environmental experiences. In sum any proposed relationship between biochemical changes in the metabolism of neurotransmitters of the brain and certain observable behaviours or sub-jective experiences has yet to be proven and currently there is no firm evidence that links chemistry to behaviour. It is likely that mental disorders are so complex with so many intervening variables that they are not likely to have a single cause (Cicchetti, 1984; Rutter, Moffitt & Caspi, 2006).

NEUROPHYSIOLOGICAL MODEL

This model assumes that the aetiology of abnormal behaviour resides in brain structures that are inher-ited, congenital or acquired. It maintains that normal cognitive and behavioural functioning depend on the anatomical and physiological integrity of the brain and that defects, insults or damage that violate this important organ provide the physical basis for disordered thinking and behaviour (Stein & Ludik, 1998). To a great extent, this model overlaps with both the genetic and biochemical views, since it acknowledges the crucial role of genetic transmission or aberrations as well as metabolic and biochemical changes in affecting brain function. But the neurophysiological model is broader and in some ways more general than the others, because it also includes a wider array of aetiological causes such as congenital anomalies, acquired injuries, toxicity or disease: for example, prenatal effects of drugs and alcohol, toxaemias of pregnancy, premature births and traumatic brain insults during or after birth. The relationship between any of these events and the emergence of abnormal behaviours is often associated but does not indicate a direct cause and effect (Andreasen et al., 1997).

RESEARCH METHODS USED IN THE NEUROPHYSIOLOGICAL MODEL

Brain lesions (injuries) produced by cooling, radiation, electrolysis or chemical means and the ablation (removal) of brain tissue have been used to study the effects of brain damage on behaviour (Uhl, 1998). For therapeutic purposes, lesions have been produced in humans (epilepsy), but for obvious ethical reasons, creating lesions in living humans is prohibited as an investigative tool. Therefore animals are used, based on the premise that the data obtained would be applicable to humans. The general procedure involves the lesioning or excising of a specific brain area followed by an examination of the behavioural effects. After the initial observations are completed the animal is humanely euthanized and a post-mortem study of the tissue (histology) is done to verify the lesion sites (Uhl, 1998).

Electrical stimulation of the human brain has been used as both a therapeutic measure and an investigative device to study brain mechanism and function in relation to abnormal behaviours. The triggering of seizures through the stimulation of appropriate brain areas has provided useful information concerning the sources of epilepsy. During the seizure activity electrical implants can monitor brain activity as it correlates with human behaviour. With this type of method there are a number of ethical issues related to the use of electrical stimulation in humans: (a) experimental control rather than therapy, (b) destruction of tissue along the path of the implant, and (c) the intensity of stimulation used, which is greater than that which would naturally occur in the brain (Uhl, 1998). There have been many criticisms of this type of research as it is believed that the results are unjustified and that the manifestations of cortical stimulation may be drastically modified by alterations in the stimulus parameters or prior stimulation, therefore all conclusions should be viewed with caution (Vickers et al., 1997).

The last type of neurophysiological research is the EEG. The EEG or electroencephalogram is an instrument used to record electrical activity of the brain by means of electrodes attached to the scalp. With the aid of EEG tracings, researchers have tried to differentiate mental patients from normals and to obtain information about the reactivity of the central nervous system of disordered persons (Nunez & Srinivasan, 2006). Unfortunately, the EEG has not proved useful in diagnosing most psychiatric conditions, although it has been effective in identifying epilepsy and organic brain lesions, and in diagnosing those hyperactive children who respond well to stimulant medication (Linden, Habib & Radojevic, 1996). Increased technical sophistication has made it possible to use the EEG to measure cerebral responses evoked (evoked potential) by sensory stimulation, such as flashes of light, electric shock, or auditory clicks.

These evoked responses have been found to be associated with a wide range of psychopathology, although very little specificity in the response characteristics has been evident thus far (Shagass, Roemer, Straumanis & Josiassen, 1985). The methodological problems of this approach include the difficulty in obtaining an adequate baseline by which to measure electrophysiological changes resulting from stimulus presentations, and the difficulty in removing all sources of extraneous electrical activity coming from either the subject (muscle activity) or outside sources such as the equipment itself (Connolly & Gruzelier, 1986).

A relatively recent and complicated type of cortical response that has been associated with attention is called the contingent negative variation (CNV) (Tecce, 1972). It is marked by a slow rise in negative potential when the subject anticipates the presentation of a stimulus, but it is not evident when the subject is unaware that the stimulus will occur. The procedure consists of instructing the subject to perform a response (press a bar) when a particular stimulus such as an auditory click is presented (S2). However, prior to the presentation of S2, another stimulus (S1) such as a light flash is presented much like the arrangement found in classical conditioning. When S1 is presented the subjects' EEG tracings show a slow negative shift in potential until the S2 appears. In other words, the subject's brain surface becomes increasingly negative after S1 is presented and this cortical response serves as an indication that the person is attentive and anticipating the presentation of S2. CNV can be thought of as reflecting a transitory state of increased arousal that is terminated after the response to the imperative stimulus (S2) is made. The technique has revealed CNV differences in children with learning disabilities, and it is being used currently in the study of psychotic children to reveal impairment in the central system that underlies such mental processes as attention, expectation and motivation (Dainer et al., 1981).

Peripheral measures of the autonomic nervous system have also been used to make inferences about mental activity. One such index, skin conductance (GSR), measures the change in skin resistance resulting from alternations in sweat-gland activity, which is thought to indicate arousal or emotionality. A landmark study conducted by Mednick and Schulsinger (1968) looked at skin conductance in children of schizophrenic mothers and found that the skin conductance response is predictive of later schizophrenia.

Issues of neurophysiological methods used to examine the aetiology and course of abnormal behaviour are inundated and plagued by problems of diagnostic inaccuracies, confounding effects of institutionalization and medication and the incomplete understanding of the intricacies of the human brain. We know less about neuropsychological factors and their implications for abnormal behaviours than the variables associated with either the genetic or biochemical models.

Table 2.2   Research methods used in the neurophysiological model

Type	Description
Brain lesions/Ablation	Studies the effects of brain damage on behaviour by creating a brain injury or removing brain tissue
Peripheral measures – skin conductance – GSR	Measures the change in skin resistance that is caused by the autonomic nervous system and indicates arousal or emotionality
Triggered seizures	Specifically triggered seizures that enables the study of brain mechanism and function in relation to abnormal behaviours
EEG or electroencephalogram	Used to record electrical activity of the brain by means of electrodes attached to the scalp and measures variations in the brain
Evoked potential – CNV	A special type of EEG to measure cerebral responses caused by sensory stimulation

PSYCHOANALYTIC MODEL

Created and modified by Sigmund Freud, the psychoanalytic model rests on two essential assumptions: psychic determinisms and the unconscious (Gedo, 1988). Freud believed that every human act whether it is directly observable (such as a smile) or only noted through self-report (such as a fantasy), occurs as a function of prior mental events and not as a matter of chance. Previous events and experiences (both internal and external to the organism) determine all facets of a person's behaviour. Therefore, one of Freud's major tasks consisted in trying to find and then eliminate the psychic determinants of abnormal behaviours (Gedo, 1988).

The other basic premise of psychoanalytic thinking is the unconscious, an inference made early by Freud to explain the thoughts, wishes, memories, information and experience of which his neurotic patients were unaware. He proposed that people banish (repress) unpleasant experiences and unacceptable feelings from consciousness because of their threatening nature. In addition, he suggests that the unconscious contains memories of preverbal infantile experiences and informally acquired information that are almost impossible to recover. Similar memory difficulties are encountered with repressed (emotionally charged) material, because the person has learned to use a variety of psychological defences to prevent it from becoming conscious. Freud also proposed another level of accessibility called the preconscious to account for mental content that was presently unavailable to the person, but which could readily be brought into awareness. Recognizing the difficulty in obtaining direct evidence to demonstrate the unconscious (since we can only know about the material after it has been transformed into consciousness), he nevertheless argued for proof of its existence through inferences made from other behaviours such as slips of the tongue, misplacing of objects, jokes, neurotic symptoms, recurrent patterns that led to negative consequences, or excessive protestations. He used the technique of free association as a way of uncovering unconscious material. He interpreted lateness and missed appointments as signs of unconscious resistance to treatment, and focused on the hidden (latent) content of dreams to understand the unconscious (Sandler, Holder, Dare & Dreher, 1997).

Anxiety plays a central role in Freud's theoretical view. It may arise from fear of the real dangers in the external world, fear of punishment for the expression of libidinal drives, and from feelings of guilt about acting in ways that are discrepant with the values of society and the family. Anxiety is a tension state determined by external factors that serves as a danger signal and as a motivator to reduce the tension through such acts as withdrawing from a dangerous situation, inhibiting an unacceptable impulse, or following a moralistic course. The responsibility for coping with anxiety resides with the ego, which utilizes a variety of defence mechanisms for this purpose. All people, both normal and abnormal, use defences to reduce anxiety, although the abnormal personality relies heavily on a smaller repertoire of defences than the healthy personality (Peterfreund, 1983).

Freud believed that the relationship between the ego and the id gives rise to the abnormal behaviours characteristic of neurosis and the failure of the ego to deal with the environment (the outer world) that results in the loss of reality and psychosis. More specifically, he viewed neurosis as arising from the ego's rejection (through repression) of the expression of an instinctual impulse. The repressed impulse persists in seeking expression until it finds a substitutive way of gratification (a symptom) that the ego is unable to control. However, this manoeuvre threatens the integrity of the ego, and the ego fights back against the symptom as it had previously struggled to prevent the expression of the original impulse. This intrapsychic conflict between the ego and the id represents the essential basis of the clinical manifestations of a neurosis (Peterfreund, 1983).

Freud viewed psychosis as originating in the ego's inability to cope with the demands of the outside world, and creating instead a world of its own, a world that is less threatening, more gratifying of primitive impulses, but quite removed from reality. In a psychosis, reality is replaced by the new world the ego has substituted for it.

Freud's view is one that is full of tension and conflict which at best can only be temporarily reduced and resolved with both past and present problems contributing to continued discomfort. Difficulties encountered in handling the various stages of psychosexual development lead to enduring personality traits and to immature and inappropriate sources of sexual gratification that heighten anxiety and prevent attempts to find more mature ways of obtaining satisfaction. Weak ego development or an excessively strict superego, for example, also increase the likelihood of intrapsychic conflict requiring too much psychic energy to resolve and still deal effectively with reality. Present day-to-day living is hardly possible without tension and intrapsychic conflict. These arise from the individual's demand for instinctual gratification on the one hand, and society's many restrictions and prohibitions against sexual satisfaction on the other. The struggle between the id seeking immediate gratification and the superego striving for moralistic and ideal behaviour is ever present (Gedo, 1976).

The psychoanalytic model has had little empirical support. The model's inclusiveness and generality along with its substantial number of interacting components make it impossible to test with most if not all research methods.

OTHER INTRAPSYCHIC/PSYCHOANALYTIC MODELS

Carl Jung proposed a distinction between extroverted and introverted personalities and introduced the concept of the collective unconscious which in addition to the personal unconscious (storehouse of the individual's past experiences forgotten or repressed), he viewed as a storehouse of innate memories of human beings' shared experiences throughout history. He used the collective unconscious and the ideas that people everywhere share a common set of instincts as well as universal developmental patterns to account for the similarities found among people of different cultures. His belief of abnormal behaviour arose from a complicated inability to integrate the personality (Stevens, 2001).

Alfred Adler stressed environmental and social forces as important determinants of behaviour. He conceived of healthy people as social animals who were motivated by the need to meet their communal obligations, love others and fulfil their work objectives. He attributed abnormal behaviours to inferiority feelings (inferiority complex) that arise from the person's real or imagined failure to achieve self-fulfilment and self-actualization (Adler, 1964).

Harry Stack Sullivan viewed disordered interpersonal relationships as the primary source of internalized anxiety which produced aberrant behaviours.

The psychoanalytic model assumes that the aetiological origin of abnormal behaviours stems from internal conflicts (intrapsychic) associated with early childhood experiences.

ENVIRONMENTAL MODELS

The environmental model focuses almost exclusively on external variables (sociocultural and psychological) as the primary determinants of abnormal behaviours. The consistency of these broad categories may appear flawed by the persistence of some environmental models in considering aberrant behaviours as disease in spite of the fact that the similarity of causes (between neurophysiological defects and problems in living) is faulty.

Whether they ignore or acknowledge the innate and biological characteristics of the individual, researchers and theorists within the environmental camp believe in the potency of cultural mores, social systems, economic influences and unique life experiences in shaping (through the learning process) personality patterns. In choosing another aetiological orientation, they tend to explore different variables with different investigative tools and designs, and to look for remedial and preventive solutions (Bronfenbrenner, 1986).

SOCIOCULTURAL MODELS

These models emphasize the importance of culture and social systems as determinants of human behaviour. They study the effect of such global and pervasive variables as the family, race, socio-economic levels, rural versus urban living, religious affiliation and cultural attitudes on personality development, while often making inferences from correlational data. Sociocultural models tend to oversimplify complicated relationships, since they are prone to deal in broad generalities or in incomplete analysis of specific variables. Yet, there are few who would discount their contributions in highlighting the important role played by sociocultural factors in personality development.

Emile Durkheim pioneered the view that society precedes the individual in the sense that people are born into society that controls and provides form and meaning to their existence. People do not create societies (although they may be instrumental in bringing about changes in them), but rather, cultures exist as greater and more powerful forces than humans. For example, this is evidenced by the predictable impact of social class on so many important aspects of human life, ranging from an individual's style of clothing, physical appearance and mannerisms, language, how much and what kind of education one receives, the nature of child-rearing practices, type and adequacy of diet and religious affiliation. The standards of society occur in three stages of development: (1) learning to respect the social rules, (2) becoming a member of and identifying with several subgroups of that society i.e. family, peer groups, etc. and (3) behaving independently in accordance with the society's rules (Craib, 1997).

Durkheim also introduced a concept, which he called anomie, that refers to the breakdown of societal controls and that the socially defined standards of conduct no longer serve as effective guidelines for behaviour. Anomie occurs when (a) social norms are no longer commonly shared by members of the society, (b) there is a decline in the application of sanctions against violations of these standards or (c) members of the society are not morally obligated to conform to them. It is manifest in periods of social disorganization and change, and when members of a society have limited access to valued goals as illustrated in the struggle of the poor to acquire material wealth. It also occurs when alternative social norms are simultaneously present, as in the case of subcultural groups living side by side (Alexander & Smith, 2005).

Anomie is associated with psychopathology because the social chaos is a source of alienation and is characterized by anxiety, uncertainty, insecurity, lowered self-esteem, identity confusion and a sense of powerlessness. There is evidence suggesting that alienation in our society is a growing problem that is correlated to personality disorganization, acts of violence and a rising crime rate. During recent years, our society has seen a great deal of alienation, largely in adolescents who have attempted to resolve conflicts with their families and society through membership of groups that abuse drugs and alcohol and participate in random acts of violence against property and individuals. These new groups appear to satisfy strong needs for acceptance, affiliation, security and self-worth but they also serve to reinforce behaviours that are maladaptive. Perhaps the riots are an example of anomie that is experienced by certain groups in British society. Although some of the rioting was used for material gain, the vast majority appeared to stem from a need to generate random acts of violence with the sole goal being the destruction of property.

Societies or individuals in transition from one culture to another increase the probability of behavioural disorders because the traditional bonds of practices and values that hold families and communities together are disrupted. Immigration can play a large role in entire groups of individuals being ostracized from the main community. Research has indicated that people living in areas isolated from their cultural group had a higher rate of behaviour disorders than those who were members of their dominant group (Draguns, 1995).

While the sociocultural perspective calls attention to important variables affecting human behaviour, it is limited by its almost total emphasis on environmental forces to the exclusion of the internal characteristics of individuals. Durkheim and other sociologists built their view on the erroneous assumption that society precedes and is independent of people, even though a social structure does not or cannot exist without people. The sociocultural position does not account for individual differences or attend sufficiently to the human's capacity to think and act in a social context.

The possibility of new life and increased access to data for the sociocultural models comes from the field of community mental health. The major objective is to place care and responsibility of the mentally ill into the community and integrate them with society. Gruenberg (1973) constructed a sociocultural model and used the term 'social breakdown syndrome' to describe the deterioration in social functioning associated with mental disorders which can be prevented both by less harmful responses to those disorders and by changed community attitudes toward the mentally ill and their treatment.

There are seven steps in the development of social breakdown syndrome which can lead to abnormal behaviour. The first step begins with transient experiences that everyone encounters, namely the discrepancy between what one can do and what one is expected to do. The second step is the failure to meet these expectations, especially when they persist and the failure is recognized both by self and others. The third step is that the failures result in self-doubt and increased uncertainty. The fourth step is that the individual initiates actions to meet the demands of the situation but these are usually unsatisfactory and result in failure. The fifth step is that the person then reacts with feelings of being misunderstood and of anger. The sixth step is that these actions and reactions eventually lead to social exclusion or withdrawal. Finally the individual is labelled as being mentally ill. The labelling results in admissions and treatment where the environment fosters the further development of social breakdown syndrome. Institutionalization brings with it compliance to the hospital's rules and isolation from family and community. In the end, the individual identifies with other patients, and the individual's capacity to cope with ordinary social interactions and work tasks deteriorates (from disuse) (Gruenberg, 1967).

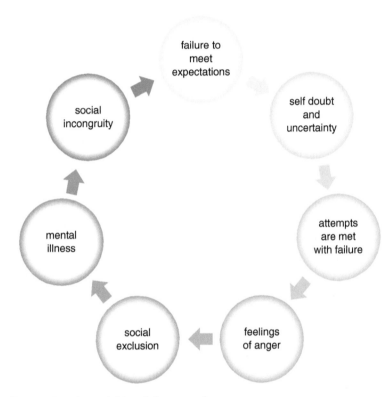

Figure 2.7   Seven steps to social breakdown syndrome

LEARNING MODELS

In contrast to the medical-disease models, the learning approach views both normal and abnormal behaviours as primarily determined by learning and in changeable through the appropriate applica-tion of learning principles (Kolb, 1984). Abnormal behaviours are learned maladaptive responses that can be either eliminated or altered in favour of more adaptive ones, without having to make any additional assumptions about an underlying disease process. In general, learning models reject the Freudian notion of the unconscious and its emphasis on symbolism in psychopathology, and the medical position of disease entities in preference to the idea that aberrant behaviour is either a failure to learn a response or the acquisition of a maladaptive response (Kolb, 1984).

In neurosis, the individual is unable to reduce the tension of the conflicting drives, but continually seeks responses that tend to reduce his or her suffering (subjective state of misery). Any response (symptom) that successfully reduces neurotic misery is reinforced, although it is not likely to solve the original conflict. Further reinforcement of the symptom increases the probability of its occurrence and strengthens it as a learned habit. For example, we are not born with an innate fear of spiders. We learn to fear them because we are taught by adults that they are something to be feared. Phobias, intense and persistent fears, are learned and avoidance responses are reinforced by the reduction in the strength of the fear drive. The original stimulus of the fear is frequently learned in childhood but new intense fears transfer to new cues through stimulus generalization over the course of time. Phobias persist because those affected usually manage to avoid the phobic situation with behaviours (withdrawal and avoidance) that reduce the fear but do not resolve the basic and underlying problem.

According to the social-learning view of Julian Rotter, abnormal behaviours are learned and maintained because the individual has a relatively high expectancy that these types of behaviours will lead to a reinforcement of value or avoid or reduce some potential punishment. Moreover, most abnormal behaviours can be thought of as avoidance behaviours attributable to expectations of punishment or low expectancies of achieving important reinforcements (Rotter, 1972).

For example, if a child places a high value on athletic success but expects that he or she will not achieve this end, then the child is likely to employ avoidance behaviours or symptoms such as withdrawal from peer relations (especially those involving opportunities for athletics). The avoidant behaviour eventually leads to the child's failure to develop competency which, in turn, tends to facilitate the development of other deviant behaviours. Withdrawal behaviour reduces practice opportunities that could increase the youngster's athletic competence, and, instead, may lead to excessive and unrealistic fantasy activities about his or her extraordinary athletic prowess.

Another possible consequence of high need value may result in the person distorting reality or in his or her failure to make appropriate discriminations among social situations. If a need is excessive, every occasion becomes an opportunity for its attainment without regard for the appropriateness of the situation. In these circumstances behaviour is likely to be inappropriate and to elicit negative reactions from others, which, in the end, will lower the person's expectations about receiving the rewards.

With regard to other aspects of abnormal behaviour, Rotter's theory substitutes either low expectancy for success or high expectancy for failure for what is clinically considered anxiety. In addition, it rejects the dichotomy between neurosis and psychosis implied in the medical model and diagnostic classification system and it attempts to deal specifically with certain forms of abnormal behaviour, such as obsessions, compulsions and depressive reactions (Rotter, 1972).

Bandura's social-learning view relies heavily on instrumental conditioning and imitation learning. Bandura believed that abnormal response patterns are learned and maintained by a flawed conditioning process. In some instances, the faulty prior learning involves a behavioural deficit in which there is a failure to acquire adequate responses that would enable the person to cope effectively with the demands of the environment. The failure to learn the requisite skills arises from inadequate modelling and reinforcements. The failure may lead to further adverse affects of impoverished performance, because insufficient rewards are given for the skills the individual has, while, at the same time, the behavioural deficit is negatively reinforced. Bandura suggests that the low levels of responsiveness of psychotic children and adults are manifestations resulting from behavioural deficits of this sort (Bandura, 1976).

Deviant response patterns also may be attributable to the failure to respond discriminately to important stimuli in people who possess normal responses. In the course of development, children learn to differentially respond to stimuli in terms of the consequences that are associated with particular stimuli (Bandura, 1976). For example, they may consistently receive approval (reinforcement) for shedding their clothes at bath or bedtime and consistently receive disapproval (punishment) for undressing at other times that are inappropriate, e.g. when there are guests in the house. The introduction of a discriminating stimulus and different schedules of reinforcement will bring the behaviour of inappropriate undressing under stimulus control. Through faulty training or a disruption of previously acquired discriminative responses, behaviours that are inappropriate to the situation may occur. Deviant (abnormal) responses are evident in psychotic individuals in the form of inappropriate or impoverished affect, delusions and cognitive dysfunction (Bandura, 1976).

In addition, deviant behaviours may arise when inappropriate stimuli acquire the capacity to produce intense emotional responses. If a formerly ineffective conditioned stimulus occurs in conjunction with another stimulus which is capable of eliciting unpleasant autonomic responses, the former stimulus itself gradually acquires the power to evoke the same aversive emotional response pattern. These deviant behaviours are manifested as somatic complaints and in psychophysiological disorders such as asthma, ulcers and hypertension. In addition, conditioned emotional reactions of phobias and other avoidance patterns are acquired in this way (Bandura, 1976).

Bandura also described the faulty prior learning of either defective or inappropriate incentive systems as a condition that results in abnormal behaviours. In this instance, he referred to pleasurable but culturally unacceptable stimuli (sexual, alcohol, drugs), which in themselves function as strong positive reinforcers, that become associated with behaviours considered deviant in our culture (Bandura, 1976).

In addition, Bandura discusses how aversive behaviours such as aggression are acquired. Experimental studies have shown that aggressive, punitive parents are likely to produce aggressive children, especially if the parents (models) are highly successful in controlling rewards. Frustrated children, who under ordinary conditions respond with aggression, can be taught new patterns in which they exhibit unaggressive and inhibited behaviour after they observe the inhibited behaviour of a model. Observers can also be influenced if the aggressive behaviour of the model is rewarded or punished. Those who observe aggression rewarded are more aggressive than the children who observe aggression punished (McCord & McCord, 1961).

Research has also shown that positive reinforcement increases the child's aggressive behaviour, and that the effects of this reinforcement transfer to new social situations. As expected, punishment tends to inhibit aggressive responses, although a great deal of punishment training may lead to aggression directed towards objects or persons who are not the punitive agent (Vitaro, Brendgen & Tremblay, 2002).

HUMANISTIC MODELS

The humanistic models blend together the elements of sociocultural models and the mechanisms of learning theories to provide a model that has existential elements to its orientation towards personality and abnormal behaviours. They are environmental positions because they stress experience and the individual's reaction both to self and the external world as essential determinants of behaviours. However, instead of being concerned with the exploration of a person's unconscious, or recounting and restructuring past learning experiences, or the basis of disease or injury, this model attempts to understand the whole person in terms of present functioning and capabilities for the future. The humanistic model is embedded in the philosophical idea that regards human nature in a positive light and that respects the worth of every person and their right to make choices about how they will live their lives (Schneider, Bugental & Pierson, 2001).

According to Abraham Maslow, one of the pioneers of the humanistic movement in psychology, an individual is always striving for perfect self-actualization. Individuals are moulded and shaped into humanness. The role of the environment is to help individuals actualize the potential that they are born with (Maslow, 1973).

For Maslow every person has an essential biological inner nature that is within limits unchangeable and which is partly unique and partly common to the species. The needs, emotions and human capacities of this inner nature are either intrinsically neutral or good suggesting that people are not innately evil but manifest such behaviours as destructiveness, cruelty and sadism as violent reactions to the frustration of their inner core. Maslow viewed the inner nature as weak and delicate and readily denied and overcome by habit and external forces although it persists in striving for survival first and then actualization (self-fulfilment). Maslow emphasized the presence in all people of inherent tendencies for survival and for self-actualization. If these tendencies are not inhibited they will eventually lead to both the maintenance and enhancement of life. Needs associated with the survival tendency include physiological demands, safety, belongingness and love. The actualizing tendency incorporates the need for self-actualization and the need for cognitive understanding (Maslow, 1973).

When either of these tendencies is blocked, the person becomes sick or evidences maladaptive behaviours. In the course of living, people continually face the conflict between the defensive forces of survival and the forces of growth. At times they must choose between safety or growth. Healthy people are those who are free to choose growth, while those who are sick are held back by the fears and anxieties of survival. The needs associated with the survival tendency (including safety needs) must be gratified before the growth needs can be met and before the person can feel safe enough to take the next step (Maslow, 1973). For example, the young child can only venture forth to explore the surrounding environment when the mother–child relationship is secure, safe and intact. However, if the mother–child relationship is impaired and uncertain, the child will cling to the mother and be unable to take the growth step of freely interacting with the environment. The maladaptive responses can best be treated when the therapist respects the fears of the sick person and provides the security and safety needed for the person to be bold enough to choose a growth direction.

Carl Rogers, one of the earliest and best known phenomenologists, conceptualized self-actualization as the core tendency of human personality. Rogers believed that every person is born with inherent potentialities and that life experiences are perceived by the individual as either favourable or unfavourable in terms of self-actualization. The developing child gains a conscious sense of self by learning that it is highly desirable to be favourably regarded by parents, relatives and others (the need for positive regard). The need for positive regard is internalized into the merging self through approval and disapproval received from others, while the child develops another important need, the need for positive self-regard. Under unusual circumstances, a person may receive unconditional approval from others, in which case unconditional positive self-regard is developed, resulting in an ideal person who experiences no discrepancy between his or her self and potentialities. Less ideal, but more the rule, is the probability that the individual will receive conditional positive regard. This leads to a less favourable outcome in the sense that the person develops conditions of worth that give rise to anxiety about the occurrence of unworthy behaviours. Defences are constructed to deal with the anxiety and to ward off threats to the self. However, when defences are inadequate, anxiety increases and abnormal behaviours appear (Rogers, 1961).

The existential view holds that human understanding cannot come from approaches that focus on the specific mechanisms of learning or the unconscious. To focus on these mechanisms is to lose sight of the existing human being, and give precedence to these methods. Existentialism is an attitude and an approach to humans instead of a theory or a special ideological school. It stresses the person's unique pattern of potentialities and their relationship to them as the person struggles to deal with being and non-being. The major task that each person must deal with is to become self-aware. They must reach a conclusion about 'who' they are and what is the purpose of their life. In this process, the person discovers that human existence is purposeless, which gives rise to angst, a subjective state of dread or anxiety over the possibility of nonbeing that also serves as a basic source of motivation. A second motivational force, the will to power, permits the person to deal with angst through self-knowledge. However, the anxiety that comes from the potential of non-being may at times be too high for some people to tolerate and too intense to prompt self-awareness. Therefore, many people choose self-deception because the more they seek self-knowledge the more they heighten the dread of non-being which in turn causes abnormal behaviour (Loewenthal, 2011).

To achieve self-awareness individuals must accept the discomfort of non-being and find the courage to persist by recognizing that they have the power to create their own meaning and existence. This sense of human dignity not only recognizes and accepts the limits set by biological and social forces but also permits the individual to examine those remaining possibilities for freedom of action. People who see no options or alternatives in their life circumstances feel trapped and confuse the actual limits of the situation with the possible degrees of freedom that may be available. These reactions form the basis of psychopathology in which the individual blames. They become unwilling to assume the responsibility as well as take the necessary action that would achieve self-awareness. In this sense, psychopathology involves cowardice and self-deception and a refusal to use one's higher mental processes of symbolization, imagination and judgement to construct alternatives (Loewenthal, 2011).

In general, humanistic models, while popular with the clinical practitioner/psychologist/therapist, have incurred their share of criticism on the grounds of being vague and incomplete; for example, they provide few, if any specifics with regard to the nature of inherent potentialities. The idea that an individual would be a constructive, rational and socially conscious being free from the malevolent distractions of society is based on unsupported assumptions about the nature of human beings.

CRITIQUE OF THE NON-BIOLOGICAL MODELS

Whereas medical models assume abnormal behaviours are caused by some sort of biological pathogen, the environmental models make no assumption about an underlying disease process. Instead these models represent a diverse set of views that primarily emphasize environmental forces (factors external to the organism) as determinants of aberrant response patterns. To the extent that this is true, they can be criticized for not adequately considering the internal state of

Table 3.1   Models of psychopathology

Medical disease model	Assumes that the pathological process occurs within the organism be it genetic, biophysical or psychogenic in nature.
Genetic model	The view that genetic factors are primarily responsible for psychopathology and that heredity disposes the person to abnormal behaviour.
Biochemical model	The view that genetic vulnerability provides the basis for biochemical changes underlying abnormal behaviours.
Neurophysiological model	This model assumes that the aetiology of abnormal behaviour resides in brain structures that are inherited, congenital or acquired.
Psychoanalytic model	The psychoanalytic model assumes that the aetiological origin of abnormal behaviours stems from internal conflicts (intrapsychic) associated with early childhood experiences.
Environmental model	The environmental model focuses almost exclusively on external variables (sociocultural and psychological) as the primary determinants of abnormal behaviours.
Sociocultural model	These models emphasize the importance of culture and social systems as determinants of human behaviour.
Learning model	This approach views both normal and abnormal behaviours as primarily determined by learning and is changeable through the appropriate application of learning principles.
Humanistic model	This model blends together the elements of sociocultural models and learning theories that has existential elements to its orientation toward personality and abnormal behaviours.

an individual and its influence on behaviour, and for viewing people as passive, without any real impact on the environment. Both the sociological and humanistic models deal in variables that are vague and too broad to be either predictive or testable, and neither sufficiently attends to developmental principles or processes. The learning views tend to be mechanistic, molecular and too often generalized from data generated from animal studies. Their attention to childhood usually takes the form of retrospective reinforcement histories that cannot be reconstructed with either the accuracy or precision needed to test their formulations. In their focus on behaviour, both normal and abnormal, they too tend to disregard the internal processes of the individual and to discount and oversimplify the psychopathological process itself.

Although the environmental models can be additionally criticized for using correlational data for making cause-and-effect interpretations, these models (like the medical models) have not only significantly contributed to our understanding and treatment of abnormal disorders, but they also have kept open alternative and promising avenues for investigating the aetiological factors involved in psychopathology. It is unlikely that any single approach will provide the necessary data that will enable us to understand this very complex field. There is every reason to encourage the further development of these and other models in spite of their methodological limitations.

CONCLUSION

Going back to our case study of Gemma we could apply the medical model and hypothesize that Gemma's problems began as a result of premature birth. It is possible that during the course of foetal development something had gone wrong causing her depression or a biological inability to adapt to her environment. However what is more likely based on an assessment and application of the various models, is that Gemma's adjustment problems are rooted in early but long-standing parent–child relationships rather than brain pathology or genetic transmission. Gemma's mother's over-protectiveness and her strong inclination to keep Gemma as dependent as possible appears to have impeded her social maturity. Gemma's father is virtually non-existent in Gemma's life. In his dedication to provide an income for the family he abdicated his parental responsibilities and thus he is a distant, ineffective father figure for Gemma, allowing his wife to assume full responsibility for Gemma's care and welfare. Gemma did have a few school friends but when these friendships drifted her mother did not encourage her independence and growth when she attempted to go to university. Therefore her peer relationships were weak, and her dependency on her mother increased. When Gemma failed she returned home where she could be close to her mother and fed and nurtured by her. Gemma's feelings of frustration and being trapped led to her extreme weight gain and need for medical intervention. Gemma's condition more closely parallels the humanistic model and therefore treatment would be in the form of getting Gemma to become more independent and lose weight so that she has more energy and can interact with her environment on a more positive and self-actualized basis.

Summary

This chapter focuses on the various models of abnormal behaviour and helps students conceptualize the various ways in which abnormal behaviour is classified. Each model was discussed and the various applications of that model were applied to the case study of Gemma. The application provided an understanding of how a model influences assessment and treatment of abnormal behaviour.

Key terms

Conceptual models – a framework that can guide research by providing a representation of theoretical constructs

Concordance rate – a rate established by computing the percentage of cases in which both members of a twin pair manifest the trait in question

Cross-fostering adoption approach – a type of research where a group of children from biologically normal parents are placed in foster homes in which one or both of the adopted parents are affected by a disorder. They are then compared with a group of children placed in normal foster homes whose biological parents evidence the disorder under study

EEG (electroencephalogram) – an instrument used to record electrical activity of the brain by the use of electrodes attached to the scalp

Family risk method – utilizes large samples of relatives of index cases to assess the degree to which a trait is related to blood times and then compares the incidence rates with those found in the normal population

Genotype – the genetic potential of an individual

GSR (Galvanic skin response) – a peripheral measure of the autonomic nervous system that measures the change in skin resistance resulting from alterations in sweat-gland activity

Pedigree studies – consists of tracing the incidence of a trait in all family members over several generations in order to make inferences about the genotype

Phenotypes – the physical features and behavioural patterns of an individual

Study guide
1   Evaluate the differences between the environmental models and the medical models.
2   Research how the various models have been applied to our current mental health system.
3   Investigate what model has been mainly applied to the Mental Health Act.
4   Explore what latest research advances support or refute the neurophysiological model.

Case study in focus
Apply two different models to Gemma, and compare and contrast the various tenets of these theories. How do these models affect Gemma, and does it change our perceptions of her? How would her treatment be different under these two models?

Personal development

Investigate all the models presented in this chapter, observing the advantages and disadvantages of each, and decide which model would be the most stigmatizing and which would be the least damaging to a person who is diagnosed as mentally ill.

Suggested reading

Bandura, A. (1999) *Self-efficacy in changing societies*. Cambridge: Cambridge University Press.

Coll, C.G., Bearer, E.L. & Lerner, R.M. (eds) (2004) *Nature and nurture: The complex interplay of genetic and environmental influences on human behaviour and development*. New York: Taylor & Francis.

Read, J. Bentall. & R. Mosher, L. (2004) *Models of madness: Psychological, social and biological approaches to schizophrenia*. New York: Taylor & Francis.

Rogers, A. & Pilgrim, D. (2006) *A sociology of mental health and illness*. Berkshire: Open University Press.

Rogers, C.R. (2004) *On becoming a person*. London: Constable & Company.

Psychology of Disorders

3

Learning aims

At the end of this chapter you should:

- Understand how stress affects physical and mental health
- Understand the positive and negative aspects of having a mental illness
- Understand suicidal behaviour and how it affects mental illness
- Be aware of the various issues surrounding care and the community

INTRODUCTION

CASE STUDY

Sara is a 42-year-old successful solicitor at a well-established law firm. She has been employed for 11 years and is married with two children aged nine and seven. She was referred by her GP because of her history with ulcer disease. In the past five years she has had nine separate attacks and three required hospitalization. Her upper gastrointestinal tract shows evidence both of an active ulcer and of scarring secondary to previously healed ulcers. Sara felt that although her job was difficult she didn't find it stressful and instead found it challenging. When questioned about her home life she felt that she had a wonderful loving husband and family. She felt it was 'perfect'. However when she began discussing her home life she became visibly anxious and unhappy. She described one incident where her son was being bullied in school and she had to take time off work to attempt to sort out the situation, while her husband who was also a solicitor remained at his job. In the end she decided to move him to a private school, which again took endless amounts of time because the job of locating a new school and getting her son moved was left to her. Sara described how she often felt 'a bit' frustrated because the household chores were left to her on the weekend and even though she had hired a housekeeper, she still had to sort everything out. As she spoke of her children, she became more and more visibly upset and eventually admitted that she often felt like a single parent and her life really wasn't that perfect. Although her career was easy to manage she found that being a parent with very little help from her partner was overwhelming and the only time she found relief was when she had been hospitalized. She felt depressed and sad most of the time and the only relief she felt was when she was at work. She dreaded going home, which then made her feel guilty because she didn't feel as competent as a mother as she was a solicitor.

INTRODUCTION

Psychological factors both influence and are influenced by physical functioning. Mental health and physical health are inseparable and one affects the other. How can psychology contribute to the understanding and management of positive or negative mental health? What are the physiological bases of emotion and how do they relate to health and illness? Can the biopsychological risk factors for illness be identified and what are their mechanisms of action? How does stress affect physical and mental health?

WHAT DOES A MENTAL ILLNESS 'FEEL' LIKE?

The question is as difficult to answer as 'what does cancer feel like?' Do individuals feel 'mental pain'? In general, the feeling of having a mental illness is different for every individual and each person will cope with the progression and treatment of mental illness in a different manner. Mental illness is as individualistic as the people it affects. Symptoms will be similar in certain types of disorders e.g. anxiety, depression etc. but a person's experience of the disorder will be different. Some will recognize that they are losing touch with reality. Some won't; some will recognize that they need to seek professional help, others won't and some will fluctuate from normal states to abnormal states. Others appear normal until they began acting in abnormal ways and never seem to recover, while yet others will have a complete break from reality, become hospitalized and then recover. Every individual will experience the disorder in different ways and it will affect different areas of their lives.

MENTAL HEALTH BEHAVIOUR

Becker and Maiman (1975) proposed a framework in which to predict and manage health-related behaviour which is applicable to mental health. Health behaviour can be seen as an individual's subjective state of readiness to take action and engage in health-related behaviours. The engagement or action is a function of many different factors. The first is the individual's beliefs or perceptions of his or her likelihood of susceptibility to an illness and the perception of the probable severity of the consequences of having the illness. Consequences can be both social and physical. The second is the perceived benefit of the action, in contrast to the perceived barrier to acting. A person's evaluation of the health behaviour, both in terms of its gains or potential benefits in reducing the possible susceptibility and/or severity as well as the possible costs or barriers in terms of physical, psychological or financial distress is important in determining whether a person will engage in a given health behaviour.

A third factor involves access to cues for action. Cues to action are stimuli that trigger appropriate health behaviours. Cues can be either internal, that is perception of bodily states or external, that is stimuli from the environment, such as interpersonal interactions or the mass media. The three factors can be influenced by demographic and psychosocial factors. Diverse demographic, ethnic and social factors as well as personality, can influence health motivations and perceptions and indirectly influence the occurrence of health behaviours.

This health proposal has been useful in predicting health behaviour before illness as well as compliance with medical regimens or prescribed therapies in physical health but its application and usefulness to mental health is also implied. Both preventive and sick-role behaviours can be predicted. It has been argued by Becker that his theory provides a useful framework for intervention. Becker suggests that by assessing which components are below a level presumed necessary for compliance

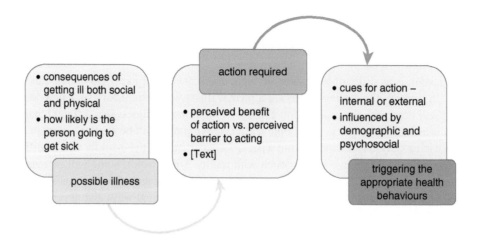

Figure 3.1   A mental health behaviour framework

for a given patient, the health care professional may be able to individualize an intervention to suit the particular needs of the patient. This formula could prove useful for future mental health care and placement in care in the community where individuals need to be assessed for compliance, level of care needed and intervention (Becker & Maiman, 1975).

For example, if an individual perceives that they are susceptible to anxiety and/or depression, when they become depressed it will significantly interfere with physical/mental functioning but generally are unable to activate the cues to action (medication, counselling, seeing the GP) by themselves. A mental health worker can intervene helping the individual and family to recognize early signs and to seek help before the depression becomes problematic and hospitalization is required. In this case, all that may be necessary is to get the family to remind the individual to continue taking their medication or engage in counselling to remain mentally healthy.

THE RELATIONSHIP BETWEEN STRESS, HEALTH AND PSYCHOLOGY

Social and psychological factors are important in the aetiology and maintenance of many illnesses and in the treatment of these disorders. Psychological sources of stress not only diminish our capacity for adjustment, but can also adversely affect our health. Stress increases the risk of various types of physical illness and mental illness ranging from digestive disorders and heart disease to mental disorders such as anxiety and depression (Speilberger, 1979).

The field of psychoneuroimmunology examines relationships between psychological factors, especially stress, and the workings of the endocrine system, the immune system and the nervous system. Psychoneuroimmunology researches the effects that stress may have in the aetiology and treatment of various physical and mental illnesses (Daruna, 2004). How does stress effect the exacerbation and maintenance of various illnesses and their associated social psychological consequences? The majority of research on stress as a response to illness has emphasized the cognitive factors associated with the modulation of the stress response, rather than emphasizing the stress response itself or the nature of the specific environmental stressors (Joiner, Wingate, Gencoz & Gencoz, 2005).

STRESS ASSOCIATED WITH ABNORMAL BEHAVIOURS

Generally the word stress refers to force or pressure applied to something. In psychology, we use stress to mean demand or pressure that is placed on an individual to adjust or adapt. Stress can cause people to respond in abnormal ways or behave in ways that are abnormal in an effort to cope with the circumstances. Stress can also exacerbate current existing mental health conditions. A stressor is a source of stress. Stressors include psychological factors, such as divorce, family problems and unemployment. They also include a variety of other types of issues such as physical illnesses, extreme temperatures (either too hot or too cold) and noise levels. The term stress should be distinguished from distress which refers to a state of physical or mental pain or suffering. Some degree of stress does not appear to be detrimental and for some, a certain amount of stress keeps them active

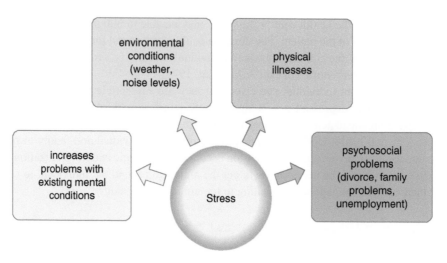

Figure 3.2

and alert. Research on stress has shown that not all individuals have negative reactions to stress (Weinstein, Brown & Ryan, 2009). A certain number of individuals who are exposed to extreme stress do not succumb to stress disorders (Jimenez, Niles & Park, 2010). Stress–illness correlations are small and it appears that there is considerable variability across individuals in the degree to which stress is associated with illness (Belsky & Pluess, 2009). However, for some individuals, prolonged stress that is intense can overwhelm the ability to cope and lead to physical complaints such as fatigue and headaches as well as emotional distress which can further lead to mental health disorders (Cohen & Wills, 1985).

STRESS AND THE ENDOCRINE SYSTEM

Stress can also have a significant effect on the endocrine system, the body's system of glands that release their secretions, called hormones, directly into the bloodstream. When the levels of hormones are too high, they can cause significant health issues. The endocrine system consists of glands distributed throughout the body. Several endocrine glands are involved in the body's response to stress. The hypothalamus, which is a small structure in the brain, releases a hormone that stimulates the pituitary gland to secrete adrenocorticotrophic hormone (ACTH). The release of ACTH then stimulates the adrenal glands which are located above the kidneys. The outer layer of the adrenal glands, called the adrenal cortex, then releases steroid hormones. This group of hormones has a number of different functions. First they boost resistance to stress and foster muscle development. They also stimulate the liver to release sugar, which provides energy for responding to a threatening stressor in an emergency situation. Finally they help the body defend against allergic reactions and inflammation (Tsigos & Chousos, 1996; McEwen, 2000).

The sympathetic branch of the autonomic nervous system or ANS, stimulates the inner layer of the adrenal glands, called the adrenal medulla, to release a mixture of ephephrine and norepinephrine. These substances function as neurotransmitters in the brain but in the body they function as hormones when released into the bloodstream. The two substances together activate the body to deal with an immediately threatening stressor by accelerating the heart rate and stimulating the liver to release stored glucose, making energy available where it can be of use. The stress hormones produced by the adrenal glands help the body prepare to cope with an impending threat or stressor. Once the stressor has passed, the body returns to a normal state. When stress is constant the body regularly produces and releases stress hormones and activates other systems, which over time can strain the body's resources and impair health. Chronic stress can damage many bodily systems including the cardiovascular system and the immune system (Chrousos, 2000).

STRESS AND THE IMMUNE SYSTEM

The immune system is the body's system of defence against disease. The immune system prevents your body from being invaded by microbes that can cause illness and disease. The first line of defence is the mucus membranes which trap and destroy microbes. Microbes that get through are then located and destroyed by the millions of white blood cells, or leukocytes. The leukocytes are specialized to systemically envelop and kill the pathogens like bacteria, viruses and fungi, worn out body cells and cells that have become cancerous. Leukocytes recognize invading pathogens by their surface fragments, called antigens. Some leukocytes produce antibodies, specialized proteins that attach to these foreign bodies, inactivate them and mark them for destruction. Special memory lymphocytes are held in reserve rather than marking foreign bodies for destruction and can remain in the bloodstream for years and form the basis for a quick immune response to an invader the second time around (Rabin, 1999).

Though occasional stress may not impair our health, chronic or repetitive stress can weaken the body's immune system over time. A weakened immune system increases our susceptibility to common illnesses such as colds and flu and possibly increases risk of developing chronic diseases, including cancer. Research indicates that there is evidence that psychological factors affect the course of cancer once established (Sklar & Anisman, 1981; Fox, 1978). Studies have also found a relationship between the loss of a close and important person (Levav et al., 2000) and reduced immune competence and long-term stress and the aetiology of cancer (Jiong et al., 2002; Kvikstad & Vatten, 1998).

Exposure to physical sources of stress such as cold or loud noise, especially when intense or prolonged, can dampen immunological functioning. Other types of psychological stressors have been proven to cause compromised functioning in the immune system from the sleep deprivation that occurs with a newborn baby to final examinations for students. Medical students, for example, show poorer immune functioning during exam time than they do a month before exams, when their lives are less stressful (Moffat et al., 2004). Traumatic stress, such as exposure to earthquakes, hurricanes or other natural or technological disasters, terrorist attacks or other forms of violence can also dampen immunological functioning (Freedy et al., 1992).

Researchers have discovered that one way chronic stress damages the body's immune system is by increasing levels of a chemical in the body called interleukin-6. Sustained high levels of this chemical are linked to inflammation, which in turn can contribute to the development of many disorders, including cardiovascular disease, cancer and arthritis (Lou et al., 2000; Fishman et al., 1998; Yudkin et al., 2000).

Life stressors such as marital conflict, divorce and chronic unemployment can also take a toll on the immune system. Chronic stress also makes it take longer for wounds to heal. Negative emotional states such as anxiety and depression are sources of emotional stress that also contribute to longer wound healing. Social support appears to moderate the harmful effects of stress on the immune system. Newly separated and divorced people also show evidence of a suppressed immune response, especially those who remain attached to their ex-partners (Pennebaker, Kiecolt-Glaser & Glaser, 1988).

Exposure to stress has even been linked to an increased risk of developing a common cold. We are constantly being bombarded with microbes and the immune system can easily fend off the majority of these pathogens, however stress can compromise the system and allow common viruses to overwhelm it. A study conducted by Cohen et al. (1991) found that people who reported high levels of daily stress, such as pressures at work, showed low levels in their bloodstreams of antibodies that fend off cold viruses. Another study found that exposure to severe chronic stress lasting a month or longer was associated with a greater risk of developing a common cold after exposure to cold viruses (Kiecolt-Glaser et al., 1996).

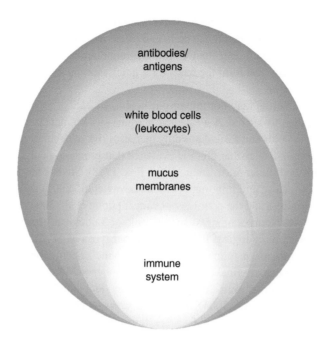

antibodies/
antigens

white blood cells
(leukocytes)

mucus
membranes

immune
system

Figure 3.3

Social support has been linked to boosting the immune system and providing greater resistance to infections and viruses. Researchers found that people who have more varied social relationships with spouses, children, other relatives, friends, colleagues, members or organizations and religious groups, were less likely than others with limited social networks to come down with a cold after exposure to cold viruses. And when they did get sick, they tended to develop milder symptoms. In addition to social support, expressing emotions through writing about stressful or traumatic events may enhance both psychological and physical well-being and perhaps even boost immune system responses (Austenfeld, 2004).

Mental illness has been linked to stress both increasing the chances of developing a mental illness and exacerbating the condition. The brain catecholamines involved in stress are also involved in various mental illnesses such as depression, anxiety and schizophrenia. Regional changes of norepinephrine in the brainstem have been reported to correlate with stress or induced depression of motor activity. In addition, individuals suffering from mental illnesses have been found to have limited social support and an inability to express their emotions on two levels, the emotions connected with the circumstances of having a mental illness and the emotions as a result of suffering from a mental illness (Link & Phelan, 1995).

PSYCHOBIOLOGICAL STRESS

It wasn't until the work of Cannon (1935) that the idea of stress and illness became formalized. Cannon was among the first to use the term stress and clearly suggested that it included both physiological and psychological components. He viewed stress as a potential cause of medical problems and felt strongly that emotional stress could cause disturbances of a physiological nature. He provided a simple description of the sympathetic nervous system in which a threatened organism readies itself for 'fight or flight' producing a heightened arousal state. Cannon believed that stress caused disruption of emotional and physiological stability as well as aiding the organism in survival. The fight-or-flight reaction helped our ancestors cope with the many dangers they faced from a hostile environment and predatory animals. Generally the stress reaction was not one of prolonged activation and once a threat was eliminated, the body reinstated a lower level of arousal and returned to the normal, non-aroused state. The innate sensitive alarm reactions increased the organism's chances of survival and were therefore beneficial.

Selye's stress model is based on his idea of a non-specific stress response that is the reverse of Cannon's ideas which were threat-specific. Selye coined the term 'general adaptation syndrome' to describe a common biological response pattern to prolonged or excessive stress. Selye pointed out that our bodies respond similarly to many kinds of unpleasant stressors, whether the source of stress is an invasion of microscopic disease organisms, a divorce or the aftermath of a flood (Cooper & Drewe, 2004).

The GAS consists of three stages: the alarm reaction, the resistance stage and the exhaustion stage. As an individual becomes aware of a stressor or the presence of noxious stimulation, the alarm reaction is experienced. The individual prepares to resist the stressor. Adrenal activity and cardiovascular and respiratory functions increase and the body is made ready to respond. When reserves are ready, the organism then enters a stage of resistance, applying various coping mechanisms and typically

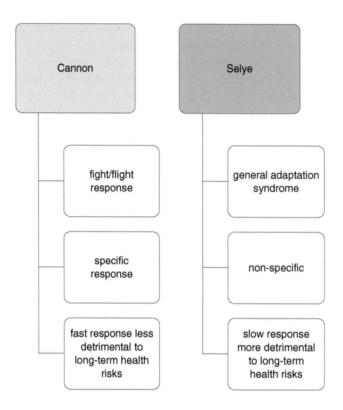

Figure 3.4

achieves suitable adaptation. During this stage, there is a relatively constant resistance to the stressor, but a decrease in resistance to other stimuli. When these reactions are repeated many times or when they are prolonged because of a recurring problem, the organism may be placed at risk for irreversible physiological damage. Selye believed that this is the result of the third stage which is exhaustion. Adaptive reserves are depleted by long-term or repeated conflict with stressors and resistance is no longer possible. The result of the exhaustion phase is likely to be the onset of diseases of adaptation, and illnesses such as kidney disease, arthritis and cardiovascular disease can occur. As the long-term stress response compromises immune function, chronic stress can damage our health, leaving us vulnerable to a range of disease and other physical health problems (Selye, 1955).

PSYCHOLOGICAL FACTORS AND PHYSICAL DISORDERS

Psychological factors can influence physical functioning; physical factors can also influence mental functioning. Physical disorders in which psychological factors are believed to play a causal or contributing role have traditionally been termed psychosomatic or psychophysiological. Disorders that involve psychological components range from asthma and headaches to heart disease. A few different psychophysiological disorders will be discussed.

Ulcers are traditionally identified as psychosomatic disorders. An ulcer is a lesion or sore in the lining of the stomach or in the upper part of the small intestine or duodenum that lies immediately below the stomach. Ulcers are quite common in the general population and it is believed that most are caused by stress. They often go undetected for a period of time because they cause no pain or discomfort until they become chronic. During the intermediate stages the individual will feel mild discomfort ranging from a 'burning sensation' to cramps but will dismiss it as overindulgence. When the ulcer is accompanied by nausea and vomiting the individual becomes aware that there is a problem. If the ulcer perforates (blood vessels break in the walls of the stomach), vomiting of blood will occur which can be serious and always requires hospitalization. Stress causes an overproduction and excessive secretion of acid that is used to digest food. Excessively high levels of gastric secretion of hydrochloric acid are produced outside of the digestive process. The walls of the duodenum and the stomach have a protective mucous lining that is normally able to resist mildly corrosive action. However, if the acid is secreted when food is no longer present, it may begin to eat away the protective mucous lining and an ulcer will develop (Sarafino, 1998).

Another disorder that is quite common and often psychophysiological is headaches. Headaches are symptoms of many medical and mental health disorders. Any type of persistent pain problem, including head pain, can be exacerbated or maintained by psychological factors. When they occur in the absence of other symptoms, however, they may be classified as stress related. The most common type of headache is the tension headache. Stress can lead to persistent contractions of the muscles of the scalp, face, neck and shoulders giving rise to periodic or chronic tension headaches. Such headaches develop gradually and are generally characterized by dull, steady pain on both sides of the head and feelings of pressure or tightness (Holm & Lamberty, 1997).

Most other headaches, including the severe migraine headache, are believed to involve changes in the blood flow to the brain. The migraine headache is a bit different and typically this type of head pain consists of two phases. The first phase is where prodromal symptoms occur. Prodromes are described as visual blind spots, flashing lights or fortification spectra, abdominal pain, vertigo and parathesias of the face or the hands. The second phase is the head pain. This is characterized by the onset of a throbbing or pulsating unilateral pain. The pain occurs most often in the temporal (top of head), orbital (around the eyes) or occipital (back of the head) regions. The head pain is usually accompanied by nausea, photophobia and constipation or diarrhoea. Typical migraines can last for hours or days. They may occur as often as daily or as seldom as every other month (Theoharides, Donelan, Kandere-Grzybowska & Konstantinidou, 2005).

The underlying causes of headaches remain unclear and subject to continued study. One factor contributing to tension headaches may be increased sensitivity of the neural pathways that send pain signals to the brain from the face and head. With migraines, investigators suspect an underlying central nervous system disorder involving nerves and blood vessels in the brain. The neurotransmitter serotonin is also implicated. Falling levels of serotonin may cause blood vessels in the brain to contract and then dilate. This stretching stimulates sensitized nerve endings that give rise to the throbbing, piercing sensations associated with migraines (Fanciullacci, Alessandri & Fanciullacci, 1998).

Many factors may trigger a migraine attack. These include stress; stimuli such as bright lights; changes in barometric pressure; pollen; certain drugs; the chemical monosodium glutamate, which

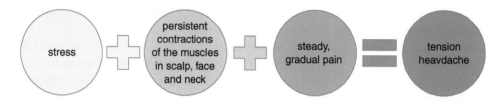

Figure 3.5

is often used to enhance the flavour of food; red wine and even hunger. Hormonal changes before and during menstruation can also trigger attacks and the incidence of migraines among women is about twice that among men (Stewart et al., 1992).

STYLES OF COPING

Why are some individuals profoundly affected by stress, yet others seem to adapt? Even in extreme situations such as a natural disaster a certain number of individuals will be overwhelmed at the event yet others will simply pick up the pieces of their lives and rebuild. The answer is in our coping responses. Coping is defined as the cognitive and behavioural efforts necessary to manage environmental and internal demands and the conflicts around them. Coping is dependent on a wide variety of factors. These factors affect the way we interpret the stressor(s) and include environmental, social and psychological variables. In addition, we must consider the severity of the stressor, the types of adjustment required as well as perceptions of control over the stressor and the positive or negative events. For example the loss of a spouse is a stressor in itself but it also has a variety of life changes associated with that loss; there may be major and significant role changes, financial implications, the necessity of moving house, change in social activities, sleeping habits, eating habits, holiday plans and changes in relationships with others. Depending on how the spouse was lost, e.g. cancer vs. murder, can also affect the individual's perception of the stressor (Carver, Scheier & Weintraub, 1989).

Cognitive factors are assumed to play a major role in emotion and adaptation. If cognitive factors influence the effects of stressful events, the choice of coping patterns and the cognitive, physiological and behavioural reactions to stressors will also be affected. It is the individual's evaluation that determines whether a stressor is benign, harmful or potentially harmful. The evaluation is partly a function of the resources available to the individual to neutralize or tolerate the stressor. The individual continually re-evaluates judgements made about demands and constraints characteristic of various interactions with the environment and the various options and resources they have for meeting the demands. Cognitions about the stressor will determine the individual's stress reaction, the emotions they will experience and the adjustment or adaptive outcome. The extent to which an individual experiences psychological stress is determined by the evaluation of both what is at stake and what coping resources are available (Lazarus & Folkman, 1984).

Table 3.2   Techniques for stress management

Progressive relaxation training	Successive tensing and relaxing of various muscle groups to ease stressful reactions
Relaxation response	The use of a mental device (sound, word or phrase) to activate deep relaxation in a quiet environment, sitting in a comfortable position
Meditation procedures	The use of yoga – consists of a sequence of postures where the person gains substantial control over individual muscle groups
Hypnosis	Use of hypnotic induction to induce deep relaxation
Biofeedback	Utilizing specialized equipment – a person learns to reliably influence physiological responses that are not under voluntary control, i.e. blood pressure, heart rate
Stress inoculation training	Self-instructional method for teaching individuals to cope with stress
Pharmacological treatment	The use of psychopharmacological intervention such as anti-anxiety medication to manage the physiological stress response

Perceptions of control are related to coping. Events that are seen as unchangeable may also be seen as uncontrollable. When control is not possible or when a stressor is seen as unpredictable, greater costs to the individual are likely. Perceived control is associated with fewer or less severe consequences of exposure to stressors which suggests that uncontrollable stressors are more likely to affect health adversely (Lazarus & Folkman, 1984).

When control is not available and if the response-outcome is prolonged, individuals may learn that they cannot affect outcomes and stop trying to do so. Repeated exposure to uncontrollable events 'conditions' individuals to expect the worst and the reaction that this produces is called learned helplessness. Research has found that individuals with learned helplessness experience motivational loss, emotional disturbance and cognitive impairment as a function of repeated exposure to an uncontrollable situation. Research on mental illness and learned helplessness and control has established that one of the biggest problems with putting individuals into institutions for care is that they lose their sense of control over their surroundings which exacerbates the mental condition as they feel that they have already lost control of their mental capacities and now have lost complete control over their lives. If control and learned helplessness are important factors in negative styles what are more positive styles (Lazarus & Folkman, 1984)?

POSITIVE COPING TRAITS

Hope

Hope is the overall perception that an individual's goals can be met, whether this applies to recovering from a physical illness, mental illness or a personal goal or competition. Snyder (2000) defined hope as having three necessary ingredients; goal oriented thoughts, pathways to achievement and agency thoughts.

Figure 3.6

Goal oriented thoughts are clear non-random behaviours that are directed by a goal that can either be long term or short term. The goal must be of sufficient value that it occupies conscious thought and be attainable but also challenging. Pathways to achievement are the routes that are planned to achieve the chosen goal. Goal-directed behaviour will have multiple pathways so that when an obstacle is faced during the course of goal-directed behaviour an alternative plan has been generated. The construct of agency thoughts is the motivational component to hope. Individuals believe that they can initiate and sustain the pathways to the chosen goal. Snyder's emphasis was on thinking and not emotions but the emotional component is a by-product of hope as positive emotions equalled perceived success in achieving the chosen goal and negative equalled perceived failure. Studies looking at hope as a psychological coping mechanism found that individuals with high hope had higher academic and athletic performances, were better adjusted and had better coping mechanisms in dealing with health issues and pain management. The level of hope people have is also related to their perceptions about themselves and their goals. People with higher levels of hope remember more positive comments and events about themselves (Snyder, 2000).

Psychological hardiness

Psychological hardiness is another element to coping and refers to a cluster of traits that may help people manage stress. Three key traits distinguished psychological hardiness: commitment, challenge and control. Commitment is described as a belief in the 'rightness' of what one is doing and rather than feeling alienated from tasks and situations, hardy individuals involved themselves fully.

Challenge is the idea that change was the normal state of things, not sterile sameness or stability for the sake of stability. Control is described as having an internal locus of control and feeling effectual rather than powerless in managing the rewards and punishments of life (Lambert & Lambert, 1999).

Psychologically hardy people appear to cope more successfully with stress by using more active, problem-solving approaches. They are also likely to report fewer physical symptoms and less depression in the face of stress than non-hardy people. Kobasa (1979) suggests that hardy people are better able to handle stress because they perceive themselves as choosing their stress-creating situations and feel they have an element of control. They perceive the stressors they face as making life more interesting and challenging, not as simply burdening them with additional pressures. A sense of control is the key factor in psychological hardiness.

Optimism

The relationship between optimism and health is another positive style of coping. Research suggests that seeing the glass as half full is healthier than seeing it as half empty. Studies looking at this variable have found that optimism is associated with less emotional distress with pain patients, lower likelihood of postpartum depression and higher infant birth weights (Carver & Gaines, 1987; Ferreira & Sherman, 2007). Heart disease patients with more optimistic attitudes showed less depression when evaluated a year later and patients undergoing coronary artery bypass showed better outcomes than pessimistic patients (Kubzansky, Sparrow, Vokonas & Kawachi, 2001; Scheier et al., 1989). If optimism has been linked to physical elements it is likely that this factor can also play a role in mental illness. Another positive psychological trait is resilience.

Siebert (1996) indicated that survivor personalities were characterized by optimism, acceptance of their situational fate, creative problem solving, and the integration of right-brain abilities of intuition and holistic thinking with left-brain analytical thinking.

Resilience

Psychological resilience refers to an individual's capacity to withstand stressors and not manifest psychology dysfunction, such as mental illness or persistent negative mood. Resilience is the ability to avoid psychopathology despite difficult circumstances. There are three basic types of resilience: unique characteristics of individuals who cope well with stress or trauma, the process by which resilience is attained through developmental and life experiences and the different cognitive mechanisms which govern resilient adaptation (Rutter, 1987). The central process involved in building resilience is the training and development of adaptive coping skills. When a stressor occurs the individual makes a cognitive assessment and decides whether the stressor is a threat; when it becomes apparent that the stressor is a danger, coping responses are triggered. Coping strategies can either be focused on the problem or on the emotions that the stressor elicits. Individuals with high resilience cope well with stress and are more likely to see problems as opportunities for growth. Resilience is a dynamic quality where individuals demonstrate active self-renewal, whereas less resilient individuals feel overwhelmed and negatively impacted by stressors (Rutter, 1987).

Table 3.3   Psychological resilience

Terms	Characteristics
Adaptive coping	Ability to 'bounce back'
Hardiness	Have a 'where there's a will there is a way' mentality
Life orientation	Ability to 'hang tough'
Resourcefulness	Have a healthy social support network
Self-esteem	Have a wide comfort zone
Self-concept	Have a wide comfort zone
Thriving	Able to recover from trauma

Community efforts to develop resilience through intervention programmes have been increasingly seen as proactive, preventive and positive approaches to minimizing psychological dysfunction. Low resilience has been correlated with anxiety disorders and illness severity (Rosenbaum & Covino, 2005; Marsh et al., 1996).

CHALLENGES OF MENTAL ILLNESS

Stigma

Suffering from a mental illness causes isolation and sets the person apart from their peers, family and ultimately their community. Mental illness is often a sign of disgrace and shame, often the condition of the individual is kept a secret as it generally makes others feel uncomfortable. Mental illness is not treated with the same concern as other types of illnesses. Friends and family of a person suffering from mental illness do not enquire politely about the progress and treatment. Society often stereotypes people with mental illness. Depictions in the media are rarely positive and generally individuals with mental illness are mocked, ridiculed or feared. Images and derogatory language in the media maintain negative beliefs about mental illness. Due to a lack of factual information and the influence of stereotypes in media, the general public tend to view the mentally ill as unpredictable, responsible for their bizarre beliefs and behaviour, incapable of rational thought, and probably dangerous. When these beliefs filter through society at so many different levels it is not surprising that the mentally ill often find themselves socially excluded and isolated. Their illness causes their friends, family and community to reject them. In their attempts to avoid feelings of disappointment from the people in their lives, they begin to limit and finally avoid all social contacts.

An individual suffering from mental illness often goes through a process called 'labelling'. Labelling is a procedure where the individual becomes known by their diagnosis which then becomes a self-fulfilling prophecy and a life-altering projection (Heatherton, Hebl, Hull & Kleck, 2003). Certain types of mental illness are more acceptable in society than others, for example we are less likely to stigmatize anxiety disorders than psychotic disorders. Anxiety disorders such as post-traumatic stress disorder are viewed by the general population as an illness where the individual is not directly responsible especially if they became ill while serving their country as a soldier. Society generally treats these individuals with respect and dignity and provides treatment and resources to speed their recovery. However a label of schizophrenia is a different matter entirely. We believe these individuals are deviant and somehow responsible for their mental illness. Once a person is designated mentally ill of a schizophrenic type, society, friends and family feel free to disregard their social obligation to the individual which in all likelihood exacerbates the mental illness. The person soon feels excluded and the pressure negatively affects their condition which in turn provokes further negative reactions from those in their immediate environment. The labelling will have long-standing and unhappy consequences for the individual and probably will last their entire lifetime even after they may have recovered fully (Heatherton, Hebl, Hull & Kleck, 2003). Often individuals living with mental illness are discriminated against and they lack funds for services and education and have difficulty finding employment securing housing, or even going on holiday abroad because they are unlikely to qualify for any type of travel insurance.

Care in the community

Resent enthusiasm for these services is the result of a general reaction against the isolation of mental patients from their families and society at large. An individual who is admitted into a mental institution is subject to degradation, shame and humiliation and often must assume a dis-identifying role. Generally, their privacy is violated, their personal environments are invaded and they are required to divulge facts and feelings to strangers. They must adapt to collective sleeping arrangements and doorless toilets. These types of living conditions are not likely to relieve feelings of anxiety, increase self-esteem or enhance treatment. Institutional care can disrupt families, interrupt education and employment activities and cause stigma. It is now generally agreed that the mentally disturbed person should, if at all possible, be treated in the community to minimize stigma and life disruption as well as positively affecting their treatment. The availability of community help can result in a person obtaining treatment as early as possible. Care in the community can also ease the period of readjustment if a person requires hospitalization.

Ideally public mental hospitals should operate within the framework of the local community mental health programme. These services include everything from outpatient clinics to day centres and halfway houses. Trends in health care have seen many changes that have shifted pressure onto community caregivers with these centres now providing complex care.

Health care provided in the community or home setting is multidisciplinary and can include home care nurses, home support workers, dietitians, social workers, speech therapists, occupational therapists and physiotherapists.

The growth of the community mental health concept underscores two fundamental developments. First, the idea that mental health hospitals should not be asylums and placed away from and outside the community. The emphasis should be placed on the treatment of individuals within the community, in facilities ranging from office and outpatient treatment to halfway houses and recreation centres, day hospitals and night hospitals. Second, the nature and degree of the emotional disturbances that require long-term hospitalization has changed with the new types of pharmacological treatment (Mandelstam, 2010).

Each of these two trends has had support from different interest groups. The more traditional mental health or mental hygiene movement has been particularly concerned with mental hospitals and was founded in 1908 by Clifford Beers. Beers was a former mental hospital patient who found his own treatment dehumanizing and wrote a book about his experience. His movement stresses the humane treatment of people suffering from obvious psychotic disorders as well as improving facilities and developing more tolerant attitudes towards present and former hospitalized patients. Unlocked wards, home visits and concern with the families of patients are all part of these newer trends that have grown from this movement.

The second element is that changes and advancements in our care or treatment in terms of new drug therapies have been able to improve the lives of individuals. Mental illness encompasses many conditions including depression, anxiety, phobia, anger management etc. Many of these illnesses are treated successfully outside a hospital environment. Over the past decade research has developed many medications, which help stabilize the mental state of those suffering from conditions like depression. Those who previously required hospitalization have been able to benefit from less restrictive treatment regimes with the help of the newer types of drugs (Means, Richards & Smith, 2008).

The newer movement of 'care in the community' tends to regard mental problems as medical illnesses. Although this appears to be an improvement over the archaic institutional model, it does come with two incorrect assumptions. The first is that physicians (GPs) can distinguish between those who are mentally well and those who have varying degrees of mental illness and that specific disease entities can be expressed in a standardized diagnostic vocabulary that everyone in the health profession will follow. Second, that the sick person's own actions correspond to the physician's diagnosis of their current state of illness and that the individuals who become worse will immediately seek out medical help. Often the safety and well-being of mentally ill individuals is directly dependent upon the patient taking his/her medications as directed and following medical directives. This is where the biggest problem with care in the community comes into play. Many mentally ill patients are not consistent with medications and fail to keep medical appointments and sessions with counsellors. Many more abuse alcohol and/or drugs rendering the prescribed medications ineffective or even dangerous. Frequently, for example, as a schizophrenic patient begins to feel better, he/she decides he/she no longer needs the medicine and begins drinking instead. This results in decompensation or a return of mental symptoms (Sharkey, 2006).

Unfortunately, in programmes where care has been shifted to various community agencies there tend to be difficulties in managing patient care and consistency in care. If an individual changes their current residence, they may no longer be eligible for certain types of services or those services may not be available in their new residence. Another issue is that the more care facilities that are involved in the individual's care the greater the risk that no specific agency will take responsibility for care management. What tends to occur instead is that there is no agency in charge of the individual and their mental health care. Often family and friends give up trying to help out of frustration in trying to maintain and manage care for the mentally ill person. These individuals can then end up homeless or shuffled from one rooming house to another as they are evicted for inappropriate behaviour or failure to pay their rent. Counsellors and social workers with high caseloads find it difficult and frustrating to keep up with the high demands of difficult-to-manage individuals who are mentally ill.

Ideally, care in the community represents a more humane and liberal treatment of mental illness in community-based settings. It may even over time change our stereotypes concerning the mentally

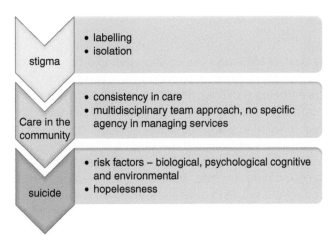

Figure 3.7   Challenges of mental illness

ill as we have more positive contact and see beyond stereotypes. However, in order to be successful there will need to be a growth in facilities staffed with adequate mental health workers to ensure patients take their prescribed medication and function as well as possible. What will be needed in order for this type of care to be successful is to build and staff safe living facilities where individuals suffering from mental illness can be cared for and closely monitored while maintaining their dignity and privacy.

THE EXPERIENCE OF MENTAL ILLNESS

Melinda was found crying at the altar of a church by the priest. She told the priest that God was punishing her and that she was being split into two people. One person was someone she didn't recognize and the other person was her. She told the priest that the bad person was eating her up and soon there would be nothing left. The priest called Melinda's parents and they came and picked her up and took her home. Melinda came to the church so often that the priest eventually asked Melinda's parents to restrict her to once a week. She was constantly found praying and crying and asking God for forgiveness.

When Melinda started university, she began telling her parents of odd incidents; one day when she was walking, she had heard birds talking about her. Another day she said an invisible person was following her. As Melinda became more ill with her mental illness the laughing, happy daughter was changing into someone her parents did not recognize. She spent more time alone, had difficulty interacting with family members and her friends stopped calling and coming over. People complained about Melinda's 'weirdness'.

(Continued)

(Continued)

During the early days of Melinda's illness she often told her parents that she was afraid that she was losing her mind. They often found her crying and distraught. But they dismissed her feelings as being a difficult transitory period between adolescence and young adulthood and thought that eventually Melinda would find her way.

But Melinda never did and in the end she lost all of her dreams of getting married, having children, becoming a nurse, finishing her degree course. Her parents mourned when friends and family members' daughters of the same age graduated from university, got married and became mothers. Instead, their daughter was often hospitalized, spent her days rocking in a chair and smoking cigarettes, and had to be reminded to bathe and eat and take her medication. She did embarrassing things in public and the family didn't like taking her anywhere so she was usually isolated and alone in the family home. They even planned their holidays around her hospitalizations. Eventually she became too ill to be kept at home and was transferred to a long-term care facility.

What does it feel like to have a mental illness? Physical suffering can often be relieved by various pain remedies such as tablets, but mental suffering is never ending. How do you provide relief for a broken/damaged brain? Various drugs are available for symptoms such as hallucinations or anxiety, but they are not cures and at best, provide only temporary relief; the basis for the illness remains unaltered. Melinda, during the early part of her illness, found herself slipping ever closer towards insanity and mourned the mental changes she knew were happening even if others around her didn't yet understand.

A mental disorder involves multiple losses for the individual who is affected. Severe mental health disorders cause losses and/or impairments in personal functioning in a variety of areas such as: vocation, social relations, self-care and independent living skills. There is also a critical change in social roles as mental illness often damages the individual's ability to function in previous roles, such as student, parent, daughter/son, wife/husband or employee (Corrigan & Watson, 2002).

Individuals suffering from a mental illness also experience a loss of purpose and meaning in their lives. Where they were previously working and getting on with their life goals, their mental illness changes their plans and creates a situation where they are destined to be unable to accomplish their goals. Various hospitalizations and the stigma of having a mental illness will force life changes that are unwelcome and unwanted (Link, Struening, Neese-Todd, Asmussen & Phelan, 2001).

An individual who is diagnosed with a mental illness is exposed to many different problems that are caused by being labelled. Generally individuals with mental illness are vulnerable and have fewer coping skills and yet are thrust into situations that are made even more complicated by their disorder: they are abhorred by a society that is fearful of individuals with mental illness; they are often degraded by others and held responsible for their illness; they are denied employment and frequently provided with substandard housing (Erikss, Agerbo, Mortensen, Niels & Westergaard-Nielsen, 2010).

Receiving a diagnosis for a psychological disorder generally means that the individual is branded for life. If they recover, it is still impossible to remove the tarnish; individuals find they are discriminated against and unable to seek employment in many professional occupations even after they have made a full recovery. Employment is often how we define ourselves; teacher, plumber, solicitor, nurse – what we do as work is often part of our self-identification and status. To be denied employment and occupational opportunities is to limit the value we place on ourselves (Dunn, Wewiorski & Rogers, 2008).

Wahl (1995) found that as a result of the damaging consequences of having a mental illness many people are reluctant to seek, accept or reveal psychiatric treatment, since those who do seek treatment or are forced into treatment encounter rejection, discrimination and restriction of opportunity. Rodin and Price (1995) found that once an individual was stigmatized by a mental illness, the individual continued to suffer degradation and was less valued than others and even if they overcame the flaw it did not restore the individual to an unblemished status.

For individuals with mental illness there is a feeling of lost opportunities, loss of pre-illness goals and aspirations, and loss of current abilities with some losing the ability to control their minds and intellect. This often creates a sense of hopelessness and a feeling that they are losing their ability to control their illness and more importantly their lives. Decisions are made for them, often by strangers such as social workers, psychiatrists and other health care professionals. They are prescribed medication with significant adverse side effects. There is a sense of hopelessness, and helplessness and forced dependency are the realities of individuals with severe mental health issues. There is a loss of privacy and respect; they are expected to divulge their most private thoughts and habits, cohabit with outsiders and share personal space.

People who face a persistent mental illness often feel a sadness that they are losing the sense of who they are. There is a loss of self-identity and self-esteem; individuals suffer a heightened sense of negativity, illness and personal failure. Often they feel responsible for their mental illness and feel ashamed. They are also very conscious of being treated and perceived differently by individuals around them (Livingston & Boyd, 2010).

Melinda's family limited her contact with the outside world because they found her behaviour embarrassing and felt it brought shame on the entire family. The family is an important social entity and we expect unconditional acceptance and support, after all, if our families reject us, how can we expect society to be accepting? Research has indicated that the family plays a critical role in recovery. Rejection by one's family must represent the ultimate condemnation and is likely that individuals who suffer this absolutely devastating loss are liable to feel totally abandoned.

Family members are also at risk of social rejection because of the attitudes of society of being contaminated by the affected relative. Phelan, Bromet and Link (1988) found that approximately 50 percent of family members of first admission psychiatric patients concealed the hospitalization from friends and family and when the information was revealed they were avoided and ostracized.

Vellenga and Christensen (1994) found that patients with serious mental illness reported a radical separation from others and an impoverishment of their lives. These individuals also experienced the onset of acute distress that did not relent or diminish; in addition they experienced a loss of self-esteem, relationships and employment. Flanagan (1978) found that individuals with mental illness often found the most important needs in life were not met and that they were mostly dissatisfied with their lives. Perese (1997) had similar findings to Flanagan and additionally found that individuals with chronic mental illness also reported not having and maintaining friendships, felt they had no role in life, no occupation, no employment, no self-identity and were outcasts in their families and communities.

The family of a mentally ill individual are frequently exposed to embarrassing and painful experiences. Torrey (1998) analysed what he believed to be the three main causes for the family to experience ostracization by the community and society. The first is the actual presence of a mentally disturbed individual in the home which makes the home a dangerous, offensive and embarrassing place. The second is that the public blames the family for causing the member's mental health problems either through poor parenting skills or some flawed family dynamic. The various publications by professionals and articles in the popular media often imply or affirm that the family did indeed generate the disorder or are otherwise responsible. Many families have reported their anger, despair and feelings of stigmatization after interactions with clinicians ranging from studied evasion to outright hostility. The third is contamination, the belief that the family acquires some of the characteristics of the affected member and is also tarnished and devalued. The family generally pays a penalty for the association with the mentally ill person and are suspect by the community from that point onward. Under these circumstances the stressors placed on the family are significant. Often they are fearful of community discrimination; there is frequently a lack of professional support and information, which contributes negatively to the family's problems. For parents there is the additional burden of long-term care and future prospects; many parents look forward to the time when their children are self-supporting which is generally not the case with a child who has long-term mental illness.

Another significant dilemma for an individual with mental illness is housing. It is not uncommon that their disorder results in homelessness. Often if they were home owners they are unable to meet their financial obligations due to hospitalizations and unemployment and the result is that they lose their homes. If they were living in social housing, the frequent absences due to hospitalization cause them to lose their benefits. If they reside within families, the toll of multiple hospitalizations and stigma often result in the individual being removed from the family home and placed in social care. The psychological effects of a home and being in familiar surroundings are profound. A home facilitates a sense of security, and provides a physical sanctuary from the external world. Having a permanent home is the primary arena for experiencing companionship and to receive social support from family and loved ones. A home promotes a sense of social connectedness and belonging. When this is disrupted, significant interpersonal losses and despondency can occur. Losing one's home is an emotionally traumatic event that often generates fear, anger, bitterness, mistrust, alienation, anxiety and insecurity as well as loss. The psychological effects are just as damaging as the loss of hope is pervasive with individuals who become homeless as a result of mental illness (Rosenheck, 2012).

To conclude, what does mental illness feel like? It feels lonely, hopeless, and threatening to every aspect of an individual's life. There is a physical and mental separation from family members and the community and it changes the individual's roles. Plans for the future are often destroyed or irrevocably altered. There is a loss of opportunity, employment and future prospects. There is a loss of privacy and respect. Every element of the person's life is in some way damaged or changed. There is a sense of a multitude of losses, and loss of self-identity. The internal and external life of an individual victimized by mental problems is often overwhelming.

SUICIDE

Suicidal behaviour is not a psychological disorder in itself. But it is often a feature or symptom of an underlying psychological disorder, usually a mood disorder. Suicidal thoughts are very common in times of great stress and many people contemplate the ideology of making the pain and problems end. National statistics for the UK reported that in 2009 there were 5,675 suicides; more males than females committed suicides in 2009, 4,304 males to 1,371 females. The suicide rates are the highest among males aged 15–44 and the rate for this group is 18 per 100,000 (Office for National Statistics, 2010).

Who commits suicide?

Generally our attention and focus is on the tragedy of youthful suicide without recognizing that elders are just as vulnerable but less publicized. Despite life-extending advances in medical care, some older adults find the quality of their lives less than satisfactory. As we age we become more susceptible to diseases such as cancer and dementias, which can leave feelings of helplessness and hopelessness that, in turn, can give rise to suicidal thinking. Many older adults also suffer a mounting accumulation of losses of friends and loved ones, leading to social isolation (Juurlink et al., 2004; Waern, Rubenowitz & Wilhelmson, 2000).

These losses, as well as the loss of good health and the feelings of inadequacy may wear down the will to live. Society appears to have an increased acceptance of suicide in older people and it has become an increased risk in this population.

More women attempt suicide, but more men succeed. Males tend to succeed in large part because they tend to choose quicker-acting and more lethal means, whereas women tend to use longer-acting and less lethal means which allows a greater percentage to survive or for someone to intervene. Gender differences in suicide risk may mask the underlying factors. The common finding that men are more likely to take their own lives may be due to the fact that men are also more likely to have a history of alcohol and drug abuse and less likely to have children in the home (Bray & Gunnell, 2006).

Hopelessness and exposure to others who have attempted or completed suicide may contribute to the increased risk of suicide. Adolescents at greatest risk tend to be reared in communities that are isolated from the society at large. They perceive themselves as having relatively few opportunities to gain the skills necessary to join the workforce and are more prone to substance abuse, including alcohol abuse. In addition the knowledge that peers have attempted or completed suicide renders suicide a highly visible escape from psychological pain (Brent et al., 1988).

Why do people commit suicide?

Suicide appears to be such an extreme act that many people cannot understand how someone could focus on a situation or problem to the extent that it would mean taking their own life. The act of suicide would indicate that only someone out of touch with reality would commit such a final act. However, suicidal thinking does not necessarily imply loss of touch with reality, deep-seated unconscious conflict, or a personality disorder. Having thoughts about suicide generally reflects a narrowing of the range of options people think are available to them (Webb, 2010). They cannot find answers to deal with their problems and are often discouraged and see no other way out.

The risk of suicide is greatly elevated among people with severe mood disorders, such as major depression and bipolar disorder. As many as one in five people with bipolar disorder eventually commit suicide. Many psychologists believe that greater efforts toward the diagnosis and treatment of mood disorders would result in lower suicide rates (Chen & Dilsaver, 1996).

Attempted or completed suicide is also linked to other psychological disorders, such as alcoholism and drug dependence, schizophrenia, panic disorder, personality disorders, post-traumatic stress disorders, borderline personality disorder and a family history of suicide. More than half the suicide attempters in a recent study had two or more psychological disorders (Conwell et al., 1996).

Not all suicides are connected with psychological disorders. Some people suffering from painful and incurable physical illness seek to escape further suffering by taking their own lives. These suicides are sometimes labelled rational suicides in the belief that they are based on a rational decision that life is no longer worth living in the light of continual suffering. However, one element in these cases is that the person's judgement and reasoning ability may be influenced by an underlying and potentially treatable psychological disorder, such as depression (Werth & Holdwick, 2000). For example it is not uncommon for depression to be a symptom in many physical types of illnesses such as dementia, multiple sclerosis and cancers.

Other types of suicides are motivated by deep-seated religious or political convictions, such as in the case of people who sacrifice themselves in acts of protest against their governments or for a cause they believe in, or who kill themselves and others in homicide bombings in the belief that their acts will be rewarded in an afterlife.

Suicide attempts often occur in response to highly stressful life events, such as the death of a spouse, close friend, or relative; divorce or separation; a family member's leaving home; or the loss of a close friend. People who consider suicide in times of stress may lack problem-solving skills and be unable to find alternative ways of coping with stressors. Underscoring the psychological impact of severe stress, researchers find suicides to be more common among survivors of natural disasters (Weyrauch et al., 2001; Krug et al., 1998).

The classic psychodynamic model views depression as the turning inward of anger against the internal representation of a lost love object. Suicide in this perspective represents inward-directed anger that turns murderous to the self. Suicidal people do not want to destroy themselves, instead want to vent their rage against the internalized representation of the love object and in doing so end up destroying themselves in the process. Freud believed that suicide was motivated by the death instinct to return to a tension-free state that existed before birth. Existential and humanistic theorists relate suicide to the perception that life is meaningless and hopeless and this is supported by research that finds that suicidal people report that they find life duller, emptier and more boring than non-suicidal people (Ellis and Ratliff, 1983).

In the early nineteenth century, Emile Durkheim, who extensively studied suicide and social environments, noted that people who experienced anomie (lack of social norms), and who felt lost, had no identity and lacked social and community bonds were more likely to commit suicide (Durkheim, 1957). Sociocultural theorists similarly believe that alienation plays a major role in the number of

Table 3.4   Types of suicide

Types of suicide	Description
Those connected with psychological disorders	Depression, schizophrenia, drug and alcohol abuse and various other psychological disorders are linked to suicide
Those connected with physical illnesses	Incurable illnesses such as motor neurone disease, dementias, multiple sclerosis – also called rational suicide
Those connected with terrorism	Individuals who intend to cause great harm usually with explosives/bombings and kill themselves in the process
Those connected with religious convictions	Individuals who sacrifice themselves for their beliefs and make a statement by ending their lives
Those connected with highly stressful life events	Divorce, death of a spouse, loss of job/employment – create despair and individuals want to end their lives

suicides in any given community and/or environment (Taylor, 1982). Our modern society is no longer composed of long-term residents in small intimate communities. Instead people frequently work and go to school in one community and live in a different one. They may commute twenty-five or more miles every day and therefore have very little time to play involved roles in the community where they reside. As a result of active lifestyles and mobility many more people are socially isolated or cut off from their support groups. It is now no longer custom and practice to find extended families living in the same house let alone the same neighbourhoods and communities. City dwellers tend to limit or discourage informal social contacts because of crowding, and fear of crime. It is therefore not unusual when individuals report that they do not have support systems in place at a time of crisis. In other cases family support is available but not helpful. Family members may be perceived as part of the problem, not part of the solution.

Learning theorists focus largely on the lack of problem-solving skills for handling significant life stress (Farber, 1977). Individuals who attempt suicide desire an escape or release from unbearable psychological pain and often believe that the only relief is in the final act of suicide. People who threaten or attempt suicide may also receive sympathy and support from loved ones and others which can become conditioned learning, perhaps making future and more lethal attempts more likely. It is important to be aware that people who threaten suicide are not merely seeking attention and their suicide attempts or gestures should not be ignored.

Social-cognitive theorists suggest that suicide may be motivated by positive expectancies and by approving attitudes toward the legitimacy of suicide (Farber, 1977). There have been many copycat suicides after the death of public figures (Stack, 2003). People who kill themselves may expect that they will be missed or eulogized after death or that survivors will feel guilty for mistreating them. Social-cognitive theorists also focus on the potential modelling effects of observing suicidal behaviour in others, especially among teenagers who feel overwhelmed by academic and social stressors. A social contagion, or spreading of suicide in a community, may occur in the wake of suicides that receive widespread publicity. Teenagers, who seem to be especially vulnerable to these modelling effects, may even romanticize the suicidal act as one of heroic courage (Lewinsohn et al., 2006).

THEORETICAL PERSPECTIVES ON SUICIDE

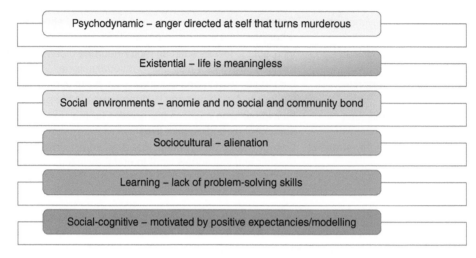

Figure 3.8

Predicting suicide

Friends and family members often respond to the news of a suicide with disbelief or guilt that they failed to pick up signs of the impending act. Often the reality is that even trained mental health professionals find it difficult to predict who is likely to commit suicide. Research has indicated that the crucial factor in determining and predicting suicide is statements concerning the helplessness of the future. Beck et al. (1990) found that psychiatric outpatients with hopelessness scores above a certain cut-off point were 11 times more likely to commit suicide.

Individuals who commit suicide often tell others of their intentions or provide clues. Shneidman (1994) found that 90 percent of the people who committed suicide left clear clues before committing the act, often to mental health professionals. It is not unusual for individuals to sort out their affairs when they become committed to ending their lives; individuals have been found to leave notes and wills and dispose of property and possessions. Family and friends often indicate that the person was in distress but in the days before the suicide appeared to be resolved and calm. Individuals who have made unsuccessful attempts reveal that they felt relieved because they would no longer have to confront the difficulties they faced.

Causal factors of suicide

Suicidal behaviour has at least four categories of causal factors: biological, psychological, cognitive and environmental. Suicidal behaviour is one of the most difficult to understand and is complex in its detail and explanations. It is very individualistic and relies on multiple factors in a variety of combinations that are constantly in flux. The four categories of risk factors can accumulate with enough negative force to result in suicidal ideation and behaviour (Kraemer et al., 2001).

Biological risk factors

There are three lines of research into the biological factors of suicide that clarify the role that they play in suicidal behaviours. The first is research on the functioning of the brain at the cellular level. The second is research into possible genetic bases of suicidal behaviour. The third is research into behaviours associated with gender.

Research has documented a high correlation between suicidal behaviour and clinical depression. Although suicide is also committed by individuals who are not clinically depressed and not all clinically depressed individuals attempt suicide, there is a great deal of evidence indicating that the same areas of the brain responsible for depression are responsible for suicidal ideation. Research has recognized that serotonergic neurons and their target receptors are impaired and that a localized reduction in serotonin could be the underlying predisposition for clinically depressed individuals to act on suicidal thoughts (Arango et al., 2002).

The second line of research into the biological aspects of suicidal behaviour raises the possibility of a genetic basis. Research in this area examined suicide among monozygotic twins and across generations in families. Voracek & Loibl (2007) conducted a meta-analysis of the literature on family history and genetics as they relate to suicide. The authors concluded that the incidence of suicidal behaviour among relatives of suicidal person is higher than in the general population. One study reviewed showed that half of a sample of psychiatric in patients who had a family history of suicide had attempted suicide themselves. They also reported that the results of co-twin studies ruled out exclusively psychosocially based explanations for more frequent completed suicides among monozygotic than dizygotic twin pairs. Their overall evidence strongly suggested genetic contributions to liability for suicidal behaviour.

The third avenue of research into possible biological bases of suicide is found in the gender differences research. One clear behavioural difference between the genders is the fact that, in all developed countries, males complete suicide at higher rates than do females. Suicide is an aggressive behaviour. Research on aggression clearly finds that males tend to be on average more aggressive than females whether this is a result of social or biological behaviour. Therefore the differences in gender may be a result of the aggression directed at the self and biological in nature (Canetto & Sakinofsky, 1998).

Psychological risk factors

Psychological risk factors refer to feelings and behaviours that contribute to suicidal ideation. There are at least four general categories of psychological risk factors that emerge from the literature on suicide. These include depression, feelings of hopelessness and helplessness, low self-esteem and poor coping behaviours (Cheng, Chen, Chen & Jenkins, 2000).

Depression is the psychological classification most often associated with suicidal behaviour. People who are depressed suffer from low self-esteem and show varying levels of hopelessness and helplessness. Although many studies have shown that depression, hopelessness and low self-esteem are positively interrelated, hopelessness is the factor that appears to be the best predictor of the level of the lethality of a suicide attempt. Taken together, these studies indicate that people who dislike themselves and are generally depressed as well as feeling hopeless about the future are at the greatest risk for taking their own lives. The last psychological factor is the lack of healthy coping skills. Often individuals rely on avoidant behaviour such as the use of alcohol and drugs that reflect poor coping abilities and are frequent correlates in the lives of suicidal individuals (Vandivort & Locke, 1979).

Cognitive risk factors

Cognitive risk factors play a major role in suicidal behaviour. Individuals create their identities from their self-concepts of themselves and their views of the world and evaluate their present, past and future options. Studies in the area of cognitions find that suicidal individuals are more rigid and dichotomous in their thinking and narrow their cognitive focus to suicide as the best and sometimes only answer to their problems. Suicidal individuals appear to be unable to consider more positive alternatives and learn new coping techniques. They tend to focus only on the bad or negative events and ignore the positive ones. Suicidal individuals also tend to overgeneralize, having a tendency to apply negative thoughts to all current and future possibilities and to see no hope in their lives. Finally the cognitions of suicidal individuals tend to reinforce misery by giving themselves continuous negative messages relating to their inferiority, hopelessness and helpless state (Beautrais, Joyce & Mulder, 1999).

Environmental risk factors

Many factors in the external environment can increase the risk of suicide. There are three major categories of environmental factors that have clearly been shown to be related to suicidal behaviour. These include negative experiences in the family, loss, and negative life events (Brent, 1995).

Research into child and adolescent suicide have shown that chaotic home lives, the presence of child abuse, alcoholism, unstable parental relationships and divorce are all correlated with increased depression, self-destructive behaviour and suicide. Suicidal behaviour is also more frequent among adults from broken or turbulent homes (Afifi, Boman, Fleisher & Sareen, 2009).

Loss is a clear factor increasing the risk of suicide, and cumulative loss increases it dramatically. The normal reaction to loss is grief, and one of the most typical characteristics of grief is depression. When a normal person loses something that is valued, that person will generally experience mild to severe depression. If multiple losses occur in rapid succession, before an individual has had time to work his or her way through the normal grieving process, their cumulative effect may predispose to suicide (Mitty & Flores, 2008; Conwell & Thompson, 2008).

Negative life events inevitably will lead to loss. Examples of such events are accidents, losing one's job, not being promoted, failing examinations and so on. Each of these negative events has the power to make people examine their prior assumptions. Generally, such examinations lead individuals to lose some of their faith in a just world, their self-esteem, their basic sense of trust, and positive outlook. Paykel (1976) found that negative life events (e.g., separation, divorce and death) differentiated suicidal depressed from non-suicidal depressed individuals more than any other type of loss.

Suicidal ideation, triggering events and warning signs

Suicidal ideation, triggering events and warning signs form an interrelated triad that is present in many suicides. Some individuals will provide no warning signs and have no apparent triggering events. It must be remembered that each individual's circumstances will vary. Suicidal ideation, including the making of specific plans, is usually a first step with the exception of the impulsive suicides. There is a wide variation in the time frames during which suicidal individuals contemplate suicide. They can range from a few minutes to many years. Usually suicidal ideation moves from the general to the specific. The individual begins to consider suicide as a possible coping behaviour and ends by accepting it as the only solution. Once plans are formed, warning signs may be evidenced. The most common warnings signs are verbal threats, self-injurious behaviours and conversations/ statements of closure such as saying good-bye or giving away prized possessions. These warning signs may precipitate a triggering event. A negative life event may occur and become the triggering event, which may or may not be accompanied by warning signs (Holmes & Holmes, 2005).

CONCLUSION

Our case study documents that the cognitive components of stress can cause physiological reactions. In Sara's quest for perfection she became so stressed that she began to suffer from stress-related ulcers. The stressful elements of Sara's job were not what caused the reaction. Instead it was her own belief that she was letting her children down and being a 'bad' parent and her anger at her spouse's lack of contribution. Once she is able to resolve these issues, with more appropriate types of cognitive coping skills, getting her partner to help in the household chores and care of the children, she would no longer use her illnesses to escape.

Summary

This chapter focused on the impact that abnormal behaviour has on the individual. Mental illness is often debilitating and isolating, further complicating the coping styles of the individual. This chapter described how stress affects physical and mental health. The chapter provided an understanding about the 'experience' of a mental disorder and showed how individuals not only have to cope with a compromised mental functioning but that the additional stresses of coping with everyday life events must also be considered by individuals who are already struggling.

LEARNING TOOLS

Key terms

Adrenal medulla – the inner layer of the adrenal glands

Adrenocorticotrophic hormone – one of a group of steroid hormones that is synthesized and secreted by the HPA axis for the metabolism of energy

Autonomic nervous system – part of the peripheral nervous system that is in control of the systems controlling the visceral functions such as heart rate, digestion and respiration rate

Epinephrine – a hormone and neurotransmitter which increases heart rate, constricts blood vessels and is part of the stress response.

General adaptation syndrome – biological response pattern to prolonged or excessive stress

Hope – the overall perception that an individual's goals can be met

Hypothalamus – a specific area of the brain located below the thalamus, responsible for regulating the endocrine system and goal-directed behaviours such as eating and drinking.

Leukocytes – white blood cells which protect the body from invading pathogens

Norepinephrine – a hormone and neurotransmitter which triggers the release of glucose, increases blood flow to skeletal muscle and increases the brain's oxygen supply. It is also part of the stress response.

Psychoneuroimmunology – the study of the psychological elements and the immune system

Psychological hardiness – a cluster of traits which may help people manage stress

Resilience – an individual's capacity to withstand stressors and not manifest psychology dysfunction.

Stress – demand or pressure that is placed on an individual to adjust or adapt.

Study guide

1 Examine the current research in the treatment of suicidal ideation.
2 Compare and contrast the two fundamental developments in the growth of the community mental health concept.
3 Investigate the process of labelling and how the media contributes to this process.
4 Research the phenomena of copycat suicides and explore the various public figures who have committed suicide and how this has affected their fans.

Case study in focus

Identify various other types of risk factors – if Sara lost her job, what elements of risk would she be vulnerable to? What would you say are Sara's positive coping skills? What techniques could she utilize?

Personal development

Clifford Beers is considered to be the founder of the mental hygiene movement. His book *A mind that found itself* details with his struggle within the mental health system of the 1900s. Investigate what types of community health would be available to you in your community. Do you think that the abuses that happened in the 1900s could ever happen again?

Suggested reading

Beers, C. (2010). *A mind that found itself: An autobiography* (4th edn). New York: Forgotten Books.

Lukas, C. & Seiden, H.M. (2007) *Silent grief: Living in the wake of suicide*. London: Jessica Kingsley.

Means, R., Richards, S. & Smith, R. (2008) *Community care: Policy and practice* (4th edn). New York: Palgrave Macmillan.

Palmer, S. & Puri, A. (2006). *Coping with stress at university: A survival guide*. London: Sage.

Physiology of Abnormal Behaviour

Learning aims

At the end of this chapter you should:

- Understand the basics of neuronal structure
- Comprehend neuronal communication
- Understand brain physiology
- Be familiar with the various structures of the brain.

INTRODUCTION

CASE STUDY

Rosemary Kennedy was the sister of the American President John F. Kennedy and the third child out of nine born to Joseph P. Kennedy Sr. and Rose Fitzgerald. There are many different accounts of the level of Rosemary's mental disability but all of them document that she was compromised in some way. Whatever her difficulty may have been she was able to function adequately as she had an active social life and attended school. She kept a diary that records various outings, going to the opera, social events, parties and lunches. As a young child she was reported to be placid and easygoing but as she became an adolescent and young adult she was subject to violent mood swings and the family often had difficulty controlling her behaviour. In 1941, when Rosemary was 23, her father was told of a 'cure' which turned out to be the prefrontal lobotomy. Without consulting the rest of the family he took her to the two most famous individuals who were performing the procedure all over the United States: Walter Freeman and James Watts. The pair discussed the surgery and told Mr Kennedy that the procedure would help to calm Rosemary's mood swings. Believing that his daughter would be cured, he agreed. During the surgery Rosemary had a mild tranquillizer but was awake, and Dr Freeman asked her to recite the Lord's prayer or sing 'God Bless America' or count backwards so that he could estimate how far to cut based on her verbal responses. When she became incoherent he stopped the procedure. Rather than being a cure Rosemary was reduced to an infantile mentality that left her incontinent and staring blankly at walls for hours. Her verbal skills were reduced to an unintelligible babble and she required constant care. She was kept at the Kennedy home for a period of time but was moved eight years later to an institution for the mentally handicapped where she remained until her death in 2005.

PSYCHOBIOLOGY

Psychobiology refers to the influence of psychological events upon biological functioning. The interaction between the two is continuous and they should never be viewed as being independent from one another. In combination with personality factors, environmental factors and social factors, all of these elements interact and form the basis for individual behaviour both normal and abnormal. This chapter will describe and discuss the various brain structures as well as what can take place when these structures do not function properly. Abnormal behaviour is a product of biology, psychology and environmental interaction and it is often difficult to delineate the specific contribution that all three provide. Where possible, examples will be given, but most of these involve medical conditions rather than exclusively psychological factors. However, it is important in the understanding of abnormal psychology as well as an appreciation that medical conditions generally have psychological interactions. For example, cancer is a strictly medical condition, but the disease process influences the cognitions and psychological processes of the individual. It is not unusual for a cancer sufferer to experience extreme anxiety and depressive conditions concerning their condition and the possibility of their demise.

The nervous system

The nervous system controls every move we make and every bit of awareness we experience throughout our lives. It is in control of our mental faculties, psychological interpretations of our environment and biological functioning, and maintains our automatic physiological processes such as breathing and digestion. The nervous system is a means of communication between the body, the brain and the outside world. The nervous system utilizes the bodily senses to collect information that is processed and assimilated and then integrated into memory and response. An intact and properly functioning nervous system allows us to perceive events, incorporate them with previous experiences and other incoming sensations, and then process and integrate the various elements into one complete experience (Bear, Connors & Paradiso, 2006). When a structure or chemical does not work properly as in the case of injury or disease or if the nervous system is genetically flawed, an individual will exhibit abnormal behaviour.

Central and peripheral nervous system

The nervous system is divided into two systems; the central nervous system (CNS) and the peripheral nervous system (PNS). The central nervous system is made up of the brain and spinal cord. The CNS is the system responsible for processing information that is received internally and externally and then provides responses and direction for action. The main function of the spinal cord is to transmit information back and forth from the brain to the PNS (the rest of the body).

The brain is bilaterally symmetrical with most structures being duplicated on the both sides. The majority of the brain systems are crossed, so that neural structures on the left are functionally related to body structures on the right and vice versa; this is also referred to as contralateral (opposite side) (Fitzgerald, Gruener & Mtui, 2011)

The central nervous system (CNS) consists of the brain and spinal cord. The brain weighs 1,400 grams and is approximately 2 percent of the average body weight. The brain is dominated by the cerebral hemispheres which sit on top and surround the brainstem. Brain tissue is different from other types of body tissue in its overall chemical composition. Brain tissue has significantly more lipid (fatty substances) and less protein than muscle and most other organs (Fitzgerald, Gruener & Mtui, 2011).

The inorganic salts, also known as the electrolytes, are present in ionic form in brain tissue and form approximately 1 percent of brain weight. The major electrolytes are sodium (Na+), potassium (K+) and chloride (Cl-), with smaller amounts of calcium (Ca++), magnesium (Mg++) (Lieberman, 2009). Electrolytes are important because they help electrical signals to be conducted in an efficient manner. All our vital bodily functions occur as a direct result of electrical signals being sent from the brain. When this is out of balance, the brain is unable to function as effectively. Electrolytes can be affected by a variety of things such as poor diet, stress, medications and illness (Lieberman, 2009).

The condition of anorexia, aside from known characteristics of weight loss and psychological elements, involves changes that occur in the electrolytes known as electrolyte imbalance as a direct result of lack of dietary contribution. There is a change in the balance of minerals such as magnesium, calcium, potassium and phosphate which in turn causes changes in the electrical signals in the brain. One critical change that affects individuals in a profound way is calcium and potassium which are essential for maintaining a normal heartbeat. An imbalance can cause life-threatening changes and the heartbeat and blood flow are at particular risk. Even after the individual begins to put on weight the possible damage done to the heart and cardiovascular system can be permanent as well as pathological changes in the brain. Research has indicated that parts of the brain undergo structural changes and abnormal activity due to the changes in electrical signals and electrolyte imbalance such as seizures, disordered thinking and peripheral neuropathy (Nussinovitch, Gur, Kaminer, Volovitz, Nussinovitch & Nussinovitch, 2012). There is evidence that even after recovery some of the damage may be permanent (Manzato, Mazzullo, Gualandi, Zanetti & Scanelli, 2009).

The PNS is divided into two parts, sensory and motor. The sensory section carries information to the brain and spinal column from the external environment and from the body's internal organs. The motor section transmits nerve impulses from the brain and spinal cord to activate muscles and glands.

The motor portion of the peripheral nervous system is further divided into two separate systems: the somatic nervous system and the autonomic nervous systems. The somatic nervous system controls the skeletal muscles, which allows voluntary behaviour like talking and walking. The autonomic nervous system (ANS) controls the internal organs of the body: the blood vessels, glands, heart muscle and viscera. The functions of the ANS, unlike those of the somatic nervous system, are generally not under voluntary control, and emotional responses are often reflected in changes in autonomic functioning (Bear, Connors & Paradiso, 2006). For example, when a person is tense or nervous, blood pressure, heart rate and stomach activity change.

The ANS is further divided into two components: the sympathetic nervous system and the parasympathetic nervous system. The two systems are responsible for the regulation of internal organs and glands but it is believed that the parasympathetic system maintains the body at rest while the sympathetic nervous system is responsible for up and down regulation (Bear, Connors & Paradiso, 2006).

Psychosomatic and stress disorders can bring about lasting damage to the body in the form of heart attacks, ulcers and various types of gastrointestinal disorders. How this occurs is that any type of stressor whether it is environmental in the form of temperature or cognitive (psychological stress) requires a form of adaptation or adjustment and produces a stress response. The response is a complex reaction that is composed of physiological, cognitive and behavioural components. Sympathetic and parasympathetic activation have been observed in response to stress. In addition to these responses stress causes a release of hormones and neurotransmitters which exert a variety of effects that in turn cause the physiological disorders. Some affect glucose metabolism and increase blood flow which increases the output of the heart, increasing blood pressure and possibly contributing to cardiovascular disease. When there is long-term secretion of hormones due to stress these secretions can cause harmful effects such as steroid diabetes, infertility, and suppression of the immune system. Stress can also promote the formation of gastric ulcers by increasing hydrochloric acid and weakening the gastrointestinal tract that defends against acid secretion (Haque, Sobhani & Ahmed, 2011). Consequently, the autonomic nervous system is of special importance in psychopathology and abnormal behaviours.

Glia

The CNS (both the brain and the spinal cord) are composed of nerve cell bodies or neurons and non-neural glia cells as well as a variety of other types of cell making up blood vessels, tissue and membranes. Ninety percent of the cells in the brain are glial cells with only about 10 percent being nerve cells. Glial cells are smaller than neurons and have a lower cellular respiration. Glial cells are produced throughout our lifetime whereas neuronal regeneration does not occur in the same quality and quantity, and although it has been extensively documented in lower invertebrates, it has only been hypothesized in human brains under specific laboratory conditions (Ziegler, Segal-Ruder, Coppola, Reis, Geshwind, Fainzilber & Goldstein, 2010).

Glial cells are extremely important in maintaining various functions in the brain. Glial cells provide structural support for the neurons that are similar to the supportive function that connective tissue provides for internal organs in the body. Glial cells also provide a nutritive role by supplying a pathway from the vascular system to the nerve cells that deliver raw materials to the neurons for the synthesis of complex compounds. Glial cells also regulate the balance of ions and contribute to the metabolism of synaptic transmitters (Verkhratsky & Butt, 2007).

When the brain is damaged glial cells migrate to the sites of injury or disease and remove debris as well as dead cells. Glial cells have become an area of clinical interest because it is believed that they may form many of the tumours that occur in the brain. Research has not yet determined why this occurs but it appears to be correlated with brain injuries in the same areas (Ziebell, & Morganti-Kossmann, 2010). Glial cells can also be detrimental instead of helpful as they sometimes respond to brain injury by changing their size and shape which can cause oedema, further damaging neurons and brain structures (Denes, Thornoton, Rothwell & Allan, 2010).

Finally, glial cells provide neurons with myelin. Some glial cells wrap around axons, forming myelin sheaths. The production of the glial wrapping is called myelination. The sheathing of the axons affects the speed of conduction of neural impulses. In between the segments of myelin are small gaps in the coating. Such a gap, where the axon membrane is exposed, is called a node of Ranvier (Verkhratsky, 2007).

Anything that interferes with the myelin sheath can have tragic consequences for the individual as it can cause various types of diseases such as multiple sclerosis which is caused by loss of myelin on the axons of the brain. Multiple sclerosis results in loss of muscle control, vision, balance and sensation. In the disease the body's immune system destroys the myelin sheath that is wrapped around the axon, sheath insulating the nerves and assisting in the conduction of nerve impulses. Although the myelin can regenerate, it isn't able to restore itself rapidly enough to replace the deterioration that occurs (Olek, Hohol & Weiner, 2004).

Multiple sclerosis gets its name from the build up of scar tissue called scleroris. The scar tissue builds up and disrupts or halts electrical signals and it is the breakdown of communication between the motor neurons that causes the vast majority of the symptoms. The types of MS and severity and course vary widely but generally the location of the scarring and extent of demyelination is directly correlated to the severity of the symptoms (Olek, Hohol & Weiner, 2004).

The psychological effects of MS cannot be ignored and are important to consider because the stress of living with a chronic illness can lead to emotional instability in the form of depression and anxiety. The psychological elements can affect the course of the disease and it becomes cyclical, causing further immune suppression and progressive demyelination.

NEURONS

A complete cell with its cell body and fibres is called a neuron. The word nerve refers to a collection of nerve fibres not including the cell bodies. Collections of nerve cell bodies are called nuclei if they are inside the CNS and nerves if they are outside the CNS. The neurons in the CNS are highly specialized and do two things:

1 receive information in the form of electrochemical impulses from sensory receptors and other sensory neurons, and
2 transmit electrochemical impulses called nerve impulses to other neurons or to effectors in the muscles and glands (Nicholls, Fuchs, Martin & Wallace, 2001).

The neuron is responsible for communication/information that is both chemical and electrical in nature. Although there are many different types with different specializations they all work in combination to keep the organism healthy and functioning correctly. When something goes wrong at this level there are generally widespread symptoms depending on area of the brain that is affected.

A conventional neuron inside the central nervous system consists of three structures: a cell body which contains the nucleus and is referred to as the soma, branched extensions called dendrites, which receive information from other cells and a long fibre that transmits activity to other neurons or to effectors (muscles and glands) which is called the axon. Neurons can come in many different shapes and varieties depending on the specialized jobs they perform (Nicholls, Fuchs, Martin & Wallace, 2001).

The most common type of neuron in the CNS is the multipolar neuron but there are other types. In a multipolar neuron the somatic membrane gives rise to the trunks of many dendritic trees. In bipolar neurons the somatic membrane gives rise to one axon and one dendritic tree at opposite ends. Unipolar neurons have only one stalk that leaves the soma and divides into two branches a short distance away (Nicholls, Fuchs, Martin & Wallace, 2001).

Unipolar and bipolar neurons detect and transmit sensory events and information occurring in the environment and communicate this information to the central nervous system. All this information is sent electrochemically which means that chemicals cause an electrical signal to be generated. We will first discuss the structure of the neuron and then discuss how the communication is transmitted.

The structure of the neuron

Within each neuron is a nucleus, a membrane that surrounds the cell and an internal fluid environment called the cytoplasm. The nucleus contains the chromosomes which consist of long strands of deoxyribonucleic acid (DNA). DNA is the hereditary material in humans and you can think of it as being the 'blueprint' for all the individual characteristics that make up who you are. Chromosomes are the structures that contain our genes. Genes contain the formulas for the synthesis of individual proteins which are important in cell function. Proteins are important as they provide structure for the cell and also serve an enzymatic function within the cell. They can cause particular molecules to join together, split apart or remain intact. They also determine what will be produced from the raw materials depending on the needs of the cell. Genes contain the individual instructions that tell our bodies how to develop and function as well as governing our physical characteristics such as eye colour (Davies & Morris, 2006).

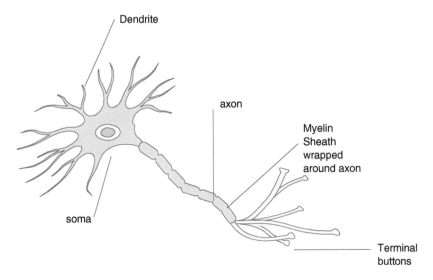

Figure 4.1

Humans have 23 pairs of chromosomes and a change in this number can cause serious problems with growth, development and function. An example of having an extra chromosome is the condition known as Down's syndrome. Downs's syndrome is characterized by specific physical abnormalities (flattened nose, small ears and mouth, upward slanting eyes), cognitive abnormalities that can range from profound mental retardation to mild and abnormal physical conditions (heart abnormalities, gastrointestinal abnormalities, eye problems and hypothyroidism). Down's syndrome is the most common single cause of human birth defects (Wynbrandt & Ludman, 2008).

Individuals who have too few chromosomes will have a condition called Turner's syndrome. Turner's syndrome affects only females and is found in about one in every 2,500 births. It has varying effects that are dependent upon how many of the body's cells are affected by the changes in the missing chromosome but it is characterized by growth problems, sexual development issues, kidney abnormalities, high blood pressure, heart problems, diabetes and thyroid problems. Common physical features that occur are a 'webbing' of the neck, drooping of the eyelids, ears that are set lower than usual on the sides of the head (Wynbrandt & Ludman, 2008).

Neuronal communication

The basic message an axon carries is called an action potential. The action potential is a brief electrical/chemical event that starts at the end of the axon next to the cell body and travels towards the terminal buttons. Nerve impulses cross the interconnections between nerve cells (synapses) in only one direction, from the axon of one cell to the cell body or fibres of another. Axons have a surrounding myelin sheath which is important for the proper functioning of the nerve cell and the speed of the nerve impulses and is produced by the glial cell. The initial portion of the axon is unmyelinated as it leaves the cell body and is called the axon hillock. The presynaptic axon terminals at the distal end are thin and unmyelinated as they branch and terminate adjacent to other neurons. The point of contact between the tip of the axon of one neuron and a dendrite of another is called a synapse. The axon tip is called a terminal button and does not quite touch the dendrite of the next neuron, at the synapse; a tiny gap, the synaptic cleft, separates them. Information is transmitted from the axon to the dendrite (of the nearby neuron) by the release of a chemical from the terminal buttons called neurotransmitters. This chemical either excites or inhibits the receiving cell and helps to determine whether a nerve impulse will occur in the axon of an adjacent cell (Levitan & Kaczmarek, 2001). We will discuss neurotransmitters a bit later in the chapter; first it is necessary to discuss the specifics of how an action potential begins.

An individual neuron receives information from the terminal buttons of axons of other neurons and the terminal buttons of its axons form synapses with other neurons. A single neuron may receive information from dozens or even hundreds of other neurons, each being capable of forming a large number of synaptic connections. The neurotransmitters diffuse across the synaptic gap and reach a corresponding nerve impulse in the dendrite of the adjoining cell (Levitan & Kaczmarek, 2001).

TRANSPORTATION OF SUBSTANCES

Proteins are also involved in the transportation of substances within the cell in order to create the chemicals needed in neurotransmitters. Long protein strands called microtubules help to transport substances from one end of the axon down to the terminal buttons. In the manufacturing of some neurotransmitter substances, terminal buttons need some items that can only be produced in the soma. In these instances the microtubules transport these items rapidly and efficiently through the axoplasm (Levitan & Kaczmarek, 2001).

Substances can be moved either from the soma to the terminal buttons called anterograde (moving forward) axoplasmic transport or from the terminal buttons back to the soma called retrograde (moving backward) axoplasmic transport. Energy for both forms of transport is supplied by adenosine triphosphate (ATP) which is produced by the mitochondria. The mitochondria is located in the cytoplasm of the cell and its major function is to produce ATP, break down nutrients such as glucose and to provide the cell with energy (Levitan & Kaczmarek, 2001).

The outside of the cell is also immersed in a fluid which is called extracellular fluid. The extracellular fluid is made up of fluid and plasma and provides energy and nutrients to the cell and then carries the waste products away. The fluid on the inside of the cell is called intracellular fluid and has a slightly different chemical make-up from the extracellular fluid that is outside of the cell. The cell membrane is not equally permeable to all substances inside and outside the cell; there are slight differences (Levitan & Kaczmarek, 2001). The difference in chemical structure between extracellular and intracellular fluids is important for understanding how neurons work and how they communicate.

Both the extracellular fluid and intracellular fluids are made up of the following elements but in differing amounts: sodium (Na+), Potassium (K+), Calcium (Ca2+), chloride (Cl-) and hydrogen carbonate (HCO3-26). Each element has a charge associated with it, called an ion. These charges can be either negative or positive and just like magnets, ions of the same sign repel each other and ions of opposite signs attract each other. Each element is electrically active and whether an ion is positive or negative determines the influences that it exerts, i.e. the direction of its movement in the solution. The effect of such attraction and repulsion is that if there are no other factors operating to move them, electrical charges become evenly distributed inside and outside the cell (Levitan & Kaczmarek, 2001).

The membrane potential

As a result of the unequal distribution of ions on each side of the membrane, there is a small electrical voltage across the membrane that is negative. This is called the membrane potential and because it is negative it is polarized. The membrane potential functions very much like a battery and provides power to the cell. The membrane potential is held at a stable value and this is called the resting potential. This voltage, a magnitude of –60 mV to –70mV (mV = millivolt or one-thousandth of a volt) tends to cause slight movement of ions across the cell membrane.

The intracellular fluid of the cell is composed slightly differently than the outside so the interior of a cell is negative with respect to the outside of the cell. As a result of the membrane potential, positive ions such as sodium and potassium tend to move from the outside of the cell to the inside and negative ions tend to move out (Levitan & Kaczmarek, 2001).

Concentration gradient

As well as the membrane potential there is another force that moves substances across the membrane of the cell and that is a concentration gradient for sodium and potassium. The concentration gradient tends to move sodium into the cell and potassium will tend to move out of the cell. The concentration gradient is always specific to a given substance. The net force of moving an ion across a membrane depends upon both the voltage and the concentration gradient for that ion. Sodium and potassium will move across the membrane to the extent that there is not a stronger force pulling them in the opposite direction and the membrane is permeable to them. Typically the cell membrane will permit a slight flow of sodium and potassium; however, the permeability to potassium is slightly greater than sodium (Levitan & Kaczmarek, 2001).

Pumps

Because the concentration gradient tends to continuously move potassium out of the cell, the cell would eventually become unbalanced with all the sodium on the inside of the cell membrane and all the potassium on the outside of the cell membrane. To correct this imbalance there is an additional process involved in each cell which is called the sodium-potassium pump. Across the membrane of the neuron, the pump expels sodium from the cell and pulls in the potassium. Over time, this pump will counter the tendencies to break down the differences in ion concentration between inside and outside as well as across the cell.

The sodium-potassium pump is not really a mechanical pump. Instead it is a chemical reaction that requires enormous amounts of energy to maintain the difference in ion concentration and this energy is provided by the mitochondria (Levitan & Kaczmarek, 2001).

TRIGGERING AN ACTION POTENTIAL

An action potential can be triggered by the movement of positive ions into the neuron, which moves the membrane potential in a positive direction away from the negative resting potential: this is called depolarization. The positive movement shifts the membrane potential from a negative charge towards zero moving away from the polarized value. At some point the voltage reaches the threshold and the action potential is triggered. A change starts to occur which characterizes the action potential. The change consists of a rapid move of the voltage across the membrane from a negative value, through zero to a positive value and then a rapid return to the original negative value. Incoming sodium makes the inside of the cell more positive, which increases sodium and sodium permeability, causing even more sodium to move inside the cell (Nicholls, Fuchs, Martin & Wallace, 2001).

The action potential moves along the axon influencing adjacent locations to open sodium channels, which moves the membrane potential in a positive direction, causing a new action potential to occur in a neighbouring location. The new action potential appears just as the instigating action potential is dying out. The action potential causes the release of the neurotransmitters across the cleft and produces electrical changes in the postsynaptic membrane (Nicholls, Fuchs, Martin & Wallace, 2001).

Many different neurotransmitters have been identified in the brain, including acetylcholine, dopamine, serotonin and glutamate to name just a few. The electrical changes in the postsynaptic membrane determine whether the postsynaptic cell will be excited or inhibited. The surface of the postsynaptic membrane is different from adjacent regions of the membrane. It contains special receptor molecules that capture and react to molecules of the neurotransmitter. Numerous synapses cover the surfaces of dendrites and of the cell body (Nicholls, Fuchs, Martin & Wallace, 2001).

LAW OF AXONAL CONDUCTION OR THE ALL-OR-NONE LAW

The all-or-none law states that an action potential either occurs or does not occur; once it is triggered, it is transmitted down the axon to its end.

An action potential always remains the same size, without growing or diminishing. A single action potential is not the basic element of information, rather the frequency of action potentials is represented by an axon's rate of firing. The all-or-none law is supplemented by the rate law. The glial cells provide the axons with myelin. Myelin speeds up the rate that the action potentials are transmitted along the axon. Along the axon are gaps at evenly spaced intervals that are called the nodes of Ranvier. At the node of Ranvier, the axon is unmyelinated and comes into contact with the extracellular fluid. The axon then moves the impulse to the next node of Ranvier so it is able to hop from node to node. The impulse is conducted passively and gets re-triggered at each node. The advantage is that the action potential is faster because the transmission between the nodes is very rapid (Nicholls, Fuchs, Martin & Wallace, 2001).

NEUROTRANSMITTERS

Neurotransmitters are manufactured in the cell body of the neuron and then transported down through the axon, packaged and stored in the axon terminal where it waits to be released through an electrical/chemical impulse. Neurotransmitters are a chemical that is released by neurons and is used for communication. These chemicals are released from one neuron at the presynaptic nerve area and then cross the synapse where they interact with the next neuron at a specialized site called a receptor. The action may either be excitatory (depolarization) or inhitory (hyperpolarization). An excitor makes it more likely that an action potential will occur (Wang & Sobie, 2008).

There are two basic types of neurotransmitters: small and large. The small neurotransmitters are made up of several different types of materials whereas the large neurotransmitters are all peptides. Small-molecule neurotransmitters are synthesized in the cytoplasm of the terminal buttons and packaged in the synaptic vesicles. Once filled with neurotransmitter, the vesicles are stored in clusters right next to the presynaptic membrane. The larger peptide neurotransmitters are assembled in the cytoplasm of the cell body and then packaged and transported by microtubules to the terminal buttons (Wang & Sobie, 2008).

An electrical nerve impulse is carried down the axon to the terminal buttons which then causes the release of the neurotransmitter substance into the synaptic cleft and on to an adjacent postsynaptic neuron. The neurotransmitter then activates the receptors on the postsynaptic neuron. The neurotransmitter is then released back into the synaptic cleft where it is either metabolized (degraded) or taken back up into the terminal of the presynaptic cell (Wang & Sobie, 2008).

The differences between the smaller neurotransmitters and the larger neurotransmitters (peptides) are in the patterns of release and receptor bindings which suggest that they serve different functions. The smaller neurotransmitters tend to be released into specific synapses and then activate either ionotropic or metabotropic receptors that act directly on ion channels. Ionotropic receptors are quick acting while the metabotropic are slower. The larger neurotransmitters tend to be released diffusely and bind to metabotropic receptors that act through second messengers. The function of the smaller neurotransmitters appears to be the transmission of more rapid, brief excitatory or inhibitory signals to adjacent cells, while the function of the larger neurotransmitters is the transmission of slow, diffuse, longer-lasting signals (Wang & Sobie, 2008).

Understanding the various neurotransmitters, their receptors, locations and interactions with each other as well as how the environment affects them has been central in the design of medications for the treatment of mental illness. Therefore they play a vital role in the discussion of abnormal behaviour.

TYPES OF NEUROTRANSMITTERS

There are four classes of small-molecule neurotransmitters: the amino acids, the monoamines, the soluble gases and acetylcholine. The large-molecule neurotransmitters act as neurotransmitters as well as neuromodulators and have little direct activity by themselves, but rather modulate action of other neurotransmitters. Large molecule are derived from proteins formed in the cell body and are first processed in the endoplasmic reticulum and moved to the Golgi apparatus before being secreted. They are generally a combination of two or more amino acids joined by peptide bonds. There have been more than 50 peptides that have been identified (Wang & Sobie, 2008).

Examples of large-molecule neurotransmitters are: Substance P that is active during inflammation and pain transmission in the PNS and endorphins that are endogenous opiates that suppress pain, cause euphoria and regulate responses to stress.

Amino acid neurotransmitters

The amino acids are the molecular building blocks of proteins. This group of neurotransmitters are generally fast-acting and are directed synapses in the CNS. Glutamate and GABA are examples among others in this classification. Glutamate is the most prevalent excitatory neurotransmitter in the central nervous system and GABA is the most prevalent inhibitory neurotransmitter. GABA is the neurotransmitter that helps stimulate relaxation and sleep and stabilizes the brain and is generally an inhibitory neurotransmitter. GABA helps to control anxiety and has been found to be at lower levels in people with disorders such as multiple sclerosis. Individuals with panic anxiety, depression and bipolar disorders have been found to have low GABA levels. Glutamate is important for learning and memory and helps to enhance signal transmission between neurons, which is important with long-term memory. Glutatme is responsible for brain development and must be present in the right concentrations, in the right areas, at the right times. Glutamate is the neurotransmitter most responsible for the occurrence of epileptic seizure activity (Powis & Bunn, 1995).

Monoamine neurotransmitters

Monoamines are a class of small molecule neurotransmitters and are probably the transmitter substances that most students are familiar with because they are most associated with mental illness when they do not function properly. Monoamine neurotransmitters are slightly larger than amino acid neurotransmitters, and their effects tend to be more diffuse. The monoamine group is divided into two classifications; the catecholamines and the indolamines.

Under the catecholamine classification are the neurotransmitters dopamine, norepinephrine and epinephrine. Each of these is synthesized from the amino acid tyrosine.

Dopamine is involved in cognition, motivation, sleep, mood, attention and learning. Dopamine is the neurotransmitter most associated with motivations as well as addictive behaviours. Attention deficit disorders are associated with dopamine and it is the neurotransmitter most associated with schizophrenia and Parkinson's disease. Individuals with Parkinson's dis-

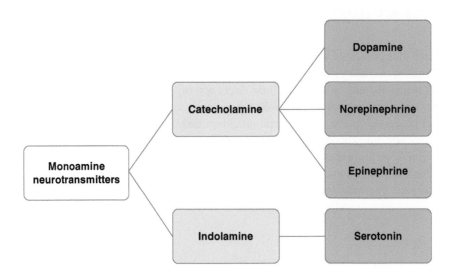

Figure 4.2   The monoamine neurotransmitters

ease have too little dopamine in their systems. Individuals with schizophrenia have too much or have receptors that are extremely sensitive. Dopamine levels can be affected by stress, sleep disorders and poor sleeping habits (Powis & Bunn, 1995).

Norepinephrine and epinephrine are the neurotransmitters that are most associated with the fight-or-flight response, which are adaptive short-term activation/stress responses. Norepinephrine is also associated with learning and memory and influences the metabolic rate. Both norepinephrine and epinephrine play a role in increasing heart rate and blood flow to the skeletal muscles, and triggering the release of glucose for energy.

There is only one neurotransmitter in the indolamines classification, which is serotonin. Serotonin is manufactured from the amino acid tryptophan and plays a role in mood and sleep. This neurotransmitter is responsible for the normal patterns in sleep, regulating memory, learning, blood pressure as well as appetite and body temperature. Low levels of serotonin are associated with depression, aggressive behaviour, obsessive-compulsive disorders and anorexia/bulimic disorders (Powis & Bunn, 1995).

Soluble-gas neurotransmitters

The soluble gases are another group of small molecule neurotransmitters. The two most important soluble-gas neurotransmitters in this classification are nitric oxide and carbon monoxide. Nitric oxide functions as a regulator and mediator of many processes in the nervous system, immune system and cardiovascular system. Nitric oxide also functions in memory formation in the brain, increases glutamate release and is a vasodilator. It is somewhat different as it is not synthesized in advanced and packed and instead is formed on demand and acts immediately. Its action is extremely brief and then combines with oxygen and water to form inactive nitrates. It is the neurotransmitter that has been implicated in stroke and neurodegenerative diseases. Carbon monoxide plays a role in neovascular growth and acts as an anti-inflammatory. It also plays an important role in modulating physiological functions such as the release of hypothalamic hormones and regulating vascular tone, and serves as a protective factor in hypoxia (Xue, Farrugia, Miller, Ferris, Snyder & Szurszewski, 2000).

Acetylcholine

Acetylcholine was the first neurotransmitter to be discovered, in 1914. It is a small molecule neurotransmitter that is created by adding an acetyl group to a chorine molecule. Acetylcholine is not made from amino acids like the other neurotransmitters and instead the building block, choline, is taken directly from food. Acetylcholine functions in the PNS and the CNS and has a wide variety of functions. In the PNS it activates muscles and plays a major role in the autonomic nervous system. In the sympathetic and parasympathetic nervous systems it is used to signal muscle movement. In

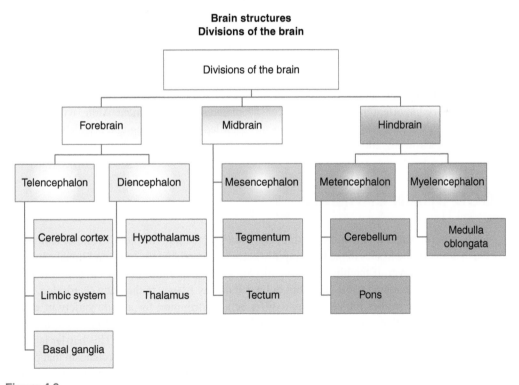

Figure 4.3

the central nervous system it plays a role in arousal, sensory perceptions and attention. Acetylcholine is the neurotransmitter that is also plays a large role in learning and memory and is important for the formation of declarative memories (memories that are consciously recalled). Some of the many functions that this neurotransmitter regulates are: the regulation of neuroendocrine function, the regulation of REM sleep cycles and the conduction of pain. Acetylcholine is the neurotransmitter most associated with Alzheimer's disease (Powis & Bunn, 1995).

STRUCTURES OF THE BRAIN

Why are the structures of the brain important to abnormal function? Understanding the various structures is important to understanding why abnormal behaviour occurs and allows us to understand the structures involved when things go wrong. The various structures have specialized arrangements and functions. Therefore it is important to understand the significance of each structure and how it functions and how it is interrelated to the various other structures in the brain. All of our emotions, thoughts and feelings such as love, hate, fear, anger and sadness are controlled by the brain. The various structures receive, interpret and direct sensory information that is transmitted from the external environment, encoded and then processed by the brain. Every area has a specialized function and although there is some overlap, each area is specialized and developed for a purpose.

The CNS is encased in bone with the brain covered by the skull and the spinal cord is encased by the vertebral column. The brain is the most protected organ of the body; not only is it encased in a bone covering but it is also surrounded by a fluid to protect it from injuries. The brain is a very delicate structure and has the texture of jelly. It is easily damaged. When the brain is removed from the skull the fluid drains and it folds upon itself much like a dried sponge. The fluid surrounding the brain is very important in maintaining a consistent and safe environment. Along with the protective structure and fluid, the brain is also chemically guarded by something that is called the blood-brain barrier (Frackowiak, 2004).

BLOOD-BRAIN BARRIER

Early experimenters found that when blue dye was injected into the bloodstream of animal subjects the majority of the tissues in the body rapidly became stained, but the brain and spinal cord remained unstained. However, if the blue dye was injected directly into the fluid of the brain the dye would circulate throughout the entire brain but did not stain any tissues in the body (Pardridge, 2006).

Various other studies found the same differential distribution for a wide variety of compounds and it was noted that a special barrier existed between blood vessels and brain tissue which prevented the diffusion of many substances from the body into brain tissue. This barrier is termed the 'blood-brain barrier'. The blood-brain barrier can be viewed as a safety mechanism that protects the brain and maintains a stable chemical environment. Without this mechanism damaging substances could freely enter the brain through the bloodstream causing significant injury to the neurons and various structures (Pardridge, 2006). For example, without the blood-brain barrier, even the slightest viral infection such as flu could enter and attack the delicate structures of the brain causing permanent damage. Encephalitis is a relatively rare condition that is caused by a viral infection that crosses the blood-brain barrier and causes irritation and swelling of the brain. This is often a life-threatening condition as the brain will sustain damage that destroys nerve cells and causes bleeding.

The blood-brain barrier is selectively permeable and has capillaries that fit very tightly together so that most substances cannot leave the blood. Some substances must be actively transported through the capillary walls by special proteins. Other substances such as lipid soluble compounds, oxygen and carbon dioxide are allowed to pass freely, while others such as sodium and potassium have long delays so that the chemical balance of the brain is maintained and the transmission of information between the neurons is not affected (Pardridge, 2006).

METABOLISM

Neurons have a very high rate of metabolism and no viable means of storing nutrients, so they must be constantly supplied or they will quickly die. When food is ingested it is broken down into component substances by the processes of digestion and then transported to all the cells in the body via the bloodstream. The most common food substance carried by the blood is glucose which is a sugar derived from natural carbohydrates. The actual process of metabolism occurs separately in all individual cells of the body. Each cell contains the structures to break down glucose for the production of energy. The cells of the body are able to store energy in the body tissue but brain cells do not have this ability. The energy requirement of brain tissue is constant and if anything disrupts the flow of nutrients and oxygen the brain is unable to function for very long.

If oxygen is withheld from the brain, the supply of nutrients and oxygen will be depleted in approximately 10 seconds and shortly thereafter neuronal death will begin to occur. Although the brain is about 2 percent of the entire body weight it consumes about 25 percent of all the oxygen. The brain's metabolism is almost entirely restricted to the utilization of glucose. The brain is very dependent on stable and adequate supplies of oxygen and glucose and can be easily damaged and lose function when the supplies are withheld and/or depleted (Dwyer, 2002).

PERIPHERAL NERVES

The nerves lying outside the spinal cord are called peripheral nerves and contain both incoming sensory fibres and outgoing motor fibres. The incoming sensory fibres are called afferent fibres and carry information from receptors in the skin, muscles and joints to the spinal cord. The outgoing motor fibres are called efferent fibres and communicate activity from the spinal cord and brainstem motor neurons to muscle fibres in the body. These nerves help to process information from the external environment and direct and process it to the appropriate structure in the brain (Frackowiak, 2004).

MENINGES

The CNS is covered by three layers of tough protective connective tissue called the meninges. The function of the three layers is to protect the central nervous system; however they also provide the brain with nourishment and a cushioning effect. The meninges also support the large network of veins and arteries that carry blood from the brain to the heart and throughout the CNS circulatory system. The outer layer is very thick, tough and flexible and is called the dura mater, which means 'hard mother'. The middle layer is called the arachnoid membrane and derives its name from its spider-web appearance. The last layer is closely attached to the brain and follows every surface convolution and is called the pia mater. The smaller surface blood vessels of the brain and spinal cord are contained within this third layer. Between the pia mater and arachnoid membrane is a gap called the subarachnoid space which is filled with a liquid called the cerebrospinal fluid. This is the fluid that protects the brain inside the bony skull (Frackowiak, 2004).

CEREBROSPINAL FLUID AND THE VENTRICLES

The brain is suspended in liquid inside the bony skull and because of its weight, density and fragility it is unable to support its own weight. The brain is surrounded by the pia mater, the gap contains the fluid and then the middle meninges layer is on top of the fluid. The brain floats in the fluid within the gap, and because it is completely suspended the net weight is reduced. If you think of someone on a plastic inflatable toy in the middle of a swimming pool, it is the same principle in terms of weight support. The fluid called the cerebrospinal fluid serves two purposes; it protects the brain and spinal cord from sudden head movements and reduces the pressure of its weight on the brainstem.

Inside the brain is a series of four hollow, interconnected structures called ventricles which are filled with cerebrospinal fluid. The fluid is a filtrate of blood and also aids in bringing nutrients to the brain and removing waste from the system. Each ventricle has a special structure called the choroid plexus which is rich in blood vessels and is able to extract fluid from the blood and then manufacture the cerebrospinal fluid. The newly manufactured cerebrospinal fluid is then circulated through the ventricles, through the gap between the meninges, bathes the brain and then is reabsorbed into the blood supply to be reprocessed and re-circulated. The cerebrospinal fluid is circulated in a specific pattern, moving from the lateral ventricle to the third and from the third to the fourth. At the fourth ventricle it passes into the subarachnoid space where it circulates around the outside of the brain and spinal cord. Cerebrospinal fluid is regenerated several times every twenty-four hours (Frackowiak, 2004). When there is an overproduction of cerebrospinal fluid due to disease or injury, the ventricles swell and put damaging pressure on the tissues of the brain. Cerebrospinal fluid is also analysed to check the health of the brain and to make a diagnosis for certain types of diseases such as multiple scleroisis. A small sample is taken from the spinal cord in a procedure called a spinal tap or lumbar puncture.

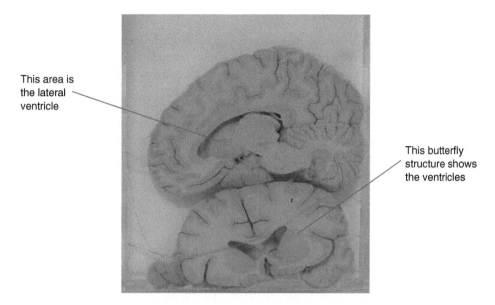

This area is the lateral ventricle

This butterfly structure shows the ventricles

Figure 4.4

DIVISIONS OF THE BRAIN

Forebrain

The forebrain is the most highly evolved, specialized and complex section of the human brain and provides us with the ability to speak, think and plan. It contains two parts: the diencephalon and the telencephalon.

The diencephalon is divided into the thalamus and hypothalamus. The telencephalon is the largest and most advanced part of the brain and contains the cerebral cortex, basal ganglia and the limbic system among other structures.

Thalamus

The thalamus is a complex cluster of nuclei that act as relay stations to the cerebral cortex. The thalamus consists of a pair of egg-shaped masses of grey matter located below the cerebral hemispheres. All the sensory pathways, except olfactory pathways, lead through the thalamus to the overlying cerebral cortex. The sensory information enters the thalamus, where neurons send the information to the overlying cortex. The cortical cells then innervate the thalamus. The thalamus also has interconnections with the reticular formation and with certain areas of the cerebral cortex.

The hypothalamus

The hypothalamus actually refers to a grouping of small nuclei that are positioned in the ventral (middle) portion of the cerebrum at the intersection of the midbrain and thalamus. It regulates the secretion of hormones from the pituitary gland, maintains and moderates endocrine function in conjunction with other internal organs and glands. The hypothalamus is relatively small, but it is packed with many distinct nuclei that have vital functions. The hypothalamus is a control centre for sexual drive, anger, hunger, thirst and pleasure. It is also involved with the functions of the autonomic nervous system, particularly with the sympathetic division. The hypothalamus interconnects with many regions of the brain and is also involved in aspects of behaviour such as emotion, motivation and reinforcement (Frackowiak, 2004).

Basal ganglia

Is a group of large nuclei that are positioned in the central regions of the cerebral hemispheres. They partially surround the thalamus and are covered by the cerebral cortex and the white matter. This group of nuclei plays a role in the control of movement and has connections with the cortex, thalamus, hypothalamus, reticular formation, portions of the midbrain and the spinal cord.

Limbic system

The limbic system contains the hippocampus and the amygdala among other structures and is involved in learning and memory with the amygdala being involved in emotions. The amygdala is specifically associated with fear and fear responses. This structure allows you to process information and then provides an instant sympathetic response. It is involved with the conscious emotional response to an event, whether positive or negative, and is the structure that is believed to be most associated with PTSD in combination with the hypothalamus. The limbic system is also involved in the experiencing of pain and pleasure and aggressive behaviours (Frackowiak, 2004).

The cerebrum and the cerebral cortex

The cerebrum is divided into two hemispheres by a clearly visible deep groove running from front to back. The cerebral hemispheres and the cortex overlie the brainstem and the cerebellum. The cortex of the human brain is wrinkled and folded, which greatly increases its surface area. The ridges of tissue are called gyri and are separated by grooves called sulci and even larger grooves called fissures. Approximately two-thirds of the cerebral cortex surface is hidden in the depths of these folds. The cerebral cortex consists mostly of glia and the cell bodies, dendrites and interconnecting axons of neurons, has a greyish-brown appearance and is called the grey matter. Millions of axons run beneath the cerebral cortex and connect its neurons with those located elsewhere in the brain. The large concentration of myelin around these axons gives this tissue a whitish appearance, hence it is called the white matter (Frackowiak, 2004).

The cerebral cortex performs sensory, motor and association functions. The sensory function receives information from the sense organs (eyes, ears, touch, taste and smell) and translates them into coherent and useful patterns. The motor function controls the movements of the body. The association function is the most complex and consists of the types of abilities such as reasoning, planning, and problem solving.

The major segments of the cerebral hemispheres are the frontal, parietal, temporal and occipital regions or lobes. Some of the boundaries of the lobes are defined by the large folds such as the temporal lobe; others are less well defined such as the parietal lobe. The outer shell of the hemispheres is the cerebral cortex.

The frontal lobes are responsible for the planning, intention and organization to carry out long-range strategies. The frontal lobes are also involved in problem solving and abstract thinking. The temporal lobes are responsible for processing visual information as well as containing the auditory cortex. The parietal lobe is involved in the initiation of muscular action as well as the recognition of objects by the sense of touch. The occipital lobe contains the primary visual cortex and is responsible for analysing the information from the eyes providing us with the ability to see (Snell, 2009).

The two hemispheres

The two cerebral hemispheres perform slightly different functions even though the structures are very similar. Some functions are lateralized, located primarily on one side of the brain while other

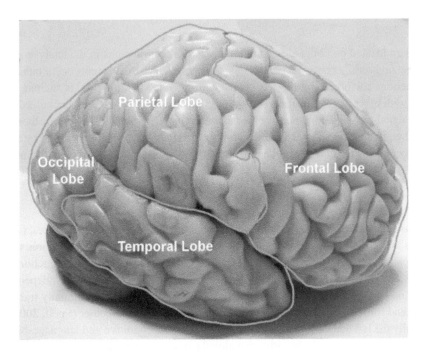

Figure 4.5

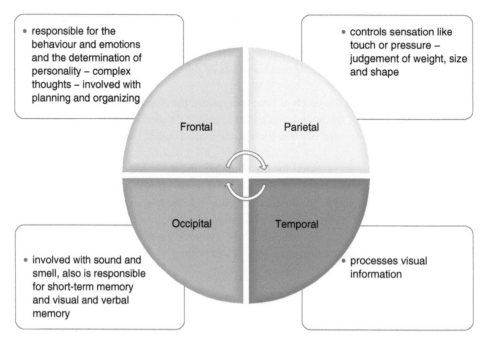

- responsible for the behaviour and emotions and the determination of personality – complex thoughts – involved with planning and organizing

- controls sensation like touch or pressure – judgement of weight, size and shape

Frontal   Parietal

Occipital   Temporal

- involved with sound and smell, also is responsible for short-term memory and visual and verbal memory

- processes visual information

Figure 4.6   The four lobes of the cerebral hemisphere

functions are located on both sides. The left hemisphere participates in the analysis of information and recognizing serial events and behaviours, those events where elements occur one after the other. Serial functions performed by the left hemisphere include verbal activities such as having a conversation with other people, reading and writing. The right hemisphere is specialized for synthesis, putting isolated elements together to make an entire picture, such as drawing or the ability to read maps. Although the hemispheres function slightly differently they are still unified by a large band of axons that connects the two cerebral hemispheres together called the corpus callosum (Snell, 2009).

Corpus callosum

The corpus callosum connects corresponding parts of the left and right hemispheres, i.e. the left temporal lobe to the right temporal lobe. The corpus callosum is a band of nerve fibres which transmit information between the two sides. The two hemispheres undertake different functions even though they have similar structures. Each hemisphere has the capacity to carry out independent learning, memory and perceptual functions. The corpus callosum functions to continually transmit information back and forth between the two hemispheres and links them together (Snell, 2009).

Generally the left hemisphere is responsible for analytic, cognitive and language-based processes while the right hemisphere deals with more global perceptions such as those involved in spatial relationships or emotional responses. The right hemisphere is better at the comprehension of language while the left is better at expression. Most right-handed people have their language functions in the left hemisphere and imagery and spatial relations in the right.

Disorders in this area of the brain create a situation where the hemispheres are unable to communicate and can cause changes in motor coordination, difficulties on multidimensional tasks, appropriate motor responses to visual information, and to process complex types of information such as language or spatial patterns. There is some research linking dyslexia to abnormalities of the corpus callosum (Elnakib, Casanova, Gimelfarb, Switala & El-Baz, 2012).

Midbrain

The midbrain (mesencephalon) is the most anterior extension of the brainstem that still maintains the basic tubular structure of the spinal cord. It merges into the thalamus and hypothalamus. The back portion of the midbrain (the tectum) contains two pairs of important structures for the visual and auditory systems called the superior and inferior colliculi. Other important motor centres in the midbrain are the substantia nigra which contain neurons that release the neurotransmitter dopamine and the red nucleus which communicates with motor neurons in the spinal cord. The midbrain is also a relay station and sends visual and auditory information to other areas of the brain. Finally the midbrain contains the reticular activating system (RAS), which functions as the brain's waking centre. This area of the brain is most closely associated with Parkinson's disease. The substantia nigra is the major area for dopamine and it has been found that when this structure begins to deteriorate, there is a corresponding decrease in the amount of dopamine which causes the majority of motor symptoms found in Parkinson's disease (Snell, 2009).

Hindbrain

This is the most primitive part of the human brain and controls vital life-preserving activities such as heart action, breathing, internal organ function, gastrointestinal activity, and coordination of motor activity. The hindbrain is divided into two sections; the metencephalon which contains the pons and the cerebellum and the myelencephalon which contains the medulla oblongata.

The pons is the upward continuation of the brain stem and contains ascending and descending fibre tracts. A large bundle of transverse fibres lies in the middle of the pons and these interconnect the brain stem and cerebellum as well as housing the pyramidal fibres going from the cortex to the spinal cord.

The cerebellum overlies the pons and has a convoluted appearance. The cerebellum is primarily concerned with the regulation of motor coordination and muscular activities. There are connections between the cerebellum and nearly all the other parts of the brain, including spinal sensory fibres and areas concerned with hearing and vision as well as the thalamus and other parts of the brainstem. The cerebellum with its two hemispheres resembles a miniature version of the cerebrum. Damage to the cerebellum impairs standing, walking, or performance of coordinated movements (Snell, 2009).

The myelencephalon contains one major structure, the medulla oblongata, also referred to as the medulla. It contains part of the reticular formation that controls the cardiovascular system,

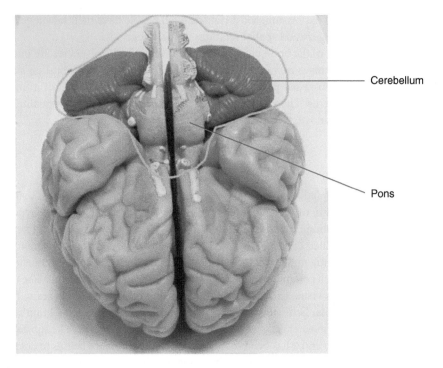

Cerebellum

Pons

Figure 4.7

respiration and skeletal muscle tonus. The majority of the cranial nerves have their entrances and exits from the medulla and pons. The medulla forms the bottom of the brainstem and marks the transition from brainstem to spinal cord. The medulla maintains vital body functions and regulates breathing and heart rate (Snell, 2009).

The hindbrain is essential to maintain life functions and if this section of the brain is damaged, individuals will lose control over fundamental life functions. The hindbrain is responsible for the autonomic function of the nervous system which encompasses the involuntary muscles including the heart and lungs, blood pressure, and respiration.

Reticular system

The reticular system is a core of tissue that is made up of a network of fibres and neurons; it is involved with arousal and attention and is located on the back of the brainstem. It is of special interest as it appears to act as a filter for incoming stimuli and alerts the higher functions as to whether the information may be important. Damage in this area will cause problems with the sleep/awake cycle, balance, and the abilities to filter incoming stimuli and to discriminate between important and irrelevant stimuli (Snell, 2009).

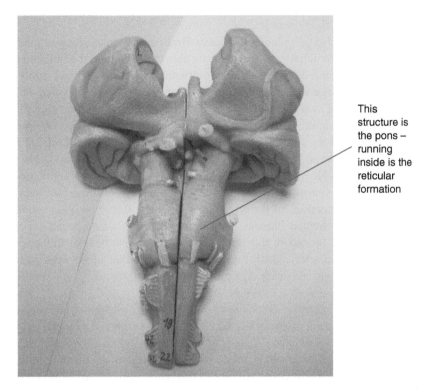

This structure is the pons – running inside is the reticular formation

Figure 4.8

SUMMARY

The various structures have been defined and discussed and although the way the brain functions is very complicated it is important in the understanding of abnormal behaviours and how this impacts mental illness. The next section will discuss the history of brain surgery and how this has impacted on psychopathology.

Psychophysiology and the treatment of psychopathology

Psychosurgery is the highly controversial surgical technique of altering human behaviour and mood and is different from the type of brain surgery that is used to remove a tumour or repair tissue after a stroke. Psychosurgery is used to alter normal brain tissue in an effort to modify behaviour. The issue of psychosurgery should be evaluated on two different levels; the research that indicates that psychosurgery is beneficial and the ethics involved in altering brain tissue in an effort to change human behaviour.

History of psychosurgery

Phineas Gage was the first accidental lobotomy. Brain injury was not uncommon, but rarely did anyone survive long enough for physicians to be able to understand the function of the damaged structures. Generally, the damage was so significant that the individual rarely regained consciousness. Phineas Gage was a railroad construction foreman who survived a terrible accident where a large iron rod was blown through his head, completely destroying his left temporal lobe in 1848. Before his accident he was described as being capable and efficient. He was well respected by his workers and described as well-balanced. After his accident his personality was radically changed and his friends described him as 'no longer Gage'. He was not physically or mentally capable of returning to his job as foreman and worked various menial jobs until his death twelve years after his accident. Gage's injury confirmed for many physicians at the time that certain functions of the brain were localized. Based on observations and writings by the physician who treated Phineas, Dr Harlow, neuroscientists began experimentation on the effects of surgical lesions in the brain. One important element of Phineas's accident was that he survived his injuries, which reinforced the belief that large areas of the brain could be removed without causing death or major impairment (Damasio, Grabowski, Galaburda & Damasio, 1994).

In 1884 the first brain surgery for the removal of a tumour was performed successfully. Radical surgery of this type was not often performed because of the high risk of mortality, most likely due to infection and/or brain swelling.

The idea that brain surgery could be used as a means of improving mental health began in 1890. It was a logical conclusion that if we could repair and removed diseased tissue in the body, the same could be done with mental disease.

The first surgical procedures used to change behaviour rather than remove diseased tissue began in 1888 with Gottlieb Burchhardt. He was forced to stop performing the surgeries because of the high mortality rate and the fact that the procedure did not alter behaviour in his schizophrenic patients and instead caused constant grand-mal seizures in the patients who survived. Despite the high mortality rate, the remaining patients were reported to be calmer (Kucharski, 1984).

In 1890 Friderich Golz began procedures on animal subjects, removing portions of dog temporal lobes which he found made them calmer. In 1935, Carlyle Jacobsen tried frontal and prefrontal lobotomies on chimpanzees and found them to be calmer after the procedure (Greenblatt, 1996).

About the same time Antonio Moniz became interested in the idea of psychosurgery and decided to conduct his own experiments. Moniz was already well known as a very productive and famous researcher, who had previously invented several significant improvements to brain x-ray techniques. Moniz found that cutting the nerves that extend from the frontal cortex to the thalamus in psychotic patients who suffered from repetitive thoughts 'short-circuited' the problem. He devised a surgical technique that he called leucotomy in 1935, which involved drilling two small holes on either side of the forehead, inserting a special surgical knife and severing the prefrontal cortex from the rest of the brain. Moniz found that he had mixed results with this type of brain surgery; some of his patients did become calmer, but others did not improve. This indicated to Moniz that other brain structures were involved in psychotic behaviour and that simply severing the frontal lobes from the rest of the brain was not the solution researchers had been looking for in controlling abnormal behaviour. Again his research in altering behaviour in psychotic patients was less than convincing as a viable method of curing mental illness. Once again the high mortality rate as well as the often debilitating effects on intellectual performance frequently produced more damage than the original abnormal behaviour. He advised extreme caution and stated that this type of surgical procedure should only be used in extreme cases where everything else had been tried (Dorman, 1995).

In 1936 two American physicians, James Watts and Walter Freeman, began doing the procedure in America and were so satisfied with the results that they went on to advocate their use, conducting thousands of operations and essentially ignoring Moniz's warning. Initially they began using Moniz's surgical procedure but then altered the technique and changed the name to lobotomy. Dr Freeman had became impatient with the difficult surgical methods and found that he could insert an ordinary ice pick above each eye of a patient, drive it through the thin bone with a light tap of a small hammer, swish the pick back and forth and perform the surgical operation in minutes instead of hours. Others followed Freeman and Watt and between 1939 and 1951 over 18,000 lobotomies were performed in the United States. The procedure was used indiscriminately, and rather than being applied to extreme cases it was being used to control unruly children, convicts, psychiatric patients and anyone else who was deemed to be behaving outside the norm (Kucharski, 1984).

Based on the publications and research conducted on these procedures, there is no convincing evidence that anyone recovered from serious mental disorders with this type of treatment. The ethical conditions at the time these procedures were being conducted were less than rigorous. Today, these operations would not be carried out in this fashion as no clinical trials had been conducted, and the procedure was hypothesized and then performed directly on humans. The high rate of mortality and disability would prohibit these procedures from being performed. In addition, there is the issue of violating individual rights and ethics when performing possibly life-threatening procedures on patients who are unable to give full consent.

Techniques of psychosurgery

Psychosurgery has been applied to a variety of psychological problems. It has been used for such varying patient populations as schizophrenics, depressives, people with chronic anxiety, and those with severe obsessive-compulsive behaviours. From the mid-1940s to mid-1950s thousands of prefrontal lobotomies were performed on schizophrenic patients with no reliable reports that any of these surgeries were successful. More precise contemporary techniques have included the destruction of specific portions of the thalamus for aggressive or obsessive-compulsive behaviour, destruction of part of the limbic system for obsessional and anxiety states and destruction of part of a cerebral hemisphere for depression. The tissue has been destroyed by various methods, sometimes using direct surgical cutting, other times with the implantation of radioactive material and/or the use of ultrasonic waves (Pressman, 2002).

There is widespread agreement that the early use of prefrontal lobotomies was not justified. The introduction of tranquillizing drugs in the mid-1950s generally slowed down the use of this approach. Chlorpromazine and other antipsychotic medications alleviated many psychotic symptoms with relatively fewer side effects and it was reversible. The effect of psychosurgery on violent and/or aggressive behaviour was not supported in the research and was not clear. What was clear was the destruction. Individuals undergoing these procedures no longer had the ability to synthesize signals from the environment, assign priorities or make balanced decisions. The control made possible by the frontal-limbic connections was weakened, and their behaviour often became erratic and unpredictable. After these procedures many of these surgical patients would participate in endless rounds of purposeless activity, or would sit for hours staring blankly at walls (Pressman, 2002).

Today, psychosurgery is still being performed; it is referred to as cingulotomy and has been utilized as late as 2003 for the treatment of severe depression, bipolar disorder, obsessive-compulsive disorder and generalized anxiety disorder. The target is more specialized and is the cingulated gyrus which is a thin ribbon of grey matter that is believed to play a role in human emotional states. Rather than using an ice pick, cingulotomy is performed in surgical theatres, using sterotaxis to advance an electrode into the structure and then applying electrical current (Cosgrove & Rauch, 2003). It has been reported in the literature that this type of psychosurgery has been effective with severe disorders that are resistant to medication.

CONCLUSION

What happened to Rosemary? The ice-pick method was not used on Rosemary. Instead Freeman and Watts performed what was called the precision method. They would first make holes in the side of the head, to allow a more direct assault on the white matter of the brain. An instrument with a narrow steel blade, blunt and flat like a butter knife, was inserted into one of the holes and then aimed at the other. Once inside Rosemary's brain the blade would be swung in two cutting arcs, destroying the targeted nerve matter. Watts was even quoted as saying 'It goes through just like soft butter'. The damage would occur from tearing of the brain, bleeding and bruising. They could not see what they were doing and untold damage would have been done. Rosemary's deterioration could have been from a number of problems, ranging from internal bleeding to damaged tissue and/ or infection. What is clear is that she went from a young adult with minor behavioural problems to an individual who required long-term intensive care and was no longer able to function as an independent person. Instead of being a saviour Dr Freeman condemned her to a lifetime of institutions and misery.

What happened to Dr Freeman? The fact that the lobotomy did not hold the cure it had been deemed to have, the number of failed lobotomies that ended in incapacitation and sometimes death, and the introduction of anti-psychotic medications, meant that the lobotomy fell out of favour as a treatment for mental illness. In 1967, while Dr Freeman was performing one of his 'ice-pick' lobotomies, he tore a blood vessel in the brain of his patient and she died. Shortly afterwards his surgical privileges were revoked and he was no longer allowed to practise. He continued to be an advocate of the procedure, but died from cancer at the age of 77 in 1972.

LEARNING TOOLS

Key terms

Adenosine triphosphate (ATP) – nucleotide used in cells for energy and as a coenzyme

Anterograde transport – movement of substances in the cell from the cell body to the synapse

Autonomic nervous system – part of the peripheral nervous system that is in control of those functions below the level of consciousness such as heart rate, digestion and respiration rate

Central nervous system – the nervous system that consists of the brain and the spinal cord

Cytoplasm – a thick liquid residing between the cell membrane

Deoxyribonucleic acid (DNA) – a nucleic acid that contains the genetic instructions for all living organisms

Glia – non-neuronal cells that maintain homeostasis for the neurons in the brain and also form myelin around the axons

Ionotropic receptors – fast acting receptors that directly open ion channels

Metobotropic receptors – slow acting receptors that do not form an ion channel and instead involve a range of second-messenger chemicals

Myelin – formed by the glial cells and is composed of proteins and lipids

Neurons – cells that process and transmit information electrically/chemically and are the core components of the nervous system

Nodes of Ranvier – are the gaps between the myelin sheaths on the axons of neurons

Peripheral nervous system – nerves and ganglia outside of the brain and spinal cord

Retrograde – movement of substances in the cell toward the cell body from the synapse

Study guide

1 Explore the latest research on the neurotransmitters and what new advances there have been in this area.
2 Investigate how drugs affect neurotransmitter activity.
3 Research how the corpus collosum has been implicated in the disorder of schizophrenia.
4 Evaluate how the lobes of the brain influence our perceptions of the environment.

Case study in focus

Discuss the ethical implications involved in modern-day psychosurgery; could another case like 'Rosemary' happen? Investigate similarities and differences between the prefrontal lobotomy and cingulotomy.

Personal development

Investigate how psychosurgery influenced and changed how we treat mental illness.

Suggested reading

Orrison, W. (2008) *Atlas of brain function*. New York: Thieme Medical publishers.

Chiao, J.Y. (2009) *Cultural neuroscience: Cultural influences on brain function*. 178 (Progress in brain research). Elsevier: UK.

Whitfield, P.C., Thomas, E.O., Summers, F. & Whyte, M. (2009) *Head injury: A multidisciplinary approach.* Cambridge, UK: Cambridge University Press.

Richards, D., Clark, T. & Clarke, C. (2007) *The human brain and its disorders*. Oxford: Oxford University Press.

Genetics and Environmental Factors

5

Learning aims

At the end of this chapter you should be able to understand:

- Mendel's laws
- Various genetic disorders
- How the environment interacts with genetics
- The genetics of abnormal disorders.

INTRODUCTION

CASE STUDIES

Michael's story

An unfortunate wrongful adoption case highlights the important role that genetics can play in the lives of people and the decisions that they base on genetic information. A young New York couple adopted an infant from the Louise Wise Adoption Services. At the time of the adoption they were told that the birth mother had completed two years of college. She was placing her child up for adoption because of unfortunate circumstances. Her fiancé had died suddenly and in her grief she had become pregnant in an impulsive rebound love affair. It was a nice story but the entire background of the child was a lie. The child's birth mother was actually living in a mental institution, was diagnosed with schizophrenia and had been given a frontal lobotomy in an attempt to control extreme aggressive and self-harming behaviour. The biological father was also a long-term resident at the same psychiatric institution and had also been diagnosed with schizophrenia.

As the Jumans' adoptive son matured into a teenager he began to have numerous mental health problems and was finally diagnosed with schizophrenia. As soon as Michael's problems became apparent the family sought additional information from the adoption agency and eventually the agency did disclose that the birth mother had some problems with depression but chose not to disclose the severity of her mental illness. The adoptive son, Michael, struggled with his mental illness into young adulthood and then died as a possible suicide. After their adoptive son died, the Jumans found out the truth about Michael's background. The family sued the adoption agency, stating that they had fraudulently misrepresented the significant and severe psychiatric, psychological and medical history of the adopted son's natural birth parents and that if this information had been known to them at the time of the adoption they would have chosen not to adopt Michael because of the genetic links to severe mental illness.

Susan and Sharon

Simon and Caroline were comfortably middle class, Caroline was employed as a bank teller and Simon was a manager at a large supermarket chain. They had purchased a nice house in an affluent neighbourhood. They were overjoyed when they learned that Caroline was pregnant with twins. Caroline had an uneventful pregnancy and gave birth to two identical girls who were so difficult to tell apart that when they came back from the hospital the parents painted a toenail on one of the girls to keep them straight. The two little girls thrived. They were intelligent and outgoing and prone to tricks, often swapping places in each other's school classes, and took delight in the fact that very few people could tell them apart. They shared a room, even though their house had four bedrooms as the girls liked to stay close together. They had the same friends, and did all the same things, they were always together. As they entered their teen years, they began to want to be distinctive from one another and Susan cut and bobbed her hair while Sharon kept her hair long. When Sharon began to become more withdrawn, it was only Susan who really noticed the difference in Sharon's behaviour. Their parents and friends didn't realize that Sharon was changing and Susan worried constantly about her sister. It was only when the girls entered university and the stress of new friends and new challenges began to affect Sharon that other people noticed the changes in her behaviour. Eventually, Sharon could no longer cope, dropped out of university and over time became more ill. Shortly after her return home she was diagnosed with schizophrenia. Susan, however, completed her university course and went on for a PhD. in microbiology. She never showed any signs or symptoms of mental illness.

Were the Jumans correct in believing that Michael would inherit schizophrenia from his biological parents? If they are correct, why didn't Susan become ill when her sister did? Communities and individuals have embraced the idea that mental illness was inheritable and therefore families would become secretive, often hiding ill relatives or sending them far away so that they would not taint the remaining family members. Novels and plays are filled with tragic stories of families who were terrified that they would be the next casualty to the mental illness that plagued their family or that their secret would be exposed and the entire family would face ostracization by the community. Hereditary and mental disorders are often very difficult to understand. This chapter will begin with an introduction to genetics in order to provide knowledge of how biological elements interact with environmental conditions to cause psychological disorders. It is believed that most of the psychological disorders have some basis in genetics. Therefore it is imperative that an appreciation and understanding of genetics be reached before discussing the psychological disorders. This chapter will utilize examples of genetic disorders that are not considered mental disorders. These examples will provide important elements of information that can be applied to the more complex genetics of mental disorders.

GENETIC HISTORY

Humans learned early in history how to improve domestic animals and crops by crossbreeding and inbreeding. The mule was a man-made hybrid cross between a male donkey and female horse and was created even before the ancient Greeks. These crossbred animals were well known for their stamina, sure-footedness, intelligence and quiet temperament. Many preferred mules over horses as they were hardier, less sensitive and were capable of heavier loads. However, they were difficult to breed as they were sterile and could only be created using horses and donkeys.

Ancient writing has detailed how some children resembled their mothers, some resembled their fathers and some would even skip back a generation to resemble a grandparent, but no one was sure why or how this occurred. The common thought was that the 'spirit/essence' of the relative whether dead or alive would inhabit the child and create the likeness (Cummings, 2010).

These facts would continue to pose a quandary and since no genetic laws were known, bizarre crossbreeds were the subject of myth and legend. It was thought that men and animals could be paired up to create animal/human crossbreds. The fabled Minotaur was an example of a crossbreeding that supposedly took place between the wife of Minos and a bull. This type of magical thinking continued until the time of Aristotle.

Aristotle was the first scientist to have carefully thought over the nature of heredity outside of mythical tales and abstract reflections. He believed that the males and females came together and gave form and power to imperfectly blended ingredients, creating life. For 2,000 years no one had a better idea; many early scientists believed that mixtures weren't even always necessary and that the simpler forms of life could arise by spontaneous generation. Worms, flies, and crawling things took shape from putrid substance, ooze and mud (Magner, 2002).

In 1677 the Dutch lens maker Anton van Leeuwenhoek discovered living sperm which he called 'animalcules' in the seminal fluid of various animals and humans. Followers used his crude microscope and believed they saw within each human sperm, a tiny creature, the homunculus or 'little man'. This little man was the future human being in miniature. Once implanted in the female womb the homunculus would grow into a child. During the same decade Regneir de Graaf described for the first time the ovarian follicle, the structure on the surface of the ovary in which the human egg cell forms. Although the actual human egg was not seen for another 150 years, its existence was accepted. This led to the belief that Eve had contained within her body all the unborn generations yet to come, each egg fitting inside like hollow blocks, that each female generation would contain one less egg than the previous generation, and that after 200 million generations all the eggs would be spent and human life would come to an end (Magner, 2002).

By the nineteenth century the most widely held hypothesis was Aristotle's blending inheritance. On the basis of this theory one could predict that the offspring of a black animal and a white animal would be grey and once blended could never be separated. Charles Darwin realized that this concept was insufficient to describe the changes in animals and that it also ignored the phenomenon of traits skipping a generation. Instead, Darwin formalized his own theory based on evolution and natural selection. Although Darwin's theories did account for some important genetic elements that were previously missing, his theories did not explain some key factors. These would be discovered by Gregor Mendel whose theories would eventually change the way we attributed genetic contribution (Magner, 2002).

MENDELIAN GENETICS

Mendel was born into a peasant family in 1822 and entered a monastery to receive an education. He attended the University of Vienna for two years pursuing studies in both mathematics and science. Unfortunately for Mendel, but happily for the field of genetics, he failed his tests for the teaching certificate and returned to the monastery where he eventually became abbot. Mendel still interested in mathematics and science, carried out genetic experiments in the monastery garden. His contribution was never to be recognized in his lifetime and his research was largely ignored until after his death (Henig, 2001).

Mendel's contribution to genetics was to demonstrate that inherited characteristics are carried as discrete units, which are distributed out in different ways, or re-assorted in each generation. These discrete units eventually became known as genes. Mendel was successful where others had failed because he had planned his experiments carefully and chose to study measurable hereditary differences in a single simple species. He was also the first to apply mathematics to the study of biology and his experiments were carried out in a precise scientific way. Mendel followed a very specific pre-planned model in a series of logically designed experiments (Mawer, 2006).

Rather than choosing animals in his experiments, Mendel chose to use plants. In flowers and plants the pollen develops in the anther and the egg cells in a structure called the ovule. Pollination occurs when the pollen grains, trapped on the stigma, germinate and grow down to the ovule. Pollination in most species involves the pollen from the plant being caught on the stigma of another plant, called cross-pollination; this generally occurs via insects but can also occur by the physical force of the elements such as wind. Mendel liked plants because he could easily manipulate the pollination and the growth period from seed to adult plant was relatively short.

Mendel chose pea plants for a variety of reasons: they were commercially available, easy to cultivate and more importantly the sexual organs of the pea plant are entirely enclosed by the petals so the flower normally self-pollinates. By using pea plants, Mendel could control the process without fear of contamination or pollination from nearby plants. The structure of the pea plant was such that crossbreeding could not accidentally occur to confuse the experimental results. The different varieties of pea plant also had clear differential characteristics which 'bred true', reappearing in crop after crop (Mawer, 2006).

Mendel began his experiments with 32 different types of pea plants which he studied for two years to determine their specific characteristics. He selected seven traits that appeared noticeably different. Mendel began to crossbreed the seven different types of pea plants. He found that in every case, one of the alternate traits disappeared completely in the first generation. For example, when he crossbred smooth pea seeds with wrinkled pea seeds, the wrinkled seeds completely disappeared and all the plants from the two parents had smooth seeds. The disappearance of one of the traits was a puzzle. All the plants in the first crossing produced smooth seeds even though one plant had smooth seeds and the other plant had wrinkled seeds. The traits that remained in the pairings, Mendel called dominant. For the second set of experiments Mendel let the pea plant itself carry out the next stage by permitting the plants to self-pollinate. The traits that had disappeared in the first generation reappeared in the second generation. The traits which originated in the parent generation were present somehow in the first generation even though it was not physically apparent. Mendel called these traits recessive. After many experiments the dominant and recessive traits appeared in constant proportions of about three to one. It was at this point that Mendel realized that the appearance and disappearance of the traits and their constant proportions could only be explained if hereditary characteristics were separable factors (Henig, 2001).

Mendel had correctly assumed that the factors occurred in the offspring as pairs, one factor inherited from each parent. The pairs of factors would separate again when the mature offspring produced the sex cells resulting in two types of gametes, with one gene of the pair in each. This premise is known as Mendel's first law or the principle of segregation.

The two factors in a pair might be the same, in which case the self-pollinating plant would breed true. Or the two factors might be different in which case the dominant pair would carry the physical attribute. The forms came to be known as alleles. Smooth-seededness and wrinkled-seededness, for instance, are determined by alleles, different forms of the gene factor for seed form. When the genes of a gene pair are the same, the organism is said to be homozygous for that particular trait; when the genes of a gene pair are different, the organism is heterozygous for that trait.

When gametes are formed, genes are passed on to them, but each gamete contains only one of two possible alleles. When two gametes combine in the fertilized egg, the genes occur in matched pairs again. One allele may be dominant over another allele; in this case, the organism will appear as if it had only one type of gene. This outward appearance is known as its phenotype. However, in its genetic make-up, or genotype, each allele still exists independently and as a distinct unit, even though it is not visible in the phenotype, and the recessive allele will separate from its dominate partner when gametes are again formed. Only when the two recessive alleles come together, one from the female and one from the male, will the phenotype show the recessive trait.

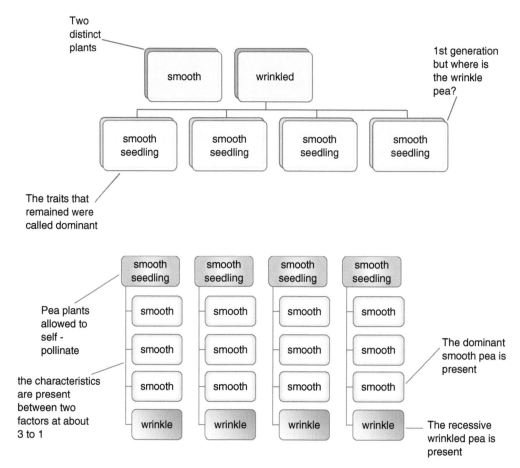

Figure 5.1   Mendel's first experiment

Principle of independent assortment

In a second series of experiments, Mendel studied crosses between pea plants that differed simultaneously in two characteristics; for example, one parent plant had peas that were round and yellow and the other had peas that were wrinkled and green. Mendel had found in previous pairings that the round and yellow traits were both dominant and the wrinkled and green were both recessive. All the seeds produced by the first pairing were round and yellow. When these seeds were planted and the flowers were allowed to self-pollinate, 556 seeds were produced, 315 of which showed the two dominant characteristics (round and yellow) but only 32 of which combined the recessive traits (green and wrinkled). All the rest of the seeds were unlike either parent plant; 101 were wrinkled and yellow and 108 were round and green – a mixture of the dominant and recessive traits had occurred. In Mendel's new experiment a totally new combinations of characteristics had appeared. The new

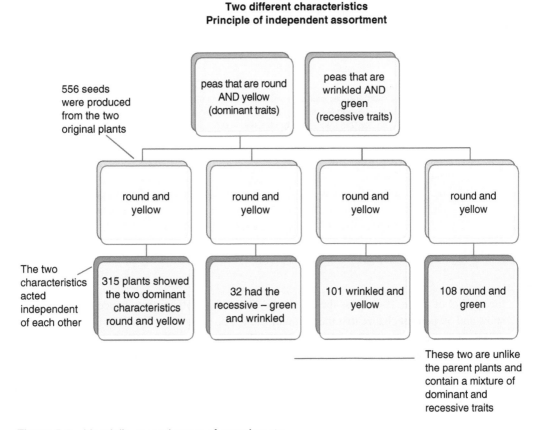

Figure 5.2   Mendel's second group of experiments

experiment did not contradict Mendel's previous 3:1 results. The round and wrinkled pea seeds still appeared in the same proportion as well as the yellow and green. However the round and the yellow traits and the wrinkled and the green ones which were originally combined in one plant, behaved as if they were entirely independent of one another. From these new experiments Mendel formulated his second law, which was the principle of independent assortment (Henig, 2001).

MENDEL AND THE LAWS OF CHANCE

The principle of independent assortment was basically applying the laws of chance to genetic theory. For example, a 10p coin has two sides, one with the face of the Queen and the other side with

50% chance that a lion or the Queen will show when you toss the coin in the air

 Add another coin and with each toss is still 50% that either the lion or the Queen will show – but now you have 2 coin tosses and you must factor this into your coin tosses – $0.5 \times 0.5 = 0.25\%$

 Add another coin – now there are 3 coin tosses so each toss is still 50% – but the odds become $0.5 \times 0.5 \times 0.5 = 12.5\%$ for 3 queens to appear

Figure 5.3

the symbol of a lion. If you toss the 10p in the air there is a 50 percent chance that the Queen will show and 50 percent chance that the lion will show. The chance that it will turn up one or the other is certain, or one chance in one. If you add another 10p coin and toss them both up in the air the chance that one will turn up with the Queen is again 50 percent and the chance that the second coin will show the lion symbol is also 50 percent. The chance that they will both turn up with the symbol of the lion at the same time is 0.5 x 0.5 or 0.25 or 25 percent. The probability of two independent events occurring together is the probability of one occurring alone multiplied by the probability of the other occurring alone.

When Mendel planned his experiments he made two assumptions; first that an equal number of male and female gametes are produced and second that the gametes combine at random. The larger the sample or in this case the more flips of a coin, the more closely it will conform to results predicted by the laws of chance (Henig, 2001). In our genetic examples we will apply these basic genetics principles to human physiology and psychopathology, but first we need a brief discussion about how traits are passed from parent to offspring.

MENDEL'S CONTRIBUTION

Mendel's findings were ahead of his time. He first reported his findings in 1865 before a small group of people at a meeting of the Brunn Natural History Society. It is apparent that no one really understood his experiments but they published his paper the following year in the Proceedings of the society, which was a journal that was circulated to libraries all over Europe. This would later be important because after Mendel's death, the new Abbott burned all of Mendel's papers and nothing existed except his publication. Although Mendel's work was widely published, the findings remained unrecognized. Mendel himself understood the importance of his findings and continued throughout his lifetime to send copies of his paper to other biologists including Darwin but no one became aware of the significance of his experiments until much later (Henig, 2001).

While Mendel's experiments awaited discovery, scientists were continuing to explore human physiology. Sperm and egg cells had been recognized as the hereditary links between parents and offspring but the specifics were not yet known. However, developments in microscopes and techniques for microscopic observation had improved to such a degree that the biology of genetics was beginning to be understood. In 1875 the German zoologist Oscar Hertwig witnessed the fertilization of the egg of a sea urchin and noted that the fertilized egg contained two nuclei, one from the sperm and one from the egg. More and more scientists began to focus their attention (and their new microscopes) on the 'coloured bodies' which would later be known as chromosomes (Magner, 2002).

CHROMOSOMES

Chromosomes are organized structures called deoxyribonucleic acid (DNA) which contain all the genetic instructions for an organism. You can imagine that DNA is like the software in a computer. The DNA carries all the information that programs what a person will become. When the software in your computer stops working or has some sort of glitch in the program in the computer will not run properly even though the hardware is unaffected. This is similar to when there is something wrong with the DNA or it does not transfer properly. When the genetic information is not correct there will be difficulties that will appear within the organism.

The number of chromosomes per cell in the tissue of any particular organism is the same from cell to cell. Individuals belonging to the same species have the same number of chromosomes per cell. Chromosomes occur in matched pairs and each species has a characteristic number of pairs in each of its body cells. The genes (alleles) that control each trait are situated at the same locus, one on each chromosome of a particular pair.

Humans have 23 pairs, 22 autosomes which contain all the genetic material and one pair of sex chromosomes. The sex chromosomes or gametes are better known as eggs and sperm and have exactly half the number of chromosomes. The number of chromosomes in the gametes is referred to as haploid and the number in the autosomes as diploid. When a sperm fertilizes an egg, the two haploid nuclei fuse and the diploid number is established (Gardner, Sutherland & Shaffer, 2011).

MEIOSIS

The process of cell division that produces gametes (egg cells and sperm cells) is called meiosis. In meiosis, the chromosomes divide, and one chromosome of each pair goes to each of the two gametes that results from the division. As a result, each gamete has only half the usual number of chromosomes (twenty-three in humans); when a sperm cell and an egg cell combine during fertilization the fertilized cell has the full complement of chromosomes (Klug, Cummings, Spencer & Palladino, 2009).

In 1902 William Sutton was studying the formation of sperm cells in grasshoppers. While observing the process of meiosis, he noticed that the chromosomes that paired with one another at the beginning of the reduction had physical similarities to one another. In diploid cells, chromosomes came in pairs which were only obvious at meiosis, but the discerning eye could find the homologues in the unpaired chromosomes when they became visible during mitosis. Homologues separate during the first meiotic division then when the gametes come together at fertilization each chromosome from the sperm cell would meet a new homologue which was the corresponding chromosome in the egg. Sutton hypothesized that the homologues were replicas of the homologous chromosomes that had come together to make the fertilized egg. If one homologue of a chromosome pair came from the mother then the other homologue must have come from the father. The two had been copied accurately in cell division and then after the division they went through several stages of development until the time of meiosis when they were once again separated. Sutton believed that alleles occurred on homologous chromosomes. The alleles could always remain independent and so could separate at meiosis, with new pairs of alleles forming when the gametes came together at fertilization (Magner, 2002).

Mendel's second group of experiments and his law of independent assortment could now be explained by Sutton's experiments. If you remember, Mendel had two groups of pea plants that had elements of dominant and recessive traits and were unlike either parent plant. In Mendel's experiments some of the plants had wrinkled and yellow seeds and some were smooth and green and Mendel did not understand how this occurred. The answer to Mendel's puzzle was meiosis, which is the basis of independent movement of chromosomes. This will be important when we discuss the complicated factors of genetics and psychiatric disorders.

CHROMOSOME STRUCTURE AND REPLICATION

We have discussed the various elements of genetics and now we will discuss how chromosomes influence psychiatric and developmental disorders. Each chromosome is a double-stranded molecule of deoxyribonucleic acid (DNA). Each strand is a sequence of nucleotide bases attached to a chain of phosphate and deoxyribose; there are four nucleotide bases: adenine, thymine, guanine and cytosine. It is the sequence of these bases on each chromosome that constitutes the genetic code. The two strands that compose each chromosome are coiled around each other and bonded together by the attraction of adenine for thymine and guanine for cytosine. The specific bonding pattern has an important consequence as the two strands that compose each chromosome are exact complements of each other. So for example adenine is always paired with thymine (Gardner & Sutherland, 2003).

Replication is a critical process of the DNA molecule. Without it, mitotic cell division would not be possible. The process is relatively straightforward, two strands of DNA start to unwind, the now exposed nucleotide bases on each of the two strands attract loose complementary bases from the fluid of the nucleus. When the unwinding is complete, two double-stranded DNA molecules exist where there had been one.

Although the process of replication is uncomplicated, errors occasionally occur. These are often called gross errors and can take the form of accidental alterations in individual genes. Down's syndrome is an example of a gross error where there is an extra chromosome in each cell. This genetic alteration causes a cluster of physical and mental impairments that are characteristic of Down's syndrome (Gardner & Sutherland, 2003).

Many of the developmental disorders of childhood are caused by mutations, deletions and other alterations in genes or chromosomes. Gene mutations are random and are factors of errors that occur during the polymerization of the second strand of DNA (Cooper & Krawczak, 1993). One specific category, called expansion mutations, is characterized by long expansion mutations of the trinucleotide sequences, for example cytosine, adenine and guanine (CAG). These mutations have been implicated in more than twenty genetic disorders. In addition to developmental disorders it is believed that expansion mutations may also be involved in psychiatric disorders (Chiurazzi & Oostra, 2006). The first and most well known developmental disorder in this category which has been identified as the leading known genetic cause of autism is fragile X syndrome which is characterized by intellectual disabilities, distinctive facial features and stereotypical movements. Males with this disorder are more severely affected than females and there is a correlation between the length of the expansion mutation and the severity of the syndrome (Garber, Visootsak & Warren, 2008).

Expansion mutations have also been beneficial in the explanation of a genetic conundrum that involved the question as to why some disorders produced a more severe phenotype at earlier ages in each successive generation in an affected family. The answer was in the mutation of the sequence. It is now known that the triplet repeat sequences that are long enough to cause disorders are unstable and tend to grow longer from generation to generation (Caskey, Pizzuti, Fu, Fenwick & Nelson, 1992). Therefore, the initial mutation that would have produced a relatively mild disorder, after two or three generations as the mutation repeats became longer, becomes more severe. This phenomenon has been called anticipation. Anticipation has been found in some families affected by bipolar disorder and schizophrenia but the phenomenon has yet to be elucidated (Ponnudurai & Jayakar, 2010; Swift-Scanlan, Coughlin, Lan, Potash, Ingersoll, DePaulo, Ross & McInnis 2005; Muir & McKechanie, 2009; Hegde & Saraph, 2011).

CHROMOSOMES, REPRODUCTION AND LINKAGE

All other cell division in the body occurs by mitosis (cell division). Meiosis is a special type of cell division that occurs only with the sex chromosomes. Just prior to mitotic division, the number of chromosomes doubles so that when the division occurs, both divided cells end up with the full complement of chromosomes (Klug, Cummings, Spencer & Palladino, 2009).

Meiosis accounts for much of the genetic diversity within each species. In humans, for example, each meiotic division produces two gametes; each gamete contains one chromosome from each of the twenty-three pairs contained in each body cell. Because each of the twenty-three pairs is randomly sorted into the two gametes, each human can produce gametes with 223 (8,388,608) different combinations of chromosomes. When we apply these numbers to humans and their offspring, one can understand how siblings can often appear unlike each other and unlike their parents. However, there are genes that link together.

The first comprehensive study of linkage was published in 1915 by Thomas Morgan in his study of fruit fly genes. He found that there are four different clusters of fruit fly genes. If the gene for one trait in a cluster was inherited from one parent, that fruit fly had a higher probability (greater than 0.5) of inheriting genes for other traits in the cluster from the same parent. Because fruit flies have four pairs of chromosomes, Morgan concluded that linkage occurs between traits that are encoded on the same chromosome (Magner, 2002).

If genes are passed from generation to generation on chromosomes, why are the genes on the same chromosome not always inherited together? The linkage between pairs of genes on a single chromosome varies from almost complete (close to 1.0) to just above chance (just over 0.5). Morgan believed that crossing over provided the solution to the mystery of partial linkage (Magner, 2002).

During the first stage of meiosis, after the chromosomes have replicated, they line up in their pairs. Then they usually cross over one another at random points, break apart at the points of contact, and exchange sections of chromosome. As a result, parents rarely pass on intact chromosomal clusters of genes to their children. Each of your gametes contains chromosomes that are a unique spliced-together combination inherited from your mother and father, unless of course you are an identical twin.

The phenomenon of crossing over is important for two reasons. First, by ensuring that chromosomes are not passed intact from generation to generation, crossovers increase the variety of subtle changes in a species. Second, the study of crossovers was the first means by which geneticists could construct chromosome mapping or gene maps. Gene mapping allowed scientists to locate genes and diagram their relationship to one another. Crossing over also provided the irrefutable fact that genes occur along the chromosome in an ordered linear array. Crossovers occur at a random point along the length of a chromosome – the degree of linkage between two genes indicates how close they are together on the chromosome. Crossovers rarely occur between adjacent genes, and they frequently occur between genes at opposite ends of a chromosome (Gardner & Davies, 2009).

SEX CHROMOSOMES AND SEX-LINKED TRAITS

There is one exception to the rule that chromosomes always come in matched pairs. That exception is the sex chromosomes, the pair of chromosomes that determines an individual's sex. There are two types of sex chromosomes, X and Y, and the two look different and carry different genes. Females have two X chromosomes, and males have an X and a Y. We characterize the two sexes as XX (female) and XY (male). Traits that are influenced by genes on the sex chromosomes are referred to as sex-linked traits. Virtually all sex-linked traits are controlled by genes on the X chromosome because the Y chromosome is small and only carries genes that are responsible for individuals to develop into males. Traits that are controlled by genes on the X chromosome occur more frequently in one sex than the other. If the trait is dominant, it occurs more frequently in females. Females have twice the chance of inheriting the dominant gene because they have twice the number of X chromosomes. In contrast, recessive sex-linked traits occur more frequently in males. The reason is that recessive sex-linked traits are manifested only in females who possess two of the recessive genes, or one on each of their X chromosomes. The traits are apparent in males because they have only one X chromosome (Gardner & Davies, 2009).

GENE EXPRESSION

As we have discussed, genes come in many different types and play many different roles. Genes can be responsible for eye colour or can even play a role in how we interact with our environment and research is showing that gene expression is involved in psychological disorders (Post, 1992). The best way to discuss how mental disorders can be influenced by the environment is by a discussion of another group of genes. These are called the structural genes and contain the information necessary for the synthesis of a single protein. Proteins control the physiological activities of cells and are important components of their structure. All the cells of the body, hair, bone and brain contain the same structural genes. What makes them different is that another category of genes, called operator genes, determines how the structural genes will be expressed, develop and function. Operator genes function like switches: they can be on or off. Once they are on they can be turned up, or down or when they are finished, turned off. Operator genes are regulated by DNA proteins and are influenced by signals that are received by the cell from the environment. This is the most important way that genes interact with the environment to influence development (Klug, Cummings, Spencer & Palladino, 2009). It is hypothesized that the genes that are responsible for psychiatric disorders work in combination with the structural genes. These genes are the most sensitive to the external environment and could explain why there is a complexity between the relationship of genetic factors and mental illness, and how individuals with high risk, such as Sharon in our case study develop schizophrenia, while her identical twin Susan did not. The next section will discuss genetic disorders and how all the elements that we have previously discussed are applied to various disorders that affect people's lives.

GENETIC DISORDERS

Imagine you were told that there was a possibility you had a genetic disorder that would eventually cause you to lose control of your body and cause a painful lingering death. Or that you were told of a possibility that any children you produced could develop a terrible disease, be born mentally retarded or pass on a genetic disorder that may afflict your grandchildren in a terrible way. What would this information mean? If you suspected a genetic illness in your family would you get tested? Is it easier to not know? Medical science has reached a point where genetic testing can confirm or rule out many different types of suspected genetic conditions or help determine the person's chance of passing on a genetic disorder.

The easiest way to understand genetics and the implications of genetic testing is by the application and explanation of genetic disorders. This section will begin with an explanation about single gene disorders and then will discuss the complexity of mental disorders. Single gene disorders are the easiest to understand and although these types of disorders mostly affect the physiology of an individual there are psychological elements to any physical disorder. We will begin with physical disorders and then discuss the more complicated types of genes that can cause mental abnormalities such as schizophrenia and mood disorders.

Cystic fibrosis

Cystic fibrosis is an inherited recessive, single gene disorder. This disorder does not involve psychopathology, but because it is a life-threatening disorder it does impact the individual in terms of quality of life. This condition mainly affects the lungs and pancreas, but can affect other parts of the body including the liver, nose and sinuses, reproductive organs and sweat glands. The cells in these specific areas of the body make mucus. Individuals affected with cystic fibrosis have cells that do not function correctly and make mucus and secretions that are thicker than normal which can cause a variety of symptoms and problems. The genes that are responsible for this disorder control the way cells handle sodium and chloride ions. There are many different abnormalities of the cystic fibrosis gene but basically they all stop the cell from handling sodium and chloride properly (Wynbrandt & Ludman, 2008).

The gene responsible is recessive and CF develops only in homozygous individuals (those who inherit a CF gene from both their mother and their father). Just like Mendel's experiments with pea plants humans can be carriers of the disorder but it takes two copies of the gene for the disorder to be manifested. The carrier parents do not suffer from the condition.

For an example let us label the recessive CF allele (c) and the dominant normal allele (C). Suppose that each parent has a dominant allele C and a recessive allele c, in other words they are both carriers of the disorder, but are not affected. In the production of gametes (sperm and eggs) of each parent there is a 50:50 distribution of alleles. Each sperm or egg will have either the dominant C or the recessive c. There are four possible combinations that can occur in their children. On average, only 25 percent of the phenotypes correspond to manifest CF (cc) and a further 25 percent are totally unaffected (CC). However on average 50 percent of the phenotypes

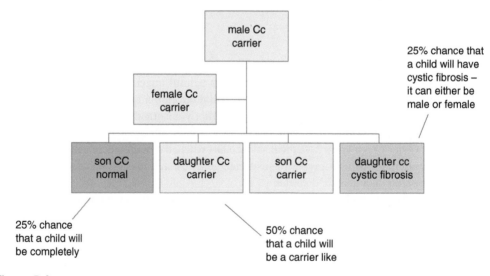

Figure 5.4

manifest no signs of CF but carry the allele c (Cc). These individuals will be carriers and are potential contributors to the disorder in subsequent generations. The probability of acquiring the condition is rare, but the probability of finding a person who is a carrier of the allele is much higher.

This disorder is not sex-linked, so the gender is not important and any child that is produced by two carriers will have a 25 percent chance of having the disorder. If you were counselling a couple who genetically tested as carriers, what would you say about their chances of having a child with cystic fibrosis? The ramifications of having a child with the disorder are severe; on the other hand, they have a 75 percent chance of having a child without the disorder, but a 50 percent chance of passing on the gene.

Huntington's disease

Huntington's disease is another single gene disorder but in this case it is dominant. Again this not a psychological disorder but will affect an individual's quality of life as well as possible decisions about reproduction. In the past an individual could not be certain whether or not they had Huntington's disease until they passed child-bearing years. Today, genetic testing allows us to know if someone has the gene that will eventually cause a lingering illness and their eventual death and can make a decision whether they want to take a chance of passing the disease to their children.

Approximately eight out of every 100,000 people in the UK have HD (Morrison, 2010). Huntington's disease is a neurodegenerative disease that causes certain nerve cells in the brain to waste away or degenerate. Huntington's disease affects a wide range of brain activities that become obvious in middle age. The personality changes can occur as much as ten years before the movements are noticed. It is a progressive illness with symptoms worsening over time. Death usually occurs 15 to 20 years after the appearance of the first symptom(s). The abnormal movements are typically rapid, jerking movements over which the person has no control. Other abnormal movements include slower, writhing movements of the arms and legs, strange postures due to muscle spasm called dystonia and slowing of voluntary movements in a manner similar to another neurodegenerative disorder, Parkinson's disease (Wynbrandt & Ludman, 2008).

Huntington's disease is a single gene disorder but unlike CF it is dominant. There are no carriers and this disorder is either present or absent. If you remember the 10p coin there is a 50 percent chance when you flip the coin of getting the symbol of the lion and a 50 percent chance of getting the picture of the Queen. This is exactly the percentages of Huntington's disease. When one parent has the disorder and the other does not, each child has a 50 percent chance of inheriting the disorder. In order to be at risk an individual must have at least one parent with the disorder. Going back to our example; let us call the recessive and normal allele (h) and the dominant and abnormal allele (H). If we have a parent with the disorder (Hh) and a parent without the disorder (hh), every child will have a 50:50 chance of getting the dominant and abnormal allele. The dominant allele will cause the disorder; it does not need two copies from each parent.

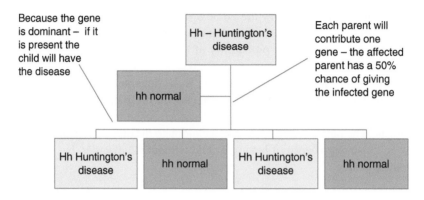

Because the gene is dominant – if it is present the child will have the disease

Hh – Huntington's disease

Each parent will contribute one gene – the affected parent has a 50% chance of giving the infected gene

hh normal

Hh Huntington's disease

hh normal

Hh Huntington's disease

hh normal

Figure 5.5

SEX-LINKED DISORDERS

We have discussed inheritance of genes on the basis of a male and a female contributing with equal probability to any effect. The sex-linked disorders take into account the aspect of gender. Previously we have described chromosomes and their alleles coming together at fertilization without specifying which parent contributes the chromosome and which allele is carried by that chromosome. In sex-linked disorders the allele is carried specifically by that chromosome, therefore gender is important in these disorders as to whether the child will be affected or be a carrier.

Haemophilia

Haemophilia is a disease in which the blood does not clot normally. Prevalence is approximately 10 in 100,000 males in the UK. When an individual gets a cut, the body naturally protects itself and sticky blood cells called platelets go to the open wound and clot in order to stop the bleeding. The next step in the process is that when the platelets begin to clot, they release chemicals that attract more sticky platelets and then activate various proteins in the blood known as clotting factors. These proteins mix with the platelets to form fibres making the clot stronger which facilitates in stopping the bleeding. Our bodies have 12 clotting factors that work together in this process (numbered using Roman numerals from I through XII). Having too little of factors VIII or IX is what causes haemophilia. A person with haemophilia will only lack one factor, either factor VIII or factor IX, but not both. There are two major kinds of haemophilia, haemophilia A and haemophilia B, depending on which factor is missing. About 80 percent of all cases are haemophilia A which is a factor VIII deficiency (Wynbrandt & Ludman, 2008).

Treatment is managed with clotting factor replacement therapy, periodic infusions of the deficient clotting factor into the bloodstream and a medication called recombinant factor VII that helps patients with inhibitors. The medication also activates another part of the coagulation process directly and bypasses the deficiencies (Wynbrandt & Ludman, 2008).

Haemophilia is X-linked recessive. The disorder is carried on the X chromosome and because it is recessive, will be much more common in males than females. In the following diagram are two examples of how sex-linked disorders that are recessive are genetically passed from parents to offspring.

In the diagram in Figure 5.6 a father with haemophilia will always have daughters that are carriers but because the disease is recessive and carried on the X chromosome, none of his sons will be affected. The next diagram will provide an example of a carrier.

When a daughter is a carrier she will give birth to sons with a 50:50 chance of being affected. This is termed 'skip-a-generation' phenomenon. Haemophilia is determined by a recessive allele carried on the X chromosome. Since males have only a single X chromosome, contributed by their mother, if the X also has the affected allele they will have the disorder. In order for females to have haemophilia they would need to inherit the allele on both of their X chromosomes, one from the father and

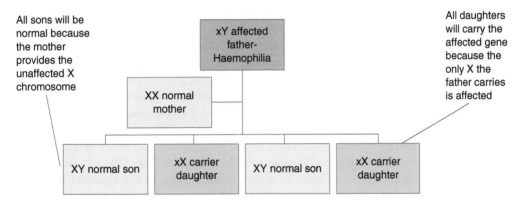

Figure 5.6

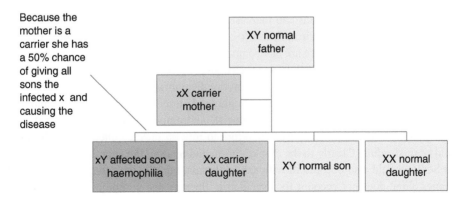

Figure 5.7

one from the mother. In this case the mother would either have to have the disorder or be a carrier and the father would have the disorder.

The diagram shows that with a carrier mother there is a 50:50 chance of a daughter being a carrier, whereas each son will have a 50:50 chance of having the disorder.

COMPLEX CHARACTERISTICS AND GENETICS

Characteristics such as height, weight, intelligence are elements that we considered to be genetic traits but they are also complex because they can be profoundly affected by the environment. In complex characteristics alleles do not act in a simple all-or-none dominant or recessive way, but rather two different alleles might add their effects or it may take four or five alleles in the right combination (structural genes) that additionally require specific environmental stimuli. This appears to be the case with psychiatric disorders. Genes are assumed to influence the development of mental disorders in three distinct ways: they appear to have a complex multiple genetic basis; they are likely to be responsible for abnormalities in a person's development before or after birth, and they are suspected of influencing a person's susceptibility to a mental disorder (Nettle, 2009). In addition to these genetic factors, variations in the environment interact with the genetic information creating complex reactions and conditions. This is referred to as polygenic, which means that there are multiple genes acting in combination rather than a single gene that is causing the psychological disorder. In these cases, genes are more correctly seen as giving a probabilistic bias towards a psychiatric condition (Pritchard & Korf, 2007).

In our case history of Michael, it would appear that genetics played a major role in Michael's illness, but how did Michael's environment contribute to his disorder, if at all? Was he genetically predetermined to eventually succumb to schizophrenia because both his parents had the disorder regardless of his environmental conditions? Was Michael at greater risk because both of his parents had the illness? What about Susan and Sharon; they both had identical environments, identical genes and yet one twin developed schizophrenia and the other twin did not, and neither of their parents were affected by the disorder.

Research in this area is providing more information that multiple gene interactions in combination with environmental interactions can increase a person's vulnerability to mental disorders (Nettle, 2009). Outside of certain environmental triggers, the genetic combination might not increase the risk and it is possible that there are environmental elements that provide immunity.

There are other examples such as gene–environment correlations where a gene might bias a person to seek a certain environment and that environment might exert an effect that could cause a psychological disorder. For example, a gene might lead an individual to seek new and novel types of entertainment, which could then lead to high-risk environments and behaviours that could then lead to drug-taking and substance abuse. Therefore to rely on purely genetic or environmental factors could be misleading. Clearly in the case of Susan and Sharon, the genetic component would dictate that Susan should also become ill with schizophrenia, but this isn't the case. As we will discover, genetics alone does not account for psychiatric illnesses and combinations of genes appear to be responsible only for small effects.

COMPLEX GENETIC INTERACTIONS AND PSYCHOPATHOLOGY

What we think, do and feel is influenced by factors from two sources, ourselves and our environment. The environment is an omnipresent, multidimensional and dynamic source of change. However, to a large extent we determine what we experience in terms of our environment. Interaction with our environment is an exercise in learning and experience as well as exposure. Our parents, their lifestyle and their access to the environment will profoundly influence our own interactions with the environment. For example someone who lives in an affluent suburb in London, from a prosperous family will have a different experience from an American who lives in rural Mississippi and comes from an impoverished background. Each person will have access to a different set of environmental conditions. When combined with their genetics and their lifestyle this will influence a different range of experiences and possibly trigger different genetic combinations which could provide an increased risk for mental illness (Nettle, 2009).

Research has documented that schizophrenia occurs in higher rates in families with impoverishment than in families of affluence, and it is believed that the stress from day-to-day living also increases the risk factors in individuals with a predisposition for mental illness (Kohn, 1976).

Our unique combination of attributes inherited from our biological parents will also guide us in our interaction with our environment. Our experiences will be shaped through our strengths and weaknesses. Genes direct the course of human experience, but experiential opportunities are also necessary for development to occur. Individual differences can arise from restrictions in environmental opportunities such as education.

Genes and the environment both play important yet different roles in our development. The environment provides the context in which growth occurs while our genotype gives direction to that growth. An example of an environmental trigger and a genetic disorder is the relationship of photosensitive epilepsy and modern society. Individuals appear to be born with a genetic flaw in the central nervous system that results in epilepsy when it is triggered by specific visual stimuli such as flashing lights, flash bulbs or quick moving visual stimuli that can be part of videogames (Bureau, Hirsh & Vigevano, 2004). Until these individuals are exposed, the condition remains undiscovered. These individuals would not be at risk for this type of epilepsy in the 1800s because technology could not create a situation that provided the environmental condition necessary for the central nervous system to react in a detrimental way. Therefore this type of epilepsy is a perfect example of how genetic elements and environmental stimuli can conflict causing a significant life-altering problem.

Another important element in how we perceive our environment can be determined and influenced by our expectations, attitudes and belief systems. In terms of psychopathology an individual may have inherited traits that increase their risk of alcoholism, but if they are born in a community that does not allow the sale of alcohol and they also have religious beliefs that forbid the consumption of alcohol at any time, their inherited traits may never be triggered and their specific environmental factors will moderate the genetic factors (Nettle, 2009).

The potential for our genetic make-up to affect behaviour is no different from any other causative factor; its importance depends on a number of considerations, such as the nature of the problem and the presence or absence of other mediating or competing factors. Genetic factors may affect events in a way that we are not normally aware of. This does not mean that they are the cause behind a particular disorder. An individual's genetic make-up may play a minor role or perhaps no role at all. Additionally, it is important to remember that heritability is not absolute, nor is it unchangeable (Nettle, 2009).

GENOTYPE AND ENVIRONMENTAL RELATIONSHIPS

There are three ways in which genes influence what we experience; first there is a passive effect that occurs when our genes and environment come from the same source. This happens primarily during infancy when a child's parents provide both the genes and the environment for the development of a particular trait. This type of effect is referred to as a passive genotype–environment relationship because it occurs independently of the individual. In other words, the child has nothing to do with determining either his or her genetic make-up or his or her environment. Neither of these elements are influenced by the individuals themselves but instead by the circumstances of birth (Plomin, DeFries & Lohehlin, 1977).

The development of musical abilities is an example of a passive effect. An individual's ability to sing will be influenced by his or her inherited ability. This is further influenced by the availability of musical instruments and additional musical training. Parents who listen to music and provide their child with musical opportunities are more likely to encourage their children to become musically proficient. In this example, there are elements of genetic and environmental interaction. Children who are born with a genetic talent such as perfect pitch, singing ability, will be able to learn, recite and hear music more easily than those who are not born with this ability. It is impossible to separate out those elements that are most important in a child's musical development because the child's genes and the rearing environment provided by the parents are all related.

A reactive genetic effect, on the other hand, occurs when our genotype elicits different types of responses from our social and physical environment. The beautiful baby will receive more attention and social stimulation than a child that is deemed to be unattractive. Glocker et al. (2009) found that unattractive babies as compared with cute babies had higher interaction rates. This type of effect extends beyond the environment provided by our parents and includes teachers, peers or other adults who respond to attractiveness by providing special opportunities for an attractive child's development.

A third and final type is referred to as an active genotype effect, which occurs when we seek out environments that are compatible with or supportive of our genetic potential. A skilled athlete may seek out opportunities so they are able to excel in sports. An intellectually gifted child may pursue environments and friends who can foster their intellectual growth. Each choice will be determined to a large extent by environmental opportunities and social values. There are many stories of the gold-medal-winning athlete who pursued their dream by training in less than ideal circumstances and through diligence, talent and fortitude won a spot in a team and then finally came to the world's attention by winning a gold medal in the Olympics. However, no amount of education, training or environmental support can make an athletically inept individual a gold medal winner, or a child with a developmental disability a genius. For this reason it is said that the active genotype effect is the most direct expression of genotypic influences on individual experience.

HERITABILITY AND PSYCHOPATHOLOGY

Heritability is defined as the extent to which differences in genotype and environment contribute to the development of phenotype (an observable characteristic which can be measured). The issue of heritability is whether individual differences in behaviour are influenced by genetic differences and if so, what is the relative influence of heredity and environmental factors (Nettle, 2009).

Genes do not directly cause behaviour; they work indirectly via physiological systems. Genes control the production of proteins which then go on to determine anatomical, biochemical and physiological characteristics in association with the internal and external environments. The outcome of all these processes may include some effect on normal behaviour (Sesardic, 2005).

Preliminary questions concerning heritability may look at how many genes and which chromosomes are involved in the expression of a particular behaviour, but genes and chromosomes alone do not necessarily determine the final outcome. Other elements that are considered are the developmental course of these particular genes, the type of gene action, the interaction with the environment, and how these will affect behaviour. Further complicating heritability is the general rule that a single gene can affect more than just a single phenotype. Genetic variation among individuals can result from either a single gene or the combined effect of several genes (Nettle, 2009).

The ways that behaviour, genes and environment interact are often incredibly complex. Our understanding of environmental risk and psychological disorders generally does not come from genetic research, rather from longitudinal studies of at-risk cohorts and with the examination of large-scale populations.

Adoption studies, in which psychiatric conditions occur more often in adoptees who have biological relatives with the same illness than in those who do not, offer powerful evidence for genetic transmission of many of these disorders. A second type of evidence occurs in twin and family studies in which individuals more closely related to the one with the disorder are more likely to demonstrate evidence of the illness. If a certain disorder appears more frequently in identical (monozygotic) twins of affected individuals than in non-identical (dizygotic) twins, the difference is attributed to genetic factors rather than family environment. This increased susceptibility is often found in monozygotic twins, who are expected to show greater concordance than dizygotic twins. Various psychiatric disorders such as schizophrenia, autism, attention-deficit/hyperactivity disorder, bipolar disorder and major depressive disorder have shown clear differences between monozygotic twins and dizygotic twins.

Crossover between the major diagnostic groupings of mental disorder (schizophrenia and affective disorders) is small and thus implies genetic specificity of each disorder (Cardno & Gottesman, 2000). Research in the prevalence rates of schizophrenia indicates that the first-degree biological relatives (parent, sibling or child that shares approximately 50 percent of their genes) have a 10 percent increased risk of developing the disorder when compared to 1 percent of the general population, whereas an identical twin of a person with schizophrenia has a 40–50 percent risk (Moyer & Sadee, 2011).

First-degree relatives of a person diagnosed with major depression were four times as likely to develop depression as individuals in the general population. Specific genetic factors are thought to account for 37 percent of a person's risk for depression with environmental factors accounting for the remaining 63 percent (Sullivan, Neale & Kendler, 2000). Studies of individuals with bipolar depression have found that a monozygotic twin of an affected individual has a 75–85 percent chance of developing the disorder (McGuffin, Rijsdijk, Andrew, Sham, Katz & Cardno, 2003). Twin studies have also indicated that certain abnormalities in brain hormone levels and brain structures are implicated in a person's susceptibility to acute stress disorder and post-traumatic stress disorder following exposure to trauma (Stein, Jang, Taylor, Vernon & Livesley, 2002). Various studies have implicated genetic determinants in anxiety and stress disorders. Roy, Neale, Pedersen, Mathe & Kendler (1995) found the heritability of generalized anxiety disorder to be approximately 0.32 in first-degree relatives and there were established links to agoraphobia and a high susceptibility to panic disorders.

HERITABILITY IS NOT ABSOLUTE

It is generally accepted that causal factors for any disorder can be categorized in three ways: (1) necessary and sufficient, (2) necessary but not sufficient and (3) facilitating or predisposing (Nettle, 2009). An example of the first category is a particular genotype that causes Huntington's disease. In this case, the presence of the single gene is both necessary and sufficient for the development of the disease.

Fortunately, the number of disorders for which a single causative factor is both necessary and sufficient is relatively rare in medical conditions and non-existent in psychological disorders. Many more factors fall into the second, or necessary but not sufficient category. In fact, in the majority of physical infectious diseases multiple factors are involved, of which all are necessary but one alone is not sufficient to cause the disorder. For example, a group of people can be exposed to the H1N1 virus (also known as swine-flu). However, only a small percentage will show clinical evidence of contagion. Many factors will come into play such as stress, resistance to the disease, previous illnesses, compromised immune system, age and possibly a genetic predisposition. All of these factors can influence the exposure to the virus and determine who will succumb to illness. In this case exposure is necessary but not sufficient for the illness to develop.

The third category includes factors that are facilitating or predisposing. Here the link between the cause and its effect is much less direct. For example, being placed in foster care as a young child is related to the development of a number of psychological problems even though it is neither necessary nor sufficient to produce psychological disorders. In this case the presence of other causative factors or moderating variables will determine the clinical outcome.

Psychiatric disorders appear to fall in either the second or third categories. Schizophrenia is thought to be a psychological complex illness involving multiple aetiologies, which include genetic, developmental, psychosocial and possibly even infectious factors. An analysis of various twin and adoption studies suggest that approximately 60 percent of the variance in predicting schizophrenia can be accounted for by genetic factors, leaving 40 percent to the environment, which is still a large variation when attempting to reduce environmental risk factors (Sullivan et al., 2003; Cardno & Gottesman, 2000).

An additional factor that complicates causative factors is that not all psychiatric syndromes appear to have all the same symptoms, which leads to the question of whether this indicates a role for different genes or different environments or the diagnosis for the disease is not reliable enough to discriminate among different types. Thus the evidence for the heritability of psychiatric disorders coupled with equally strong evidence for an important environmental role suggests that the genetic basis for mental illness, while important, is still only relative in terms of its effect (Smoller, Shiedley & Tsuang, 2008).

Alcoholism is another complex psychiatric disorder that has genetic implications as well as environmental influence. Goodwin (1979) adapted techniques utilized in the study of schizophrenia and mood disorders to research substance abuse disorders. Children of alcoholic, biological parents who were reared by non-alcoholic, adoptive parents were followed and a control group that consisted of individuals who were reared by their non-alcoholic, biological parents. Goodwin found that the incidence of alcoholism in the offspring of alcoholic parents reared in non-alcoholic, adoptive homes was 22 percent while only 4.4 percent of the children in the control group became alcoholic.

While this research suggests that heritability is a factor for some people, it does not show that genes are either necessary or sufficient to cause alcoholism. Many people who become alcoholic appear to lack a genetic basis for the disorder. Furthermore, even if they have a genetic make-up that predisposes them towards alcoholism, abstinence will ensure that they do not become alcoholic. In fact alcoholism appears to be linked to a number of other variables, including life stress, peer groups, depression, as well as social and cultural influences, so that our genetic make-up is seen as playing a facilitating or predisposing role only.

HERITABILITY DOES NOT MEAN UNCHANGEABILITY

Even in the worst-case scenario in which an inherited trait is both necessary and sufficient, the environment still plays a crucial role, as there are many examples of how environmental factors can affect or modify even the most debilitating genetic disorders. Going back to our example of cystic fibrosis, this disorder would be representative of the necessary and sufficient category since it is transmitted by a genetic mutation. Individuals are able to take enzyme pills to help digest food as well as eat a suitable diet and maintain a good body weight, easing the pressure on the pancreas and causing the overall body less distress. So although the genetic factors vary in terms of their degree of influence, they are also flexible in terms of their ability to be influenced by environmental factors.

Another example of why heritability does not mean unchangeability is intellectual ability. Intelligence is made up of many different factors such as creativity, logical abilities and spatial abilities to name a few. The ability to read and/or remember factual information is one variable that defines intelligence but it is not the sole definition. Individuals who grow up in impoverished environments will not do as well on tests of intelligence as those who have the benefit of a good education, good nutrition, literate family members and social reinforcement for learning, but these elements do not necessarily make them more intelligent. Consequently, it may be misleading to attribute differences in intelligence between groups of people unless environmental factors are also taken into account.

On the other hand, it would be equally misleading to assert that genetic factors play no role whatsoever. While the average level of intelligence may be affected by environmental considerations, individual variability may be determined to a large degree by genetic factors. For example, adopted children may generate IQ scores that are above those of their biological parents. Yet the correlation of their scores with those from their biological parents is higher than the correlation of scores from their adoptive parents.

There are fundamental reasons why it is important not to credit genetic factors with more influence than is deserved. Genetic determinism can provide a basis, but our genotype exerts an influence that is relative in its effect and somewhat impressionable in terms of outcome. If we consider the various psychological disorders, there is not one single gene that appears to be responsible for any specific psychological disorder; rather it appears that a complex system which is also reliant on the environment triggers the presence of psychopathology (Smoller, Sheidley & Tsuange, 2008).

RESEARCH, GENETICS AND PSYCHOLOGICAL DISORDERS

The relationship between genes and environment occurs in three basic ways. In the case of a passive effect, our genetic make-up and environment are linked by a common factor, our biological family. The term 'passive' is used to indicate that the individual does not contribute to this situation; it is provided without asking and usually without our thinking about it. Nevertheless, this effect can be extremely important, especially during the very early years of development. The second or reactive effect extends beyond the family to include anyone with whom we come into contact. This type of effect involves the different ways people respond to us because of our physical attractiveness, temperaments or natural abilities. Consequently, the reactive effect is most important during early childhood when basic skills and competencies are being developed and our sense of identity is being established. This developmental step paves the way for an active effect in which the individual seeks out those experiences that are important for the realization of our inherited abilities. This effect becomes more pronounced throughout adulthood. Furthermore, an active effect is not limited to our interaction with other people but can entail any sort of environmental circumstance, social or physical, that enables us to realize our genetic capability.

The research into psychological disorders is complicated and although genetic contribution has been implicated there is a great deal of environmental overlap. In addition there are five factors that add to the complexity of the relationship between genetic factors and psychiatric disorders. The first is psychiatric nosology. This refers to the classification system that is used for mental disorders. Currently the psychiatric/psychological community tends to rely on the Diagnostic and Statistical Manual of Mental Disorders (DSM) published by the American Psychiatric Association to provide a classification system. However, many would argue that this classification system may not accurately diagnose and classify mental disorders, as it is based on superficial symptoms, lists of behaviours that may or may not be observed with very little validity that is entrenched in research. It is possible that some of the current diagnostic labels may represent groups of related syndromes rather than a single diagnostic entity. Even more damaging is the possibility that various psychiatric disorders that appear to be closely related in terms of symptoms may not be.

The second factor is that classifications of mental disorders are reliant upon the diagnostician's human judgement and evaluation of an individual's behaviour or appearance. This category is fraught with possible inconsistencies such as education level, experience, and the possibility that not all symptoms are visible at the time the diagnosis is made. Unlike other fields of medicine there are no definitive tests for bipolar disorder or schizophrenia. We cannot take a sample of blood, urine or any other biological material from the individual and perform a test that will be conclusive. There are no laboratory tests that can provide definitive answers and although we can utilize diagnostic questionnaires they do not have the same degree of precision or objectivity that laboratory findings can provide.

The third factor is that mental disorders involve more than one gene. Various studies have shown that one mental disorder can be caused by different genes on different chromosomes. Weinberger (2004) estimated that the current number of gene variations linked to schizophrenia may be as high as ten. Although many genes have been identified as being related to schizophrenia, they only appear to predispose the individual. Research has shown that various environmental factors have also been associated, such as birth complications, high stress experiences in early life, illnesses and drug use (Jones, Rantakallio, Hartikainen, Isohanni & Sipila, 1998; Corcoran, Walker, Dobbs, Huot, Mittal, Tessner, Kestler & Malaspina, 2003; Tyrrell, Parry, Crow Johnstone & Ferrier, 1979). The fourth factor is that genes associated with mental disorders do not always show the same frequencies for a gene to produce its effects within a specific group of people. In other types of genetic disorders such as Down's syndrome there is a characteristic patterning of mental and physical abnormalities, and although they are on a spectrum from mild to severe, the patterns are relatively stable. In psychiatric disorders this patterning has greater variability, sometimes to the point that some symptoms are not identifiable. So for example, one characteristic of schizophrenia is hallucinations, but what type of hallucinations? Auditory? Visual? Olfactory? Can they occur in combination or is one type primary? Do they involve themes? People? Places? There are no patterns or characteristic behaviours that can be identified as being entirely characteristic of schizophrenia. To further complicate matters, many types of brain disorders, tumours and injuries create similar hallucinations to those experienced by individuals who have received a diagnosis of schizophrenia.

The fifth and final factor is the possibility that genetics is overlooking the potential role of 'protective genes' in psychiatric disorders. Various researchers have documented that there appear to be particular genetic markers which prevent mental illness from manifesting within individuals who are otherwise genetically and environmentally predisposed to develop it. Furthermore, these individuals posses a distinct genetic trait that possibly influences wellness and provides a resilience to cope with the constitutional vulnerabilities that lead to psychopathology (Cowan, 1988; Garmezy, 1985; Rutter, 1990).

CLINICAL APPLICATIONS OF GENETICS TO PSYCHOLOGICAL DISORDERS

There are basically four possibilities of clinical applications to psychological disorders; genetic counselling, medication selection and dosage, environmental intervention and psychopharmacogenetics. Although currently it is possible to engage in genetic counselling with individuals who have been identified as being at high risk for psychiatric disorders, the science is not quite capable of specifically identifying the prevalence of individual risk factors that are identifiable with a disorder such as Huntington's disease.

However, once the genes are identified, individuals whose parent is known to have a psychiatric disorder or when there is a family history of a psychiatric disorder could be tested and provided with genetic counselling that would include information concerning the disorder, mitigating environmental circumstances, medication and reproductive choices. Intervention could take place before the individual began to show symptoms and it is possible that many of the debilitating aspects of having a psychiatric illness, such as; low self-esteem and social stigma, could be diminished.

In terms of medication selection and dosage, if the specific genetic markers were identified in psychiatric disorders it would possible to identify through DNA testing an individual's responsiveness to psychiatric medications, eliminating unnecessary side effects, as the genetic testing would simplify the present process of trial-and-error prescribing of drugs.

Genetic testing could also help in the identification of individuals who are at risk and changes in lifestyle and circumstance could help to mitigate the psychiatric illness. Individuals could be identified at younger ages before they succumbed to the disorder and helped at an earlier stage in their development.

Finally there is psychopharmacogenetics where medications are developed that target individuals with a particular genetic profile.

THE HUMAN GENOME PROJECT

Finally, our chapter concludes with a brief discussion of the Human Genome project which began in 1990 and was completed in 2003. It was a collaborative project between the United States, the Wellcome Trust (UK) and various other countries which contributed to the aims and objectives of the undertaking. The project was able to identify all of the 25,000 genes in human DNA and determine the sequences of the 3 billion chemical base pairs. It provided this information in a database that is being used for genetic research and the improvement of related technologies (US Department of Energy Genome Programs, 2008). This project has provided researchers with new techniques and a means to decipher the intricate complexities of the interactions between the environment and genes in psychiatric conditions, possibly providing in the near future the answers to many questions concerning psychiatric disorders and gene expression.

CONCLUSION

In our first case study it is clear that genetics played a role in Michael's own mental illness. Both of Michael's birth parents were diagnosed with schizophrenia so his own probability of risk was high. We don't know anything about other predisposing factors, so although it is likely that he carried a genetic predisposition to schizophrenia, the environmental triggers are unknown. Michael could have had a traumatic birth, there could have been infectious illnesses, he could have used drugs as an adolescent, all of which could have increased his chances of mental illness. Perhaps if his adoptive parents had been provided with the information about his birth parents they could have raised Michael with a different awareness and provided changes in his environment that may have lessened his risk. Unfortunately we will never know. What is important is that the laws have changed to provide prospective adoptive parents with medical histories of the birth parents if they are known, and the genetic contribution to mental illness has been acknowledged. If we looked upon this as a positive method of helping people avoid the manifestation of mental illness instead of stigmatizing individuals, this could be constructive in the treatment and identification of high risk individuals. What about Susan and Sharon? We can eliminate to a certain degree environmental factors as both girls were exposed to similar environmental stressors. Perhaps this case provides more evidence for the 'protective gene'? What is different about Susan and Sharon is that one twin was protected from schizophrenia and the other wasn't. Perhaps one day we will be able to help children like Michael, Susan and Sharon and change heritability to changeability.

Summary

The chapter initially provided an introduction to the history of genetics as well as a basic understanding of genetics, chromosomes and heredity. The interaction (nature/nurture) was discussed and how these elements were applied to abnormal behaviours and psychophysiology. Students were provided with examples of genetic disorders and how the interaction of genes and the environment impacted abnormal disorders and behaviour.

LEARNING TOOLS

Key terms

Crossing over – The exchange of sections between pairs of chromosomes during the first stage of meiosis

Deoxyribonucleic acid (DNA) – Double-stranded, coiled molecules of genetic material chromosomes

Dominant trait – a trait that will outwardly appear in the offspring if one of the parents contributes it

Gametes – egg cells and sperm

Gene – A unit of inheritance

Gene maps – Maps that indicate the relative positions of genes along a chromosome

Linkage – The tendency for traits that are encoded on the same chromosome to be inherited together

Meiosis – a type of cell division that produces gametes with half as many chromosomes

Mitosis – The process of cell division that produces cells with the same number of chromosomes as the parent cell

Mutations – Abnormal genes that are created by accidents of chromosome duplication

Recessive trait – an inherited trait that is outwardly obvious when two copies of the gene for that trait are present

Replication – The process by which the DNA molecule duplicates itself

Sex chromosomes – The pair of chromosomes that determine an individual's sex: XX for a female and XY for a male

Sex-linked traits – Traits that are influenced by genes on the sex chromosomes

Structural genes – Genes that contain the information required for the synthesis of a particular protein

Study guide

1   Research a different recessive single gene disorder from the two presented in this chapter, detailing how the disorder affects the three basic elements of functioning.
2   Explore the relationship of mood disorders to sex-linked genetic disorders.
3   A family would like to adopt a child but has found out that one parent and two siblings have a diagnosis of schizophrenia. What can you tell them with regard to the possibilities that this child will be affected with a mental disorder?
4   The tongue-rolling ability seen in seven out of ten people is transmitted by a dominant gene. Would both your parents have to have this gene for you to have this ability?

Case study in focus

Discuss the reasons why Sharon become ill and Susan did not. What possible variations could have occurred? Would genetic testing and counselling have helped in this case? What about Michael? Identify the positives and negatives involved with genetic testing and how they would be similar or different to the two case studies.

Personal development

Investigate whether race and ethnicity have a genetic factor that is unique to a certain group of people. How does this relate to genotype and environmental relationships, and does this element affect mental illness?

Suggested reading

Bazzett, T. (2008) *An introduction to behaviour genetics*. New York: Sinauer.
Faraone, S.V. & Tsuang, M.T. (2002) *Genetics of mental disorders: What practitioners and students need to know.* New York: Guildford Press.
Jang, K.L. (2005) *The behavioral genetics of psychopatholgy: A clinical guide*. London: Routledge.
Joseph, J. (2006) *The missing gene: psychaitry, heredity and the fruitless search for genes*. New York: Algora.

Assessment, Diagnosis, Research Methods and Ethics

Learning aims

At the end of this chapter you should understand:

- The process of diagnosis
- How assessment contributes to the process of diagnosis
- What types of research methods are used in psychpathology
- Ethical issues in abnormal psychology.

--- **INTRODUCTION** ---

CASE STUDY

Mr Janson had recently retired from his job as an accountant. He had been looking forward to retiring and finally getting a chance to go on some long fishing trips. He planned and went on a three-week trip and was very successful in catching a couple of trophy fish that he had stuffed, mounted and placed in his study. His family was a bit puzzled when he suddenly seemed to lose interest and didn't plan any more trips. He seemed to be a bit down and they thought it was due to his retirement and that perhaps he was missing his work colleagues and a steady schedule. As time passed it was clear that Mr Janson was becoming depressed; he began to sleep a lot and when he wasn't sleeping would sit for hours in front of the television watching random programmes. When his personal hygiene began to slip his wife decided it was time to visit the GP. The local physician did a routine physical, checked his blood pressure and cholesterol levels and asked Mr Janson a lot of questions. Mr Janson responded by telling the physician that he just did not feel very happy, he couldn't elaborate any further but said that although he enjoyed his fishing trip he just didn't have the energy to plan another one and that he simply didn't have a reason to get up in the morning. Dr Moffit diagnosed Mr. Janson as having mild depression, prescribed anti-depressants and sent him home. Mr Janson came in three months later and said he felt worse and that the medication was not helping, he was sleeping more and felt very sad and depressed most of the time. Dr Moffit felt that that Mr Janson was having difficulty coping with his life changes, changed the prescription to tricyclic antidepressants and made a referral to a psychologist. Mr Janson faithfully took his medication and began attending therapy sessions, but he seemed to be deteriorating. He never got dressed any more except to attend his therapy sessions, he spent all of his time asleep, his personal hygiene was deplorable, and he refused to speak to anyone. His doctor changed his medication again, explaining to Mrs Janson that this new medication had special dietary requirements which should help Mr. Janson feel more like himself. Dr Moffit prescribed MAO inhibitors. Again, Mr Janson seemed to be making no improvements. Two months after Mr Janson had been taking the new medication he collapsed at home and began having seizures. He was taken to hospital where medical tests found that he had a benign brain tumour. It was surgically removed and Mr Janson made a complete recovery, he no longer suffered from depression and began planning his next trophy fishing trip.

What went wrong in Mr Janson's case? Why was his medical condition not immediately recognized and treated? Was it medical negligence? All too often initial symptoms can be part of many different types of physical and/or psychological problems. What appears to be one type of illness can change over time as other symptoms surface during the course of the illness and it becomes clear that the original conclusion was incorrect. Often decisions about treatment must be made on the basis of what is currently happening and affecting the individual; the care provider may not have the luxury of waiting until all the symptoms are present before deciding the course of treatment. However, in Mr Janson's case you may have wondered how a psychological disorder was first diagnosed when the actual cause of his symptoms was physical, i.e. a tumour. This chapter will discuss the various issues surrounding psychological assessment and diagnosis and we will return to Mr Janson and discuss what went wrong.

DIAGNOSIS

What is a diagnosis and why is it important? A diagnosis is not an entity; it is a process. It begins with a statement of the problem. Diagnosis is a medical term that is defined as the act of identifying a disease from its symptoms. The medical model proposes that for each disease/illness there is an underlying cause responsible for a specific set of symptoms that is unique to that cause. By observing and classifying various symptoms the physician can identify the illness/disease and then provide treatment (Widiger & Mullins-Sweatt, 2008). This is the process of making a diagnosis. A diagnosis is important because for many types of illness there is a specific treatment procedure. Making the wrong diagnosis could mean that the wrong medication is given and the individual does not make a full recovery until the right diagnosis is made and the right treatment is provided. A medical diagnosis and a psychological diagnosis basically follow the same procedures. First, there is the initial statement of the problem; the next step is information gathering, information analysis, the use of medical tests/assessments, organization and integration of all the information, and finally classification and treatment (Choca & Denburg, 1996).

When a health professional makes a diagnosis they utilize a classification system that incorporates a method of disease deduction. This means that they eliminate what it isn't before they arrive at the conclusion as to what it is. Using a medical example, the body's immune system responds to pathogens in a similar pattern usually with the onset of a fever, and many diseases/illnesses begin with a fever before other symptoms are evident. The physician must narrow down the possible category and classification of the illness and this can only be done by a systematic method of elimination. In some cases, if the fever is high and possibly life threatening, the symptom is treated before the actual illness is diagnosed, but the process continues until the disease is identified and the correct treatment protocol is provided (Drabick & Kendall, 2010).

When a mental illness is diagnosed the same procedure is followed. There is an initial assessment of the problem, what symptoms are currently present, how the illness began, what other symptoms may be present that the individual does not feel are important or relevant and hasn't mentioned in the original problem. The clinician will have a general idea of what the problem is and psychological tests may be conducted to narrow down the classification. All the information is organized and classified and finally a diagnosis is made. Once the mental health problem is identified a course of action can be undertaken (Drabick & Kendall, 2010).

Psychological disorders are different from physical illnesses because of the interaction between mental and physiological symptoms. Often physiological disorders will affect mental functioning and mental disorders can affect physiological functioning. For example, many of the stress disorders begin with physiological symptoms, e.g. breathing difficulties, pain in the chest, heart racing, dizziness, etc. The physiological symptoms must be assessed first as the problem could be medical and life threatening. Once it has been established that the problem is not medical the psychological issues are examined and evaluated (Beinart, Kennedy & Llewelyn, 2009).

Psychological disorders are usually not characterized by the presence of a single symptom or a single biological indicator and can be complicated to diagnose. If psychological disorders are difficult to categorize why classify them at all? The main answer is that by placing various disorders in classification groups, the treatment protocol will be easier to implement. Although there may be very little difference in the physiological treatment of stress disorders, i.e. medication, the psychological treatment may be very different (post-traumatic stress disorder vs. agoraphobia) (Carr & McNulty, 2006).

There are four basic reasons for categorizing and diagnosing mental disorders. The first is the organization of clinical information. This helps to structure the symptoms in a way that is coherent, conscious and retrievable by others. If every psychologist had to structure and organize all the information for every client, the process would be time consuming and each patient would be a new and different problem with treatment developing out of trial-and-error experimentation, possibly to the detriment of the individual with the psychological disorder (Hoff & Morgan, 2010).

The second most important reason is the communication among professionals. A diagnosis can enhance effective exchange of information. Without labelling and organizing patterns of abnormal behaviour, researchers could not communicate their findings to one another and the progress towards understanding these disorders would significantly slow down.

The third reason is the prediction and selection of treatment. Important decisions are made on the basis of classification. Certain psychological disorders respond better to one therapy than another or to one class of drugs than another. Classification can also help to predict the course of the mental illness and what time lines can be expected for a full recovery. Finally a diagnosis helps to reduce undesirable variability among identified disorders. Classification helps researchers identify populations with similar patterns of abnormal behaviour. By classifying groups of people with a particular mental disorder, researchers might be able to identify common factors that help explain the origins of that mental disorder. The diagnosis of psychological disorders represents a way of classifying patterns of abnormal behaviour on the basis of their common symptoms. No psychological disorder always looks the same and no patient's behaviour can be predicted with certainty, but it is helpful to have an idea of what to expect during the course of treatment (Hoff & Morgan, 2010).

Is the diagnosis of psychological disorders always clear? No, most diagnoses are based on the extent that they depart from normal functioning. For example, if someone is suffering a bereavement, at what point does this depart from normal and expected grieving to abnormal grieving and depression? There is no absolute criterion for making a determination when a normal behaviour becomes abnormal. If we are making a determination of abnormal behaviour in terms of grieving, would we base this on time? Is it abnormal to grieve after one month? One year? Or ten years? Does it matter what the relationship to the person was? Some cultures and religions have different time lines for grieving; how would this be accounted for in terms of abnormal behaivour? Evaluation of actions as normal or abnormal can often depend on accepted social conventions. Individuals who are diagnosing psychological disorders must be sensitive not only to variables such as psychological orientation but also to individual value systems, societal norms and values (Antony & Barlow, 2010).

How are psychological disorders classified? Classification involves the arrangement of various forms of abnormal behaviour into specific categories. The descriptive categories help organize our thinking concerning the causes, symptoms and treatment of abnormal behaviour. The most familiar and most utilized of the various classification systems is the Diagnostic and Statistical Manual of Mental Disorders first published in 1952 by the American Psychiatric Association. Although there are others, this system is one that is widely recognized and most often utilized in the classification and research of mental disorders (Cave, 2002).

DSM

The German psychiatrist Emil Kraepelin is credited with developing the first systematic and widely accepted classification system of mental disorders. Kraepelin viewed mental disorders as diseases of the mind and noted that certain symptom patterns occurred with regularity, allowing it to be identified and classified. He believed that once various forms of mental illness had been distinguished and classified, medical research could begin looking for agents responsible for the disease and it could then be cured. The classification system Kraepelin created greatly influenced the field of psychiatry and it served as a broad framework when the DSM system was initially developed (Robertson & Walter, 2007).

In the late 1940s increased interest in classification models for psychiatric diagnosis began to be discussed. The American Psychiatric Association's initial effort was to classify mental disorders in a glossary that provided descriptions of diagnostic categories. Mental disorders in this early version are primarily described as reactions to psychological, social and biological factors (Wilson, 1993).

The DSM was revised ten years later and during this revision it was decided to organize it into a classification system that was similar to the World Health Organization's classification of diseases and morbid conditions called the ICD (The International Statistical Classification of Diseases, Injuries and Causes of Death). The intention of the changes was to enable mental health professionals throughout the world to compare types of disorders, incidence of occurrence and other relevant data concerning mental disorders. The DSM adopted the ICD coding system so that the two systems could be used to share information about the prevalence and characteristics of particular disorders (Wilson, 1993).

The aims and objectives of the third and fourth revision of the DSM were to provide a diagnostic criterion that would allow for reliable classification through the use of explicit and carefully defined criteria. The third revision was released in 1980 and the fourth revision was published in 1987. The fourth revision, called the DSM III-R, improved the reliability and clinical usefulness of the third edition.

In 1994, the fifth revision was published and called the DSM IV. This revision enhanced the diagnostic structure by adding clinical significance criteria as well as relating the various diagnoses to clinical practice (Goldman, Skodol & Lave, 1992). The DSM-IV-TR was published in 2000 and updated some of the information provided on the various classifications as well as changing some of the diagnostic codes to maintain consistency with the ICD. The next edition, called the DSM-5 (no roman numeral) is currently in planning and preparation and the date for its release is May 2013. A few of the changes planned for this new edition include: a section to include a binge eating disorder, a more formal process for suicide risk, combining substance abuse with dependence, aligning the autistic disorders and an inclusion of self-injury as a maladaptive coping mechanism (APA, 2011).

HOW DOES THE DSM WORK?

The DSM is descriptive, not explanatory; the definitions consist of descriptions of the clinical features of the disorders. It describes the diagnostic features and makes no attempt to explain the origins of the disorders nor does it adopt any particular theoretical framework. The clinician arrives at a diagnosis by

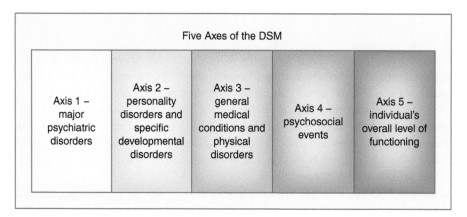

Figure 6.1

matching a client's behaviours with the criteria that define particular patterns of abnormal behaviour. The DSM is a multiaxial approach to classification and diagnosis. The individual is evaluated on five different aspects that are called axes that are believed to have high clinical independence from each other.

Axis I is the aspect that includes the major psychiatric disorders with the exception of the personality disorders and developmental disorders. Axis II is for reporting all the various personality disorders (adults) and specific developmental disorders (children and adolescents). Axis III is for the classification of general medical conditions and physical disorders that may be significant to the management of the individual's psychological disorder. Axis IV is for the reporting of specific psychosocial events, for example the loss of a job, a financial hardship etc. This axis is for reporting any psychosocial and/or environmental problem that may affect the diagnosis, treatment and prognosis of the psychological disorder. The final axis is for reporting the clinician's judgement of the individual's overall level of functioning and is done using the global assessment of functioning scale. This information is useful in planning treatment, measuring the impact of the psychological disorder and making a prospective prediction of outcome (Wilson, 1993).

The multiaxial approach of the DSM reduces the probability that a single diagnostic category will classify an individual's psychological disorder. The DSM classification system is intended to reduce the undesirable variability in the diagnostic evaluation process and standardize the categories of psychological disorders. Although the multiaxial system allows for individuals to be classified by both categorical and dimensional components, there are still issues with this type of system (Lewis, 2006).

PROBLEMS WITH DIAGNOSIS

Some of the criticism of classification systems and diagnosis is that it can be unreliable and often not useful. The course of a psychological disorder is often unpredictable and the basis for making a diagnosis is not always a consensus by health care providers. Additionally the psychological, physical or environmental factors responsible for many of these disorders are not known, so a diagnosis does not usually help in identifying them. Moreover, the diagnosis of psychological disorders has not been useful in creating effective treatment for many psychiatric disorders such as schizophrenia. It has also been suggested that diagnostic labels can be used as powerful tools to disenfranchise or otherwise injure individuals and that the classification of people and their behaviour is unnecessary, harmful or degrading (Cooksey & Brown, 1998).

Although these criticisms are valid, categorizations are inevitable and how a system is justified is determined by how accurately it facilitates the prediction, control and understanding of behaviour. Any system used in the classification of abnormal behaviour will have advantages and disadvantages for the individual and understanding and recognizing the appropriate reasons may help to protect against their misuse.

ASSESSMENT INSTRUMENTS AND PSYCHOPATHOLOGY

Assessment is part of the diagnostic process and there are many types of assessments for many different purposes, completed by many different professions. This section on assessment is going to discuss psychologists using assessments for the diagnosis of psychological disturbances.

One of the most common diagnostic problems to confront the psychologist is that of distinguishing between a disorder caused by a physical disease and/or injury to the central nervous system and a psychological disorder (Carr & McNulty, 2006). A psychological disorder such as schizophrenia and an organic disorder such as a brain tumour or degenerative neurological condition can be difficult to distinguish when both are in the early stages and the symptoms do not differentiate between the two. Assessments are used to collect meaningful information about an individual for the purpose of helping narrow a diagnosis. They should never be used in isolation nor should they be used without other information when making a determination about an individual. They should be used to help with problem clarification, information gathering, and the understanding of what information has been assessed (Lewis, Gould, Habib & King, 2010).

The very first personality inventory to assess psychological disturbances was the Personal Data Sheet developed by Robert Woodworth in 1920. This inventory was used as a screening device for identifying seriously disturbed men who were not suitable for military service. This instrument was found to be very useful and other types of assessments were then created for the purpose of identifying abnormal behaviours from the normal population (Beinart, Kennedy & Llewelyn, 2009).

Assessments have developed out of a need to find a more objective and efficient method of collecting information about people in a short amount of time. The clinical interview is one of the most useful and effective tools used by a trained professional in order to gather individual information and should always precede any other psychological assessment. The clinical interview is the first step in the assessment process and is involved in problem clarification. The interview process allows the clinician to make decisions in terms of what other psychological assessments should be utilized. Once a link between a reported problem and a content area has been implied, various psychological tests can be considered to access further information before a final diagnosis is completed (Lewis, Gould, Habib & King, 2010).

THE CLINICAL INTERVIEW

What is a clinical interview and how is it different from any other type of interview? The clinical interview is different because its sole purpose is to provide information for the determination of a psychological abnormality. The clinical interview is a basic method of psychological assessment that is effective for exploring and defining specific concerns, feelings and problems an individual may be experiencing. There are many issues with the validity of the clinical interview as the organization tends to vary with the vast majority of interviews being very informal and unstructured.

The advantage of the clinical interview is that the professional is able to ask questions and change direction easily and quickly while trying to understand the initial issue. The disadvantage is that it makes it impossible to compare content and material between individuals and professionals. Another disadvantage of the clinical interview that has been well documented in the literature is the differing experiences and clinical skills of the interviewers. The level of experience and clinical skills does make a significant difference in these informal, unstructured assessments (Goldberg, 1968).

Even though clinical interviews are unstructured, they should cover three basic areas, although not necessarily in any particular order. The first is the individual's leading complaint and present difficulty. The questions of when, where, and under what circumstances did their disorder develop should be part of the interview. The next area will be the individual's personal history, which involves an exploration of each period − infancy, childhood, adolescence and adulthood for adequacy of social, sexual, psychological and vocational functioning. The third area will be the individual's personal relationships with others. This would include the individual's parents and siblings, friendships and intimate relationships, the nature of relationships with various people and the role they have played in past and present psychological turmoil (Rogers, 1980).

What other elements make up the clinical interview? Clinical observations are part of the clinical interview as they provide additional information during the interview although its limitations are more pronounced. Clinical observations are subject to the biases of the clinician and there is always a danger of distortion. A psychologist might overlook or underrate various behaviours. There is also the danger of subject bias; most individuals will want to create a good impression and may temporarily adopt behaviours that mask behaviours that may be important in making the correct diagnosis. Some may be guarded and defensive because they fear being studied or fear the prospect of being viewed as crazy. Any of these conditions will make the individual's behaviours during the interview difficult to accurately interpret and assess. Clinical observations can be useful in five categories:

1   general physical appearance and attire;
2   emotional gestures and facial expressions;
3   gross and fine motor acts;

4   the quality of the relationship between the interviewee and interviewer; and
5   the individual's verbalizations (Rogers, 1980).

Many professionals encourage structured elements to be included in the clinical interview as they can provide a more systematic approach in the assessment process and a way of providing a brief assessment of the individual's current functioning. One widely used structured assessment is called a mental-status examination and generally has six elements of evaluation:

- appearance and manner;
- speech characteristics;
- level and quality of mood,
- content of thought
- the assessment of the patient's orientation, memory and learning, attention and concentration (Rogers, 1980).

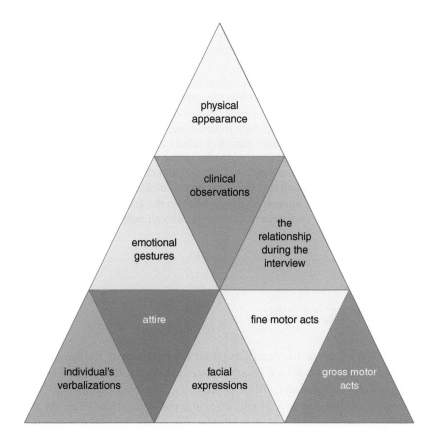

Figure 6.2   Elements of the clinical interview

Table 6.1   Mental-status examination

1 **Appearance and manner**	How facial and body expressions match with the conversation, i.e. sad face with sad conversation.
	Overall impression of the person.
	How the individual relates to the interviewer.
	Does the conversation flow?
2 **Speech characteristics**	Are there difficulties? Does the person follow normal speech patterns, conversation too fast or too slow?
	The presence of any of the following; neologisms, flight of ideas, difficulty finding words, hesitation, use of non-words.
3 **Level and quality of mood**	The interviewer must be alert to a variety of possible moods, including sadness, depression, grief, suspicion, anxiety, fear, panic, hostility, elation, ecstasy and tranquillity. The level and quality of the patient's mood are extremely sensitive reflections of emotional disorder.
4 **Content of thought**	The substance of the conversation can indicate thought processes. It is important to pay attention to the individual's subtle thought content, both normal and abnormal, as a means of assessing unconscious influences on thinking.
	The presence of hallucinations and faulty perceptions, delusions and illusions, obsessive thoughts and phobic ideas are diagnostic.
5 **Assessment of the patient's orientation, memory and learning, attention and concentration and general information**	This section is an indication of how well the individual is processing and utilizing data from the environment. The functions are often impaired in acute brain disorders (intoxication and acute brain trauma). Such individuals may not know where they are, what time it is or how they came be where they are. Chronic brain disorders are often characterized by profound disorders of memory, especially recent memory.
6 **The interviewer evaluates the individual's insight and judgement**	This section evaluates whether the individual can distinguish themselves as incapable of functioning without help from others.

PSYCHOLOGICAL TESTS

Once the clinical interview has been conducted the next step in the decision-making process is whether psychological tests should be administered and what tests should be used. Psychological assessment is a very complex and difficult procedure as it involves the appraisal of personality which is multifaceted and has a variety of meanings and characteristics. There are five different ways of collecting information about an individual's personality: trait, phenomenological, psychodynamic, situational and interactional. The five different elements can also be thought of as paradigms (Groth-Manat, 2003).

The trait paradigm assumes that human behaviour may be ordered and measured along a dimension of defined traits, e.g. responsibility, affiliation, and that individuals can be classified and characterized by these defined traits. Traits are defined as elements that are the main determinants of behaviour and represent a person's tendencies to behave in certain ways regardless of environmental conditions. Traits are believed to be inner dispositions that are relatively consistent across a variety of situations. Assessments in this category are often referred to as objective assessments. Objective tests of personality and behaviour require direct self-reports of memories, attitudes, beliefs and feelings about past, present and future behaviour to portray personality and predict behaviour (Wiggins & Schwartz, 2005).

The phenomenological paradigm focuses on the individual's subjective perceptions and experiences of the world and is also concerned with person factors such as self-concept and subjective experiences. This element focuses on the interaction between the individual and the environment and again is believed to be relatively consistent across different situations. Very few assessments are designed to measure the various components in this complicated paradigm, which is difficult to measure or quantify (Wiggins & Schwartz, 2005).

The psychodynamic paradigm assumes that personality is made up of specific elements and associated motives and instincts that cause a person to behave in certain ways. This paradigm does not focus on external information and believes that all sources of behaviour are within the individual and that this behaviour is relatively stable across a variety of situations and can be accessed through the individual's responses to vague or ambiguous stimuli. Projective tests assess behaviour by indirect or disguised means in an effort to capture unconscious, forgotten or suppressed behavioural memories (Wiggins & Schwartz, 2005).

The situational model defines personality in terms of the individual's actual overt behaviour. Behaviour is believed to be a function of prior experiences. The individual's personality is defined in terms of what he or she does and therefore personality is considered to be composed of a pattern of behavioural responses that the individual makes with some consistency. Individuals completing these types of assessments are asked to perform some tasks in a given situation and then the specific behaviours are discussed in terms of excesses, deficits and appropriateness (Wiggins & Schwartz, 2005).

The interactional model assumes that human behaviour tends to be influenced by many determinants both in the person and in the situation. This model emphasizes person–situation interactions in personality and suggests that behaviour involves a continuous interaction between individuals and situations. This type of paradigm has been difficult to quantify as it must simultaneously take into account the individual's responses and the varying situations as well as the interaction between the two (Wiggins & Schwartz, 2005).

In terms of the application of these five paradigms the vast majority of psychological assessments utilized for the assessment and diagnosis of psychological disturbances are the trait model and objective assessments.

An example of an objective assessment: the MMPI

The MMPI (Minnesota Multiphasic Psychological Inventory) is one of the most widely used of the objective measures of behaviour, and illustrates the major strengths and weaknesses of most of these types of assessments. There are many other tests in this category such as: the NEO personality inventory, the Personality Assessment Inventory, and the OMNI Personality Inventory. The MMPI is a self-report scale consisting of true or false statements and is scored according to ten basic psychiatric-personality scales and three validity scales. A subject's pattern of responding to the test items can be converted into a profile which shows whether the responses were deviant on any of the ten basic scales. The MMPI has been proven to be very reliable which means that a person taking the test on different occasions will be likely to give about the same answer each time. The MMPI has proved valuable when attempting to distinguish normal from abnormal behaviour and when trying to distinguish between psychotic and neurotic. On the negative side, the MMPI has not proved consistently useful in differentiating between types of psychotic disorders which is a very important clinical decision for psychologists to make when narrowing down a specific diagnosis among the subtypes of schizophrenia (Ayers, Templer & Ruff, 1975).

The Rorschach and the TAT: two projective tests

The two projective tests most frequently used are the Thematic Apperception Test (TAT) and the Rorschach inkblot test. Unlike the MMPI, which asks direct questions that are to be answered as either true or false, these assessments require the individual to apply their own perceptual structure to an ambiguous stimulus. The Rorschach test requires that the individual looks at a set of random inkblots and then reports what they see, which can be people, places or things. The TAT solicits the respondent to tell a story after looking at a picture of people engaged in undefined, ambiguous behaviour. The story may or may not stick closely to the original picture and may or may not involve the subject. In both these tests, the subject must project his or her own fantasies, perceptions and thoughts onto a stimulus that is deliberately left vague in order to complete the assessment (Rath, 2001).

Behavioural assessments

Behavioural assessments involve self-observation from the person being tested or can be observations and perceptions of other people. Examples of these types of tests are ratings of behavioural statements, ranking types of behaviour from highest to lowest, noting frequency of the behavioural occurrences. Specific assessments are: Adult Behaviour Checklist, Behavioural and Emotional Rating Scale and the Scales for Assessing Emotional Disturbance (Groth-Manat, 2003).

Projective vs. objective vs. behavioural assessments.

Studies that have directly compared the three different types of assessment find that the behavioural assessments have the highest reliability and validity with projective assessments having the lowest valid and reliable measures. The reason for this is that behaviour assessment procedures are directly tied to treatment with the ideology that the assessment should directly tie into treatment plans. Many objective assessments are reliable but do not necessarily integrate diagnosis and treatment (Bornstein, 1999; Ivnik, 1977).

RESEARCH METHODS

Research validates hypotheses and theories and adds to our knowledge of psychological disorders. Consequently it is important to be familiar with a few of the research methods that are used in assessment, psychological therapies and psychopathology. This section is just a brief introduction to the various research methods used and is not written as a comprehensive guide.

Psychological research has often been criticized in that the studies are of limited value to the general population. What this means in technical terms is that the research has low validity. There are two types of criterion used to evaluate research design; external and internal validity. External validity is the extent to which the results of a study generalize to other subjects and situations (Mook, 2001). For example, how does studying victims of an earthquake disaster in Argentina relate to studying victims of a flood in North Yorkshire? The types of disaster are different, the locations are different but the responses people have in general to natural disasters will be similar. Individuals in both situations will probably have similar feelings and fears and have to cope with the rebuilding of their lives. These two studies can be generalized to individuals of any type of natural disasters.

Internal validity refers to the extent to which the researcher has controlled for all the other explanations that could be responsible for the results of the study (Mook, 2001). Does the study measure what it was designed to measure and to what level do the results account for the experimental treatment? In other words, did the variable being studied actually produce the observed results? Internal validity in a study is essential because without this element the results of the study are meaningless. We cannot trust that the study has reliably examined and reported the results accurately because other factors could be responsible for the results. Table 6.2 lists common extraneous variables that can confuse the results of a research study.

Psychological research can be defined as belonging to one of two primary categories: observational studies and experimental studies. In an observational study there is no direct manipulation of the variables within the study and data (information) is simply collected on groups of participants. The researcher collects information on the attributes and makes no effort to influence or manipulate it. Depending on how the information was collected, this type of study can have high external validity (it can be generalized) but more than likely will have low internal validity as many other factors can interfere and contribute to the final result(s) (Mook, 2001).

In an experimental study the researcher directly influences the events in order to draw conclusions regarding the impact of the influence on the variables. The researcher samples from a population and randomly assigns subjects to two or more groups. The use of randomization, if done correctly, ensures that participants in the intervention and control groups are similar at the start of the study. The groups are then exposed to identical conditions during the course of the study, and any factors that may influence the variables are controlled or kept constant across groups. At some point during the course of the experiment the researcher introduces the experimental manipulation, also called the independent variable. At the end of the study the groups are compared to examine whether any differences have occurred. If the groups differ, then the researcher can conclude that the difference was caused by the experimental manipulation (independent variable) (Mook, 2001).

Table 6.2   Common extraneous variables in research

Internal validity	History	Specific events occurring between the first and second measurement in addition to the experimental variable
	Maturation	Process within the respondents operating as a function of the passage of time, i.e. growing older or becoming bored with study
	Testing	Effects of taking a test upon the scores of a second testing
	Instrumentation	Changes in the calibration of a measuring instrument or changes in the observers or scorers used may change the obtained measurements
	Statistical regression	Tendency for measures to drift toward the mean or average – often occurs when groups have been selected on the basis of their extreme scores
	Selection	Biases resulting in differential selection of respondents for the comparison groups
	Experimental mortality	Differential loss of respondents from the comparison groups
External validity	Reactive/interactive effect of testing	Pre-test might increase or decrease the respondent's sensitivity or responsiveness to the experimental variable
	Interaction effects	Selection biases interacting with the experimental variable
	Reactive effects of experimental arrangements	May preclude generalization about the effect of the experimental variable on persons exposed to treatment in non-experimental settings
	Multiple-treatment interference	Likely to occur whenever multiple treatments are applied to the same respondents

Experimental study designs are the strongest of the research designs as they allow inferences regarding causation to be made because participants are randomly assigned and any differences will be the result of the effects of the conditions. The randomization procedures are important since the validity of the results depend on not biasing the allocation of participants to either the test or control conditions. If random assignment is not employed and groups are established by some other means, such as using a previously existing group, then the research is not a true experiment but is instead called a quasi-experiment (Haworth, 1995).

Quasi-experimental research does not permit the investigator to draw causal conclusions because the researcher has not been able to control all the elements of the study. Experimental research does allow the researcher to make confident conclusions about the study because the elements of the study have been controlled during the course of the experiment. However, experimental research must still be evaluated by the two types of criterion: internal and external validity. If subjects or situations in the experiment are non-representative of the subjects and situations that the results will be compared to, then the experiment will have low external validity (Clark-Carter, 1997).

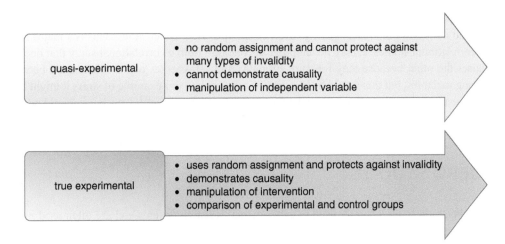

Figure 6.3   Differences between quasi and true experimental design

CORRELATIONAL RESEARCH

In a correlational study the researcher measures two or more variables in order to measure the strength of the relationship between them, for example how life stress is related to psychological problems. The levels of these factors are not determined, and instead are just measured as they naturally occur and are believed to be independent of one another. A statistical test is used to determine whether the variables have an effect on each other. Correlational studies measure relationship and do not have the ability to determine cause and effect. A positive correlation between variables indicates that where one variable increases the other variable also increases. For example, many studies have found that as an individual's stress levels increase psychopathology also increases, and although a positive relationship exists, one cannot imply that stress causes psychopathology. A negative correlation indicates that as one variable decreases, the other variable decreases (Greene, 1991).

Correlational research can be modified to examine more complex relationships among variables. These include the multiple correlational study and factor analysis. Multiple correlation studies measure the association between a criterion (condition) variable and a set of predictor variables. For example, if a psychologist wished to study stress, the researcher would consider numerous variables that may be correlated with stress; stress would be the criterion variable. A multiple correlation coefficient can be calculated between an individual's stress levels and a set of predictors including household income, mortgage payments and household debt (Greene, 1991).

Factor analysis is a multivariate technique that examines the interrelationships among a large number of variables in an attempt to identify the basic dimensions that contribute to scores on the variables. For example how household income, mortgage payments and household debt are related to each other as well as stress levels (Greene, 1991).

Although correlational studies measure the strength of an association between many variables, they do not permit the investigator to draw cause and effect conclusions. This is a major limitation of correlational studies. It may be tempting to conclude from a correlational study that one variable causes the other because they measure strengths and weaknesses of the relationship between and among variables, but this would be incorrect. Going back to our example of stress it might be that in our research we find that household debt accounts for higher stress levels, but it would be incorrect to say that this is what is causing the higher levels of stress (Greene, 1991).

PLACEBO STUDIES

Placebo studies are generally used in experimental research designs and are often used in psychological and medical studies. A placebo is an inert or inactive treatment that should not have any therapeutic effect. The placebo study is an experiment that determines whether a treatment causes more improvement than a placebo. Placebo studies in psychology are often used in determining the effectiveness of new forms of treatment. In a placebo study participants are randomly assigned to groups; one group will receive the treatment and the other group will receive the placebo. Individuals in the research are unaware whether they are receiving the placebo or the new treatment. Once the treatment has been administered both groups are measured to see whether there are any changes in the variable under study. By comparing the new treatment to the placebo the researcher can determine whether the treatment is more effective than a placebo. An example of this type of research might be the following: a psychologist plans to research a new type of therapy for phobias. The researcher

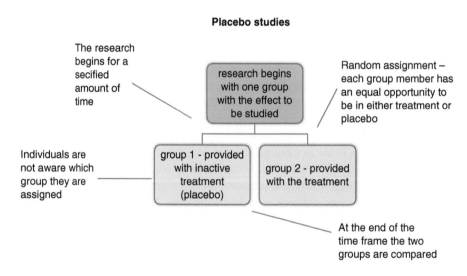

Figure 6.4   Placebo studies

randomly assigns individuals into two groups without telling the participants which group is the treatment group and which is the non-treatment (control) group. The treatment group receives the new therapy while the other group watches educational movies on the environment that have nothing to do with phobias and could not be considered therapy or treatment. At the end of the research both groups are measured to determine whether the therapeutic group has received any benefit (Peters, 2001).

ANALOGUE STUDIES

Analogue studies are specific types of research studies that are often used in psychology because there are practical and/or ethical issues that limit access to a clinical population. Analogue studies are often used to examine correlates, antecedents and even the causal influences of mild levels of particular symptoms in a sub-clinical population without harming the population that may be vulnerable. Psychologists often use analogue studies in research on causal models of abnormal psychology to examine the precursors of a mental disorder (McLeod, 2003).

There are many practical reasons for using analogue studies which include: the difficulties in obtaining an adequate number of subjects, funding for research and random assignment of individuals to various treatment groups. Ethical considerations in experimental research, such as withholding treatment or using treatments that may be ineffective or harmful when other more effective treatments are available, are generally not factors in analogue studies as the population is not high risk and more than likely not receiving any type of treatment. The disadvantage of analogue research is the question of external validity: specifically, do the research findings apply to the actual clinical population? The fewer clinical symptoms studied in a certain classification of disorder creates a problem for generalizing the research findings to the clinical population (Leong & Austin, 2005).

An example of an analogue study is the following. A researcher wishes to examine the antecedents of eating disorders. Rather than interrupt the treatment of individuals with an eating disorder by assigning them to treatment and control groups − both of which could be life-threatening and unethical − they examine a group of college students who have tested positive for elements of eating disorders but have not been diagnosed with an eating disorder. In other words, they are individuals who are showing a few positive symptoms of the disorder, but currently do not meet the full criteria for a diagnosis of an eating disorder. This example could allow a researcher to examine the antecedents of eating disorders without breaching ethical guidelines or endangering a clinical population by interrupting their treatment.

SINGLE-CASE STUDY

The single subject research design is a research method that focuses on a single research subject. This type of research focuses on a specific element, e.g. depression, and is often conducted over a period of time. When this type of research design is utilized in the study of psychopathology, the focus is usually a detailed investigation of the subject's response to treatment. Information is gathered concerning the subject's history, symptoms and relationship to others. The experimental procedure would be the treatment and how the individual responds over a period of time. Single-case studies are useful because a large amount of detailed information is obtained that would probably not be collected otherwise (Kazdin, 2010).

The depth and detail of a case study is useful in hypothesis generation and theoretical development as elements may be exposed that might not have surfaced in other types of research. In addition, case studies are useful for providing evidence for furthering a research area. Large group studies can be expensive and time consuming; single case research can be used to pilot test an area before embarking on a large-scale study. Single-case studies can also be helpful in generating research funds for further research in a particular area of psychopathology. Another practical motive for using a single-case study is to investigate rare or unusual cases. The psychological condition may be so rare that it is impossible and/or impractical to attempt to design a research study (Morgan, & Morgan, 2008). An example is the psychological disorder of dissociative identity disorder which is extremely rare and thought to occur in about 0.01–10 percent of mentally ill populations across the world. Attempting to study this condition on a large scale would be impractical.

The single subject design does have its disadvantages. They have poor internal validity, because the observations may be subject to bias and the subject design does not allow researchers to control for or rule out alternative interpretations. These types of studies also have questionable external validity, because the research subject may be so unique that the results cannot be generalized to others, i.e. a single subject research design on an individual with dissociative disorder would be so rare that generalizing the results to any other type of psychological disorder would be inappropriate and outside of clinical interest and therefore of of little value to a practising psychologist (Kazdin, 2010).

Traditional case studies are described as having a simple AB research design. The A corresponds to the condition of the individual before the intervention and B represents the condition of the individual following the intervention. As noted above, this design does not provide much support for the claim that the treatment in state B actually caused the observed changes because the experimenter does not manipulate any elements or control for outside variables (Kazdin, 2010).

One way that the single-case subject design has been improved is the ABAB reversal design. This method establishes a baseline period prior to the treatment phase (A), then there is the implementation of the treatment (B), removal of the treatment and return to a baseline condition (A), and finally a re-implementation of the treatment (B). If the individual's condition improves during the first treatment period, worsens when treatment is removed, and improves once again when treatment is restored, then the researcher has more confidence that the treatment may be causing the improvement. However, there is still the possibility that an unknown factor working in conjunction with the treatment has caused the improvement (Kazdin, 2010).

Another improvement over the original case study is the multiple baseline design. This design can be used when the researcher has identified a number of discrete symptoms to be studied. The researcher establishes a baseline period for each of the symptoms under investigation. Treatment is then introduced for one symptom. If this symptom improves while the others do not, the researcher then moves to the second symptom under study. This pattern is repeated until each symptom has received treatment independently of the others. If each symptom improved when it was receiving the treatment then the researcher has more confidence than in the traditional case study that the treatment caused the improvement (Morgan & Morgan, 2008).

When employing a single-case design the researcher should obtain stable measures of the dependent variable(s) during the baseline phase before manipulating the independent variable (treatment) regardless of which design they intend to employ. This will assure some degree of internal validity and can strengthen the premise that the change is more likely to be related to the intervention. However, this type of research design will always have limitations in terms of making a definite cause–effect statement (Morgan & Morgan, 2008).

GENETIC RESEARCH

Three types of genetic research methods are used in psychological research: the family study, the adoption study and the twin study. The family study is the simplest of the three designs and has the lowest internal validity. This type of genetic study determines whether a specific characteristic or trait is present in a family group and has a higher probability rate than the general population. The disadvantages of this type of study are that the genetic and environmental influences are confounded. This type of study can demonstrate that a trait is present in a family but it cannot explain why this trait exists, in other words it does not prove a genetic basis. If these types of genetic studies don't actually prove a genetic influence, why use them? The rationale for these genetic studies is that they are less expensive and less time consuming and if they show that a trait is present, they can serve as a pilot study for further genetic research (Fieve, 1975).

The second type of genetic research method is the adoption study. The adoption study determines the relative similarity of adoptees to both their adoptive and biological families. This method relies on the fact that adoptees are reared in environments alongside adoptive family members with whom they share no genes and researchers are able to separate genetics from the environment (Fieve, 1975).

Adoption studies can be conducted in two different ways. The researcher can identify adopted-away offspring of parents who possess the trait of interest or they can begin with adoptees who exhibit the trait of interest. The researcher then determines the degree to which this trait appears in both the adoptive and biological families and then makes comparisons to the general population or to the adopted-away offspring of parents who do not possess the trait. Adoption studies attempt to separate the genetic and environmental influences that are confounded for most people. However, adoption studies do not completely distinguish between these two influences. For example, children are placed for adoption at different ages: those placed for adoption at older ages may have shared a significant amount of early environment with their biological parents. If these adoptees are later found to resemble their biological parents, it may not be easy to determine whether this resemblance is due to genetic or early environmental influences. Even if the adoption study is limited to children placed for adoption in the first weeks of life there is still a confounding of genes and environment as children will be exposed to the biological environment prenatally, i.e. drug and alcohol abuse while pregnant, prenatal care etc. which could influence later development (Boomsma, Busjahn & Peltonen, 2002).

The third type of genetic research is the twin study. In a twin study the relative similarities of identical and fraternal twins are compared. The twin study is the opposite of the adoption study as twin studies hold the environment constant and vary genetic similarity while the adoption studies hold an individual's genetic make-up constant and vary the environment. There are two types of twins: identical twins who have identical genetic make-up, develop from a single fertilized egg and are called monozygotic and fraternal twins, who share one-half of their genes, develop from two separate fertilized eggs and are called dizygotic. This type of genetic research is important because identical twins have a common environment and all of their genes in common, whereas the fraternal twins have only half of their genes in common and a common environment. This allows the researcher to be relatively certain that differences that occur are as a direct result of genetic contribution. External validity issues such as socioeconomic status, parental personality and parental style of interacting with the children should be balanced. Twin studies have been very useful for the genetic influence of psychopathology, intelligence and personality characteristics. A variation on the twin studies has been research that has compared twins who have been reared apart. This is a combination of the twin and adoption methods (Smoller, Sheidley & Tsuang, 2008).

All of the genetic studies have issues with external and internal validity. The adoption and twin studies are not true experiments as there cannot be random assignment for ethical reasons. In the adoption studies children who are placed for adoption may not be representative of all children in the general population as there may be a variety of reasons why children are placed for adoption. As a result of these many issues, genetic studies cannot provide conclusive evidence of genetic causation, but the twin studies do provide a significant amount of evidence of all the various types of research studies (Joseph, 2006).

Table 6.3   Types of genetic studies in psychology

Type	Description	Validity	Disadvantages	Advantages
Family study	Studies whether a specific characteristic or trait is present	Lowest internal validity	Genetic and environmental influences are confounded	Less expensive, less time consuming and can serve as a pilot study for other types of research
Adoption study	Determines similarity of adoptees to their adoptive and biological families 2 types of adoption study	Moderate internal validity	Variations in adoptees and families – environmental influences still confound the research	Attempts to separate genetics from the environment
Twin study	Opposite of the adoption – hold the environment constant 2 types: monozygotic and dizygotic	Highest validity of the genetic studies	No random assignment Some external issues such as parental personality, parental style	Separates the genetics from the environment

ETHICS

Ethics is a construct that directs the beliefs of right and wrong and defines our principles of behaviour towards other living things. They are the rules we apply to ourselves and others in terms of treatment and behaviour. Ethical codes are moral guides to self-regulation and attempt to ensure the appropriate use of skills and techniques which have been defined for a specific profession and individuals who are part of that profession. Ethical codes are principles that specify the rights and responsibilities of professionals in their relationships with each other and with the people they serve, as well as stating prescriptive, normative values reflecting the consensus of the profession. Codes of conduct are the highest and lowest standards of practice expected of the individuals who define themselves by a specific profession. They are guides to the legal enforcement of ethical behaviour and to the punishment of unethical violations. No single code or specific guidelines exist that govern the ethical treatment of individuals who are mentally ill. Instead each profession involved with the treatment and care is governed by their own ethical codes that not only apply to mentally ill individuals but to anyone who is under their care (Koocher & Keith-Spiegel, 2008).

Generally, all professions have the same basic goals which are: to sensitize members to an ethical way of professional life, the provision of a structural guide and alerting mechanisms to ethical issues and dilemmas. Ethical guidelines attempt to prescribe how to protect the welfare of a variety of publics including patients, students, supervisors, employees, employers, employing agencies, human and animal research participants and society in general.

Despite the wide variety of people involved with the care of individuals with mental disorders all professional ethical codes confirm similar themes: to promote the welfare of people served, to maintain competence, to protect confidentiality and/or privacy, to act responsibly, to avoid exploitation and to uphold the integrity of the profession through exemplary conduct (Koocher & Keith-Spiegel, 2008).

If we have guidelines and ethical codes of conduct, why do ethical issues occur? Sometimes individuals wilfully, even maliciously, engage in acts they know to be in violation of the ethical standards of a profession. In other cases, greed, convenience and other self-serving motives can blur judgements and boundaries. Some elements that appear to be less malevolent but nonetheless still violate ethical codes of conduct can be: a problem that is unforeseen or inadequately anticipated, incompetence, lack of adequate training or inadequate guidelines that do not exist or may have not been anticipated for a specific situation (Knapp, 2011).

What are common ethical violations?

The basic patterns of ethical violations committed against individuals who are mentally ill fall into four basic categories: exploitation, insensitivity, incompetence and irresponsibility (Knapp, 2011).

Exploitation can happen whenever a professional takes advantage of a patient by abusing a position of trust, expertise, or authority, e.g. making decisions about hospitalization without consulting the family or patient.

Insensitivity involves harm caused by a lack of regard or concern for the needs, feelings, rights or welfare of others. Specific examples include rude or abusive behaviour directed inappropriately towards patients, biased attitudes towards minority groups which adversely affect the quality of treatment provided.

Incompetence occurs when a professional is not fully capable of providing the services being provided for reasons ranging from inadequate training/inexperience to personal unfitness, such as an emotional disturbance, or alcohol or substance abuse problem.

Irresponsibility can occur from lack of reliable or dependable execution of professional duties, negligence or dereliction of duty, attempts to blame others for one's mistakes, shoddy or superficial professional work, or excessive delays in delivering necessary feedback, assessments, reports, or services.

Other ethical considerations

Professionals working with mentally ill individuals who are unfamiliar with the social, economic and cultural pressures confronting women, the elderly, children, minority group members and the poor has been cited as unethical behavior (Koocher, 2007). These specific groups may be socialized in a manner that may accustom them to having their individual rights to self-determination denied and may not be aware that they have rights in their mental health treatment and choices. In addition, an untrained professional may fail to recognize the impact of being a member of one of these groups, which can cause further negative impact on their psychological problems escalating additional problems with care and treatment (Koocher, 2007).

Individuals who are mentally ill may not be compliant, understand or take direction. As a result of their illness they can be difficult to work with and as such are often targets of abuse and neglect. When working with the mentally ill, professionals must remain cognizant of their professional and personal limitations. Mentally ill individuals can be verbally abusive and/or physically abusive to themselves, other patients and health professionals. Ethical issues can easily occur when attempting to provide safety and security for the individuals in distress, the protection of others and themselves and often there is a fine line between control and retaliation (Irons, 2009).

Ethical considerations related to assessment and diagnosis

Ethical issues can develop from the use and potential abuse of psychological tests and assessment techniques. As we have discussed, psychological tests are often used to diagnose and classify individuals and are designed for a specific purpose to which they have been normed and standardized. A test, which is reliable, valid and quite useful for one purpose, may be useless or inappropriate for another. Another problem can occur when an instrument that is quite adequate for its intended use in the hands of a trained examiner could be subject to substantial abuse in the hands of a less well-trained user especially when that test is used for a diagnosis that could mislabel an individual (Knapp, 2011).

Assigning a diagnostic label to a client can have extremely serious consequences for him or her. Anyone using psychological test data as the basis for applying diagnostic labels should be appropriately cautious and sensitive to potential alternatives. It is also inappropriate to establish a diagnosis about an individual based solely on one assessment without the consideration of other factors. Without the assimilation of multiple pieces of information and data, a misdiagnosis can occur which can remain for a long time, to the individual's detriment (Schminke, 2010).

The value of a psychological assessment technique develops because it provides a means for assessing a standard sample of behaviour. Standardization implies a specific testing environment, adherence to administration rules, and specific scoring criteria. When a deviation occurs, the psychological test may lose its effectiveness. Training in psychological assessment is also important as it should be evident that there is more involved in the appropriate use of psychological tests than simply recording responses and adding up the score. Many standardized psychological instruments are deceptively easy to administer and score, requiring little or no formal training. Nevertheless, the accurate interpretation and application of these instruments is another matter entirely (Schminke, 2010).

Ethical considerations in regard to treatment

The issue of informed consent and the right to refuse treatment is important. In the past, individuals who were mentally ill were denied any rights and past history of the mistreatment of the mentally ill is well documented. Individuals were often subjected to extreme abuse and forced to undergo treatment that often was life-threatening and in some unfortunate cases died at the hands of those who were suppose to safeguard their care (Palmer & Barnes, 2001).

As a direct result of these many abuses, individuals now have the right to full disclosure concerning the effects of treatment and if they are unable to give consent, someone who does not have a conflict of interest is able to view the risks and benefits and decide on their behalf. Patients now have the right to refuse treatments, especially those involving physical interventions (e.g. drugs, psychosurgery and electroconvulsive shock therapy) (Jenkins, 2002).

Children are a special population that presents different types of ethical issues. When a child wishes to refuse treatment, they are not able to do so, even if the proposed treatment involves inpatient confinement and physical interventions. It is believed that some decisions are too difficult intellectually and emotionally to expect children to make independently. The courts have tended to assume that the mental health professional contacted to hospitalize or to treat the child at the parent's request is an unbiased third party who can adequately assess what is best for the child. Some have argued that the best interests of parents are not necessarily those of their children, and that mental health professionals are not always able to function in the idealized, unbiased, third-party role (Hart & Brassard, 1987; Daniels & Jenkins, 2010).

Researchers' responsibilities towards vulnerable study populations

Ethical guidelines related to research with human beings are easiest to apply to individuals who are fully functioning, competent and able to make rational decisions. However, these individuals do not generally contribute to our understanding of abnormal behavior. Understanding abnormal behavior and mental illness requires that research be conducted within this population. A major issue of concern is that often individuals in this population are vulnerable and may not be legally competent to consent to participate in a research study. Individuals in restrictive environments, hospitals, prisons etc. must be safeguarded because they are vulnerable to exploitation. Competent but lonely or bored individuals residing in care homes may be willing to engage in a research project in return for attention which may or may not be in their best interest (Jenkins, 2002).

Other problems with this type of research may be false beliefs that are mistakenly presumed to be objective or theoretical about a study population's characteristics; such beliefs which influence investigators' perceptions of the morality of research questions and experimental procedures. Conscious or unconscious biases against a study population may affect the research question or increase the risks to which the participants are exposed in such a way as to cause harm to the participants themselves or perpetuate or create unfair or inaccurate generalizations about the entire study population (Jones & Hill, 2003).

The ethics of specialized treatment, techniques and devices

Some types of treatment, techniques and devices involve a substantial degree of control over the individual's environment. Treatment and techniques such as operant conditioning, aversive therapies, physiological monitoring etc. as well as devices such as biofeedback machines and certain instrumental procedures may push the boundaries towards the violation of an individual's rights. Some individuals may be incompetent to consent to such techniques, for example, individuals with compromised intellectual ability or severely psychotic individuals. Individuals who are institutionalized, incarcerated or incompetent should be shown careful concern for ethical issues as often these individuals are not fully able to assert their rights and are fearful of reprisals if they do not participate. When an individual is incompetent to consent fully, special ethical consideration and procedures should be put into place to guarantee safety and protection. Professionals employing these techniques and devices must avoid using unsafe or unproven devices, not to mention those that might prove dangerous to clients through electric shock or other hazards. When implementing operant conditioning programmes, great care must be taken to ensure that there is no confusion on the distinction between the concepts of 'punishment' and negative reinforcement. No programme or technique should be undertaken without a firm theoretical foundation and scientific basis for anticipating benefits for the individual who is participating (Tribe & Morrissey, 2004).

Ethics involving research

Usually researchers are individuals who are practising in a profession as well as conducting research so they are typically part of a professional body who have ethical codes and standards. However someone who is not affiliated with a profession is unregulated in the sense that anyone can conduct research and attempt to publish it. Researchers outside of a profession are not required to attain certain degrees or to pass exams or to obtain other proof of competence, therefore peer and self-regulation of quality and ethical research practices are especially important (Israel & Hay, 2006).

Table 6.4   Incompetent ethical practices in psychology

Assessment	1	Improper use of standardized testing conditions
	2	Poor reliability and validity of the tests used
	3	Untrained examiner
Diagnosis	1	Applying inappropriate diagnostic labels
	2	Hurried diagnosis based on an interview
	3	Reliance on insufficient evidence, assessments and documentation
Treatment	1	Limited or no disclosure to the client concerning effects of treatment
	2	Children and vulnerable populations not protected and not allowed to have an unbiased third party (guardians) to protect their rights
	3	The use of special techniques and devices that are unsafe or unproven
	4	Individuals denied the right to refuse treatment
Research	1	Poorly designed
	2	Improperly interpreted
	3	High risk for participants

The ethical consequences for research that is poorly designed or improperly analysed or interpreted is being recognized as ethical violations even if the researcher is outside of a profession, and legal ramifications are being used to make sure that participants and the general public are protected. Using human beings or animals in a flawed project cannot be justified on any grounds. At best, the participants' efforts are wasted and at worst, they could be harmed. Examples of the ethical issues include: exposing participants to excessively risky procedures, using samples of convenience in a trivial manner, designing and/or executing research carelessly or hurriedly. The best way to illustrate a violation of ethical codes in research is to profile a case (Israel & Hay, 2006).

WHEN RESEARCH GOES BAD: A CASE STUDY IN RESEARCH

An example of research that violated many different types of ethical codes is the controversial research that was conducted on autism and the MMR vaccine. In 1998 a respected British medical journal published research by a physician who had claimed that he had found a connection between the MMR vaccine and autism. The MMR vaccine is a combined immunization injection against measles, mumps and rubella that is administered to children at 12 months and then a booster is administered before the child begins school at age five. The researcher, Andrew Wakefield and 12 other physicians claimed that eight out of the 12 children studied developed behavioural symptoms within two weeks of receiving the MMR vaccination that were antecedents to autism. Dr Wakefield later made statements at a press conference calling for the suspension of the triple MMR vaccine until more research could be conducted.

Investigations were conducted and multiple ethical violations were found by the lead researcher, the hospital and the actual research participants. Dr Wakefield was found to have multiple undeclared conflicts of interest; one particularly damning piece of evidence was that some of the parents of the 12 children were recruited and paid by a UK lawyer who was preparing a lawsuit against the MMR manufacturers. The hospital had been paid £55,000 to conduct the research on-site and Dr Wakefield had personally been paid more than £400,000 to oversee the research. Further investigations found that Dr Wakefield had manipulated the data to suggest a connection between the MMR vaccine and autism. Ten out of the 12 co-authors published a retraction of the interpretation, and the study's findings have never been replicated. The research was eventually declared to be fraudulent in 2011. The author/physician Andrew Wakefield was found guilty by the General Medical Council of serious professional misconduct and was struck off the Medical Register.

The long-term ramifications of this flawed and inaccurate study have continued long after the research has been dismissed and all individuals involved disciplined for ethical violations. The general public who were previously unaware of any potential danger real or exaggerated became alarmed, with thousands of concerned parents choosing not to immunize their children. MMR vaccination compliance dropped from 92 percent in 1996 to 84 percent (European Centre for Disease Prevention and Control, 2009). The result was that the incidence rates in the UK of two of the three diseases increased from 56 confirmed cases of measles in 1998 to 449 in 2006, with a death occurring in 2006 for the first time since since 1992 (MacMahon, 2006). In 2008, measles was declared endemic meaning that the disease was sustained within the population for the first time in 14 years. The cost to society has included outbreaks of previously controlled diseases, death and unnecessary medical expenses (Poland & Jacobson, 2011).

What is the truth about the MMR vaccine and autism? To date, not a single research study has found a link and there is no evidence that the vaccine is related to the development of autism. Although supporters have pointed out that the cases of autism have increased since the 1990s and the creation of the MMR vaccine, the increase is believed to be as a result of changes in diagnostic practices as well as changes in education and training in the recognition of early symptoms.

As the flawed research above demonstrates, ethical codes are important in protecting individuals who are participants in research as well as how the research is disseminated into the general population. The long-term ramifications can be significant.

CONCLUSION

In our case study it is clear that Mr Janson did not receive the right diagnosis, but how did it go so wrong? It is difficult to determine when Mr Janson's tumour began, but many of the inital symptoms coincided with his retirement. It is not unusual for individuals to go through a period of readjustment, especially if it is a major life change. Retirement for many individuals means a major change in life circumstances and often people plan what they intend to accomplish once they no longer have to work, but quickly become bored if the plans are transitory. The physician as well as Mr Janson's family believed that he was going through a period of adjustment. They became increasingly worried when Mr Janson did not make the adjustment and began exhibiting what they believed was a mood disorder. Mr Janson's doctor made an appropriate diagnosis based on the information he collected. Until neurological signs were exhibited, Mr Janson's physician would not have tested for this physical issue as there were no symptoms that indicated that he should and the symptoms Mr Janson was experiencing were pointing at a psychological issue. Dr Moffit did conduct a general physical exam to rule out any physical problems. As you can see, once the diagnosis was made, no one questioned its validity and assumed that the medication was not being effective. It wasn't until Mr Janson began having seizures that the neurological problem was detected. Once the tests had been conducted and the correct diagnosis and treatment provided, Mr Janson made a complete recovery. What if Mr Janson had not begun having seizures? It is likely that the diagnosis of depression would have persisted and Mr Janson could have continued with the wrong treatment for years.

Summary

The chapter initially provided an introduction to diagnosis, the contribution of psychological tests and assessment, and finally discussed the most utilized classification system of the DSM. The chapter then discussed various research methods that are common in the study of psychopathology and ended with a discussion about ethical codes and guidlines for individuals with psychological disorders.

STUDY GUIDES

Key terms

Analogue – in research it refers to a population under study which resembles a different population to which a researcher wants to generalize a study

Autism – a range of disorders characterized by impaired social interaction and communication, often referred to as autism spectrum disorders

Dependent variable – a variable that is observed when the experimental variable is manipulated or changed in some way

Independent variable – a variable that is manipulated by the researcher to determine its relationship to the dependent variable

Multiple correlation studies – measure the association between a criterion variable and a set of predictor variables

Placebo – an inert or inactive treatment that does not have any effect

Reliability – in assessment, indicates that the test dependably measures what it is supposed to measure and the results are repeatable

Standard error of measurement – is a score interval that has a certain probability of including any indivdiual's true score

Validity – the concept of whether a reliable test does in fact measure what it is suppose to measure

Study guide

1   Explore classification systems other than the DSM. Why are these systems not as popular as the DSM for diagnosis and classification of abnormal disorders?

2   Psychological diagnosis has been criticized as not being appropriate for mental disorders. Explore the reasons why there are individuals who are against the classification of psychological disorders.

3   The Rorschach test was originally designed as a free association test but has undergone a variety of scoring systems. Investigate one of the many scoring systems and how this compares to objective assessments.

4   The British Psychological Society publishes its own ethical codes and guidelines. If Dr Wakefield had been a psychologist, what principles would he have violated?

Case study in focus

Discuss the repercussions that Dr Wakefield created when he reported his research on autism. How many ethical violations did he commit? Were participants harmed during the course of his research? What about children who were not participants in his research. How did his research change autistic research in the future? If you had a small child, how would this research change your behaviours concerning the MMR vaccine?

Personal development

You have been hired to determine the effects of aerobic exercise in the treatment of patients with mild depression. How would you design this research so that you could report with confidence the cause–effect of your research findings?

Suggested reading

Cave, S. (2002) *Classification and diagnosis of pscychological abnormality*. New York: Taylor & Francis.

Davey, G. (2008) *Psychopathology: Research, assessment and treatment in clinical psychology*. Oxford, UK: Blackwell Publishing.

Graham, J.R., Naglieri, J.A. & Weiner, I.B. (2004) *Handbook of psychology: Assessment psychology*, Vol. 10. Hoboken, NJ: John Wiley & Sons.

Koocher, G.P. & Keith-Spiegel, P. (1998) Ethics in psychology: Professional standards and cases. New York: Oxford University Press.

Child Development and Abnormal Psychology

7

Learning aims

At the end of this chapter you should understand:

- The various child developmental factors
- How developmental norms are used to determine abnormal behaviour in children
- The innate factors of personality and how this is influenced by environment
- Psychological theories and how they relate specifically to children.

INTRODUCTION

CASE STUDIES

Jon's story

Jon was the middle child out of three children born to a housewife and a forklift truck driver. Jon's elder brother was born with a cleft palate which led to communication and behaviour problems, such as tantrums, physical aggression and screaming. Jon's younger sister was also born with developmental problems that affected her emotionally as well as learning difficulties and she also had tantrums. Jon's elder brother and younger sister attended special schools and required a great deal of his parents' time and attention. Having two disabled children put an additional strain on a troubled relationship and Jon's father was constantly moving in and out of the family home. The family was in constant flux, sometimes they moved in with Susan's parents, sometimes they were an intact family and sometimes Susan and the children lived on their own. Both Neil and Susan had histories of clinical depression before they met and both continued to have issues with depression throughout their relationship.

At the age of seven, Jon began to have behavioural difficulties; he was not diagnosed with developmental issues himself but had begun to mimic his elder brother's behavioural problems. Jon would throw tantrums, throw himself on the floor and scream as well as throw anything he could get his hands on. Susan his mother was also prone to frustration and often took her anger and dissatisfaction with her life out on Jon and would physically and verbally abuse him. Often when she was angry with the other two children she would take out her feelings on the one child she felt she could discipline. During particularly stressful times she would place Jon in temporary foster placement which caused him to feel insecure and fearful that his mother would place him in permanent care and he would lose his home. When Jon entered school he was teased and bullied. He was eventually moved to a different school because his behaviour was difficult to manage by his teachers and at the school. The new school held Jon back a year because of his immaturity and problematic behaviour. Jon immediately paired up with another boy with behavioural problems who had come from an extremely physically abusive home. The two boys brought out the worst in each other and bullied their classmates, often singling out other children who were weak or easy targets and picking on them.

When Jon was 11 his teachers documented that he had extreme attention-seeking behaviour. He would rock back and forth in his chair and make odd noises in the classroom. His behaviour became increasingly erratic and he began engaging in self-abuse. He would bang his head on the furniture and against the wall, throw himself on the floor and couldn't be trusted with anything sharp such as scissors, because he would cut himself and his clothing. He was hyper, easily distracted and had difficulty learning. More troubling was that he began to act violently towards other children, throwing things and attacking them in front of the teachers. Even after all of these behaviour problems his teachers still reported him as a basically 'sweet kid' who needed attention and came from a very difficult home life.

Marshall's story

Marshall was the only child born to Debbie and Marshall (his namesake) and spent the majority of his childhood in constant confusion and disorder because of his dysfunctional family dynamics. His father had difficulty maintaining employment and as a result the family was constantly moving in with relatives, and then being forced out when they could not help pay for expenses and food. The family was never able to stay in any one place for any length of time and often kept their clothes in bin bags. Debbie and her husband moved constantly from one substandard housing situation to the next and it wasn't unusual for the family to stay in their car until they could find another relative who was willing to take them in. The father eventually abandoned the family before Marshall turned two years old and his mother had a series of relationships with various men that did not change their circumstances and they generally remained homeless and impoverished. As a single mother Debbie was eventually able to secure benefits which made their lives a little less miserable but she suffered from depression and anxiety and began abusing prescription drugs as well as drinking and smoking cannabis.

Marshall changed schools so frequently that he was not easily accepted and had difficulty making friends. His teachers reported him to be aloof and a loner. Marshall didn't really reach out to his peers because he felt it would only be a matter of time before he would be uprooted and moved to another place. Because he was an outsider and a bit underweight and small for his age he was constantly bullied. At one point he suffered such extreme physical violence at the hands of a classmate that he was hospitalized for his injuries.

Marshall was a poor student and was held back three years until he finally left school at the age of 17. Marshall's childhood had no stability: they relocated constantly, often his mother did not pay utilities so it wasn't unusual for the home not to have heat and it was not uncommon for there to be very little food available. Most of their money was spent on drugs and alcohol. Marshall experienced inconstancy in parenting and at times his mother was physically abusive.

Debbie married three more times with all three relationships being volatile, abusive and erratic, all three ending shortly after the marriage. Debbie had a son with her second husband and life became even more difficult with a young child that needed care. At the age of ten, Marshall began stealing his mother's prescription drugs and became addicted to vicodin and valium. During an investigation into child abuse for Debbie's younger son a social worker made comments that she believed Debbie suffered from various serious mental disorders including severe depression and that the children were at high risk for abuse, but no further action was taken.

The early life of these two children would be considered disorganized, unstable and dysfunctional. Unfortunately many children grow up with less than nurturing home environments. How does this affect development and does it cause abnormal behaviour later in life? In the two case studies presented both boys have similar backgrounds, but as you will find out at the end of the chapter, very different conclusions.

CHILD DEVELOPMENT AND PSYCHOPATHOLOGY

This chapter will provide a basic framework for the understanding of normal personality development in children and adolescence as it is important to understand what is normal before moving on to what is abnormal. All too often abnormal behaviour in children is compared to abnormal behaviour in adults. Children are not 'mini-adults' and to simply describe the various childhood psychological disorders without the relevance of the basic principles of development would be insufficient to provide an overall picture of childhood psychopathology (Berk, 2008).

In our society, we highly desire children to be above average in physical, mental, emotional and social development, and we become concerned when the child is below average without understanding that not every child can be above average in every element and at every developmental period in their lives. However, for some parents with exceedingly high expectations being average is not acceptable. The only atypical element in children that is desirable is exceptionality. All else brings unhappiness, disappointment, problems and even misery to parents (Patton, 2011). Some parents will spare no expense in an effort to shift their child from average to above average, but how realistic is this expectation?

At various developmental stages we have a range of measures for what is expected at a certain age and what is considered above average, average and below average and refer to these as developmental norms (Berk, 2008). These developmental norms are always easier to define when they involve tangible elements such as height and weight rather than more elusive factors such as cognition. For example, for a newborn there is a certain birth weight that falls between what is normal and what is abnormal. Because every newborn is weighed at birth, long established patterns of development has been charted and are widely accepted. Low birth weight is not only considered below average, but is a concern as it is regarded as a health risk. High birth weight is considered healthy and robust and a newborn can never be too high. During the developmental period from birth to 12 months, the baby is constantly being weighed and measured; a low weight at one measurement period can quickly change with the next period of measurement. Weight is also balanced out with length. As the child develops and their bodies begin to change, the chubby baby becomes a toddler and at this point in a child's development we change our perceptions of what is too high. A child that is overweight will not be able to balance and will be unable to walk properly and at this point high weight becomes abnormal and the child is judged to be obese (Smith, Cowie & Blades, 2011).

In early childhood development we only become concerned when something interacts or interferes with a child's development and progression to the next developmental stage, through adolescence and ultimately adulthood. The same principle is applied to behaviour; an extreme in either direction could be considered abnormal, but again without taking the process of development into account we may be inaccurate in our perceptions (Smith, Cowie & Blades, 2011). It is important to have a basic understanding of normal development so that we are able to recognize deviant behaviour (Empson & Nabuzoka, 2003). For example, most children are toilet trained before the age of three; a child that is still bed-wetting at the age of eight significantly deviates from developmental norms. In general, the greater the deviation from developmental norms, the higher the agreement will be with regard to the abnormality of the behaviour.

Factors of determining normal patterns of behaviour and child development are: frequency of behaviour, intensity and duration (Wilmshurst, 2008). Behaviour must be evaluated in terms of these three factors and they are best explained with an example. Consider the question: is the behaviour of pulling hair from one's head abnormal? Most people would answer this question as yes as it isn't normal behaviour to pull out one's hair. What if the hair pulling occurred only once or at most twice? The frequency of the event would probably lead us to say no – the behaviour, although not desirable, would probably not be abnormal. If the hair pulling was a frequent event the answer would definitely be yes. What if the hair pulling behaviour only occurred during a temper tantrum? It is not unusual for children in the midst of a rage to pull out a handful of hair. Consider the difference if the hair pulling occurred once or twice but over 75 percent of the hair on the head was removed in large clumps? What if the hair pulling occurred every day and resulted in a damaged scalp? Most of us would view this behaviour as abnormal. When behaviours are evident in extremes of intensity or degree they usually fall outside of the bounds of normal behaviour. The greater the persistence of deviant behaviours, the more likely they are to be considered as falling within the domain of abnormality. Another aspect of these dimensions is the absence or rarity of a response may be just as significant as high frequency.

But not all developmental deviations reflect abnormality in the sense of impaired or insufficient progress. Some children walk unaided at an earlier age than the norm, or have vocabularies and linguistic skills that far exceed the average. Most, but not all instances of rapid or early development are looked upon as positive indications of exceptional abilities. It is at the slow end of the continuum where developmental deviations have their major significance as a negative criterion of abnormality in children (Empson & Nabuzoka, 2003).

CHILD DEVELOPMENT

Development is an active process that consists of two important components: a structure with pre-existing capacities; and the concept of a sequential set of changes in the system that provide permanent additions to the structure as well as its process and function (Berk, 2008). We think of development as involving sequential and orderly changes over time in an individual's physical and mental structure and functioning. There are many factors affecting development:

- biological (which includes heredity), congenital factors, maturation, temperament, prenatal and postnatal care, drugs and nutrition;
- cognitive, including intelligence, thinking, memory and knowledge;
- social and psychological, emphasizing race, social class, cultural context, family, school, peer relationships as well as early neonatal experiences (Lindon, 2010).

Developmental factors have been shown to have positive relationships with the development of psychopathology (Rolf, Masten, Cicchetti, Nuechterlein & Weintraub, 1990; Masten & Coatsworth, 1998).

One of the most important aspects in development is maturation. Maturation refers to physical alterations in size and qualitative changes in tissues or in anatomical and physiological organization (Lindon, 2010). With respect to child development, maturation is extremely important because these physiological transformations make it possible for new behaviours to emerge, that is, the child is biologically ready to acquire a new behaviour without a great deal of practice or preparation (Eccles & Midgley, 1989). Maturation provides the physiological structures necessary for cognitive development to occur.

In conjunction with maturation is intellectual development. Cognitive development is the process of basic to advanced acquisition of intelligence, thought, language and problem-solving ability (Neaum, 2010). Cognitive development describes the child's progress from a totally dependent individual to a distinctive and independent person. Cognitive development is impossible without maturation and the two form the basic components for all the other factors of child development. The intellectual dimension of development is difficult to measure because how do we reliably measure thinking and the process of developing cognitive abilities?

Cognitive development is an interactive process between the infant and their external environment (Meggitt, 2006). As a newborn ages and matures, they explore and learn through sensory and motor investigation about their own bodies, intimate others and the environment around them. Objects are identified for them, sounds become language and they are shown how to interact with every new element in their environment. While they are exploring and interacting with people and things in their surroundings they are simultaneously beginning to develop a self-concept and proficiency to cope without assistance. As they become increasingly successful in their adventures they become more inclined to think and act on their own and their cognitive abilities are advancing (Winnicott, 1960).

Babies that have had positive interactions with their environment and many successes are more self-confident, and have fewer emotional outbursts than infants who have had negative interactions (Bronfenbrenner, 1986). As the infant matures over time they progress from a helpless, dependent, emotionally unstable and undifferentiated self to a more independent, emotionally controlled and distinctive self. This process continues throughout the child's development until they mature into adults (Winnicott, 1960).

Cognitive malfunctioning is apparent when a disparity exists between ability and actual performance in such areas as attention, comprehension, judgement, learning, memory, thinking and perception. The larger the difference between a person's capabilities and actual performance, the greater is the likelihood of abnormal behaviour (Oates & Grayson, 2004).

An example of how maturation and cognitive abilities must be congruent is toilet training. Parents who begin the process too early, before the child is mentally and physically ready will meet frustration and engage in a losing battle causing unnecessary anxiety and conflict for all individuals involved. Understanding and knowledge concerning maturation can go a long way in minimizing needless parent–child strife and in increasing the child's chances of successful acquisition of new behaviours (Issenman, Filmer & Gorski, 1999).

As the child matures and develops they begin to form new relationships and extend from intimate family to others outside of their immediate environment. Their environments begin to expand and they begin learning how to interact with the new surroundings (Wood, 1997). Children begin to develop relationships with others through play groups and interactions with extended family members. Humans are social animals who require relationships with others for normal development to occur (Berbert, 2002). In order to function adequately in society, a child must acquire the capacity to interact with others on a friendly and cooperative basis and maintain relationships of mutual respect, agreement and responsibility. These skills are learned in the social environment (Wood, 1997).

An important competence in relationships is emotional expression. During the course of development, children learn to alter the way they express emotions, from the infant's demanding cries to the capability of emotional control. Children learn to assess environmental cues in terms of what emotion is appropriate and what manner is acceptable for its expression. Misjudgements are met with social condemnation and individuals who display too much emotion or too little emotion are subject to criticism and disapproval (Calkins & Bell, 2009). Emotional dysfunction is another factor that helps determine abnormal social behaviours from other kinds of deviant interactions. When emotional instability is present along with deviant interpersonal behaviour, the social interaction is more likely to be abnormal (Greenberg & Kusche, 1991). Difficulties in interpersonal relationships such as social withdrawal and isolation, suspiciousness, fear, hatred of others and uncooperativeness can lead to psychopathology (Parker et al., 2006; Lynch & Cicchetti, 1997). In addition, emotional regression or the use of emotional expressions evident in an earlier period of development may indicate abnormal behaviour (Harris, 1989). Temper tantrums in a 16-year-old who has since learned to express anger verbally is a sign of emotional regression and emotional immaturity. Here again the greater the deviation from normal developmental patterns the greater is the likelihood that the behaviour would be regarded as abnormal. Extremes or sudden fluctuations of moods, infantile, inappropriate, or lack of emotional expression, and irrational but persistent fears are some of the emotional signs of personal instability (Suveg et al., 2007).

NATURE–NURTURE

Research has documented the role of heredity versus environment as determinants of child development (McCrae et al., 2000; Collins et al., 2000; McCall, 1981). Various environmental elements interact with genetics on a continuum that can have an influence on behaviour. For example, the genetic effects of a debilitating and irreversible condition such as Down's syndrome will significantly limit the opportunities of positive environmental factors to influence the developmental outcome. A child with severe Down's syndrome, even if exposed to excellent learning environments, will only be able to engage to the degree that their physical limitations allow. Alternatively the physiological effects of attention deficit hyperactivity disorder have a potential effect that is less extensive than Down's syndrome since there is the opportunity for environmental conditions to control the outcome, i.e. medication, therapy and educational services. This interactional effect between the environment and the person is termed 'Nature–nurture'. While past inquiry emphasized the relative contributions of either nature or nurture, this approach has been replaced by an interactional one in which the potential impact of each factor varies on a continuum, allowing for greater or lesser interplay of the other factors in determining behaviour (McCrae et al., 2000).

The environment can contain a multitude of factors that can influence development on a continuum from direct to indirect (Keating, 2010). One major category that can change the course of development is organic accidents. Organic accidents can happen at birth such as birth complications, e.g. prolonged delivery, which can seriously impair the baby's oxygen supply (anoxia) leading to the destruction of brain cells and the direct consequence of mental retardation. In contrast, less direct influence on intellectual development may occur in children who have acquired sensory defects (visual or auditory) and for whom educational opportunities and enrichment may be restricted by their social environment (Keating, 2010).

In this interactional context, heredity may be thought of as providing the basic biological organization by which the organism's physical structure and personality can develop. However, environmental factors can change the course of development. Genetic factors can determine exclusively such physical characteristics as eye colour and blood type. It can account for other human characteristics that can be affected by experience such as height and intelligence. Genetics can also account for certain types of psychological disorders. Schizophrenia is one such disorder where genetics provides a predisposition that can manifest in the presence of certain types of stimuli depending on the environment as well as the individual's reaction to their environment. Therefore, it is important to keep in mind that people are uniquely different in both their genetic make-up (except for monozygotic twins) and in their environmental experiences, making it unlikely that they will develop in the same way or be capable of responding in the same manner to similar experiences.

TEMPERAMENT

Temperament is a concept referring to individual differences that are innate and characterize particular behavioural styles which can be affected by environmental forces and are part of the process of child development. Research has identified specific infant reaction patterns that have consequences for personality development and has also suggested relationships between temperament and childhood behaviour disorders (Joyce et al., 2003).

Early research in infant and child temperaments was conducted by Thomas, Chess and Birch (1977). Over a period of approximately 20 years they collected information on the temperaments of infants and established nine categories of infant behavioural style or temperamental reactivity. Using the ratings of these nine reactive patterns, the investigators showed that after the first ten years of life, children were remarkably stable and consistent in temperamental reactivity. For example, the 'easy' child rated positive on the approach and withdrawal category at one year of age, and would approach a stranger without fear and could easily sleep in new surroundings, while at ten years the same child went to camp happily, loved new activities and was willing to attempt any new experience without feeling threatened or insecure. The 'difficult' child type included those children who had irregularity in biological function (poor sleeping, eating and toileting behaviour), negative withdrawal responses to new stimuli, frequent and loud crying periods, slow adaptability to change, and experienced frequent tantrums when frustrated (Thomas, Chess & Birch, 1977). While these groupings are broad and imprecise, it is significant that in their study, 70 percent of the children from the original population who were classified as difficult later evidenced emotional problems and needed psychiatric attention. Conversely, in the same population, 18 percent of the children identified as easy had psychological problems. Difficult children represented 10 percent of all the children sampled by these investigators (a figure that corresponds to other estimates of occurrence of abnormal behaviours in children), while 40 percent fell into the easy category (Thomas & Chess, 1977).

These findings suggest that temperament may be useful to determine at-risk children and that it may be possible through the use of early temperament measures to intervene at a critical time in their development and lower the risk of psychiatric disorders. In this context, Thomas and Chess (1977) emphasize the goodness of fit between the child and the environment. They theorized that when there is a significant discrepancy between the child's temperamental dispositions and environmental demands, severe stress and psychopathological development are likely to occur.

Although recent research in child temperaments suggests that there is some overlap in Thomas, Chess and Birch's nine categories, finding four to six variations, all the research has documented the existence of infant temperaments (Buitelaar, Hizink, Mulder & Visser, 2003; Kagan, Snidman, Arcus & Reznick, 1994; Seifer, 2000).

Buss and Plomin (1975) suggested that individual differences are governed by four temperaments: activity, emotionality, sociability and impulsivity. These are depicted as dimensions (each ranging from one extreme to the other). The potential to occupy some place on the dimension of each of the four temperaments is inherited, although the final form the initial inherited tendencies takes depends on environmental influences. Every person represents some combination of the four temperaments that are the basic building blocks of personality. Buss and Plomin claim that the proposed nine temperaments of Thomas et al. have not been substantiated as truly inherited, and that if this criterion were applied, both views would identify similar temperaments. This view has been substantiated by other researchers (Rothbart, 1981; Bates, 1989). Further research in this area concurs that the nine types of temperament originally researched by Thomas, Chess and Birch have a significant overlap.

Research on temperaments has added to the understanding of individual differences, of the interplay of heredity and environment in the stability of reactive patterns over time, and of the early identification of psychopathology (Holmes, Slaughter & Kashani, 2001; Center & Kemp, 2001; Lysaker & Davis, 2004; Calkins, 1994; Maziade et al., 1990). But equally importantly, inquiry on temperament has called attention to the influence of temperamental reactivity on parental responses to the child (Dunn & Kendrick, 1980). For too long, theorists have focused on the effect of only the mother and development of personality and now research is concentrating on both mother and father as well as the multidirectional components of parent–child interactions.

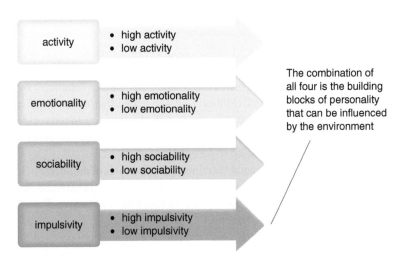

Figure 7.1 The four temperaments

Table 7.1   Thomas, Chess and Birch (1977) nine categories of temperament reactivity

Activity level	The proportion of active to inactive periods
Rhythmicity	Regularity of biological functions: sleep, hunger
Approach	Moving towards or withdrawing from new situations and people
Adaptability	Ability to become accustomed to new situations
Responsiveness	The intensity of stimulation needed to evoke a response
Intensity	Intensity of a reaction – the energy of the response
Quality	The amount of pleasant, friendly and joyful behaviour versus unpleasant, unfriendly and crying behaviour.
Distractability	The degree to which extraneous stimuli change behaviour
Attention	Attention span and persistence – time spent on an activity and the effect of distraction on that activity

PARENTAL RELATIONSHIPS AND PERSONALITY DEVELOPMENT

Our strongest relationships and influences come from the family and the parental relationships. Each area of our lives is shaped and altered by our interactions with our parents (Barnes, 1995). These relationships are a focal point in child development and can significantly alter the presence or absence of psychopathology dependent upon the various factors of biological elements.

Child as stimulus

The child can act as a stimulus and an active opponent in the parent–child relationship modifying the behaviours of adults either positively or negatively. The effect of the infant on its caretaker and child-rearing has been the subject of increasing study. Early studies conducted by Bell (1968) examined the autonomy–control issue of child-rearing and found that active children elicit upper-limit control behaviour from parents presumably as a means of reducing and redirecting the behaviours of the child that exceed parental limits, whereas parents set lower-limit controls for lethargic children in order to stimulate their behaviour up to parental expectations.

Brazelton (1969) found that parental reactions are a function of an interaction between their preconceived notions of child-rearing and the nature of the infant. In addition, he found that babies manifest unique qualities that are obvious to the parents from birth onwards and that these qualities set the tone of parental reactions to the child.

Thomas and Chess (1984) similarly observed that to a large extent parental responses are a function of the child's temperamental constellation, which determines the smoothness or turmoil of management routines. Mothers prefer children of the easy child type because these youngsters reassure them that they are adequate, healthy and loving mothers, whereas difficult children tend to make mothers feel threatened, resentful or anxious. Various studies have linked difficult infants to annoyance/irritation in primary caregivers and the high probability of abuse (Bugental, Blue & Cruzcosa, 1989; Frodi & Lamb, 1980; Cicchetti & Toth, 1994).

In terms of linking early child relationships to parental responses and the links to later psychopathology, Rapee (1997) documented that rejection and control by parents may be positively related to later anxiety and depression. Cirulli, Berry and Alleva (2003) found that early disruptions resulted in changes in the nervous system in infants with the high possibility of behavioural changes that could result in psychopathology in later life. Teerikangas et al. (1998) found that children described as difficult in infancy were found to predict psychiatric symptoms in adolescence.

The effects of early mothering

During infancy, the baby's primary caregiver becomes a powerful reinforcer, an influential stimulus as well as the object of the baby's responses. The primary caregiver provides for the infant's needs by feeding, comforting or easing pain; stimulating the child through talking, moving and playing; and allowing the child to explore its environment. It is during these various interactions that the infant becomes attached to the primary caregiver and gains sufficient sensory stimulation and need gratification for the development of a healthy personality (Sroufe, 1985).

Early researchers documented the importance of early mothering on later personality development. Sensory experiences (tactile, kinaesthetic and auditory stimulation) provided by the mother (primary caregiver) were critical for stable personality development, and the mother's failure to provide these vital sensory experiences would result in both biological and psychological damage to the child (Ribble, 1944).

The most significant experimental advance in this area was the research conducted by Harry Harlow. Harlow (1962) examined tactile stimulation as a principal ingredient in the mother–child relationship. Infant monkeys were reared with two types of inanimate surrogate mothers: a wire-mesh one and one covered with terry-cloth material. The baby monkeys preferred the cloth mother, and spent more time clinging to her than to the wire mother. In addition, the monkeys with a cloth mother evidenced a sense of security that enabled them to explore a fear-arousing stimulus, whereas the monkeys with the wire mother exhibited fear and avoidance. Harlow also discovered that tactile stimulation was not the only important variable for normal development. Regardless of which surrogate mother the monkeys had, those raised in isolation from peers later showed abnormal behaviours that included aggressiveness, self-mutilation, withdrawal and social indifference (Harlow, 1962).

Another area of study that has been closely linked with psychopathology in later life has been maternal deprivation (Sanchez, Ladd & Plotsky, 2001). Various studies have documented that infants in deprived institutional settings showed both profound intellectual and motor retardation and a higher incidence of disease and mortality (Johnson, 2000; Morison, Ames & Chishom, 1995; Cermak & Groza, 1998; Glennen & Masters, 2002).

While the mother–child relationship traditionally has been viewed as unique and of critical importance to later personality development, research has documented that other individuals in the infant's environment are also important. Ainsworth (1985) found that infants could establish strong bonds with those who do not provide caretaking. This research suggests that other persons can play an important role in the child's early development. The popular idea that mother is the most important figure in the infant's life because she spends the most time with the infant is unsupported by research data, which show that the time spent in interacting is a poor predictor of the quality of the relationship between infant and parent (Barglow, Vaughn & Molitor, 1987). In fact, the most important factor is the quality of the relationship as evidenced by the intact relationships found between working mothers and their children. Working mothers often rely on childcare in order to continue working, often this caretaking can be for the greater amount of the infant's day. However research has found that a minimal amount of interaction is necessary to allow attachment to form with working mothers and that it was the quality of time not quantity that was a more important factor (Ainsworth, 1985; Barglow, Vaughn & Molitor, 1987).

The effect of father

Until recently, the role of the father in child development and psychopathology has not been considered or researched because of the emphasis placed on the importance of mother–infant relationships. It was believed that primary caregiving was provided by the mother and that the father would merely serve as an occasional mother substitute in nurturing the child before the age of three. However, recent research has indicated that fathers do play an important role in child development and may be a factor in later development of psychopathology. Palkovitz (1987, 2002) found that the early and strong father–infant bonding is qualitatively different than the mother–infant attachment and although fathers spend less time with their infants, many (but not all) are responsive to their cues, enjoy interacting with them and become early and enduring central figures in their social worlds. Phares & Compas (1992) found that there is a substantial association between clinically referred paternal characteristics and child and adolescent psychopathology and that the degree of risk associated with paternal psychopathology was comparable to that associated with maternal psychopathology.

Santrock and Warshak (1979) found that both IQ and achievement scores were most depressed for boys whose fathers died when the child was between the ages of six and nine, while the other forms of father absence had the most detrimental effect on cognitive development during the period from birth to two years for both girls and boys. Boys whose fathers were absent consistently scored lower than either father-absent girls or father-present boys. Additionally, when fathers who were absent because of divorce, separation, or desertion were replaced through remarriage during the first five years of the child's life, the effect on the cognitive development of boys was positive but not for girls. In addition, Hoffman (1971) studied the relationship of father absence to moral development in seventh-grade boys and girls from low and middle socioeconomic level homes. He found clear evidence that father absence had a detrimental effect on conscience development in boys but not in girls.

Using measures of parent–child relations, internal–external locus of control and self-concept, Moerk (1973) compared the test scores of the sons of imprisoned fathers and of divorced fathers with those of juvenile delinquents and normal youngsters. Profiles of sons of imprisoned fathers were more similar to those of juvenile delinquents and less similar to the normal controls than were the profiles of the sons of divorced fathers. Absence of father has also been linked with alcoholism in young men whose fathers were in the home until they were 15 years of age, with hospitalized female alcoholics evidencing serious behaviour problems and with suicide attempts and drug addiction in both males and females (Knoester & Eggebeen, 2006; Eggebeen & Knoester, 2001; Isohanni, Oja, Moilanen & Koiranen, 1994).

Further research on the relationship between daughters and fathers found that girls who had grown up without a father felt insecure and apprehensive in relating to male peers and adults and girls of divorced parents reported more heterosexual activity while those whose fathers had died tended to be more sexually inhibited. Higher self-esteem and positive feelings about father were noted more frequently for daughters whose fathers had died as compared to those whose parents were divorced (Hetherington, 1973).

Paternal nurturance seems to be more highly correlated with the cognitive competence of boys than of girls and father absence before the age of five seems to be particularly damaging to the cognitive functioning of young boys (Scott-Jones, 1984). For both sexes, authoritarian paternal behaviour or intense paternal involvement in the problem-solving activities of the child are related to reduced academic competence (Amato, 1999).

Fathers do well at many of the traditional feminine tasks of child care, but unlike mothers, they tend to provide more physical stimulation for their babies than verbal stimulation. Baby boys seem to benefit more than girls from interactions with their fathers not only cognitively but in social situations as well. In fact as early as five months, baby boys show less fear of strangers or less apprehension on being left alone when fathers have taken care of them and played with them (Ban & Lewis, 1974).

THE TOTAL INTERACTING SYSTEM – THE FAMILY

So far, we have discussed the one-child family unit as single component of a complex interacting system, although we have considered each (the child, the mother and the father) as influencing and being influenced by each component. This section will discuss the family as an entire unit. Throughout a person's life the family provides a sense of security that facilitates adaptive and effective functioning within society and it is rare that ties to the family are completely broken or abandoned.

Dysfunctional families have long been thought to play an important part in psychopathology in later life. The family environment has the greatest impact on the child's personality and social development (Barnes, 1995). Several different types of dysfunctional families have been described as occurring in families that evidence psychotic or other abnormal conditions. One example of severe dysfunction is the situation where a parent exerts undue pressure on a child to take sides with one of the two warring parents; this type of forced alliance can seriously impede identification with either parent since each is depreciated by the other. This type of dysfunctional family situation has been found to cause psychopathological disorders in later life (Emery, 1982; Amato, 2000; Guidubaldi & Perry, 1985).

Another dysfunctional family environment is one characterized by parental mental illness. Research has shown that parents suffering from mental disorders often have difficulties in parenting, and parent–child interactions. Children from these families are at higher risk for a full range of psychological disorders (Downey & Coyne, 1990; Beardslee, Versage & Gladstone, 1998).

The family dynamics of a parent having a mental illness have been studied as they appear to be very different in these types of dysfunctional family environments. Generally these families are characterized by one parent having a severe abnormal disorder, e.g. bipolar disorder, while the other parent passively submits and appeases the disturbed spouse to keep the marriage intact. The normal parent is reluctant to leave the relationship and attempts to stay to help the spouse and take care of the children. This tends to place the normal spouse under a great deal of pressure and it is not unlikely to find the normal spouse succumbing to clinical depression. This situation provides a family environment for children in which abnormal behaviours and unrealistic views of the world are implicitly, if not explicitly, sanctioned. Children are often caught in the struggle and invest a great deal of energy in keeping the family intact rather than focusing on their own development. Various researchers have documented that this environment creates children who are unhappy, tense, experience considerable situational problems and show more maladaptive patterns of aggression towards peers and adults (Davenport et al., 1984; Zahn-Waxler et al., 1984).

Ross and Compagnon (2001) found that 74 percent of children with a schizophrenic parent met diagnostic criteria for a psychological disorder. The most common diagnostic categories included attention deficit/hyperactivity disorder (40 percent), any anxiety disorder (23 percent), and any depressive disorder (12 percent). Psychosis was present in 9 percent of this childhood sample; of those children with a psychiatric diagnosis, 47 percent demonstrated current moderate or severe impairment.

THE SCHOOL

Apart from the family, no institution has a greater and more continuous impact on the child's social and personality development than the educational system (Faulkner, Littleton & Woodhead, 1998). When we consider that children spend half of their waking lives for many years in some type of teaching institution, it is not surprising that it becomes the centre for not only academic instruction but also for the acquisition of social skills and competence. Cohen (1976) likens the school to the family in its form and mode of operating (although not in content), since in both situations the child is placed into a relatively self-contained unit and is expected to be responsive to adult controls. Entrance into the school environment usually represents the child's first prolonged separation from the familiar and comforting family environment. In this new setting, demands are made to do things that are not always rewarding and greater independence is required (Birch & Ladd, 1996).

What the child experiences, how the child perceives school, whether school will positively or negatively affect the child's motivation to learn, to persevere, to act independently, to cope with frustrations, and to acquire a sense of competence and self-worth will depend largely on teacher–pupil relationships and then secondly on peer relationships (Faulkner, Littleton & Woodhead, 1998).

PEER RELATIONS

As children grow and develop the parent's exclusive control of them decreases and gives way to other sources of influence, specifically peer groups. Peer groups and peer relationships become increasingly important as a source of influence in social and personality development. The opportunity for peer interactions provides children with normative standards by which they can compare and to some extent modify their own feelings, thoughts and actions. Peer groups begin to form early in middle childhood as the child extends his or her interpersonal ties beyond the immediate family. Initially these groups consist of informal and tenuous associations that over time evolve into more structured, stable, and cohesive organizations which sometimes involve special rituals and paraphernalia. The peer group is an alternative social unit to the family (Howe, 2010).

Peer groups offer companionship in age-appropriate interests and activities and provide opportunities for children to explore new experiences that are group sanctioned. Sometimes peer values conflict with those held by parents, in which case the resolution will likely depend on the relative strength of the child's relationship to the parents and the group. Finally, peer relationships serve to foster a sense of responsibility and commitment to others necessary for adaptive functioning within our society (Kupersmidt & Dodge, 2004).

Consequently, membership in a group affords social status and enhances self-esteem, whereas rejection from a group can have serious negative effects. Children can be cruel and insensitive so that a child's limitations or some other characteristic might be the basis for his or her exclusion from a peer group and the justification of the continued torment he or she receives from the group in the form of bullying. Such a child is likely to feel angry, alienated, threatened and devalued to the point where he or she is apt to actively avoid almost any further social interactions with peers (Howe, 2010).

Deater-Deckard (2001) researched the role of peer groups and friendship and found that various processes were involved with the development of psychopathology in childhood and adolescence which included: peer rejection, social withdrawal, avoidance of peer interaction, internalizing problems and the socialization of deviant behaviour. Other research has further documented the process of peer rejection in predicting loneliness and depressed mood in children and adolescence (Boivin, Hymel & Bukowski, 1995; Bagwell, Newcomb & Bukowski, 1998). Considering that peer relationships play an important role in adjustment problems in later life, how does bullying affect child development and psychopathology?

BULLYING

Bullying is a specific type of peer rejection and is an explicit dysfunctional peer relationship with the sole intent of causing deliberate harm to another individual. Bullying comes in a three different types: emotional, verbal and physical with a variety of combinations that can occur. A victim can be subjected to one type, a combination of various types or be subjected to all three forms. Bullying is abusive treatment that is repetitive in nature with generally the same person becoming the victim/ target for the abuse. Although bullying can happen anywhere it is more common in the school environment where children have easier access to each other and interact with each other in a variety of activities (Williams, Forgas & Von Hippel, 2005).

Bullying can take the form of physical aggression; shoving, poking, throwing things, slapping, choking, punching, kicking, hair pulling, scratching, biting and pinching. It can involve various types of social aggression such as refusing to socialize with the target, being critical of the individual's manner of dress, or the individual's race, religion, disability or sexual orientation, staring, giggling, laughing at the individual, mocking, name-calling and spreading gossip/lies/rumours in a variety of ways (Crothers & Levinson, 2004).

Children have been socialized that adults will protect them from harm, therefore when children report the bullying behaviour to teachers and the bullying continues, the harm that is caused is significant (Nansel et al., 2004). Research is finding that the teacher's response to bullying is vital in how the victim responds and the high risk of psychiatric symptoms if the child believes that the adults involved are not protecting them (Yoon, 2004). In terms of school and teacher response there appears to be a great deal of variability among teachers when bullying is uncovered, ranging from telling the victim to ignore the bully, not understanding the extent of the bullying, lack of appropriate consequences to the bully when caught doing the behaviour, and a general permissive attitude towards the perpetrator (Craig, Henderson & Murphy, 2000; Stephenson & Smith, 1989; Song & Swearer, 2002).

Klomek et al. (2007) found that frequent exposure to victimization or bullying others was related to a high risk of depression, suicidal ideation, and suicide attempts compared with adolescents not involved in bullying behaviour. Infrequent involvement in bullying behaviour was also related to increased risk of depression and suicide, particularly among girls. Additionally the most troubled adolescents were those who are both victims and bullies and psychopathology was associated with bullying behaviour both in and away from school.

Kokkinos & Panayiotou (2004) examined a sample of 202 adolescents between the ages of 12 and 15 and examined the association between bully–victim problems and disruptive behaviour disorders. The difference between bullies and their victims was that conduct disorder was predictive of bullying, whereas low self-esteem and oppositional defiant disorder were predictive of victimization.

Children who were victims of bullying displayed more internalizing symptoms; depression, suicidal ideation and attempts, predisposition to psychotic experiences, post-traumatic stress syndrome, paranoia and dissociation, whereas children who were bullies demonstrated more externalizing symptoms; delinquency, aggression, psychiatric symptoms as well as an inability to function socially (Ivarsson et al., 2005; Kim et al., 2001; Campbell & Morrison, 2007).

A relatively new form of bullying that far outreaches the confines of the school environment is cyberbullying. Cyberbullying involves using the internet, mobile phone or other digital technology for the purpose of causing harm. Few studies have investigated this new form of bullying, but Kapatzia & Sygkollitou (2008) found that the harm was increased because children felt overwhelmed as they were unable to escape the bullying and were targets even in what should be the relatively safe confines of their own homes.

PSYCHOLOGICAL THEORIES OF CHILD DEVELOPMENT

Cognitive-developmental theories

The cognitive-developmental approach in contrast to psychoanalytic theory stresses the higher mental processes and intellectual factors. This group of theories does not compartmentalize development into discrete areas of experience nor does it make assumptions about unconscious processes or major systems of the developing child. We begin by discussing Piaget.

Piaget

Piaget's theory stresses the universal nature of intellectual development and views development as an evolutionary process that is innate and fixed. Piaget believed that development progresses through successive stages for all children, but that the rate of progress varies from child to child. Piaget's cognitive theory begins with the idea that motor action is the source from which mental operations develop. Infants begin life with innate reflexes, some of which are modifiable through experience and become the behavioural elements that more complex forms of cognitive behaviour develop. While the child is developing they begin to learn to organize all experiences of a particular type into a cognitive structure which can change with learning. Piaget believed that intelligence is the ability to adapt and adaptation depends on the dual learning processes of assimilation and accommodation. Assimilation refers to the tendency to incorporate external reality into some meaningful structure (schema), while accommodation is the process by which a schema changes so the child is better able to adapt to the assimilated reality (Piaget & Inhelder, 1972).

Piaget divided cognitive development into the following four stages that roughly correspond to age periods: the sensorimotor stage (birth to approximately two years); the preoperational stage (two to seven years); the stage of concrete operations (seven to eleven years); and the stage of formal operations (eleven to fifteen years) (Piaget & Inhelder, 1972).

Piaget divides the sensorimotor stage into six sub-stages beginning with the infant's use of reflexes and progressing to the acquired behaviour patterns of voluntary movements and active exploration. The child progresses from a very self-centred existence to one that is object-centred. It is during this stage that the concept of object permanence is important as an explanatory base of the child's mental images (memory) of objects beyond their immediate sensory experiences (Piaget & Inhelder, 1972).

The preoperational stage is a period of language acquisition and development. This stage is where the child begins to shift from a total reliance on motor activity to an increased use of symbolic activity (cognitive), ranging from problem solving to concerns dealing with the environment. During the early period of this stage the young child will have egocentric thoughts that are specific to the situation and reflect only their point of view. As they progress through this stage they begin to view the world less objectively as their perspective gradually widens. The child's reasoning is still distorted during this phase as they still have a tendency to attend to one essential feature of a problem while neglecting other important aspects. For example if water from a tall glass is poured into a short broad glass, the child believes that the tall glass contained more water, even though the water is the

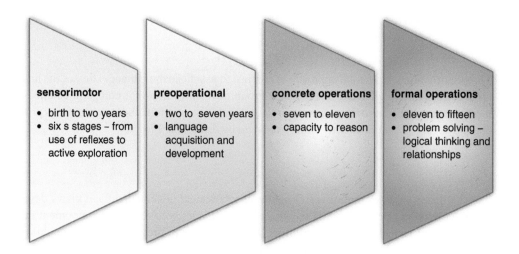

Figure 7.2   Piaget's four stages of child development

same. The child will only focus on the height of the glass without attending to the other dimensions in reaching the conclusion that the taller glass contained more water (Piaget & Inhelder, 1972).

The concrete operations stage is the beginning of the child's capacity to reason. For the first time, the child can produce a mental representation of a series of actions and can recognize the notion of conservation, seeing volume, weight, length and number as constant even when minor changes in their external appearance are introduced. The child at this stage is able to identify that water poured from a tall glass to a short, wider glass contains the same volume of water (Piaget & Inhelder, 1972).

The last stage in Piaget's theory is formal operations. In this stage the adolescent is capable of thinking about all of the possible solutions to a problem by systematically exploring the possibilities and checking the effectiveness of each particular application. Adolescents are able to think in hypothetical terms and are capable of forming abstractions and dealing with symbols. For Piaget, the capacity to formulate hypotheses and to handle logical relationships brings intellectual growth to its highest point (Piaget & Inhelder, 1972).

Kohlberg – moral development

Another example of a cognitive-developmental theory is Kohlberg's theory dealing with moral development and concepts of reason and judgement in child development. Kohlberg's research is largely an outgrowth of the earlier work of Piaget, who viewed morality as a system of rules for conduct which the child forms from the influence of the child's parents and other significant adults and the child's own experiences (Kohlberg, 1981).

The pinnacle of Kohlberg's theory is that moral development involves a component of cognitive growth and development. In general stage theorists such as Freud, Erikson Piaget and Kohlberg hold

Table 7.2   Kohlberg's stages and judgement levels of moral judgement

Judgement levels	Stages of development
1 – moral value is in external factors – bad acts	Stage 1 – obedience and punishment – objective responsibility
	Stage 2 – vaguely aware of others but mainly satisfying one's own needs
2 – moral value resides in performing good or right roles	Stage 3 – orientation to approval and to pleasing and helping others
	Stage 4 – authority and social-order – showing respect for authority
3 – moral value resides in conformity to shared standards, rights or duties	Stage 5 – recognition of rules or expectations – avoidance of rule violation
	Stage 6 – conscience – orientation to not only rules but principles of choice and orientation to conscience as a directing agent and to mutual respect and trust

a maturational view of development in which biological factors play a central role in the sequential and orderly unfolding of behaviour. In contrast, learning theorists emphasize environmental conditions which give rise to the acquisition of behaviour and those that maintain or produce changes in behaviour (Kohlberg, 1981).

LEARNING THEORY

Learning pervades nearly every aspect of a child's developmental functioning. It plays a role in eating, bowel and bladder control, language development, interpersonal relations, emotional expression, motivation, thinking, remembering, perceiving, motor skills and in the formation of attitudes and values. Although limited by biological factors, learning is the process by which environmental forces bring about lasting changes in behaviour through practice (Illeris, 2008). For example, the child who is born deaf will be unable to learn normal speech patterns but will be able to silently read and no amount of practice will enable a child with advanced muscular dystrophy to learn to play football, although they will be able to memorize the rules.

   Learning results in long-lasting behaviour change, as distinguished from temporary alterations that occur from fatigue, drugs or adaptation. Practice or experience is essential to differentiate learning from the effects of physical maturation and biological factors, such as brain injury or damage. Changes in behaviour that result from learning may be either desirable or undesirable since the process of acquisition makes no distinction between good and bad behaviours (Illeris, 2008). These learning principles often play a role in many of the psychiatric disorders, such as drug addiction and anxiety disorders.

Types of learning

Learning is a hypothetical construct because it cannot be observed directly and is the variable that intervenes between stimuli and response and that links the stimuli and response together. Underlying the link of stimuli and response is the assumption of associationism that assumes that internal connections (learning) are most likely to occur when objects, behaviours or experiences are close together in time and space (Lutz, 2005). Classical conditioning, first introduced by Ivan Pavlov, found that reflexes not only occur to innate factors but could also occur to learned ones as well. His famous experiments proved that dogs could learn to salivate to a neutral stimulus such as a bell when they associated the neutral stimulus with an unconditioned stimulus that triggered a reflexive innate response.

Pavlov showed that through successive temporal pairings of the conditioned stimulus (CS), the onset of the sound of a bell, with the unconditioned stimulus (UCS) which serves as the reinforcer (the sight of meat powder), the conditioned stimulus would come to elicit a specific response of salivation, called the conditioned response (CR). Through this simple procedure Pavlov showed that a new stimulus–response connection could be established through learning. He also showed that a CR could be diminished and eventually be eliminated through the absence of the UCS. The progressive weakening of a CR under these conditions is known as extinction, although there are special occasions (referred to as spontaneous recovery) when an extinguished CR re-appears (Jarvis, Holford & Griffin, 2003).

Another principle uncovered by Pavlov, stimulus generalization, provides an explanation for our ability to respond appropriately to new stimuli as long as they are similar to familiar ones. Generalization occurs when a stimulus which is similar but not identical to the original one elicits the same response. The closer the similarity to the original stimulus, the more completely the new stimulus will substitute for it (Jarvis, Holford & Griffin, 2003). For example if a child is scratched by a Siamese cat, the child will not only avoid all Siamese cats but also any other types of cats as they will identify them as a group of animals that are harmful and mean.

The effect of generalization can be reduced through a process known as discrimination, in which the association between a particular conditioned stimulus and a conditioned response is reinforced through conditioning; while the conditioned responses are similar, conditioned stimuli are eliminated through extinction. In this way, the organism learns to discriminate between stimuli and to respond to the appropriate one. After a CS acquires the ability to elicit a CR, it may be successfully paired (this time serving as the UCS) with a new CS, which eventually will also elicit the same CR. This higher-order conditioning is an important finding because it extends the possibilities of learning through conditioning in our daily lives (Jarvis, Holford & Griffin, 2003). Classical conditioning is important to understand because it is the basic building block to the next step in learning, which is operant conditioning.

Operant conditioning

Operant conditioning is different from classical conditioning as it employs a different sequence of events where reinforcement is provided after the organism makes the appropriate response. The

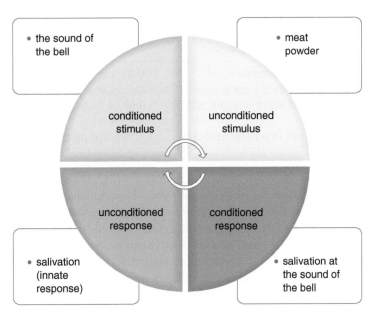

Figure 7.3   Classical conditioning

organism is 'acting' on its environment in order to make the reinforcement occur. In operant conditioning the action is active, whereas in classical conditioning the action is passive. However, responses that are classically conditioned are considered to be elicited and under direct stimulus control in that they are reflex- like and specific to the UCS, such as salivation to food or an eye blink to a puff of air (Baum, 1994).

In contrast, operant responses are emitted in the sense that they are available in the organism's response repertory and they appear spontaneously rather than as a response to a specific stimulus. The stimulus situation in this kind of learning is non-specific as in an operant chamber (sometimes called a Skinner box) where the hungry animal must by chance make a bar-pressing response before it receives food as a reinforcer. In this way, the animal's behaviour of bar pressing operates on the environment to produce the effect of obtaining food. Much like everyday situations, operant condition can and does occur without the reinforcer following the responses every time (continuous reinforcement). In fact, experimental studies have used different schedules of intermittent reinforcement in which reinforcement may occur after a fixed number of non-reinforced responses at fixed time intervals following the last reinforcement, after variable numbers of non-reinforced responses, or at variable time intervals between reinforcements (Baum, 1994).

An example of this is the use of fruit machines versus vending machines. Our expectation is that if we put money into a vending machine we expect the machine to produce chocolate (continuous reinforcement). If the machine takes the money without producing chocolate, very few of us will

Table 7.3   Classical conditioning vs. operant conditioning

	Classical conditioning	Operant conditioning
Type of response	Reflex, involuntary	Unprompted, voluntary
Reinforcement	Occurs before the response (paired with the innate action)	Occurs after the response (can be negative or positive – and is called the reinforcer)
Role of subject	Passive (the person reacts)	Active (the person does something)

continue the behaviour. However, if we put our money into a fruit machine (gambling) very few of us will expect to win on the first try and we may believe that more than one try is useful for producing the results we hope to achieve. Our expectation of this machine is very different, therefore we may continuously put money into the machine even though it may never provide us with the positive reinforcement. This is a schedule of partial reinforcement. The behaviour is exactly the same (putting money in a machine) but our expectation will be very different and therefore our behaviours will change.

Many of the principles found with classical conditioning such as extinction, spontaneous recovery and generalization apply equally well to operant conditioning. In addition, novel or new responses which are not already available in the organism's repertory can be learned through a procedure known as shaping. Initially, approximations of the wanted response are reinforced, followed by the reinforcement of responses which are increasingly similar to it, until only the appropriate response is reinforced (Baum, 1994).

An example that links classical conditioning and phobias is the following. A strange man has taken to lurking in a secluded corner under a staircase in a woman's apartment building. Every time someone knocks on her door, he shrieks in a weird maniacal voice. The effect includes a number of very obvious fear responses. Eventually, the man is arrested, but the woman continues to react with fear every time someone knocks on her door.

Learning and reinforcement

The concept of reinforcement is extremely important in a discussion of the learning process. If the occurrence or removal of an event or condition leads to the strengthening of a stimulus–response (S–R) connection or to the increased probability that a response will be emitted, the event or condition may be referred to as a positive or negative reinforcer. Positive reinforcements are usually thought of as a reward and they can come in primary (food, water) or secondary (praise, money) form. A secondary reinforcement is one that has been learned or paired with a primary. Negative reinforcement involves the removal of an unpleasant or aversive consequence that strengthens avoidance or escape behaviour. In many instances, reinforcement is difficult to identify until after learning has taken place. In this sense, it is not independent of learning, but is inferred from it. When we deal with complex human behaviours we don't always know what specific reward will reinforce learning (Gross, 1997).

In contrast, punishment is a condition or event that is presented after a response occurs that will decrease the probability that the response will be emitted, that is, it will weaken the S–R association. Punishment is rarely given with either sufficient intensity or suddenness to have more than transient effects. For example, if a child learns to steal sweets and eats them before they are caught, and is then punished, the child will continue stealing but will learn to avoid getting caught. In order for punishment to be effective, the child must be punished every time the act is committed. The action of stealing has been positively reinforced by the eating of the sweets. The punishment will not be able to negate the positive reinforcement that the child has received from their action and instead will strengthen sweet-stealing behaviour and the incentive to not get caught. In this case what is reinforced is illicit behaviour because in most cases the act becomes a secondary reinforcement (excitement of not getting caught). In most cases, punishment is not administered at maximum strength initially. Parents typically begin to correct their child's behaviour by gentle verbal reprimands that may escalate into screams, and eventually spanking, without much success in curing the unwanted behaviour. If punishment is to be used, the most extreme form should be employed at the outset, but the ethical and moral problems involved keep most of us from doing what should be done when we choose to use punishment as a way of changing behaviour (Gross, 1997).

Imitation learning or modelling

Now that we have detailed classical and operant conditioning we can apply these principles to specific types of learning. One type of learning that has had major applications in the area of child development and abnormal behaviour is modelling. This type of learning takes place by observing another person, or a model, make a response or a set of responses. For the developing child, the opportunities for imitation learning are almost limitless in such obvious behaviours as emotional expressions and in more subtle behaviours such as attitudes toward others.

Bandura's social learning theory

Combining the principles of imitation learning with the procedures of operant conditioning, Bandura and Walters (1963) introduced a social learning theory that accounted for the acquisition of novel responses in children and adults. They emphasized the importance of imitation (modelling) in the learning of both deviant and conforming behaviours, and they provided numerous examples where modelling occurs, such as sex-linked roles, vocational roles, child-rearing practices and learning to perform specific acts. Imitation learning may occur through direct modelling, or through symbolic modelling, although the mode of modelling will affect the rate and level of learning. Bandura describes imitation as an active process that is determined by four interrelated concepts: attention, retention, motoric reproduction and incentive and finally motivation.

Attention is necessary since imitation would not be possible if the observer failed to attend to the model or failed to notice the specific actions of the model's behaviour. Retention is necessary for the reproduction of the actions without the continued presence of the external model. The process of motoric reproduction, although complex, must be available in order for the child to actually perform the modelled behaviour. Finally, incentive and motivation must be present if overt perfor-mance of the modelled sequence is to occur. Behaviour is maintained through direct reinforcement given to the individual or through vicarious reinforcement given to the model, or through self-reinforcement in which the individual administers self-rewards or self-punishments (Bandura, 1976).

Bandura and Walters (1963) provided research that supported their social learning theory and found that aggressive-punitive parents are likely to produce aggressive children, especially if the parents (models) are highly successful in controlling rewards.

Rotter's social learning theory

Rotter (1972) hypothesized three basic concepts of social learning theory: behaviour potential (B.P.), expectancy (E.) and reinforcement (R.V). Rotter arranged these concepts in an equation without making any mathematical assumptions about the relationship between expectancy and rein-forcement value.

$$B.P. = f(E. \ \& \ R.V.)$$

His formula states that the probability of the occurrence of a particular behaviour in a specific situation is a function of both the subjectively held probability, that the behaviour in question will be reinforced and the value of the reinforced and the value of the reinforcer to the responder. The psychological situation was the fourth basic concept and was used to reflect the stimulus complex to which the organism reacts and to acknowledge the selectivity of reactions to diverse kinds of stimu-lation. Rotter believed that reinforcement (either internal or external) as any event that changes the potential for occurrence of a given behaviour, while reinforcement value as the relative preference for one of a number of reinforcements to occur if the probability of occurrence for all of them was equal. Expectancy is the subjectively held probability that a specific or set of reinforcements will occur in a given situation (Rotter, 1972).

For example, a child acquires a number of expectancies as they attempt to satisfy a need for atten-tion from a parent. If the child fails to gain attention and affection from a parent they soon develop a generalized expectancy of rejection. If the child's need to engage the parent is strong they are likely to persist in their efforts although the expectancy for achieving the goal is low. If a child's need for the parent is reduced through interactions with their peers their attempts to gain a parent's attention will drop considerably. However, the child carries the generalized expectancy into new situations so that they are likely to expect reflection in a new encounter with adults.

PSYCHOANALYTIC THEORY

Psychoanalytic theory of child development emphasizes the ideology that external behaviour is an exterior characteristic determined by symbolic significance and internal psychic meanings and that all our early experiences with our parents shape our development (Elliott, 2002).

According to psychoanalytic theory the personality consists of three major systems: the id, the ego and the superego. The id is the inherited component and is present at birth and represents the world of subjective reality with its activities being governed by what Freud termed the 'pleasure principle'. Freud viewed the newborn infant as a pleasure-bound organism seeking immediate gratification of impulses without regard for or knowledge of objective reality, which he believed was evidenced by the screaming cry that only stopped when the baby was given food. In seeking immediate gratification, the id largely functions by a primary process that includes motor actions or mental images of the desired object if the image isn't immediately available. In addition, the id's demands for immediate satisfaction are likely to lead the infant into dangerous conflicts with the external environment (such as the baby getting hurt when reaching for a desired object or touching a hot cooker), since the id is cut off from the external world and knows nothing of ensuring the organism's survival. Finally, as the caregiver tries to foster self-control skills in the child by gradually withholding immediate and continuous gratification, the infant is forced to deal with the demands of the environment (Tyson, 1993).

The self-control skills that the infant learns are how the ego develops and they enable the child to achieve pleasure for the id that is within the bounds of objective reality. The ego emerges from the id with the help of the environment and becomes the component of the personality that is concerned with reason. Guided by keeping experiences within external constraints, the ego applies a secondary process that distinguishes the subjective from the objective world of reality to delay tension states until an appropriate way or object is found that satisfies the need. The ego also protects the child by making use of the sensations of anxiety as warning signals of danger that in turn prompt safer responses (Elliott, 2002).

The superego is the last system of the personality to develop and it is the moral component of the personality. The superego first assimilates the values and culture of the parents or caregivers and then, as the child develops, assimilates the traditional values of the society. The superego is recognized by its judicial functions (the conscience) in judgements about right and wrong and its strivings for perfection. In trying to control the impulses of the id, the superego seeks to permanently block the id's gratification. This is in contrast to the ego's effort to postpone gratification. The superego keeps a careful watch over the ego, attempts to direct it and threatens to punish it for id gratification. When the ego and the superego are in complete agreement, there is little to distinguish them, but when the ego fails to block the impulses of the id, tensions flare up and the superego becomes visible as pangs of conscience. As the executive of the personality, the ego controls cognitive and intellectual functioning and acts as a mediator between id impulses and the demands of reality and between the id and the superego (Gaddini & Limentani, 1992).

In addition to the description of these essential components of the personality, Freud's major contribution to child development was his view of infant sexuality and its connection to a temporal series of differentiated stages by which personality develops. He believed that excessive frustration or indulgence of the child's needs were the two primary causes of pathology and that fixation and regression were the ways that personality development became permanently halted at a particular stage of development. The first stage, known as the oral period, occurs during the first 18 to 24 months of the infant's life in which stimulation of the erogenous zones of the lips and mouth by objects such as nipples, toys and fingers provide pleasure and relieve libidinal tension. During the second period, called the anal phase, the anus becomes the site of sexual stimulation and gratification. This stage extends from about 18 months to approximately three years (roughly corresponding to the period of toilet training) during which time the child seems to derive sensual pleasure from both the retention and expulsion of faecal matter (Gaddini & Limentani, 1992).

The phallic stage occurs between the third and fifth year of the child's life when the genitals become the primary focus of sexual excitation and pleasure. Shortly after the phallic state the child enters the oedipal period, when the libidinal source of gratification becomes an external object. The opposite sex parent becomes the object of libidinal pleasure instead of the child's own genitals and body. The child views the parent of the same sex as an obstacle and as a source of interference with the sexual desire for the other parent. The child's wish to replace and eliminate the same-sex parent arouses guilt and fear of retaliation, as well as a sense of inadequacy at an inability to successfully accomplish this desire. This period is conflictual and tumultuous for the child, but is eventually resolved through a process of identification with the same-sex parent (Gaddini & Limentani, 1992).

The longest psychosexual stage of development, known as the latency period, begins at about age six and extends through pre-adolescence. It is a stage where sexual tensions and activities are dormant, where the child can recover from the turmoil of the oedipal phase, and where further identification with the same-sex parent occurs. The final period, the genital stage, takes place during adolescence at a time when the sexual drive is heightened and the opposite sex becomes the sexual object for those who have developed normally. Freud viewed homosexuality as abnormal behaviour and an individual who had been halted at a previous stage of development (Gaddini & Limentani, 1992).

The psychosexual stages of development are significant not only as focuses of sensual pleasure but also as important sources of parent–child interactions in which enduring patterns are established

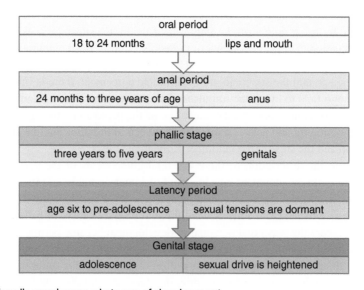

Figure 7.4   Freud's psychosexual stages of development

for the gratification of the child's needs. According to Freud, the manner in which libidinal needs are satisfied or frustrated has important implications for the child's social development and for the formation of specific character traits. For example, Freud proposed bipolar personality traits that were associated with each stage of psychosexual development and believed that manifestations of either extreme of the trait reflected fixation (caused by indulgence or frustration) at that particular developmental level. Thus, an excessively indulged person fixated at the oral level would evidence traits of optimism, gullibility and admiration, while the orally fixated person would show pessimism, suspiciousness and envy. In this way, Freud's theory described the means by which specific personality attributes are initially acquired and more broadly suggested that the nature of the child's experiences during each stage of development determines the form that personality structure will take (Fonagy & Target, 2002).

ERIK ERIKSON

Erikson used a Freudian psychoanalytic orientation to create a different view of personality development. Erikson placed greater emphasis on the ego than the id in personality development, stressed

Table 7.4   Erikson's eight stages

Hope	Birth to 18 months	Trust vs. mistrust	Trust is the foundation of the personality – enables the infant to feel comfortable while distrust can lead to psychoticism
Will	18 months to 3 years	Autonomy vs. self-doubt and shame	Self-doubt occurs in the absence of parental regulations and controls – a combination of freedom and regulation attains success
Purpose	3 to 6 years	Initiative vs. guilt	Initiative is encouraged that includes both approval and regulation – guilt occurs because the superego id developed at this time
Competence	6 to 12 years	Industry vs. inferiority	Time for mastering new skills and work on the development of work habits that will be important later – inadequacy can occur if they are not successful
Fidelity	12 to 18 years	Identity vs. role confusion	Rapid physiological changes along with the challenge of adult tasks create conflict in adolescence about their role
Love	19 to 40 years	Intimacy vs. isolation	The task is establishing intimate relationships and establishing a permanent relationship with a spouse
Care	40 to 65 years	Generativity vs. stagnation	Develop strong marital union and guiding the next generation by having and raising children
Wisdom	65 onward	Ego integrity vs. despair	Adults learn to accept and adapt and go forward without despair and unafraid of death

the importance of social and cultural influences beyond the mother–father–child triangle, and adopted a more optimistic view of human nature. Erikson saw various developmental components as conducive to growth and not necessarily detrimental, leading to personal and social crisis. He proposed eight stages of development that include the adult years, reflecting his belief that the individual constantly redevelops his or her personality in passing from one phase to the next. Erikson believed that development followed a universal course and that each person was required to face and master a central problem at each stage. An individual's success at each developmental phase would contribute to ego strength, while failures were carried over as problems that impaired attempts to resolve new problems at later phases (Erikson, 1995).

CONCLUSION

Going back to our two case studies – the first example at the beginning of the chapter was of Jon and his family. Clearly Jon's family was dysfunctional and his early family environment provided Jon with a developmental history that would have poorly prepared him to cope in a social environment that became more demanding on Jon's limited resources. What happened to Jon? Unfortunately Jon's situation had a tragic conclusion. Jon Venables and his schoolfriend Robert Thompson abducted, tortured and murdered two-year-old James Bulger. At the time of the murder the boys were ten years old. The both served eight years and were released on lifelong licence. Jon had a great deal of difficulty when he was released and very quickly found himself in trouble again, he was convicted and imprisoned for downloading and distributing child pornography and will be considered for parole sometime in 2012.

The case study of Marshall was about a dysfunctional family environment and a disorganized developmental background. What happened to Marshall? Marshall Mathers, better know as Eminem, became a famous rapper, record producer and actor. He has won a multiple awards for his albums and music. He has sold over 12.5 million records in the UK and has a net worth of approximately £93 million. He is involved in charity work providing donations to food banks and youth groups and has founded his own charity to help disadvantaged youths.

Although these are extreme examples, they are interesting as both boys suffered similar dysfunctional backgrounds. Both the boys had parents with mental illness. Both boys had unstable home lives, so what modified the outcomes and what was different about the two boys? We can only speculate concerning infant temperaments, but it appears that Jon was a more difficult infant than Marshall and additionally his mother's resources were stretched as she was also caring for two other children who had behavioural difficulties. Jon's mother suffered with clinical depression and when Jon became too difficult to handle she placed him in foster care, which would in all likelihood trigger abandonment issues. In terms of peer relationships, Jon was able to forge a close friendship with another child who had a similar dysfunctional background, whereas Marshall's family moved so often that he stopped trying and did not rely on peer group interactions. Another difference was that Jon was a bully, while Marshall was a victim of bullying. In terms of psychological theory and child development, many different models can be applied. Using psychoanalytic theory, Jon's violence could be explained in terms of his id not having any type of self-control and lack of a superego development. Jon was unable to assimilate the values from his parents and therefore had no conscience. Marshall applied his frustration and aggression to his music and channelling his creativity, therefore perhaps more closely modelling Bandura's social learning, as he was imitating individuals he admired and creating his own music.

Summary

This chapter focused on the child development issues of abnormal psychology. The section concentrated on the various factors such as: personality development, nature vs. nurture, temperament, environmental factors and interactional systems such as the family, the school and peer relationships. The chapter then finished with a brief discussion of various developmental psychological theories.

LEARNING TOOLS

Key terms

Conditioned response – learned response to a stimulus

Conditioned stimulus – stimulus used to provoke a conditioned response

Conduct disorder – a group of behaviours that involve chronic behaviour problems such as defiant, antisocial behaviour and impulsivity

Negative reinforcement – taking away of an aversive stimulus to increase a desired behaviour or response

Oppositional defiant disorder – a pattern of disobedient and hostile behaviour generally directed at authority figures

Paranoia – a thought process influenced by the irrational idea of perceived threat, anxiety or fear

Personality – a combination of emotions, attitudes and behavioural response patterns of an individual

Positive reinforcement – anything that occurs after a behaviour that increases the likelihood that the behaviour will reoccur

Post-traumatic stress syndrome – a severe anxiety disorder that can develop after exposure to any traumatic event

Psychosis – loss of contact with reality which generally includes a false perception of reality such as delusions and hallucinations

Punishment – a negative or unpleasant stimulus that is utilized to decrease a specific behaviour or response

Temperament – elements of an individual's personality which are regarded as innate

Unconditioned response – the unlearned response that occurs naturally in response to the unconditioned stimulus

Unconditioned stimulus – a stimulus that unconditionally, naturally and automatically triggers a response

Study guide

1 Explore the differences between temperament and personality. How are these two concepts related?
2 Investigate whether there are disadvantages or advantages to being an only child and how this affects personal development.
3 Kohlberg provided one theory of moral development in children. Research the other theories and compare/contrast them to Kohlberg's model.
4 Investigate the moral and ethical issues surrounding punishment. Can it be used in ways that are useful in child development?

Case study in focus

Apply the various psychological theories to the two case studies. Which theories would provide more explanation for the behavioural differences? Which theories would account for the criminal behaviour?

Personal development

Explore how cyberbullying has become such an important issue in the lives of adolescents and the significant differences between bullying and cyberbullying. Why can't teenagers simply turn off the technology?

Suggested reading

Lindon, J. (2010) *Understanding child development: Linking theory and practice* (2nd edn). Abingdon: Hodder.
Gibbs, J.C. (2009) *Moral development and reality: Beyond the theories of Kohlberg and Hoffman* (2nd edn). New York: Pearson.
Rothbart, M.K. (2011) *Becoming who we are: Temperament and personality in development*. New York: Guildford Press.
Friel, J. (1991) *Adult children: Secrets of dysfunctional families*. New York: Health Communications.
Williams, D., Forgas, J.P. & Hippel, W.V. (eds) (2005) *The social outcast: Ostracism, social exclusion, rejection and bullying*. New York: Psychology Press.

Child Disorders and Psychopathology

8

Learning aims

At the end of this chapter you should:

- Be familiar with the variety of psychological disorders in childhood and adolescence
- Understand how pervasive developmental disorders affect children
- Understand how learning disabilities can impact the developmental stages of a child
- Be able to identify the variety of factors that are responsible for mental retardation.

INTRODUCTION

CASE STUDY

Marc and Debra had the perfect middle-class suburban life. They lived in a nice house in a pleasant, quiet neighbourhood; they had two kids, Jasmine and Jacob. They went on family holidays and took weekend trips on their motorcycles and were often seen playing ball with their children in the back garden. Family, friends and neighbours described the family as wonderful and they never seemed to argue or disagree about anything. Marc made a comfortable living for the family and was employed as an instrumentation technician in the oil and gas industry; his wife was a stay-at-home mum but had plans of starting a business of her own in reiki and had begun to take classes. She had wanted to be available for her children as they grew up and then had plans once they were teenagers to start her new business. By all reports they were a loving, caring family that treated their children with love and respect. Marc and Debra were described as parents who were fair and caring and not overbearing. No one has ever reported that Marc and Debra abused their children in any way.

Jasmine appeared to be normal in every aspect; she decorated her room with stuffed animals and had a canopy bed. She went to a Catholic school and was a good student. She was a normal, well-adjusted girl who made new friends easily. She was described by her friends as doing all the regular things; going to the mall, watching movies, having sleep-overs with friends and going swimming. When she turned 12 she became interested in Goth culture and music. She soon began wearing black clothes and heavy make-up and associating at the mall with a local Goth group that consisted of a few dozen individuals of varying ages. It was at this point that she began to change; she stopped hanging around with her school friends who didn't really approve of the new Goth image. She appeared to enjoy her new image and often intimidated others and became aggressive. Jasmine seemed to grow up overnight – and looked much older than her 12 years, the dark make-up and Goth clothes made her appear four to five years older. Her new Goth friends did not know she was 12 and thought she was much older. She began to put various profiles on the internet, always stating that she was much older than she actually was. Her parents disapproved of her new friends and Jasmine found it easier to sneak around and not tell them anything about her activities. As Jasmine became more rebellious her mother attempted to gain control: Jasmine's grades began to drop and the school kept complaining that she was constantly breaking school rules. Both Debra and Marc started telling friends they were having problems with their daughter but everyone assumed it was normal teenage trouble and that it was just a period most teenagers go through.

Then Jasmine met Jeremy. Jasmine's new boyfriend Jeremy came from a completely different background. He was a 23-year-old man who had left school at an early age and had difficulty remaining employed for any length of time. He was living with his mother in a caravan park; she had been diagnosed with a terminal lung disease, and the pair had a subsistence living that was unexceptional. Jeremy's childhood had been very dysfunctional and physically abusive. Jeremy's father and mother were both alcoholics and Jeremy's father would come home drunk and beat his son and his wife. When Jeremy's mother eventually split up with him she married another man who was also an alcoholic and an abuser. The family was in constant turmoil and moved around a lot, never remaining stable. Jeremy had a difficult time in school, where he was constantly bullied and called names. He was described by friends and family as being odd, having a quick temper as well as being mentally young. They were concerned when he began dating girls who were five to six years younger and felt his behaviour was often inappropriate around young girls. On his various internet sites he described himself as a 300-year-old werewolf and stated that he had fantasies about killing and drinking blood. Jeremy began using alcohol and marijuana at the age of 14 with his mother's approval as she felt he was easier to live with when he was under the influence of drugs. Earlier in his life he had attempted to go 'Goth' but it hadn't caught on yet and he had quickly given it up. When he was 21 he tried again. This time it was different – there were a lot more people to hang out with and the group was accepting of Jeremy's odd behaviour. The younger Goths adored him since many were under-age and he could buy them alcohol and provide rides for them in his car. For the first time in Jeremy's life he had authority and respect.

When Jasmine's parents found out about Jeremy they attempted to prevent Jasmine from having any further contact with him, angering both Jasmine and Jeremy. Jasmine and Jeremy told friends that they were going to kill Jasmine's parents so that they could be together, but no one took either one seriously and thought it was bravado.

Late one night Jasmine telephoned Jeremy and asked him to help her sneak out so that they could be together; Jeremy arrived at her house, drunk and high on cocaine and confronted Jasmine's parents. Jeremy stabbed Debra 12 times and her father Marc was stabbed 24 times while Jasmine waited upstairs with her eight-year-old brother. Jasmine could hear what was going on downstairs but did not call the police for help. Jeremy dragged both of them to the basement where they bled to death. It is unclear who actually killed Jasmine's eight-year-old brother as both would later blame the other. What is known is that he was stabbed four times and his throat was cut. After the family were murdered, Jeremy left Jasmine's house and went home, leaving Jasmine behind. Again the story as to why this happened is convoluted, but what is fact is that Jasmine did not call for help, and did not call the police. Instead, after being left behind she decided to join Jeremy at his house. She retrieved her mother's purse to get enough money to hire a taxi. When she realized that there wasn't enough money she walked to the local convenience store where she withdrew some cash, then walked back home and ordered the taxi. Again, she didn't tell anyone what had happened and made no attempt to call for help. She joined Jeremy at his house where they drank alcohol, smoked cannabis and engaged in sex. They were quickly caught and charged with the murders and both were convicted. Jasmine became the youngest person to be convicted of murder in Canada; she was 12 years old when her family was murdered.

What happened to cause Jasmine to participate in the death of her brother and parents? We will come back to the case and discuss it in terms of child psychopathology.

THE CHILD STUDY MOVEMENT AND CHILD PSYCHOPATHOLOGY

Child psychopathology began with G. Stanley Hall who became interested in learning about children and abnormal behaviours and how it related to psychopathology. He was the first to design various research techniques to study and systematically observe children's behaviour. Hall's early studies marked the beginning of child psychology and embraced the conviction that this area of study was important to the understanding of abnormal adult behaviour. The first task in this specialized field was the establishment of the necessary developmental norms by which behaviours could be judged so that the second element of psychopathology could be determined (Senn, 1975).

Previously, psychopathology was predominately viewed as an organic disease. Hall instigated a new line of thinking which proposed that early developmental factors were the cause of abnormal behaviour and that frustrations and emotional conflicts of early childhood and daily living could be the basis of mental illness instead of parenting practices and/or personality flaws (Senn, 1975).

Psychoanalytic theory had greatly influenced the fields of child psychology and child psycho-pathology through its emphasis on the critical role of early-childhood experiences for both normal and abnormal personality development. Freud established the significance of past experiences for the understanding of present behaviour and promoted the importance of childhood. Freud had constructed psychoanalysis as a theory and a treatment method intended primarily for neurotic adults, but he expanded his theories to children when he analysed the famous case of little Hans (Tyson, 1993).

Freud believed that his theories concerning infantile sexuality and the psychosexual stages of development were directly revealed in little Hans who was a five-year-old boy suffering from a horse phobia. Little Hans's father provided Freud with detailed information about the boy's past history and current behaviours from which Freud was able to confirm some aspects of his theory as well as to formulate the nature of Hans's unconscious sexual conflict which had presented itself in the form of fear of horses. Freud demonstrated that psychoanalysis could be effectively used in treating a phobic reaction in a very young child (Wolpe & Rachman, 1960).

BEHAVIOURISM, LEARNING AND CHILD PSYCHOPATHOLOGY

Another major component in the field of child psychology was Pavlov's classical conditioning. Although Pavlov's work influenced scientific inquiry on both humans and animals and at all levels of development, its major impact on child psychology was to provide an experimental procedure that made infants and young children suitable subjects for psychological study. Pavlov showed that learning can occur if a previously neutral stimulus is paired successively with a stimulus already known to elicit the response in question.

John B. Watson introduced behaviourism, in 1913, as a reaction against psychology's chief interest at that time in studying consciousness and in its use of methods designed to provide information about what was going on inside the individual. Watson adopted the view that psychology as a science need only concern itself with behaviours that can be directly observed and measured. He believed that through the analysis of stimulus–response (S–R) connections, the more complex forms of human behaviour could be understood. He argued for an environmentalist position in which environmental forces play a dominant role in influencing and shaping personality and he intended for child psychology to be the focus of his theories on behaviourism (Senn, 1975).

Watson established an infant laboratory and on the basis of his research on emotional conditioning, wrote a book dealing with the psychological care of infants which greatly influenced child care and training practices. Watson and Rayner (1920) used the Pavlovian paradigm to demonstrate the acquisition of a fear response in an 11-month-old boy named Albert. Prior observations of Albert indicated that he was not afraid of a white rat but that he showed a fear of loud noises which is innate in young children. The experiments paired presentations of a white rat followed closely by a loud noise until Albert demonstrated a fear reaction to the presentation of the rat alone (Senn, 1975).

B.F. Skinner's research in operant conditioning provided another important experimental paradigm for learning. His methodical research primarily with pigeons not only contributed significantly to the understanding and prediction of human behaviour but also had enormous application to education and the treatment of abnormal conditions such as mental retardation. Skinner's operant conditioning involves the strengthening of a stimulus–response bond by reinforcing (rewarding) the response when it occurs, and by making the reinforcement contingent on the emission of the proper response (Senn, 1975).

These various ideologies combined with various experimental methods made it possible to study a wider range of factors in children of various ages, abilities, emotional reactions and cognitive processes. The research in these various areas contributed new knowledge about children's abilities and the orderly changes in their behaviour that come with maturity.

MENTAL HYGIENE MOVEMENT AND CHILD PSYCHOLOGY

Progress for the intellectually disabled and handicapped child was fostered by the emergence of psychological tests to measure intelligence and other abilities and by the research on normal child development. In addition, parent groups awakened the public to the special needs of impaired and disordered children by advocating community and legislative involvement. The need to train other child specialists was dramatized by the mental hygiene movement (Donaldson, 1986).

Psychoanalysis continued to dominate the field as Freud's student Melanie Klein and his daughter Anna Freud introduced modifications in the 1920s, making his theory and treatment method more applicable to children. Klein replaced free association with play techniques on the grounds that play was a natural activity of children and that it revealed the same sources of anxiety and unconscious conflicts as words did for adults. Anna Freud used play, especially drawings as well as dreams, to understand and treat children's problems and she elaborated on her father's notions of the ego and its defensive functions. Then in 1950 Erik Erikson's book *Childhood and Society* made an enormous impact on the field as he analysed the human life cycle and identity in terms of a psychosocial stage theory as contrasted to Freud's psychosexual states of development (Holder, 2005).

Paediatric medicine became interested in the psychological aspects of child care largely as a result of the influences of psychoanalytic theory, the mental testing movement, normative data from child psychology and Watson's environmental view of learning. Paediatricians who were thrust into the position of giving advice about child-rearing practices now could offer suggestions that were based on the important psychological ingredients of development (Cullen, 2011).

MENTAL RETARDATION

History

Mental retardation was the first childhood disorder to arouse public attention. Mental defects in children were easy to identify and were viewed as abominations and the families that produced these children were stigmatized. In ancient Greece and Rome mental defects were treated with contempt and persecution. Often the mother was blamed for producing a defective child and in early civilizations there were many rules as well as preventive remedies to guard against producing a child with mental and physical deformities. With the rise of Christianity, the public attitude shifted from disdain to pity and often individuals with mental dysfunctions were taken in and cared for by the Church. During the dark ages the intellectually disabled served as amusement for others and were given the most difficult and dirty jobs that no one else in the community wanted to do and lived on the fringes of society. Many were abandoned by their families in the wilderness to die or be killed by wild animals as they did not want the stigma and shame of producing a mentally deficient child (Scheerenberger, 1983).

The Renaissance period provided an era of enlightenment in medicine and science and the question of physical and mental abnormalities became of interest for scientific inquiry. Individuals with mental defects were housed with individuals with mental illness and were often classified as one and the same. The Renaissance period began separating various disorders and identifying those with mental illness and those with mental retardation. Sir Thomas Willis in 1672 studied the various mental conditions and labelled it as feeble-mindedness. He gave the first detailed description of its varying degrees of mental incapacity, helping to classify and categorize different stages of impairment. The first interest in the actual treatment of mental retardation came with Jean Itard in 1800 (Scheerenberger, 1983).

Itard attempted to educate and re-socialize a young boy who had been found by hunters in a town called Aveyron. When the boy was found the people believed he had been raised by animals, but what is more likely is that he had been abandoned and had lived on the outskirts of society scavenging and stealing food to survive. At the time of his capture the boy was filthy, speechless and unsocialized. He was brought to Paris to be examined by a variety of physicians who decided that he was profoundly retarded and a hopeless case and sent him to live in the national institution for deaf mutes. Itard, who was a physician working with the children in the institution, believed that the boy (whom he named Victor) was educable and that his strange and retarded development was the result of prolonged sensory deprivation and isolation from human contact. After five years of intensive tutoring, Itard abandoned the project because Victor remained mute and showed little progress in speaking but was able to read simple words and appeared to understand simple language. Although the experiments with Victor appeared to be unsuccessful, the educational programmes that Itard had developed to educate Victor did benefit other children with mental retardation. Soon, many institutions were implementing Itard's programmes and began training intellectually disabled children (Lane, 1976).

Itard's work in mental retardation soon gave way to biological beliefs and the interest in Mendelian genetics as the findings of pedigree studies suggested that mental retardation was an inherited disease. Unfortunately this view also led to the enactment of eugenic laws that permitted the sterilization of intellectually disabled adults and children as well as to justify their isolation in prisons and institutions (Rosen et al., 1976).

Although newer and more specialized facilities (residential schools) began to appear during the early part of the twentieth century, segregation of the intellectually disabled persisted. Institutions were often constructed in remote geographical areas away from the public which made visits difficult and a deterrent for parents who wanted to maintain close ties with their institutionalized youngsters. Children who were born retarded were often either forcibly taken away from parents or in the case of the middle and upper classes. Parents were shamed into hiding their progeny to avoid the stigma attached with producing a genetically deficient individual. Genetic information had increased the stigma of producing a mentally retarded child and parents were blamed as being genetically inferior (Scheerenberger, 1983).

Definition

Mental retardation has been provided with many different names and terminology over the years: mental deficiency, feeble-mindedness, mental handicap and the new DSM 5 termination, intellectual disability (soon to be called intellectual developmental disorder) all refer to a heterogeneous condition involving many different patterns of cognitive limitations with a wide diversity of aetiologies. The most current and accepted definition is that it refers to significantly sub-average general intellectual functioning existing concurrently with deficits in adaptive behaviour and manifested during the developmental period (Grossman, 1973; APA, 2011).

While this definition emphasizes intelligence, it also acknowledges that it is neither sufficient nor an exclusive criterion of mental retardation. The additional criterion of deficits in adaptive behaviour restricts reliance on measures of intelligence and requires evidence of a broader and more consistent nature. Not completely basing the definition on intelligence safeguards the misdiagnosis of children who for various reasons cannot be assessed accurately by traditional assessments of intelligence (Grossman, 1973).

Adaptive capacity is difficult to measure because it rests with social change and is dependent on the individual's life situation. Developmental norms are important in determining the level of adaptive behaviour in context with the social demands placed upon an individual at the various points of development. Children who are intellectually below average can cope successfully with the minimal social demands made during infancy while at a later age the demands become more complex, making adaptation more difficult. It is usually at these stages that the child is identified (Luckasson, Schalock, Spitalnik & Spreat, 2002).

If adulthood has been reached without prior evidence of mental retardation, clinicians are inclined to look upon impaired adaptive behaviours as manifestations of an abnormal condition other than mental deficiency.

Mental retardation and intelligence tests

As an outgrowth of interest in mental retardation, the mental testing movement was begun in 1904 by the French minister of education to assure the best training possible for children and to construct a test that would identify feeble-minded youngsters (Anastasi, 1965). A psychologist by the name of Alfred Binet was asked to develop a device for measuring this. Binet introduced the concept of mental age by grouping test items according to the chronological age at which children usually answered them correctly. Children whose test performance matched their chronological age were average. Those who exceeded their chronological age were considered brighter than average whereas those with a mental age lower than their chronological age were below average in intelligence. Binet developed a procedure that provided a frame of reference relative to the chronological norms for

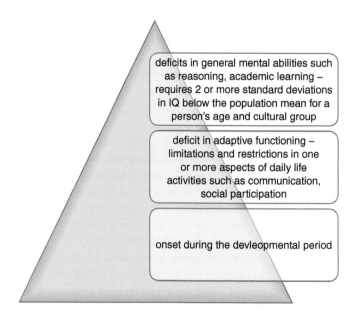

deficits in general mental abilities such as reasoning, academic learning – requires 2 or more standard deviations in IQ below the population mean for a person's age and cultural group

deficit in adaptive functioning – limitations and restrictions in one or more aspects of daily life activities such as communication, social participation

onset during the devleopmental period

Figure 8.1   The DSM-5 criteria for intellectual developmental disorder

the interpretation of intelligence. Public acceptance of mental tests encouraged the development of newer measuring devices purporting to assess academic achievement, personality, special aptitudes, abilities, interests and brain damage (Anastasi, 1965).

Levels of retardation

Mental retardation is classified by four degrees of severity; mild, moderate, severe and profound. The IQ score is reflected in most classification systems and very few take adaptiveness into consideration because of its fluid nature; however the proposed revision of the DSM-5 will no longer rely on specific IQ levels (APA, 2012).

There are two major issues with the use of IQ scores. First, mental retardation is expressed by a range, corresponding to a standard deviation unit that describes the distribution. Because the IQ score is subject to errors of measurement it can be expected to vary from one time to another. Therefore, it is arbitrary and misleading to regard an IQ score near the top of one range as fixed since in actuality it may reflect the individual's capacity to function in the lower portion of the next higher category (Zigler, Balla & Hodapp, 1984).

Another issue associated with the classification of mental retardation is the use of scores to draw inferences about the child's future behaviour, in spite of the fact that test scores and IQs only reflect present performance. The danger in inferring future potential lies in the possibility that planning for the child will be limited by his presumed capacity, which may preclude opportunities for education and training beyond this predicted level. In the absence of any preconceived notion about a child's limited potential, achievement can reach heights that exceed prior expectation. Consequently scores

Table 8.1   Levels of mental retardation

IQ score	Low	High	Abilities
Mild	50–55	70	Can hold unskilled jobs, adequate social and vocational adjustment – supervision of social and financial affairs
Moderate	35–40	50–55	Slow to learn, conceptualization skills are limited, typically cannot read or write, capable of self-care behaviours, require close supervision in almost all aspects of living
Severe	20–25	35–40	Learning capacity is very limited – motor, speech and social development are severely affected, need constant supervision
Profound		20–25	Very little evidence of learning, require constant supervision and frequent medical care, central nervous system disorders, sensory and motor disturbances and other physical disabilities

and levels of retardation must be interpreted as indicative of present functioning, rather than as a stereotyped and fixed prediction of the child's future limitations (Zigler, Balla & Hodapp, 1984).

The new changes in the DSM-5 have based the definitions on both an intellectual deficit and a deficit in adaptive functioning with the onset during the developmental period. It no longer bases the diagnosis on IQ level (APA, 2012).

Aetiological considerations

Mental retardation is not a category of abnormal behaviour that appears in the same form, to the same degree at the same time. It is not always produced by the same causal factors and can result from one circumstance or from the interaction of a number of circumstances before, during or after birth. Mental retardation also varies in severity and in the behavioural characteristics of those affected. It has been estimated that there are more than 300 known or suspected causes of mental retardation (Leonard & Wen, 2002).

Heredity and experiential factors interact and both contribute to human development and behaviour. Many forms of mental retardation are known hereditary diseases or chromosomal abnormalities. It is important to remember that the interaction of both biological and environmental factors contributes significantly to these disorders. Even in children born with a genetic defect the effects of early stimulation on both the rate and quality of development and the influence of many environmental factors on primary areas such as learning, memory, thinking, perception and personality formation are important in the ultimate outcome of the disorder (Knight & Schmid, 2010).

Treatment

The various disorders that cause mental retardation are irreversible and treatment is not an option. However, remedial approaches that focus on care, education and rehabilitation and facilitate the capabilities of the individual are crucial. Success in remedial approaches greatly depends on the

Table 8.2   Hereditary diseases and chromosomal abnormalities in mental retardation

Recessive genetic disorders	Amino acid metabolism disorders	Phenylketonuria Menke's syndrome Hartnup's disease	Characterized by either a faulty or lack of enzyme that is needed to break down substances that are then improperly utilized by the body and its accumulation in the bloodstream; causes brain damage and mental retardation
	Lipid metabolism disorders	Taysach's disease Niemann-Pick disease	Faulty metabolism of fatty compounds needed for the development of the central nervous system
	Carbohydrate metabolism disorders	Galactose	Impairs the infant's ability to metabolize carbohydrates
	Endocrine function disorders	Hypothyroidism	Aberrant conditions of the thyroid that are associated with mental retardation
Chromosomal abnormalities	Down's syndrome		An autosomal syndrome associated with an extra group-G chromosome
	Klinefelter's syndrome		A group of disorders associated with chromosomal abnormalities of the sex chromosome. This condition affects only males and there is an extra X chromosome
	Turner's syndrome		Abnormalities of the sex chromosome that only affect females
Other biological factors	Toxins	Foetal alcohol syndrome	Interferes with brain-cell metabolism causing mental retardation
	Infections	Rubella, encephalitis	Array of cognitive problems
	Trauma, injury, physical agent	Birthing process, prolonged labour, hazards with umbilical cord	Brain damage
	Premature birth		High incidence of physical and mental disorders
	Nutritional deprivation	Malnutrition	Physical and intellectual deterioration

extent of the attitudes and values held by the community towards mental retardation. Individual families will not have the resources available and most rely on community support. Therefore attitudes and values will greatly influence the basic policies and programmes selected and how they are implemented. Comprehensive health services, special education, sheltered workshops, hostels for community living and residential facilities are important for the proper care of individuals. It is important to consider the aptitude and abilities a retarded person may have and not focus simply on the IQ score as a measure of future possibilities (Luckasson, Schalock, Spitalnik & Spreat, 2002).

No type of retardation in itself indicates the need for residential care and the child's placement is greatly influenced by the availability and strength of the educational programmes, vocational training and placement opportunities along with other resources in the community. The principles of behaviour modification have been widely utilized to teach children a wide variety of self-care behaviours so that they are able to profit from and enjoy a wider range of experiences (Baroff & Olley, 1999).

The parents of a mentally handicapped child also play a major role and are an important influence in shaping the life of both the family and the handicapped child. It is essential that the parents maintain a positive outlook and that their child's potential and future outlook is far from dismal and hopeless while at the same time managing goals and expectations in a realistic perspective (Emerson, Dickson, Gone & Hatton, 2012).

LEARNING DISORDERS

The period of childhood that ranges from three to pre-adolescence is a time of transition for both parents and child in which the child's world is extended from the home to new situations and relationships. Children are called upon to acquire new skills and behaviours in order to cope with the demands of a more complex environment. The attitudes, values and stimulation within the home along with peer relationships affect the development of the child (Silver & Hagin, 2002).

The extent to which children successfully adapt is not only dependent on the impact of new experiences, but also on the influence of prior biological and environmental conditions. The school's emphasis on academic achievement is communicated early to students. Those who are capable of succeeding are motivated to achieve higher levels while those who are slow learners are stigmatized. Repeated failures to achieve often result in poor motivation, avoidance of academics and withdrawal. It is this period that previously tolerated or unnoticed behaviours, as well as newly acquired ones, surface as trouble signs that indicate some impairment of academic success and social adjustment (Silver & Hagin, 2002).

Learning disabilities is only one of many labels used interchangeably for a large category that refers to a discrepancy between anticipated and actual academic achievement in children who otherwise are not handicapped in intelligence, sensory processes, emotional stability or opportunities to learn. This large grouping encompasses reading disorders (dyslexia), disorders of written expression, dysgraphia, dyspraxia, dyscravia and mathematics disorders (dyscalculia). There is frequently a strong genetic component to these disabilities (Pennington, 1995; Plomin & Kovas, 2005).

Learning disabilities are not a single, relatively well-defined entity or syndrome. They are an extremely heterogeneous group of learning problems with diverse characteristics that can result from a variety of biological influences, including genetic factors, environmental insults to the brain and possibly extreme lack of early environmental stimulation. As a result, the multifaceted field of LD is complex and often contentious, with many competing theories, definitions, diagnostic procedures and suggested avenues of intervention (Lerner, 2000).

Historical development

Early research into children's learning disabilities coined the term 'minimal brain dysfunction' to describe children of normal intelligence who exhibited a combination of hard or soft signs

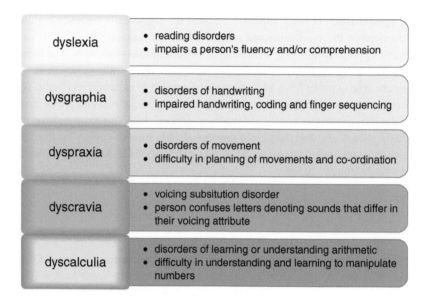

Figure 8.2   Categories of learning disabilities

of neurological deficiency concomitantly with educational and sometimes with behavioural disorders (Mercer, 1991). Minimal brain dysfunction was believed to be responsible for deficits resulting in disorders of receptive and expressive language, reading, writing, mathematics, physical skill development and interpersonal adjustment (Lerner, 1993).

Prevalence

Prevalence rates are difficult to determine as a result of the stringency of identification criteria and have varied from as low as 1 percent to as high as 30 percent in the school age population (Lerner, 1993). The primary factors for the discrepancies in the prevalence of learning disabilities are the lack of clear-cut definitions, the multitude of types of learning disabilities and lack of classification procedures (Thomas & Woods, 2003).

Aetiology

It is believed that learning difficulties are a result of central nervous system dysfunction in specific portions of the cerebral cortex. Learning disabilities that are primarily reading disorders or dyslexia are being linked to measurable differences in brain function. Research has been conducted by computerized tomography scan, static magnetic resonance imaging, electroencephalographic studies, studies of evoked potentials, positron emission tomography and functional magnetic resonance imaging reveal-ing various differences in structures of the brain in the parietal lobe and corpus callosum as well as subcortical thalamic abnormalities (Galaburda & Kemper, 1979; Hynd, Marshall & Gonzalez, 1991; Temple, Deutsch, Poldrack Miller, Tallal, Merzenich & Gabrieli, 2003; Vallar, Burani & Arduino, 2010; Elnakib et al., 2012).

A number of neuroimaging studies lend preliminary support to the view that phonological pro-cessing takes place primarily in the language areas of the frontal region; that letter recognition occurs primarily in the occipital lobe; and that words are processed primarily in the temporal lobe (Shaywitz et al., 1997; Shaywitz, 1998; Kraus, 2012; Nittrouer, Shune & Lowenstien, 2011).

Studies indicate that dyslexia is not a unitary disorder related to dysfunction in a single region of the brain, but rather a heterogeneous disorder that involves a widely distributed aggregate of brain functions (Szmalec, Loncke, Page & Duyck, 2011). Galaburda (1993) hypothesized that a genetic predisposition is probably the main aetiological factor in the cerebral asymmetry observed in many individuals with dyslexia and that observed structural abnormalities are produced by genetic, immu-nological or undetermined factors which alter the normal pattern of neuronal migration and cortical organization sometime during the fifth to seventh month of gestation. Galaburda and his colleagues have since identified a number of susceptibility genes that are associated with dyslexia (Currier, Etchegaray, Haight, Galaburda & Rosen, 2010).

Normal brains show asymmetrical development, generally larger on the left, of structures impli-cated in language and reading. A most striking convergent finding from many studies has been that of symmetry or even reversed asymmetry in these critical brain regions in approximately 65–75 percent of dyslexic subjects (Haslam, Dalby, Johns & Rademaker, 1981; Heim, Grande, Meffert, Eickhoff, Schreiber, Kukolja, Shah, Huber & Amunts, 2010). MRI studies have shown that sym-metry or reversed asymmetry is associated with general neurolinguistic deficits (Hynd, Marshall & Semrud-Clikeman, 1992; Chiarell, Welcome & Leonard, 2012). Correlating information from CT scans with measured IQ documented lower verbal than performance in those dyslexic subjects who demonstrated symmetry or reversed asymmetry of the posterior region (Shaywitz et al., 1992; Payne, Moharir, Webster & North, 2010).

Environmental factors

Environmental factors appear to play a role in prenatal development (DeLong, 1993; Abu-Saad & Fraser, 2010). Silver (1989) found that brain development may be affected by severe deficits in maternal nutrition if they occur before the 24th week of gestation or if essential proteins or specific micronutrients are missing. Maternal use of tobacco during pregnancy produces babies with lower birth weight, which increases the risk of developmental difficulties, including learn-ing disabilities (NIMH, 1993; Anderko, Braun & Auinger, 2010). Alcohol consumption during pregnancy has been shown to have damaging effects on the neuronal development of a foetus, leading to problems with learning, attention, memory and problem solving, as well as foetal alco-hol syndrome, general intellectual impairment and learning difficulties (Thackray & Tifft, 2001; Guerri, Bazinet & Riley, 2009).

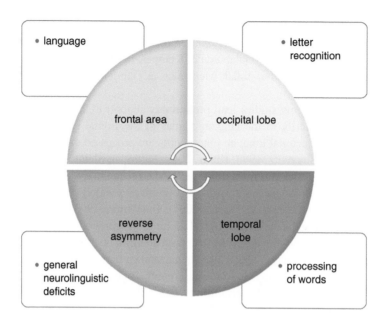

Figure 8.3   Structures of the brain involved in learning difficulties

Genetic factors

In the last 40 years research has provided strong support for genetic factors in some forms of learning disabilities. The familial occurrence of reading, spelling and writing disabilities has been investigated via several methodologies, such as study of family members and pedigree analysis, determination of concordance rates among identical and fraternal twins, comparison of linear regression reading scores between identical and fraternal twins and chromosomal analysis of family members (Yoshimasu, Barbaresi, Colligan, Killian, Voigt, Weaver & Katusic, 2010; Geary, 2010; Petrill, Hart, Harlaar, Logan, Justice, Schatschneider, Thompson, DeThorne, Deater-Deckard & Cutting, 2010).

Family studies/Twin studies

The earliest widely cited family pedigree study of reading disorder conducted by Hallgren in 1950 consisted of a statistical analysis of dyslexia in 112 families. He found that among first-degree relatives, the risk for co-occurrence of this disorder was 41 percent which is much higher than the usual prevalence estimates for the general population of 5–10 percent.

A study conducted by Gilger and his colleagues (1991) conclusively proved a link through family studies. They compared the reading abilities of 125 reading-disabled children and their family members to those of 125 matched control children who were not reading-disabled and their family members. The results demonstrated that reading disorders are familial in nature. Scores for siblings of learning disabled subjects were significantly lower than scores for siblings of control subjects on measures of both reading and symbol-processing speed. A similar pattern of significant results was observed for the parents of subjects and controls.

An extensive study conducted by DeFries & Fulker (1985, 1988) which examined reading disability in 101 pairs of identical twins and 114 pairs of fraternal twins found a concordance rate of 52 percent for identical twins while the rate for fraternal twins was 33 percent, providing strong evidence for a genetic factor in the aetiology of reading disabilities. Further research has found that reading deficits are substantially due to genetic factors (Astrom, Wadsworth, Olson, Willcutt & DeFries, 2012; Kovas & Plomin, 2008).

Treatment

Various interventions and learning programmes have been suggested for children with learning disabilities. These include the psycholinguistic-process or specific abilities approach (Kirk & Kirk, 1971); behavioural approaches, including direct instruction and data-based instruction (Marston & Tindal, 1995); cognitive approaches, including constructivism and instruction in learning strategies (Butler, 1989); and neuropsychological approaches (Rourke, Fisk & Strang, 1986).

It is suggested that LD intervention should be combined into a functional, multidimensional treatment programme beginning with a careful assessment of the strengths and weaknesses of the individual, then educational intervention with a strong emphasis on academic development with specific information-processing skills that should be developed (Marston & Tindal, 1995; Swanson, Hoskyn, 1998). The learner's innate cognitive strategies for acquiring and retaining information and individuals should be taught specific strategies including perceptual aids, study skills and compensatory strategies. LDs should be understood as complex phenomena ranging from mild to severe with even mild LD having the potential for a devastating impact on the academic, emotional and general life adjustment of affected individuals (Vellutino, 1979; Vellutino, Fletcher, Snowling & Scanlon, 2004).

LANGUAGE DISORDERS/COMMUNICATION DISORDERS

Normal speech emerges during infancy following a period of vocalizations of nonsense sounds. Once the child begins to use language, the number of spoken words dramatically multiplies. At the age of five, depending on developmental and environmental factors the child is capable of combining words into sentences that reflect a mastery of the complex structure of language. As a result of language being a vital skill, children with speech problems come to the attention of professionals at an earlier age than most other forms of abnormal behaviour. There is also a higher frequency of speech disorders in boys or approximately − 3 to 1 as compared to non-language problems (Paul, 1995).

Language is a complex function that is significantly dependent on the brain, and the anatomy of many structures involved in the formation and production of speech, such as lips, tongue, palate and vocal chords. Hearing is intimately related to speech. A child who is unable to hear will be unable to voice and articulate sounds. Injuries, illnesses and congenital defects can all lead to speech problems but the consequences will differ as to what aspect of language is disabled. An intellectually developmentally disabled child may show language delays and slow speech development because of cognitive damage, while a child with cerebral palsy will have articulation problems because of damage to the musculature structures involved in the formation of words (Caplan, 1992).

Research has documented that the vocabulary of young children can be significantly increased by reading to them which suggests that some instances of delayed speech may arise in families where there is insufficient verbal stimulation (Krashen, 1993; Mol, Bus & deJong, 2012). In addition, emotional trauma, illness and hospitalization, birth of a sibling, parental rejection and negativism are among the psychogenic factors implicated in speech disorders (Baker, 2008).

Aphasia (from the Greek, meaning without speech) is a term used to designate an impairment of symbolic language, not only of speech, but also of other types of language modalities (gestures and writing), and of comprehension of language. Aphasic children frequently manifest multiple problems that include perceptual, learning, behavioural and emotional difficulties (Alajouanine & Lhermitte, 1965; Ceccaldi, Joanette, Tikhomirof, Macia & Poncet, 1996).

The literature dealing with the relationship between speech disorders and intelligence consistently indicates that the lower the intelligence level, the greater the incidence of defective speech. While the relationship between low intelligence and speech disorders has been well documented, it should not be taken to indicate that speech problems are only found in mentally handicapped children as they can occur in children of all levels of intelligence (Felsenfeld & Plomin, 1997; Pennington & Bishop, 2009).

Articulatory problems are the most prevalent of all speech aberrations. Defective articulation and the degree of imprecision in producing speech sounds are determined by listening to phonetic behaviour. With the exception of the high incidence of faulty articulation found in intellectually disabled children, intelligence at other levels bears no significant relationship to articulatory proficiency (Whitacre, Luper & Pollio, 1970).

A particular type of articulatory problem is stuttering. Stuttering refers to a particular breakdown in speech fluency characterized by blocking (inability to articulate), repetition and prolongation of speech sounds. Stuttering begins between the ages of two and five and almost always before eight. It occurs more frequently in boys, and it is extremely rare in adult females. Socioeconomic factors and intelligence are unrelated to stuttering. Persistent stuttering is found in only 1–2 percent of the population, while transient stuttering appears in 4–5 percent. Most cases of stuttering are temporary; more than 50 percent recover by puberty without treatment and 80 percent have normal speech by the time they reach their late teens (Van Riper, 1982).

Aetiology

Neurological deficits that affect hearing or impair intellectual functioning are generally responsible for the majority of delayed speech and language retardation (Pennington & Bishop, 2009). Paul (1995) found that many children with delayed speech, particularly those who are brain damaged, are impaired in their ability to handle the complex process of analysing auditory sequences. They also have difficulty reproducing them from memory in a comprehensible form.

If environmental factors are responsible for language disorders, they are most significant in delayed speech and articulation problems. In these circumstances a child is capable of learning the basic systems of language but generally reflects difficulties in their vocabulary, grammar and articulation (Paul, 1995).

No single explanation has been found for the aetiology of stuttering. The search for biological or constitutional factors has been unsuccessful. Psychological interpretations have focused on stuttering being a symptom of anxiety. The most viable viewpoint seems to be that stuttering is learned, although different theorists have not always emphasized similar environmental conditions and learning paradigms (Guitar, 2005).

One hypothesis is that stuttering has a psychological component. Dysfluencies can occur in the normal speech of children, which often causes negative reactions by the parents. Through this type of interaction, stuttering becomes a learned avoidance reaction in which the child struggles to avoid all instances of dysfluencies and subsequent negative reactions from parents. Failure to achieve fluent speech is inevitable and this in turn heightens anxiety and the likelihood of more interruptions in the flow of speech (Van Riper, 1982).

Treatment

Behaviour modification procedures have been employed with children with language disorders. Imitation, verbal stimulation and differential reinforcement have been used to teach children correct grammatical usage. It is important that parents encourage and positively reward correct verbalizations. The majority of articulation problems can be appropriately treated by professionals and research has revealed no consistent evidence that either parents of children or the child manifests emotional disturbances as a result of articulation problems (Bloom et al., 1978; Ward, 2006).

Whenever social and personal adjustment problems are associated with articulations, speech therapy and psychological intervention may be an effective remedial combination (Guitar, 2005). Learning principles have been increasingly applied to the construction of techniques employed to modify articulatory problems. The procedure involves the same set of steps that are applicable to the modifications of a wide variety of unwanted behaviours. In order to change behaviour, it is necessary to select an unwanted behaviour (the target) that can be reliably observed and manipulated (increased or decreased). Then instructional or other cues should be provided to elicit the desired response and consequences should be found that will strengthen it and weaken the target behaviour. Records of response frequencies prior to, during and following the intervention must be kept in order to assess the effectiveness of the modification (Bloom et al., 1978; Lees & Stark, 2005).

Treatment plans and procedures for stutterers are numerous and diverse. Programmes that combine psychotherapy and speech practice under conditions of progressive stress (similar to desensitization) have proved effective in reducing or eliminating stuttering in 50 percent of the cases that were followed up five years later (Van Riper, 1982). A wide variety of delayed auditory feedback techniques in which very brief delays in hearing one's own voice to improve or eliminate (during practice) speech dysfluencies have been employed both to study organic components of the disorder and to treat the condition (Andrews, 1964; Onslow, 2003).

Early studies demonstrated that the frequency of stuttering can be operantly manipulated. Flanagan et al. (1958) showed that principles derived from operant conditioning have been shown to modify stuttering behaviour.

PERVASIVE DEVELOPMENTAL DISORDERS

The pervasive developmental disorders share certain clinical features but have diverse aetiologies and progression. These disorders are generally diagnosed in infancy or early childhood and are characterized by deviant patterns in the areas of social, affective and communicative development. The term of 'pervasive' emphasizes that this group of disorders are invasive and persistent over a wide range of abilities from extreme impairments in human relationships, to inadequate perceptual and conceptual responses, abnormalities of psychomotor behaviour and communication to unusual preoccupations. All the categories of disorders in this classification are varied; however, the children affected by these disorders will have substantial disparities in the framework of their personalities (Matson & Sturmey, 2011).

Autism

Kanner (1943) first described the disorder now known as autism as early infantile autism and based his description on case histories and clinical observations. Kanner found that a few of the cases that had been referred to him as either deaf or intellectually disabled were very different from the usual presentation of either of these disorders. One of the most striking presentations with these children was their inability to relate to people. He called this 'extreme autistic aloneness' and described it as having no interest in people or their conversations, rarely, if ever, making direct eye contact with others and sitting motionless staring into space for hours. Additionally these children had a very active interest in and fondness for inanimate objects, peculiar eating habits and food preferences with an insistence on the maintenance of sameness in their environment (Vokmar, Paul, Klin & Cohen, 2005).

Kanner's original descriptions of the disorder remain relatively unchanged; however more information about the disorder has been accumulated. Research has indicated that although the condition appears in infancy, it can sometimes appear within the second or third year of life, but rarely after age three (Short & Schopler, 1988). The prevalent feature of the disorder is lack of socialization in any form or level. Children with this disorder display a lack of reciprocity in social contact, appear unable or unwilling to make attachments, and lack social communicative skills. In a normal infant their neurological development predisposes them to engage caregivers in social interaction at a very early stage, by smiling and reaching for affection, whereas young autistic children do not. Typical forms of early nonverbal interchange are deviant and they appear to lack a differential preference of speech sounds (Klin, 1992; Matson & Sturmey, 2011).

In terms of cognitive abilities many autistic children are also intellectually disabled although autistic children differ from children with primary intellectual disability disorders in terms of cognitive processing abilities, with autistic children having scattered vs. even scores (Klin, Carter, & Sparrow, 1997). Subsequent research has also revealed that IQ is strongly correlated with severity of the social impairment and other aspects of the disorders (Cohen et al., 1987; Volkmar, Bregman, Cohen, Hooks & Stevenson, 1989; Bolte, Dziobek & Poustka, 2009), and that it is a potent predictor of ultimate outcome in the autistic child (Lockyer & Rutter, 1969; Lotter, 1978; Billstedt, Gillberg & Gillberg, 2011).

Language development in autism differs from developmental language disorders in the pervasiveness of the communicative deficits. Autistic children's disability encompasses both verbal and nonverbal communication and higher social deficits, and their use of whatever linguistic ability is available to them is deviant (Fay & Mermelstein, 1982; Hodge, Makris, Kennedy, Caviness, Howard, McGrath, Steele, Frazier, Tager-Flusberg & Harris, 2010). Their speech is often characterized by inappropriate use of intonational patterns and stress (Menyuk, 1978; Diehl & Paul, 2012), monotonic or pedantic delivery and preverbal vocal output (Ricks & Wing, 1975; Nadig & Shaw, 2011). Semantic difficulties are often reflected in the form of extreme literalness, as well as a scarcity of conceptual words (Fay & Schuler, 1980; Ketelaars, Hermans, Cuperus, Jansonius, & Verhoeven, 2011).

Neurobiological studies suggest the operation of some as yet unspecified neurobiological factor or factors in the pathogenesis of autism as it is common for autistic children to develop seizure disorders and other neurobiological abnormalities consistent with as yet unspecified underlying organic aetiology (Volkmar & Nelson, 1990; Fatemi, Folsom, Reutiman & Thuras, 2009).

Genetic studies indicate that the frequency of autism in siblings is nearly 3 percent, signifying that the frequency of the disorder is higher than the expected prevalence in the general population (August, Stewart and Tsai, 1981; Vokmar, Paul, Klin & Cohen, 2005). Folstein and Piven (1991) reported that monozygotic twins are more likely than dizygotic twins to be concordant for the disorder.

Prevalence of autism

Rates of autism have suggested between two and five cases within 10,000 children (Bryson, 1997; King & Bearman, 2009). Most studies indicate that autism is usually four or five times as common in males as in females; however, girls who are affected may exhibit a more severe form of the disorder, particularly in terms of having lower IQ. The significance of the observed sex difference is unclear, but it may reflect the operation of underlying genetic mechanisms (Lord & Schopler, 1987; Rivet & Matson, 2010).

Childhood disintegrative disorder

In 1908, Theodore Heller first observed a disorder in six cases of children who had developed normally until three to four years of age and then exhibited a striking behavioural and developmental deterioration with a negligible recovery. He called the condition 'dementia infantilism' which was later changed to Heller syndrome and is now referred to as childhood disintegrative disorder (Matson & Mahan, 2009).

The disorder is extremely rare with less than 100 cases reported worldwide and begins with the child being described as being normal, meeting all developmental norms and language development. At a certain point a profound developmental regression occurs that appears to be similar to autism except the deterioration continues to progress and the prognosis is irreversible and discouraging with the majority requiring constant care and supervision (Volkmar, 1992; Homan, Mellon, Houlihan & Katusic, 2011).

Rett syndrome

Rett (1966) first described this pervasive developmental disorder from observing it in two patients and then consequently identifying it in 22 other children who exhibited similar symptoms. Although the disorder has some characteristics of autism, e.g. seizures and language difficulties, it differs in several distinct ways. The autistic-like phase is relatively brief with stereotyped motor behaviours that resemble washing or wringing movements. There are also abnormalities in gait and the associated intellectual developmental disability is more profound. The disorder is gender specific and appears to only affect females. The initial presentation is normal to early growth and development followed by developmental regression in the first months, deceleration of head growth and loss of purposeful hand movements. The period of normal development is shorter than those observed in childhood disintegrative disorder. Prevalence rates are estimated at 1 in 15,000 girls affected (Naidu, Murphy, Moser & Rett, 2005).

This disorder is being recommended to be removed from the DSM-5 because of the specificity of its aetiology, which is a genetic mutation on the X chromosome (APA, 2012).

Asperger disorder

Asperger disorder was named after Hans Asperger who described a group of individuals who exhibited social and behavioural abnormalities that interfered with social interaction and communication in spite of having adequate intellectual skills.

The abnormal social characteristics of Asperger's are similar to autism but are less severe and include: paucity of empathy, poor nonverbal communication, pedantic and monotonic speech, inappropriate one-sided social interaction, inability to form friendships, social isolation, clumsy and ill-coordinated movements and odd posture, and intense absorption in circumscribed topics that are learned in rote fashion that reflect poor understanding. The onset of the disorder is later than that of autism and reflects better-preserved language and cognitive abilities (Attwood, 2008).

Treatment

Almost every form of treatment has been tried with children of pervasive developmental disorders including individual psychotherapy, behaviour therapy, milieu therapy, electro-convulsive shock treatment, drug therapy and sensory deprivation, but no treatment approach has been successful in bringing about major improvements in any significant number of children (DeMyer et al., 1981; Rutter, 1985; Attwood, 2008). There are anecdotal case studies but no longitudinal studies or large studies indicating that any therapies have produced any long-term results. Behaviour modification approaches still offer the best options in terms of altering and/or controlling behaviours that make these children more manageable at home and in school (Attwood, 2008).

The psychosocial factors of having a child with a pervasive developmental disorder generally have a profound effect on families (Schopler & Mesibov, 1984). Families must cope with the severity of the social, communicative, adaptive impairments and unusual behaviours which will vary over time and require flexibility in caring and community resources that are more responsive to the family's specific needs (Morgan, 1988; Attwood, 2008).

ADHD

Attention-Deficit/Hyperactivity Disorder or ADHD is a term used to collectively reflect a syndrome rather than a specific disorder. ADHD is among the most common disorders of childhood and it is estimated that it affects between 3 and 5 percent of the school-age population. The term hyperactivity is used for describing a heightened activity level. This terminology has no norms and is difficult to quantify because children vary considerably in activity output, across different situations and among themselves in specific situations. However, hyperactivity in children is harassing, frustrating, exasperating and extremely troublesome to others, especially to parents and teachers who must deal with it on a daily basis (Terrell & Passenger, 2006). The attention-deficit component is highly correlated to the level of activity and reflects a short attention span and restlessness when attempting to keep focused especially in highly ritualized environments. This disorder also has a component of impulsivity that affects children's interaction with all elements of their environment. Their behaviour is often uneven, unpredictable and inconsistent (Terrell & Passenger, 2006).

ADHD is a disorder that arises from the interaction between temperamental traits and the demands placed upon the child by the environment. The disorder is a combination of factors, the temperament of the child that is innate, and the environmental conditions that modify and determine the level of severity (Selikowitz, 2009).

Voeller (1991) believed that ADHD was a cluster of different behavioural deficits set on a continuum of severity and should not be viewed as a single behavioural abnormality with associated comorbidities and that ADHD represented a distinct disorder from other disorders of childhood and adulthood.

The practical definition contains five components with the first, impulsivity, considered to be a contributing factor in shaping the other four components. These are detailed in Table 8.3.

Table 8.3 The five components of ADHD

Impulsivity	Difficulty thinking before acting; does not factor in consequences of behaviour or actions; difficult to follow rule-governed behaviour.
Inattention	Difficulty remaining on task and focusing their attention; problems with tasks that are repetitive, effortful and not of their choosing.
Over-arousal	Excessively restless, overactive and easily aroused emotionally, with the speed and intensity to the extreme.
Difficulty with gratification	Requires immediate, frequent, predictable and meaningful rewards; difficulty in maintaining a long-term goal.
Emotions and locus of control	They go from either extreme: happy–sad, tend to develop an external locus of control and project blame on others, unwilling to recognize and accept responsibility.

Aetiology

Goodman and Stevenson (1989) demonstrated a concordance rate of 51 percent in 39 identical twin pairs and 30 percent in 54 non-identical (fraternal) twin pairs which produced an overall heritability estimate of 0.64.

Research involving difficult temperaments in infants has noted that these specific types of infants do not handle changes in routines and follow-up studies of these types of infants have found that as many as 70 percent develop school problems and are at higher risk than others for receiving a diagnosis of ADHD (Terestman, 1980). Infants with difficult temperaments also have a significant negative impact on their developing relationships with caregivers. These relationships are critical in predicting children's life outcomes because parents tend to report more negative feelings about parenting and higher stress levels with these types of children (Donenberg & Baker, 1993; Katz, 1997). Additionally children with ADHD are more likely to develop speech and language problems (Baker & Cantwell, 1987), and to display a wide range of behavioural problems (Cantwell, Baker & Matison, 1981).

Treatment

The preferred treatment for ADHD is a combination of behaviour modification and drug therapy. Stimulants increase attention span and improve academic performance allowing the child to manage key symptoms and improve daily functioning. Research has mostly focused on methylphenidate which was found in placebo-controlled double blind trails to demonstrate a 75–80 percent positive response compared to a 30–40 percent positive response to the placebo (Kratochvil et al., 2002).

Educational interventions including positive and negative contingent teacher attention, token economies, peer-mediated and group contingencies, time out, reductive techniques based on reinforcement and cognitive-behavioural strategies can be effective in managing the behavioural components of the disorder in the classroom. Finally, it is suggested by many researchers and psychologists that a combination programme of education and counselling for the parents be implemented to help parents understand and manage their child's ADHD issues within the home environment, which also helps to add in consistency in all social environments (Pfiffner et al., 2007).

CONDUCT DISORDER/OPPOSITIONAL DEFIANT DISORDER

These disorders involve a child or adolescent's relationship to authority, social norms and rules of social conduct. In both conduct disorder and oppositional defiant disorder aggressive or antisocial behaviour is the focus. Oppositional defiant disorder is usually apparent by about age six, while conduct disorder tends to be seen by age nine with both disorders being closely related. Prevalence rates of CD range from about 2 to 16 percent in boys and from less than 1 percent to 9 percent in girls (Robins, 1991; Matthys & Lochman, 2009).

Conduct disorder and oppositional defiant disorder are psychological terms that are closely related to behaviours seen in criminal antisocial behaviour which may or may not be illegal. Delinquent behaviour is a legal term, not a psychological term and refers to the commission of an act by a minor that would be regarded as criminal if committed by an adult, but it also involves acts that only apply to minors such as running away (Kazdin, 1995).

Different social agencies and disciplines generally formulate their own views of antisocial behaviour. For example a police constable may view bicycle riding on the pavement as youthful behaviour and provide a warning while regarding criminal damage as more serious and forego a warning even though the bicycle riding probably puts more people in harm's way. The school system may view antisocial behaviour as academic underachievement, and disruptive and unmanageable behaviour in the classroom, none of which are illegal, while a psychologist may be inclined to think of antisocial behaviour as a manifestation of something more serious, such as fire setting.

There is substantial evidence to indicate that oppositional defiant disorder is a separate diagnostic category and not a milder form of conduct disorder (Stringaris, Maughan & Goodman, 2010). Individuals displaying oppositional defiance disorder are generally engaged in nonviolent and non-delinquent behaviour, i.e. argumentative toward authority, school rule breakers. These individuals have a normal personality structure and function and their inclination towards antisocial

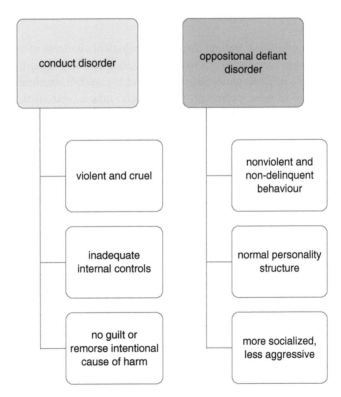

Figure 8.4   Conduct disorder vs. oppositional defiant disorder

behaviour is usually part of their socialization within a delinquent group. These children tend to be the product of inadequate parental supervision, families in which there is little cohesion and there is no discipline and control within the family unit. Oppositional defiant disorder children tend to be resistant to authority – arguing with parents and teachers and refusing to follow rules, disrupting classes, throwing tantrums, nonviolent bullying behaviours and running away. The behaviours although annoying to individuals in authority tend to be more socialized and less aggressive (Loeber, Burke, Lahey, Winters & Zera, 2000; Kazdin, 1995; Matthys & Lochman, 2009; Rutter, 2011).

Conduct disorder tends to refer to those who have inadequate internal controls over their impulses and who are likely to display open hostility towards others. These children tend to be self, defiant, self-indulgent and inclined to act out without feelings of guilt or remorse. They are also characterized by internal conflict and anxiety stemming from an overly developed tendency to inhibit the expression of feelings and impulses. Their antisocial behaviours are considered to be manifestations of severe internal conflicts. Their actions are intentionally aggressive, often cruel and meant to commit physical harm (Robins, 1991; Liabo & Richardson, 2007; Decety, Michalska, Akitsuki & Lahey, 2009).

Aetiology

Conduct disorder/oppositional defiant disorder's biological elements of innate temperament place the child at risk for environmental factors exacerbating and elevating the severity of behaviour problems. The child's difficult temperament can lead to insecure attachments because parents find it difficult to engage in good parenting. Additionally, infants with difficult temperaments are at high risk for ineffective parenting, rejection, harsh and inconsistent discipline and parental neglect (Loeber, Burke, Lahey, Winters & and Zera, 2000).

Studies have reported a genetic predisposition of low verbal intelligence, mild neuropsychological problems and difficult temperament in conduct disorder. When these genetic predispositions are combined with environmental factors such as inconsistent/poor parenting, deficiencies in self-control functions and impulsive behaviours they can increase the probability antisocial behaviours and a diagnosis of conduct or oppositional defiance disorder (Moffitt, 1993).

A number of broader psychosocial and sociocultural variables increase the probability that a child will develop conduct disorder: low socioeconomic status, poor neighbourhoods, parental stress and childhood depression and anxiety (Frick et al., 1992).

Social learning theory explains deviant antisocial behaviour as a result of copying behaviours of role models who are held in high esteem and who provide rewards. If children base their behaviour on role models who are involved in criminal activity or support acting out behaviour it is highly likely that such children will be more likely to engage in similar activities (Miller & Prinz, 1990).

Research has found that parents of conduct disorder/oppositional defiant disorder children provide inconsistent discipline, show little regard for how their children act in social environments and frequently behave in antisocial ways themselves (Frick et al., 1992). Rutter (1994) found that parents' poor behaviour management and inconsistent discipline were major factors in the lives of children and a significant consequence of poor parental control is that the children developed little if any impulse control. Studies have further indicated that there is a high correlation with family discord; unstable, dysfunctional families which have difficulty providing children with consistent guidance, acceptance or affection, and display hostility, were primary factors in conduct disorder/oppositional defiant disorder. Children are trained by the family in antisocial behaviour directly by coercive interchanges and indirectly by lack of monitoring or consistent discipline (Rutter, 1994).

Another influential explanation is blocked opportunity theory. This theory considers antisocial acts to be violations of conventional societal norms that are expected activities in a deviant subculture. A delinquent subculture pressures members to engage in deviant behaviours. Blocked opportunity theory maintains that delinquency occurs because youths face barriers to achieve approved economic and social goals. Conforming to social norms merely produces frustration; therefore they become antisocial to reduce anxiety and frustration (Cloward & Ohlin, 1960).

It has been hypothesized that one of the major differences in the development of conduct disorder rather than oppositional defiant disorder is that children who are aggressive and socially unskilled are often rejected by their peers and adults, leading to isolation and alienation which in turn leads to emotional and behavioural difficulties that are projected outwards, and that the anger they feel is directly projected towards others (Loeber, Burke, Lahey, Winters & Zera, 2000).

Conduct disorder and oppositional defiant disorder takes a different form in girls than in boys. Girls are more likely to be involved in lying, truancy, running away, substance abuse and sexually acting out (Berger, 1989). Shaw & Riley (1989) found that girls with a combination of low parental supervision and association with delinquent friends were 15 times more likely than other adolescent females to participate in antisocial behaviour and acts. Konopka (1966) found that girls who participated in antisocial behaviour were lonely, had feelings of helplessness and estrangement and desperately wanted to feel accepted. They participated in antisocial behaviour to feel powerful and to fit into a social group, often to secure a love relationship. One way of reducing these emotions and feeling secure was in the fantasy of a love relationship. Being rescued provided intensely fantasized relief and the girls deeply resented anyone who questioned the reality of the fantasy relationships.

TREATMENTS AND OUTCOMES

Society tends to take a punitive rather than rehabilitative attitude toward an antisocial aggressive youth. Such treatment appears to intensify rather than correct the behaviour. Longitudinal studies indicate a moderately strong relationship between children with conduct disorders and those who have antisocial personality disorder as adults (Zoccolilo, Pickles, Quinton & Rutter, 1992). Robins' (1966) study found that 20 percent of the children in his study with a diagnosis of conduct disorder later developed antisocial personalities as adults.

Treatment programmes for children with conduct disorders and oppositional defiant disorder have had mixed results with behavioural programmes based on education and skills development having the highest success and talking therapies having the lowest (Kazdin, 1993; Dodge, 1993; Dretzke et al., 2005). Other forms of behavioural management and treatment have focused on the family, utilizing parenting skills, behaviour therapy techniques, anger management and control techniques which appear to be moderately successful in shaping behaviour (Scott, Spender, Doolan, Jacobs & Aspland, 2001). These techniques focus on family relationships by helping parents modify their parenting techniques from punitive to positive reinforcing helping to modify the environmental conditions that have been reinforcing maladaptive behaviour. Changes can occur when parents consistently accept and reward their child's positive behaviour and stop focusing attention on the negative behaviour, which can change their perception of and feelings towards the child, leading to the basic acceptance that the child needs (Nelson, Finch & Hart, 2006).

FEEDING AND EATING DISORDERS OF INFANCY OR EARLY CHILDHOOD

Pica

This disorder occurs in children over the age of one and generally disappears in the fourth or fifth year. It involves the consumption of substances not ordinarily considered edible, such as clay, plaster, hair, paper and coins. Children with pica prefer these unnatural substances and purposefully seek them out, which distinguishes this disorder from normal youngsters who indiscriminately mouth almost everything they touch as part of the normal developmental process (Young, 2011).

In general this disorder is not considered life-threatening, but can lead to serious health hazards because of gastrointestinal blockages and possible accidental poisoning as well as ingestions of dangerous substances such as lead-based paint that can cause brain damage and mental retardation (Young, 2011).

Pica is not restricted to any specific intelligence level but is more commonly found in intellectually disabled children, who it is believed are unable to discriminate between food and non-food substances. Children with pica also appear to manifest other oral activity such as thumb sucking, nail biting and oral disturbances such as feeding problems. In addition these children often show a variety of other symptoms including rocking, head-banging, hair pulling, enuresis, nightmares, temper tantrums, and phobias (Young, 2011).

Research has found that pica is highly correlated to environmental factors such as family disorganization, broken homes, parental neglect, poor physical environment and poverty conditions (Mace & Knight, 1986; Lanzkowsky, 1959).

Treatment

Pica tends to disappear in children of normal intelligence by the age of five with proper diet and careful supervision. Pica beyond the age of six is rare but generally a sign of severe psychopathology requiring professional attention and intervention. Persistent pica is usually considered a symptom of some other type of serious abnormal disorder and the choice of treatment is usually tied to the eventual diagnosis and not to the specific eating problem (Mace, 1986; Lankzkowsky, 1959).

ELIMINATION DISORDERS IN EARLY CHILDHOOD

Enuresis

Enuresis is difficult to define because of the variability in young children's ability to establish bladder control. However, it is subject to age limitation and most consider lack of bladder control (primarily during night-time sleep) in children past the age of four or five that is not linked to any demonstrable organic pathology to be abnormal. Most children develop the necessary physiological and social maturity by the age of 15 to 18 months for controlling the bladder, although parental practices differ widely as to when training is initiated and how the control is taught (Schaefer, 1993).

The question of how often wetting must occur to be regarded as abnormal is not easily answered and is an area of some controversy. Some writers accept the frequency of once a month, while others consider weekly or more frequent wetting as satisfying the criteria for enuresis. While daytime wetting (diurnal) is known to occur and to properly fit the definition of enuresis, nocturnal wetting during sleep is far more frequent and common. Daytime wetting happens at times when the child is so engrossed in play that time out is not taken to go to the toilet, or when the child is under nervous tension that tends to exaggerate the urgency to urinate (Schaefer, 1993).

Research has found that enuresis is found in all levels of intelligence, but it rarely occurs as an isolated symptom. Instead, clinical observations indicate that it is highly associated with general immaturity (manifest in such behaviours as whining, moodiness, irritability, restlessness, overactivity, excitability, stubbornness, disobedience and oversensitivity), and a wide array of acting-out behaviours (that include temper tantrums, nail biting, fear reactions, encopresis, tics, health concerns, thumb sucking, stuttering, stealing and truancy) (Blackwell, 1995; Hagglof et al., 1997).

Most instances of enuresis are thought to be the product of psychological and environmental conditions, primarily of faulty habit training in which the regulation is started too early, too late or with training practices that are inconsistent and emotionally charged (Blackwell, 1995).

Encopresis

Involuntary defecating not directly caused by physical disease that occurs in children beyond the age of about two or three years is known as encopresis or faecal soiling. In addition to soiling, encopresis is almost always associated with constipation in which alternating periods of loss of bowel control and withholding of faeces are characteristic. As objectionable and aversive as the soiling may be to parents, it is far less hazardous physiologically to the child than constipation. Persistent withholding results in impacted faeces, enlarged colon (megacolon) and loss of tone and sensitivity of the colon which eventually leads to its improper functioning. Unlike enuresis, encopresis is primarily a diurnal phenomenon that more often occurs after bowel control has been established. Incidence estimates are infrequently cited in the literature, and those that are available vary considerably depending on such factors as the

Table 8.4 Aetiology of conduct/oppositional defiant disorder

Innately difficult temperaments	Insecure attachments
	Difficulty engaging in good parenting
Psychosocial variables	Low socioeconomic status
	Parental stress
	Childhood depression and anxiety
	Parents behaving in antisocial ways themselves
	Inconsistent discipline
	Family discord/dysfunction
Social learning	Copying behaviours of role models engaged in criminal activity
Blocked opportunity theory	Individuals face barriers and react with frustration

size of the sample, the age of the children, the frequency of soiling and the criterion used with regard to withholding.

Support for its psychogenic origin comes from the finding that encopretic children who have experienced the emotional stress of separating, arrival of a new sibling or the illness of mother also evidence regressive behaviour, feeling problems and temper tantrums (Bellman, 1966; Cohn, 2006; Schaefer, 1993).

Treatment of enuresis and encopresis

Whatever the primary cause or causes, it is generally agreed that enuresis/encopresis is a problem that is not only troublesome to all concerned, but also may contribute to serious adjustment difficulties in the affected child. Treatment begins with first eliminating any physiological issues the child may have that are causing lack of bladder/bowel control and then psychological issues such as anxiety and depression as well as psychosocial variables such as family dynamics and environment; finally behaviour modification programmes are implemented to help parents reward the child for appropriate toileting behaviour (Hjalmas et al., 2004; Levine, 1975; Cohn, 2006).

OTHER DISORDERS OF INFANCY, CHILDHOOD OR ADOLESCENCE

Anorexia nervosa

Anorexia nervosa is an eating disorder, primarily of females in affluent societies obsessed with looking thin, distorted body image and a fear of weight gain. Individuals suffering from anorexia nervosa or bulimia tend to come from societies that emphasize a certain type of appearance, status and achievement (Levine & Smolak, 1992; Malson, 1997; Pike, Hilbert, Wilfley, Fairburn, Dohm, Walsh & Striegel-Moore, 2008). Key transitional events in an individual's life also present risk factors for developing an eating disorder, for example the maturation changes that occur from childhood to adolescence. Young adolescent females become sensitive to cultural values about desirable feminine body weight and appearance (Rutter, 1990; Wentz, Gillberg, Anckarsater, Gillberg & Rastam, 2009).

Anorexia nervosa typically begins in early or middle adolescence and is thought to affect less than 1 in every 200 individuals in the general population. Anorexia nervosa tends to be found more often in females than in males with one estimate that females outnumber males 20:1. Males with the disorder appear to be clinically similar to females; however they appear to be less concerned with weight and more concerned with attaining the idealized masculine shape that probably reflects cultural values in terms of body image (Darcy, Doyle, Lock, Peebles, Doyle & Grange, 2011; Noshpitz, 1991).

Typically the profile is of an adolescent who is striving for praise and acceptance from peers and family. They generally begin a weight loss programme because they adopt an image portrayed in the media as being thin which translates to high self-esteem, popularity and success. As the individual begins to lose weight, they receive praise on their appearance and become fearful of weight gain, seeing it as the ultimate loss of control while staying thin means being perfect (Levine & Smolak, 1992; Grabe, Ward & Hyde, 2008; McCabe & Ricciardelli, 2011).

The weight loss programme and dieting become an obsession as well as a compulsion. They balance calorie consumption with a strenuous excessive daily exercise regime. They refuse to maintain body weight that is normal for their age and height and intensely fear obesity. They tend to have distorted perceptions of their body shapes. Anorexics tend to engage in peculiar food behaviours and obsessions such as calorie counting, spending a great deal of time cutting food into tiny pieces, rearranging food on their plates, and attempting to dispose of food rather than eating it. Despite their excessive weight loss and emaciated appearances they deny that they have an eating problem and continue to express worry that they are fat (Garfinkel & Garner, 1982; Giordano, 2007).

The physical effects of anorexia nervosa are widespread and affect almost every organ in the body – difficulty regulating body temperature, reduced oestrogens levels, delayed puberty, they stop menstruating if they have reached puberty, cardiovascular problems, kidney dysfunction; it can contribute to osteoporosis later in life and cause electrolyte imbalances (Garfinkel & Garner, 1982; Swain, 2005).

Bulimia nervosa

Where anorexia is a restrictive regime, bulimia is a disorder of purging. Bulimia means 'binge eating' the rapid consumption of a great quantity of food. Individuals with bulimia nervosa consume large amounts of food in one seating, generally feel out of control during a binge and then purge the food consumed by vomiting, the use of laxatives and/or diuretics with some individuals utilizing all three methods of purging. These individuals then feel shame and guilt after purging behaviours but maintain their preoccupation with body shape and weight which originally caused the abnormal relationship with food. The bulimic unlike the anorexic appears normal and will eat in public but will hide the binge-and-purge episodes. Generally it is not the bulimics who seek help with their disorder, rather it is a friend or family member who observes them in a binging/purging frenzy (Russell, 1979; Cooper, 2009).

Although there are also males who suffer from bulimia nervosa it tends to be a disorder of females, under the age of 30 with the eating disorder beginning in late adolescence following a series of unsuccessful diets. The major difference in the psychological aspects of bulimia is that the anorexic does not believe there is a problem, whereas the bulimic recognizes the issue and attempts to hide it from others (Russell, 1979; Cooper, 2003).

Bulimics often experience difficulties in interpersonal relationships, possess low self-esteem, experience high levels of anxiety, and engage in compulsive behaviour. Purging behaviour has physical effects such as damaged teeth and gums, lacerated hands, cracked and damaged lips and irritated or ruptured oesophagus. Bulimics also have fluid and electrolyte imbalances which can produce serious medical problems such as heart disorders, kidney injuries, bladder infections and renal failure. Excessive use of laxatives and diuretics can damage the lower intestinal tract (Fairburn & Beglin, 1990; Robinson, 2009).

Treatment of anorexia/bulimia

Treatment programmes using cognitive behavioural techniques emphasizing an alteration in an individual's belief system have been found to be effective in the treatment of both anorexia and bulimia. Evidence suggest that residential, rather than outpatient programmes have greater success in altering the maladaptive behaviour but success relies on the individual's ability to gain control of eating behaviours once they leave a residential programme. Residential programmes have proven more successful than outpatient as they can implement a wide variety of nutritional programmes, diet, and psychological aspects of the disorders simultaneously (Whitney & Hamilton, 1987; Rolfes & Debruyne, 1990; Cooper, Todd & Wells, 2008).

Bulimics tend to be more cooperative in treatment as they comprehend that their behaviour is abnormal whereas anorexics have difficulty accepting their maladaptive behaviour. One of the biggest obstacles to overcome in developing treatment programmes for bulimics is the identification of the triggering mechanisms that control binge-eating episodes (Fairburn & Beglin, 1990; Cooper, 1995).

CONCLUSION

What happened to Jasmine? Was she born bad? Looking at the case from a psychological viewpoint, Jasmine by all accounts was a normal teenager in a normal family. There do not appear to be any dysfunctional elements although no environment is perfect. Jasmine's change in circumstances began when her physical maturity (many people commented that she looked year older than her 12 years) enabled her to fit into a group of older adolescents and young adults. Emulating their behaviour and dress would have been easy for her, but her emotional maturity was still that of a 12-year-old girl. Had she not met Jeremy, we can hypothesize that the most trouble that Jasmine would have attracted would have been typical delinquency issues in the form of drug and alcohol abuse, truancy, authority issues, and sexual acting out. Her relationship with Jeremy was like adding fuel to the fire. Jeremy clearly had all the elements of an antisocial personality disorder which probably stemmed from conduct disorder when he was an adolescent; his impulsivity, lack of guilt and remorse were exacerbated by his dysfunctional, abusive background that caused him to react in a violent manner. Although he would probably have always acted in violent antisocial ways his behaviours might not had such a motivating target. If we focus on the behaviours outside of the actual murder (which is difficult because the heinous aspects of their crimes) both reacted in a way that indicated their levels of immaturity.

The ultimate goal for both was to be together, which meant moving the obstacle (Jasmine's family) out of the way. Once her parents had been removed there were no further plans; Jeremy simply went home without Jasmine, who eventually followed. They did not attempt to hide their crimes and their half-hearted attempt at escape in which they brought two of Jasmine's friends further indicate that neither really comprehended what 'being together' actually meant. The reality after the crimes had been committed for both individuals was confusion and indecision. They did not feel guilt or remorse because they were focused on a flawed internal belief system that revolved around self-indulgence. If we look at Konopka's research on the fantasy relationship, is one explanation of what occured in this case. Jasmine deeply resented her parents from allowing her to be with Jeremy and Jeremy was willing to do anything Jasmine asked for her love and the physical aspects of the relationship. Once they were incarcerated for the crimes, the focus was again not on their acts of murder but instead the content of their fantasized relationship which was evident in their letters to each other. What happens now? Jeremy will probably never be released from prison as he was sentenced to life without parole for a minimum of 25 years and under Canadian law Jasmine must be released in 2015 at the age of 22. Time will tell if Jasmine will be able to integrate all the elements of her behaviour into a positive psychological outcome.

Summary

This chapter focuses on the various disorders of childhood and adolescence. The section began with a brief history of child psychopathology and the field of child psychology. It then focused on the various disorders such as: mental retardation, learning disorders, language disorders, elimination disorders, pervasive developmental disorders and eating disorders.

LEARNING TOOLS

Key terms

ADHD – Attention deficit hyperactivity disorder – a developmental disorder that is characterized by hyperactivity and attentional issues

Aetiology – refers to the causes or origins of disease/disorders

Anorexia nervosa – eating disorder that is restrictive; individual refuses to maintain a normal body weight and has an obsessive fear of weight gain and distorted body image coupled with low self-esteem

Aphasia – class of language disorders that ranges from having difficulty remembering words to an inability to speak, read or write

Asperger disorder – pervasive developmental disorder characterized by difficulties in social interaction, along with repetitive patterns of behaviours and interests

Autism – pervasive developmental disorder characterized by severely impaired social interaction and communication, along with restrictive and repetitive behaviour

Bulimia nervosa – an eating disorder that is the combination of binging and purging of food. It is often seen in combination with the use of laxatives and diuretics.

Conduct disorder – a group of behaviours that involves chronic behaviour problems such as defiant, antisocial behaviour and impulsivity

Dyslexia – learning disorder that impairs a person's fluency or comprehension with reading and/or spelling

Encopresis – involuntary faecal soiling in children who have previously been toilet trained

Enuresis – inability to control urination usually during the night when the individual has the physical ability to maintain bladder control

IQ – Intelligence quotient – a score that is derived from assessments measuring intelligence

Oppositional defiant disorder – a pattern of disobedient and hostile behaviour generally directed at authority figures

Pica – a disorder characterized by the eating of substances that are non-food items

Prevalence – a measurement of all individuals affected by a disorder and/or disease within a particular period of time

Stuttering – articulation disorder that refers to a particular breakdown in speech fluency characterized by blocking, repetition and prolongation of speech sounds

Study guide

1   Detail how the area of testing and assessment affected the various disorders of childhood and adolescence.
2   Discuss the issues associated with the classification of mentally retarded children solely based on intelligence.
3   Consider the differences between conduct disorder and oppositional defiant disorder
4   There are five components of ADHD, impulsivity is one of those components. Detail how this element affects the other four.

Case study in focus
Research the differences between oppositional defiant disorder and conduct disorder and our case study of Jasmine and Jeremy. What theories apply? In this case are the two disorders distinctly different? In what ways are they similar?

Personal development
Individuals with dysfunctional cognitive/mental abilities have been documented as having remarkable mental skills such as rare musical talent, and mathematical abilities. Investigate the savant syndrome and how this applies to pervasive developmental disorders.

Suggested reading
Baron-Cohen, S. (2008) *Autism and Asperger Syndrome (The facts)*. New York: Oxford University Press.

Smith, M. (2005) *Menal retardation and developmental delay: Genetic and epigenetic factors*. New York: Oxford University Press.

Hughes, L.A. & Cooper, P.W. (2007) *Understanding and supporting children with ADHD: Strategies for teachers, parents and other professionals*. London: Sage.

Matthys, W. & Lochman, J.E. (2009) *Oppositional defiant disorder and conduct disorder in children*. Oxford: Wiley-Blackwell.

Schizophrenia and Other Psychotic Disorders

9

Learning aims

At the end of this chapter you should:

- Understand schizophrenia and other psychotic disorders
- Be familiar with the various types of schizophrenia
- Comprehend the psychosocial and biopsychological models of schizophrenia
- Be able to identify the various treatments used in schizophrenia

INTRODUCTION

CASE STUDY

In his own words: 'My schizophrenia experience'

Thirty years I've been a schizophrenic and like many people – I'm still lonely, isolated and socially excluded. Life plainly isn't fair but schizophrenia does include a cruel twist; society's ongoing myth states that schizophrenics can't be trusted – like the British weather – but it also declares that they are a real danger to society.

Two years after I was diagnosed with schizophrenia – the passing of the 1983 Mental Health Section Act enabled my doctor to lock me up in a closed hospital ward – against my will – so that society could be protected from me. There, at 18 years of age my hefty initial schizophrenic medication i.e. depixol depot injections – resulted in severely debilitating side effects – like parkinsonism and being constantly over-sedated. In other words, 'society' drugged me up and left me to rot. OK! Now, at 46, I've got some good news to tell you. I'm no longer 'locked up' and I'm only taking 40 percent of the overall comparable strength of my original medication; this positive transformation has been due mainly to my persistent pursuit and application to long-term counselling and long-'term therapies which I received as part of my disabled students education allowance. This counselling and therapy – which I will need to continue with for the rest of my life – includes Cognitive Behavioural Therapy (CBT), hypnotherapy, psychotherapy and of course, plain straightforward counselling.

Schizophrenia is indeed a double disablement; it is a devastating condition and it also has to battle against society's preconceived prejudice, ignorance, fear and discrimination.
By Shuresh Patel

CASE STUDY

Tom aged 32 had a relatively normal childhood. He was the oldest of three boys born to a mechanic and his stay-at-home wife. They had a comfortable life. Tom was an average student and his teachers and parents did not report any abnormalities; he didn't really have very many friends and was just a very quiet lad who kept himself to himself. He got along well with his brothers, he was helpful, but he appeared to be shy and preferred to be in his room with a book. After he finished school he got a job at a bank and got his qualifications in accounting. He met his wife who was a bank teller at the same bank. The two got married, bought a nice bungalow in a quiet neighbourhood and began their family. Karen became pregnant after their first year of marriage and although she worked up until her delivery day decided she wanted to be a full-time mother and gave up her job permanently at the bank. They added two more children to their family in four years. Tom appeared to be happy; the dual income had allowed them to put a large down payment on the house and the mortgage was easily affordable on his single salary. Tom worked long hours at the bank and loved the quietness of simply processing all the various bank documents, deposit slips and cheques. He soon was in charge of the accounting department and was very good at his job as he kept everything in complete order. Tom loved order, and he lived a very ordered life. He would wake up exactly at 6 a.m., always had porridge for breakfast and then walked to the bus at 7.15 where he would arrive at the bank at 8.45 and then begin work promptly at 9 a.m. Tom arrived at home at 6.15 when the family ate dinner. Karen was an excellent mother and wife. She kept their home clean and tidy and although she sometimes complained that Tom wasn't very interactive, they seemed to have a good life. Karen was very busy with the kids and drove them to all their school activities. They gardened in the summer and Tom built intricate model boats and aeroplanes. Tom was never late to work and he was never sick. All his co-workers liked him but found him aloof; he rarely talked, ate his lunch at his desk and appeared visibly uncomfortable when anyone attempted to socialize with him.

Tom and Karen lived happily in this manner for years and then the bank decided to close the branch office. Although they made offers to relocate all the employees, Tom refused and was made redundant. Tom worked until the very day that the doors of the bank were locked. He even continued to return to the building for weeks after the branch office had closed and appeared to be lost and confused. Although Tom got a large redundancy payment which was sufficient to pay all their bills for six months, he immediately became depressed. Karen told her friends she was worried and concerned. Tom had taken to the guest room and often refused to come out; she would occasionally catch him sneaking out late at night to stock up on food, and then he would retreat immediately. Their friends and family thought it would pass and that Tom was reacting to losing his job and felt that he would eventually snap out it once he got a new job, but Tom didn't get better; instead he got worse. When Karen attempted to talk to Tom through the locked door of the guest room, he would respond by saying he knew who she was – and that it was only a matter of time before the authorities would find out. The room began to smell and Karen decided to move out because Tom's behaviour was becoming more and more erratic.

Once Karen and the children had moved out, when friends and family members attempted to stop by the house, Tom would not answer the door. He had painted all the windows with black paint. His parents would leave bags of food by the door that would disappear so they knew that at least Tom was getting food. Eventually Tom was arrested by the police at the local skip; he was attempting to steal the old televisions and had them loaded in his car when he was stopped. Tom's behaviour was so erratic at the holding unit that he was suspected of being high on drugs and the police decided to search his home for stolen property and illegal drugs. The door wasn't locked and they found that the house was in complete disarray. There was garbage everywhere, and the place smelled. They did not find drugs or stolen property but what they did find was disturbing. Tom had painted large eyes in black paint on everything; all the walls were covered as well as the ceilings. He had also collected a large number of television sets which also had large eyes painted on them and had them scattered throughout the house as well as elaborate structures created out of aluminium foil. Tom was quickly evaluated by a psychiatrist and sectioned.

SCHIZOPHRENIA

This disorder is known by its abnormal behaviour patterns and has the closest relationship with the term 'insanity'. No other mental disorder has symptoms that are so readily apparent to the general public and although they may be unaware of the specifics of the mental illness, watching an individual interact with people and things that no one else can hear or see is typically what a normal person would classify as insane. Schizophrenia is one of the psychoses in which the sufferer is no longer fully in touch with reality. The signs and symptoms associated with schizophrenia are many and diverse. In general, schizophrenia involves the disturbance of personality, thought processes, bizarre perceptions and delusions and inappropriate emotions (Read, Bentall & Mosher, 2004).

History of schizophrenia

The actual term 'schizophrenia' (meaning split mind) has only recently been used and describes a group of symptoms that mostly involve disturbances of perception (Bewley, 2008). The disorder can be traced back to the earliest writings in history beginning with written documents of ancient Egypt that asserted that the disorder was a disruption in the connection between the heart and mind. Plato believed that mental illness stemmed from an unhealthy balance between the intellect and desire. Aristotle's belief was that mental illness originated from an unhealthy balance between the mind and primitive urges whereas Hippocrates introduced the idea that mental conditions had a physical cause. Following from Hippocrates, Galen proposed the idea of the four humours as being responsible for mental illness. According to Galen, the four humours were: sanguine (blood), choleric (yellow bile), melancholic (black bile) and phlegmatic (phlegm) and these four humours needed to be balanced or the individual would become either physically or mentally sick. The four humours could become imbalanced by the change in location by the individual, diet, occupation, as well as a wide range of psychosocial factors. At the same time, interwoven among these individuals and their attempts towards the scientific origins of mental illness was the enduring belief that insanity was caused by the supernatural, possession of demons and/or witchcraft. Eventually the scientific explanations would triumph as a result of the advancements in technology and mental illness would be regarded as a defect of the mind. At this point, all brain ailments from injuries, birth defects, mental retardation and mental illness would be combined as one broad category and treated by isolating the individuals away from the general population in asylums (Porter, 2002).

It wasn't until 1887 when Emile Kraepelin began to systematically identify symptoms and place them in categories that anyone had given much thought to the different types of mental illness and mental injuries. Kraepelin found in his studies of large groups of patients that the main symptom in many with mental illness appeared to be a mental deterioration. He was unable to explain the loss of intellectual capacity as a result of injury or illness and since no anatomical lesion could be discovered, he believed it had to be functional in origin. Kraepelin was puzzled by the inability of his patients to perform efficiently on intellectual problems when he had reason to believe that at one time they had been able to do so. This apparent dementia was one of the marked symptoms, and as a result he labelled the disease dementia praecox. Kraepelin believed that dementia praecox was a specific disease which developed in early life and then led to a rapid mental deterioration (Bewley, 2008).

Kraepelin believed that the common core of dementia praecox was the destruction of the internal connections of the psychic personality. This damage then led to a major impact on the emotional and volitional aspects of mental function. Kraepelin did not hold environmental factors responsible for two basic reasons; his own experiences of a clear hereditary predisposition evidenced by a family history of the illness in preceding generations, and the fact that the disease had antedated the civilization process. Kraepelin believed that the underlying aetiology was organic and the course of the disease was progressive deterioration which was similar to a disease. Kraepelin justified the grouping on the bases that (1) each disorder typically affected patients in early life; (2) the course of each was invariably chronic and deteriorating, and (3) each seemed to be a manifestation of a metabolic and possibly an endocrinological disorder (Bewley, 2008).

Upon more careful study of his cases he found a wide variety of differences in symptoms in his single classification and consequently subdivided dementia praecox into specific types. Although originally he had many different types he eventually settled on three major categories; paranoid schizophrenia, catatonic schizophrenia and hebephrenic schizophrenia (Bewley, 2008).

KRAEPELIN'S ORIGINAL CATEGORIES

Hebephrenic schizophrenia

Kraepelin found that inappropriate laughter and silliness were the two most regularly found characteristics in this category and called it hebephrenic which was the combination of two Greek words that meant 'youthful mind'. This classification showed typical emotional deterioration with the individuals being indifferent to anything in their environment that would arouse an affective reaction in a normal person. Although they did not lack perceptual ability, they were simply not interested in what was going on around them and took very little interest in it (Kraepelin, 2010).

Catatonic schizophrenia

Kraepelin described this grouping as catatonic which was an alternation of excitement and stupor with the latter being the predominant characteristic in this classification. He believed that this category resembled a manic-depressive psychosis as it had elements of withdrawal and retreat from reality as well as the excitement element. The progression was relatively quick in comparison to the hebephrenic and paranoid categories (Kraepelin, 2010).

Paranoid schizophrenia

This category dealt exclusively with the nature, development and content of delusions. Kraepelin found that the paranoid schizophrenic had delusions that had obvious gaps in the way information

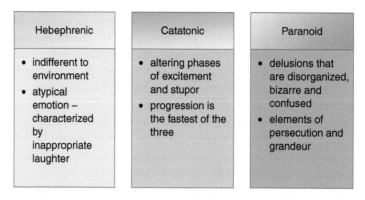

Figure 9.1   Kraepelin's three categories

was put together without any clear relationship to facts or reality. He found that individuals in this classification had delusions that were disorganized, bizarre and confused. They often contained delusions of both persecution and grandeur. Progression for this category was a slow onset in which the withdrawal and disintegration was not as prominent as the other two types (Kraepelin, 2010).

BLEULER AND THE TERM SCHIZOPHRENIA

Bleuler followed Kraepelin and coined the term schizophrenia to replace dementia praecox. Bleuler found that the dementia that Kraepelin described was not a dementia at all and instead a disorder of personality integration. Bleuler used the term schizophrenia to indicate what he believed to be the outstanding characteristic of the disease which was the splitting of the personality. It should be kept in mind that his use of 'splitting' did not mean that the personality split into two separate personality segments. Rather, Bleuler's split-off was the division of the affective patterns of behaviour from the more intellectual or motor patterns of behaviour. The terminology that Bleuler used is really better described as a lack of integration or a disintegration of the personality rather than splitting. Bleuler also believed that schizophrenia was not a single disease and that there were a number of disorders manifesting a splitting of the personality, with the different forms being based on different personality maladjustments. Bleuler's conceptual ideology of schizophrenia had some elements that were very different from Kraepelin's. Although he believed the disorder had some elements of biology, the disease itself was not caused by an organic deterioration but instead followed more closely with the ideology of Sigmund Freud and was more characteristic of different psychic functions that could be re-integrated. He also added a fourth schizophrenic subtype that he called simple (Berrios, 1996).

Simple schizophrenia

This category includes the mildest forms of regression which are severe enough to be considered pathological. The outstanding symptom is something that is termed 'emotional dilapidation' or an emotional collapse which leaves the person with a permanent emotional indifference and an inability to overcome life obstacles. The individual with simple schizophrenia had no other symptoms of any consequence, no substantial hallucinations or delusions, and did not show any further regression, rather they failed to progress in any direction (Black & Boffeli, 1989).

The 4 As

Bleuler attempted to organize the multitude of symptoms by distinguishing between what he called fundamental and accessory symptoms, also referred to as primary and secondary symptoms. Bleuler believed that the fundamental (primary) symptoms were found to some degree in every schizophrenic patient, while the accessory (secondary) symptoms were seen in some but not others. Bleuler considered the disturbances of associations and affect as well as audible thoughts and thought diffusion to be pathognomonic (characteristic for the disorder). The need for simplification

Table 9.1   Bleuler's fundamental and accessory symptoms

Fundamental 4 As	Autism	Preoccupation with internal stimuli – escape into a complete internal world – social withdrawal – loss of contact with reality
	Associations (loose)	Illogical or fragmented thought processes – no clear link between actions and ideas, incoherence
	Affect (inappropriate)	External manifestations of mood – little or no expression – flat/blunted/restricted – affect and thought content are contradictory
	Ambivalence	Simultaneous, contradictory thinking about self and others – presence of two conflicting feelings, emotions or thoughts
Accessory	Neologisms	Creating and using new words generally only known by the individual using them
	Poverty of ideas	Restriction in plans, opinions or thoughts
	Catatonic posturing	State of inertia or stupor – rigidity of the muscles
	Hallucinations	Perceptions of people and things that are not real
	Delusions	A false or mistaken belief or idea
	Audible thoughts	Thoughts that are spoken aloud
	Thought diffusion	Thoughts that are scattered, broadcast, inserted or removed

in the area of mental disease and illness, along with Bleuler's own theoretical interests, resulted in disordered associations becoming the distinctive and unifying construct that defined schizophrenia (Read, Bentall & Mosher, 2004).

Eventually Bleuler's classification, definition and designation was broadened to include most forms of thought disorder while at the time acknowledging that it was localized in the area of cognition. The somatic process was still the central source of the disorder, but the main effect and defining characteristic was the dissociative thinking.

SYMPTOMS

Positive and negative symptoms

Bleuler's and Kraepelin's early contributions helped to organize and classify the considerable array of symptoms. However, another individual who was just as influential and helped to restructure and reorganize the symptoms for the purpose of treatment and classification was Kurt Schneider. Schneider classified symptoms that he called 'first rank symptoms'. His classification of symptoms is still widely used and highlighted the importance of what is called positive and negative symptoms. Positive symptoms represent a change in behaviour or thoughts such as delusions and hallucinations. Negative symptoms represent a withdrawal or lack of function that you would normally expect to see in a normal functioning individual such as emotional expression, social relationships and communication skills (Bentall, 1992).

Individuals with schizophrenia show a wide variety of disordered behaviours. Some of these appear characteristic of the disorder, while others are better explained as reactions to the stress and turmoil that is created in their social environments. Many individuals show a poverty of action in all areas; movement, speech and affect. Individuals who are profoundly affected by the disorder are often described as showing abulia (no will), alogia (no words) and athymia (no feelings). Individuals have difficulty generating the appropriate behaviour required at a specific place and time, but additionally often fail to suppress inappropriate behaviour. It is not unusual for them to repeat recent actions (perseverate) or produce responses that are irrelevant to external stimuli (Belitsky & McGlashan, 1993).

Frith (1987) found that disorders of action correlated with schizophrenia typically can be classified into three categories. The first is poverty of action, where the individual is unable to produce any appropriate behaviour in response to external stimuli. The second is perseveration, where the same action is repeated inappropriately time after time even when it is clear that the action is ineffective. The third is that when actions do occur they are completely inappropriate to the context. All three of these disorders of action are observable in the language of individuals with schizophrenia.

Language and mode of thinking are among the most obvious indication of the seriousness of the disorder. Although the cognitive disorders take a variety of forms, they are all strikingly deviant from normal thought patterns. The cognitive disorders do not follow the rules of logic, their word associations may be based upon similarities of sounds, and they often make up words (neologisms) to create new patterns that only they understand. In general language loses much of its communicative value and individuals demonstrate disruptions in the continuity of their thoughts (Kasanin, 1944). Meehl (1990) called this phenomenon cognitive slippage and described it as a specific type of thought derailment in which the individual's mental processes and cognitive sequence slipped off the track.

Research in the area of memory and schizophrenia has found that they do not form the assemblies by which memory is organized. As a direct result they have poor recall, and appear unable to organize information in any systematic way so that they are able to easily recall or form new assemblies.

Table 9.2   Positive and negative symptoms of schizophrenia

Positive symptoms	Negative symptoms
Agitation	Alogia – lack of speech
Tension	Amotivation
Associated disturbances	Anhedonia – lack of pleasure
Delusions	Blunted affect
Hallucinations	Poor grooming and hygiene
Ideas of reference	Poor social skills
Illusions	Poverty of speech
Insomnia	Loss of interest in people and things
Paranoia	Lack of concentration

They tend to rely on a rigid conceptual process without adequate constraint from perceptual data; when they do attend to sensory aspects of stimuli it is in an automatic processing fashion and they show significant deficits in the formation of schemata (Goldman-Rakic, 1994). Table 9.2 outlines the various positive and negative symptoms.

CORE FEATURES OF SCHIZOPHRENIA

Hallucinations

The primary feature of schizophrenia is hallucinations. These are typically defined as perceptions that occur in the absence of any appropriate stimulus. Generally hallucinations involve hearing human voices with approximately 20 percent reporting hallucinations in other sensory modalities such as vision, touch, or olfactory (Bentall, 1990). Various explanations have been put forth as to why individuals with schizophrenia have pervasive hallucinations. One major theory that has been suggested is input theory (Frith, 1992). This theory states that hallucinations occur as a result of external stimuli being misperceived and that the abnormality lies within the cognitive processes that affect perception. Another possibility for the hallucinations is a failure of discrimination (Cutting & Murphy, 1987). The ideology behind this theory is that two stimuli appear more similar to the individual with schizophrenia than to individuals without the disorder and are therefore more likely to be confused. However, there has not been concrete evidence for this and it has been hypothesized that if hallucinations are due to discrimination problems, the issue would be in the nervous system of the individual and not the external environment (Frith, 1992). Finally the last theory is that misperceptions occur because of a change in bias. External stimuli have many different interpretations that are dependent upon our ability to discriminate but also on our preconceived notions of what the stimuli represent. Therefore they would reflect the individual's expectations and preoccupations. However, if hallucinations truly are misperceptions it remains unexplained how many of the characteristic auditory hallucinations such as hearing one's own thoughts would be explained by this bias (Frith, 1992).

Delusions

Delusions are typically defined as false perceptions and beliefs. Maher (1974) felt that delusions occur when an individual applies normal logic to an aberrant experience or perception. For example, someone who is hearing voices will create a reason or explanation for the voices. When non-schizophrenic individuals experience an unusual event, they do not have to create delusional explanations to explain the event. For the individual who is suffering from schizophrenia some information is ignored while the rest is over-emphasized and they are attempting to apply logic in circumstances where normal people would not (Andreasen & Olsen, 1982).

Communication and language in schizophrenia

The language and quality of speech in an individual with schizophrenia often reflects the imperceptible cognitive disturbances. The quality of language and speech is varied; for some it is barely understandable for others it is clear and logical. Schizophrenic speech can also be deviant without being incomprehensible. Approximately 16 percent of individuals with a diagnosis of schizophrenia have incoherent speech (Andreasen, 1979). Andreasen et al. (1998) investigated three different aspects of language in individuals with schizophrenia: syntax (grammar), semantics (meaning), and discourse (how phrases and sentences are linked together) and found that individuals showed specific impairments only at the level of discourse. They also found that individuals were defective in their use of rules governing how sentences are combined in order to construct a complete idea set. Murphy and Cutting (1990) demonstrated that individuals with severe schizophrenia were impaired in the use of prosody (variations in the pitch, intensity and rhythm of speech) for the expression of emotion and they had difficulty with the metaphorical meaning of words and sentences relative to other psychotic patients. In addition their research found that in schizophrenia language errors can be explained as the consequence of higher-level processing failure and the language abnormalities are expressive rather than receptive.

Individuals with schizophrenia have been described as having odd and distinctive language. The peculiar speech that is often observed in individuals with schizophrenia is categorized as thought disorders. Thought disorders describe the peculiar things that schizophrenic individuals say as a consequence of the peculiar thoughts they are experiencing. The ability to put these abnormal thoughts into language is unimpaired (Chapman & Chapman, 1973).

The abnormalities of language commonly follow the division of positive and negative symptoms. Poverty of speech and poverty of content would be considered negative; other features such

Table 9.3   Types of communication disorders (based on Frith, 1992)

Poverty of speech	Monosyllabic answers
Poverty of content of speech	Replies of adequate length supplying little information
Tangentiality	Irrelevant replies
Derailment	Lack of proper connection between phrases and ideas
Incoherence	Unintelligible lack of proper connection between words
Illogicality	Incorrect reasoning
Loss of goal	Failure to follow a chain of thought through to its natural conclusion
Perseveration	Persistent repetition of words or ideas
Self-reference	Repeatedly referring the subject under discussion back to the self
Neologisms	Newly created words that typically only have meaning to the person who uses them
Clang associations	Characterized by words that are associated by sound rather than meaning

as incoherence and derailment would be considered positive (Frith, 1992). Poverty of speech describes the lack of speech production while poverty of content implies many words but few ideas (Frith, 1992). Poverty of content also arises because the individual often repeats the same words and or produces words that are unusual or inappropriate in the linguistic context. Spontaneous speech is also characterized by the use of unlikely words and in some cases they generate new words that only have meaning to the person who creates them (neologisms) (Frith, 1992). Covington et al. (2005) defined a language impairment they called schizophasia which was composed of dysphasia-like impairments such as clanging (association of words based on sound rather than concept such as house/mouse), neologisms and unintelligible utterances. Other researchers have hypothesized that individuals with schizophrenia generate new words as a way of expressing themselves because they are unable to use existing words that are applicable to the feelings they want to convey (Abu-Akel, 1998; Byrne, Crow & Griffin, 1998).

NEGATIVE SYMPTOMS

Negative symptoms are defined as deficits in the normal emotional responses and focus on the individual's social skills and ability to associate with others. Negative symptoms are more strongly associated with a more chronic course and are often accompanied by intellectual deterioration and a poor response to antipsychotic medication. Negative symptoms are also associated with various neurological dysfunctions such as movement disorders and cognitive impairment. The disruption of social relationships is believed to contribute to the decrease in attentional capacity and other cognitive impairments (Andreasen, 1982b).

Involuntary movements are also characteristic of individuals with schizophrenia and are considered negative symptomatology. Individuals have been documented as making peculiar movements, specifically strange grimaces with their lips and mouth. They also engage in stereotypic movements. It was originally thought that these movements were caused by long-term treatment with antipsychotic drugs that caused extrapyramidal reactions (parkinsonism, dystonias, akathisia, tardive dyskinesia). However, it is now clear that certain individuals develop movement disorders whether they are being treated with antipsychotic medications or not, although medication can make these movement disorders worse for those individuals that are more susceptible to them (Owens, Johnstone & Frith, 1982; Andreasen, 1982a; Manschreck, Maher, Rucklos & Vereen, 1982).

One of the most characteristic negative symptoms of schizophrenia is flat affect. This is defined as having very little emotional expression, an absence of emotional facial expression and the person is uninvolved and does not respond even if circumstances would evoke an emotional response. Affect refers to our emotional expressiveness; people with flat affect appear apathetic and often speak in a monotone and do not vary their pitch or frequency (Gur, Kohler, Ragland, Siegel, Lesko, Bilker & Gur, 2006). They also appear nonresponsive to the emotions of others. Research in this area has shown that schizophrenic individuals are poor at identifying emotional expressions and appear to perceive faces in an abnormal way (Berenbaum & Oltmanns, 1992).

Table 9.4   Schneider's first rank symptoms (Schneider, 1959)

Traditional symptom classification
Person hears voices speaking his or her thoughts aloud
Person hears voices discussing or arguing about him or her
Person hears voices describing his or her activity
Person gives special or highly personalized significance to an accurate and normal percept
Person experiences bodily sensations he or she interprets as originating outside him or herself
Person experiences his or her own thoughts as being placed in his or her mind by an external force
Person believes that someone or something is taking away his or her thoughts
Person believes that others can hear his or her thoughts and he or she has no control over the process
Person believes his or her emotions and feelings are being imposed or controlled by others
Person believes his or her desires and impulses are being controlled or imposed by others
Person believes his or her motor activity is being controlled or imposed by others

Braun et al. (1991) found that schizophrenic individuals have difficulty in using their faces to express emotion.

DIAGNOSIS, PROGNOSIS AND OUTCOME

Although the categories and classifications appear to be straightforward, this is far from the case in a clinical setting. Individuals present with some symptoms and not others, or have a presence of symptoms at different times; some regress, some remain constant and some make good progress. Some appear to cycle through various symptoms and others are stable and consistent. Some are able to function in their communities and some require lifelong residential care (Mueser & Jeste, 2011).

The problem of diagnosis is further complicated by the uncertainty of the disorder's prognosis. Research has evidenced that the presence of negative symptoms is related to poor prognosis, however many of these symptoms focus on social skills and interpersonal aspects of the individual and not the more physiological elements of the disorder presented in the positive symptoms (Tsuang, Woolson, Winokur & Crowe, 1981). Brown (1959) found that social factors appear to be important prior to and following a schizophrenic episode, with the patient's premorbid adjustment predictive of length of hospitalization.

Other significant predictors include acute onset, clear precipitating factors, married, good premorbid adjustment, presence of depressive features, lack of schizoid features, feelings of guilt, presence of disorientation or confusion on admission, above average IQ, absence of marked emotional blunting during hospitalization, and no schizophrenia in blood relatives. These findings indicate that the interpersonal aspects of the person's adjustment are the best predictors of a poor prognosis (McCabe, Fowler, Cadoret & Winokur, 1971).

DSM-5 AND RECLASSIFICATION OF SCHIZOPHRENIA

The changes that are being implemented are the elimination of the schizophrenia subtypes while the characteristic symptoms will remain unchanged (APA, 2012). The subtypes are the following: Paranoid, disorganized, Catatonic, undifferentiated and residual. The diagnosis under the DSM categories is that two or more of the following symptoms must be present for a majority amount of time during a one-month period; delusions, hallucinations, disorganized speech, disorganized or catatonic behaviour and negative symptom (APA, 2012).

Table 9.5   Prognosis and outcome

Feature	Good prognosis	Poor prognosis
Premorbid functioning	High	Low
Precipitating factors	Present	Absent
Age at onset	Above 21	Below 21
Onset of symptoms	Sudden	Insidious
Family history	Mood	Schizophrenia
Interpersonal relationships	Stable/married	Single
Affective symptoms	Wide range	Blunted affect
Behavioural features	Positive	Negative
Response to antipsychotics	Good	Poor
Audible thoughts	Absent	Present
Delusional perceptions	Absent	Present
Depersonalization	Absent	Present

MODELS OF SCHIZOPHRENIA

Three basic models or approaches to schizophrenia will be discussed; the medical model, the social model and the psychological model. The adoption of a model provides a frame of reference with a broad but cohesive way of understanding and explaining the characteristics of a disorder. It also includes who will be identified, the type of criteria used, treatment and the public's attitudes towards those identified individuals.

MEDICAL MODEL

This perspective supports the ideology that schizophrenia results from abnormalities in brain structure. These abnormalities can be as a result of biochemical and physiological differences in the central nervous system, injuries, infectious disease, systemic disease characterized by a known or unknown organ dysfunction, all affecting the central nervous system. These elements may be solely responsible or could precipitate the disorder in persons with a genetic predisposition. Schizophrenia is seen as a discrete disease state that is aetiologically and symptomatically distinct. Efforts to identify the pathogenic factors have subsequently relied most heavily on morphological, neurohistorical and biochemical techniques.

Physical factors

There are a number of specific physical factors of possible aetiological significance that have been identified in the medical literature, although the specific mechanisms by which they induce schizophrenia are unclear. It is a possibility that the various factors could predispose the individual to the disorder and then the environmental elements increase the likelihood that the disorder will occur.

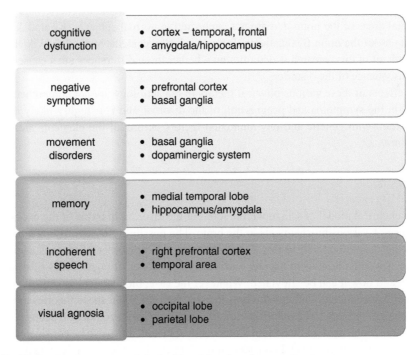

cognitive dysfunction	• cortex – temporal, frontal • amygdala/hippocampus
negative symptoms	• prefrontal cortex • basal ganglia
movement disorders	• basal ganglia • dopaminergic system
memory	• medial temporal lobe • hippocampus/amygdala
incoherent speech	• right prefrontal cortex • temporal area
visual agnosia	• occipital lobe • parietal lobe

Figure 9.2   Brain structures associated with schizophrenia symptoms

Identified factors have been: viral infection, birth injuries, neurological disease, and neuroanatomical abnormalities (Read, Bentall & Mosher, 2004).

It has been established that viruses are capable of producing mental disorders that can remain latent for years and may show a particular affinity for the limbic system; however no virus has been definitely associated with schizophrenia. Studies have found the presence of viral antibodies in schizophrenic patients as well as antibodies for cytomegalovirus in the cerebrospinal fluid which has been linked to CT abnormalities (Rantakallio, Jones, Moring & Von Wendt, 1997).

Birth injuries are also thought to precipitate schizophrenia particularly in those that are genetically predisposed with the pathogenic cause being neonatal hypoxia (Kim, 2008). Mednick and Schulsinger (1967) found that children of schizophrenic mothers who experienced complications during pregnancy or birth were five times more likely to develop symptoms of the disorder than children of schizophrenic mothers who had uncomplicated deliveries and healthy children.

Neurological disease has been linked to schizophrenia as a result of a number of syndromes having symptoms that are typical of schizophrenia, i.e. encephalitis, temporal lobe epilepsy and Huntington's chorea. In addition, research looking at neurological dysfunction has found that schizophrenics exhibit neurological signs, but have no evidence of neurological disease (Cox & Ludwig, 1979).

Neuroanatomical abnormalities have been examined between schizophrenic individuals and normals in relation to weight, thickness or size of various structures in the central nervous system. Several studies have found that the corpus callosum of schizophrenics is thicker than normals (Foong et al., 2000), an increased number of myelinated interhemispheric nerve fibres that link functional areas of the brain that are not connected in normal subjects (Konrad & Winterer, 2008) and atrophy of the brain (Oxenstierna, Bergstrand, Bjekenstedt, Sedvall & Wik, 1984). The major issue with all of this research is determining whether these differences are a cause of schizophrenia or a consequence of the disorder.

The effects of these various physical factors in the aetiology are not comprehensive or adequate to explain the symptoms and progression of the disorder and it is highly likely that they work in combination with genetic and environmental factors before all the elements are present to cause schizophrenia.

Biochemical factors

The biochemical model of schizophrenia looks at the disorder in terms of the excess, deficiency, or imbalance of various biochemicals in the brain. The possibility of identifying a biochemical problem would enable research to target the aetiology of the disorder. If there is a specific biological disorder it would allow us to narrow down the vast number of possibilities of what is causing the disorder and how it can be alleviated. Whatever the case, biochemical models of schizophrenia are still highly speculative. Perhaps the best that can be said about these theories at this point is that schizophrenia appears to be manifestation of adrenergic and serotonergic pathways connected in a series in the limbic system. In addition, biochemical factors must also be considered in terms of their interaction with environmental considerations. And finally, it is probably unrealistic to expect any biochemical theory to explain schizophrenia in its entirety (Donaldson, 1998).

Early hypotheses

An early medical model of schizophrenia suggested that the disorder resulted from the production of toxic compounds in the brain. Osmond & Smithies (1952) observed that the synthesis of epinephrine required an enzyme and that mescaline, a powerful hallucinogen is a derivative of the catecholamines that utilized the same enzyme and caused similar symptoms of schizophrenia in users. Another observation found that methylated indoleamine derivatives were capable of producing schizophrenic-like symptoms. Consequently these theories were called the transmethylation hypothesis and it was suggested that schizophrenia results from an over-accumulation of enzymes that either do not break down themselves or do not appropriately break down neurotransmitters (Nestoros, Ban & Lehmann, 1977). Research in this area has attempted to find evidence in bodily fluids and to identify the enzymes that might be responsible for the aberrant metabolic process but to date has not found any evidence to substantiate the hypothesis.

The Dopamine hypothesis theorizes that schizophrenia is caused by an excess of dopamine-dependent neuronal activity in the brain. In support of this theory is that antipsychotic medications exert their therapeutic effect by reducing dopaminergic activity (Carlsson, 1988; Meltzer & Stahl, 1976). The ability of phenothiazines to bind to dopamine rectors is highly correlated with their clinical effectiveness (Carlsson, Persson, Roos & Walinder, 1972). In addition, a side effect of antipsychotic medications is a syndrome that resembles Parkinson's disease and tardive dyskinesia. These conditions are believed to be the result of dopaminergic supersensitivity resulting from the tonic blockage of postsynaptic dopamine receptors. Other compounds, structurally similar to the catecholamine, such as amphetamines can induce or exacerbate psychotic symptoms.

Antipsychotic drugs are capable of antagonizing all three types of dopamine rectors so it is difficult to know which of the three are important in schizophrenia. The possibility that antipsychotic medications have an effect on all three receptor types explains why these drugs produce adverse as well as therapeutic effects (Keefe, Silva, Perkins & Lieberman, 1999). In spite of the knowledge of how the antipsychotic medications affect dopaminergic activity, there is still no direct evidence that schizophrenia is caused by a defect in the dopaminergic transmission system (Laruelle, Abi-Dargham, Gil, Kegeles & Innis, 1999).

Also it must be noted that the antipsychotic drugs have a significant effect primarily on the positive symptoms with very little effect on negative aspects of the disorder, such as poverty of speech and flatness of affect (Leucht, Corves, Arbter, Engel, Li & Davis, 2009). Consequently dopamine receptor activation, if present in schizophrenia, must be responsible for only some aspects of the disorder, namely those seen in the acute stage. Chronically, dopamine may not be involved at all although it may contribute to negative symptomatology through inhibition or underactivity rather than excitation or overactivity (Leucht, Corves, Arbter, Engel, Li & Davis, 2009).

Another early theory of schizophrenia implicated monoamine oxidase (MAO), which is the primary catabolizing agent for the catecholamines. Watt et al. (1973) compared the MAO activity in blood platelets in 13 monozygotic twins discordant for schizophrenia and in 23 normals. There was an inverse correlation between the degree of schizophrenic symptomatology and MAO levels with a high positive correlation between the twins suggesting that the MAO levels were genetically determined and not the consequence of the disorder itself. This in turn suggested that MAO levels could serve as a genetic marker for vulnerability but were not directly involved in the disorder.

Various other studies investigating this line of research have failed to prove the MAO theory (Tsuang, Bucher & Fleming, 1982; Carlton & Manowitz, 1984).

However, there is still the possibility that MAO levels are related to medications, diet, activity, hospitalization, sex, age or non-specific effects of stress or psychoses rather than the disorder itself. In addition, the finding that patients suffering from both schizophrenia and affective disorder exhibit lower levels of MAO activity than controls suggests that MAO may be involved in these types of disturbances generally but not schizophrenia specifically (Bleich, Brown & Van Praag, 1991). On the other hand, the MAO theory complements both the dopamine and transmethylation hypotheses since MAO metabolizes all of those compounds.

Interactional hypotheses

Although the dopamine hypothesis appears to be the most probable for the explanation of schizophrenia, it is likely that no single agent is completely responsible and that a number of other systems are involved, hence the variations in symptoms and the various types of the disorder. It has been suggested that the basic defect in schizophrenia involves a lack of inhibition of the GABA-ergic system and that antipsychotics work by preventing an overload of dopaminergic impulses normally dampened by that system (Roberts, 1977; Ashton, 1987).

Another hypothesis involves an imbalance between dopaminergic and cholinergic activity, with there being a relative predominance of the former over the latter (Carlsson, 1990). Davis (1974) proposed a two-factor theory in which one factor, an unidentified biochemical compound, turns on schizophrenia while the second factor, dopamine, 'turns up the gain'. Both factors must be in operation for a schizophrenic episode to be expressed. The phenothizines block the dopaminergic stimulation while dopaminergic stimulants, such as amphetamine and methylphenidate, turn up the gain in persons with the first factor. In terms of this model, the antipsychotic agents work by turning down the gain.

Psychophysiological factors

Scientific investigations in the area of psychophysiology of schizophrenia have relied on a variety of responses and methods with the majority of research being conducted in the areas of orienting response and evoked potentials. Electrodermal measures have focused primarily on schizophrenic hyper and hypo responsivity to simple stimuli, while studies involving evoked potentials have examined the tendency for individuals to augment rather than reduce their perception of simple stimuli.

Orienting response

The electrodermal orienting response (also referred to as the orienting reflex) is one of the more widely studied psychophysiological variables in schizophrenia. The electrodermal orienting response is thought to be triggered by change or movement of a stimulus in the perceptual field that signals a divergence between the sensory input and a neuronal model of that field (Bernstein, 1987). If schizophrenia is characterized by an impairment in response to the external world, then a flaw in orienting response function would be expected.

It has been proposed that both the hypo and hyper-responsivity shown by individuals with schizophrenia relate to a dysfunction in the limbic system, particularly in the amygdaloid or hippocampal areas (McGuiness & Pribram, 1980). Spohn and Paterson (1979) suggest that disturbances in the balance of cholinergic activity account for this dysfunction, providing basically a biochemical substrate for these functional 'lesions'. The limbic dysfunction hypothesis can also be linked to the dopamine hypothesis or a combination of the two.

Research in this area clearly indicates that schizophrenics tend to respond inappropriately and it is believed that the orienting response function does reflect different stages or phases of the disorder with hyper-responding associated with positive symptomatology and hypo-responding negative symptomatology (Dawson et al., 1994)

Evoked potentials

Evoked potentials are averaged electroencephalographic waveforms recorded from subjects stimulated by light flashes, tones, electric shocks, or any sensory event that has an onset fast enough to produce adequate synchrony of the brain's response. Evoked potentials complement the use of the electrodermal orienting response by demonstrating the presence of reliable differences across individuals. One of the major areas in this line of research has been the concept of augmenting and reducing, which refers to the way that individuals vary in the extent to which their nervous systems either amplify or diminish the effects of stimulation. Work with evoked potentials using light as a stimulus has found that augmenters exhibit elevated evoked potential amplitudes with increasing flash intensity while reducers show either smaller increases or even reductions with increments in intensity (Blackwood, Whalley, Christie, Blackburn, St. Clair & McInnes, 1987).

Silverman (1968) suggested that the states of chronic withdrawal seen in schizophrenia represent an excessive narrowing of attention resulting as a defensive manoeuvre against threatening or otherwise intense stimulation – the reducing effect. This hypothesis has been supported by the finding that acute schizophrenics not on medication tend to be reducers in terms of visual and somatosensory evoked potentials (Keefe et al., 1999) Other investigators have also demonstrated that schizophrenics show deviant types of responding when the strength of the sensory stimulus is progressively varied (Yamada et al., 2011; Huang et al. 2011).

The two conclusions that may be derived from the EP studies of schizophrenia are that, first, many schizophrenics seem to be reducers, a finding that is compatible with the stimulus overload hypothesis. The second conclusion is that schizophrenics may exhibit a paradoxical profile of response that is different from that of normals. More specifically, when physiological arousal is very low, sensitivity to environmental stimuli seems much increased. In normals, the level of attentiveness to external stimuli is more directly related to level of arousal.

Hemispheric factors

Hemispheric research has emphasized the brain's horizontal organization and is closely associated with information-processing of schizophrenics and expands on the detection and integration of environmental stimuli. Temporal-limbic dysfunction of the left hemisphere in schizophrenics has long been suspected with some evidence coming from the observation that a higher proportion of mixed or reversed dominance in schizophrenics than in normals (Shenton, Kikinis, Jolesz, Pollak, LeMay, Wible, Hokama, Martin, Metcalf, Coleman & McCarley, 1992). The strongest data supporting a left-located cerebral dysfunction in schizophrenia come from studies employing EEG, neuropsychological and behavioural measures. Research has indicated that schizophrenic psychoses are associated with left hemisphere lesions, whereas affective disorders are associated with right hemisphere pathology (Yu, Cheung, Leung, Li, Chua & McAlonan, 2010). Additionally, schizophrenics are more likely to be left-handed than normals, suggesting that they did not use the left hemisphere as dominant, in comparison to normals (Deep-Soboslay, Hyde, Callicott, Lener, Verchinski, Apud, Weinberger & Elvevag, 2010). Schizophrenics have higher right ear auditory thresholds and weaker right side halvanized skin responses, suggesting impaired left hemisphere function (Breska, Moaz & Ben-Shakhar, 2010; Jansen, Hu & Boutros, 2010).

Schizophrenics appear to have a particular problem processing information presented to the left, normally language-dominant hemisphere indicating the possibility that the problems of language and flight of ideas imply an overactivation of left hemisphere functions, whereas sluggish thinking and speech, impoverished sometimes to the point of muteness, which characterized the group with larger right-hand response, implies a reduction in left hemisphere activation (Turetsky, Bilker, Siegel, Kohler & Gur, 2009).

Mohr et al. (2008) have linked hemispheric dysfunction to deficiencies in information-processing highlighted by the attentional models of schizophrenia, proposing that the left hemisphere attends to contralateral stimuli while the right attends to both contralateral and ipsilateral stimuli. The evidence for left hemispheric dysfunction, however, is inconclusive, particularly since it is extremely difficult to place dysfunction definitely in either hemisphere.

The genetics of schizophrenia

The genetic explanation is not solely a medical model. It is a combination of the medical-social model. Nearly all genetic theorists believe that the psychological condition is stressed by the environment in order to produce the disorder and does not occur without both elements. Some genetic factors interact with some non-specific and possibly universal environmental factors to produce phenotypic schizophrenic behaviour. There are three main approaches to the study of the genetics of schizophrenia: the concordance approach, the adoption approach and the high-risk approach (McGuffin, Owen & Farmer, 1995).

The concordance approach compares the rate of schizophrenia across groups that differ in terms of their biological relatedness. First-degree relatives share approximately 50 percent of their genes, while second-degree relatives only share 25 percent of their genes. The greatest probability of being schizophrenic is if both parents are schizophrenic. The least probable are those relatives most removed genetically, such as uncles and aunts. Across the general population there is an incidence

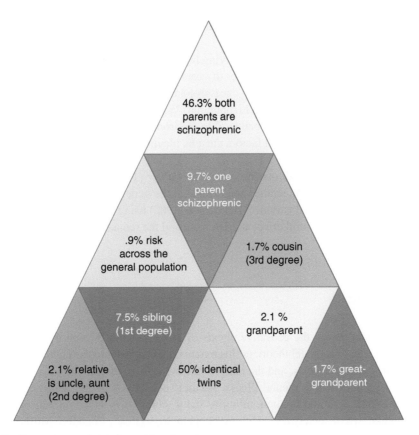

Figure 9.3 Percentage of risk for schizophrenia

rate of approximately 0.9 percent. The risk for a third-degree relative is 1.7 percent, for a second-degree relative with schizophrenia it is 2.1 percent. The risk for schizophrenia rises to 7.5 percent for children with a schizophrenic sibling, 9.7 percent for the children of one schizophrenic parent and 46.3 percent if both parents have schizophrenia (Rosenthal, 1971; Gottesman & Shields, 1982).

ADOPTION APPROACH

Adoption studies assume that similar genotypes are exposed to differential rearing patterns. One form of adoption approach focuses on children of a schizophrenic parent who have been adopted at an early age. The relative contribution of the child's genetic make-up can be compared with that of the rearing environment. Research has indicated that biological relatives are as much as ten times more likely to be diagnosed as schizophrenic than the child's adoptive relatives (Kety, Rosenthal, Wender & Schulsinger, 1968). Individuals whose biological parents are normal but who are adopted by a schizophrenic parent do not develop schizophrenia at an increased rate (Rosenthal, 1971).

The high-risk approach involves identifying high-risk individuals such as children of schizophrenics and following them for a number of years. Mednick and Schulsinger (1968) found that a large proportion of subjects exhibiting excessive autonomic lability at an earlier assessment had developed full-blown symptoms of schizophrenia. Venables (1978) found that genetically high-risk children exhibited a greater 'openness' to environmental stimuli. It is believed that these studies indicate that environmental factors must be playing a significant role in the development of schizophrenia as well.

Twin studies indicate a high concordance rate. Fulker (1979) conducted a meta-analysis on the various twin and adoption studies and estimated the genetic variance at 73 percent, leaving 27 percent for environmental variance. Henderson (1982) using only twin data estimated genetic variance at 71 percent, cultural effect at 20 percent and the remaining 9 percent as a result of the twin environment itself.

SOCIAL MODEL

The social model places the causative agents of schizophrenia outside of the individual and within the society. This model theorizes that external and environmental factors act upon an individual causing extreme stress, and the result is the breakdown of the individual's ability to cope and therefore a retreat into mental illness. Factors such as population density, socioeconomic level, educational level, occupation, minority status, community isolation, unemployment, and general breakdown of society all lead to psychopathology (Read, Bentall & Mosher, 2004).

PSYCHOLOGICAL MODEL

The psychological models postulate that the cause of schizophrenia resides within an individual's internal psychological processes. Although the origin may differ depending on the theory, the common element is that they are all internal processes that are causative factors in the aetiology of schizophrenia (Read, Mosher & Bentall, 2007).

Psychoanalytic theories hypothesize that the underlying intrapsychic conflict gives rise to the neurosis that eventually becomes schizophrenia when the internal psychic functions are unable to resolve the conflict. Covert symptoms give information about the conflict, the defences and the character structure, but they are not primary in treatment. The belief is that symptom removal (delusions, hallucinations) without the resolution of the basic conflict only leads to symptom substitution and soon other symptoms will appear. Therefore the principal task is to resolve the intrapsychic conflict which will in turn resolve the clinical symptoms of schizophrenia (McWilliams, 2011).

The behavioural perspective in contrast to the psychoanalytic view believes that cultural, social, environmental and family factors are important. The primary task for the behaviourist is to determine which factor(s) are acting in a maladaptive response pattern and causing maladaptive behaviour. Therefore the behaviourist is concerned if the hallucinations that a schizophrenic is experiencing are due to the way the person is responding to private stimuli or public stimuli. The behaviourist does not dismiss the fact that there may be a biochemical flaw that produces hallucinations, but the primary focus is in conditioning the individual to function in spite of the hallucinations. Therefore, the behavioural mechanism plays a role in understanding the causes of schizophrenia, the factors that maintain it and the factors that could be applied to change that disorder. In other words, no matter what may be the mixture of magnitudes of cause in producing schizophrenia, the near cause is always a behavioural one. Furthermore there is no guarantee that the factors that caused schizophrenia are the same as those that presently maintain it or that could be used to eliminate or attenuate it (Swerdlow, 2010).

SCHIZOPHRENIA TYPES

The DSM previously recognized five different types of schizophrenia, however beginning with the DSM-5 this will no longer be the case. As a result of other classification systems and the controversy with these subtypes, this chapter will detail the five types. Four of the types involve the active phase and one involves the residual phase. This chapter will detail the different types in terms of prognosis and response to treatment.

Paranoid type

Individuals with the paranoid type of schizophrenia show patterns of increasing suspiciousness and difficulties within interpersonal relationships. Persecutory delusions are the most frequent and generally involve a wide range of bizarre plots and ideas. Frequently their delusions revolve around law enforcement agencies or military organizations and they become convinced that they are being watched, followed, talked about or poisoned. Often they engage in elaborate methods to hide themselves and/or their activities (Lauriello & Pallanti, 2012).

Individuals of the paranoid type also have themes of grandeur, meaning that they place themselves in positions of power and/or greatness, such as believing that they are regularly consulted by the prime minister, or they are the world's greatest spy or believing that they are famous people such as movie stars, military generals or politicians. They tend to have vivid auditory and visual hallucinations, but their cognitive skills and affect are relatively intact. The weaving of delusions and hallucinations into a paranoid composition often results in a loss of critical judgement and in erratic, unpredictable behaviour. They generally do not have disorganized speech, have a higher level of adaptive coping and typically a better prognosis than people with other forms of schizophrenia (Leonhard, Beckmann & Cahn, 1999).

Disorganized type

This type of schizophrenia was called hebephrenic schizophrenia by Kraepelin and Blueler. Individuals with this type tend so show noticeable disruptions in the pattern and intonation of their speech and extreme disordered behaviour, as well as flat or inappropriate affect. Often their affect will fluctuate between blunted and inappropriate, e.g. laughing in a loud and childish manner that is unsuitable for that time and/or place or not responding to sad situations. Their delusions and/or hallucinations tend to be fragmented and incoherent. Often they involve immoral practices, voices that call them vile names, delusions that are hypochondriacal, disorganized and fantastic. They tend to exhibit peculiar mannerisms and other bizarre forms of behaviour, often appearing obsessive in nature (e.g. constantly waving their arms before speaking, making odd facial grimaces). They are often indifferent to real-life situations and are erratic and unpredictable. Age of onset is typically early and chronic without remissions that often characterize other types of schizophrenia (Lauriello & Pallanti, 2012).

As the disorder progresses their affect tends to be more severely disturbed and their speech often becomes disjointed and incomprehensible. They tend to use similar-sounding words called clanging (house-mouse), a derailing of associated thoughts, the use of neologisms (new words) and in some instances they become unintelligible. The prognosis is generally poor and no specific type of treatment or combinations have been found to be useful (Mueser & Jeste, 2011).

Catatonic type

The new antipsychotic medications have made this type relatively uncommon. The main characteristic is pronounced motor signs, either of an excited or a stuporous type. In addition these individuals sometimes display odd mannerisms with their bodies and faces, including grimacing. They often repeat or mimic the words of others (echolalia) or the movements of others (echopraxia). The main feature of this disorder is unusual motor responses of remaining in fixed positions which fluctuate from extreme rigidity to engaging in excessive activity. Catatonic patients may pass suddenly from states of extreme stupor to great excitement, during which they seem to be under great pressure of activity and may become violent. Age of onset is typically early, and it becomes chronic and progressive. Treatment is in the form of antipsychotic medication (Mueser & Jeste, 2011).

Undifferentiated type

This is the most common type of schizophrenia. The primary feature is the presence of prominent psychotic symptoms, delusions, hallucinations, incoherence and grossly disorganized behaviour that cannot be classified in any other type. Individuals in this classification type do not clearly fit into one of the other types because of a mixed symptom pattern. People in the acute, early phases of a schizophrenic breakdown frequently exhibit undifferentiated symptoms as do those who are in transitional phases from one to another of the standard subtypes, who are then later reclassified once their symptoms become more stable and pronounced. Individuals who show this type of chaotic, undifferentiated pattern typically do not have the early and slowly developing onset characteristic of the other types. Instead they tend to have sudden psychotic breakdowns that are surprising as they have previously shown no history of a psychotic disorder. Generally these incidents occur in conjunction with a period of notable stress that tends to quickly resolve itself in a short period of time (less than six months). Treatment is generally antipsychotic medication with supportive types of therapy (Mueser & Jeste, 2011).

Residual

This is a classification that is generally reserved for individuals whose symptoms have improved to a degree that they cannot be classified by the other four active types. Although individuals have improved, they are not typically symptom free and are not classified as recovered. They may have elements of the positive and negative symptoms but they differ from the other four subtypes as they are not as severe, incapacitating, organized or persistent. It is also hypothesized that this category may represent a transitional phase between the other four subtypes and complete remission (Lauriello & Pallanti, 2012).

OTHER TYPES OF PSYCHOTIC DISORDERS

Schizophreniform disorder

This category is a classification for schizophrenia-like psychoses of less than six months' duration. It may include any of the symptoms of delusions, hallucinations, incoherence or disorganized behaviour but can also include some of the blunted/flattened affect and paranoid ideation. Brief psychotic states may or may not be related to subsequent psychiatric disorder and generally sudden or recent onset cases with no previous history of a psychotic disorder are first given a schizophreniform diagnosis. The prognosis for this disorder is better than a formal diagnosis of schizophrenia. Individuals with this disorder who do not progress to a diagnosis generally have an early and lasting remission from a first episode of a breakdown. The prognosis where it is a manifestation of recent-onset is better than the established forms (Fujii & Ahmed, 2007).

Schizoaffective disorder

Individuals with this diagnosis generally present with a mixed picture of symptoms of schizophrenia (disturbed thought patterns, hallucinations, delusions) as well as symptoms of mood disorders (anxiety, depression) and have characteristics that belong in both categories. The prognosis for individuals with this disorder is similar to those with schizophrenia as they do not tend to get better without medical/psychological intervention and usually continue to experience major life difficulties for some time to come. Individuals with this classification may not suffer from delusions or hallucinations but generally show some disordered patterns of thought disturbance and negative beliefs. Other symptoms can include social withdrawal, inactivity, lack of motivation and blunted/flat affect.

Onset typically begins in late adolescence or early adulthood with the prognosis being somewhat more favourable than those diagnosed with schizophrenia. Treatment consists of antipsychotic medication and lithium if there are clear manic symptoms. If the depressive symptoms are more unipolar in nature, adding an antidepressant does not appear to be helpful (Olfson et al., 2009).

Delusional disorder

This disorder is characterized by a persistent delusion that is not the result of an organic factor such as brain seizures of any severe psychotic disorder. Individuals with these delusions tend not to have most of the other problems associated with schizophrenia. For example, they do not have the flat affect or the other negative symptoms of schizophrenia; but importantly, they may become socially isolated because of their suspicion of others. Their delusions will often be long-standing, sometimes persisting over several years. These delusions differ from the more bizarre types often found in people with schizophrenia because in delusional disorder the imagined events could be happening but aren't. While not accurate representations of the situation, they reflect situations that could occur in real life. Delusional disorder appears to be relative rare, affecting between 1–4 percent with identified psychological disorder (Freudenreich, 2007).

The onset of this disorder is relatively late compared to other disorders, with the average age of first admission to a psychiatric facility falling between 40 and 49 years of age. However because these individuals may not seek help earlier and because many people with this disorder can lead relatively normal lives, this later age of admission for treatment may not represent the beginning of the delusions but rather the point at which the symptoms become most disruptive. There seem to be more females than males with this disorder (between 45 and 55 percent of the affected population). Often this disorder is precipitated by extremely stressful situations. Typical delusions found in delusional disorder include being followed, poisoned, infected by disease, or loved by someone the person has never met (usually a person who is famous) or being chosen for some important mission or providing the world with important information. Generally these delusions are well systematized. This means that apart from the particular topic involved in the delusion, the person's thinking seems to follow logical patterns and that he or she is able to function at least relatively effectively in other areas of life. Antipsychotic medication is often used. Appropriate psychosocial treatments include cognitive therapy and general supportive therapy to enhance the fragile self-esteem common in these individuals (Fujii & Ahmed, 2007).

Shared psychotic disorder

This disorder is extremely rare and information concerning the condition has generally only been available in single-case studies in clinical settings. The condition typically affects two people, who share the same psychotic disorder; they are almost always from the same family and live together in comparative social isolation. One generally takes/plays a dominant role with the

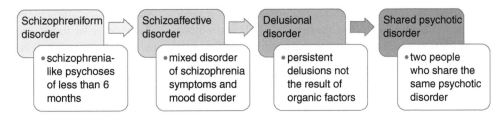

Figure 9.4   Other types of psychotic disorders

other person being more passive and taking the beliefs of the first. If the two are separated, the secondary person tends to abandon the delusion. The content and nature of the delusion depends on the dominant person's delusions. Treatment would first separate the two individuals with the dominant psychotic individual being treated with antipsychotic drugs and the secondary individual provided with psychological support to compensate for the loss of the relationship (Silveira & Seeman, 1995).

TREATMENT

Treatment for schizophrenia should involve all elements of an individual's life; physical, psychological, social and environmental and should be guided by a multidimensional interaction model that considers stress, vulnerability and protective factors (Vaccaro & Roberts, 1992). An individual who is struggling with psychotic disorder is not only attempting to cope with their illness but is also faced with a bewildering and threatening world. The result of these experiences can lead to a number of secondary adaptive processes that in many cases are more debilitating than the positive symptoms characteristic of the early stages of the disorder (Freudenreich, 2007).

Consequently, it is clear that the treatment of the schizophrenia must proceed along two parallel lines – appropriate medication and an active psychosocial intervention, which can provide education to individuals and caregivers about schizophrenia as well as teaching practical ways of coping with the illness which can reduce the risk of relapse. The benefit of a multidimensional model of treatment is to strengthen the individual's coping capacities and social support system as well as a wide spectrum of therapeutic goals and objectives such as emotional insight, skill development and family problem solving (Vaccaro & Roberts, 1992).

Treatment should also consist of education about the illness, assistance with access to support and rehabilitation in the community, and generally foster an alliance between the individual and the team providing treatment. Clinicians and disability support workers in a multidimensional model would assist individuals with persistent cognitive impairment by providing help with problem solving, budgeting, and activities of daily living. Interventions based on cognitive behavioural programmes or more finely tuned cognitive rehabilitation can also help improve their quality of life and prevent relapses that require long-term hospitalization (Perris & McGorry, 1998).

Vaccaro & Roberts (1992) suggest organizing psychosocial treatments according to their focus, locus and modus as well as therapeutic goals and objectives. They describe focus as being the individual, the locus being the actual place where therapy takes place (clinic, hospital) and modus being the theoretical orientation that is utilized.

Research has indicated that a community, whether it be in a hospital or in a family is of paramount importance in helping individual cope with their illness. A positive community environment can enable the individual to reach equilibrium between an optimal amount of activity which is stimulating and an optimal amount of routine and order which helps to induce calm and control. In addition to a supportive community environment the individual should be provided with therapy that functions in two ways: supportive and therapeutic. The success of the individual is contingent upon the organization of an active community and opportunities for the individual to improve their quality of life and feel in control (Hofmann & Tompson, 2002).

Social skills training

Another beneficial therapy is the use of social skills training. This type of training uses learning theory principles to improve social functioning. The goal of this type of training/therapy is to improve the individual's social skills, which in turn will help to remediate the problems in daily living, employment, leisure and interpersonal relationships thereby reducing relapse and minimizing hospitalization (Bellack and Mueser, 1993).

There are three forms of social skills training: the basic model, the social problem-solving model, and the cognitive remediation model. In the basic model, complex social repertoires are broken down into simpler steps, subjected to corrective learning, practised through role playing, and applied in natural settings. The social problem-solving model focuses on improving impairments in information-processing that are assumed to be the cause of social skills deficits. The model targets domains needing changes including medication and symptom management, recreation, basic conversation and self-care. In the cognitive remediation model, the corrective learning process begins by targeting more fundamental cognitive impairments, like attention or planning. The assumption is that if the underlying cognitive impairment can be improved, this learning will be transferred to support more complex cognitive processes, and the traditional social skills models can be better learned and generalized in the community (Bellack and Mueser, 1993)

Deficits in social and independent living skills are prevalent with individuals with a psychotic diagnosis (Bellack, Turner, Hersen & Luber, 1984; Brown & Munford, 1983). Typically individuals with psychotic disorders (in particular schizophrenia) have deficiencies in non-verbal communication skills, poor eye contact and inadequate problem-solving abilities. Social skills training in these areas would help to improve these deficits by using in-vivo experiences and homework assignments in order to encourage generalization to real life experiences. Group formats provide opportunities in vicarious learning and a peer support network for helping in the completion of homework and positive peer reinforcement (Wallace & Liberman, 1985).

One particular type of social skills training is the successful living approach created by Hierholzer (Hierholzer & Liberman, 1986). In this specific type of social skills training programme individuals are taught specific problem-solving skills necessary for the negotiation of daily living. This programme has been successfully used to set treatment and rehabilitation goals. It has also been used as an ongoing intervention programme designed to generalize the effects of the more structured social skills training programmes (Vaccaro & Roberts, 1992).

Medication

The use of medication for this disorder has changed the reality of many individuals from hopelessness to one of optimism and possibility. Psychopharmacology has helped to remove some of the more debilitating elements and in turn change the attitude of individuals suffering with the disorder, caregivers as well as the general public. It has provided many individuals with positive symptom reduction so that they could function outside of institutions and in some cases become employed, secure professions and establish stable relationships (Temte & Greist, 1992).

Antipsychotic medications have assumed a major role in the treatment of schizophrenia, particularly in its acute phase. The effectiveness of the antipsychotic medications in the treatment of schizophrenia has been demonstrated and many studies report consistently favourable outcomes, although for a small percentage of individuals this is not the case (Lieberman, Stroup, McEvoy, Swartz, Rosenheck, Perkins, Keefe, Davis, Davis, Lebowitz, Severe & Hsiao, 2005). Once an individual is in remission, antipsychotic drugs substantially reduce the risk of relapse, but they appear less effective for individuals in an acute phase. Most individuals with psychosis will show a moderate to substantial reduction in their positive symptoms after treatment with antipsychotic drugs, but approximately 30 percent of hospitalized individuals will not respond to medication and those with predominantly negative symptoms are even less responsive to drug treatment (Leucht, Corves, Arbter, Engel, Li & Davis, 2009).

For those individuals who have a positive response to medication, the greatest limitation of treatment with antipsychotic drugs has been their side effects (even though they have been improved over the earlier traditional types). Individuals with schizophrenia have had to balance the negative side effects for the reduction in symptomatology. In particular, they had to tolerate disabling and distressing extrapyramidal side effects such as parkinsonism, akathisia (restlessness in the legs and body), acute dystonia, and tardive dyskinesia (involuntary movements, often of the tongue and face but also of the fingers, hands, legs, and trunk) (Bebbington, Angremeyer, Azorin, Marwhaa, Marteau & Toumi, 2009).

However, with careful management of side effects, the accumulated data on the effectiveness of antipsychotic drug treatment in schizophrenia is positive and when used in combination with psychosocial interventions provides the most comprehensive programme with many individuals being able to return to productive lives with a minimal amount of intervention and intrusion (Gray, Wykes, Edmonds, Morven & Gournay, 2004).

Hansen & Bebbington, (2005) found it is particularly important to use the in-patient experience to establish a solid foundation for subsequent treatment efforts with one of the major goals being the most effective use of medication with the best possible aftercare planning and initiation of long-term treatment efforts. Medication can only alleviate the positive symptoms, the negative symptoms are more troublesome and upwards of 40 percent of individuals who are compliant with medication still relapse within a year, therefore it is important to combine therapies for successful adaptation to community life (Hogarty, 1984; Falloon & Liberman, 1983).

Case management

The introduction of antipsychotic medication has been very effective in the treatment of schizophrenia with many individuals no longer needing long-term hospital care and therefore being released back into their initial social environment with care being provided by various community programmes. Unfortunately, many individuals with schizophrenia lack the level of cognitive and social competence to consistently follow-through with medical regimes and therapy which increases their stress levels, decreasing the likelihood that they will get their needs met and increasing the risk of relapse and hospitalization. In addition many individuals are often ill-prepared to find and maintain the multiple services they need in order to function in the community. Case management has been a programme/service that has been identified as being crucial to the success of the individual to prevent re-hospitalization of individuals at risk for relapse through the provision of comprehensive integrated community services. Typically a person is assigned to one multidisciplinary team member (case manager, social worker, psychologist, nurse, etc.) who functions by contracting any services that are needed by the individual, arranging the appointments and monitoring all elements of their medical, social and psychological functioning (Scott & Dixon, 1995).

Psychosocial interventions

Even when the antipsychotic medications do work, the individual struggling with schizophrenia must still face the daily problems and stress in living that proved so difficult to cope with in the initial stages of the disorder's onset. It has been estimated that as many as half of medicated patients still are unable to adapt to living successfully in the community at discharge (Kern et al., 2009; Dixon et al., 2010; Drake, Bond & Essock, 2009; Waldheter et al., 2008). Consequently, there has been a shift in focus and treatment strategies with various forms of psychotherapies to attempt to improve the social adaptation, vocational functioning, and subjective well-being of individuals with schizophrenia (Wu & Lingyu, 2009). At the same time, the appropriate increase in emphasis on providing necessary information to patients and families about the nature of the illness, the available treatments, and their respective benefits and risks has also influenced the nature of psychosocial strategies. The following sections provide a brief overview of the various successful psychological treatments.

Family therapy

Therapeutic approaches involving families have shifted from viewing the family as a factor in the aetiology of the condition to recognizing the potential influence of the family on the course of illness and providing strategies to assist in promoting the positive aspects of that influence.

Pharoah, Mari, Rathbone & Wong (2006) found that contrary to expectations, discharged patients who returned to live in their marital or parental home were more likely to relapse, showed more disturbed behaviour and remained unemployed longer than patients living either with siblings or by themselves. Large hostels were also predictive of poor adjustment. One of the explanations of high relapse rates was that these family/social environments had high expectations and were highly emotionally charged, which added extra stressors onto the individual attempting to cope with their illness after hospitalization.

In response to research on the family, broad-spectrum, family-centred treatment approaches have been advocated to reduce the stress involved in complicated social situations. Using medication in conjunction with family therapy can help reduce the individual's disturbed behaviour at home and/ or at work and may therefore reduce the level of emotion expressed by others, which can be debilitating to the individual struggling with schizophrenia. In addition self-management training in terms of medication can play an important role in helping the individual take control of their illness and providing positive coping strategies (McFarlane, 2011).

A large body of evidence has demonstrated the superiority of a variety of family therapy interventions that employ behavioural and psychoeducational techniques over customary outpatient care or individual therapy in terms of the primary outcome measures of psychotic relapse and re-hospitalization (Gerson, Davidson, Booty, McGlashan, Malespina, Pincus & Corcoran, 2009). On average, relapse rates among schizophrenic patients whose treatment involves family therapy are approximately 24 percent as compared to about 64 percent among those who receive routine treatment (Rait & Glick, 2008).

Factors that should be assessed before the individuals released from an in-patient setting are: the family's ability to cope, assessment of the family's problem-solving effectiveness, an analysis of the family system as a unit, and sessions devoted to educating the family on the diagnosis, aetiology, management and course of schizophrenia. Other components include communication training, training in structures problem-solving, and behavioural strategies, such as self-management skills (including medication adherence training), social skills (including job-finding and job interview training), and anxiety management training (Rait & Glick, 2008).

Cognitive behavioural therapy

Cognitive behaviour therapy has been used with individuals, particularly those who continue to experience psychotic symptoms despite medication. The principal aims of cognitive behaviour therapy for medication-resistant psychosis are to reduce the intensity of delusions and hallucinations, reduce stress and promote the active participation of the individual in reducing the risk of relapse and levels of social disability (Kingdon, Turkington & John, 1994). Cognitive behavioural interventions focus on rationally exploring the subjective nature of the psychotic symptoms, challenging the evidence for these, and subjecting such beliefs and experiences to reality testing. Tai & Turking (2009) found that patients receiving cognitive behaviour therapy demonstrated a significant reduction in overall symptoms as compared to standard treatment alone but they did not find a specific reduction in psychotic symptoms. Bechdolf et al. (2010) found a reduction of delusions and hallucinations with the use of cognitive behaviour therapy compared to supportive counselling and routine care. In acutely psychotic in-patients, Turkington et al. (2008) found that cognitive behaviour therapy in combination with antipsychotic medication resulted in a significantly faster and more complete recovery from the psychotic episode.

These studies suggest that the therapeutic benefit of cognitive behaviour therapy is not simply attributable to non-specific psychological intervention, but rather to the elements that are specific to cognitive behavioural therapies and interventions.

Summary

This chapter focused on the psychotic disorders. The discussion began with a historical perspective of schizophrenia and mental illness. The various symptoms and classification systems of schizophrenia were discussed and then the various models of schizophrenia were considered with respect to the possible aetiology of the disorder. The chapter then discussed other types of psychotic disorders and finished with a discussion about treatment.

LEARNING TOOLS

Key terms

Anhedonia – inability to experience pleasure from activities formerly found enjoyable

Contralateral – affecting the opposite side of the body, biological structure

Depersonalization – a feeling of not being in control of your body, or being able to watch it from afar

Dystonia – a movement disorder in which sustained muscle contractions cause twisting and repetitive movements – muscle spasms

Electrodermal orienting response – a method of measuring the electrical conductance of the skin

Evoked potential – an electrical potential recorded from the nervous system following the presentation of a stimulus

Extrapyramidal symptoms – various movement disorders that usually occur after taking dopamine antagonists

Ipsilateral – affecting the same side of the body, biological structure

Neologism – using words that only have meaning to the person who is using them

Pathognomonic – characteristic for a disease

Premorbid – refers to the condition of an individual prior to the onset of a disorder

Tardive dyskinesia – disorder that has a slow onset resulting in involuntary, repetitive body movements

Study guide

1 Compare and contrast the differences between Kraepelin's and Bleuler's definitions of schizophrenia.
2 Describe and discuss the 4 As of schizophrenia.
3 Diagnosis, prognosis and outcome have been discussed in terms of the positive and negative symptoms of schizophrenia. Describe what these are and how they affect the individual.
4 Detail one of the treatments and how it is implemented for individuals with schizophrenia.

Case study in focus

Discuss the various ways we could classify our case study of Tom. What models could be applied? Detail what symptoms are present, what would be considered negative and what would be considered positive. What would you say is Tom's future prognosis?

Personal development

Genetics have been discussed in terms of the medical-social model. Bill and Sue would like to adopt a child who has one parent that has schizophrenia. What would be the implications of their decision? Include all elements that should be considered and how this could affect all of their lives.

Suggested reading

Beck, A.T., Rector, N.A., Stolar, N. & Grant, P. (2009) *Schizophrenia: Cognitive theory, research and therapy*. London: Guilford Press.

Mueser, K.T. & Jeste, D.V. (eds) (2008) *Clinical handbook of schizophrenia*. London: Guilford Press.

Burton, N. & Davison, P. (2007) *Liviing with schizophrenia*. London: Sheldon

Jones, S. & Hayward, P. (2004) *Coping with schizophrenia: A guide for patients, families and caregivers*. Oxford: Oneworld.

Mood Disorders

10

Learning aims

At the end of this chapter you should:

- Be familiar with the various models associated with mood disorders
- Comprehend the aetiology of mood disorders
- Be aware of the assessment and treatment of mood disorders
- Appreciate the various other types of mood disorders.

INTRODUCTION

CASE STUDY

Charlie is a 69-year-old man who was supposed to be undergoing facial reconstruction surgery to correct a breathing problem, but he was refusing to sign the papers and kept telling the doctors that he wanted to die. Without the surgery it was likely that he would die as he kept getting lung infections. Charlie had until recently been a farmer. He had a farm that had been in his family for five generations but unfortunately it had been repossessed by the bank to pay off a defaulted loan.

The land had been broken up into pieces and each piece had been sold. Charlie was very bitter and angry and said that the bank had made ten times the profit and they should have given him at least one more chance to make good. Charlie said he didn't want to have the surgery because he had nothing to live for and if they fixed his breathing problem this time it would only be a matter of time before he tried to take his life and this time he would be successful, so he wanted to save everyone the time and trouble. Charlie said his life was in ruins and he was a failure at everything including his own suicide.

Charlie's life began happily enough, he was an average student, but his real love was his family farm and his work with the animals. When he was a boy he would wake up early to help his father with the farmyard chores. He had been born in the middle of the Second World War and he was nearly five years old when his father had come home from the services. For the next 25 years life was perfect. There were ups and downs on the farm but they were good farmers and usually made a profit which his father squirrelled away to balance out off years. Then his father passed away, he missed him but carried on with the farm. At the age of nearly 40 he met a woman and fell in love, it was a short courtship but Charlie was sure she was the right woman. Her love was horses and she loved the farm. His mother decided that it was time for her to move into town and left Charlie and his new bride the farm. At first things were perfect, but then his wife started spending money. She needed a new wagon for her horses, then it was more money for more horses, then post and rail fence as the sheep fencing was dangerous, and soon Charlie's bank account began dwindling. When the money was not as forthcoming as she thought it should be, they would quarrel. She soon began to spend more time at distant horse competitions than she spent at home and it wasn't long before Charlie began to hear rumours that his wife was cheating. Charlie realized that his relationship was failing apart, he began to drink and eventually filed for divorce and that, according to Charlie, was when the trouble began. He was stunned and surprised to learn that she was claiming half of the farm. When the divorce finally ended, Charlie lost half of his savings and had to buy 25 percent of the farm. He didn't have the money and had to get a loan from the bank. Charlie struggled as he had no cushion and he began to drink to help him forget his woes. Between the drink and a few bad years he couldn't make the payments on the loan and the bank foreclosed on his farm. On the last day that he was supposed to vacate the premises he attempted suicide by putting his shotgun under his chin and pulling the trigger but somehow it had gone wrong and he hadn't died instantly or bled to death as he should have. The postman was delivering a package and had found him and called an ambulance which had saved his life. So here he was. He couldn't breathe very well, kept getting recurrent infections and pneumonias. He had lost an eye in the shooting so he was nearly blind, he was in constant pain, his livestock all sold, his farm repossessed, he had no money and no place to live. His last statement ... I have nothing, wouldn't you want to die?

INTRODUCTION

The mood disorders are a category of disorders that all have depression as the distinguishing feature. One of the primary criteria for the identification is a dysphoric mood characterized as depressed, sad, blue, hopeless, low or irritable (Wetzel, 1984). Everyone has moments when they feel a bit 'down' which can be caused by a number of factors and life circumstances. But when does feeling 'down' become a problem? We will all experience a time in our lives when things aren't going as well as we want: stressful job, financial difficulties, interpersonal relationship difficulties with partners, family and friends, but the expectation is that these will be transitory, and the depressive feelings will pass within a relatively short span of time.

What about when we are grieving? Situational depression usually lasts longer than a normal depression and although we feel the loss, it reflects good reality testing. All is not hopeless and with time people recover and move forwards with their lives. Again, time is a factor as well as the intimacy felt towards the lost loved one. A close relationship will take longer to mourn than a relationship with a casual friend or distant family member.

Clinical depression is grossly out of proportion to any life event and affects cognitive and psychomotor processes. It is diagnosed according to its severity. In depression the primary mood is one of sadness or apathy; whereas in mania, euphoria or irritability predominates. Affect is used to connote emotional feeling and the outward manifestations of that feeling (Blatt, 2004).

Individuals suffering from affective disorders manifest a variety of other signs and symptoms in addition to the abnormality of mood. The mood disorders encompass a diverse range of syndromes reflecting a variety of states (Freidman & Anderson, 2010).

The aetiology of depression is not specifically known and given the many forms of depression it is likely that a number of factors are involved. It must also be recognized that some of these factors may interact with each other. This chapter will discuss the various theories associated with the aetiology of affective disorders.

PREVALENCE

Depression is a critical problem of personal and social significance. It is the third most common psychiatric disorder in the UK, with two-thirds of adults experiencing a level of severity of depressed mood to interfere with their daily lives (Mitchell & Vaze, 2009). Singleton et al. (2001) found that in the year 2000 the prevalence rate for depression among those between 16–74 years of age was 2.5 percent. Moussavi et al. (2007) in a WHO study found a prevalence rate for depression of 23 percent in people with two or more chronic physical disorders whereas depression was reported at 3.2 percent in healthy controls.

HISTORY

Literary descriptions of clinical depression have been documented in early historical documents in various civilizations. The first person to formally describe depression was Hippocrates. He coined the term melancholia which referred to a pathological form of despondency that he attributed to a condition where the individual had an excess of black bile. Several centuries later Artaeus, who was trained in the Hippocratic tradition, decided that if black bile moved upwards to the stomach it caused melancholy as a result of the production of flatulence which sent rumbling wind downward, disturbing the understanding. He was also the first to recognize that melancholia and mania could occur in the same individual (Millon & Davis, 1996).

In the 1800s Falret described a type of circular insanity in detail; the clinical syndrome he depicted is very similar to what we would now call bipolar illness. Kraepelin in his evaluation of various types of mental illness separated the major functional psychiatric syndromes into dementia praecox and manic-depressive psychosis. He made this distinction chiefly on the basis of outcome; patients with dementia praecox nearly always had a chronic downhill course, whereas those with manic-depressive illness tended to recover. Dementia praecox would later be called schizophrenia but his terminology for bipolar disorder would remain with many physicians and researchers for years to come who were uncertain as to whether this was an illness of psychosis or depression (Millon & Davis, 1996).

Freud adopted a very different view of depression and outlined his theory of the psychodynamic basis of depression. Freud believed that the predisposition for depression was a depression-prone personality that had resulted from unresolved earlier losses during childhood and was a combination of oral and anal characteristics. The precipitating event for depression would be the loss of a love object that would trigger the feelings of depression in the depressive-prone personality. During childhood, earlier losses and the threatened withdrawal of parental support and affection were incorporated early on into one's own ego where they remained. When a loss occurred in adulthood there was an over-identification with the lost loved one, unconscious hatred for the lost loved one and then depression would become hatred turned inwards and directed against one's own ego (Erwin, 2002).

Freud believed that depressive episodes within and across individuals share a common set of characteristics, originate from a common cause and respond to one type of treatment. This is contrasted with a multidimensional perspective that would later be developed under cognitive and behavioural theorists (Erwin, 2002).

The development in the late 1930s of electroconvulsive therapy constituted a major breakthrough in the treatment of both depression and mania and expanded the idea that depression was not unidimensional. The conceptual explanations of depression began to shift from analytic to biological models. In the late 1950s the first effective antidepressant drugs were introduced, followed a decade later by lithium carbonate, the first specific anti-manic medication. This resulted in an enormous increase in research seeking to identify biological and genetic factors associated with the aetiology and treatment of the disorder as well as the psychological and interpersonal aspects (Millon & Davis, 1996).

CLINICAL FEATURES

Depression is defined as a persistent and deviant lowering of mood and/or a loss of interest in usual activities, accompanied by a variety of distinctive signs and symptoms. The depressed mood differs from normal sadness or unhappiness by its inappropriateness to the situation, intensity, duration and the effect it has on the life of the person who is experiencing it so that it interferes with normal living. The signs and symptoms of depression can be divided into four distinct groups: affective, cognitive, somatic and behavioural (Blatt, 2010). Table 10.1 summarizes the various symptoms under the four headings.

Table 10.1   Symptoms of depression

Affective symptoms	Lowered mood	Nervousness
	Sad feelings	Self-blame
	Apathy	Guilt
	Anhedonia	Irritability
	Anxiety	Poor reality testing
Cognitive symptoms	Difficulty concentrating	Indecisiveness
	Worthlessness	Hopelessness
	Helplessness	Never recover
Behavioural symptoms	Neglect personal appearance	Change in style of dress
	Neglect personal hygiene	Social withdrawal
	Psychomotor retardation	Difficulty with conversations
	Agitation	Tension
	Physical hyperactivity	Restlessness
Somatic symptoms	Sleep disturbance	Change in appetite
	Change in weight	Gastrointestinal complaints
	Constipation	Dry mouth
	Loss of libido	Menstrual irregularity
	Headache	Aches and pains

AFFECTIVE SYMPTOMS

The most prominent feature of depression is the abnormally lowered mood. These feelings are associated with crying or a feeling of wanting to cry but being unable to do so. Other feelings are apathy (not caring any more) and anhedonia (inability to derive satisfaction from activities). Most depressed individuals have feelings of anxiety, nervousness or irritability and may experience feelings of self-blame, worthlessness and guilt that are disproportionate to reality and irrational often referred to as poor reality testing (Blatt, 2010).

The affective feelings may fluctuate and be worse at certain times of the day with the majority of individuals feeling worse in the early morning hours than evening. This fluctuation is referred to as diurnal variation and implies that normal biological rhythms may be disturbed in some cases (Blatt, 2010).

COGNITIVE SYMPTOMS

A variety of cognitive changes or abnormal thinking is present in depression. Difficulty concentrating, indecisiveness and not thinking clearly are common elements.

Individuals often believe that only 'bad' things will happen, they frequently feel helpless and unable or unwilling to take any action that could improve their situation.

Feelings of self-blame, worthlessness, hopelessness and helplessness become so severe that they take on a delusional quality. Depressed individuals frequently believe that they will never recover and they will spend the rest of their lives depressed and unhappy (Beck & Alford, 2008).

BEHAVIOURAL SYMPTOMS

Individuals with depression often display behavioural signs that are indications of their apathy and depressed mood. Often they neglect their personal appearance, change their style of dress to an unkempt look and some will neglect personal hygiene. Social withdrawal is common and in severe cases can lead to total isolation. Depressed individuals also have psychomotor retardation which refers to the slowing down of thoughts and physical activities. Conversations appear to be difficult, or at times impossible. In extreme cases psychomotor retardation can lead to depressive stupor where the individual is mute and does not move at all. Some individuals will display a slowing of behaviour while others become agitated. They experience anxiety, tension and/or restlessness associated with physical hyperactivity. In the milder forms individuals may fidget and have difficulty being still; more severely agitated individuals may wring their hands, pace or participate in other nervous types of behaviour (Martell, Dimidjian & Herman-Dunn, 2010).

SOMATIC SYMPTOMS

Somatic symptoms are common and include: sleep disturbance, change in appetite and weight, gastrointestinal complaints, constipation, dry mouth, heavy feelings in the abdomen, loss of libido. Women may experience menstrual irregularity, aches and pains, tingling or numbness in the extremities or headache, and they often have many different somatic or hypochondriacal concerns with some bordering on the delusional (Blatt, 2010).

MODELS/THEORIES

Psychoanalytic model

Freud emphasized the dominant role of the loss of self-esteem in depression. He proposed that depression resulted from a symbolic loss and not necessarily the actual loss of a loved object. He proposed that the withdrawal of love and support by a significant figure during a crucial stage in development predisposes an individual to depression later in life. When this withdrawal of love occurs during the oral stage of psychosexual development, the individual becomes fixated at that stage of development and tends, as an adult, to become very dependent on other people, as well as to seek oral types of gratification. The depressed individual redirects feelings of hostility that they had previously felt towards the lost person or love object and instead, channels that anger towards themselves. A number of psychoanalysts have made further contributions to this premise and emphasized that the loss of self-esteem in depression usually results in a consciously perceived discrepancy between an individual's desires and reality. Although Freud made major contributions to the understanding of depression, the explanations did not apply to the various types of depression, for example depressed individuals may direct anger towards others rather than themselves (Erwin, 2002).

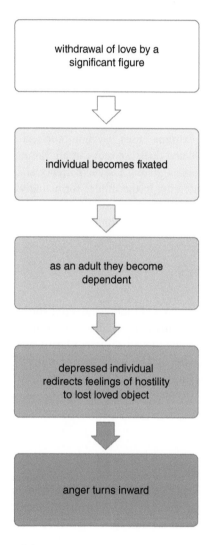

Figure 10.1   Psychoanalytic model

Social model

The major premise is that psychological factors interact with environmental conditions causing depression. Each individual will react within their environment to situational events and most will adapt. When an individual is unable to adapt either as a result of a lack of resources or innate ability, depression is the result. For example, unemployment may make it difficult for a person to obtain what they need from their environment. If there is an added element such as low socioeconomic status, they may have also been denied the opportunity to further their education, increasing the likelihood that they will have a difficult time gaining employment. The environment may further complicate the picture by going into a recession so that all job opportunities in the area are further eroded; they become depressed because of their feelings of helplessness and hopelessness. The social model emphasizes the importance of the relationship between the social environment and the likelihood of developing depression and loss of self-esteem when expectations are not fulfilled (Goldberg & Huxley, 1991).

Behavioural model

Behaviourists have sought to understand depression by attempting to quantify and analyse the observable behaviours of individuals who exhibit depressive symptoms and relate them to causal behaviours. Behaviourists believe that at the core of depression is a decrease in the rate of the response-contingent reinforcement. An individual becomes depressed as a direct result of not being able to obtain sufficient satisfaction from their environment or positive reinforcement for actions and behaviours. This could be as a consequence of a variety of factors, such as decreased participation in pleasurable activities, a tendency to rate the pleasantness of activities lower than non-depressed individuals, inadequate social skills and/or living in an unfavourable environment that does not provide positive reinforcement (Martell, Dimidjian & Herman-Dunn, 2010).

An alternative approach is that depression is the analysis of the precipitants and consequences of depressed feelings and behaviour. Individuals learn to exacerbate their feelings in certain conditions that are then reinforced by the environment. Some behaviour theorists feel that depressed individuals characteristically fail to perform behaviours that would elicit positive feedback behaviours that would elicit positive feedback from their environment. This lack of support from others may tend to make the depressed individual feel more depressed which leads to further withdrawal and a vicious cycle (Martell, Dimidjian & Herman-Dunn, 2010).

Cognitive model

The cognitive model of depression views the disorder as a multidimensional problem composed of a complex pattern of responses with a multiplicity of causes. Individuals with depression display abnormal patterns of thinking. These include tendencies towards low self-esteem, excessive self-criticism, frequent self-commands and exaggerated concepts of responsibility. Although there are many different elements to the cognitive model all assume that the main cause of depression is the individual's negative thinking or cognition patterns and that these are the basis of the affective and motivational symptoms that are present in depression (Beck, Rush, Shaw & Emery, 1979).

Beck (1991) hypothesized that the depression-prone person developed a depressive schemata in childhood and adolescence as a result of traumatic events, repeated negative events, the judgements of others or imitation of depressive models. A normal cognitive schema is a generalization about a particular domain of experience that organizes information and incorporates it into the individual's belief system as well as selectively categorizing new information into the schema. The schema then determines how that information is to be perceived, coded and organized for storage in memory and subsequent recall. Therefore, the depressive schemata was a compilation of negative events and situations that the individual believes involve real or potential losses of personal attributes, relationships with others, objects, goals or ideals that the person considers to be pertinent to their happiness and/or self worth. When an individual encounters a negative event it further strengthens the depressive schema resulting in a circular feedback system. The cognitive schema is evaluated in terms of what Beck called the cognitive triad, which is the individual's view of themselves, the world and their future. Depressed individuals have a negative view of themselves, perceive their worlds as permeated by the experience of loss and have negative expectations about future events.

Seligman's (1975) learned helpless model characterized depression as the individual's negative perception of behaviour that resulted from negative expectations. The individual's belief system was that neither positive nor negative events were contingent on behaviour and there was a high expectation that negative events were highly probable or likely to occur and the individual was helpless. Individuals would then develop an expectation that future events would also be out of the individual's control at which point a depressive affect would develop as well as apathy. The source of the depressive paradox would be simultaneous self-blame and a belief in personal helplessness.

Abramson (1982) believed that depressed affect was proportional to the importance of the expected negative event and the person's certainty that the event would occur. Since helplessness is a necessary correlate of pronounced hopelessness, intensely depressed affect would be accompanied by intense cognitive and motivational deficits. A person attributing helplessness to causes that are relatively stable or unlikely to change produces longer-lasting expectations of future helplessness than attributions to less stable causes, because the person will expect a stable cause to be functioning which causes helplessness to continue for an indefinite period. Attributions that are relatively global or general lead to more generalized motivational and cognitive deficits than attributions to more specific causes, since a person is likely to expect a more general cause to produce future helplessness in a wider variety of situations.

Biochemical model

A variety of biochemical theories of depression have been proposed. However, no specific model has been found to be completely responsible for depression. Correlations between depth of depression and biological variables as well as inter-correlations between the physiological variables themselves remain low (Licinio & Wong, 2005). There are two main biochemical theories of depression: the catecholamine theory and the indoleamine theory (Deakin, 1986). The biochemical theories began in the 1940s when clinicians noticed that some drugs that were being used to treat tuberculosis appeared to elevate the patient's mood. Researchers began to examine what other drugs had this effect and what other clinical populations would benefit. They discovered that a drug called iproniazid reduced symptoms of psychotic depression in clinical populations. Iproniazid inhibits the activity of monoamine oxidase, an enzyme which destroys excess monoamine neurotransmitters within terminal buttons, increasing these neurotransmitters in the synapse. Further evidence that supported the theory came from the drug reserpine. This drug was found to be effective in the 1950s for treating high blood pressure, but caused severe depression in patients. After investigating these side effects it was found that reserpine depleted the brain of catecholamines. These findings led Schildkraut to publish his paper on his theory of the catecholamine theory of depression. Schildkraut (1965) stated that depression was the result of reduced neurotransmission of catecholamines, particularly noradrenaline, at certain synaptic sites in the brain. One major criticism of this theory was that it underestimated the importance of serotonin in clinical depression.

The indoleamine theory of depression

The critical evaluation of the catecholamine theory led researchers to look specifically at the neurotransmitter serotonin. There are several different lines of evidence that indicate that depression is affected by levels of serotonin (Wichers & Maes, 2004). This is referred to as the indoleamine hypothesis of depression. The main evidence comes from the effectiveness of selective serotonin re-uptake inhibitors in lifting clinical depression. Serotonin's action in the synapses is terminated by re-uptake of the neurotransmitter by the presynaptic cell. The selective serotonin re-uptake inhibitors stop serotonin from being removed from the postsynaptic membrane. The removal of transmitter substance stops its effect on the postsynaptic membrane, keeping more serotonin active and allowing it to have a greater effect. Just as an increase in serotonin decreases depressive symptoms, the removal of selective serotonin re-uptake inhibitors decreases serotonin levels and increases depressive symptoms (Anderson, 2000).

Reward system

The reward system of the brain contains various brain structures that are involved in the regulation and control of pleasure and external stimuli. It functions as a positive reinforcing feedback system and was discovered by Olds and Milner in 1954. The system is composed of neural structures located in the medial forebrain bundle and periventricular areas of the central nervous system (CNS) which are innervated by noradrenergic and dopaminergic fibres that provide numerous connections with the arousal system in the reticular formation of the brain stem. There are also pathways to both the psychomotor system and the stress-neuroendocrine system, particularly the hypothalamic-pituitary-adrenal axis. The system has a common pathway which is the culmination of various processes converging in areas that modulate arousal, mood, motivation and psychomotor function utilizing dopamine as the main neurotransmitter that is most active in these regions. The premise is that depression results when the interaction of several factors such as genetic vulnerability, developmental events, social support, physiological stressors and personality characteristics as well as the reward system do not produce a positive reinforcement contingent (Akiskal & McKinney, 1973, 1975). This explains how a disruption of normal functioning in the reward system can result in a range of diverse effects involving arousal endocrine function and psychomotor activity.

Genetics

Research indicates that affective disorders appear to have a genetic basis and affective disorders tend to run in families. The morbidity risk of developing a major depression for first-degree biological relatives of persons with unipolar depression is 28 percent compared to 9 percent for the general population (Cadoret & Winokur, 1975; Merikangas, 1990). The average concordance rate for monozygotic twins in various studies is approximately 70 percent whereas the rate for dizygotic twins is approximately 20 percent (McGuffin, Rjsdijk, Andrew, Sham, Katz & Cardno, 2003; Schur et al., 2009). These studies support the premise that environmental factors do play an important role in the development of affective disorders although genetics and biological factors result in higher vulnerability to mood disorders.

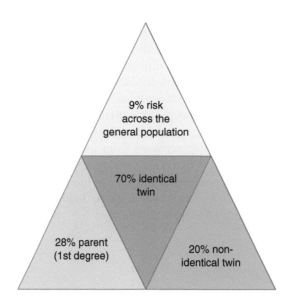

9% risk
across the
general population

70% identical
twin

28% parent
(1st degree)

20% non-
identical twin

Figure 10.2   Percentage of risk for unipolar depression

PSYCHOPHYSIOLOGY

A number of investigators have studied the electrical activity of the brain in affective disorders by the use of the electroencephalograph (EEG). Research has been conflicting in determining inconsistencies between depressed subjects and normals in most areas with the exception of the research in wake and sleep. Research in this area has revealed that depressed subjects take longer to fall asleep, have more spontaneous awakenings, have less stage 4 (deep sleep) and tend to wake earlier in the morning than normals (Steiger & Kimura, 2010).

Several investigators have studied evoked potentials in which the EEG changes in response to a stimulus such as a bright light or a loud noise are evaluated. Schizophrenic and bipolar depressed patients have both been shown to produce evoked potentials that are significantly different from normal; unipolar depressed patients do not appear to differ consistently from normals (Souza et al., 1995; Himani, Tandon & Bhatia, 1999).

The electromyograph (EMG) which measures the electrical activity of muscles has also been used to study depressed patients. Most investigators have reported a generalized increase in muscle tension in depression as measured by the EMG (Dimberg, 1990; Sloan, Bradley, Dimoulas & Lang, 2002). Schwartz et al. (1976) found that EMGs of the facial muscles of depressed patients frequently reflect an unhappy facial expression even when their faces do not appear sad to the observer.

CLASSIFICATION

Attempts to categorize subtypes of depression have been marred by controversy with the only major classification unanimously accepted being the bipolar–unipolar distinction. Rosenthal and Klerman (1967) have divided the various conceptual viewpoints of unipolar depression into three groups: the unitary, the dualistic and the pluralistic. The unitary view posits that depressive episodes within and across individuals are marked by a common set of characteristics (a syndrome) and a common aetiological pattern, and should respond to a particular treatment programme. The pluralistic viewpoint assumes that depressive episodes within and across individuals are multifaceted with a variety of variables, that require a variety of treatment. The dualistic viewpoint attempts to subcategorize unipolar depressives into three dichotomized groups. The relevant dimensions are: endogenous-reactive, psychotic-neurotic, and primary-secondary (Paykel, 2008).

The dichotomized distinction is useful to the degree that it reminds us that affective disorders are never the same in individuals and each person will present with different aetiologies, treatment and progression of the disorder. Most individuals will appear to lie intermediate on the continuum; few will be at the extremes.

The first dimension deals with depression that appears to be biologically based (endogenous depression) as opposed to those forms that seem to result from the person's interaction with his or her environment (reactive depression). Endogenous depression is considered a genetically based disorder which results primarily from biological factors. The physiological characteristics or symptoms are most prominent, although they will be accompanied by other characteristics. Endogenous depression usually requires hospitalization and is characterized by progressively severe symptoms that are primarily vegetative in nature. Endogenous individuals tend to respond positively to the somatic therapies such as antidepressant medications and electroconvulsive therapy (ECT). Reactive depression, on the other hand occurs in response to external events, and may be characterized by any of the identifying factors in depression. Reactive depression is thought to be more responsive to psychosocial interventions. Endogenous and exogenous have differential responses to treatment. Traditional forms of psychotherapy are essentially useless in cases of endogenous depression (Caspar, 2003).

The second dimension in the dualistic viewpoint is the distinction between psychotic and neurotic depression. Neurotic depressions are presumed to be reactive to traumatic environmental circumstances involving loss. Psychotic depressions are usually thought of as endogenous, although there are probably instances in which reactive depressions assume psychotic proportions. The term psychotic depression is best used to describe a depression characterized by disordered reality testing, which is usually manifested by hallucinations or delusions. In contrast the neurotic depression reflects good reality testing, appears relatively mild, is characterized by intrapsychic conflict and is usually precipitated by an environmental stressor (Paykel, 2008).

The third dimension in the dualistic viewpoint is the primary vs. secondary depression. This distinction was originally proposed by Robins and Guze (1972), who defined a primary depression as a type of mood disorder that occurs in an individual who has had no previous psychiatric disorders, with the exception of mania or a prior episode of depression. The secondary dimension was defined as a mood disorder that has been preceded at some time in the individual's life by a non-affective mental disorder, for example obsessive-compulsive disorder. This distinction has considerable clinical utility, for example a schizophrenic individual who becomes depressed is likely to be very different from an individual with primary depression. Individuals with depression secondary to some other condition might not necessarily differ from primary depressives.

BIPOLAR AFFECTIVE DISORDER

This disorder is characterized by depression with the pathognomonic presence of elevated or irritable mood (mania). At least one episode of mania must occur in order for a diagnosis of bipolar to be given. The clinical picture of a manic episode can vary but it generally contains three cardinal symptoms: elevated mood, flight of ideas and psychomotor overactivity. Individuals generally have a mixed presentation of what is called 'cycling', which consists of an episode of depression, a normal state and then a manic or hypomanic phase with the individual returning to normality and the cycle resumes. Individuals are different in terms of cycling with some being rapid cyclers and others being extremely slow. The pattern within the cycle can also vary with manic phases being shorter or longer than the depressive episodes (Yatham & Maj, 2010).

The prevalence of the disorder is a gross approximation because this disorder is often misdiagnosed as unipolar depression until the individual has the presence of a manic phase. Therefore, the data on lifetime prevalence currently suggest a figure near 1 percent in the general population (Merikangas et al., 2010). This figure is considerably lower than the reported rates for unipolar disorder.

The depressive element of bipolar disorder is similar to the depressive states experienced in unipolar depression with some subtle differences. Kraepelin (1921) was the first individual to separate the categories of depression according to severity and documented the element of mania into his groupings. The resulting groups were: melancholia simplex, stupor, melancholia gravis, paranoid melancholia, fantastic melancholia and delirious melancholia. The first three classifications are characteristic of what we typically diagnose today as unipolar depression. The classification of melancholia gravis is typically classified as schizoaffective disorder. His last two categories are more characteristic of symptoms often seen in bipolar disorder with elements that classified it as a psychosis rather than a neurosis (Kraepelin, 1921).

Kraepelin documented that the individuals he classified as dementia praecox regressed and did not recover while the individuals that he classified as having psychotic types of melancholia did not regress and would eventually recover. As a result of the element of psychosis, bipolar affective disorder was often categorized as a 'functional psychosis'; it was not attributed to physical conditions, and the person did not degenerate. Rather they were able to function relatively normally in between these psychotic episodes and often remained relatively intact during their psychosis (Yatham & Maj, 2010).

Although the depression in bipolar disorder appears similar to unipolar depression, there are slight differences. Bipolar individuals typically have minimal anger, few somatic complaints, more hypersomnia and display more psychomotor retardation. In contrast unipolar depressed individuals appear to have more anger directed at self or others, present more frequently with multiple somatic complaints as part of their depression, experience hyposomnia, and have higher levels of psychomotor agitation (Detre et al., 1972; Beigel & Murphy, 1971).

The episodes of mania are the defining characteristic of bipolar disorder and are divided by severity into hypomania and mania. Hypomania is characterized by the loss of ability for goal-directed work and incapacity to complete a definite series of thoughts. The rate of thought production is accelerated but derailment does not occur. The mood is cheerful, but irritability may appear at the slightest provocation. Self-confidence is high and actions may be impulsive. Psychomotor activity is increased with characteristic energy. Speech rate may be minimally increased and the individual is often verbose and bombastic (Grieco & Edwards, 2010).

Mania is usually preceded by a period of hypomanic signs and symptoms and gradually increases in severity. It has a number of characteristic signs and symptoms that are different from hypomania in quality. Individuals in acute mania are extremely physically active and report boundless energy. Generally the activity is purposeful in nature and if the individual was involved in creative activity the production will be increased. Manic individuals are unusually socially active in a variety of other ways such as joining clubs and organizations, calling old friends at odd hours of the day or night and generally acting in an intrusive, demanding and domineering manner (Goodwin & Jamison, 1996).

Individuals in a manic phase are nearly always more talkative than usual, frequently speaking very rapidly, and tend to keep on talking without making normal pauses (pressure of speech). They exhibit what is called 'flight of ideas', the tendency to jump from one topic to another, although a logical connection between the thoughts is usually apparent to the observer (in contrast to the idiosyncratic speech characteristics of schizophrenia). Individuals in a manic phase can become easily

Table 10.2   Characteristic signs and symptoms of mania

Increased activity	Boundless energy
	Physical hyperactivity
	Extreme socialization/sociability
Talkativeness	Speak rapidly
	Pressure of speech
	Interrupt others
	Increased volume of speech
Flight of ideas	Jumping from one topic to the next
	Puns and playful use of words
	Easily distracted by external stimuli
	Rapid change of topics
Inflated self-esteem	Grandiosity
	Unusual abilities
Decreased need for sleep	Sleep disturbances
	Decreased total sleep time
	Early morning awakenings
Poor judgement/lack of insight	Does not recognize any problems of behaviour
	Unable to realize consequences

distracted by external stimuli and may change their topic of conversation based on random stimulation. Individuals also display inflated self-esteem and believe that they have unusual abilities. They often display poor judgement and lack of insight, becoming involved in activities without recognizing the high potential for negative consequences, for example buying sprees, stealing, and sexual indiscretions are common during this phase. The manic individual characteristically has no insight into the nature of their illness; they are elated when they are allowed to do what they want and become angry and frustrated when they are prevented (Marneros & Goodwin, 2005). See Table 10.2 for a list of characteristic signs and symptoms of mania.

Age of onset

Bipolar illness typically has a young age of onset, but rarely appears after the age of 60. When contrasted to unipolar depression, bipolar disorder has a mean age of onset between 8 to 15 years earlier than unipolar illness and has more limited age of risk. When contrasted with schizophrenia, the mean age of onset of the two illnesses is similar but the variance is much greater in bipolar disorder (Clayton, 1981).

Course and prognosis

Research is only available from individuals under treatment. For most individuals recurrences averaged approximately seven, and subsequent episodes recur at increasingly shorter intervals. The disorder is chronic in nature for the majority of individuals and continuous psychiatric or social disability is not uncommon (Goldberg, Harrow & Grossman, 1995).

Aetiology

Genetic factors and biochemical characteristics of the disorder appear to be the predominant theory, although a specific CNS structure or biochemical abnormality has not been discovered. Genetic studies have indicated that monozygotic bipolar twins had a concordance rate of approximately 70 percent, while the concordance rate for unipolar illness was 40 percent (Smoller & Finn, 2003). In dizygotic bipolar twins the concordance rate was approximately 15 percent versus 10 percent for unipolar twins, indicating an element of environmental factors (Taylor, Faraone & Tsuang, 2003). The research indicates that psychopathology in the biological parents of the bipolar-affected adoptees was in excess of that found in their respective adoptive parents. Also, the frequency of affective illness in the biological parents of the affected adoptees was no different from that found in the parents of non-adopted bipolar patients. Thus, these investigators concluded that the results support the major importance of genetic factors in the aetiology of bipolar illness and placed less importance on environmental factors (Taylor, Faraone & Tsuang, 2003).

Another area of research that has been investigated is the disproportionate number of ill females among affectively ill relatives and the absence of father–son transmission, which suggests an X-linked mode of transmission for bipolar illness. Accepting this hypothesis, several investigators have proceeded to study the linkage of various known markers on the X-chromosome and bipolar illness (Baron & Risch, 1987). An X-linked locus of the gene on the X-chromosome would allow a depressive disorder to be transmitted to female offspring by either or both parents, but to males only by the mother. Theoretically, father-to-son inheritance of the trait should not occur. The results of this hypothesis have not been supported; perhaps it is because the female relatives of bipolar patients are more likely to exhibit symptoms of a unipolar rather than bipolar disorder, or the frequency of their manic episodes.

Treatment

The treatment for bipolar depression is lithium carbonate, a metallic element which has been found to be therapeutically useful in controlling the manic phase. There is a differential response to lithium therapy with bipolar having a good response in contrast to unipolars (Prien et al., 1973; Tohen et al., 2003).

POSTPARTUM DEPRESSION

This disorder is characterized by either depressed mood or decreased interest in pleasurable activities as well as disturbances in sleep, appetite and cognition for more than two weeks after the birth of a child. Women with postpartum depression are excessively emotionally labile, i.e. cry more easily than usual or are more irritable than usual. Onset generally occurs within four weeks after delivery which corresponds to the rapid hormonal changes that are hypothesized to contribute to a vulnerability to the disorder. However because psychosocial factors also contribute to triggering the disorder many clinicians and researchers use a working definition of the postpartum period as lasting up to six months after delivery (Delatte et al., 2009).

Postpartum depression must be distinguished from the 'baby blues', which occur in the majority of new mothers. In this syndrome, symptoms such as weeping, sadness, irritability, anxiety and confusion occur, peaking around the fourth day after delivery, and resolving by the tenth day whereas postpartum depression generally does not resolve itself without treatment. Untreated postpartum depression can have long-term adverse effects. For the mother, the episode can be the precursor for recurrent depression. For the infant, a mother's ongoing depression can contribute to emotional, behavioural, cognitive and interpersonal problems later in life (Gjerdingen, 2007).

Symptoms can include despondent mood, feelings of inadequacy as a parent, sleep and appetite disturbances and impaired concentration. The patterns of symptoms in women with postpartum depression are very similar to women with major depression. The sleep disturbance is usually characterized by difficulty sleeping even when the infant is asleep and others have offered to care for the infant. Psychological difficulties include: poor interactions between mother and infant, stress and anxiety, bonding difficulties, infants' increased risk of insecure attachments, family discord, loss of income and placement of children outside of the home environment (Marcus, 2009).

Postpartum depression is believed to occur in 15 percent of women after delivery. Postpartum depression causes difficulty in infant bonding and caregiving. Women who have had postpartum depression with the birth of their first child are at 25 percent greater risk for a recurrence with the following births (Marcus, 2009; Pearlstein et al., 2009).

Risk factors include a history of major depression, a history of premenstrual dysphoric disorder, psychosocial stress and inadequate social support. The predisposition to develop postpartum depression is unrelated to psychiatric history, environmental stressors, cultural context, breastfeeding or the birthing process. The likelihood of developing postpartum depression does not appear to be related to a woman's educational level, sex of the infant, the mode of delivery or whether the infant was breast-fed (Pearlstein et al., 2009).

A high percentage of women with postpartum depression have ego-dystonic thoughts of harming their infants. The term ego-dystonic refers to thoughts that are at marked variance with what a person actually desires or believes. These thoughts are obessional in quality and are rarely acted upon in the absence of psychosis. However, when a woman with severe postpartum depression becomes suicidal, she may also consider killing her infant and young children, usually not out of anger but stemming from a desire not to abandon her children (Friedman, 2009).

In terms of aetiology, there are two major hypotheses concerning postpartum depression. The first is that the mood changes occur from abrupt hormonal withdrawal. Supporting evidence includes the finding that absolute levels of oestrogens and progesterone are unrelated to postpartum blues, but the greater the change between pregnancy and postpartum levels, the greater the likelihood of developing postpartum depression. In addition the progesterone metabolite is lower in women with postpartum depression (Green et al., 2009).

A second hypothesis is that postpartum blues occur from the activation of a biological system underlying mammalian mother–infant attachment behaviour regulated primarily by the hormone oxytocin (Skrundz et al., 2011). There is direct evidence for this effect in non-primate mammals; rodent mothers whose oxytocin-producing cells have been removed exhibit significantly less maternal behaviour than rodents in the control group (Cox et al., 2011). Indirect evidence suggests similar, but more versatile, mechanisms in humans and other primates. Under conditions of ample support and low stress, these neurophysiological changes promoted attachment between mothers and infants. However, under conditions of high stress and inadequate support, this emotional reactivity may increase vulnerability to depression by rendering a woman more susceptible to stress (Brunton, 2008).

Baby blues	Postpartum depression
• onset –24 hours after delivery resolving by the 10th day • weeping, sadness, irritability, anxiety and confusion	• onset – within 4 weeks of delivery – can last up to 6 months • does not resolve itself without treatment • emotionally labile • sleep and appetite disturbances • patterns similar to major depression

Figure 10.3

An effective assessment for postpartum depression is the Edinburgh Postnatal Depression Scale (Cox, Holden & Sagovsky, 1987). This is a 10-item questionnaire that has proved to be an effective screening tool. The severity of symptoms and the preferences of the individual influence the recommendations for psychotherapy and/or antidepressants. Antidepressants are effective for postpartum depression; while there are no absolute contra-indications to using antidepressant medications during pregnancy or lactation there is also no specific approval. In addition, data are needed about long-term physical and mental development in infants exposed to antidepressants through breastfeeding as well as prenatally. In terms of therapy, cognitive behavioural therapy has been used successfully in treating postpartum depression (Cuijpers et al., 2008; Logsdon et al., 2009; Meltzer-Brody, 2011).

CYCLOTHYMIC DISORDER

This disorder is characterized as a chronic but milder form of bipolar mood disorder which has alternating episodes of mild depression and hypomania separated by short periods of normal mood. Often the hypomania is described as euphoria and/or excitement and is difficult to distinguish from the upbeat types of moods in individuals who do not have cyclothymic disorder. Individuals with cyclothymia are never free of symptoms of either depression or hypomania for more than two months at a time. This disorder has a similar course to that of bipolar disorder with similar longitudinal course, family history and treatment response. Approximately 15–50 percent may go on to develop bipolar disorder (Cassano et al., 1999; Depue et al., 1981; Howland & Thase, 1993; Klein, Depue, & Slater, 1986; Shen, Alloy, Abramson, & Grandin, 2008).

Cyclothymic disorder is disruptive as individuals have a continual fluctuation of mood and can rapidly cycle on a daily basis. Individuals with the disorder are often unable to maintain interpersonal relationships, have sleep difficulties especially during hypomanic phases that alternate with oversleeping during depressive episodes. Self-medication with alcohol or illegal drugs is common (Howland & Thase, 1993).

The causes of cyclothymic disorder are unknown but because it is similar to bipolar it is thought that this mood disorder shares a similar aetiology. Lifetime prevalence rates are reported to be 2.4 percent but true estimates are difficult since many individuals may be undiagnosed or misdiagnosed as having other mood disorders because the hypomanic phase does not appear to be that unusual or remarkable (Merikangas et al., 2007). Genetic factors appear to be causative in cyclothymia as they do in bipolar disorders. Cyclothymia, like bipolar disorder, often occurs together in families. Cyclothymia usually begins early in life and appears to be equally common in men as in women. The age of onset for this disorder is early, generally beginning during adolescence or young adulthood (Howland & Thase, 1993).

Treatment is similar to bipolar and includes medication and psychotherapy. Individuals with cyclothymia may not respond to medications as strongly as individuals with bipolar disorder and lithium has also been found to be effective with some individuals with cyclothymic disorders (Baldessarini, Vazqeuz & Tondo, 2011).

DYSTHYMIA

Dysthymic disorder is characterized by a chronic depressed mood most of the time for at least two years. Dysthymia is diagnosed if the individual does not meet all the qualifications for a major depressive disorder and there is no evidence of hypomanic, manic, mixed episodes or psychotic disorder. In addition the disorder is not the consequence of a pre-existing, chronic, non-mood disorder or a chronic physical illness and not due to medication or illegal drug or alcohol use. The onset is typically in childhood, adolescence or early adulthood and for this reasons this disorder is often referred to as a depressive personality. In children the mood may be irritable rather than depressed and the required minimum duration is only one year rather than two for adolescents, young adults and adults. It is not uncommon for an individual to have dysthymic disorder in childhood and then later develop a major depressive episode as an adult (Moch, 2011).

In adults the disorder causes significant distress and/or impairment in social, occupation or other important areas of functioning. In childhood and adolescence it is associated with impaired school performance, poor attendance and poor social interaction. In addition, children and adolescents are usually irritable and angry as well as depressed, with low self-esteem and poor social skills. Social and or/occupational impairment in persons with dysthymia is usually mild to moderate. Another characteristic of this disorder that often makes it difficult to diagnose is that it often co-occurs with other disorders such as substance-related disorders, anxiety disorders and eating disorders. In children it is associated with attention-deficit hyperactivity disorder, conduct disorder and learning disorders (Brieger & Marneros, 1997).

Prevalence rates for this disorder have been reported as approximately 6 percent in the general population, with females two to three times more likely to develop this disorder than males. It appears to be more common among first-degree relatives of people with major clinical depression than the general population (Ryder et al., 2006). Treatment consists of medication and therapy with studies reporting good efficacy for antidepressant medication (Kevkovitz, Tedeschini & Papakostas, 2011).

SEASONAL AFFECTIVE DISORDER

Historically individuals believed that a depressed mood was caused by lack of sunlight. Aretaeus advised placing individuals who were suffering from lethargy to be placed in direct sunlight because their disease was about gloom (Porter, 2002).

Seasonal affective disorder is characterized by winter depression with remission in the spring and summer with symptoms of depression, anxiety, fatigue, lowered motivation, hypersomnia, increased appetite and weight, irritability, increased sleep duration, appetite changes, craving for foods high in carbohydrates, difficulty concentrating and reduced sociability (Boyce, 2011). Research in seasonal affective disorder has been plagued by inconsistent diagnostic criteria, although it appears to be more common in women than men. Females are four times more likely to develop seasonal affective disorder, although men tend to have more severe symptoms when the disorder is present (Lurie et al., 2006).

Seasonal affective disorder is more common in geographical areas distant from the Equator, probably due to decreased sunlight during the winter and longer days in the summer (Steinhousen, Gundelfinger & Metzke, 2009). Rosen et al. (1996) found an increasing prevalence of seasonal affective disorder across four locations moving progressively north. Mersch et al. (1999) also found a positive correlation between seasonal affective disorder and latitude of residence. Seasonal affective disorder may begin at any age, but the main age of onset is between 18 and 30 years. Other risk factors include having a family history of seasonal affective disorder which indicates the possibility of having inherited specific gene combinations that place individuals at higher risk (Boyce, 2011). McClung (2007) found that the presence of certain combinations of genes involved in the function of the circadian clock increased the risk of developing seasonal affective disorder by 25 percent.

Seasonal affective disorder also appears to occur along a severity continuum so some individuals are more affected than others. Beauchemin & Hays (1996) found that individuals suffering from depression who were admitted to sunny rooms had shorter lengths of stay than those situated in dull rooms. Partonen & Lönnqvist (2000) found that office workers who received light therapy experienced improved mood and vitality whether or not they had rated themselves as having seasonal changes in well-being. Avery et al. (2001) administered light therapy in a work situation to 30 individuals who were mildly affected with seasonal affective disorder and found that it improved mood, energy, alertness and productivity.

The physiology of SAD is based on neurotransmitter function and that mammals use changes in day length to detect seasonal changes, which in turn regulate seasonal behaviours. Although the exact mechanism of SAD is unknown and probably multi-factorial, substantial data suggests a dysfunction in normal circadian rhythms (McClung, 2007).

Seasonal light variation has been shown to affect several hormones and neurotransmitters including melatonin, serotonin, norepinephrine and dopamine. These hormones and neurotransmitters exhibit a diurnal secretion, with the catecholamines norepinephrine, epinephrine and dopamine peaking in the morning and the indoleamine melatonin peaking in the evening. Serotonin generally peaks mid-day. This daytime variation plays a significant role in levels of arousal and alertness between daytime and night. Thus, balancing the rhythm of these hormones and neurotransmitters is important in the regulation of the normal circadian rhythm (Lavoe et al., 2009).

Low levels of serotonin are associated with clinical depression and it also plays a role in the regulation of appetite, sleep, muscle contraction, memory and learning. Reduced sunlight can cause a drop in serotonin, which may lead to SAD. Research has shown that serotonin production is directly related to the prevailing duration of bright sunlight and rises with increased luminosity. Turnover of serotonin by the brain was lowest in winter. In addition low levels of tryptophan, which in turn causes low levels of serotonin, increase carbohydrate cravings, which is a symptom related to seasonal affective disorder (Lam et al., 2006). Virk et al. (2010) found that a reduction in catecholamine levels could induce a relapse in individuals who were previously in remission during the summer months indicating that catecholamines play a significant role in seasonal affective disorder.

Other explanations for seasonal affective disorder have been related to melatonin. Melatonin is a hormone secreted from the pineal gland which plays a significant role in circadian rhythms and can affect sleep patterns and mood. In seasonal affective disorder, the timing of the secretion of melatonin is altered, showing a phase delay, and changes in the onset, duration and offset of secretion. Studies have found that melatonin secretion is abnormal in individuals with seasonal affective disorder and that these individuals respond to changes in seasons by secreting melatonin longer in the winter months compared to healthy controls (Brown et al., 2010).

The most effective treatment of seasonal affective disorder has been with light therapy. Research has documented the efficacy of light therapy in seasonal affective disorder. Lewy et al. (1985) found that bright light was more effective when administered in the morning than in the evening, and stated that this supported the theory that seasonal affective disorder was a circadian phase delay. Dawn-simulating alarm clocks, that gradually illuminate over a 30–90-minute period while the individual remains asleep have proved to be effective in the treatment of seasonal affective disorder (Terman et al., 2000). Other studies have focused on melatonin supplementation to reduce depressive symptoms. One study indicated that treatment with agomelatine (melatonin receptor agonist) decreased symptoms of seasonal affective disorder in subjects (Pjrek et al., 2007). Antidepressants have been used in the treatment of seasonal affective disorder but their evidence of effectiveness is limited (Pjrek et al., 2007).

ASSESSMENT

A number of general psychological tests and specially developed rating scales have been developed for the assessment and diagnosing of depression. The following is a brief overview of various types of assessments.

Table 10.3   Examples of various assessments commonly used for depression

Personality tests	Minnesota Multiphasic Personality Inventory	Butcher, Dahlstrom, Graham, Tellegen & Kaemmer (1989)
	16PF	Cattell, Cattell, Cattell & Kelly (1999)
	Millon Clinical Multiaxial Inventory	Millon, Millon, Davis & Grossman (1997)
	Taylor-Johnson Temperament Analysis	Johnson, Taylor, Morrison, Morrison & Romoser (1966)
	Myers Briggs type indicator	Briggs, Myers, McCaulley, Quenk & Hammer (1998)
	Personality Assessment Inventory	Morey (2007)
Behavioural tests	Behavioral and emotional rating scale	Epstein (1998)
	Clinical assessment of behaviour	Bracken & Keith (2004)
	Behavioral and emotional screening system	Kamphaus & Reynolds (2007)
	Behavioral summary	Lachar & Gruber (1993)
Depression inventories	Beck Depression Inventory	Beck, Steer & Brown (1998)
	Beck Hopelessness Scale	Beck & Steer (1988)
	Postpartum Depression Screening Scale	Beck & Gable (2000)
	Hamilton depression inventory	Reynolds & Koback (1995)
	Hamilton Rating Scale for Depression	Warren (1994)
	Reynolds depression screening inventory	Reynolds & Kobak (1998)
	Hospital Anxiety and Depression Scale	Snaith & Zigmond (1983)
	Edinburg Postnatal Depression Scale	Cox, Holden & Sagovsky (1987)
Projective tests	Rorschach	Rorschach (1942)
	Draw a Person	Naglieri (1988)
	Holtzman Inkblot Technique	Holtzman & Gorham (1967)
	Thematic Apperception Test	Murray (1943)
	House-Tree-Person projective drawing technique	Buck, Warren, Jolles, Wenck, & Hammer (1966)

Among the general psychological tests is the Minnesota Multiphasic Psychological Inventory (MMPI-2), a self-rating scale which consists of 567 items that the individual responds to as either true or false. A number of subscales are derived from the answers including a scale that measures clinical depression. Specific self-rating scales have been developed solely for the purpose of measuring depression (Butcher, Dahlstrom, Graham, Tellegen & Kaemmer, 1989).

The Beck depression inventory (Beck, Ward, & Mendelson, 1961) and Zung self-rating depression scale (Zung, 1965) are two commonly used assessments in the evaluation of depression. Both require the individual to select one statement that is most applicable to their condition.

The Hamilton Rating Scale for depression is a widely used observer-rating scale. This is a 17-item test in which the interviewer rates a variety of signs and symptoms about the depressed individual (Hamilton, 1960).

Projective assessments such as the Rorschach and the Thematic Apperception Test have been used to elucidate an individual's depression and the dynamics underpinning it.

TREATMENT OF DEPRESSION

Psychotherapy

Psychological treatment of depression usually takes place in conjunction with psychopharmacological therapies. The goal is to establish a positive, accepting relationship and aid the individual in the understanding of their disorder depending on the psychotherapeutic approach (Leahy, Holland & McGinn, 2011).

Psychoanalytic psychotherapy

The goals of this type of therapy are to help the patient become aware of unconscious conflicts and their roots in childhood experiences and to help him or her learn to resolve them. Psychoanalysis is an intensive long-term procedure for gaining conscious access to repressed memories, motives, conflicts and anxieties stemming from problems in early psychosexual development and then facilitating their resolution. Psychoanalysis's utilize free association, dream analysis, interpretation of transferences and resistances as well as projective assessments to reach the unconscious (Mendelson, 1974).

Cognitive therapy

This therapy is based upon the premise that faulty attitudes and thought patterns underlie many emotional and behavioural disturbances. Therapy is based on changing the thinking process, changing attitudes and redefining problems and meanings. Rather than focusing on the emotional aspects of the individual or exploring the deeper significance of problems, this type of therapy acts 'in the moment' to change the individual's perspectives on the world and his or her place in it (Beck, Rush, Shaw & Emery, 1979).

Therapeutic goals consist of confronting irrational thoughts and replacing them with more reasonable responses. In addition to the cognitive reconstruction, many cognitive behavioural therapies use behavioural techniques to encourage individuals to identify and correct thoughts and behaviours outside of the therapeutic environment. In cognitive behavioural therapy the therapist is generally more active and directive than in psychoanalytic psychotherapy. The goal is to help the individual become aware of the cognitive distortions and negative thoughts that may be contributing to the depressed mood. The final goal is to help the individual learn to adapt and cope with the distortions and negative thoughts in a more appropriate manner (Blackburn & Davidson, 1995).

Behaviour therapy

This therapy is based on the principles of classical and operant conditioning as a way of eliminating problem behaviours that are related to depressive affect. The goal is to encourage the individual to obtain more positive reinforcement from the environment. The therapist helps the individual to identify the possible environmental precipitants and consequences of depressed feelings and behaviour and to change their behaviour in more ways that will enable them to get positive reinforcement and feedback. One specific method often used in behavioural therapy that shows good efficacy is social skills training, which helps the individual to develop skills in their positive socialization with others (Martell, Dimidjian & Herman-Dunn, 2010).

Electroconvulsive therapy (ECT)

Electroconvulsive therapy has had a somewhat dubious history. The early use of seizures was based on the false observation that schizophrenia and epilepsy seldom co-occurred in the same patient. Initially malarial infections were deliberately given to schizophrenics at the turn of the century in order to induce high fevers and seizures which had limited success and often fatal consequences. A physician named von Meduna noted that epileptic seizures caused psychotic patients to improve and hypothesized that the violent storm of neural activity somehow improved the patient's mental condition. He then used various drugs such as such as camphor monobromide to produce seizures and reported that he was achieving success with long-term schizophrenic patients (Abrams, 2002).

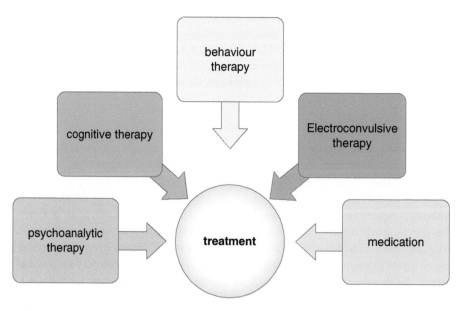

Figure 10.4

A procedure involving electricity was initially tested on animals until they realized that if the electricity was passed through the brain rather than the heart the procedure was relatively safe. Ugo Cerletti, who was researching the idea that criminals were physiologically different from normals, decided to apply the electric treatment to an individual who was catatonic and had remained mute for 15 years. After the treatment, the individual began to speak and engage in conversation which endured after the sessions were stopped (Abrams, 2002).

ECT has proved to be effective for quickly reversing a depressive state and is often used when medication has proven to be ineffective. Antidepressants are thought to be more effective in preventing recurrences but ECT has been found to have a good response. The procedure for receiving ECT is, the person is first anaesthetized, which paralyses the muscles, preventing injuries that could be produced during a seizure. The next step is that ECT is then given either either bilaterally or unilaterally. Unilateral treatments appear to result in less memory impairment. Electrodes are placed on the individual's scalp to the non-speech-dominant hemisphere to avoid damaging verbal memories; and then the person is given a jolt of electricity strong enough to trigger a petit mal seizure. The side effect of ECT is two types of memory loss, both short and long term (Abrams, 2002).

Medication/antidepressant drugs

There are basically four types of medications used to treat depression; MAO inhibitors, tricyclic antidepressants, serotonin re-uptake inhibitors and serotonin-norepinephrine re-uptake inhibitors. Monoamine oxidase inhibitors exert their effect by inhibiting an enzyme that is responsible for metabolizing and inactivating the excess release of monoamines (noradrenaline, dopamine and serotonin). Consequently these three monoamines are left in the synaptic cleft where they are able to continue to interact with various structures in the CNS. The major problem with MAO inhibitors is the large number of side effects, many of which are caused by interactions with various foods and drinks that contain tyrosine. Tyrosine is an amino acid found in many high-protein foods such as cheese, turkey, fish, milk, most nuts and soy products. Tyrosine is broken down into tyramine which is a naturally occurring monoamine-releasing agent. MAOs interfere with this metabolism and result in hypertensive effects (Kelsey, Nemeroff & Newport, 2006).

Tricyclic antidepressants have a different mechanism of action than the MAOs. The tricyclic antidepressants produce their effect by preventing the re-uptake of monoamines. Re-uptake is the main way that monoamines are removed from the synaptic cleft. The tricyclic antidepressants block the re-uptake pump and increase the levels of monoamines, particularly noradrenaline. Although the tricyclic antidepressants are generally regarded as safer than the MAOs they are not free from side effects. Tricyclic antidepressants can produce cardiovascular problems, including irregular racing heartbeats and hypotension; they are also lethal if taken in an overdose. Tricyclic antidepressants are preferred over MAO inhibitors and are effective 60–70 percent of the time (Kelsey, Nemeroff & Newport, 2006).

Selective serotonin re-uptake inhibitors are often called 'second-generation antidepressants' and have a different mechanism of action than either the tricyclic antidepressants or the or the MAOs as they only bock the re-uptake of serotonin. The selective serotonin re-uptake inhibitors are similar to the tricyclic antidepressants in their efficacy in treating depression, but they are safer. The side effects are limited and include sexual dysfunction, weight gain and drowsiness. Selective serotonin re-uptake inhibitors, like the tricyclic antidepressants, have a high overdose disadvantage and can cause a variety of symptoms when the dosage is too high, such as hallucinations, fluctuating blood pressure, seizures and irregular heartbeats, with a high possibility of a lethal condition developing (Kelsey, Nemeroff & Newport, 2006).

Serotonin-norepeinephrin re-uptake inhibitors act on two neurotransmitters and inhibit the re-uptake allowing increased concentrations to build in the synaptic cell which in turn allows for greater neurotransmission in the CNS. This group appears to have a slightly higher efficacy than the SSRIs. Side effects are similar to the SSRIs and include loss of appetite, sleep disturbances, negative sexual side effects, anxiety and elevated blood pressure. Table 10.4 details medications that are commonly prescribed for depression in the UK.

Table 10.4   Drugs commonly prescribed for depression in the UK

Category	Generic name	Trade name
Monoamine Oxidase inhibitors	Isocarboxazid	Marplan
	Phenelzine	Nardil
	Tranylcypromine	Parnate
	Selegiline	Eldepryl, Emsam
	Moclobemide	Manerix
Tricyclic antidepressants	Amitriptyline	Elavil, Endep, Tryptizol
	Clomipramine	Anafranil
	Doxepin	Adapin, Sinequan
	Imipramine	Tofranil
	Trimipramine	Surmontil
	Desipramine	Norpramin
	Dosulepin	Prothiaden
	Lofepramine	Gamarnil
	Nortriptyline	Allegron
Serotonin re-uptake inhibitors	Fluoxetine	Prozac, sarafem, symbyax
	Citalopram	Celexa, cipramil
	Paroxetine	Paxil, Aropax, Seroxat
	Sertraline	Zoloft, Lustral
Serotonin-norepinephrine re-uptake inhibitors	Duloxetine	Cymbalta, Yentreve
	Milnacipran	Ixel
	Venlafaxine	Efexor

St John's Wort (Hypericum perforatum)

Hypericum perforatum is sold over the counter and is a popular herbal supplement. Research has indicated that this herb is effective in treating mild to moderate depression and is comparable to conventional antidepressant therapy (Linde et al., 1996; Shelton et al., 2001). Its mode of action is similar to the tricyclic antidepressants and St John's Wort inhibits the re-uptake of the monoamine neurotransmitters. The side effects are similar to those of the tricyclic antidepressants. Several studies have shown that *Hypericum* is effective in reducing depression in subjects with seasonal affective disorder (Miller, 1998; Hammerness et al., 2003). The major issue with this medication is that it is not regulated and can be sold in a variety of dosages and interactions between prescribed medicines (Barnes, Anderson & Phillipson, 2010). Many individuals believe that because this is 'natural' it is safer than the other types of manufactured antidepressants. An interesting conundrum with this type of thinking is: belladonna is also a natural herbal plant, with rather deadly consequences. Just because something is produced and packaged under a 'natural' label does not necessarily make it a safer and better alternative.

Lithium

Lithium is a metallic element used primarily for the treatment of bipolar disorder and its anti-manic effects. In 1949 John Cade discovered the effects while he was researching sleep and dreaming. The mode of action of lithium is that it inhibits protein kinase C activity in the brain (Yildiz et al., 2008).

Lithium also competes with the four most abundant, positively charged ions in the biological tissue – sodium, potassium, magnesium and calcium and ion transport processes that relay and amplify messages carried to the cells of the CNS. Alteration of the function of any or all of these actions in the CNS can result in widespread neuronal effects. Lithium has a differential response; bioplars are likely to have a good therapeutic response whereas unipolars do not. Lithium also appears to prevent further episodes of affective disturbance. Lithium does have side effects, and can cause nervous system and renal system failure that can result in death. Lithium toxicity occurs at high levels so there is a need to monitor blood-lithium levels periodically. Lithium overdose can result in decreased appetite, diarrhoea, vomiting, ataxia, confusion and cardiovascular failure (Miller 2004).

CONCLUSION

If we return to our case study, what would you say to Charlie? His life does appear rather hopeless. In terms of models, Charlie had a happy childhood and does not report any affective disorders. His parents do not appear to be affected by any type of mood disorder, so there is no family history. He doesn't appear to have any unresolved issues from childhood. Which model best explains Charlie's depression? Charlie more closely follows the cognitive model of depression. We could blame everything on the ex-wife – but the reality is that although she appears to be the catalyst of what happened to Charlie, what is more important is the cognitions that are behind what happened. The treatment goal is to change Charlie's thinking process, help him change his attitude and therefore redefine his problems and solutions.

Summary

This chapter discussed affective disorders and began with a discussion about unipolar depression, the various models and aetiology as well as symptoms. The chapter discussed the various affective disorders and then finished with a discussion of therapies and medications.

LEARNING TOOLS

Key terms

Affect – emotional feeling and the outward manifestations of that feeling. Frequently used interchangeably with mood, emotion

Affective disorder – a disorder marked by a persistent abnormality of mood and associated with a variety of other characteristic signs and symptoms

Agitation – a subjective feeling of anxiety or tension accompanied by physical restlessness or hyperactivity

Anhedonia – inability to experience pleasure

Apathy – a state of indifference, suppression of emotion

Bipolar affective disorder – a disorder marked by episodes of both mania and depression

Dysphoric mood – being afflicted with a general feeling of unhappiness.

Electroencephalograph – an instrument used to study the electrical activity of the brain

Electromyography – an instrument used to measure the electrical activity of muscles

Euphoria – an affect; a profound sense of well-being and happiness

Grandiosity – inflated self-esteem, which may be delusional

Hypomania – less severe form of mania

Mania – a disorder marked by a persistent feeling of euphoria or irritability, accompanied by a variety of characteristic signs and symptoms

Pressure of speech – used to describe speech in which normal pauses are lacking

Psychomotor retardation – a condition in which thinking, speech and physical activity are slowed down

Schemata – a mental model that is structured in order to allow the individual to process experiences and information

Study guide

1   Discuss the differences between clinical depression and situational depression.
2   Describe the differences and similarities between bipolar depression and unipolar depression.
3   Detail how electroconvulsive therapy changed how various mental illnesses were viewed.
4   Describe and discuss the affective disorder of seasonal affective disorder.

Case study in focus

Discuss the various models of treatment; how would each one be applied and what would be the targets of therapeutic intervention? In the circumstances would you allow Charlie not to have his operation? Do you think in this situation that Charlie should be allowed to make a surgical decision that could profoundly affect his future?

Personal development

Bipolar disorder has been termed 'the functional madness'. Many individuals throughout history are thought to have suffered from bipolar disorder. Describe and detail why bipolar disorder is called the functional madness and then identify a famous individual and match their symptoms and behaviours.

Suggested reading

Beck, J.S. (1995) *Cognitive therapy: Basics and beyond.* New York: Guilford Press

Jones, S. & Bentall, R. (eds) (2006). *The psychology of bipolar disorder: New developments and research strategies.* London: Oxford University Press.

Kleiman, K. (2008) *Therapy and the postpartum woman.* New York: Routledge.

Partonen, T. & Pandi-Perumal, S.R. (eds) (2009) *Seasonal Affective Disorder: Practice and research.* London: Oxford University Press.

11

Anxiety Disorders

Learning aims

At the end of this chapter you should:

- Recognize and understand the aetiology and symptoms of anxiety disorders
- Be familiar with the various types of anxiety disorders
- Understand how the psychological and biological components can cause a class of abnormal disorders
- Be aware of the various types of treatment for anxiety disorders.

INTRODUCTION

CASE STUDY

Caroline was a 37-year-old businesswoman. She was a manager and co-owner of a large legal corporation that managed the practices of twelve solicitors. She was completely responsible for two departments: accounting and collections, as well as constantly helping to expand the corporation by engaging new law firms. Caroline had always been an overachiever, earning very good marks in school, and then continuing on to university in business studies and earning a first-class degree. She was initially hired at entry level at a legal firm, but her attention to detail and hardworking attitude moved her up into management very quickly. Caroline worked long hours, often 50–60 hours a week in the office as well as taking work home at the weekend. Her life revolved around her job and her social life was mostly occupied with entertaining clients or prospective clients. She loved her busy intensive life. When her mother became ill with cancer and could no longer live alone, Caroline as the only child moved her mother into her apartment. Her father had passed away a few years previously and before her illness, her mother occupied her time with friends and church activities. Caroline's relationship with her mother had always been strained and when her father passed away, Caroline spent as little time as possible with her mother. Caroline's mother did not approve of her life. She thought it was inappropriate that her daughter was unmarried and childless at the age of 37. Caroline's mother was a very devout Catholic and most of their phone calls ended in arguments about Caroline's lifestyle. When her mother moved into her apartment, their arguments became bitter and often Caroline would retreat into the bathroom to get away.

Her mother's cancer progressed quickly and she was in the terminal stages after only a few months of moving in with Caroline. Caroline hired care workers to stay with her mother during the day, but she felt guilty for not spending more time with her mother, so she provided the care herself in the evening. The stress at times was overwhelming, compounded by the fact that Caroline's mother was resentful of the time Caroline spent at her job and the fact that she would never be surrounded by the grandchildren she had wanted all her life. Caroline wanted to be the perfect daughter but her mother would constantly remind her of her shortcomings. The time between the two of them was spent uneasily. Once her mother entered the final weeks of her life she lost control of her bowels and bladder and Caroline spent most of her evenings changing soiled bed linen and cleaning her mother, changing her clothes and putting her back to bed. Caroline had always been meticulously clean and the smell was repugnant to her so she ended up taking hot showers and scrubbing herself after every episode. Even when she was at work she often thought she could smell soiling on her hands and would go to the bathroom and scrub them until they were raw. Her mother soon passed away, but Caroline's feelings about soiling continued. She spent hours cleaning her apartment, and then when she was finished scrubbing, would spend time in the shower until the water went cold, scrubbing her skin with a brush until it was red raw. She would focus on her hands and could still see soiling under her nails; she began to use stronger soaps, then household cleaners, and when that wasn't enough she began to use bleach and a kitchen scrub brush until her hands would bleed. Even though she was getting up at 3 a.m. to clean she found herself running out of time because after each job she had to wash her hands.

Caroline's productivity began to fall and co-workers noticed that she was coming in late. She began to make comments about some health issues and skin problems, and spent more time away from her job. Eventually, her partner in the business confronted Caroline and realized that something was terribly wrong. Although she attempted to hide her hands, he could see that they were bleeding, raw and covered in scabs. When he demanded to know what was going on, she burst into tears and said 'I can't stop'.

WHAT IS ANXIETY?

Anxiety is characterized as a basic feeling or an emotional state that is distressing (Starcevic et al., 2009). Emotion is defined as a complex reaction, that is an individual's private meanings and interpretations which are often revealed by verbal and/or facial expressions. The term emotion is used to designate a collection of responses triggered from parts of the brain to the body (Damasio, 1998). People attach importance to circumstances surrounding their personal domain. The character of a person's emotional responding is contingent upon whether they perceive events as adding to, subtracting from, endangering or impinging on their domain (Bedrosian & Beck, 1980).

Therefore, anxiety is an emotional reaction that integrates physiological, cognitive and behavioural components and is usually a normal reaction to a stressor (Starcevic et al., 2009). A stressor can be external, such as outside temperature, crowding, interpersonal difficulties with other people, or it can be internal such as an illness or pain. Stressors represent stimulus events that require some form of adaptation or adjustment (Selye, 1956). How do we tell the difference between fear and anxiety? A distinction is generally made in terms of a realistic danger. Fear is generally referred to as a feeling of apprehension about a tangible and existent danger, whereas anxiety commonly refers to the feelings of apprehension that are difficult to relate to a tangible source. Anxiety is usually defined in a broader sense as an emotion that is aroused by a conditioned stimulus associated by previous experience with physical or psychological discomfort and/or pain (Amstadter, 2008).

FEAR AND ANXIETY

Fear and anxiety have long been regarded as fundamental human emotions. Darwin first described the typical manifestations of fear in his book *The Expression of Emotion in Man and Animals*, first published in 1872. Darwin provided a clear description of the typical manifestations of fear as well as documented that an important adaptive characteristic of fear was that it varied in level of intensity dependent upon the situation. Darwin believed that the potential for experiencing fear was an inherent characteristic in humans and animals that had evolved as an adaptive mechanism over the evolutionary process. Fear reactions were shaped through a process of natural selection and its gradations went from mere attention, to start of surprise and finally to extreme terror and horror. Those organisms that were successful in coping or escaping refined the fear reactions to better enable them to cope with the various dangers of survival (Darwin, 1965).

Fear has four main components: the subjective experience of apprehension, associated physiological changes, outward expressions of fear and attempts to avoid or escape certain situations (Griskevicius, Goldstein, Mortensen, Sundie, Cialdini & Kenrick, 2009). Facial and related expressions register only certain kinds of fear, particularly those of an acute and episodic nature; diffuse and chronic fears are less visible. We can easily observe signs of fear in an individual with a spider phobia, but may not recognize it in a person who is afraid of dying.

There are many types of fear and a major division can be made between acute and chronic fears. Acute fears are generally provided by tangible stimuli or situations and subside when the frightening stimulus is removed or avoided. A less common type of acute fear is the sudden onset of panic which seems to have no tangible source. Chronic fears tend to be more complex but are like the acute types in that they may or may not be tied to tangible sources of provocation. Examples of chronic intangible fears are difficult to specify, one simply feels persistently uneasy and anxious for unidentified reasons (Griskevicius, Goldstein, Mortensen, Sundie, Cialdini & Kenrick, 2009).

Repeated or prolonged exposure to fearsome stimulation can give rise to enduring changes in behaviour, feelings and psychophysiological functioning. The major causes of fear include exposure to traumatic stimulation, repeated exposure to threatening situations, observations (direct or indirect) of people exhibiting fear and receiving fear-provoking information (Gower, 2005).

Fear is the emotional reaction to threat and is the motivating force for defensive behaviours. Defensive behaviours are designed to protect the organism from threat or harm. Biopsychological research on emotion has focused to a large degree on fear. One reason for this focus is the major role played by chronic fear in the development of disease (Turk & Wilson, 2010).

Efforts to identify the neural mechanisms of fear have focused on the study of fear conditioning. Maren (2001) found that bilateral lesions to the medial geniculate nucleus blocked fear conditioning to a tone but bilateral lesions to the auditory cortex did not, indicating that for auditory fear conditioning to occur it was necessary for signals elicited by the tone to reach the medial geniculate nucleus, but not the auditory cortex.

Another structure indicated in the neural mechanisms of fear has been the amygdala. The amygdala receives input from all sensory systems and is the structure whereby emotional significance of sensory signals is learned and retained. Lesions of the amygdala blocked fear conditioning. The amygdala assesses the emotional significance of the sound on the basis of previous encounters with it, and then activates the appropriate sympathetic and behavioural response circuits in the hypothalamus and peraqueductal grey (Davis, 1992).

THREAT, EMOTIONAL AROUSAL AND STATE ANXIETY

The perception of threat refers to a person's subjective evaluation of an event as potentially harmful. When the cues associated with a situation are seen as signs of impending danger, the situation will be experienced as threatening. In addition the perception of threat is influenced by the objective facts of a situation. The individual may have thoughts or memories that are stimulated by the situation, the context in which a potential danger is encountered, as well as the individual's coping skills and previous experience all of which will influence the extent to which a situation is appraised as threatening. Therefore, a potential danger may be threatening at the first encounter but if it is successfully negotiated, the next encounter will be less fear inducing. However, if the potential danger was unsuccessfully negotiated the next encounter will compound the threat and danger (Foa & Kozak, 1986).

The experience of threat has two characteristics: it is future oriented, that is, it generally involves the anticipation of a potentially harmful event that has not yet happened; and it consists of mental processes, which include perception, thought, memory, and judgement (Feinstein, Adolphs, Damasio & Tranel, 2011). When threat reactions are based on a realistic appraisal of present or future danger, they serve an adaptive function in producing a state of emotional and physiological arousal, which operates as a danger signal to mobilize an individual to take action to avoid harm or what was termed the 'fight-or-flight' response (Jansen et al., 1995).

Cannon (1929) observed that stressful stimuli evoked intense states of physiological arousal that mobilized 'fight-or- flight' reactions. In his laboratory research he found that the physiological arousal was a complex response of the sympathetic adrenal medullary system of humans and animals. Cannon observed that there was a homeostatic characteristic to 'resist distortion' and maintain the original state before exposure to some 'external force' or disturbing stimulus.

As a result of the physiological mechanisms, whenever an event or situation is seen as threatening, irrespective of whether the danger is real or imagined, the sense of threat will lead to an arousal of the 'fight-or-flight' response. The appraisal of a situation as threatening will evoke an emotional reaction proportional in intensity to the magnitude of the perceived danger or threat (Cannon, 1929).

PHYSIOLOGICAL ELEMENTS OF ANXIETY

The physiological systems associated with stress include the central nervous system, catecholamine, immune, endorphin-enkephalin, hypothalamic-pituitary-adrenocortical and the sympatho-adrenomedullary systems (Dunn & Berridge, 1990).

The sympatho-adrenomedullary system is activated during active coping (flight or fight), which usually involves physical exertion in terms of avoidance or defence. This system increases metabolic activity in response to threatening stimuli. Measures of norepinephrine and epinephrine are typically used to indicate the activity of the sympatho-adrenomedullary system (Dunn & Berridge, 1990).

Measures such as EEGs, neuroendocrine responses, heart rate, electrodermal responses, blood pressure, eye pupil size, muscle blood flow and electromyographic activity all provide evidence of an anxiety disorder (Lader, 1983). These systems are also implicated in many physical disorders and attention should be directed as to whether the physiological aspects the individual is experiencing are a result of anxiety or a medical condition. Table 11.1 lists common medical conditions that often imitate anxiety disorders.

Physiological symptoms are important as they can cause responses that can create further problems. This can occur when the body's homeostatic mechanisms become constantly disrupted or exhausted under conditions of prolonged anxiety. Chronic anxiety can affect the health of an individual in two ways; the body's organs may become damaged by prolonged overaction and the immune system can become so weakened that the body is susceptible to infectious diseases. Acute stress increases the steroid hormones known to be lymphatic, which suppresses the immune response. This system is under a different physiological system (Roy-Byrne et al., 2008). The hypothalamic-pituitary-adrenocortical system plays a role in the organism's response to emotionally stressful situations in which active coping is not possible. The response includes heightened activity of the anterior pituitary and the adrenal cortex. Although the response is relatively constant, regardless of type of stimulus, the degree of response may vary as a function of the intensity of the demand for adjustment. Adrenocorticotropic hormone and corticosteroids are often measured as they are thought to be involved in negative feedback loops in the hypothalamic-pituitary-adrenocortical system (Selye, 1976).

Table 11.1   Medical conditions that imitate anxiety disorders

Cardiovascular	Myocardial infarction (heart attack)
	Dysrhythmia
	Hypertension
	Congestive heart failure
Respiratory system	Hypoxic conditions
	COPD – chronic obstructive pulmonary disease
Metabolic/endocrine	Hypoglycaemia
	Hypothyroidism
	Hypoadrenalism (Cushing's or Addison's disease)
	Diabetes mellitus
Neurological system	Brain tumour
	Migraine headache
	Seizure disorders
	Multiple sclerosis
Hematologic system	Anaemia

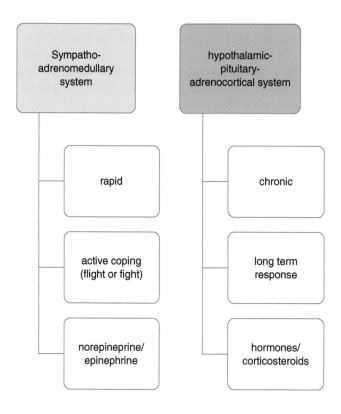

Figure 11.1

Anxiety may be secondary to or concurrent with other psychological disorders, particularly depression. In some cases, the symptoms of anxiety or panic disorder may precede and be symptomatic of a major depressive episode. The serotonergic and noradrenergic systems are thought to be involved in stress anxiety and depression. It is believed that norepinephrine depletion in the central nervous system disinhibits cortisol-releasing factor secretion in the hypothalamus, which contributes to cortisol-releasing factor secretion in the hypothalamus and to the hypersecretion of cortisol which demonstrates disturbances similar to depression (Ressler & Nemeroff, 2000).

HORMONAL RESPONSE TO ANXIETY

Epinephrine affects glucose metabolism, causing the nutrients stored in muscles to become available to provide energy for strenuous exercise. Along with norepinephrine, the hormone also increases blood flow to the muscles by increasing the output of the heart. In doing so, it also increases blood pressure, which over the long term contributes to cardiovascular disease (Bonnet et al., 2005).

Another stress-related hormone is cortisol, a steroid secreted by the adrenal cortex. Cortisol is also referred to as a glucocorticoid because it helps break down protein and convert it to glucose, making fats available for energy, increasing blood flow, and stimulating behavioural responsiveness. The secretion of cortisol is controlled by neurons in the paraventricular nucleus of the hypothalamus. These neurons also secrete a peptide called corticotrophin-releasing factor which stimulates the anterior pituitary gland to secrete adrenocorticotropic hormone which stimulates the adrenal cortex to secrete more cortisol. All this has various muscle and tissue targets. Corticotrophin-releasing factor is also secreted in the central nervous system where it serves as a neuromodulator/neurotransmitter, especially in regions of the limbic system that are involved in emotional responses (Brown, Varghese & McEwen, 2004).

HERITABILITY OF ANXIETY DISORDERS

Can psychophysiological elements be inherited or are certain people more susceptible than others? Could there be a genetic predisposition that places people more at risk for the development of an anxiety disorder? Although there is little evidence that biological factors are of critical importance in the development of the neuroses, constitutional predisposition may contribute to a genetically determined lack of resistance, making some people more vulnerable to the onset of neurosis than others.

Torgersen (1983) found the frequency of anxiety disorders to be twice as high in monozygotic twins as in dizygotic twin pairs (60 percent and 33 percent) and three times as high in the monozygotic twins if generalized anxiety disorder was excluded (45 percent and 15 percent). In addition, panic attacks were five times more likely among the MZ sets. Giampaolo et al. (1997) confirmed much of the Torgersen study with a higher concordance rate among monozygotic twins vs. dizygotic twins (73 percent vs. 0 percent).

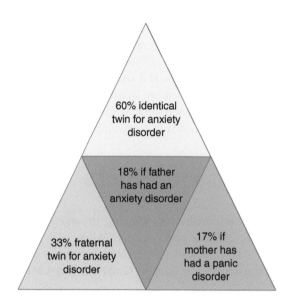

Figure 11.2   Percentage of risk for anxiety disorder

Noyes et al. (1987) compared the family histories of 112 patients with anxiety neurosis to 110 surgical controls and found that the morbidity risk for first-degree relatives of anxiety patients was 18 percent as compared to 3 percent among the control relatives. Relatives of the anxiety patients were also found to be at higher risk for developing alcoholism.

Crowe et al. (1983) found that the incidence of panic disorder for first-degree relatives was 17 percent with an additional 7 percent with probable symptoms that compared to the control group of 1.7 percent and 0.4 percent. They concluded that panic disorder is a familial disease that appears to affect women twice as often as men and does not appear to be associated with an increased risk for other types of psychiatric conditions.

A meta-analysis of genetic epidemiology of anxiety disorders concluded that obsessive-compulsive disorder, panic attack and generalized anxiety disorder have significant familial aggregation and that genetic inheritance appears to explain the result although the role of family environment in generalized anxiety disorder is uncertain as there are no large-scale twin studies. In addition, the role of non-shared environmental experience is significant, emphasizing the importance of identifying environmental risk factors that predispose individuals to anxiety (Hettema et al., 2001).

NEUROSIS AND ANXIETY – PSYCHOANALYTIC EXPLANATION

The original meaning of neurosis was designated to describe a neurological disorder or loss of function of a bodily organ that was attributed, mistakenly, to a disorder in the function of peripheral nerves or nervous tissue. With advances in scientific knowledge, it became apparent that the neuroses were caused by psychological rather than neurological problems. The concept of neurosis as a type of emotional disturbance was popularized by Freud who viewed it as a pattern of behavioural and psychological disturbance produced by conflict within the personality structure (Fenichel, 1996).

The most common symptoms of a neuroses are: anxiety, worry, nervousness, irrational fears, depression, obsessions and compulsions, dissociated states, conversion reactions and a wide variety of somatic complaints of a vague and indefinite character such as indigestion, headaches, insomnia, dizziness, shortness of breath, trembling, and heart palpitations, paralyses and asthenia without any organic basis. The personality of individuals who exhibit neurotic disorders generally contains feelings of inadequacy and insecurity, hypersensitivity to criticism, and strong needs for affection and approval. Neurotic persons also display markedly inadequate emotional adjustment, feelings of inferiority, excessive worry, inability to adapt to everyday life, and numerous other psychological, somatic and behavioural symptoms (Fenichel, 1999).

Psychological stress is one of the major factors in producing neurotic symptoms. Generally the adaptive style of a neurotic person does not result from any one incident but tends to gradually develop as a consequence of emotional maladjustment to environmental stress and life circumstances. The pattern of symptoms in neurosis often varies from person to person but anxiety is always a pervasive underlying issue. Most neurotic symptoms are either manifestations of anxiety or reflect defences against anxiety. The different types of neuroses are distinguished primarily by the particular symptoms which dominate the disorder. Research in the aetiology of neurosis indicates the involvement of a variety of psychosocial factors such as death, bereavement, interpersonal relationship difficulties, financial issues and illness (Adler, 1964).

DEFINITIONS OF ANXIETY: STATE–TRAIT PROCESS – BEHAVIOURAL PERSPECTIVE

The definition of anxiety as a complex psychophysiological process must be added to the conceptual distinction between anxiety as a transitory state and individual differences in anxiety proneness as a personality trait. The term anxiety also refers to relatively stable individual differences in anxiety proneness as a personality trait. This is referred to as trait anxiety (t-anxiety). Trait anxiety is not directly manifested in behaviour, but may be inferred from the frequency that a person experiences elevations in state-anxiety. Persons who are high in trait-anxiety are more vulnerable to stress and respond to a wider range of situations as dangerous or threatening. Since individuals who are high t-anxiety are more disposed to see the world as dangerous or threatening, they re-experience state-anxiety reactions more frequently, and often with greater intensity than do people low in trait-anxiety. Persons who are high in trait-anxiety are more vulnerable to stress and respond to a wider range of situations as dangerous or threatening (Spielberger, 1996).

State-anxiety is a complex psychophysiological process which involves stressors, mediating cognitive, physiological and emotional reactions and behavioural consequences. The unpleasant experience in an anxiety state (s-anxiety) includes feelings of apprehension, tension, nervousness and worry. In addition to worrisome thoughts about physical or psychological damage that might result from real or imagined dangers related to the specific circumstances that arouse state-anxiety, unrelated worry cognitions may also come to mind, stimulated by the general level of emotional arousal. Conceptions of anxiety as a process generally imply a temporally ordered sequence of events. This process may be initiated by a stressful external stimulus or by internal cues that are interpreted as dangerous or threatening; the appraisal of danger is immediately followed by a state-anxiety reaction, or by an increase in the intensity of state-anxiety. Thus an emotional state of anxiety is at the core of the most process definitions (Spielberger, 1996).

MODELS OF ANXIETY

A model as discussed in other chapters makes reference to the overall way of ordering or conceptualizing a specific area of study, in this case anxiety disorders. A model of abnormal behaviour is distinguished from a theory because it explains behaviour instead of hypothesizing how it could occur. There are three main models of anxiety disorders: biological, learned and psychological.

Most biological models elucidating anxiety disorders begin with the basic principle that psychological anxiety can bring about physiological malfunctioning and actual tissue change. There are two basic views; the first is that individuals have a genetic vulnerability or somatic weakness which leaves bodily systems more susceptible to damage from stress. The vulnerable or weakened somatic area is further damaged when harmful psychological stress conditions occur and persist (Rodgers, 1997).

The second biological model specifies that people are different in their physiological reactions to stress and these specific patterns are likely to be genetic in origin. Autonomic reactivity to anxiety is characteristic of these specific patterns and the individual pattern tends to be consistent and similar from one stressor to another. On the basis of their specific autonomic response patterns to anxiety, individuals are considered as primarily stomach reactors, heart reactors, skin reactors etc. For example stomach reactors are individuals who are likely to respond to anxiety with increased secretion of stomach acid which in turn make them more vulnerable to stomach ulcers (Heller et al., 1995).

The learning model is a combination of classically conditioned anxiety and operant conditioned avoidance, also called the two factor theory (Rachman, 1976). If a stressor is determined to be dangerous or threatening, an anxiety reaction will be evoked and the intensity of this reaction will be proportional to the amount of threat the situation poses for the individual. The duration of the anxiety reaction will depend on the persistence of the evoking stimuli as well as the individual's experience in dealing with similar circumstances. Stressful situations that are frequently encountered may require a person to develop effective coping responses that quickly alleviate or minimize the danger, reducing the level of intensity (McAllister, 1995). Observational learning, also called vicarious learning or modelling, involves the same processes except that instead of experiencing the stressful stimulus the individual observes others, which can occur by watching movies and television, reading or information from others (Marks, 1987).

Children can learn fearful behaviour by the modelling of fearful behaviour by parents; therefore entire generations can learn to be afraid of objects or things having never understood the basis of their fears (Olsson et al., 2007).

The psychoanalytic model views anxiety as a relationship between certain personality traits and intrapsychic conflicts. Freud conceptualized anxiety as the fundamental problem in neurotic symptom formation. Anxiety was simply not the central problem in neuroses, but the understanding of the aetiology of anxiety as being fundamental to the treatment of the individual. Freud considered the physiological changes and behavioural symptoms to be essential components but focused on the subjective, experiential qualities of neurosis. Using the introspective methods of psychoanalysis Freud believed that these methods would enable the therapist to discover the childhood experiences which connected anxiety reactions with the external stressors that evoked or reactivated them (Freud, 1936).

Freud regarded anxiety as an internal emotional reaction that served as a signal to indicate the presence of a danger situation. He differentiated between objective and neurotic anxiety which was based on whether the source was from the external world or the individual's own repressed impulses. Objective anxiety was normal and adaptive whereas neurotic anxiety was not. Neurotic anxiety was the individual's own repressed impulses that were punishment for the expression of normal sexual and aggressive impulses especially during early childhood and often resulted in objective anxiety being converted into neurotic anxiety. The process of converting objective anxiety into neurotic anxiety begins when internal stimuli are associated with previously punished behaviours that arouse objective anxiety. Since objective anxiety is unpleasant, coping behaviours attempt to reduce the feelings in the subconscious or repression of the internal cues. Repression is never complete and fragments of symbolic representation erupt into awareness. When the partial breakdown in repression leads to the perception of danger from one's own impulses, a neurotic anxiety reaction will occur (Compton, 1972).

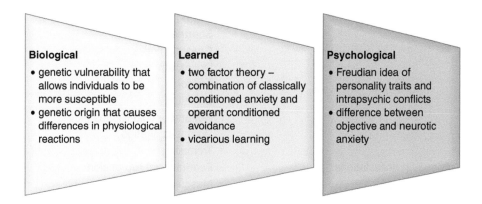

Figure 11.3   Three main models of anxiety disorders

ANXIETY DISORDERS

Anxiety states

The anxiety states are the most common of the various types of anxiety disorders. In addition to chronic anxiety, the predominant symptoms of anxiety states are: inability to concentrate, sleep disturbances, autonomic hyperactivity and sustained muscle tension, hypersensitivity and excessive vigilance and scanning behaviour that results in difficulty in concentrating. It is often undifferentiated and free-floating (not anchored to a particular object or event) feelings that carry the dreadful expectation of impending doom or catastrophe. The anxiety is the central symptom and it goes beyond the apprehensions and fears experience considered to be normal. It is more severe and usually unrelated to external reality, although it may be triggered by a variety of events such as interpersonal relationships, financial worries etc. (Clark, 1989).

Phobic disorders

The term phobia is from the Greek word phobos, meaning fear or dread, It refers to intense fear (state-anxiety) reactions and avoidance behaviours that are evoked by an object or situation which

Table 11.2 Symptoms of anxiety

Psychological symptoms	Worry
	Agitation
	Fear of losing control
	Dread that something terrible is about to happen
	Irritability
	Feelings of detachment
Physical symptoms	Racing heart beat (palpitations)
	Shortness of breath
	Chest tightness
	Dry mouth
	Tremor
	Sweating
	Hot and/or cold flashes
	Dizziness, vertigo
	Trembling
Behavioural manifestations	Fearful facial expression
	Muscular tension
	Lack of energy
	Fatigue

is generally harmless or at the worst could result in sight harm. When exposed to a feared object or situation, the phobic individual experiences a sudden increase in state-anxiety which leads them to take elaborate steps to avoid the phobic object. In phobias, intense fear reactions may become attached to specific objects or situations as the result of a learning process (Buchanan & Coulson, 2012).

This form of neurosis consists of persistent, severe and irrational fear of which the individual is aware but from which he or she cannot free himself or herself. Some observers regard the irrational nature of the fear as the important element in distinguishing phobias from ordinary fears, while others contend that the experience of fear is the same regardless of whether its origins are real or imagined. The ingredient of severity is probably more important since a phobia is usually so debilitating that it interferes with the individual's daily functioning. In addition, a phobia has an obessional quality in that the individual ruminates about it and cannot completely free his or her thoughts from it (Marks, 1970).

In young children, fears and phobias are particularly difficult to distinguish, because fears occur with regularity during the course of normal development (Muris, 2009). All infants have a startle response (freeze reaction) to loss of support or to any sudden and loud noise. Later, during the first year of life babies evidence a fear of strangers in which they react with fear-like panic to unfamiliar people, objects or situations and will begin to scream and cry seeking comfort from the familiar (Muris, 2009). Between the ages of two and three, fear of animals tends to appear, while beginning with the third year of life, children become fearful of the dark, perhaps because they feel alone and vulnerable to outside forces they can't control (Morris & Kratochwill, 1982). Animal fears increase during the preschool years as animals become part of frightening dreams and as children become more aware of the powerful and dangerous aspects of animals (i.e. fear of being eaten) (Ollendick & March, 2004). Frequently, animal fears are learned and heightened by contagion that is through parent's, siblings and intimate others in the environment transferring the anxiety and fear of animals. 'Don't get too close that dog could bite' is only one of many illustrations of people communicating fear to children who may not have been previously affected. A full-blown animal phobia occurs when the fear of the animal becomes unwarranted, intense and persistent (Muris, Zwol, Huijding, & Mayer, 2009).

Phobias tend to endure because they cause the phobic person to invest a considerable effort in avoiding the feared object or situation. By avoiding the frightening situation that originally evoked the intense anxiety reaction, the phobic person is prevented from discovering that the situation is in fact relatively harmless. Therefore, he or she continues to experience an increase in state-anxiety whenever cues associated with or similar to the original traumatic experience are encountered. Additionally, each time the phobic object is successfully avoided, anxiety is reduced, thus rewarding and further enhancing the phobic individual's determination to avoid the feared situation (Marks, 1970).

It appears that no single factor is sufficient to explain the development of all phobias. Not all phobias are caused by or associated with traumas, and it appears that a number of factors are involved and phobias can develop when any of several combinations of factors occur (Buchanan & Coulson, 2012).

For example, many children in the course of playing have either been accidentally or purposefully locked into a small space, closet, box etc. The longer they are confined the more likely they are going to experience intense state-anxiety. After the child is released they may experience terrifying dreams and memories of the event, intensifying the state-anxiety. As a result, small enclosed areas will trigger the anxiety cue and the child will soon develop avoidance behaviours. As the child avoids these triggers, the positive reinforcement for this type of behaviour increases and it is more likely that a phobia of small places will develop. This anxiety reaction can then be generalized to other types of small spaces such as lifts. As an adult the individual cannot ride in a lift because of the anxiety and fear that it causes.

Again it should be emphasized that not all children develop a phobia when trapped in a small space; many children and adults have been trapped for long periods of time in small enclosed places without developing a phobia. It appears that the most important variable in the development of a phobic response is the person's perception of the situation and their experience of the relationship of the events (Gournay, 2010).

Specific phobia

Specific phobias are more prevalent than any other type of phobic disorder. When suddenly exposed to the phobic stimulus, an individual who suffers from a simple phobia experiences a rapid increase in state-anxiety which resembles a panic attack. The most common specific phobias typically involve small animals; for example, insects, spiders, snakes, mice and dogs. However, there are other types such as injections, water, lifts, flying, heights, enclosed places and dentists (Antony & Barlow, 1998). Table 11.3 documents the more common phobias.

Social phobia

The fundamental characteristic in social phobias is an intense, irrational fear of, and a compelling desire to avoid, situations in which an individual may be exposed to scrutiny and evaluation by others. The individual feels highly anxious when they must enter into certain types of situations in

Table 11.3   Common phobias

Apiphobia	Fear of bees/wasps
Aquaphobia	Fear of water
Arachnophobia	Fear of spiders
Chiroptophobia	Fear of bats
Claustrophobia	Fear of being enclosed in with no escape
Coulrophobia	Fear of clowns
Cynophobia	Fear of dogs
Dysmorphophobia	Fear of having a real or imagined body defect
Nosophobia	Fear of contracting a disease
Ophidiophobia	Fear of snakes
Scoleciphobia	Fear of worms
Xenophobia	Fear of strangers

which they may be embarrassed or humiliated by a poor performance. These social events generally involve a group of people such as: public speaking, crowds, interacting with members of the opposite sex in a social situation such as a pub or club, eating in public places and using public restrooms. Social phobias tend to not be as incapacitating as other types of phobias but they often interfere with professional advancement and the achievement of educational goals as individuals choose their environment carefully in order to avoid placing themselves in a situation where social cues will trigger anxiety (Liebowitz, 1987).

Agoraphobia

This anxiety disorder is probably the most stressful and incapacitating of all the phobic disorders. The basic underlying problem in agoraphobia is an intense fear of personal catastrophe in a public place that is generally meaningful to the person involved, e.g. illness, stress, heart attack, being physically attacked, losing control of bowel or bladder functions. It involves an intense fear of social areas or open spaces, and typically includes multiple fears of crowds, public transport, enclosed spaces, travel, being alone and an intense fear of 'losing control'. Individuals also have a variety of physiological symptoms such as fainting, being unable to breathe, and panic attacks (Magee et al., 1996).

Agoraphobics have an intense need to control their immediate environment and intense fear of being away from familiar surroundings. The normal activities of persons suffering from agoraphobia are greatly constricted because their fears and avoidance behaviours come to dominate their lives. The agoraphobic individual generally becomes housebound, often refusing to leave his or her home unless accompanied by a family member or friend and often the phobia continues to develop so that even companionship is not enough for them to leave familiar surroundings. The initial phase of the disorder often consists of recurrent panic attacks and then anticipatory fear of having an attack which causes the individual to refuse to enter situations in which such attacks were previously experienced. It is not unusual for their social space to become even more restricted as the intense fear slowly erodes more and more social places. These environments become even more restricted when the individual feels that they can only control their familiar and immediate environment (Craske & Barlow, 1993).

Generalized anxiety disorder

This anxiety disorder is a chronic disturbance characterized by two types of symptoms; persistent, diffuse anxiety and panic attacks. Most individuals report that they are frequently tense, anxious and fearful and live much of their lives with a feeling of 'impending doom'. The subjective distress is accompanied by a variety of physical symptoms and autonomic nervous system reactions (Fricchione, 2004).

A panic attack is a specific episode in which intense anxiety and physiological symptoms are suddenly experienced. In panic attacks, the sudden onset of intense apprehension, fear and terror is often associated with terrifying feelings of fear. Individual panic attacks may vary in length from a few seconds to many hours. These attacks interrupt all other activity and thought. Frequently the individual feels as if they are going to die. Panic attacks can occur from once a year to several times a day (Clark, 1986).

There are two types of symptoms; panic and diffuse anxiety which can be found in varying combinations, ranging from recurrent mild anxiety to chronic anxiety with occasional panic attacks to frequent panic attacks interspersed with mild or severe anxiety (Fricchione, 2004).

Obsessive-compulsive reaction

The essential features in this disorder are obsessive thoughts that repeatedly intrude into awareness, and irrational compulsive behaviours that an individual feels compelled to perform. In this particular type of neurotic reaction, the anxiety is isolated from its origin (the unacceptable impulse) through recurrent thoughts (obsessions) or acts (compulsions) or both that the individual must perform in spite of the fact that the ideas or the behaviours seem silly or unreasonable. Although the individual is unaware of the original source of the anxiety, it is very much tied to the maintenance of obsessions and compulsions in that the individual experiences marked apprehension when something or someone interferes with their completion (Hollander et al., 2003).

Obsessions can be so bizarre that they can be difficult to distinguish from being delusional. The most common obsessions involve: thoughts of being harmed or of harming others, feelings of responsibility for protecting others from harm and obsessions about contamination that may involve thoughts of becoming infected by shaking hands, or contracting a disease from touching doorknobs, toilets, or other objects in public places. Obsessions are recurrent, persistent ideas, thoughts, images or impulses that are not experienced as voluntarily produced, but rather as thoughts that invade consciousness and are experienced as senseless or repugnant.

Examples of obsessions involving aggression and violence are: recurrent thoughts of beating, shooting, choking or injuring one's parent, sibling, spouse or child; shouting obscene words at work or at home or thoughts of suicide. Individuals can also experience obsessional doubts or have recurrent thoughts about having committed unacceptable acts (McElroy, Phillips & Keck, 1994).

Compulsions are repetitive behaviours that are somehow tied to the obsessions; they generally have meaning only to the individual who is participating in them. They tend to be stereotyped behaviours that have a ritualistic quality and must be performed in a very specific manner. Like obsessions, they are viewed as irrational and unwanted but the individual is driven to perform them. The repetitive behaviour is not an end in itself, but is designed to produce or to prevent some future event or situation. However, the activity is not connected in a realistic way with what it is designed to produce or prevent and is generally clearly excessive (Bobes et al., 2001).

Compulsions generally take two forms; corrective activity and checking. Corrective activity most frequently involves cleaning or hand-washing to undo the effects of contamination. Checking appears to be aimed at preventing something from happening. The most common forms of pathological compulsions are hand-washing, counting, checking and touching. Compulsive acts may vary from relatively innocuous behaviours, such as not stepping on cracks in the pavement, to elaborate, time-consuming compulsive rituals that grossly interfere with job performance and social activities. Counting to oneself, memorizing licence plate numbers or street signs, or reciting innocuous words or phrases, requires concentration, and thus diverts attention from more distressing thoughts or memories (Hollander et al., 2003).

Minor obsessions and compulsions occur in all individuals and in many different forms, such as bedtime rituals that must be played out in proper sequence, categories and organization of tools, software, DVDs or the reverberation of a tune or a jingle in one's thoughts. These reactions are distinguishable from the obsessive-compulsive individual in severity and in the degree to which they affect functioning. In addition, obsessive-compulsive disorder is frequently marked by several other manifestations such as depression. The symptoms of obsessive-compulsive disorder often appear first during bouts of depression. Periods of relatively severe depression seem to recur more frequently than is the case with many other disorders and the obsessive-compulsive symptoms typically become more acute during those times. Depression is typically accompanied by negative self-evaluation, self-criticisms, lowered belief in one's competence and excessive guilt (Coryell, 1981).

In addition to specific obsessions and compulsions, many obsessive-compulsives exhibit what is referred to as a compulsive personality. This is a general style of behaviour which involves excessive orderliness and neatness and a meticulous overattention to details. These individuals often have extreme difficulty making decisions, ruminating endlessly about the pros and cons of even small matters. Another common characteristic is primary obsessional slowness. OCDs often appear to be living in slow motion, taking excessive amounts of time to perform even the simplest of acts such as washing and dressing (Pollak, 1979).

Obsessive-compulsive disorders are the most difficult to explain. They seem to share common features with other anxiety disorders but are unique in the persistent obsessive thoughts. Research indicates that there is a common theme which is that they appear to be on guard against making errors or doing something wrong. The consequence of the error appears to be of less concern than a feeling of being responsible for the error (Bobes et al., 2001).

Post-traumatic stress disorder

The fundamental characteristic of this disorder is the recurrent experiencing of a traumatic stressful event that previously produced intense anxiety and fear. PTSD is caused by a situation and/or event in which a person experienced, witnessed or was confronted with an incident that involved actual or threatened death or serious injury or a threat to the physical integrity of self or others that provoked a response that involved intense fear, helplessness or horror. The level of state anxiety evoked by the stressor is so intense and painful that cues associated with the traumatic event become conditioned to the emotional reaction. Subsequent thoughts about the traumatic situation stimulated by memories or cues associated with the original circumstances initiate a cognitive and psychophysiological reaction causing the individual to re-experience the traumatic event and the intense emotions that were associated with the event as if it was happening in the here and now (Wolf & Mosnaim, 1990).

The symptoms of PTSD can start after a delay of weeks, or even months. They usually appear within six months of a traumatic event but may not happen until years later, or they may come and go over many years. The course of chronic PTSD usually involves periods of symptom increase followed by remission or decrease, although some individuals may experience symptoms that are unremitting and severe (Wolf & Mosnaim, 1990).

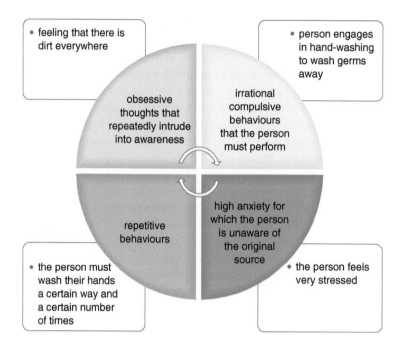

Figure 11.4   Obsessive-compulsive cycle of behaviour and thoughts

Whether or not a traumatic experience will cause post-traumatic stress disorder will be influenced by the duration and severity of the stressor and by the personality structure, coping skills and past experience of the person. The level of trait-anxiety also influences the extent to which psychological dangers are appraised as threatening. Persons high in trait-anxiety tend to be lacking in self-confidence and are more vulnerable to traumatic events that pose threats to self-esteem. Nearly every individual who is involved in a traumatic incident will display signs of stress but over time the symptoms of an acute stress reaction will begin to decline (Wolf & Mosnaim, 1990).

The stressors that produce this syndrome are generally more painful, dangerous or threatening than stressful experiences commonly experienced in everyday life. Military combat, being the victim of rape or assault, serious accidents, and natural disasters such as earthquakes or floods, are examples of the types of stressors that may produce post-traumatic stress disorder. Because the situation is generally extremely dangerous and life threatening, the individual is overwhelmed by intense anxiety. Types of trauma appear to be a factor as well, with trauma generally being more severe and long lasting when it is of human design (such as being raped or in a terroristic attack) than being traumatized by an environmental disaster. The literature is also inconclusive over whether physical injury at the time of the initial trauma is more causal of PTSD (Jones, 1990; McFarlane & Atchison, 1997).

The recurrent dreams, recollections of the event and flashback episodes are pathogenomic for PTSD and create intense psychological as well as physiological distress. In addition individuals become hyper-aroused and feel constantly 'on guard' and on the lookout for danger. As a result they have difficulty sleeping, concentrating and remaining focused. Other symptoms associated with this disorder are avoidance of the situation or anything that is remotely associated with the trauma. They often over-engage in activities or work in order to keep themselves intensely occupied. Individuals are often reluctant or unwilling to admit they are in distress and often deny symptoms and difficulties (Miller, 2003).

PTSD is also characterized by a sensation of emotional numbing; individuals have a difficult time expressing their feelings about the incident, lose interest in activities and have a difficult time within interpersonal relationships. They generally have a diminished responsiveness to the external world, feelings of detachment or estrangement from others and general emotional constriction. As a result of the extreme emotions and fatigue, avoidance and numbing are maladaptive coping strategies employed in an attempt to keep the number of replays to a manageable level (Feeny, Zoellner, Fitzbibbons & Foa, 2000).

The clinical picture also includes symptoms of anxiety, which may vary in intensity from mild apprehension to panic attacks when the traumatic situation is recalled. The number of recurrent episodes varies and can occur from many times a day to once or twice a year but always brings emotional distress and alarm, leaving the individual physically and mentally exhausted. Symptoms of post-traumatic stress disorder can be terrifying, disrupting the individual's life and making it impossible to continue with daily activities (Taylor, 2009).

Secondary symptoms as a direct result of the primary symptoms are not uncommon as the individual attempts to cope with the emotional trauma. Drinking or 'self-medicating' with drugs is a common way many cope with upsetting events to numb themselves and to try to deal with the difficult thoughts, feelings, and memories related to the trauma. The events often undermine the belief systems of individuals resulting in insecurity and anger issues. It is not uncommon for individuals with PTSD to experience depression. Individuals feel hopeless and participate in self-blame, guilt and shame concerning the incident (McFarlane, 1998).

As a result of the psychological symptoms as well as the biological changes, PTSD frequently occurs in conjunction with problems of memory and cognition and other problems of physical and mental health. In addition it impairs the person's ability to function in social or family life, family discord, difficulties in parenting, marital problems and divorce, occupational instability and physical aggression and abuse towards others (Ehlers & Clark, 2000; Ray & Vanstone, 2009).

Various studies have indicated that pre-existing personality factors may play a role in the development of PTSD. Individuals who tend to brood about their feelings were more likely to go on to develop PTSD (Breslau, Davis & Andreski, 1995; Ullman, 1995; McFarlane, 1989). There is also evidence that early traumatic experiences (e.g. during childhood), especially if these are prolonged or repeated, may increase the risk of developing PTSD after traumatic exposure as an adult (Shalev, Peri, Canetti & Schreiber, 1996; Ehlers, Mayou & Bryant, 1998). PTSD is also more likely if passive defences, such as freezing or dissociation, are used rather than active defences such as fight or flight (Birmes et al., 2000).

There appear to be biological changes in the brain associated with PTSD as MRI studies have found evidence of hippocampal damage in veterans with combat-related PTSD. In a study by Gurvits et al. (1996) the volume of the hippocampal formation was reduced by over 20 percent and the loss was proportional to the amount of combat exposure the veteran had experienced. Others have found similar findings with a variety of individuals who have survived trauma (Bonne et al., 2001; Bremner et al., 1997, 2003; Carrion et al., 2001).

Certain professions are at higher risk than others for PTSD, such as fire-fighters, police and various crisis frontline personnel (Haslam & Mallon, 2003; Carlier et al., 1997; Bryant & Harvey, 1996). Various researchers have documented that approximately 25 percent of fire-fighters will develop PTSD at some stage in their careers (Bryant & Guthrie, 2007; Corneil et al., 1999; Del Ben, Scott, Chen & Fortson, 2006).

Mueser & Fox (2002) proposed a model which indicated that individuals with a previous mental health disorder were more likely to develop PTSD after a traumatizing event. In addition, having PTSD predisposed individuals to developing other types of mental health disorders such as phobias, generalized anxiety disorders, drug and/or alcohol addiction and clinical depression (Cox et al., 2007).

The negative elements of being exposed to a trauma have been well documented. An aspect of this that is only recently being acknowledged is the negative effects of vicarious traumatic exposure to individuals who are first responders.

Vicarious traumatization

Vicarious traumatization (also called secondary traumatic stress) is defined as the negative effects that occur to individuals who work in certain types of professions that are constantly exposed to the distress and suffering of others (McCann & Peralmann 1990). Continuous exposure to the trauma of others can erode belief systems and make individuals susceptible to post-traumatic stress disorder and acute stress disorder even though they are not directly involved in the trauma.

The psychological elements of vicarious traumatization are important to understand. Although individuals are not directly being harmed or in danger, it is their psychological processes that are being damaged. Human beings have a need to create meaning out of the context in which events occur; when faced with random acts of violence and situations with impossible explanations such as accidents, meaning cannot be understood or extracted. When individuals cannot balance the trauma with an internal explanation, the individual begins to question their fundamental view of the world causing psychological distress (McCann & Peralmann, 1990).

Figley (1983) documented that vicarious traumatization symptoms are nearly identical to those of post-traumatic stress disorder, with the exception that the person has not been directly exposed to trauma, but vicariously exposed to the traumatized person. The negative effects of being exposed to the suffering of others by professional health care workers have long been recognized and various studies have documented damaging psychological reactions following vicarious exposure to victimized populations (Collins & Long, 2003). Intervening in severe crises or the constant observation of human tragedy erodes psychological resilience. Psychological resilience refers to an individual's ability to endure stressors and resist negative psychological dysfunction and disorders such as stress, depression, helplessness or anger as well as disorders such as post-traumatic stress disorder, acute stress disorder, anxiety disorders and clinical depression (Brooks & Goldstein, 2004).

Farrar (2002) found that 10 percent of people who had worked with trauma survivors had symptoms of re-experiencing the event, avoidance and hyper-arousal as well as intrusive thoughts and emotional numbing. The effects of vicarious traumatization can include: severe, debilitating anxiety that persists for months and sometimes even years following the event: nightmares; depression; anger or aggressive behaviour; substance abuse; physiological reactions such as constant severe headaches; exhaustion and gastrointestinal distress (Baird & Kracen, 2006). Individuals working in the various professions that place them at risk will experience symptoms and distress which often goes undiagnosed and undetected because they were not directly involved in the event (Wasco & Campbell, 2002). However, since 9/11 and the well documented reactions of the diverse professions that were involved in the disaster it is becoming increasingly recognized that vicarious traumatization, left untreated, can have a profound effect on individuals and the importance of self-care models and training (Bauwens & Tosone, 2010; Piotrkowski & Telesco, 2011).

Research has documented that many professions are at high risk for vicarious traumatization such as: ambulance services personnel (Clohessy & Ehlers, 1999), fire-fighters (Argentero & Setti, 2011), police officers (Shaffer, 2011), social workers (Bride, 2004), disaster response workers (Connorton, Perry, Hemenway & Miller, 2011), psychologists and mental health workers (Jordan, 2010), rescue workers (Ricciardi, Valsavoia, Russo, Ferraro, Alloro, Messina, Dolce & Barbera, 2011), clergy (Hendron & Taylor, 2012) and nurses (Sabo, 2006). This growing body of research indicates that individuals in helping professions are at risk not only of experiencing stress, but also of developing pathological responses to learning of another's traumatic experiences (Cunningham, 2003).

Mental health professionals such as counsellors, social workers and psychologists are not usually present at the disaster/trauma but are exposed to the event when a victim retells a traumatic incident and gives an account of their experience and feelings. It is not unusual for these mental health workers to experience intense emotions concerning the event and the health and welfare of their client (Harrison & Westwood, 2009). Therapists are at risk for vicarious traumatization as a result of their empathetic engagement with clients who are survivors of trauma. Similar to the ways in which trauma impacts the survivors themselves, exposure to the traumatic material of clients can affect a therapist's sense of meaning, identity, world view, and beliefs about self and others. They begin to experience a change in their psychological belief systems and question their safety and the safety of loved ones (Lybeck-Brown, 2003).

Support resources for people who are indirectly affected by a traumatic event are on the rise and the negative effects of exposure to trauma are only beginning to be recognized (Bober & Regehr, 2005). To date the following have been identified as mediating the effects for those individuals in professions who will be exposed to secondary trauma: history of previous trauma, previous psychological well-being, social support, age, gender, educational achievement, socioeconomic status and styles of coping (Williams, Helm & Clemens, 2012). Another well supported aspect in preventing vicarious trauma is in the training and development of adaptive coping skills and building psychological resiliency (Russ, Lonne & Darlington, 2009; Zander, Hutton & King, 2010; Ben-Porat & Itzhaky, 2009). Support networks have been identified as important to help maintain self-efficacy and wellness and as a non-threatening way of helping to provide self-awareness about stress and anxiety (Cohen & Hoberman, 2006).. Finally education and debriefing have been suggested to offset the negative effects of exposure (Trippany, Kress & Wilcoxon, 2004).

ASSESSMENT

The assessment of anxiety is dependent upon the theoretical frame of reference and the purposes of the assessor. A variety of measures exist, although some are better developed and more useful in specific situations than others. The usefulness of psychological tests in the assessment of anxiety is varied because of its reliance on subjective reporting on cognitive functions such as attention and memory. Individuals may over report or under report symptoms and exaggerate various conditions for a variety of reasons (Leahy, Holland & McGinn, 2011).

The cognitive component of anxiety can only be measured by indirect means using observations which are again subject to inaccuracy and reactivity. Cognitive assessment can refer to a wide variety of criteria designed to measure thoughts, beliefs, attitudes and mood. It is important to emphasize that cognitive processes do not only represent components of the stress response, but also can influence the stress response. There are several dimensions in which cognitive processes can be assessed: these include process–content, occurrence–non-occurrence, conscious–non-conscious, meaning and validity (Kendall & Ingram, 1987).

Behavioural assessment methods are the most reliable and are the most closely tied to treatment. They include both direct observations made by the assessor and self-reports made by the individual. There are two basic types of observational methods; facial expressions and rate of speech and performance ability or adaptive functioning. Self-report questionnaires are used to indicate behaviour that may not be observable by the assessor to provide additional information on behaviour. These include activity schedules, ratings on specific behaviours and avoidance of certain stressors to name a few (Hofmann, 2008).

State-anxiety can be assessed by evaluating a person's thoughts, feelings and behaviours or by measuring the physiological changes associated with activation of the autonomic nervous system. The galvanic skin response and changes in heart rate appear to be the most popular measures. Blood pressure, muscle action potential, palmar sweating and respiration have also been given considerable attention (Shimizu, Seery, Weisbuch & Lupien, 2010). Physiological measures are ideologically attractive but complex to implement and difficult to interpret. No single measure appears robust enough to serve, on its own, as a measure of anxiety.

A number of rating scales, questionnaires and inventories have been constructed to measure s- and t-anxiety. The Hamilton rating scale, which was designed for evaluating patients diagnosed as suffering from neurotic anxiety state, is widely used. The specific types of anxiety symptoms that are rated include: anxious mood (worries, apprehension, irritability); tension (inability to relax, trembling, restlessness); fears (of strangers, animals, traffic, crowds) (Hamilton, 1959).

The state–trait anxiety inventory was developed to provide reliable, relatively brief self-report measures of both s- and t-anxiety. Since most anxiety inventories measure t-anxiety, a large number of items embodying content of proven relationship to the most widely used anxiety scales were rewritten so that each item could be administered with different instructions to measure eithers- or t-anxiety (Spielberger, 1996).

Self-report inventories and questionnaires are by far the most popular procedures for the assessment of anxiety because they are easily administrated and scored and do not require much expensive professional time.

Projective techniques such as the Rorschach inkblots and the TAT are also widely used in the clinical evaluation of anxiety.

TREATMENT

Medication

The basic psychopharmacological treatment for anti-anxiety is the benzodiazepines. The benzodiazepines were discovered by chance as chemists were searching for better muscle relaxants and accidently discovered that these variants not only relaxed muscles but also selectively reduced anxiety without causing extreme drowsiness. The advantages of this class of drug are its low abuse potential and that it continues its effectiveness as it is slowly eliminated from the body. This class of drug appears to be effective with social phobias, general anxiety disorders and panic disorders (Baldwin et al., 2005).

Antidepressants can also be used and appear to work more effectively on some types of anxiety disorders than others, such as PTSD and obsessive-compulsive disorders. Antidepressants can be used in the other types of anxiety disorders but generally as a second line of defence if the benzodiazepine class is found to be ineffective. Selective serotonin re-uptake inhibitors (SSRI) have been effectively used for PTSD. The side effects of antidepressants are more severe than the benzodiazepines; for example, monamine oxidase inhibitors have strict dietary requirements (Hidalgo et al., 2007).

Psychological therapies

Cognitive-behavioural therapy (CBT) is one type of counselling that is effective with the wide variety of anxiety disorders. The goal of CBT is to help the person understand how certain thoughts about situations and/or the environment can cause stress and anxiety, increasing the symptomatology. CBT assists individuals to change the way they think about the anxiety/trauma and its consequences. The individual learns to identify thoughts about the environment/trauma that creates emotional distress and replaces those thoughts with less distressing thoughts. CBT also helps the individual learn coping mechanisms to deal with feelings such as anger, guilt and fear (Dugas & Robichaud, 2007).

One cognitive-behavioural stress management strategy that has been particularly useful in anxiety disorders is stress inoculation training, developed by Meichenbaum. Stress inoculation training is the behavioural analogue of Orne's immunization model (Dobson & Block, 1988). The

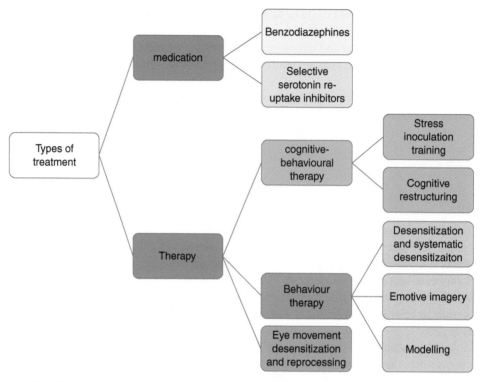

Figure 11.5   Obsessive-compulsive cycle of behaviour and thoughts

rationale underlying this approach assumes that individuals who learn ways of coping with mild levels of stress are vaccinated against uncontrollable levels of stress (Meichenbaum, Turk & Burstein, 1975). When a person is inoculated, he or she is given an opportunity to deal with a low dose of the stress-related stimulus in a controlled environment (Meichenbaum, 1972, 1977).

The experience of learning to cope with small and manageable portions of the stressor and/or stressful environment helps the person develop skills to cope with larger concerns in varied settings (Rehm & Rokke, 1988). Stress inoculation training emphasizes the need for the individual to learn to cope with a distressing event by gradually approaching the event. Stress inoculation training was successfully utilized in the control of phobias (Meichenbaum and Cameron, 1973), anger (Novaco, 1975), and interpersonal anxiety (Meichenbaum, 1973).

Meichenbaum and Turk (1976) suggested the use of Schachter's theory of emotion with anxious or phobic clients. Schachter (1966) believed that fear reactions were composed of two basic components, heightened physiological arousal and cognitive events. From this perspective, treatment can be focused on reducing physiological arousal and substituting more positive self-statements for the habitual anxiety-producing self-statements. The goal of treatment is not to eliminate anxiety, but to help the client respond adoptively in anxiety-arousing situations and to be resilient in the face of fear.

Various forms of relaxation training and cognitive coping techniques can be employed to enable the client to address these two components of anxiety-related responses. A variety of coping techniques are presented and the client may choose and practise those that he or she and the therapist agree may be most useful. The client in this type of therapy will learn as much as he or she can about the stressors to develop realistic expectations and a plan for dealing with predictable stressors. Relaxation skills and cognitive coping skills are also simultaneously developed. Problem-solving self-instructional training may be added if the client's cognitive repertoire is deficient in skills for approaching and solving problems (Meichenbaum & Deffenbacher, 1988).

Various coping strategies may include active behavioural responses as well as cognitive coping strategies. Once clients are able to describe and assess the phobic object and or stressful event, specific cognitive strategies can be designed. These strategies may include changing negative self-statements to more positive and adaptive ones and using imagined strategies to influence attention and affective aspects of the setting (e.g. guided imagery of a pleasant scene) (Meichenbaum & Turk, 1976).

Another type of cognitive behavioural technique that is useful for a variety of anxiety disorders is cognitive restructuring. Cognitive restructuring refers to the identification and modification of negative cognitive processes and structures. Common cognitive restructuring procedures include the following: evaluating the validity and viability of thoughts and beliefs, eliciting and evaluating predictions, exploring alternative explanations, attribution retraining and altering an absolutist, catastrophic thinking style (Bryant et al., 2009).

Reality therapy is a type of cognitive behaviour therapy where the therapist focuses on the present while actively and deliberately encouraging the individual to make a value judgement about his or her behaviour, to make a plan that would achieve the desired goal, and to be committed to the plan. Reality therapy assumes that when people are accountable for their actions and responsible for their behaviours they will be able to decrease the number of anxiety-producing incidents. Interpretations and attempts to provide insight are never part of the therapy in as much as these techniques serve to prompt excuses for irresponsible behaviours and to delay efforts to formulate and commit oneself to a plan of action that will change unwanted behaviours (Powers, 2008).

Behaviour therapy

Behaviourists find it unnecessary to diagnose psychopathology or use traditional assessment techniques to uncover the origins of abnormal behaviour in order to plan a corrective action for the treatment of anxiety disorders. The ideology is that they need to assess the current conditions influencing the occurrence of the unwanted behaviour in question. In addition once the factors are identified they must construct a realistic behavioural plan that will help them to extinguish the unwanted behaviours. Treatment strategies are then devised in terms of whether the desired effect involves:

1   a decrease in the emission of target behaviour;
2   an increase in the occurrence of wanted response or class of responses; or
3   a combination of increasing the rate of wanted behaviours and eliminating unwanted ones (Roemer & Orsillo, 2007).

Desensitization pairs the incompatible response of relaxation with a graded series of anxiety stimuli in such a way as to prevent the occurrence of the fear response (avoidance) and allow the anxiety to extinguish. Wolpe (1961) developed a method that involved the training of muscle relaxation and a hierarchy of fear-evoking stimuli arranged in order from the least anxiety-provoking to the most fearful. During the therapy the individual is relaxed and then is asked to imagine the least fearful stimulus, then the next in the hierarchy and so on until the individual reports that the relaxation has given way to anxiety. At this point relaxation is re-established and the process is repeated until the individual successfully goes through the entire hierarchy without anxiety (Rosqvist, 2005).

Systematic desensitization is slightly different as it is conducted in a way that maximizes anxiety arousal. This approach involves the induction of intense anxiety by exposing the client to highly threatening stimuli. The idea is to induce and sustain high levels of anxiety without relief, until the aversive reactions are extinguished (Rosqvist, 2005).

Emotive imagery uses imagery of pleasurable scenes which are incompatible with anxiety and are in effect substitutes for muscle relaxation. While the person enjoys the pleasurable fantasy, the anxiety-arousing stimulus is gradually introduced (Rosqvist, 2005).

Modelling is another behavioural technique which has been effective in reducing avoidance behaviours in children. An example of this type of technique is, a child who is afraid of dogs is exposed to another child playing and having fun with a dog. The child is then encouraged to imitate the behaviour (Rosqvist, 2005).

Eye movement desensitization and reprocessing (EMDR)

Eye movement desensitization and reprocessing (EMDR) is a trauma therapy developed by Shapiro (2001). EMDR involves recalling a stressful past event and 'reprogramming' the memory in the light of a positive, self-chosen belief, while using rapid eye movements to facilitate the process. EMDR incorporates elements of cognitive-behavioural therapy with bilateral eye movements or other forms of rhythmic, left-right stimulation. One of the key elements of EMDR is 'dual stimulation'. Individuals are asked to think and talk about memories, triggers and/or painful emotions while simultaneously engaging in bilateral stimulation. The external stimulation can also be bilateral tactile sensations and sounds (e.g. alternating hand taps or a chime that pans back and forth from ear to ear). The goal of EMDR is to 'unfreeze' traumatic memories allowing the individual to re-process the information and the person is then able to resolve them. Over time the cues associated with the trauma no longer trigger emotions and memories of the traumatic event. Research varies in terms of the effectiveness of this type of therapy and it only appears to be effective with PTSD (Maxfield & Hyer, 2002).

CONCLUSION

What happened to Caroline? Caroline probably began with a predisposition to anxiety disorders because of her temperament and the environmental factors of being exposed to parental over-concern and over-control as an only child. As previously discussed in this chapter, over-control can take either of two general forms, to either compulsively clean or check. In addition Caroline's mother was also very critical of her daughter's life choices. She was never satisfied with Caroline's accomplishments or behaviour, probably never praised or encouraged her efforts because she did not share the same types of goals. Caroline's mother appeared to be interested in 'old fashioned' attitudes of women and felt that the only vocation worthwhile was that of wife and mother, it is entirely possible that even if Caroline had chosen that direction for her life, her mother would have probably found fault. When Caroline's mother became ill, Caroline had no other choice but to take care of her mother in her apartment. Although it is very likely that Caroline previously felt depressed and anxious concerning her relationship with her mother, it was easy to ignore these feelings. Once Caroline's mother was living with her in close quarters, she could no longer ignore her feelings and could either face them or repress them. She chose to repress them and became depressed. The combination of caring for her mother, guilt, stress and anxiety resulted in the obsessive-compulsive behaviour. Even after her mother died, the reaction remained because the feelings were unresolved.

Summary

This chapter focused on the disorders characterized by anxiety. The initial discussion was on the interrelationship between the biological elements of feelings of fear and anxiety and how this interacted with psychological elements. The chapter then discussed models of anxiety and the specific disorders. Finally the chapter discussed various assessments and treatment of anxiety disorders.

LEARNING TOOLS

Key terms

Amygdala – mass of nuclei located in the temporal lobe of the brain and is part of the limbic system

Anxiety – an unpleasant, distress psychological and physiological state characterized by emotional, cognitive, physical and behavioural components

Auditory cortex – the area of the brain responsible for the processing of auditory information

Benzodiazepines – a psychoactive drug used in the treatment of anxiety

Cortisol – a steroid hormone that is released by the adrenal gland and is one of the main hormones that are released when an organism is under stress

EEG (electroencephalography) – records the electrical activity of the brain

Hypothalamico-pituitary adrenocortical system – an interdependent endocrine system that is one of the systems involved in stress and is a complex feedback system between the brain and the body

Monamine oxidase inhibitor – class of antidepressant drugs that act by inhibiting the activity of an enzyme preventing the breakdown of monoamine neurotransmitters

Neurosis – disorders of sense and motion caused by a general affliction of the nervous system

Selective serotonin re-uptake inhibitor – a class of antidepressants that act by increasing the level of the neurotransmitter serotonin

Sympatho-adrenomedullary system – involves the sympathetic nervous system and the adrenal glands and is involved with the homeostasis of stress and the stress reaction

Study guide

1 Discuss how the emotions of fear and anxiety are adaptive as well as being maladaptive.
2 Research the genetic information of anxiety disorders. Why are there differences in heritability among the disorders?
3 Compare and contrast the psychoanalytic explanation with the behaviourist's view of anxiety disorders.
4 Detail the differences between trait-anxiety and state-anxiety.

Case study in focus

Discuss the various treatments that have been described in this chapter. Which do you think would provide the best relief for Caroline? Would you say that Caroline has state- or trait-anxiety? Why would the distinction be important?

Personal development

Investigate how terrorism has impacted anxiety disorders, specifically post-traumatic stress disorders and vicarious traumatization. How has society changed in terms of belief systems and has this changed factors and elements associated with anxiety disorders?

Suggested reading

Beck, A.T., Emery, G. & Greenberg, R.L. (1985) *Anxiety disorders and phobias: A cognitive perspective.* New York: Basic Books.

Simpson, H.B., Neria, Y., Lewis-Fernandez, R., & Schneier, F. (eds) (2010) *Anxiety disorders: Theory, research and clinical perspectives.* London: Cambridge University Press.

Taylor, S. (2009) *Clinician's guide to PTSD.* New York: Guilford Press.

Wells, A. (2002) *Cognitive therapy of anxiety disorders: A practice manual and conceptual guide.* Chichester: John Wiley & Sons.

Personality Disorders

12

Learning aims

At the end of this chapter you should:

- Comprehend the classifications used for personality disorders
- Understand the different types of personality disorders
- Be knowledgeable of the various models/theories of personality disorders
- Be familiar with the various treatments utilized for personality disorders.

INTRODUCTION

CASE STUDY

Andrew's story

Andrew was referred to court-ordered counselling because of a drink driving conviction. As part of his sentencing he was required to attend 15 counselling sessions. The first five sessions were uneventful; he told the therapist that he had simply misjudged his limit and should have called a friend or taken a taxi home. He only drank the occasional pint and didn't consider himself to be an alcoholic. He did feel that his conviction was rather excessive considering all the crime that was going on, but he would pay the fine, finish the counselling sessions and would never get caught out again. He then told the therapist that having to come to the sessions was cramping his style as he was planning on moving out of the area and now he would have to wait. Andrew insisted that he did not have a drinking problem, and didn't really have any issues he needed to discuss. He avoided any discussions about family and was evasive any time the therapist brought up any conversations concerning family or intimate relationships. The sessions continued as non-eventful with Andrew mostly discussing various places where he had been on holiday. On the last session, Andrew said he had something he wanted to talk about. He then related how 'a friend' liked to pick up recently divorced women with small children who had been in difficult custody battles with their ex-husbands. His 'friend' would then be very gracious and kind, buying the woman flowers and small gifts, stuffed toys and computer games for the kids. He said his 'friend' would become the best boyfriend ever; paying bills, buying food, and very quickly his 'friend' would be invited to move in. After a few weeks his 'friend' would begin to sexually abuse the children. When his 'friend' had finished after a few months, he would cause an argument that would be a full blown fight and his 'friend' would pack up his belongings and leave, and his ex-girlfriend would find out afterwards what his 'friend' had done to her children. Andrew said his 'friend' felt safe because he knew the woman would never report what happened to the police because if her ex-husband found out she would lose her kids as he would probably take her back to court to fight for custody since she was responsible for what had happened. Andrew said his 'friend' had done this at least six times that he was aware of. The therapist sat stunned. When she asked what the friend's name was, and said that Andrew was duty bound to report him to the police as he was committing a horrendous crime, Andrew just smiled and said, 'I guess our time is up. Good bye Doc, have a nice life. It's been fun.'

Edie's story

Edie was a pretty 32-year-old who had been admitted to hospital for a suicide attempt. Her boyfriend had called the ambulance after he had found that she had ingested all the pills in the house and drunk a bottle of vodka and was unconscious on the floor in their flat. He had told the police that they had been fighting on the phone and he had come home to find her. He also said that this wasn't the first time and that he was sick of the drama and was going home to pack and leave. He then related to the police that this was Edie's ninth attempt and that whenever things became difficult in their relationship that she would attempt suicide. He was also fairly certain that the three 'miscarriages' were probably lies as well. He had been manipulated for the last time and was leaving while he had the chance and she was in the hospital.

WHAT IS A PERSONALITY DISORDER?

If a friend said to you before they introduced another person to you, they had a 'lousy personality' what would you be expecting? Someone with poor social skills? Someone who wasn't friendly? Someone who wasn't going to make the evening enjoyable? Your expectation of this new person would probably not be one of anticipation; probably more than likely you would dread the experience. However, if they described the person as having a 'great personality' you would probably expect to spend an enjoyable evening and possibly make a new friend. Having a 'good' personality is desirable, while having a 'bad' personality isn't something that anyone wants.

What is personality? Generally it is defined as the embodiment of the physical, mental, emotional and social characteristics of an individual and how these various characteristics interact and impact each other as well as being influenced by the environment (Eysenck, 1987). How is 'personality' different from the previously discussed element of temperament?

Temperament refers to innate individual differences which are characterized by particular behavioural styles and are significantly affected by the interplay of environmental forces (Thomas and Chess, 1977). Buss & Plomin (1975) felt that individual differences are governed by four temperaments which are innate: activity, emotionality, sociability and impulsivity, and that every person represents some combination of the four temperaments. Goldsmith and Rothbart (1991) proposed that behaviour manifestations of temperamental dispositions change during the course of childhood development. Thomas & Chess (1977) believed that temperament was biologically determined and modified by environmental elements. Personality is slightly different. It is also a product of the social environment; it is not innate, and it is shaped during later periods of development with the fundamental origin of personality being temperament. Personality is the result of all the influences, past and present, which shape and modify the outcome in a constantly evolving interactive process and is an integrative function of human behaviour that underlies temperament. Personality is generally referred to as the content of behaviour whereas temperament refers to intensity. Personality also refers to an individual's pattern of thoughts, feelings and behaviours; individuals may not always think, feel and behave in exactly the same way, but each person has a set of predictable patterns that are characteristic of them and can be describe by others (Pervin & Cervone, 2010).

Now that we have defined personality, what is a personality disorder? Personality disorders are different from any of the other disorders discussed. They are not diseases, but are considered to be maladaptive patterns to the affective and conative qualities of an individual. Buss and Plomin (1975) believed that after the age of ten years a child's temperament becomes relatively stable and consistent and that personality being a factor of temperament would also stabilize and become consistent during adolescence. After this point in development it is believed that personality doesn't change very much and that patterns that are developed will be applied through adulthood whether they are normal or maladaptive. The next question is: why are we concerned with personality disorders? Research has indicated that personality disorders constitute one of the most important sources of long-term impairment in both treated and untreated populations (Merikangas & Weissman, 1986).

HISTORY

Individuals with character flaws have always existed. Many books, plays and songs describe individuals who are not in control of their impulses and desires, engaged in immoral acts and cause mayhem and destruction to other people's lives as well as their own. During the nineteenth century, as other mental illnesses were being examined and classified, the disorders of personality were also being examined and re-classified. Previously they were referred to as 'moral insanity' but in 1891 Koch, a German physician, proposed replacing the label with the term 'psychopathic inferiority' which included all mental irregularities that were not classified as madness (Kellerman, 2012). Koch believed that a physical basis existed for these individuals with character impairments and that they stemmed from a congenital or acquired inferiority of brain constitution (Kellerman, 2012). Freud had a different view and believed that these individuals resulted from a psychodynamically defective constitution where the personality had not fully developed. Kernberg (1975) broke away from the more traditional psychoanalytic characterology and constructed a different framework for organizing personality types in terms of the level of their severity. While Kernberg was redefining the categories of personality disorders, the DSM was in revision and included many of the categories that Kernberg had previously redefined (Jansz & Van Drunen, 2004). The DSM III discarded psychoanalytic concepts and sought to group patients on the basis of observable symptoms with the objective of standardizing the new edition with the European classification system. This edition abandoned much of the psychodynamic view of mental disorders and the approach was based on particular underlying pathology (Jansz & Van Drunen, 2004).

As the DSM was being revised, a decision to include the personality disorders that had been earlier reclassified by Kernberg was made and the new classification system has been controversial ever since. Instead of placing personality disorders in a category or grouping them with the impulse control disorders, they were placed under the Axis II dimension which reflected the view that personality disorders were stable patterns and recalcitrant. Personality disorders were believed to be pervasive features which characterized an individual's enduring personality pattern and therefore virtually impossible to change. During the diagnosis phase, a clinician had to decide whether an individual was demonstrating a transient state that was associated with a clinical disorder or a pervasive enduring pattern (trait) or both. The new classification system enabled them to code both 'state' and 'trait' simultaneously (Benjamin, 2003).

The personality disorders continue to remain on Axis II because it is thought they are largely non-conscious, not easily altered and express themselves automatically in almost every aspect of functioning, but the placement under Axis continues to be an area of controversy (Roysamb et al., 2010).

The diagnostic criteria for personality disorders are either near to descriptions of actual behaviours or they are descriptions of traits and dispositions which could be readily operationalized and refined by behavioural referents and standardized behavioural observations. The DSM-IV-TR identifies four core features that characterize all personality disorders: extreme and distorted thinking patterns, problematic emotional response patterns, impulse control problems and significant interpersonal problems (APA, 2000). Currently the personality disorders are categorized under three main clusters: suspicious, emotional and impulsive and anxious. Table 12.1 categorizes the different groupings and disorders. There are three recurrent issues with the classification of personality disorders: the division appears to be arbitrary and not adequately justified, there is a great deal of overlap between the criteria which compromises their validity as separate disorders as well as overlap on the Axis 1 disorders, and the current three groupings have not been satisfactorily validated (Shedler et al., 2010).

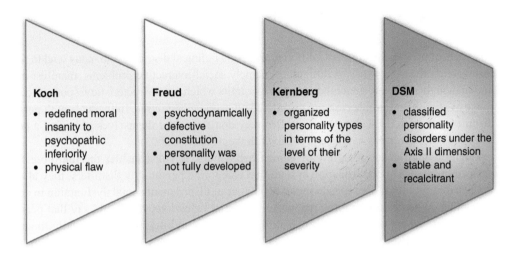

Koch
- redefined moral insanity to psychopathic inferiority
- physical flaw

Freud
- psychodynamically defective constitution
- personality was not fully developed

Kernberg
- organized personality types in terms of the level of their severity

DSM
- classified personality disorders under the Axis II dimension
- stable and recalcitrant

Figure 12.1

DSM CLASSIFICATION BY THE THREE MAIN CLUSTERS

The new changes to the DSM-5 have suggested significant changes to the current classification system including revised general criteria, provisions for clinical to evaluate a limited set of disorder types according to criteria and an overall measure of the severity of personality dysfunction. There is also a hybrid dimensional-categorical model that has been proposed (APA, 2012).

Table 12.1   DSM classification by the three main clusters

Cluster A – suspicious	Paranoid personality	Lack of trust – assume others will harm them
	Schizoid personality	Socially isolated – detached
	Schizotypal personality	Socially isolated – odd beliefs
Cluster B – emotional and impulsive	Anti-social personality	Hostile – aggressive behaviours
	Borderline personality	Intense and unstable emotions
	Histrionic personality	Drama often with somatic illnesses
	Narcissistic personality	Uniquely talented – brilliant/attractive
Cluster C – anxious	Avoidant personality	Social inhibition – sense of inadequacy
	Dependent personality	Need to be taken care of by others
	Obsessive-compulsive personality	Preoccupied with rules, regulations and orderliness

THE SOCIAL ASPECTS OF PERSONALITY DISORDERS

Disorders of personality are vastly different from other clinical disorders and many tend to see them as involving the same types of difficulties, namely social-interactive problems, manifest in action and in thought. They are general dispositions or traits which are characteristic responses to a broad range of stimuli and in this case are disordered adjustment responses. Individuals with personality disorders are often difficult to treat as often they don't consider themselves as having a problem. They see other people as having a problem with them (Sperry, 2003).

Cognitions influence a variety of human behaviours. If you consider the four core features defined by the DSM classification system that categorize personality disorders, they all tend to include disruptions of appropriate social behaviour or disorders of social dysfunction in one form or another. When examining the inappropriate social behaviour, one could say that personality disorders are an extreme lack of social skills that causes an interference with daily functioning. All personality disorders have difficulty in social behaviour; they are consistently dysfunctional or maladaptive perceptions, cognitions, or overt responses in an interpersonal context (Adshead & Jacob, 2008). There are five basic social skills: assertion, interpersonal aversion, rewardingness, social ability and affiliation (Cottrell, 2003). It is important to think of these five skills as being on a continuum of functioning. Not all personality disorders are on the extremes and not all personality disorders are flawed on all five social skills, although problematical behaviour on one tends to influence the other four. Table 12.2 describes the various social skills.

Table 12.2   Dimensions of social dysfunction in personality disorders

Social dimension	Negative	Positive
Assertion	Aggressive/manipulative/bullying/timid/ineffectual	Firm/confident/self-assured
Interpersonal aversion	Argumentative/confrontational/awkward	Pleasant/affection/attachment/fondness
Rewardingness	Selfish/greedy/egocentric	Caring/kind/altruistic
Social anxiety	Criticism/rejection/evaluation	Praise/approval/admiration
Affiliation	Aloofness/detached/distant	Alliance/friendship/association

DIMENSIONS OF SOCIAL DYSFUNCTION IN PERSONALITY DISORDERS

The first of the basic social skills is called assertion and is best described as one individual's influence over another person's behaviour (Cottrell, 2003). Assertion is dysfunctional when the behaviour is ineffective in influencing others in the desired way, or when it produces undesirable effects in others. Assertion exists on a continuum and is best described as standing up for one's rights, having oneself 'heard' over a crowd, an act of asserting or stating something, convincing others of a cause. For example, individuals in a discussion attempt to influence each other in a mutual way. A negative assertion would be talking over the other person, yelling, or in any way becoming aggressive and the opposite would be to agree with everything and not put up any defences. Both are examples of dysfunctional assertions.

The second social skill is defined as interpersonal aversion (Hutchings, Comins & Offiler, 1997). This is defined as an individual's behaviour that is consistently unpleasant or inappropriate, or when it repeatedly harms or disadvantages others. As a result of their inappropriate and unpleasant behaviour other people learn to avoid the individual's presence. This is a result of the individual's unskilled social behaviour and is defined as interpersonal aversion.

The third type of social skill is called rewardingness and is a type of social performance (Hutchings, Comins & Offiler, 1997). An individual is rewarding in their interactions with others when they are agreeable, cooperative, helpful, supportive, kind, generous, affectionate or enthusiastic. We learn these types of social interactions by appropriate modelling by our primary caregivers. These include what is often called 'social graces', e.g. saying 'please' and 'thank you'. Children are taught 'manners' – to share, be pleasant, be polite to others, to wait patiently, not to crowd in a queue. Individuals with a personality disorder are not likely to be rewarding in their interactions with others; they tend to be unpleasant and difficult and other people see them as being rude, impolite, discourteous and bad-mannered.

The fourth type of social skill is social anxiety (Csoti, 2001). Social anxiety manifests itself in a variety of forms and approaches; this includes behaviour and cognitions which are responses to a perceived threat from others, criticism from others, negative evaluation and fear of rejection by others. For example, nearly everyone will have some element of performance anxiety and people learn to adapt and conquer their fears. Individuals with high social anxiety are unable to overcome their negative attributions and cope by either becoming extremely defensive or complete avoidance of social situations.

The last dimension is affiliation (Antonello, 1996). Affiliation is defined as an association, relationship, connection, attachment with other people. Humans are social creatures and have a need to establish and maintain close interpersonal relationships with others. Individuals with personality disorders have a defect in their capacity to establish close relationships and maintain them over a period of time. They tend not to have warm and tender feelings for others and there is an indifference to praise or criticism. Dysfunctional affiliation takes a variety of forms and occurs for diverse reasons with the various personality disorders. For example, unlike the avoidant personality disorder, individuals with a schizoid personality disorder are socially isolated with no apparent desire for affiliation or social interaction; they rebuff any attempt, whereas the narcissist craves the social interaction but acts in ways that are inappropriate so that others do not want to interact with them. Appropriate social cognitions go hand in hand with effective social behaviour and dysfunctional social cognitions contribute to ineffective social behaviour (Linehan, 1993).

AETIOLOGY/MODELS

Personality disorders are believed to have their precursors in childhood although they are generally not diagnosed until adulthood as it is believed that during childhood and adolescence the personality is still developing and is malleable. The general consensus is that early experience plays a central role in shaping personality attributes. Research has suggested that a number of different interacting factors are involved in the aetiology of personality disorders. What is unknown is how much influence is important over the development of different personality disorders and how they interact with the temperament, social rearing practices, quality and type of attachments, culture, ethnicity, and family dynamics (Lewis-Fernandez & Kleinman, 1993).

Another factor that has been researched is early childhood traumas. It has been suggested that early and severe emotional trauma creates individuals who are vulnerable and when combined with temperament and environmental factors can cause personality difficulties (Ball & Links, 2009; Heim et al., 2008). Other evidence of causal factors in the development of personality disorders has been in family dynamics; research has indicated that family members with schizophrenia and manic depression are at higher risk for personality disorders (Erlenmeyer-Kimling et al., 1995; Maier et al., 1994).

What is difficult to determine is whether multiple combinations of these factors or one single factor may be much more important in the development of personality disorder. The fact that entire families or groups of siblings from high-risk families do not develop personality disorders leads us to believe that multiplicities of factors are responsible.

Figure 12.2 outlines the various models that have been hypothesized to be causal in the development of personality disorders.

Psychoanalytic model

The psychoanalytic model is based on the premise that early childhood experiences are responsible for the formation of personality disorders. The psychoanalytic model has three main approaches.

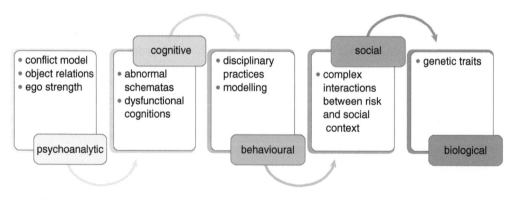

Figure 12.2

The first is based on ego strength and defence mechanisms. Individuals develop personality disorders as a direct response to defence mechanisms that are flawed and underdeveloped that interfere with the individual's ability to function. The individual develops primitive defence mechanisms that are maladaptive and cannot control the id's desires for immediate gratification without regard to reality. As a result of low ego strength the individual ignores all social norms and rules and gives into the id's desires (Clarkin, Fonagy & Gabbard, 2010).

The second approach is the conflict model and has a slightly different paradigm. It is based on personality constellations that are assumed to originate from developmental conflicts and defences that become translated into the trait structure of personality. Therefore all personality processes are the products of conflicts and compromises involving basic drives, especially sexual and aggressive impulses (Clarkin, Fonagy & Gabbard, 2010).

The last approach is the object relations premise. This approach believes that personality structures, including self and identity, are shaped by interactions with significant others. Problems arise from the failure to integrate different representations of the self or others, leading to fragmented images of self and others. Kernberg's concept of borderline personality is a classic example of how biologically determined aggressive feelings are assumed to impede integration of positive and negative object representations, resulting in splitting that leads to ego weakness. The borderline personality disorder individual displays the splitting by the intensity of emotions they often feel toward intimates (Kernberg, 1993).

Cognitive model

The cognitive model assumes that dysfunctional cognitions are at the core of an individual with a personality dysfunction. Their maladaptive patterns of cognition influence behaviour that is a product of a dysfunctional belief system and abnormal expectations. Young children are exposed to and frequently learn different and contrasting sets of perceptions, feelings, attitudes and behaviours as well as a mixed set of assumptions about themselves and others. Interactions between temperament and confusing life experiences lead to the formation of abnormal schematas which remain dysfunctional throughout the majority of adult life. Various life experiences continue to strengthen and support the abnormal schema that was formed during childhood and adolescence with the result being abnormal cognitions and behaviours (Linehan, 1993).

Behavioural model

The behavioural model is based on a broader perspective that emphasizes various factors such as inherited dispositions, organic dysfunctions and early childhood experiences as well as environmental and internal cues in the maintenance of dysfunctional behaviour. Behaviourists place emphasis on the reinforcement and punishment practices of the family as well as behaviours and attitudes modelled by parents and primary caregivers. According to the behavioural model, children are provided with little or no experience of consistent and supportive affectionate relationships when they are young and therefore never have the opportunity to model appropriate interpersonal behaviours

(Bandura, 1961). In addition, inconsistent and severe disciplinary practices of the parents make feedback irrelevant and do not provide the child with any reinforcement value. The child then fails to respond to appropriate feedback provided by others as a direct result of the feedback having no significant value to the child. Not only do they fail to develop by imitation, affectionate responses and an emotional concern for others, they are also provided with models for inappropriate, antisocial behaviours (Bandura, 1961). Research has shown that modelling is effective in producing a variety of behaviours both beneficial and detrimental. In particular, it has been demonstrated that children can acquire, via observational learning, responses such as self-controlling behaviour (Mischel & Liebert, 1966), empathy (Aronfreed & Paskal, 1970), and aggression (Bandura et al., 1963), to mention just a few of the more relevant behaviours to personality disorders.

Social model

The social model is based upon the ideology that unstable social structures and high rates of social change are factors in the development of personality disorders. Certain societies emphasize image over substance with various images projecting aggressive behaviour and antisocial attitudes as well as cultural norms which emphasize interpersonal superficiality and self-interest over appropriate social norms and behaviours. Contemporary examples of antisocial behaviour displayed as a result of flawed social structures are the recent riots in various cities in the UK.

Some of the factors shaping personality also come from outside the family, emerging out of experiences with peers and with the wider community. The social model is based on the idea that there are complex interactions between risk and protective factors and that social risk factors can be balanced by increased economic opportunities. Therefore the development of personality dysfunction is relevant to issues such as social context, social change, occupation, representation of mental illness, gender roles, social disparities, self-harm or self-threats, suicide, case identification and treatment interventions (Lopez & Guarnaccia, 2000).

Biological model

The biological model is based upon the premise that individuals are born with the genetic traits for a personality disorder which is then 'triggered' by the individual's environment. Research has not yet identified specific central nervous system structures correlated with personality dysfunction, nor has it identified gene linkages and personality disorder associations. However, there is promising research in the area of serotonergic function and the trait of impulsivity. Hernana et al. (2010) found lowered values of serotonin in the CSF of those exhibiting a variety of aggressive behaviours directed towards others and towards self (suicide). Livesley & Jang (2008) found in their research on genetically determined processes of behavioural activation, behavioural inhibition and behavioural maintenance that these behaviours were governed by the catecholamine system and subject to genetic influence.

Antisocial behaviour has been associated with high levels of neuroticism and extroversion which lead to changes in reactivity of autonomic nervous system and heightened arousal mediated by reticular activating system (Corr, 2008). Individuals with personality disorders exhibit lower

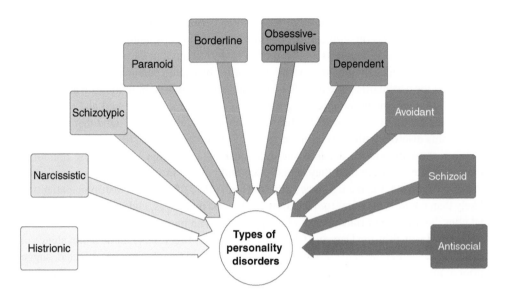

Figure 12.3

anticipatory fear as demonstrated by lower galvanic skin responses (Crider, 2008). In addition, Zuckerman (1990) found that adults with antisocial characteristics have a high level of sensation-seeking behaviour and children with conduct disorders show heightened response to reward in the form of changes in heart rate and skin conductance which is slow to fade when the stimulus is withdrawn. Other biological markers for impulsivity include defects in executive function on neuropsychological testing, as well as imaging findings pointing to dysfunction in prefrontal cortex (New et al., 2004; Soloff et al., 2003; Stein et al., 1993).

SPECIFIC TYPES OF PERSONALITY DISORDERS

Histrionic personality

The personality characteristics of the histrionic are extravagant, dramatic, overacted, and appear artificial or 'over the top', often accompanied by an air of superiority and a seductiveness designed to manipulate other people or to gain their sympathy, attention, or admiration (Alarcon & Covi, 1973). The histrionic personality tends to be very shallow and superficial in their relationships with others and is predisposed to be suggestible and easily influenced by other people in order to maintain their manipulative relationships. Individuals with histrionic personality disorder want to be the centre of attention and often will appear or become impaired and/or fragile in order to manipulate or receive attention from others. Nestadt, Romanoski, Chahal, Merchant, Folstein, Gruenberg and McHugh (1990) found that individuals with this disorder tend to use health care facilities more frequently than others.

Research has identified a positive association between somatoform disorders and histrionic personality disorders in clinical populations. Garyfallos, Adamopoulou, Karastergiou, Voikli, Ikonomidis, Donias, Giouzepas and Dimitriou (1999) found that 24 percent of patients with somatoform disorders also met the diagnostic criteria for histrionic personality disorders compared to 7 percent of the psychiatric patients with no somatoform diagnosis. Individuals with histrionic personality disorder are uncomfortable being alone and often become depressed and resentful when they are not the centre of attention. Corruble, Ginestet and Guelfi (1996) found that depression is common in this disorder with rates in the range of 15–30 percent.

When these individuals are in casual relationships, they often assume these relationships to be more intimate in nature than they actually are and behave in very egocentric ways, usually at the expense of the other person. Slavney and McHugh (1975) found that histrionic patients were more likely than controls to come from unhappy homes and marriages, and many were admitted to hospital after the breakup of romances or after arguments with partners.

Grant, Hasin, Stinson, Dawson, Chou, Ruan and Pickering (2004) found a prevalence of approximately 1 percent in the general population with males and females equally affected, suggesting that prior reports of an increased prevalence in females were an expression of gender bias found in hospital-based studies.

Torgersen, Lygren, Skre, Onstad, Edvardsen, Tambs and Kringlen (2000) found a heritability index of 0.67 in a large twin study indicating that environmental effects were minimized and that heritability played a large factor.

In terms of dysfunction in the social dimensions, the histrionic personality is a case of inappropriate assertive responding. The positive relationship between depression and lack of assertive behaviour suggests that histrionic individuals are not as skilled in assertion and become angry and depressed when they are unable to manipulate others to their intentions. Initially, they superficially appear not to have social aversion, but this is generally a tactic utilized to establish a relationship. Once this has been secured their manipulation and negative assertion generally drives the person away. They have a high need for affiliation, are not rewarding in their behaviour and seek praise and admiration from others.

Narcissistic personality disorder

This disorder is defined by extreme self-centredness, self-aggrandizement, self-indulgence, manipulation and taking advantage of others without regard for their feelings or rights. It is at the extreme other end of a continuum from altruism. Where someone would give their life for a stranger, the narcissist would expect that everyone else would sacrifice themselves for their life. Narcissists have a grandiose sense of self-importance and accompanying grandiose fantasies. They believe that they are special and unique and have a strong need for admiring attention. The cognitions are characterized by extreme self centredness and self-absorption. Individuals exaggerate their abilities and hold unrealistically high expectations for achievement, together with the expectation that others are obliged to do favours for them but with no expectation of reciprocation.. They become angry and hostile if others have any type of reciprocating expectations. They tend to be very sensitive and do not cope well with criticism, often having intense emotional reactions and outbursts (Masterson, 1999).

Individuals with this type of personality disorder are considered to be highly resistant to change; the perpetuation of narcissistic patterns especially in interpersonal relations leads to poor prognosis. The denial of problems and factors in the environment that interfere with grandiosity and narcissistic pursuits, combined with a compensatory fantasy life, and the opportunities for gratifying support of grandiose self-experience, are additional contributing factors (Millon, 1981; Kernberg, 1980).

Individuals with narcissistic personality disorder also like to be the centre of attention, but want the attention to be based on their perceived superiority over others. The most important discriminator is the inflated self-concept of the narcissist and its various manifestations of grandiosity, including exaggeration of talent, attractiveness, grandiose fantasies and sense of uniqueness (Plakun, 1987; Ronningstam & Gunderson, 1991). They are unwilling to recognize or identify with the feelings or needs of others and when they are unable to get their needs met they discard the individual and find someone who is willing to provide for them (Holdwick et al., 1998). As a consequence they have multiple failed relationships and friendships. When they are not the centre of attention they become envious and hostile toward others and often engage in dangerous and destructive behaviours in an effort to neutralize the competition. Ronningstam (2001) found that many individuals with narcissistic personality disorder also have antisocial characteristics ranging from inconsistent and contradictory moral stands to specific criminal behaviour. Blais (1997) identified a sociopathic factor in individuals with narcissistic personality disorder in terms of their lack of empathy, exploitation, envy and grandiose sense of self-importance.

The prevalence rate for narcissistic personality disorder in the general population ranges from 0.4–1 percent (Mattia & Zimmerman, 2001; Torgersen, Lygren, Oien, Skre, Onstad, Edvardsen, Tambs & Kringlen, 2007). Research has shown that narcissistic personality disorder is found more frequently among people in higher education or special professional groups and is equally prevalent in both genders (Maffei, Fossati, Lingiardi, Madeddu, Borellini & Petrachi, 1995; Crosby & Hall 1992; Plakun, 1990). Higher rates of the disorder are found in clinical populations: 32 percent among cocaine abusers (Reich, Yates & Nduaguba, 1989), 47 percent among bipolar patients (Turley, Bates, Edwards & Jackson, 1992), 21 percent among depressed patients (Sato et al., 1997).

Narcissism is a good example of aversive social behaviour. There are elements of narcissism in both the histrionic and borderline personality disorders. Narcissism is also a good example of dysfunctional assertion; exerting influence over others that is consistently exploitative to the other's disadvantage and without regard for the other's rights is frowned upon by most groups in our society. Others will have a high social aversion to them − they are not rewarding in their relationships, have a high affiliation (how else could others admire them?) and high social anxiety.

Schizotypic personality disorder

This personality disorder is characterized by individuals who are described as being odd and extremely isolated. Individuals with this disorder avoid forming close relationships and they frequently experience perceptual abnormalities and have odd beliefs, for example it is common for them to believe they are telepaths and have the ability to read other people's thoughts. Schizotypic speech involves many peculiarities, including unusual use of words or concepts, and lack of clarity of thought. These peculiarities, however, never become so severe as loosening of associations or incoherence and do not meet the diagnostic criterion for schizophrenia (Burack & Enns, 1997).

Schizotypic perceptions include recurrent illusions, depersonalization or derealization. These abnormal cognitions are generally stable, but under stress can increase in severity resulting in temporary psychosis. Individuals with schizotypal personality disorder have extreme social anxiety that manifests itself in a variety of ways such as perceived threat from others, negative evaluation and rejection (Lenzenweger, 2010). Fossati et al. (2003) found that individuals with schizotypal personality disorder have difficulty with aspects of close relationships: confidence and have great discomfort with closeness.

Individuals with schizotypal personality disorders have a poor quality of life, deprived subjective well-being, reduced self-realization, less contact with friends and family, less social support, a lot of negative life events and generally a poorer global quality than the general population (Cramer et al., 2003). Skodol et al. (2002) found dysfunction in relation to parents, siblings, family members and friends as well as occupational dysfunction. Individuals with schizotypal personality disorders appear to be emotionally constricted and indifferent, experience little or no pleasure in things, seem indifferent to praise or criticism and come across as detached, cold and unexpressive (Goulding, 2004).

Neurological studies have identified brain abnormalities in people with schizotypal personality disorder such as peculiarities in startle response and eye movement response (Cadenhead et al., 2000). Coccaro & Siever (2005) have documented distinctive behavioural patterns in family members diagnosed with schizophrenia and those diagnosed with schizotypal personality disorder suggesting these behaviours share a common genetic origin.

Prevalence studies show that schizotypal personality disorder is relatively rare and occurs in 0.7–0.6 of the general population, with a higher number of schizotypal traits found in individuals with less education, and living apart from families and partners (Maier, Lichtemann, Klinger, Heun, & Hallmayer, 1992; Torgersen, Lygren, Oien, Skre, Onstad, Edvardsen, Tambs & Kringlen, 2001; Zimmerman & Coryell, 1989).

Genetic studies indicate a specific familial and genetic relationship between schizophrenia and schizotypal personality disorder, with no other personality disorder being consistently related to schizophrenia (Torgersen, 1992; Kendler & Gruenberg, 1984).

In terms of social dysfunction schizotypal individuals' major dysfunction is in affiliation; they are detached and distant and do not want close relationships. They don't tend to be overly assertive, and instead are ineffectual; they have virtually no interpersonal aversion because they have no affiliation and are not rewarding in their relationships, although they do not display the geocentricism that other personality disorders do.

Paranoid personality disorder

This disorder is characterized by extreme suspiciousness or mistrust of people (although suspiciousness in normal social interaction is often adaptive, as the opposite of this characteristic would be naivety). Individuals with this disorder have a rigid belief system that others are out to harm them, take advantage of them, or humiliate them in some way. Even when contrary evidence and information exists they will ignore anything that does not support their original hypothesis of harm. They continuously imagine hidden motives, are constantly scanning their environment for signs of betrayal or hostility; they often read threats and menace into everyday situations and are always on their guard. They find evidence of threat and menace with no appreciation for the context in which this evidence is found and their expectations of threat are always confirmed. Those with paranoid personality disorder also may be very critical of others, argumentative and rigid in beliefs, again stemming from harbouring unwarranted suspicions about people around them. They put a lot of effort into protecting themselves and keeping their distance from others. They are known to preemptively attack others whom they feel threatened by. They tend to hold grudges, are litigious, and display pathological jealousy. Distorted thinking is evident: their perception of the environment includes reading malevolent intentions into genuinely harmless, innocuous comments or behaviour, and dwelling on past slights. Their emotional life tends to be dominated by distrust and hostility. People with a paranoid personality disorder tend to think that other people are deliberately putting them down or are out to get them. They react really badly when they have setbacks in their lives and often bear grudges, or believe in conspiracies against them that are clearly not backed up in fact (Freeman, Bentall & Garety, 2008).

Transient ideas of reference are also part of paranoia and when inevitable interpersonal conflict arises, the paranoid individual exaggerates the problem and is reluctant to come to a resolution, remaining argumentative and disagreeable (Kantor, 2008). Requests for changes in their behaviour are interpreted as criticism and confirm their ideas of threat, which precludes criticism ever being constructive. It has been observed that the course of the disorder rarely worsens or goes into remission and remains stable over time (Akhtar, 1990). Fulton et al. (1993) found that paranoid personality disorders had less psychiatric intervention, were themselves less likely to seek treatment and although extremely dysfunctional were less likely to worsen on follow-up compared to other personality disorders.

Recent studies examining the possible relationship of PTSD and paranoid personality disorder found that individuals with paranoid personality disorder had a higher rate of comorbid post-traumatic stress disorder than subjects without the disorder (29 percent compared with 12 percent) and had higher rates of physical abuse and assault in childhood and adulthood (54 percent compared with 35 percent), suggesting a possible link between trauma during early events in life and subsequent paranoid behaviour and mistrust (Golier, Yehuda, Bierer, Mitropoulou, New, Schmeidler, Silverman & Siever, 2003). In a similar study, Humphreys et al. (2001) found that in a group of drug-dependent women who had suffered physical, emotional or sexual abuse, the survivors of physical abuse in particular were more likely to be paranoid than the emotionally or sexually abused women. Bierer & Elliott (2003) found that sexual and physical abuse in childhood appeared to be predictive of paranoid and antisocial personality disorders in later life.

The prevalence rate for paranoid personality disorder was 0.5 to 2.5 percent in the general population, and more common in males (Grant, Hasin, Stinson, Dawson, Chou, Ruan & Pickering, 2004). Ramklint, Von Knorring, Von Knorring & Ekselius (2003) identified higher risk factors for individuals developing a paranoid personality disorder if they had a previous childhood substance-related disorder. Kendler (1985) identified individuals at higher risk if first-degree relatives had a delusional disorder as opposed to relatives with schizophrenia (4.8 percent compared to 0.8 percent).

In terms of social dysfunction individuals with paranoid personality disorders display extreme interpersonal aversion, negative assertions, extreme social anxiety and negative assertions.

Borderline personality disorder

The borderline personality disorder is characterized by an enduring instability of behaviour, cognition and affect. These individuals are argumentative and devalue others. They are manipulative without finesse, demanding, dependent, irritable, and sarcastic. They tend to report chronic feelings of loneliness and emptiness, and complain that their life lacks pleasure or enjoyment. Their personal history often includes depressive episodes, impulsivity, manipulative suicide attempts, alcohol and drug abuse, self-mutilation, unusual sexual behaviour including promiscuity, inappropriate intense anger, and transient stress-related paranoid ideation or severe dissociative symptoms and brief transient psychotic episodes. This disorder is characterized by repeated, intense, one-to-one relationships which are usually unstable, transient and brief (Skodol, Gunderson, McGlashan, Dyck, Stout, Bender, Grilo, Shea, Zanarini, Morey, Sanislow & Oldham, 2002; Gunderson & Links, 2008; Skodol, Gunderson, Pfohl, Widiger, Livesley & Siever, 2002). They are extremely impulsive and often act without thinking about consequences to themselves or others. Perry and Klerman (1980) describe individuals with borderline personality disorder as individuals who report feeling angry and then behave in an angry ways often directing their anger at a variety of targets. The borderline type shows several of the characteristics of emotional instability but includes problems with self-image, lack of personal clarity about preferences (including sexual) and chronic feelings of emptiness (Gunderson, 2007).

The prevalence rate for borderline personality disorders in the general population is between 0.2–1.8 percent (Swartz, Blazer, George & Winfield, 1990). Prevalence rates increase if patients within the mental health system are sampled, with 75 percent of patients diagnosed with borderline personality disorder being female and at younger ages at diagnosis than other personality disorders and with approximately 9 percent committing suicide (Frances, 1986). Individuals with borderline personality disorder tend to be single, separated or divorced (Zimmerman & Coryell, 1989). There is a high rate of reported sexual and physical abuse and borderlines have a high rate of contact with mental health services (Zanarini, Young, Frankenburg, Hennen, Reich, Marino & Vujanovic, 2002).

Genetic studies indicate a specific familial and genetic relationship of 0.69 giving a clear indication that genetic factors are crucial in the development of borderline personality disorder (Torgersen, Kringlen & Cramer, 2001). A number of psychosocial factors have been related to the aetiology which include: prolonged early separations and losses, disturbed parental involvement, childhood histories of physical or sexual abuse, and high prevalence of affective disorder in first-degree relatives (Zanarini & Frankenburg, 1997).

The effect of these environmental factors may be mediated through their influence on neurobiological development, particularly of the arousal system. In genetically predisposed individuals, developmental abnormalities in the frontal lobes may be stimulated by environmental insults, which lead to difficulty in inhibiting impulsive action (Rinne, de Kloet, Wouters, Goekoop, DeRijk & Van Den Brink, 2002).

Comorbidity with Axis I disorders is often a common feature. Skodol,Gunderson, McGlashan, Dyck, Stout, Bender, Grilo, Shea, Zanarini, Morey Sanislow & Oldham (2002) found that around 60 percent of patients are diagnosed with major depressive disorder; 30 percent have panic disorder with agoraphobia; 12 percent substance misuse; 10 percent bipolar-I; and 4 percent bipolar-II disorder.

Obsessive-compulsive personality disorder

This disorder is characterized by individuals who are governed by an extreme sense of rules and behaviours, excessive perfectionism, preoccupation with orderliness, and mental and interpersonal control at the expense of flexibility and openness (Pfohl & Blum, 1991). They display ritualistic behaviours that are generally taken to an extreme and exhibit maladaptive behaviours which become ineffective and inefficient and significantly disturb the individuals' functioning in daily life. Individuals with this type of personality disorder are preoccupied with lists and small details, to the extent that purposeful activity becomes lost in the preoccupation of perfectionism at every step. They are reluctant to delegate tasks, have inflexible belief systems and morality, are often over-committed to work at the exclusion of leisure activities and interpersonal relationships, and are prone to violent rages when they are unable to completely control their environments or there is interference (Sanislow, Little, Ansell, Grilo, Daversa, Markowitz, Pinto, Shea, Yen, Skodol, Morey Gunderson, Zanarini & McGlashan, 2009).

The behavioural features of obsessive-compulsive personality disorder are that they are generally polite and formal but keep social relationships at a distance. They often lack warmth and involvement, are loyal in relationships and organizations that they do subscribe to but remain emotionally detached. They are highly respectful to authority figures, seek approval from supervisors and individuals they deem to be at a higher social and/or occupational level and are highly critical of others they consider below them and seldom giving positive feedback (Calvo et al., 2009).

In terms of cognitive characteristics, individuals are dogmatic, overly sensitive to criticism, often lack empathy toward others, have difficulty expressing affection, love and tenderness, and have high social and performance anxiety. They fear failure and of making mistakes and are frequently dissatisfied with their performance in any arena (Nestadt, Riddle, Grados, Greenberg, Fyer, McCracken, Rauch, Murphy, Rasmussen, Cullen, Pinto, Knowles, Piacentini, Pauls, Bienvenu, Wang, Liang, Samuels & Roche, 2009).

Prevalence rate for obsessive compulsive personality disorder showed a range from 1.6–6.4 percent in the general population, and range from 3–10 percent among people referred to mental health clinics, with a mean of 5 percent (Widiger & Sanderson, 1997).

Millon (1996) hypothesized that environmental factors were important in the development of this disorder and proposed that parental over-control was responsible. Millon's premise is based on the child's fear of parental rejection and retaliation. As long as the child operates within the parental approved boundaries, the child is safe from parental punishment. The child is continuously taught to comply with rules and parental expectations and must be orderly, educated, organized, punctual and scrupulous. As a result of being continuously exposed to situations where they need to show their sense of responsibility they behave in order to avoid guilty feelings and parental disapproval.

The course of obsessive-compulsive personality disorder is relatively stable through time, tends to appear during adolescence or the beginning of adult life, and is more prevalent among individuals with methodical and detailed jobs (Robinson, 1999).

In terms of social dysfunction, these individuals are extremely high in social anxiety, moderate levels of affiliation and assertion and have slight elevations of interpersonal aversion.

Dependent personality disorder

This personality disorder is characterized by allowing others to assume responsibility for all major areas of their life. They subordinate their needs to those upon whom they depend, avoiding the necessity to be self-reliant. These individuals tend to be indecisive, lack self-confidence, are timid and ineffectual to an extreme. They have difficulty completing tasks without help, feel uncomfortable and helpless when they are alone and often go to excessive lengths to obtain support, protection and nurturance. They are often preoccupied with fears of being left alone and will immediately become involved in another relationship if the current one ends (Bornstein, 2009).

This personality is often difficult to diagnose as there are many confounding variables. For example there is support for the premise that certain individuals express dependent strivings in a flexible, modulated manner which enables them to obtain needed help and support, whereas others express dependency in ways that undermine their help- and support-seeking efforts (Bornstein, 1993). Baltes (1996) found a population-wide increase in dependent behaviour through later adulthood that is a consequence of increase in functional dependency that occurs in old age. Longitudinal research indicates stability in dependency levels. Individuals who show high rates during early adulthood continue to show high levels later in life (Abrams & Horowitz, 1996).

In marked contrast, situational variability changes dramatically in response to perceived opportunities and risks. When the dependent person believes that passive behaviour will strengthen the attachment to potential care providers, passivity develops; when the dependent individual believes that active behaviour is necessary, assertive behaviour is displayed (Bornstein, 1993).

Another important element that must be considered is the factor of culture and gender. Many cultures emphasize interpersonal attachments and gender roles more strongly than individual achievement and persons raised in these cultures and environments will show higher levels of dependency than those raised in individualist cultures that are not related to dependent personality disorder and not dysfunctional within that context (Cross, Bacon & Morris, 2000).

Research indicates that dependent personality disorder is related to genetic factors with a concordance rate in monozygotic twins of approximately 30 percent (Torgersen, Kringlen & Cramer, 2001). Currently no studies have determined what inherited factors increase dependent personality disorder but temperament has been hypothesized to be a contributing factor (Richter & Brandstrom, 2009).

The prevalence rate is estimated to be between 0 percent and 10 percent in the general population (Klein, 2003) somewhat higher in women than men (Bornstein, 1997) and between 15 and 25 percent in hospital and rehabilitation settings (Oldham, Skodol, Kellman, Hyler & Steven, 1995).

Comorbidity with Axis 1 disorders indicates substantial correlations with mood disorders, anxiety disorders, adjustment disorders, eating disorders and somatization disorders (Grodniczuk & Piper, 2001). Barber and Morse (1994) found that dependent personality disorders showed significant comorbidity with paranoid, schizotypal, antisocial, borderline, histrionic, narcissistic and obsessive-compulsive personality disorders in a mixed-sex sample of psychiatric outpatients.

In terms of social dysfunction these individuals display high negative assertions in terms of timid and ineffectual behaviour, moderate interpersonal aversion, moderate rewardingness and high affiliation needs.

Avoidant personality disorder

Another form of social anxiety is avoidance of social interaction as in the avoidant personality. These individuals withdraw from and actively avoid social interaction and any opportunities for close personal relationships despite a strong afflictive desire. This withdrawal is the result of an extremely fearful expectation of criticism, humiliation or rejection. These individuals may have one or two close friends, but only when the other person provides constant unconditional approval and acceptance: at the first sign of criticism, they will withdraw. Social phobias, or exaggerated fears of specific social situations, may complicate pervasive and general social avoidance in this personality disorder (Tillfors & Ekselius, 2009).

The major disruptive effect of social anxiety in the avoidant personality disorder is social isolation. Avoidant personality disorder is a pervasive pattern of social inhibition, feelings of inadequacy or inferiority, and hypersensitivity to negative evaluation. People with this disorder are timid, extremely self-conscious and fearful of criticism, humiliation, and rejection, which are thought to be an extreme variant of the fundamental personality traits of neuroticism. They usually feel inadequate and uncertain when meeting someone new or doing something that is unfamiliar. Despite their great desire for the warmth of companionship, they try to avoid social situations at any cost due to their alleged fear of rejection. Because of their extreme vigilance about rejection, they are afraid to speak up in public or make requests of others. Individuals with this disorder experience extreme anxiety in social situations that dominate their emotional life and interfere with their ability to function. Their high levels of anxiety cause them to avoid social situations such as parties and other social gatherings (Turkat, 1990). Individuals with avoidant personality disorders often have a very limited social world with a small circle of confidants and tend to be very restricted (Herbert, 2007).

Skodol, Gunderson, McGlashan, Dyck, Stout, Bender, Grilo, Shea, Zanarini, Morey, Sanislow and Oldham (2002) found that certain personality traits in avoidant personality disorder, such as feeling socially inept and socially inadequate, tend to remain stable over time, while other dysfunctional behaviours that serve to adapt to defend against or compensate for ineffectual traits such as social isolation appear to change over time.

The prevalent rate for avoidant personality disorder is 0.5–2 percent of the general population, and appears equally in both genders (Grant, Hasin, Stinson, Dawson, Chou, Ruan & Pickering, 2004; Jackson et al., 2004). It is more prevalent within clinical settings and reported to present 5–35 percent in psychiatric populations (Zimmerman & Mattia, 2001). Grant, Hasin, Stinson, Dawson,

Chou, Ruan and Pickering (2004) found that individuals from lower income groups, basic educational levels, widowed/divorced/separated and never married were at higher risk for the disorder.

Comorbidity with Axis 1 disorders indicates high correlations with major depression, dysthymia, agoraphobia and social phobias (Alnaes & Torgersen, 1988; Johnson & Lydiard, 1995; Mauri, Sarno, Rossi, Armani, Zambotto, Cassano & Akiskal, 1992; Schneier, Spitzer, Gibbon, Fyer & Liebowitz, 1991). Depressed individuals with both avoidant personality disorder and social phobia but not social phobia alone appear to have greater social dysfunction (Alpert, Uebelacker, McLean, Nierenberg, Pava, Worthington, Tedlow, Rosenbaum & Fava, 1997). Avoidant personality disorder is often comorbid with social anxiety disorder; however it is not clear whether these two disorders are independent or if one is the extreme form of the other (Millon & Davis, 1996; Reich 2000).

In terms of social dysfunction, avoidant personality disorder displays extreme social anxiety and although they have a high affiliation, they are unable to overcome their fears.

Schizoid personality disorder

The schizoid personality disorder is characterized by an all-encompassing pattern of detachment from social relationships and a restricted range of emotional expression. Individuals with this personality disorder avoid all social contact with others, are isolated, introverted, reclusive, unemotional, disinterested, impersonal and aloof. They are uncomfortable with all types of social contact, which includes physical and emotional and reject any type of connection with others including, family and childhood friends. They prefer to engage in solitary activities and often do not derive any pleasure from participating in these activities. Individuals with this disorder are described as being emotionally cold, uncaring, unfeeling and basically uninterested in others. They rebuff any physical contact and do not engage in any type of sexual experiences with others. They are often described as being emotionally flat and show no range of affect including anger (Mittal, Kalus, Bernstein & Siever, 2007).

Beck (1990) found that individuals with schizoid personality disorder tend to view themselves as loners who value independence, solitude and mobility above interpersonal relationships with others. Frances, First and Pincus (1995) described individuals with this personality disorder as being unable to form personal relationships or to respond to others in an emotionally meaningful way.

The few social contacts they do maintain are generally first-degree relatives who demand little intimacy and make few emotional demands (Thylstrup & Hesse, 2009). Millon and Davis (1996) found that these individuals engage in social communication only when it is perfunctory and formal and often react passively to adverse circumstances and appear unable to respond appropriately to important life event.

Schizoid personality disorders desire to be are attached to their social contacts but often have conflicted feelings about how intimate the contact will be. They appear to long for the security relationships can provide while at the same time require freedom and independence (Kalus & Bernstein, 1995). Millon & Davis (1996) describe the schizoid personality disorder as an 'asocial' pattern in which people are preoccupied with tangential matters, are apathetic, and while not intentionally unkind, have a paucity of social skills and an inability to sense the needs of the people around them. They are under-responsive to most forms of stimulation or reinforcement, often using intellectualization as a defence mechanism. Akhtar (1987) found that individuals with more normal variants were often described as being dull and uninteresting; they are able to function adequately in their occupations but avoid all types of social contact with colleagues. Individuals with this disorder will experience a low level of sadness if separated from social contacts and a low level of anxiety if they are forced into interaction with others; generally they have a lack of reactivity which results in little need for complex defence mechanisms as they engage in few complicated unconscious processes (Shedler & Westen, 2004; Millon & Davis, 1996).

Prevalence rates are estimated to be approximately 1.7 percent in the general population and appear more frequently in males who seem to be more impaired than females (Torgersen, Kringlen & Cramer, 2001; Gooding, Tallent & Matts, 2007).

Comorbidity with Axis 1 disorders indicates high correlations with drug and alcohol abuse, Asperger, social phobia and agoraphobia (Raine, 1989; Lenzenweger & Willett, 2009). On Axis II there are high correlations with avoidant personality disorders and schizotypal (Kalus, Bernstein & Siever, 1995).

Aetiological factors have not been established, however dopaminergic abnormalities have been proposed as a possible factor (Depue & Morrone-Stupinsky, 1999). Other factors hypothesize sociocultural factors, interaction of temperament and the environment (Henning, Herpertz & Houben, 2008).

In terms of social dysfunction, individuals with schizoid personality disorders have high social anxiety, moderate interpersonal aversion, low rewardingness (although not unpleasant they are not caring and altruistic) and have low affiliation.

Antisocial personality disorder

Antisocial personality disorder is characterized by a broad range of symptoms in six different domains (Arrigo & Shipley, 2001; Berrios, 1996). Table 12.3 categorizes these behaviours under the six domains.

The single most revealing trait within the description of antisocial personality disorders is their lack of guilt or remorse. When they manipulate and/or take advantage of someone they have a total

Table 12.3   Six domains of antisocial personality disorder

Behavioural organization	Lack of perseverance, unreliable, reckless, restless, disruptive, aggressive
Emotionality	Lack of anxiety, lack of remorse, lack of emotional depth, lack of emotional stability
Interpersonal attachment	Detached, lack of commitment, lack of empathy or concern for others
Interpersonal dominance	Arrogant, deceitful, manipulative, insincere, disingenuous
Cognitive	Suspicious, inflexible, intolerant, lack of concentration
Self	Self-centred, self-aggrandizement, self-justification, a sense of entitlement, uniqueness, invulnerability

Adapted from Berrios, 1996

lack of regard for their victim's feelings and assume no responsibility over their actions. They are able to consume their human victims as easily as drinking a beverage and then throwing away the empty container. Their lack of culpability is generally what others find so abhorrent. Other crucial features that distinguish these individuals are inability to profit from experience, inability to delay gratification, inability to form lasting emotional ties, stimulus seeking and superficiality (Farrington, 1991).

Earlier in our history they were called 'psychopathic' or 'sociopathic', terms that more closely defined their criminal actions. Both terms are still utilized by the general public, especially when another murderous crime spree is brought to our attention by the press, but the appropriate psychiatric/psychological term is antisocial personality disorder. Whereas schizophrenia is the disorder most closely associated with madness, antisocial personality disorder is most closely associated with inhumane crimes and criminal activity.

Individuals with antisocial personality disorders have both fascinated and horrified those who have attempted to explain the rationale behind their actions and crimes. In 1888, Koch was the first to use the term psychopath and attributed the disorder to a hereditarily determined weakness (Willis, Herve & Yuille, 2007). Freud considered these individuals to be defective rather than constitutionally inferior, believing that all antisocial individuals had failed to interject the requisite moral prerogative through the inappropriate or inadequate behaviours of their parents (Elliott, 2002). Behaviourists have focused on reinforcement and punishment practices of the family as well as behaviours and attitudes modelled by the primary caregivers. Others believe that there is a defect in the autonomic or central nervous system and use the evidence of the antisocial personality disorder's lack of emotionality.

Individuals with antisocial personality disorder have a characteristic 'emotional flatness', that is, they are less emotionally responsive than others, which many believe is why they have an inability to form affectionate relationships and lack guilt and empathy (Morizot & LeBlanc, 2005). In addition to being less emotionally responsive to others, they are also less responsive to stimuli or events that are emotionally provocative to others and as a result experience boredom more frequently (Romero, Luengo & Sobral, 2001). Boredom naturally leads to sensation seeking and various researchers have documented the antisocial's need for stimulation (Perez & Torrubia, 1985; Haapasalo, 1990; Sher, 1994).

Eysenck's (1967) personality analysis saw antisocial as being at the lower end of the cortical arousal dimension. Studies examining this dimension have consistently observed that the electroencephalographic (EEG) patterns contained a greater incidence of slow-wave activity (Deckel, Hesselbrock & Bauer, 1996; Mednick, Vka, Gabrielli & Itil, 1981; Ishikawa & Raine, 2002). Lijffijt, Cox, Acas, Lane, Moeller and Swann (2012) found that antisocials demonstrated abnormal pre-attentive filtering in pathological impulsivity. Gao and Raine (2009) found that reduced P3 amplitudes (measure of brain activity and engagement of attention) and prolonged P3 latencies reflected inefficient deployment of neural resources in processing cognitive task-relevant information. Various studies have identified lower resting levels of galvanic skin responsivity indicating a significant difference within normals and individuals identified as antisocial personality disorders and the autonomic nervous system (Lobbestael & Arntz, 2010; Schug, Raine & Wilcoz, 2007; Macintyre & Schug, 2007).

Additional support of antisocials being stimulus seekers came in vigilance tasks, in which subjects are required to watch over long periods of time, under reduced stimulus conditions, the occasional presence of a signal. The research in this area indicated that antisocials are typically under-aroused and when they are placed in a situation where they are unable to seek stimulation, they become rapidly bored and their attention to the task weakens (Orris, 1967; Lykken, 1955). Individuals with antisocial personality disorder also show a greater preference for frightening and dangerous experiences and engage in impulsive sensation seeking more often than normal subjects (Emmons & Webb, 1974; Zuckerman, 2001).

The general conclusion of these various studies is to document that antisocials are stimulus seekers because they are emotionally under-aroused. They are less responsive to stimuli that are emotionally arousing to others, and therefore slower to acquire responses that are under the control of emotional consequences. Various techniques of punishment are less effective in modifying the behaviour of the antisocial because the emotional overtones that accompany punishment as well as the emotional anticipation are lower. Antisocials do not appear to have a constitutionally defective response system to punishment; rather they have learned to be non-responsive under certain conditions and oppositional in other situations. When there is a degree of uncertainty they are responsive to punishment but only when it is relevant to them. Neurobiological evidence does point to a defect in the autonomic nervous system of antisocials, what specific elements are still unknown.

Another significant area in the aetiology of antisocial disorders is the research in the psychosocial factors of child development and parental discipline. Previous environmental and social factors, e.g. poverty, poor stimulation, overcrowding, large families, have been proved not to be causal in the development of antisocial behaviour (Raine, 2008). McCord and McCord (1963) early on demonstrated a relationship between antisocial acts and a history of inconsistent or erratic discipline. Other researchers have confirmed their findings and found that not only do the parents of children who later become antisocial use inconsistent discipline, they almost exclusively employ harsh punishment (Straus, 1999; Patterson, 1984; Patterson & Dishion, 1988; Flynn, 1999). Inconsistent punishment rapidly becomes ineffective leading to an increase in the intensity of punishment. Several studies have described the use of excessive verbal abuse and physical punishment by parents of children who later display aggressive behaviours; in addition when physical punishment is employed it is particularly harsh and generally constitutes child abuse (Feigelman, Dudowitz, Lane, Prescott, Meyer, Tracy & Kim, 2009; Winstok, 2011).

Another factor found in inconsistent parental practices was substance abuse (Fite, Colder, Lochman & Wells, 2008; Parker & Benson, 2004; Boden, Fergusson & Horwood, 2008). The parents of antisocial individuals either inconsistently vacillate between permissiveness and harshness or are persistently severe in their responses to their children (Button, Scourfield, Martin, Purcell & McGuffin, 2005). So for example, if a child is beaten and verbally abused when they are 'good' as well as when they are "bad'," punishment becomes irrelevant and will not serve to discriminate amongst behaviours, thus losing its power to control unwanted behaviours in the child. In addition, if in the context of this inconsistency, both verbal and physical punishment are excessive, then the child will gradually become desensitized to the effects of punishment, again rendering these events irrelevant in the control of behaviour. As a result of genetics, family dysfunction and inconsistent parental practices we would expect that children with a predisposition to antisocial personality disorder would have an insensitivity to both verbal and physical punishment, social and physical feedback of any form will be less provocative and these individuals will have difficulty in responding appropriately to any type of positive reinforcement and have an inability to reciprocate. Button, Scourfield, Martin, Purcell and McGuffin (2005) found that gene–environment interaction effects were highly significant in their twin study and that a risk genotype conferring susceptibility to family dysfunction was responsible for most of the variance found in their study.

Rates of prevalence for antisocial personality disorders report approximately 2–3 percent in the general population, the rate among psychiatric patients is approximately 1–2 percent and the rate among correctional offenders and substance abusers is relatively high, with approximations of 50 percent, with males outnumbering females by about 3:1 (Robins, Locke & Regier, 1991).

Individuals with antisocial personality disorder have high rates of comorbidity with substance use disorders (Hemphill, Hart & Hare, 1990; Robins, Locke & Regier, 1991). This causes more difficulty in terms of treatment issues as the combination of substance use and antisocial personality disorder is daunting. Research indicates that individuals with antisocial personality disorder engage in more disruptive behaviour during treatment, are less likely to remain in treatment and engage in more criminal activity after treatment than controls (Hemphill & Hart, 2002).

In terms of social dysfunction individuals with personality disorders have a high assertion that is combined with low interpersonal aversion. They are pleasant in their contacts with others but in a manipulative and self-serving manner. They are high in rewardingness, high in social anxiety as they do not like negative evaluations and their affiliation is moderate. Their social dysfunctions in many ways are a paradox. They are emotionally indifferent to others and insensitive to feelings, but they are able to discern their feelings well enough to charm and manipulate others to their advantage. The former is often seen as a lack of empathy and the latter as a Machiavellian skill. It is not unusual for antisocials to live with partners and to take advantage. However once the superficial interaction is over and the antisocial has used the partner for what he/she wants, they are unable to carry the relationship further. They are able to use empathy to a dysfunctional advantage and use other's emotion to sustain their own needs. Furthermore it has been shown that empathy has little to do with accurate person perception required of successful manipulators (Guterman, 1970).

ASSESSMENT

The assessment of personality disorders does not differ significantly from those disorders that are coded on Axis I and comprise the clinical disorders. There are four sources of information that are utilized in the diagnosis and assessment: observations/clinical interviews, formal rating scales and checklists, self-report inventories and projective techniques.

The clinical interview consists of the therapist asking the individual a variety of questions. A standardized type of interview has been found to be helpful as it greatly increases the reliability and validity of the interview. One specific instrument found useful for personality disorders is the International Personality Disorder Evaluation interview. This clinical interview was developed by the World Health Organization to specifically investigate personality disorders and was designed with both the ICD-10 and the DSM-IV diagnostic criteria for personality disorders. Studies employing this instrument have demonstrated good inter-rater reliability and temporal stability (Loranger et al., 1994).

Rating scales and checklists are designed so that they can be completed by anyone who is acquainted with the individual being assessed. Rating scales are easy to use and generally require that the individual filling out the scale makes a series of judgements based on behaviour and impressions. An example of a rating scale that has been used with various personality disorders with good results is the Hare Psychopathy Checklist (PLC-R) (Hare, 1999).

Self-report inventories assess individuals by their own responses. A self-report inventory typically provides an overall profile that can be used to establish baselines to evaluate treatment progress, as well as important information on current levels of functioning and dangerous behaviour such as suicidal ideation. Two assessments that have been widely used in personality disorders are the Minnesota Multiphasic Personality Inventory (MMPI) and the Millon Clinical Multiaxial Inventory (MCMI) (Millon, Millon, Davis & Grossman, 1997; Butcher, Dahlstrom, Graham, & Tellegen, 2001).

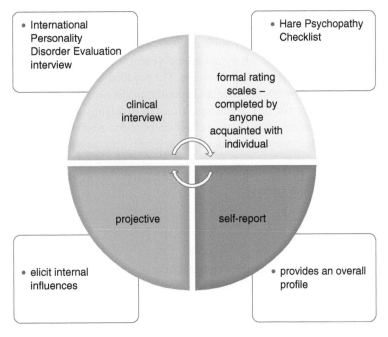

Figure 12.4   Assessment of personality disorders

The projective techniques are designed to elicit internal influences on behaviour with unstructured, vague or ambiguous situations. Two widely utilized instruments are the thematic apperception test which uses pictures of various interpersonal situations and the subject is asked to tell the story, and the Rorschach inkblot test where the individual is asked to describe what they see (Murray, 1943; Rorschach, 1942).

TREATMENT

Generally individuals with personality disorders seek treatment for three reasons: an acute crisis caused by vocational or personal failures or losses; in response to requests or ultimatums from family, employer, or court; or due to an increasing sense of dissatisfaction or meaninglessness in their own life (Benjamin, 2003). The following is a brief discussion of the various treatments utilized in personality disorders.

Psychodynamic therapy

Psychodynamic therapy is based on the premise that personality is shaped by childhood experiences, and unconscious mental functioning is responsible for behaviour, symptomatology and emotional distress. The displacement of past relationships (transference) onto present interactions with others is important to treatment and finally the therapist's emotional response back to the individual (countertransference) is a significant source of information within the treatment setting. Psychodynamic therapy focuses on symptomatic neuroses such as the behaviours that are displayed by individuals with personality disorders. The psychodynamic understanding of an individual is heavily influenced by transference and countertransference developments in the evaluation and treatment process. Personality is conceptualized as involving an ongoing attempt to actualize certain patterns of relatedness that largely reflect unconscious wishes. Psychoanalysis also studies the unique set of defence mechanisms found in each individual as a key to diagnostic understanding and treatment. Defences ward off awareness of unpleasant affect states, troubling sexual or aggressive wishes and attempts to stabilize a person's self-esteem, therefore are important in the therapeutic process (Sperry, 2003).

Cognitive therapy

This type of therapy focuses on correcting the abnormal schemas with more appropriate schemas. Individuals with personality disorders are encouraged to evaluate and modify their global, rigid, negative beliefs about themselves, others and their worlds and to develop more realistic, adaptive ideas. Each personality disorder is characterized by a specific set of dysfunctional belief and compensatory strategies. Once individuals are able to identify their abnormal belief systems, cognitive behavioural therapies then focus on a variety of emotional, interpersonal, supportive, problem-solving techniques to help them modify their maladaptive ideas and cognitions. Therapists help individuals with personality disorders to change their belief systems both at a cognitive level as well as an emotional level, exploring and modifying the meaning of significant childhood experiences. Cognitive restructuring is emphasized in order for individuals to identify their automatic thoughts and adapt their distorted cognitions into new functional behaviours. Therapists often use 'homework' assignments to elicit and help individuals to respond to maladaptive cognitions that interfere with more adaptive responses. Treatment is also used to solve problems and achieve specific goals. Often individuals with personality disorders have difficulty identifying goals or working towards problem solving behaviour, especially those who believe they are helpless or vulnerable (Beck, Freeman & Davis, 2007).

Medication

Medication is used in managing specific features of personality disorders and can help facilitate the individual's ability to use psychotherapeutic techniques and interventions. Psychopharmacological intervention appears to be used only for the treatment of specific symptoms rather than the entire spectrum of personality disorder. Research in the use of medications has indicated that it is useful in treating individual differences such as perceptual-cognitive symptoms, quasi-psychotic features, impulsivity and aggression as well as affective symptoms (Soloff, Meltzer, Greer, Constantine & Kelly, 2000; Cornelius, Soloff, Perel & Ulrich, 1990; Nose, Cipriani, Biancosino, Grassi & Barbui, 2006; Fournier, DeRubeis, Shelton, Gallop, Amsterdam & Hollon, 2008). Psychopharmacological interventions have not proved effective in dealing with distress and modification of symptoms of self and interpersonal functioning (Binks, Fenton, McCarthy, Lee, Adams & Duggan, 2006). Pharmacotherapy trials have shown efficacy for neuroleptic drugs in low dose strategy against these symptoms in borderline and schizotypal patients (Bartak, Spreeuwenberg, Andrea, Holleman, Rijnierse, Rossum, Hamers, Meerman, Aerts, Busschbach, Verheul, Stijnen & Emmelkamp, 2010). The affective and impulsive components of personality disorders appear responsive to MAOs, tricyclic antidepressants and SSRIs (Soloff, Meltzer, Greer, Constantine & Kelly, 2000; Cornelius, Soloff, Perel & Ulrich, 1990; Nose, Cipriani, Biancosino, Grassi & Barbui, 2006; Fournier, DeRubeis, Shelton, Gallop, Amsterdam & Hollon, 2008).

Combination treatment

Research indicates that the combination of psychotherapy and medication is probably the most effective in treating personality disorders (Bateman, 2009). The necessity of using psychotherapy and medication forces an examination of the principles and problems involved and the development of a rational framework for combined treatment. The combination of the two approaches ensures a more integrated, consistent and cohesive approach (Leichsenring & Leibing, 2003; Clarkin, Levy, Lenzenweger & Kernberg, 2007).

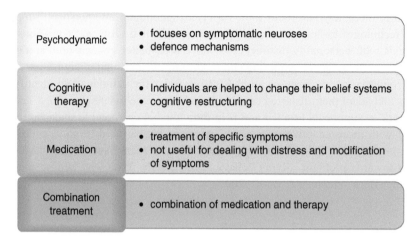

Figure 12.5

CONCLUSION

Returning to our case studies: Andrew is a disturbing dilemma; he reveals information when he knows that his court-ordered counselling sessions are over and he will no longer be required to attend. Did he really have a friend who was participating in these horrendous acts? Was it Andrew? Or did he make up the story to deliberately upset his therapist? Clearly whatever his motivations were, and whether or not he was involved in the sexual abuse of young children, he deliberately manipulated his therapist in a way to cause the most harm. His actions and behaviours are characteristic of antisocial personality disorder – he does not feel guilt or remorse – he was ordered by the court to have counselling otherwise he would not have come in of his own free will – and then he used the sessions in order to manipulate and control as well as provide himself with amusement. Could Andrew's therapist report him to the police? She could, but it is likely that they will be unable to do anything – no victim has come forward. Andrew could always say he was 'messing' with his therapist. There is no crime in making up stories during a counselling session. We can't violate Andrew's rights to privacy, so doing an investigation would be wrong. He never said HE was involved, only that he had knowledge of a friend. As troubling as this case is, unfortunately it is characteristic of individuals with antisocial personality disorder.

The second case concerning Edie is another difficult situation; clearly Edie will need some immediate intervention before she is released from the hospital. She exhibits many of the classic symptoms of a histrionic personality disorder; she uses illness to control her interpersonal relationships and is controlling and self-centred. Her boyfriend is angry and feels manipulated and it is highly likely that she did lie about being pregnant and miscarrying in order to manipulate her boyfriend. Her multiple suicide attempts appear to be designed to solicit the constant care and approval she needs. Again, Edie's personality difficulties are documented in the literature; histrionics tend to use health issues and suicidal attempts to manipulate and control. They are without finesse so eventually their intimate relationships end. The major concern is that at some point Edie will misjudge one of her suicide attempts and will not be rescued in time. In her case psychotherapy combined with medication may help her understand that her actions are causing her to lose the things she most desires, and it may be possible with cognitive behavioural therapy to help Edie learn and utilize better strategies for achieving her goals and maintaining her relationships.

Summary

This chapter began with a discussion of the classification and definition of personality disorders. It discussed the different social dimensions that are abnormal in individuals with personality disorder and then discussed the aetiology and various theories and models that have been used to clarify the development of personality disorders. The chapter then went on to discuss the specific personality disorders and provide a general overview of assessment and treatment strategies.

LEARNING TOOLS

Key terms

Affiliation – an association, connection

Altruism – concern for the welfare of others, unselfishness

Assertion – affirmation, a statement of assurance, confidence, insist on one's rights

Countertransference – the psychotherapist's reactions to the patient's feelings, complex feelings that the psychotherapist has towards the patient

Empathy – intellectual identification with another person's feelings, thoughts and attitudes

Extroversion – being concerned with things outside of the self; being concerned with the external environment rather than one's own thoughts and feelings

Interpersonal aversion – a strong feeling of dislike between persons

Prevalence – how widespread or common something is

Rewardingness – something that is given or provided – gratitude, positive return

Schemata – an underlying pattern or structure – provides the basis by which someone relates to the events he/she experiences

Self-aggrandizement – making it appear that someone is better/appear greater than they actually were/are

Social anxiety – distress concerning social events, occasions, contacts

Sociopath – a person who lacks a sense of moral responsibility or social conscience

Transference – the shift of emotions from one person or object to another – the transfer of feelings about a parent to an analyst

Study guide

1   Why is the concept of disease not suitable when discussing personality disorders?
2   What are some of the issues of the classification of personality disorders?
3   Compare and contrast two models of personality disorder.
4   Detail two out of the ten personality disorders.

Case study in focus

Discuss the various models that could be applied to Edie's behaviour. How would the psychody-namic model be different in explanation to the behaviourist's model? What models could we apply to Andrew?

Personal development

Investigate the history and legal aspects of antisocial personality disorder. How does criminally insane differ from the psychological aspects?

Suggested reading

Dobbert, D. (2010) *Understanding personality disorders: An introduction*. New York: Rowman & Littlefield.

Adshead, G. & Jacob, C. (2008) *Personality disorder: The definitive reader*. New York: Jessica Kingsley.

Rotgers, F. & Maniacci, M.P. (2005) *Antisocial personality disorder: A practitioner's guide to comparative treatments (Comparative treatments for psychological disorders)*. New York: Springer.

Moskovitz, R.A. (2001) *Lost in the mirror: An inside look at borderline personality disorder*. New York: Taylor Trade.

Substance-Related Disorders

13

Learning aims

At the end of this chapter you should:

- Understand the various models of addiction
- Understand how drugs work in the brain
- Understand the various types of drugs
- Be familiar with the various treatments that are used in substance-related disorders.

INTRODUCTION

CASE STUDY

Diane began drinking with her friends when she was 12. It started as a bit of fun but soon she found herself drinking 10 to 12 cans of cider every weekend. Her parents had recently divorced and she found that she was often left unsupervised. Her mother had gone back to work and she spent every other weekend with her father. The divorce was amicable and her parents happily went to other lives. They were solid middle-class and Diane was their only child. Diane was loved by both of her parents, her room was filled with stuffed toys, a new computer and she always had the latest phone. Diane had no specific reason for drinking, her friends were doing it and it was something to do. Diane loved the feeling that alcohol gave her and she didn't even mind when she drank too much and got sick. She was always the 'life of the party. Unfortunately during one of those parties she lost her virginity and wasn't even sure which person was responsible. After that she seemed to have lost her inhibition and began binge drinking and having sex. Her parents began to see changes in Diane. She became difficult and argumentative as well as being very secretive about her friends. Her behaviour became uncontrollable and at 16 whenever she was confronted, she simply ran away and returned after the weekend partying. Her new-found freedom came with new friends and she added smoking cannabis and using LSD to her binge drinking. She became known as a party girl and was always going from party to party on a weekend. At a party not far from her father's house she first tried MDMA, also known as ecstasy; shortly after taking the drug she went into convulsions. Her friends at the party panicked and argued about what they should do and eventually someone called an ambulance. When the ambulance arrived most of the party attendees had left. Her parents were contacted by the numbers on her phone. She went into a coma shortly after arriving in A&E and died two days later with the official cause being, anoxic encephalopathy or lack of oxygen to the brain, specifically due to MDMA intoxication.

INTRODUCTION

Deaths attributed to ecstasy overdose are rare, but the use of the drug is on the rise especially among teenagers and young adults. There has been a great deal of controversy over ecstasy and LSD with a previous governmental chief drug adviser, David Nutt, stating that ecstasy and LSD were less dangerous than alcohol. He also famously compared horseback riding deaths with ecstasy deaths and was fired over his continued comments concerning the reclassification of many illegal substances such as cannabis, LSD and ecstasy. Although David Nutt was correct, the number of deaths attributed to ecstasy in the UK is small, how does substance abuse factor into the larger question of substance-related issues? Is it simply a matter of politics? What about the psychological elements of abusing substances and becoming addicted; should we simply calculate the dangerousness of a drug based on the number of deaths per year? If we reclassified drugs would the number of substance abusers go down? Would reclassifying drugs reduce the number of substance addicted individuals?

In early June 2011 many high-profile celebrities together with lawyers and academics requested that David Cameron revisit the governmental policies, specifically the 1971 Misuse of Drugs Act. Many believe that the policy has only been effective in criminalizing people who use drugs and damaging communities, and has done nothing for reducing the number of individuals abusing substances. How does governmental policy affect substance abuse?

A report by the charity-funded UK Drug Policy Commission found that the UK has the highest levels of addiction and multi-drug consumption and the second-highest rate of drug-related deaths in Europe. Drug-related crime costs England more than £13 billion a year and damages the health of hundreds of thousands of addicts. What causes the devastation and why?

The abuse of substances usually begins with curiosity, excitement, peer pressure, or a prescription. The next steps in problematic behaviour are dose size, frequency, tolerance, and psychological dependence due to the reinforcing effects of pleasure and social-peer approval, and then finally the use of substances begins to take precedence over all other behaviours and an obsessive preoccupation with the drug occurs. The individual then begins to display drug-seeking behaviour and learns drug-abuse skills (e.g. drug acquisition, drug language, drug administration) (Bardo, Donohew & Harrington 2010).

It is believed that drug use may have begun as early as 7,000–4,000 BC with the use and cultivation of opium poppies (Bejerot, 1970; Brown, 1961; Maurer & Vogel, 1973). It is likely that recreational use and abuse of opium also began about this time when cultivation increased availability. The variety of drugs used for recreational purposes and abuse has changed throughout the years in accordance with shifting societal standards and sanctions. Although the varieties and types of drugs that have been abused have changed, drug abuse in some form has a long history. Alcohol has an even longer history and it is believed that fermented beverages existed as early as 10,000 BC (Rudgley, 1995). It is likely that as long as beverages have been fermenting there have been people who have been abusing them and a percentage of those individuals becoming addicted.

WHO USES DRUGS?

Prevalence

The British Crime Survey is a large national survey of approximately 45,000 adults who live in a representative cross-section of private households in England and Wales. The British Crime Survey enquires about a number of crime-related topics and has included questions on illicit drug use. An issue with this information is that the BCS provides valuable information from and about British households but it does not cover some important small groups such as the homeless and those living in institutions. As a result it is likely to underestimate the overall use of drugs, especially opiates and crack cocaine. However, it does provide one representation of drug use across England and Wales that is useful.

The 2009/10 survey found that 8.6 percent of 16–59 year olds had taken an illicit drug and 3 percent had used a class A drug in the past year. Approximately 3 million individuals have used some type of illicit drug use and around 1 million individuals have used a class A drug. Out of these individuals 3.3 percent were defined as frequent drug users, using a drug more than once a month on average in the last year. Cannabis was the most frequently used drugs with one in 15 adults using in the last year. An estimated 2.4 percent reported the use of powder cocaine which is approximately 0.8 million adults. The most common age for the onset use of cannabis was 18 and for powder cocaine was 18. The most common age at which ecstasy was first taken was 18 years of age.

The extent of illicit drug use was approximately that one out of every three individuals aged 16 to 59 (36.4 percent) had used illicit drugs at some point in their lives. Class A drug use was less common and cannabis was the drug most likely to have been abused. Men reported higher levels of illicit drug use than females with drug use being twice as high.

There is a clear relationship between nightclub and pub visits and illicit drug use. The levels of drug use increased with increased levels of frequent visits to a nightclub or pub. Any illicit drug use increased as the frequency of alcohol consumption increased. There is a strong relationship between alcohol consumption and class A drug use: 0.6 percent of those who did not drink in the last month had used a class A drug in the last year compared with 5.1 percent of adults who drank three or more times a week (British Crime Survey, 2009/10).

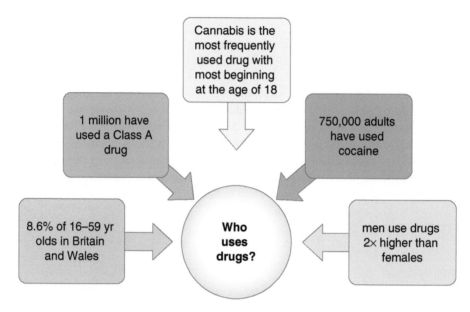

Figure 13.1   Drug use in Britain and Wales

Table 13.1   Drugs and their classification under the Misuse of Drugs Act

Classification	Drug
Class A	Powder cocaine
	Crack cocaine
	Ecstasy
	LSD
	Heroin
	Methamphetamine
Class A/B	Amphetamines
Class B	Cannabis
Class B/C	Tranquillizers
Class C	Anabolic steroids
	Ketamine
Not Classified	Glues and solvents

Table 13.2   Age and type of drug usage

	Powder cocaine	Ecstasy	Hallucinogens	Amphetamines	Cannabis	Ketamine	Solvents	Any drug
16–19	4.6	3.5	1.8	2.8	18.5	1.7	3.3	22.3
20–24	6.2	4.8	1.2	2.1	14.3	1.7	3.1	18.1
25–29	4.6	2.3	0.7	1.3	9.9	0.5	1.3	13.3
30–34	3.2	2.0	0.4	0.8	6.3	0.2	0.9	8.9
35–44	1.4	0.7	0.2	0.7	3.8	0.2	0.5	5.5
45–54	0.4	.2	0.1	0.2	2.1	0.0	0.2	2.5
55–59	0.1	.1	0.0	0.0	1.1	0.0	0.1	1.5

2009/10 British Crime Survey

WHAT CAUSES THE ABUSE OF DRUGS AND ALCOHOL?

The aetiology of drug use may be conceptualized in two interdependent categories: personal-psychological factors and social factors. Personal motives that have been identified include: satisfying curiosity, achieving a sense of belonging, expressing independence and hostility, seeking pleasure, attaining increased understanding, peer pressure, instant achievement, psychological support, rebellion, aphrodisiac effects fostering relaxation, and facilitating escape (Hawkins, Catalano & Miller, 1992; Sinha, 2008). In terms of psychological factors, psychopathology has been found to predispose individuals to drug and alcohol dependence and abuse (Mirin, Weiss, Griffin & Michael, 1991; Perry & Carroll, 2008). However, it is difficult to determine whether individuals become drug addicted as a direct result of their psychopathology or after. In other words which came first? Another psychological factor has involved medical treatment for a painful illness and then the individual becomes addicted to the drugs prescribed (Compton & Volkow, 2005).

Social factors relating to the aetiology of drug abuse are numerous: the availability of the substance, the prevalence of abusers and geographical location. Having an association with other drug users also increases vulnerability to drug use. Other contributing social factors are: single parent homes, divorce, lack of parental guidance, marginal social status, chronic unemployment, transience, war and rapid sociocultural change (Gorsuch & Butler, 1976; Andersen & Teicher, 2009).

Studies examining the family dynamics of drug-dependent individuals revealed an excessive dependency on their families. Children from drug-abusing families are at high risk for drug abuse as adults. Research has found that mothers of drug abusers or addicts fostered dependence. Addicts also appear to serve an important role in dysfunctional families allowing the family to focus on the addict's problem to the exclusion of other family problems (Chaffin, Kelleher & Hollenberg, 1996; Hemovich & Crano, 2009; Tafa & Baiocco, 2009).

TYPES OF ABUSED DRUGS

Alcohol

Alcohol molecules are small and soluble in both fat and water, invading all parts of the body. Alcohol is classified as a depressant because at moderate-to-high doses it depresses neural firing; however, at low doses it can stimulate neural firing. At moderate doses, the alcohol drinker experiences various degrees of cognitive, perceptual, verbal and motor impairment, as well as a loss of mental control. High doses result in unconsciousness; if blood levels reach 0.5 percent, there is a risk of death from respiratory depression. Alcohol intoxication also produces a red facial flush which is produced by the dilation of blood vessels in the skin. This dilation increases the amount of heat that is lost from the blood to the air and leads to a decrease in body temperature. Alcohol is also referred to as a diuretic because it increases the production of urine by the kidneys (Kuhar, 2011).

Alcohol, like many addictive drugs, produces both tolerance and physical dependence. The livers of heavy drinkers metabolize alcohol more quickly than do the livers of non-drinkers, but this increase in metabolic efficiency contributes only slightly to overall alcohol tolerance. Alcohol withdrawal often produces a mild syndrome of headache, nausea, vomiting, and shaking often referred to as a 'hangover' (Winger, Woods & Hofmann, 2004).

Individuals who are addicts will experience significant withdrawal symptoms which occur in three phases. The first phase begins about five or six hours after the individual stops drinking and is characterized by severe tremors, agitation, headache, nausea, vomiting, abdominal cramps, profuse sweating and sometimes hallucinations. The defining feature of the second phase, which typically occurs between 15 and 30 hours after the individual stops drinking, is convulsive activity. The third phase, which usually begins a day or two after an individual stops drinking and lasts for three or four days, is called delirium tremens (DTs). DTs are characterized by disturbing hallucinations, bizarre delusions, agitation, confusion, hyperthermia (high temperature), and tachycardia (rapid heartbeat). The convulsions and the DTs produced by alcohol withdrawal can be lethal (Walcott, 2007).

Long-term use of alcohol causes a great deal of physical damage. Alcohol attacks almost every tissue in the body and chronic consumption produces extensive damage and Korsakoff's syndrome. The elimination process causes extensive scarring, or cirrhosis, of the liver, which is the major cause of death among heavy alcohol users. Alcohol erodes the muscles of the heart and increases the risk of heart attack. It irritates the lining of the digestive tract and, in so doing, increases the risk of oral and liver cancer, stomach ulcers, pancreatitis and gastritis (Yoshida, 2007).

Women who drink alcohol during their pregnancies expose the foetus to the damaging effects of alcohol and the high possibility of Foetal alcohol syndrome. This syndrome can cause mental retardation, poor coordination, poor muscle tone, low birth weight, retarded growth, and physical deformity (Bagheri, Burd, Martsolf & Klug, 2009).

Alcohol has multiple mechanisms of action; it reduces the flow of calcium into neurons, increases the action of the inhibitory neurotransmitter GABA, increases the number of binding sites for the excitatory neurotransmitter glutamate, and interferes with second messenger systems inside neurons (Morgenstern & Longabough, 2000).

Epidemiology of alcoholism

Epidemiological studies of alcoholism have suggested that alcoholism may be properly considered a chronic disease or process, much like cancer and heart disease. Such studies have suggested that, like cancer and heart disease, there may be a natural history of the disorder, with certain variables that might predict its onset, a highly variable but still delimited time course and outcome (Morgenstern & Longabough, 2000; De Lint & Schmidt, 1971).

The assessment of alcoholic dependency is often difficult to diagnose and many people believe that the 'face of alcoholism' is the dirty dishevelled homeless person begging for loose change. The reality is actually quite different. Individuals who drink large quantities of alcohol per day or binge on weekends are likely to be candidates, especially if they feel that an increasing amount of alcohol is needed, suffer withdrawal symptoms when they go without alcohol, suffer blackouts during drinking or feel that whenever they drink they lose control over their drinking. These individuals are a far cry from the popularized image. Until their drinking begins to impair their ability to function, they often have families and jobs and are contributing members of the society.

Certain segments of our population are more likely to become alcoholics. Although it is not clearly established, there is some evidence that alcoholism runs in families and that it may be inherited (Walters, 2002). Human twin studies indicate that offspring of alcoholic or alcohol-preferring parents have a greater tendency to drink more or to become alcoholic (Pickens, Svikis, McGue, Lykken, Heston & Clayton, 1991). Studies of adopted children also show that adopted children with natural parents who are alcoholic are more likely to become alcoholic themselves than such children with non-alcoholic parents (Cloninger, Bohman, Sigvardsson & Von Knorring, 1985). However, it is possible that in some of these cases other influences may have been operating. For example, many parents may teach their children how much and under what circumstances to drink, and, less directly, may serve as models to their children through their own drinking practices. Another major issue with alcohol is that it does not possess the same negative connotations of other abused substances (White & Jackson, 2006). Society is more accepting of drinking behaviour than substance abuse and often does not condone extreme consumption – rather, finds the behaviour entertaining. It has become the norm within certain age groups to go on binges beginning on Friday and ending on Sunday where large quantities of alcohol are consumed. Alcohol is legal and can be easily purchased in large amounts without hardship and it is relatively inexpensive. Drinking behaviour is a socially accepted activity and many pubs and clubs are open 24 hours.

Binge drinking

Binge drinking is consistently in the news and is often the subject of television and news programmes. Former Conservative MP Ann Widdecombe recently conducted an investigation for a documentary on BBC Radio 5 Live and was unable to draw any conclusions about why this type of drinking behaviour is so prevalent in British culture. The programme did document that it isn't a problem of a specific class, profession, race, gender or age. It is an attitude towards excessive drinking that is pervasive throughout the UK. Everyone who was interviewed on the BBC programme believed that binge drinking was a way of relaxing and having a good time and it was odd when individuals didn't binge drink on a weekend. There appeared to be no shame involved in becoming 'falling down drunk' and this was perfectly acceptable behaviour. Ann Widdecombe's final solution to change binge drinking in the UK was to bring a sense of shame to this behaviour in order to stop people from binging and behaving so badly. She believed that charging individuals with a breach of the public order and requiring that they attend court would be the first step in changing positive attitudes to negative ones. But would this change attitudes and behaviours? What is binge drinking and why is it such a problem? Is binge drinking abnormal behaviour?

Recently the term has taken on a new meaning and a new life. The original term 'binge' was used to refer to someone who was alcohol dependent and went on a continuous drinking spree that ended when the individual became incapacitated and was physically unable to continue drinking. It signified shameful, negative, undesirable behaviour conducted by unsavoury individuals, who were unkempt and social outcasts. Today it has a positive connotation and is synonymous with having a good time. How did this terminology change so dramatically and how did the UK become a nation of bingers?

Binge drinking is neither a new trend nor restricted to the UK (Plant & Plant, 2006). Drinking behaviour is often defined by culture and social mores. In communities and cultures where the dominant alcoholic beverage is wine and is consumed daily as part of a meal in family settings, there are strong informal sanctions against public drunkenness. Excess drinking of alcohol is not considered acceptable behaviour and when individuals participate in this type of behaviour they are either deviant or dysfunctional. The excess drinking behaviour is never tolerated. However, when drinking behaviour is defined as an activity in and of itself, does not take place in family settings or at meals, the consumption tends to be characterized by heavier drinking patterns with drunken behaviour being more socially acceptable. Different social mores define this behaviour (Diguarde, 2009).

In the UK drinking tends to be pub-centred, individuals tend to gather at a pub and/or clubs and drink alcohol as an activity in its own right. It has been hypothesized that the idea of bingeing was reinforced by the practice of buying drinks in rounds which did two things: encouraged everyone to drink more than they would otherwise do depending on the group of friends collected at one place and to drink at the speed of the fastest drinker (Plant & Plant, 2006).

There appears to be a 'culture of intoxication' which is fashionable and involves the consumption of large amounts of alcohol as well as illegal substances to achieve at the quickest rate possible a state of altered consciousness. Binge drinking is so routine that young people have the expectation that every weekend they will meet up with friends for the sole purpose of becoming intoxicated. The current trend is that socialization revolves around bingeing behaviour and it is an integral part of the social scene (MacLachlan & Smyth, 2004). Episodes of risk and disorder that accompany binge drinking are often seen as part of the excitement of getting drunk with friends. The main objective of the binge drinker is to become inebriated as quickly as possible and individuals have reported various strategies for accelerating the process such as having a few drinks before leaving home, mixing drinks and deliberately 'downing' alcoholic drinks (Plant & Plant, 2006).

Individuals of all professions, both male and female and a vast age range are rewarding themselves for working hard during the week with a weekend of uncontrolled and uninhibited drinking and drug use (Plant & Plant, 2006). The introduction of the alcopops, shooters, shots and jelly drinks have been hypothesized to increase bingeing behaviour and allow this type of behaviour to become more acceptable. This new production of a wide range of alcoholic products aimed mostly at women but including the trendy club scene have been widely advertised as being the drink of a youthful generation. They are colourful, have stylish names, have a high sugar content, don't require mixing, are consumed directly out of the bottle and are easy to consume in large quantities (Metzner & Kraus, 2008).

Research refers to binge drinking as the consumption of more than a certain number of drinks over a short period of time, typically a single drinking session that generally lasts for a single day. There is no internationally agreed definition of binge drinking, but in the UK it is normally defined as consuming double the maximum units that is recommended as the safe limit for men and women. Units of alcohol are a measure of the volume of pure alcohol in a beverage. The maximum daily units of alcohol for men is 3–4 and for women it is 2–3 units. One unit of alcohol is defined as 10 millilitres. There are slight variations in the units that are specified because there are many factors that influence the blood alcohol levels, for example, alcohol tolerance, body weight, individual metabolism and speed of consumption (Plant & Plant, 2006).

The increase of binge drinking behaviour has a positive correlation with significant damaging health factors. The effects of binge drinking have been found to be significantly more damaging than frequently drinking small quantities of alcohol (WHO, 2002; Rehm, Room & Monterior 2004; Rehm, Gmel, Sempos & Trevisan, 2003). The NHS has reported that approximately 40 percent of individuals admitted to A&E on the weekend are diagnosed with alcohol-related injuries or illnesses, most of which are as a direct result of binge drinking (NHS, 2009). Wechsler, Davenport, Dowdall, Moeyknes and Castillo (2012) found that binge drinkers were more likely to experience serious health issues and other consequences as a result of their drinking behaviour with participants in their study possessing five or more different drinking-related problems including injuries, unwanted sexual advances, rape, violence, being physically assaulted, and engaging in high-risk sexual behaviour. Table 13.3 documents the various diseases associated with long-term bingeing behaviour.

Binge drinking affects the brain and how it functions and can affect mood, motivation, memory, learning and attention (White & Swartzwelder, 2005; Weissenborn, & Duka, 2003). It has been linked to mental illness (Meyerhoff, Blumenfeld, Truran Lindgren, Flenniken, Cardenas, Chao, Rothlind Studholem & Weiner, 2004; Haynes, Farrell, Singleton, Meltzer, Araya, Lewis & Wiles, 2005), suicides and suicide attempts in young adults (Miller, Naimi, & Brewer 2007; Schaffer, Jeglic & Stanley, 2008), significant liver degeneration in younger than expected individuals (Mathurin & Deltenre, 2008), and increasing numbers being referred for alcohol-related psychiatric problems (Jenkins, Bebbington, Brugha Farrell, Gill, & Lewis, 2000; Meltzer, Gill, Hinds & Petticrew, 1996).

Alcohol misuse is closely linked with antisocial, aggressive and violent behaviour (Brewer & Swahn, 2005; Szmigin, Griffin, Mistral, Bengry-Howell, Weale & Hackley, 2007; Ormerod & Wiltshire, 2009; Measham & Brain, 2005). Various researchers have documented that alcohol is a factor in sexual offences and street crimes (Wechsler & Nelson, 2001; Glider, Midyett, Mills-Novoa, Johannessen & Collins, 2001). Men are more likely to commit or experience alcohol-related violence, whereas women are at increased risk of sexual assaults (Abbey, McAuslan & Ross, 1998; Abbey & McAuslan, 2004).

Table 13.3   Medical and psychological consequences of binge drinking

Brain damage	Destruction of brain cells
	Shrinkage of the hippocampus
	Cognitive impairment
	Epilepsy
Alcohol poisoning	Hypothermia
	Convulsions
	Respiratory depression
	Hypotension
	Coma
	Aspiration of stomach contents resulting in choking
Gastrointestinal tract	Damage to the oesophagus
	Acute gastritis
	Acute pancreatitis
	Metabolic complications
	Cirrhosis of the liver
Cardiovascular system	Increase blood pressure
	Strokes
	Heart disease
	Arrhythmias – atrial fibrillation
Cancer	Increased risk of breast cancer
	Mouth and oropharynix cancers
	Oesophageal cancer
	Liver cancer
Accidents, violence and criminal behaviour	Drink driving
	Traffic accidents
	Fatal injuries due to falls
	Committing criminal offences
	Drowning
	Increase risk of using illegal drugs
Psychological problems	Increase in risk of alcohol dependence later in life
	Suicide
	Rape
	Unwanted/unsafe sexual activity
	Mental illness
	Depressive disorders
Skeletal muscle damage	Acute myopathy

Cannabis

The usual mode of consumption for cannabis is to smoke the dry leaves in either a rolled cigarette or pipe; but it is also effective when ingested by being added and baked into food, e.g. cakes, brownies, cookies. The use of cannabis and its resin (hashish) produces physiological, perceptual, and psychological effects (Lichtman & Martin, 2009).

The psychoactive effects of cannabis are largely attributable to a constituent called THC (delta-9-tetrahydrocannabinol). However, it contains over 80 cannabinoids (chemicals of the same chemical class as THC), which may also be psychoactive. Most of the cannabinoids are found in a sticky resin covering the leaves and flowers of the plant, which can be extracted and dried to form a dark, corklike material called hashish. The hashish can be further processed into an extremely potent product called hash oil. Tetrahydrocannabinol (THC) is the prevalent psychoactive ingredient in marijuana and hashish, so dosage levels will refer to THC content. With

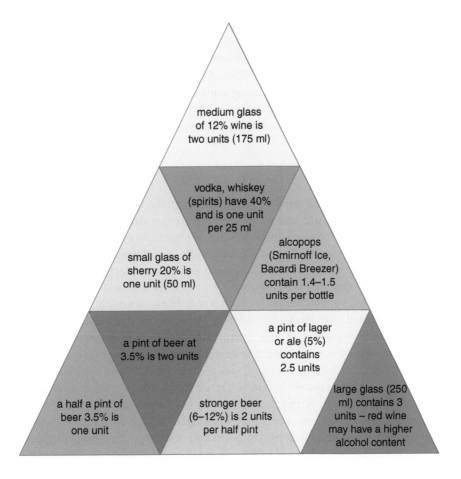

Figure 13.2 Typical units of alcohol

low doses, 5 to 25 mg. (one cigarette equals approximately 7.5 mg. of THC), typical physiological effects include bloodshot eyes, dry mouth, unusual sensations such as tingling (parasthesias), increased appetite, and craving for sweets. Heightened senses of taste, touch, smell, sound, and vision are typical perceptual effects. Psychological effects are elated mood, slowed time sense, difficulties in thinking, comprehending, and expressing and poor memory (Ashton, 2001).

At low to moderate doses the intoxicated individual may experience an increased sense of well-being: initial restlessness and hilarity followed by a dreamy, carefree state of relaxation; alteration of sensory perceptions with an increase in sense of touch, sight, smell, taste, and sound; a feeling of hunger, especially a craving for sweets; and subtle changes in thought formation and expression (Lichtman & Martin, 2009).

High doses can impair psychological functioning. Short-term memory is affected and the ability to carry out tasks involving multiple steps declines. Speech becomes slurred. A sense of unreality, emotional intensification, sensory distortion, and motor impairment are also common. Emotional responses are magnified and sensations are distorted, also hallucinations may occur (Solowij & Battisti, 2008).

A hazard of long-term cannabis use appears to be lung damage. Those who regularly smoke marijuana tend to have deficits in respiratory function and they are more likely to develop a chronic cough, bronchitis and asthma (Abramson,1974).

The addiction potential of cannabis appears to be low. Tolerance to cannabis develops during periods of sustained use. There are withdrawal symptoms for those individuals who are addicted and have high use that consist of nausea, diarrhoea, sweating, chills, tremor, restlessness and sleep disturbance. THC is fat-soluble and binds to receptors that are particularly dense in the basal ganglia, hippocampus, cerebellum and neocortex and exerts most of its effects through these mechanisms (Hall & Solowij, 2009).

Cocaine and other stimulants

Stimulants are drugs whose primary effect is to produce general increases in neural and behavioural activity. Cocaine and its derivatives are the most commonly abused stimulants. Although stimulants all have a similar profile of effects, they differ greatly in their potency and effectiveness. The drink Coca-Cola originally was formulated with small amounts of cocaine; the recipe has long since been revised and now you can choose to have the caffeinated version for the kick that was originally provided by the small infusion of cocaine or opt for the decaffeinated version and enjoy it as a soft drink (Washton, 1991).

Cocaine is prepared from the leaf of the coca bush. It is typically consumed by snorting or by injection. Cocaine hydrochloride may be converted to its base form by boiling it in a solution of baking soda until the water has evaporated. The impure residue of this process is called crack, which is a potent, cheap, smokable form of cocaine. Crack is easy to make, can be extended by the addition of additives and sold in larger quantities and as a result has become a popular street drug (Platt, 2000).

People eat, smoke, snort, or inject cocaine or its derivatives in order to experience its psychological and physiological effects. Users report feelings of self-confidence, alertness and feelings of boundless energy. Cocaine addicts tend to go on binges in which extremely high levels of cocaine usage is maintained for a short period of time. During a cocaine binge users become increasingly tolerant to the euphoria-producing effects of cocaine and larger and larger doses are required for them to achieve the same level. During these binges, extremely high blood levels of cocaine are reached and the side effects include sleeplessness, tremors, nausea, and psychotic behaviour. The binge usually ends when the supply is depleted, or when the person begins to have serious toxic effects which can come in the form of loss of consciousness, respiratory arrest, or stroke (Platt, 2000).

Tolerance develops to most effects of cocaine but repeated cocaine usage often sensitizes subjects to its motor and convulsive effects. Fatalities from cocaine overdose generally occur as a result of IV injection. Cocaine snorting can damage the nasal membranes, and cocaine smoking can damage the lungs; but both routes are safer than IV injection. Although cocaine is extremely addictive, the withdrawal effects triggered by abrupt termination of a cocaine spree are relatively mild. Common cocaine withdrawal symptoms include a negative mood swing and insomnia (Washton, 1991).

Cocaine facilitates catecholaminergic transmission. It does this by blocking the re-uptake of catecholamines (dopamine, norepinephrine, and epinephrine) into presynaptic neurons. Its ability to aid in dopaminergic transmission appears to play a role in its euphoria-inducing effects (Joseph & Quattrochi, 1997).

Amphetamines

Amphetamines were widely used for a variety of products and were once the main ingredient in diet pills. Amphetamines are extremely addictive and are usually consumed orally. The effects are comparable to those of cocaine. Recently it has been replaced by a more potent drug, methamphetamine, and the designer drugs such as ecstasy, and mephedrone (bath salts, plant food, vanilla sky, lunar wave, cloud nine) which are synthetic powders that are currently legally sold and contain various amphetamine-like chemicals (Ross, Watson & Goldberger, 2011). Low to moderate doses of amphetamine elevate mood, increase alertness and induce euphoria. Increased motor activity and respiration, agitation, insomnia and decreased appetite are common effects of moderate doses. With chronic use of high doses an intense, pleasurable feeling or 'rush' is produced, especially when intravenous (IV) administration is used. Withdrawal symptoms appear after termination of high doses; sleep, depression, hunger, and high fluid intake have been reported, although administration of amphetamines during the withdrawal stage does not restore normal physiological and psychological functions, which demonstrates there are no clearly defined withdrawal symptoms (Rasmussen, 2009).

Overdose with amphetamines resembles paranoid schizophrenia or paranoid psychotic reactions. Cardiovascular symptoms (circulatory collapse, irregular heartbeat) and gastrointestinal symptoms (nausea, cramps, diarrhoea) occur.

Death from overdose is rare, although in some instances a large increase in arterial blood pressure leads to ruptured vessels and death (Rasmussen, 2009).

Methamphetamine

Methamphetamine (meth, speed or chalk) is commonly used in its even more potent, smokable, crystalline form (ice, crank or crystal). It is a highly addictive stimulant that affects the central nervous system. The drug can be easily manufactured in small home-based kitchen labs with inexpensive over-the-counter ingredients. It is a white, odourless crystalline powder that easily dissolves in water or alcohol. Methamphetamine is slightly different from its predecessor as it requires smaller amounts of the drug to achieve higher levels of action in the brain, it is more potent and longer lasting, and alternatively it causes increased damage and significantly more negative effects in the central nervous system (Weisheit & White, 2009).

Methamphetamine causes increased activity, decreased appetite and a sense of well-being and euphoria. Chronic abusers exhibit anxiety, confusion, insomnia, mood disturbances and violent behaviour. Users can also exhibit a number of psychotic features including paranoia, visual and auditory hallucinations and delusions. Psychotic symptoms have been known to last for months or years after methamphetamine abuse has stopped. Methamphetamine abuse has a number of adverse side effects and causes a variety of cardiovascular problems; irregular heartbeat, increased blood pressure, hyperthermia and convulsions. Long-term physical effects include severe weight loss, acute acne and skin lesions and severe dental problems (Roll, Rawson, Ling & Shaoptaw, 2009).

Chronic methamphetamine abuse significantly changes the structures associated with the neurotransmitter dopamine and the major neurochemical pathway of the reward system that includes the mesolimbic and mesocortical pathway. In addition there have been reported significant structural and functional changes in areas of the brain associated with emotion and memory. Neuroimaging studies have shown that even after two years of abstinence the various structures continued to indicate significant damage. Methamphetamine is extremely addictive, withdrawal effects include depression, anxiety, fatigue and an intense craving for the drug (Thrash, Karuppagounder, Uthayathas, Suppiramaniam & Dhanasekaran, 2010; Kousik, Graves, Napier, Zhao & Carvey, 2011; Roussotte, Soderberg & Sowell, 2010).

Ecstasy

Ecstasy has been associated with a variety of counter cultures and the club scene and is generally combined with alcohol. Ecstasy is taken orally, and its effects last approximately three to six hours. Structurally ecstasy (also referred to as MDMA) resembles both mescaline and amphetamine and acts as both a stimulant and psychedelic, producing an energizing effect, distortions in time and perception and an altered state of consciousness with heightened sense of sexual pleasure. Ecstasy causes its affect by altering the activity in the neurotransmitters, specifically serotonin and norephenpehrine (Iversen, 2008).

MDMA produces a variety of adverse health effects, including nausea, chills, sweating, involuntary teeth clenching, muscle cramping, raised body temperature, dehydration, heart failure, kidney failure, arrhythmia, increase in blood pressure, loss of consciousness and seizures. Because of its stimulant properties and the types of environments where it is typically ingested, coupled with vigorous physical activity and alcohol, it creates situations that compound the adverse effects that can result in death. It is also not unusual for users to want to extend the effects over the course of an evening and take another dose which can produce unexpectedly high blood levels and the possibility of overdose. In moderate to high doses ecstasy causes the destruction of serotonin nerve endings. MDMA produces significant reductions in mental abilities with changes lasting up to one week with the possibility of long-term effects in regular users. The addictive potential is moderate and the withdrawal symptoms include fatigue, loss of appetite, depressed feelings and difficulty concentrating (Scholey, Owen, Gates, Rodgers, Buchanan, Ling, Heffernan, Swan, Stough & Parrott, 2011; Milroy, 2011; Turillazzi, Riezzo, Neri, Bello & Fineschi, 2010; Degenhardt & Hall, 2010).

The opiates: heroin and morphine

Opium is the sap released from the seeds of the opium poppy and has several psychoactive ingredients. Morphine, codeine and other drugs that have similar structures or effects are commonly referred to as the opiates. In the early 1900s, opium was legally available and consumed in great quantities in many parts of the world, including Europe and North America. Opium was available in cakes, candies, and wines, as well as in a variety of over the-counter medicinal offerings, until it was removed because of its addictive properties (Fernandez, 2010).

The effect of opiates most valued by opiate addicts is the rush that follows intravenous injection. The heroin rush is a wave of intense abdominal, orgasmic pleasure that evolves into a state of serene, drowsy euphoria. Other symptoms include decreased physiological responses: body temperature, heart rate, respiration, blood pressure, urination and deep sleep. Effects diminish in four to six hours and, as tolerance develops, the duration of euphoric effects becomes shorter. Many opiate users, drawn by these pleasurable effects, begin to use the drug more and more frequently. Then, once they reach a point where they keep themselves drugged much of the time, tolerance and physical dependence develop and contribute to the problem. Opiate tolerance encourages addicts to progress to higher doses, to more potent drugs (e.g. heroin), and to more direct routes of administration (e.g. IV injection); and physical dependence adds to the already high motivation to take the drug (Fernandez, 2010).

The opiates exert their effects by binding to particular receptors whose normal function is to bind to endogenous chemicals. The endogenous chemicals that bind to opiate receptors are called endorphins. Withdrawal symptoms occurs after five to six hours, peak in 36 to 48 hr, and lasts about ten days. Symptoms include nervousness, irritability, weakness, leg and back aches, cramps, nausea, decreased appetite, yawns, watery eyes, runny nose, constricted pupils, perspiration, goose flesh and chills. After ten days, physiological functioning slowly begins to stabilize, but complete return to pre-addiction baselines may take as long as 30 weeks. While the physical distress is serious, death is seldom associated with withdrawal. The symptoms of opiate withdrawal have been widely exaggerated and for most individuals they appear as serious as a bad case of the flu (Fernandez, 2010).

Overdose with opiates is characterized by respiratory failure and collapse of the circulatory system. Most of these adverse effects are from true overdoses, but a portion are probably the result of allergic reactions to the drug or dilutants, non-sterile syringes, opiate-induced arrhythmias, and/or failure of tolerance effects. Most risks of opiate addiction are indirect and are not as a consequence of the drug itself. Addicts must purchase their drugs from street dealers and become trapped in a life of poverty and various crimes in order to fund their addictions. They are often driven to prostitution, contract various diseases from unsafe sex and unsterile needles. In addition the majority of street drugs are cut by unknown substances which can cause toxicity and death. Overdose deaths occur when contaminated drugs are sold or when shipments of particularly pure heroin are sold (Fernandez, 2010).

Table 13.4   Comparison of amphetamines, methamphetamine and ecstasy

Amphetamines	High addictive properties
	Increase alertness and elevate mood
	Withdrawal symptoms are mild
	Death is rare and overdose resembles paranoid schizophrenia
Methamphetamine	High addictive properties
	More potent and longer lasting than amphetamines
	Sense of well-being and euphoria
	Withdrawal symptoms: depression, anxiety and intense craving for the drug
	Permanent damage to neuronal structures
	Death is common due to the cardiovascular effects
Ecstasy	Moderate addictive properties
	Combination of stimulant and psychedelic effects
	Withdrawal symptoms of fatigue, difficulty concentrating and depressed feelings
	Permanent damage to serotonin nerve endings
	Overdose is common and death can occur because of the adverse cardiovascular effects, increase in body temperature and respiration and the way it is ingested within social environments.

Barbiturates and hypnotic sedatives

All drugs within this class are central nervous system depressants. Their mechanism of action is their affinity for the GABA receptor which is the principal inhibitory neurotransmitter. They inhibit GABA and inhibit glutamate causing inhibitory affects for both of these neurotransmitters (Wong, Snowman, Leeb-Lundberg & Olsen, 1984; Henn & DeEugenio, 2006).

Addicts may stagger, slur speech, be uncoordinated, and appear drunk. They show oscillatory movement of the eyes (nystagmus) and decreased muscle tone. They may become loud, boisterous, irritable, or aggressive. Withdrawal symptoms from barbiturates is life-threatening due to the possibility of convulsions. After withdrawal of the drug for 24 hrs, anxiety, restlessness, fatigue, irritability, insomnia, and nightmares frequently occur. These symptoms may be accompanied by faintness, sweating, shivering and convulsions. Psychotic states and/or seizures are most likely to occur with chronic use of dosages of 600 mg. or more. Withdrawal symptoms are worse during the first three days; however, with some of the longer-acting compounds, seizures may not occur until the eighth day. Severely addicted individuals may display a three to five day delirious psychotic reaction marked by paranoid delusions. There is usually complete recovery from the psychotic reaction within three weeks. Hospitalization is mandatory for safe, effective detoxification from barbiturates (Adamec & Triggle, 2012).

Barbiturate overdose is frequent and probably the most prevalent cause of drug-related deaths. Accidental overdose with barbiturates is frequent among alcoholics as they substitute or mix drugs or mix barbiturates with alcohol. Death is due to circulatory failure and respiratory collapse (Houle, 2000).

Hallucinogens

The drug class hallucinogens contain diverse drugs with wide differences in chemical structure and mechanism of action. D-Lysergic acid diethylamide (LSD) is the major drug in this class and consists of two phases of dose effects, the autonomic nervous system (ANS) effects and psychological symptoms. ANS effects are decreased appetite, dizziness, increased body temperature and blood sugar, chills, restlessness, goose flesh, nausea, vomiting, and variations in pulse and blood pressure. Psychological symptoms include depersonalization, body image distortion, distortion of external stimuli, and perceptual distortion of internal stimuli (i.e. visual, auditory, tactile, olfactory, gustatory, and thermal illusions) (Fantegrossi, Murnane & Reissig, 2008).

Chronic dosage does not cause physical dependence but tolerance occurs to physical and psychological effects. Individuals having a history of psychological disturbances, living in insecure environments, or who are undergoing crisis situations frequently have adverse reactions. Psychological dependence does occur but relatively infrequently. No overdose deaths have been reported in the literature (Nichols, 2004). Lasting adverse reactions have not been adequately documented, although anecdotal reports indicate that flashbacks and panic reactions ("bad trips') occur (McWilliams & Tuttle, 1973; Millman, 1978; O'Shea & Fagan, 2012).

PSYCHOPHARMACOLOGY

Psychopharmacology is the study of the effects of drugs on the body and on behaviour. Drugs have a specific effect and site of action. Drug effects are the changes we can observe in an individual's physiological processes and behaviour. The sites of action of drugs are the points at which molecules of drugs interact with molecules located on or in cells of the body (Meyer & Quenzer, 2004).

Drugs are usually administered in one of four ways: oral ingestion, injection, inhalation, or absorption through the mucous membranes of the nose, mouth, or rectum. The route of administration influences the rate at which and the degree to which the drug reaches its sites of action (Leonard, 2003).

In terms of oral ingestion once they are swallowed, drugs dissolve in the fluids of the stomach and are carried to the intestine, where they are absorbed into the bloodstream. However, some drugs readily pass through the stomach wall (e.g. alcohol), and these take effect sooner because they do not have to reach the intestine to be absorbed. The two main advantages of the oral route of administration over other routes are its ease and relative safety. Its main disadvantage is its unpredictability. Absorption from the digestive tract into the bloodstream can be influenced by the amount and type of food in the stomach (Ettinger, 2011).

Drugs are often injected because the effects are large, rapid and predictable. The drug is dissolved in a liquid (or, in some cases, suspended in a liquid in the form of fine particles) and injected through a hypodermic needle. Drug injections are typically made three different ways; subcutaneously into the fatty tissue just beneath the skin, intramuscularly into the large muscles, or intravenously directly into veins at points where they run just beneath the skin. Many addicts prefer the intravenous route because the bloodstream delivers the drug directly to the brain. There is very little waste and the entire dose reaches the bloodstream at once. However, the speed and directness of the intravenous route presents little or no opportunity to counteract the effects of an overdose, an impurity, or an allergic reaction. Another issue of intravenous drug use is that the constant injections cause scar tissue, infections and collapsed veins (Leonard, 2003).

Drugs are also absorbed into the bloodstream through the capillaries in the lungs. The route from the lungs to the brain is very short, and drugs administered this way have very rapid effects. The two major problems of this method are that it is difficult to precisely regulate the dose of inhaled drugs, and many chronically inhaled substances damage the lungs. Nicotine, freebase cocaine and marijuana are usually smoked (Anderson & Reid, 2007).

Drugs can be absorbed through the mucous membranes of the nose, mouth and rectum. Cocaine is commonly self-administered through the nasal membranes (snorted) – but not without damaging them. This method delivers the drug into the bloodstream very rapidly and then the brain. When powdered cocaine is sniffed, it ends up in the mucous membranes of the nose and not in the lungs. Drugs can also be administered at the opposite end of the digestive tract but very few addicts prefer this method as it leaves the user exposed and vulnerable (Schatzberg, Cole & DeBattista, 2010).

Once a drug enters the bloodstream, it is carried in the blood to the central nervous system where it acts on various action points dependent upon the drug. Psychoactive drugs influence the nervous system in many different ways. Drugs such as alcohol act diffusely on neural membranes throughout the CNS. Others act in a less general way: by binding to particular synaptic receptors; by influencing the synthesis, transport, release, or deactivation of particular neurotransmitters; or by influencing the chain of chemical reactions elicited in postsynaptic neurons by the activation of their synaptic receptors (Ettinger, 2011).

HOW DRUGS WORK IN THE SYSTEM

The drugs that affect our affect behaviour do so by affecting synaptic transmission. Particular drugs can selectively affect neurons that secrete particular neurotransmitters which in turn has a specific effect on behaviour. Drugs that affect synaptic transmission are classified into two general categories. Those that block or inhibit the postsynaptic effects are called antagonists. Those that facilitate them are called agonists. The steps in the synthesis of neurotransmitters are controlled by enzymes. Therefore, if a drug inactivates one of these enzymes, it will prevent the neurotransmitter from being produced. Such a drug serves as an antagonist. Some drugs act as antagonists by preventing the release of neurotransmitters from the terminal button. They do so by deactivating the proteins that cause docked synaptic vesicles to fuse with the presynaptic membrane and expel their contents into the synaptic cleft. Other drugs have just the opposite effect: They act as agonists by binding with these proteins and directly triggering release of the neurotransmitter (Neal, 2009).

The most important site of action of drugs in the nervous system is on receptors, both presynaptic and postsynaptic. Once a neurotransmitter is released, it must stimulate the postsynaptic receptors. Some drugs bind with these receptors, just as the neurotransmitter does. Once a drug has bound with the receptor, it can serve as either an agonist or an antagonist (Neal, 2009).

The next step after stimulation of the postsynaptic receptor is termination of the postsynaptic potential. There are two main processes: re-uptake and enzymatic action. Molecules of the neurotransmitter are taken back into the terminal button through the process of re-uptake, or they are destroyed by an enzyme. Drugs can interfere with either of these processes (Neal, 2009).

DISTRIBUTION OF DRUGS WITHIN THE BODY

Drugs exert their effects only when they reach their sites of action. Several factors determine the rate at which a drug in the bloodstream reaches sites of action within the brain. The first is lipid solubility. The blood–brain barrier is a barrier only for water-soluble molecules. Molecules that are soluble in lipids pass through the cells that line the capillaries in the central nervous system, and they rapidly distribute themselves throughout the brain (Neal, 2012). For example heroin is more lipid soluble than morphine. An injection of heroin produces much more rapid effects than morphine. Both drugs perform the exact same function and act on the same sites in the brain, but heroin arrives faster giving the addict a more intense feeling which explains why they prefer heroin to morphine.

Drugs that bind with various tissues in the body or with proteins in the blood, called depot binding, delay the drug from reaching its target of action and once it arrives prolongs the effects of the drug. As long as the drug is bound to a depot, it cannot reach its site of action and cannot exert its effect. Other sources of depot binding include fat tissue, bones, muscles and the liver (Neal, 2012).

Once a drug enters the body it begins to be broken down. The actions of most drugs are terminated by enzymes and are eventually excreted by the kidneys. The liver plays an active role in breaking down drugs into its different components but there are also enzymes in the blood and brain. This process is called drug metabolism and will eliminate the drug's ability to pass through lipid membranes. The blood–brain barrier is a lipid membrane so drugs are no longer able to pass through the barrier into the brain (Neal, 2012).

Occasionally the broken-down molecules of a drug will be even more active than when it was in originally introduced into the body. It must go through at least another cycle of exposure to enzymatic deterioration before it is eliminated. In these cases the effects of this type of drug will be very long in duration (Neal, 2012).

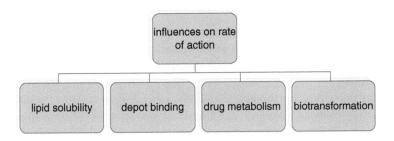

Figure 13.3

DRUG EFFECTIVENESS

Drugs vary widely in their effectiveness. A small dose of a relatively effective drug can equal or exceed the effects of larger amounts of a relatively ineffective drug. Most drugs have more than one effect. Opiates such as morphine and codeine produce a reduced sensitivity to pain but they also depress the structures that control heart rate and respiration. A measure of a drug's margin of safety is called its therapeutic index. A measure is obtained by administering varying doses of the drug to a group research subjects, generally research animals. Two numbers are then obtained, the dosage that produces the desired effect in 50 percent and the dose that produces toxic effects in 50 percent. The therapeutic index is the ratio of those two numbers. For example, if the toxic dose is five times higher than the effective dose, then the therapeutic index is 5.0. The lower the therapeutic index, the higher the chance of toxic levels occurring and extreme care must be taken when prescribing that type of drug (Katzung, Masters & Trevor, 2009). For example, barbiturates have relatively low therapeutic indexes – as low as 2 or 3. In contrast, tranquillizers such as Librium or Valium have therapeutic indexes of well over 100. As a consequence, an accidental overdose of a barbiturate is much more likely to have tragic effects than a similar overdose of Librium or Valium, especially if the user is combining drugs with other types of substances. In the case of street drugs this ratio is constantly changing because the drugs are not pure and are usually mixed with a wide variety of substances that can alter their effectiveness.

The second reason that drugs vary in their effectiveness has to do with the affinity of the drug with its site of action. Drugs vary widely in their affinity for the molecules to which they attach. Drugs that have a high affinity or readiness will produce effects at a low concentration, whereas one with a low affinity must be administered in relatively high doses for it to be effective. Two drugs with identical sites of action can vary widely in their effectiveness if they have different affinities for their binding sites. In addition, because most drugs have multiple effects, a drug can have high affinities for some of its sites of action and low affinities for others. The most desirable drug has a high affinity for sites of action that produce therapeutic effects and a low affinity for sites of action that produce toxic side effects (Katzung, Masters & Trevor, 2009).

DRUG TOLERANCE

Drug tolerance is a state of decreased sensitivity to a drug that develops as a result of use. Drug tolerance can be demonstrated in two ways: by showing that a given dose of the drug has less effect than it had before drug use or by showing that it takes more of the drug to produce the same effect (Rassool, 2008).

Exposure to one drug can produce tolerance to other drugs that act by the same mechanism which is called cross-tolerance. Tolerance can also develop to some of the drug effects and not to others. This can have unfortunate consequences for people who think they have built up a tolerance to all the effects and the drugs other effects builds to a toxic level. Drugs can affect individuals differently so tolerance may develop for some effects while it increases the sensitivity to other effects. When a drug is repeatedly taken its effects will not remain constant, in most cases it will diminish in effectiveness requiring higher doses for the same result (Rassool, 2008). For example a regular heroin user will develop a tolerance for the drug and will require higher doses to reach the same high they felt when they originally took the drug. That individual will suffer from withdrawal symptoms if they suddenly stop taking the drug.

Withdrawal symptoms are generally the opposite effect of the drug. Heroin produces a sense of exhilaration; the withdrawal symptoms from heroin will be despair. Withdrawal symptoms are caused by the same mechanisms that are responsible for tolerance. The severity of withdrawal symptoms depends on the particular drug in question, the duration and degree of the preceding drug use, and on the speed with which the drug is eliminated from the body. In general, longer exposure to greater doses followed by more rapid elimination produces greater withdrawal effects (Rassool, 2008).

PHYSICAL-DEPENDENCE THEORIES OF ADDICTION

The development of dependence begins when the initial drug effects are reduced due to tolerance and constant use. Drug craving develops and is perceived as a 'need' for the drug. The dosage is gradually increased until the level remains fairly constant and a balance is achieved. The user is able to get high and prevent withdrawal symptoms. Generally with illegal and abused prescription drugs periods of abstinence occur when the drug source becomes unavailable. Often when the drug of choice is unattainable, other drugs with similar effects are substituted which develops cross-tolerance (Skinner & Aubin, 2010).

Additional characteristics of dependence are associated with the use of illegal drugs and abused prescription drugs. The user generally becomes obsessed with drugs and spends time, money and energy finding and consuming them. The obsession leaves very little time for any types of activities that are not drug related. Often individuals participate in criminal activities to provide money for drugs, sometimes leading to incarceration. When a person reaches a point where illegal activities are undertaken in order to secure drugs, it is not unusual for them to allow themselves to deteriorate so that their health and well-being suffer as well as psychological implications such as depression, anxiety and low self esteem (Kalant, 2010).

The greatest confusion about the nature of addiction concerns its relation to physical dependence. Many people are under the mistaken assumption that addicts are people who continue to use drugs to prevent withdrawal symptoms and that it becomes a vicious cycle of drug taking. This is rather simplistic; addicts do take drugs to prevent or alleviate withdrawal symptoms, but this is not the only motivating factor for their addiction. If it were as straightforward as breaking this cycle of addiction the treatment programmes would hospitalize them until their withdrawal symptoms subsided. As we know most addicts renew their drug taking even months after abstinence (Kalant, 2010).

Treatment programmes based on the physical-dependence theories of addiction do not have a high success rate. There are two basic reasons why these types of treatment programmes have low success rates. First, many highly addictive drugs, such as amphetamines do not produce severe withdrawal symptoms. The major issues with these types of drugs appear to be psychological. Second, the pattern of drug taking involves a cycle of binges and detoxification and again the pattern involves the user's behaviour toward drug taking activities and the psychological and social factors underlying the drug taking behaviours. There are a variety of reasons for this pattern of drug usage which are mostly economical. Most drug users do not have enough money to use/supply drugs continuously (Tiffany, Friedman, Greenfield, Hasin & Jackson, 2011).

Physical-dependence theories of drug addiction attempt to account for the frequent relapses by postulating that withdrawal symptoms can be conditioned. When addicts who have remained drug free for a considerable period of time return to a situation in which they have previously experienced the drug, conditioned withdrawal effects opposite to the effects of the drug are elicited. These effects result in a powerful craving for the drug (Tiffany, Friedman, Greenfield, Hasin & Jackson, 2011).

The theory that relapse is motivated by an attempt to counteract conditioned withdrawal effects has two problems. One is that the effects elicited by environments that have previously been associated with drug administration are similar to those of the drug. The second is that addicts often display a preference for drug-predictive cues, even when no drug is forthcoming, also called positive incentive theories of addiction. For example some detoxified heroin addicts called needle freaks continue to obtain pleasure from sticking an empty needle into themselves (Pates & Gray, 2009).

The failure of physical-dependence theories to account for the major aspects of addiction has lent support to the theory that the primary reason most addicts take drugs is not to escape or avoid the unpleasant consequences of withdrawal or conditioned withdrawal, but rather to obtain the drugs' positive effects. This positive-incentive theory of addiction acknowledges that addicts may sometimes self-administer drugs to suppress withdrawal symptoms or to escape from other unpleasant aspects of their existence, but it holds that the primary factor in most cases of addiction is the craving for the positive-incentive (pleasure-producing) properties of the drugs (McAuliffe et al., 1986; Stewart, de Wit & Eikelboom, 1984; Robinson & Berridge, 2002).

Another positive-incentive theory of addiction is based on the idea that the value of addictive drugs increases (i.e. is sensitized) with drug use. The use of drugs sensitizes their positive-incentive value, thus rendering the user highly motivated to consume drugs and to seek drug-associated stimuli. It isn't the pleasure of drug taking that is the basis of addiction; it is the anticipated pleasure of drug taking. Initially, a drug's positive-incentive value is closely tied to its pleasurable effects; but tolerance often develops to the pleasurable effects, whereas the addict's wanting for the drug is sensitized. Thus, in chronic addicts, the positive-incentive value of the drug is often out of proportion with the pleasure actually derived from it: Many addicts are miserable. Their lives are in ruins, and the drug effects are not that great anymore; but they crave the drug more than ever (Nocjar & Panksepp, 2002).

REWARD CIRCUITS IN THE BRAIN

Olds and Milner (1954), discoverers of intracranial self-stimulation, argued that the specific brain sites that mediate self-stimulation are those that normally mediate the pleasurable effects of natural rewards (e.g. food, water and sex). Accordingly, researchers have studied the self-stimulation as it is believed that these areas of the brain play a major role in addiction.

The mesotelencephalic dopamine system has been shown to play an important role in intracranial self-stimulation. The mesotelencephalic dopamine system is a system of dopaminergic neurons that projects from the mesencephalon (the midbrain) into various regions of the telencephalon. Evidence that the mesotelencephalic dopamine system mediates the rewarding effects of intracranial stimulation and natural motivated behaviours suggests that it may also mediate the rewarding effects of addictive drugs (Chen, 1993; Wise, 1996; Chiara & Bassareo, 2006).

Research has found that studies support the view that the mesotelencephalic dopamine system is involved with various substances such as morphine, cocaine, amphetamine, alcohol, nicotine and THC. Various studies have documented that these structures are involved in self-stimulation and addiction (Chen, 1993; White & Hiroi, 1993; Wise et al., 1992; Kornetsky & Esposito, 1979; Koob & Moal, 2008; Di Chiara, Bassareo, Fenu, De Luca, Spina, Cadoni, Acquas, Carboni, Valentini & Lecca, 2004). The study of the mesotelencephalic dopamine system has greatly increased our understanding of the neural basis of addiction, but has not really contributed to providing treatment for addicts. The challenge is to develop specific drugs that can reduce the positive-incentive value of drugs without reducing the positive-incentive value of natural motivated behaviours.

MAJOR PSYCHOLOGICAL THEORIES OF ADDICTIVE BEHAVIOUR

Psychoanalytic theories

These theories have been derived from Freud's psychoanalytic theory of personality. Addiction is attributed to the impulse to use drugs rather than the effects of the drugs on the individual. Addiction occurs because drugs can produce euphoria and alleviate anxiety and pain. The pleasurable effects depend upon the unique psychological preparedness of the individual. Addicted individuals are assumed to have been tense, frequently depressed, frustrated and intolerant to physical and psychic pain. These characteristics and presumed history make them more susceptible to the pleasurable effects of drugs (Petersen & McBride, 2002).

Habits for dealing with reality are neglected and the individual turns to drug use. As drug effects wear off, reality becomes more painful than ever because of the contrast to drug effects. As time and experience with the drugs progress, elation diminishes and eventually only depression recurs. Because the addict cannot reproduce the pleasurable effects with the same drug dose, the dose level is increased, thus explaining tolerance development and physical dependence (Rassool, 2008).

Metabolic disease theory

The central hypothesis is that addiction is due to drug action on the body's metabolism which produces a chronic 'drug hunger', rather than to underlying psychopathology. The nature, mechanism, and duration of metabolic changes are unspecified, but are thought to be similar to a disease which is chronic and requires long-term treatment to correct the metabolic imbalance via daily dosage of insulin (Courtwright, 1997; Volkow & Fowler, 2000).

Moral models

There are five basic models of moral addiction, (1) retributive, (2) deterrent, (3) restitutive, (4), preventive and (5) rehabilitative. Although they are probably the most prevalent cause of abuse held by the general public, they are usually not as clearly expressed as the scientific models of addiction (McMurran, 1994).

The retributive model defines the addict as a criminal and the aetiology of addiction as a moral failure. Intervention involves unassisted withdrawal and punishment by society, that is, imprisonment. The deterrent model defines the addict as a bad example where the aetiology is a lack of deterrence. Intervention involves unassisted withdrawal and punishment by society with the objective of reducing addiction by frightening people. The restitutive model defines the addict as a debtor to society where aetiology is unimportant and remains unspecified. Intervention involves restitution to victims and/or society, for example, work on public projects, etc. The preventive model defines addiction as a failure of moral education where the aetiology is a deficit in moral instruction. Intervention implied is appropriate moral instruction to prevent development of addiction. The restorative or rehabilitative model defines the addict as a wrongdoer and aetiology as a moral failure due to the human condition. Intervention with all three models is similar and involves confession, repentance, prayer, meditation, reality therapy and social rehabilitation (West, 2006).

Learning theories

Learning theories are among the most influential within the models of addiction and they have generated a great deal of research on addictive behaviour.

Learning theories are based on the belief that early drug use is maintained by a variety of positive reinforcers including social reinforcement, pleasant drug effects, and relief from pain and anxiety (negative reinforcement). Once an individual comes into contact with drug use and pairs the positive reinforcements they are exposed to the pharmacological effects as well as the psychological effects. The physiological aspect of drugs becomes the positive reinforcer and drug use becomes the conditioned response. The withdrawal symptoms are negative reinforcers that the addict wishes to avoid; they acquire conditioned punishment and negative reinforcement properties which strengthen and maintain drug-seeking behaviour.

Drug seeking is reinforced by the conditioned reinforcing properties which remain (Hyman, Malenka & Nestler, 2006).

TREATMENT

The treatment of substance abuse is often a myriad of treatments and there are likely to be as many approaches as there are theories to explain the complexities of addiction. Most clinical treatment programmes involve a combination of techniques and approaches including psychotherapy, aversive condition, medication, hypnosis, physical exercise and social skills training rather than a single technique. There are three general categories of clinical treatment, pharmacological, psychotherapeutic and behavioural (Ouimette, Crosby & Moos, 1997). Often pharmacological intervention is used to reduce the anxiety and depression that may comes in conjunction with withdrawal from certain types of drugs, e.g. opiates.

Opioid antagonists

Opioid antagonists were developed to block or counteract the effects of opiates. They complete this action by binding with opiate receptor sites and prevent stimulation or displace an opiate already occupying the site. The major issue is that the vast majority of these drugs have significant side effects and cause severe withdrawal in dependent individuals (Meyer & Quenzer, 2004).

Opioid agonists – methadone

The most widely used and well-known agonist is methadone. Methadone is a synthetic narcotic that was developed in Germany during the Second World War. Methadone produces similar analgesic and sedative effects as heroin and is longer-lasting although the euphoria is less dramatic. Methadone has typically been used in hospitals to methodically detoxify individuals addicted to opiates. Withdrawal from heroin is made relatively painless by the administration of doses of methadone equivalent to their heroin dosage which is then lowered until the individual is no longer dependent (Simpson, 1997).

The methadone maintenance programme is another type of treatment utilized for heroin addiction. This treatment programme was originally created by two individuals, Vincent Dole and Marie Nyswander, in the early 1960s. Methadone is used in a similar fashion to any other prescribed medicine and normalizes the individual's functioning by replacing heroin with methadone. Research in this type of use of an opioid agonist has evidenced that some addicted individuals have been able to refrain from heroin use, secure employment, maintain relationships and family responsibilities and avoid criminal activity. This type of programme appeals to a group of addicted individuals who have not been amenable to other social intervention strategies (Erdelyan, 2009).

Detoxification

Detoxification is often used in treatment programmes to facilitate the withdrawal from substances. Detoxification is a term that was left over from an obsolete theory that addicts suffered from an accumulation of toxins. Antagonists are sometimes used for detoxification and the process is accomplished by decreasing dosages so that the individual does not experience unpleasant withdrawal symptoms. Cocaine detoxification presents a complicated dilemma because of the extreme depression that occurs during the beginning of abstinence that can lead to suicide. One additional aspect of detoxification programmes is that often addicts are willing to enter treatment because their habits have become too expensive to maintain and they are unable to continue supplying themselves with adequate amounts of the drug they have become tolerant to. They enter a detoxification treatment programme to comfortably withdraw from their addiction and are not confronted with the negatively reinforcing pharmacological and physiological aspects of addiction. The detoxification lowers their level of tolerance so that once they are released they can return to a habit they are able to maintain for a limited amount of time and then begin the addiction cycle again or are arrested for illegal activities and incarcerated (Coombs, 2002).

THERAPIES

Psychotherapy comes in many different forms but the vast majority rely on verbal communication between the individual and the therapist. This type of treatment can occur in group settings, individually or a combination of both. The nature and goals of the communication vary with the orientation of the therapist but most generally focus on the individual's background, current life situation, motives and the consequences of drug and alcohol abuse. Group therapy offers the opportunities (1) to share and to identify with others who are going through similar problems; (2) to reach an understanding of attitudes toward addiction and (3) to communicate needs and feelings more directly. In some approaches the individual can come to an understanding of what has caused the abuse. In other approaches there is an emphasis on the impact of drugs on the past, present and future rather than searching for past causes (Rapaka & Sadee, 2008).

In psychodynamic therapy the interpretation and focus is that the substance abuse is as a result of a reflection of some unresolved conflict, either conscious or unconscious. The symptoms of drug and alcohol abuse are as a result of neurotic behaviour that is tied to repressed material from early life. The psychoanalyst aims to make unconscious emotion and memories available to the individual's consciousness. The individual is then encouraged to give up the repressions belonging to their early life and replace them by reactions that correspond better to a mature condition. This is accomplished through the use of dream interpretation and free association. Another issue that may be responsible for substance abuse is that it may stem from a characterological defect that occurred in an earlier stage. In either case the substance-addicted individual is regarded as being unable to utilize defence mechanisms such as denial, rationalization and projection to cope with various threats and therefore relies on outside substances. The focus is on improving functioning at the ego level. The goal of this type of therapy is to re-interpret the past, re-establish appropriate defences and provide insight to the individual and facilitate recovery (Weegmann & Cohen, 2002).

In cognitive-behavioural therapies the goal is completely different from that of psychodynamic therapy and instead places more emphasis on increasing the individual's awareness of present and future motivators of drug use than on past or unconscious factors. The idea is that the psychological problems stem from faulty cognitions and beliefs held by the individual and the therapist attempts to dispel and correct misconceptions held by the individual and how this relates to substance abuse. By continually questioning and confronting the substance user with evidence the therapist aims to help the individual realize the illogical and flawed views they have. The major goal is to facilitate and help the individual realize why they are abusing substances and to find alternative positive ways of achieving their goals. Cognitive behavioural therapies also help the individual understand the need for substances and provide new beliefs about overcoming their reliance on substances (Beck, 2011).

Behavioural approaches are a bit different from cognitive behavioural therapies as the focus is exclusively on behaviour. The belief is that to counter current behaviour there is reinforcement of prior associations and habits previous to the learned substance taking behaviour. The idea is that the same processes can be employed to unlearn prior habits or to develop new ones. However the strength of substances as positive reinforcers and the negative reinforcement associated with withdrawal and abstinence provide conditioned responses that are often difficult to overcome. In order for behaviour modification to be effective, reinforcement must immediately follow the behaviour which is what makes behaviour modification so difficult to apply. A variety of techniques are utilized based on classical and operant conditioning which include relaxation training, covert desensitization, counter-conditioning, aversive conditioning and contingency contracting. The focus is that drug taking behaviour was learned and therefore can be unlearned (Bellack, Bennett & Gearon, 2006).

Behaviour modification can also involve the application of an aversive stimulus. One specific type of therapy that utilizes pharmacology as a method of treatment is the use of antabuse (disulfiram) with alcohol addiction. Antabuse reacts with alcohol and creates a strong unpleasant physical reaction (extreme vomiting and diarrhoea) which limits alcohol consumption and is believed to cause extreme negative reactions to drinking behaviour (Krampe & Ehrenreich, 2010).

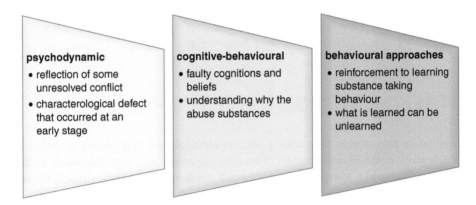

psychodynamic
- reflection of some unresolved conflict
- characterological defect that occurred at an early stage

cognitive-behavioural
- faulty cognitions and beliefs
- understanding why the abuse substances

behavioural approaches
- reinforcement to learning substance taking behaviour
- what is learned can be unlearned

Figure 13.4

TWELVE STEP PROGRAMMES

The twelve step programmes were originally created for alcoholics. The alcoholics anonymous (AA) programme was co-founded by William Wilson and Robert Holbrook Smith in 1930. The twelve step programmes require an act of surrender, acknowledgement of the addiction, the destructiveness that results, a willingness to bear witness and an acknowledgement of a higher power. The twelve step programmes are nondenominational although they feature a repentative element and many groups begin their meetings with reciting the Lord's Prayer. Within the twelve step programmes the addicted person seeks salvation through personal testimony, public contrition and a submission to a higher authority. The programme recognizes the potency of shared honesty and mutual vulnerability and supports each member on their efforts to remain substance free. The conceptual model that is utilized within the programmes is based on the disease model of addiction and that dependence is a lifelong struggle. It is never cured and there are only recovering abusers. Members are encouraged to accept the belief that they are powerless over their addiction, they cannot control their intake and therefore total abstinence is required. New members are expected to find a sponsor who has remained abstinent for a period of time and can help the new member to work through the twelve steps. The programmes have a minimum of formal organization, no power of punishment or exclusion and are always local groups that meet in community-based facilities such as churches or community centres (Brown, 2009).

Table 13.5   Different types of twelve-step programmes for substance abusers

AA	Alcoholics Anonymous
CA	Cocaine Anonymous
CMA	Crystal Meth Anonymous
HA	Heroin Anonymous
MA	Marijuana Anonymous
NA	Narcotics Anonymous
PA	Pills Anonymous (recovery from prescription pill addiction)
SA	Smokers Anonymous

DRUG TREATMENT PROGRAMMES (REHAB)

Rehabilitation programmes vary widely and are accomplished in a variety of settings: voluntary or involuntary, inpatient or outpatient. There are variations in the qualifications of the staff and the length of treatment. Most programmes have a standard course of withdrawal, physical restoration, psychological therapy in individual and group counselling and vocational training. Generally all programmes have a period of time where residents are isolated until the withdrawal process is accomplished with the support of staff and other residents. Most programmes assign work projects, and assignments and are kept busy in a highly structured environment where the expectation is to be active and cooperative in all aspects of the rehabilitation programme. Once the programme is completed the individual returns to their communities and takes part in community outpatient programmes and therapy (Benshoff & Janikowski, 1999).

SUMMARY

Treatment of all abused substances should be both physical and psychological in form. Treatment programmes should address the complex needs of the individual. Assesment should be conducted to assess the types of drugs the person has been abusing, what types of medical intervention should be provided, e.g. a detoxification programme should be followed by a multidimensional treatment programme. Programmes should provide intervention that focuses on all elements of dependency in order to maximize effectiveness. Addressing the simple elements of physical dependency will not be a long-term solution to addiction. Social, cultural, biological and psychological factors interact in both the aetiology and the resolution of substance-related problems. Social and environmental factors may be just as important in the recovery of any substance-abusing client, regardless of age, or drug of choice. Treatment goals need to take into account not just substance-use behaviour but also rehabilitation in such areas as occupational functioning, psychological well-being and social involvement. Levels of functioning in these aspects of life may have a strong influence on the likelihood of relapse. Negative effects of stressful life events can be lessened if individuals learn more effective coping responses, increase their feelings of self-efficacy and purposefully build the environmental resources available to them.

CONCLUSION

Returning to our case study, Diane's addiction began as she participated in drinking behaviour with her peers. It is possible that her psychological and physiological need was somewhat different from her peer group which caused her to seek more potent types of drugs and these led to her wanting to try out more 'party drugs' Her case is more illustrative of the positive incentive models. Her constant need to achieve 'a better high and party' led her to try ecstasy and her demise. Diane is just a single case in an ever growing societal issue of young people who are becoming addicted to substances. Each case must be evaluated as there are many different reasons why individuals begin using substances that could lead to addiction.

Summary

This chapter focused on substance-use disorders and included a discussion on the variety of problems associated with abusing substances. The chapter focused on the various theories of abuse, the biological pathways, genetic predisposition to substance abuse, physical and biological dependency and treatment.

LEARNING TOOLS

Key terms

Addicts – habitual drug users who continue to use a drug despite the adverse effects of the drug on their health and life and despite their repeated efforts to stop using it

Cross-tolerance – tolerance that develops to the effects of one drug as the result of exposure to another drug

Drug metabolism – the conversion of a drug from its active form to a non-active form

Drug tolerance – a state of decreased susceptibility to a drug that develops as a result of exposure to the drug

GABA – an amino acid, the most important inhibitory neurotransmitter in the brain

Korsakoff's syndrome – the severe memory loss and dementia that is commonly associated with alcohol addiction

Mesotelencephalic dopamine system – the ascending projections of dopamine-releasing neurons from the substantia nigra and ventral tegmental area of the mesencephalon into various regions of the telencephalon

Psychopharmacology – the study of the effects of drugs on the nervous system and on behaviour

Sensitization – an increase in the sensitivity to a drug effect that develops as the result of exposure to the drug

Sites of action – the locations at which molecules of drugs interact with molecules located on or in cells of the body, thus affecting some biochemical processes of these cells

Therapeutic index – the ratio between the dose that produces the desired effect in 50 percent of the subjects and the dose that produces toxic effects in 50 percent of the subjects.

Withdrawal symptom – the appearance of symptoms opposite to those produced by a drug when the drug is administered repeatedly and then suddenly no longer taken

Study guide

1   Compare and contrast the biological model of addiction with one of the psychological theories of addictive behaviour.
2   Explore the twelve step programme and investigate the twelve steps and twelve traditions.
3   Describe the withdrawal symptoms of barbiturates vs. opiates.
4   Olds and Milner were the first to discover intracranial self-stimulation. How does this affect our understanding of addictions?

Case study in focus

Apply two different models to Diane's drug use. What was Diane most vulnerable to? Suppose that Diane's parents were both alcohol dependent, how would this influence Diane's own substance abuse? If Diane had survived what types of treatment would have been the most useful?

Personal development

Investigate the differences between drinking normally and binge drinking. How has this affected the psychological and physiological of the person participating in this type of behaviour and what are the risks associated with this type of drinking?

Suggested reading

Miller, W.R. & Carroll, K.M. (2010). *Rethinking substance abuse: What the science shows and what we should do about it*. New York: Guilford Press.

Ghodse, H., Herrman, H., Maj, M. & Sartorius, N. (2011) *Substance abuse disorders: Evidence and experience*. Oxford: Wiley-Blackwell.

Straussner, S.L.A. & Huff, F. (2006) *Impact of substance abuse on children and families: Research and practice implications*. New York: Routledge.

Alzheimer's, Cognitive Disorders and Disorders Related to Aging

14

Learning aims

At the end of this chapter you should:

- Be familiar with how cognition is affected by the process of aging
- Understand the biological elements of cognitive disorders
- Be able to explain the various types of treatment available
- Understand the differences between various types of cognitive disorders.

--- **INTRODUCTION** ---

CASE STUDY

Mr Zeidel had been a successful businessman and had been well respected in his community. He had been a Holocaust survivor and had lost his entire family to the internment camps. His first wife had died of cancer when they were both in their late fifties. With his children now adults he remarried and he and his second wife by all accounts had lived contentedly for the past 15 years. He sold his business and at the age of 68 had settled into a comfortable retirement. His wife suffered from arthritis and was a bit frail in health and Mr Zeidel happily settled into the role of care provider. Within two years of his retirement Mrs Zeidel began to complain to family members that her husband was moody and was becoming forgetful. Her complaints were dismissed by family members as typical aging concerns and it was felt that as a result of Mr Zeidel's retirement he was constantly at home and perhaps that was causing a bit of irritation between the two of them. The family soon became alarmed when Mr and Mrs Zeidel were found by the police 120 km away from home. A concerned individual had heard a woman in distress in a parked car and had contacted the police. They found Mr Zeidel in a confused state and Mrs Zeidel crying and begging to be taken home. The pair were taken to the hospital where both were found to be in good health and escorted back home. It was at this point that Mr Zeidel's cognitive deterioration was noted. Over the course of two years, Mr Zeidel's cognitive function continued to decline and on two occasions after taking his wife for medical appointments he had forgotten where the couple lived and had driven around the town for hours until Mrs Zeidel insisted on stopping and calling her son. The stepson attempted unsuccessfully to stop Mr Zeidel from driving and many arguments occurred as Mr Zeidel refused to give up motoring. Mr Zeidel's condition continued to deteriorate and he became increasingly paranoid and felt that the Nazis were coming and his behaviour became more erratic. He began hoarding food and hiding objects of value and then would accuse his wife of stealing because he had forgotten where he had hidden the objects. Eventually he became angry and combative and was unable to care for his wife and it was felt for his own safety as well as others that he be confined to a residential treatment facility. After his separation from his wife and home he deteriorated very quickly and died.

INTRODUCTION

This chapter will mainly focus on cognitive disorders that result in permanent damage to the brain due to the aging process. There will also be some discussion of cognitive disorders that comprise the DSM-5's new classification of neurocognitive disorders. Cognitive disorders are those related to mental functions such as memory, perception, language and problem solving.

The DSM-III-R originally categorized this class of disorders in a section that was titled 'organic mental syndromes and disorders' (APA, 1987). This category was changed in subsequent revisions to reflect changes to the category. It was felt that the original category name was inaccurate and implied that non-organic mental disorders did not have a biological basis so the current category addresses those inaccuracies. The current title in the DSM-IV is 'Delirium, dementia, and amnestic and other cognitive disorders'. However the new proposals for the DSM-5 have suggested that the previous classification in the DSM-IV should be revised and titled 'Neurocognitive Disorders' (APA, 2012). This newly revised category will have three broadly defined syndromes; (1) delirium, (2) major neurocognitive disorder and (3) minor cognitive disorder. The new classification will redefine the characteristics of this group as primary deficits in cognition that represent a decline from a previously attained level of cognitive functioning. This new classification system would distinguish this class of disorders from those neurodevelopmental disorders that are present at birth or those that impede the early development of the child. The disorders in the new classification system are similar to the earlier DSM-IV categories and are attributable to changes in brain structure, function or chemistry. Those disorders whose aetiologies are known are coded into specific subtypes (APA, 2012). One new distinction in the DSM-5 has been the division of minor and major neurocognitive disorders that are based on severity. The major division is defined by a greater loss of independence in activities of daily living, while the minor is distinguished by fewer difficulties in daily living and fewer disruptions in the cognitive domains. As a result of many cognitive disorders being progressive, an individual can be initially diagnosed in the minor category and through the course of their illness progress to the major category (APA, 2012).

Recently cognitive disorders have come to the attention of the British public as a result of many famous individuals disclosing their medical statuses and some asking for a change in the laws for medically assisted death. Terry Pratchett, a famous fantasy writer has openly called for more research in neurocognitive disorders, specifically Alzheimer's and has provided £500,000 to help fund projects in the hopes that others would join in funding more research in this area. Margaret Thatcher's daughter has recently disclosed that her mother has Alzheimer's, while Ronald Reagan the American president died of the disorder. The government has responded by becoming more active in educating the public with various types of advertisement campaigns on cognitive disorders of the aged.

HISTORICAL BACKGROUND

It is well known that the aging process brings many physical and mental changes. As an individual enters their sixth, seventh and eighth decades of life they face a steady decline in their physical abilities. They become less mobile, less flexible and struggle with a variety of age-related health disorders. They must also cope with the complex mental challenges of living a long life and the losses that come with time; physical abilities, employment, the death of parents, family members and friends (Luukinen, Koski, Kivela & Paippala, 1996; Osterweis et al., 1985). They find themselves at odds with an ever changing environment. As a result of their physical and mental vulnerability they rely more and more on the help of others and unfortunately often become the targets of crime. Depression, senility and dementias within this age group are frequent.

Historically elders were held in high regard as the guardians of the local community and were sought for guidance and wisdom. They were often called upon as experts in a variety of areas from farming to the raising of children. However, in our fast moving modern society elders are no longer valued for their wisdom and instead communities and families rely on other forms of information. Libraries have become the place where history and information is stored and the internet provides instant access to a wealth of information. The older generations are no longer valued for their contribution and instead are often viewed as a liability rather than an asset. Current society has cast aside the previous high regard and often displays disinterest and even contempt for the aged (Cann & Dean, 2009).

In the not so recent past it was custom and practice for the elderly to remain as part of the nuclear family and their roles were often caregivers of younger family members. In turn they were provided with care and security within the family unit. Modern society has changed the family roles and often both parents work outside of the home while young children are cared for in day care facilities until they reach school age. Adult children rarely remain in the familial home and generally establish independent lives and homes. Older family members are more frequently being left behind to care for themselves until they become unable to do so and are then placed in residential care facilities until their deaths (Tobin & Kulys, 1981).

With these changes in roles and families, society is faced with multiple dilemmas in terms of our elder populations. The improvements in health care and the new types of drugs and antibiotics are allowing elders to live longer. The percentages of older people have been steadily increasing. In 1900 approximately 4 percent of the UK population was 65 or older. It has been projected that by 2033, 57 percent of the UK population will be 65 or older (Office for National Statistics, 2011). With the rise in the population of older individuals, there will be a parallel increase to the number of people with cognitive impairment due to the aging process. Clearly this will become a significant social issue as families will be forced to rely on health care systems for support.

An interesting element that may affect the prevalence of cognitive disorders is the increasing changes in long-term health. Although there is an increase in the number of older individuals, many factors play a considerable part in their long-term health and well-being. Our modern society has provided better nutrition, health care, education, and changes to employability. Health and safety laws are helping to prevent people from coming into direct contact with dangerous elements which prevent life threatening injuries that in the past have caused shorter life spans (Victor, 2010).

As a result of these many changes older adults are living longer and are often finding themselves dealing with medical illness, physical limitation, and/or social loss without the support of the community or family. It is common for elders to experience psychological problems such as depression, anxiety, and adjustment disorders. Suicide among the elderly is a significant and ever increasing problem. Sometimes these difficulties develop as a natural reaction to losses or limitations. However, depression and anxiety can also be associated with medical illnesses, such as heart disease, the various neurocognitive disorders and/or diabetes (Stuart-Hamilton, 2006).

Another important element when discussing neurocognitive disorders is the issue of quality of life. Poor quality of life has often been used as a basis of support for physician-assisted termination and euthanasia. Quality of life is a concept that incorporates a variety of different philosophical, political and health related definitions. Generally the basic definition of quality of life refers to the physical, functional, social and emotional well-being of an individual. Quality of life has been defined by the World Health Organization as an individual's perception of their position in life in the context of the culture and value systems in which they live and in relation to their goals, expectations, standards and concerns (World Health Organization, 1993).

Individuals suffering from neurocognitive disorders have increasingly cited their progressive disorders as diminishing their quality of life as well as not wanting to face the inevitable end and requesting the right to die with dignity and make choices before they reach a point in their illness when they are unable to do so. As a result of many outspoken individuals who have supported the cause, various countries around the world have enacted changes in legislation and legalized physician-assisted suicide. The UK has yet to make any changes and the Suicide Act of 1961 can prosecute and convict anyone assisting the suicide of another individual regardless of the reasons, who can serve up to 14 years in prison.

There is a distinction between euthanasia and assisted suicide. Euthanasia is defined as a physician intentionally killing a person by the administration of drugs at that person's voluntary and competent request. There are two types of euthanasia, active and passive. Active is the physician actively contributing to an individual's death, whereas passive is removing an individual's life support or other

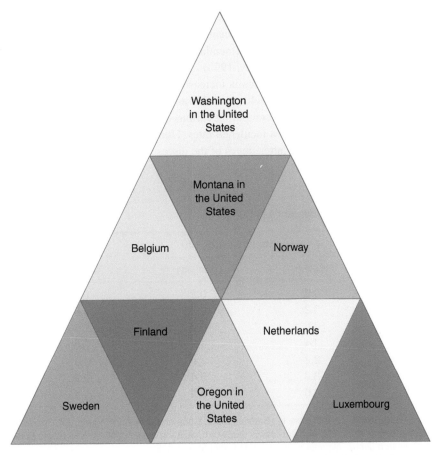

Figure 14.1   Places where euthanasia and/or physician-assisted suicide is legal

treatment if the person has signed a living will or their next of kin has requested it. Physician-assisted suicide is defined as a physician intentionally helping a person to commit suicide by providing drugs for self-administration at the person's voluntary and competent request (Firth, 2011).

PREVALENCE OF COGNITIVE DISORDERS IN THE ELDERLY

Alzheimer's Disease International estimates that there are 30 million people with dementia in the world (Alzheimer's Disease International, 2008). The exact incidence rates of dementia are difficult to obtain because methods of reporting and the criteria used for research all influence the information obtained in prevalence studies. The prevalence of dementia also varies with aging, with older groups having higher incidence rates. Between ages 65 and 70, approximately 3–5 percent may have some level of dementia. This value rises to about 5–7 percent between 70 and 75, to 7–9 percent between 75 and 80, and to about 25 percent by age 85 and over. People living into their nineties or hundreds have a reduced incidence of dementia, in all likelihood because the demented subgroups have died at an earlier age (Jorm & Jolley, 1998).

Although the incidence rates of dementia increase in populations 65 and older, younger cases do occur, even among people in the 30–40-year-old range. There are many causes of dementia and these are listed in Table 14.2. When comparing various other types of degenerative neurological disorders, Alzheimer's has the highest incidence rates. Due to the progressive nature of Alzheimer's most if not all individuals in the latter stages of the disease will require institutional care until their deaths.

Table 14.1 Prevalence of dementia in Europe

Age group	Annual incidence per 100		Prevalence (%)	
	Males	Females	Males	Females
60–64	0.2	0.2	0.4	0.4
65–69	0.2	0.3	1.6	1.0
70–74	0.6	0.5	2.9	3.1
75–79	1.4	1.8	5.6	6.0
80–84	2.8	3.4	11.0	12.6
85–89	3.9	5.4	12.8	20.2
90+	4.0	8.2	22.1	30.8

Fratiglioni, L., Launer, L.J., Andersen, K., Breteler, M.M., Copeland, J.R. & Dartigues, J.F., 'Incidence of dementia and major subtypes in Europe: A collaborative study of population based cohorts', *Neurologic Diseases in the Elderly Research Group. Neurology* 2000, 54(11 Suppl 5):S10-S15.

Table 14.2   Causes of dementia

Alzheimer's disease
Down's syndrome
Multinfarct dementia
Toxic substances (drugs, alcohol)
Metabolic deficiency (e.g. vitamin A)
Endocrine (e.g. hypothyroidism)
Infectious (e.g. neurosyphilis)
Inflammatory (e.g. vasculitis)
Post-traumatic and postanoxic
Genetic (e.g. Huntington's disease)
Degenerative (e.g. Parkinson's disease)
Cerebral tumours
Subdural haematoma
Hydrocephalus
HIV
Binswanger's disease
Pick's disease
Korsakoff's syndrome
Multiple Sclerosis
Prion diseases (e.g. Creutzfeldt-Jakob disease)

CHANGES IN COGNITION IN THE AGING BRAIN

The brain has the ability to change and adapt. This ability is called plasticity. Plasticity is most apparent during the early development of a foetus although the process to a much lesser effect will occur throughout the course of an individual's life. This ever changing ability provides the brain with the ability to be continually responsive to its environment. Through the five methods of perception, information is provided to the brain. If one of these is damaged, e.g. vision, the brain can reorganize itself so that it is better able to process information through the remaining four. This does not imply that a visually impaired person has superior qualities in other areas. Instead the plasticity of the brain allows for more information to be processed in those areas that are responsible for other types of input.

Even though the brain has the ability to adapt to changes, the neurons do not. There is some evidence that neurons do trigger a limited type of neurogenesis but neurons do not regenerate in large numbers after injury or disease and this type of recovery will be limited (Kokaia & Lindvall, 2003). Non-neuronal changes do occur in a newborn's brain such as an increased number of synapses that are formed and an increase number of glia cells that are created (Prechtl, 1984). Glia cells are supporting cells and provide physical and chemical buffers that surround the neurons and hold them in place. They also provide a role for removing the remains of neurons that have been killed by injury, disease or simply die off as a result of old age. As neurons are removed, the space left behind is filled with glia cells. As the aging process affects the changes in the structure of the brain the function of the glia cells becomes more complicated.

BRAIN REGIONS MOST SUSCEPTIBLE TO THE EFFECTS OF AGING

The regions of the brain that appear to be most affected by aging and cognitive decline are those that support higher order associative functions. Associative functions are those that are responsible for language, compassion and foresight as well as planning and guidance of behaviour.

Frontal regions

Both physiological and behavioural evidence exists for changes in frontal regions as a result of increasing age (Mann, South, Snowden & Neary, 1993). Reductions in blood flow to the brain appear to be the most noticeable for frontal regions. These changes don't just occur in the brain but are a result of the overall physical conditioning of the individual. Lack of physical exercise, and health-related illnesses such as high blood pressure and cardiovascular disease significantly contribute to the loss of blood flow in the frontal regions and the overall nervous system. These physiological changes in brain function also have behavioural consequences. One specific example is what is termed 'source amnesia'. This is the inability to remember specifically where information was learned although the specifics about the information have been retained, e.g. what year the Second World War ended (Sachdev, 2003).

Temporal regions

The temporal lobes are a region of the brain that is important in creating new long-term memories. Memory for facts and events appears to be stored in these areas – what is called the consolidation of memories. This is critically important for the ability to create new long-term memories of the declarative sort, which allows information to be used flexibly and in a variety of contexts. By the sixth and seventh decades of life, healthy older adults begin to perform more poorly than younger individuals on direct tests of declarative memory. Older persons especially have problems with recall and on tasks that require an organized search through memory to retrieve the information rather than in structured situations in which a person must only recognize information (Whalley, 2002).

IMPAIRED COGNITIVE FUNCTION

Concrete thinking is generally identified as one of the first signs of cognitive impairment. This characteristic appears as the inability to think abstractly. Individuals begin to have difficulty forming concepts, using categories, generalizing from a single instance, or applying procedural rules and general principles. These can be in the form of grammar, mathematical operations or more revealingly in the lack of rules of behaviour and/or conduct. The loss of abstract thinking results in the individual preferring to apply superficial solutions with little permanent resolution to the problem. Without resolution the problem persists and they continue to apply the same superficial solutions (Larner, 2008).

Generally individuals who begin experiencing cognitive dysfunction are unaware of the subtle underlying aspects of the problem and begin to be unable to distinguish what is relevant from what is irrelevant, essential from non-essential and appropriate from inappropriate. Their inabilities to distinguish these fine details are often translated into frustration and confusion when others do not understand. It is generally at this point that others begin to notice and the behavioural elements become more pronounced.

Another aspect to impaired cognition is conceptual inflexibility. This frequently occurs in association with concrete thinking. Conceptual inflexibility is the inability to apply flexibility in problems. A healthy individual will use trial and error until the right solution is found. An individual with conceptual inflexibility must treat each small portion of the problem and soon becomes lost and unable to distinguish what is relevant from what is irrelevant, essential from unessential, and appropriate from outlandish (Wilson et al., 2003).

As a result of being unable to conceptualize abstractly, the individual deals with each problem as if it was a new and isolated experience with unique rules. Conceptual inflexibility frequently occurs in association with concrete thinking. It may show up in what appears to be repetitive behaviour where the individual goes over the issue multiple times with no solution. Individuals displaying this level of cognitive dysfunction are unable to plan ahead, initiate activity, think creatively or adapt to the demands of changing circumstances. This type of repetitive thinking is termed 'stimulus bound behaviour'. The person is unable to shift attention from whatever is in their perceptual field. Although they are still able to live relatively independently they begin to struggle with the complexities of life.

When we think of our case study Mr Zeidel's cognitive dysfunction began with his wife noticing moody behaviour and patterns of forgetfulness. It is likely that his wife was noticing his difficulties in thinking clearly and his inability to abstract as well as his cognitive inflexibility.

Conceptual concreteness and mental inflexibility are sometimes treated as different aspects of the same disability. When they occur together, they tend to be mutually reinforcing in their effects.

PRESERVING COGNITIVE FUNCTION IN LATER LIFE

Research has indicated that cognitive functions can be preserved longer with stimulation and enriched experience throughout life. Schaie, Willis & Caskie (2004), found in their longitudinal study that contextual, health and personality variables offered explanations for individual differences in cognitive decline. They found the following factors reduced the risk of cognitive decline:

1   individuals with above-average education
2   occupations that were stimulating but involved low routine
3   above-average income
4   living in an intact family, i.e. happy in a long-term stable relationship
5   continued involvement in activities that were complex and intellectually stimulating, such as reading, travel, attendance of cultural events, continuing education and participation in clubs and professional associations
6   marriage to a spouse with high cognitive status.

Masliah et al. (1991) found that enriched life experiences preserved cognitive function and that the loss of synapses correlated strongly with the severity of symptoms in Alzheimer's disease.

THE SPECIFIC DISORDERS

Delirium

Delirium is defined as a disturbance of consciousness and changes in cognition, i.e. memory deficits, disorientation, language and perceptual disturbances. These impairments and changes are generally not attributable to dementia and 90 percent of hospital admissions are as a direct consequence to alcohol and/or substance abuse. The remaining 10 percent are typically aged 65 or older and are hospitalized because of a general medical condition that has caused the delirium. Once the condition has been addressed, the delirium will subside until the person is functioning normally (Lindesay, Rockwood & Rolfson, 2002).

Delirium is a rapid development of symptoms and will fluctuate during the course of the day. Individuals will exhibit confusion and disorientation, problems of attention or inability to shift mental sets and memory disturbance as well as impaired social and occupational functioning. With a small percentage of individuals it co-occurs because of declining health such cardiovascular disorders, diabetes etc. Once the general medical condition is addressed the individual will return to their normal state. Delirium is normally a short-term condition (Lindesay, Rockwood & Rolfson, 2002).

THE NEUROCOGNITIVE DISORDER SUBTYPES

HIV

Acquired Immune Deficiency Syndrome (AIDS) and its related conditions are caused by the human immunodeficiency virus (HIV). HIV affects both the central nervous system and peripheral nervous system. The HIV virus is responsible for the destruction of the body's immune system. The virus enters the brain and other organs throughout the body, resulting in compromised movement, memory and body functions.

One of the many complications of AIDS has been neurological disease (Krishna, Taneja & Gokhale, 2011). Navia, Jordan and Price (1986) reported that over 50 percent of AIDS patients showed some cognitive, motor, and/or psychological changes in the course of their illness. About 70–90 percent of adult AIDS patients have some neurological impairment (Levy, Bredesen & Rosenblum, 1985, 1988; Scourfield, Waters & Nelson, 2010).

Neurological disease in the HIV-positive individual can be caused by an opportunistic infection, such as toxoplasmosis or cryptococcal meningitis or from HIV infection in the brain. These illnesses cause a progressive dementing disorder called AIDS Dementia Complex and is a significant cause of disability among those in the advanced stages of the disease. AIDS Dementia Complex is a clinical diagnosis with a variable course which includes symptoms in three different areas: cognitive, behavioural and motor symptoms (Pereira-Chioccola, Vidal & Su, 2009; Brew, 2007).

Early cognitive symptoms of AIDS Dementia Complex include difficulties with concentration and memory and a general slowing of mental function. Common behavioural symptoms include social withdrawal and a generalized apathy. Early motor problems can include difficulty with balance, clumsiness and leg weakness. Another aspect is progressive multifocal leukoencephalopathy (PML) that is characterized by widespread demyelinative lesions due to infection of the oligodendrocytes by a human papovavirius. Individuals with progressive PML typically have symptoms that include behavioural, speech, cognitive, motor and visual impairment. Progressive multifocal leukoencephalopathy generally demonstrates a more rapid progression than AIDS dementia complex (Brew, 2007; Navia & Rostasy, 2005).

AIDS dementia complex is second only to sensory neuropathy as the most common of central nervous system (CNS) complications of HIV disease. Estimates of prevalence among HIV-infected individuals vary from as low as 1 percent to as high as 8 percent. Low CD4 counts (typically less than 200 cells/μL) greatly increase the risk of the disease. Evidence of HIV may be found in cerebrospinal fluid samples, but the virus can be present without causing dementia. Accurate diagnosis is important, because specific treatment is available for a number of CNS complications even though there is no standard specific treatment for either ADC or PML, although some therapies may be aimed at relief of symptoms. Early diagnosis is important in the early treatment of ADC/PML so that it can be aggressively treated, increasing the individual's lifespan. In addition cognitive status can be monitored, providing a baseline which can then be used for long-term treatment and planning (Brew, 2007; Navia & Rostasy, 2005).

Lewy body dementia (dementia with Lewy bodies)

Lewy bodies are small, spherical protein deposits that are found in nerve cells. These protein deposits disrupt two neurotransmitters, specifically acetylcholine and dopamine and cause a specific type of dementia. Research has yet to elucidate why they form and how they disrupt neurotransmitter activity. This type of dementia is unique in that it embodies two distinct characteristics that are found in Alzheimer's and Parkinson's disease and often individuals with Parkinson's also have Lewy bodies present in areas of the brain. Lewy body dementia accounts for approximately 10 percent of all dementia cases and tends to be under-diagnosed. Lewy body dementia is a progressive disease with approximately the same rate of deterioration as Alzheimer's. The disease presents with problems with memory, attention and alertness, spatial disorientation, problem solving and mental flexibility that are similar to Alzheimer's although the element of memory is less affected than

Alzheimer's. The motor symptoms are similar to Parkinson's and include changes in the strength and tone of voice, tremor, rigidity, muscle stiffness and slowness of movement. The symptoms that are only specific to Lewy body dementia are the experience of detailed and convincing visual hallucinations, dyssomnia, and restless disturbed nights generally marked with confusion. Lewy body dementia is often difficult to diagnose and often is misdiagnosed as Alzheimer's disease until the presence of hallucinations and the motoric symptoms begin to occur. Accurate diagnosis with this type of dementia is important because individuals tend to react badly to certain types of medication (Hewitt & Gabata, 2011).

Prion disease

This is a category of diseases that are also referred to as transmissible spongiform encephalopathies (TSEs) and are a related group of rare progressive neurodegenerative disorders that can affect both humans and animals. The three main human diseases in this category are: Creutzfeldt-Jakob disease (CJD), Gerstmann-Sträussler-Scheinker syndrome (GSS), and fatal insomnia (FI). The animal condition is called bovine spongiform encephalopathy (BSE) also known as 'mad cow disease' because of the way it affects the cow's nervous system causing it to behave in odd ways as well as affecting its motor movements. Humans can acquire Creutzfeldt-Jakob disease by eating beef products from cows affected by BSE, which is why there continues to be a great deal of focus on BSE in the UK, although acquiring this disease in this manner is extremely rare (Nunnally & Krull, 2003).

The central feature of this group of diseases is the spongiform changes that occur in the brain as well as neuronal loss, astrocytosis and amyloid plague formation. All of the diseases in this category are progressive and cause impaired brain function, memory changes, personality changes, and dementia. These conditions form a spectrum of diseases with overlapping signs and symptoms (Brown, 2005).

The aetiology of TSEs occurs in individuals without any known risk factors or gene mutations with only a very small percentage being genetic. In familial cases of prion disease the mutations in the PRNP gene cause the cells to produce an abnormal form of the prion protein. The abnormal prion protein builds up in the brain, forming clumps that destroy or damage nerve cells causing the characteristic sponge-like holes in the brain. Familial forms of prion disease are inherited in an autosomal dominant pattern, although a parent can become infected with prion's disease and then pass the genetic change to their offspring (Baker & Ridley, 1996).

Huntington's disease

Huntington's disease was named after George Huntington who originally described this disorder and named it chorea. Huntington's disease is a genetic disorder which commonly affects individuals in their forties and fifties. It primarily affects the brain, with a gradual loss of control of movement, memory, mental ability as well as personality changes and depression. Changes in personality or mood are usually the earliest signs of the disease, followed by problems with memory and abnormal uncontrollable movements. The abnormal movements, which gave Huntington's disease its former name of Huntington's chorea (chorea is a Greek word meaning dance), are typically rapid, jerking movements, writhing movements of the arms and legs (athetosis), strange postures due to muscle spasm (dystonia) and a slowing of voluntary movements. Current theories suggest that the protein formed as a result of the abnormal Huntington's disease gene (IT15), which codes for a protein. The exact function of the protein is unknown but somehow it prevents the neurons from protecting themselves against the toxic chemicals as well as decreasing the amounts of signalling neurotransmitters (GABA) involved in signalling, transporting materials and binding proteins (Lawrence, 2009).

Substance-induced neurocognitive disorder

There are two separate but related stages of alcohol associated damage in this category: Wernicke's encephalopathy and Korsakoff's psychosis. Both are neuropsychiatric disorders that are a direct result of a thiamine (Vitamin B1) deficiency which affects the brain and nervous system. Although this condition can be found in other disorders (anorexia nervosa, AIDS) it is more common in heavy drinkers because of their poor eating habits, frequent vomiting and inflammation to the stomach lining. The symptoms of Wernicke's include confusion, drowsiness, poor balance and memory impairment. If the disorder is treated the symptoms can be reduced but if left untreated or undiagnosed until the later phases it can result in irreversible brain damage with the possibility of death. Death occurs to approximately 20 percent of individuals with Wernicke's with 85 percent of the survivors developing Korsakoff's psychosis. Wernicke's is a more acute form of damage while Korsakoff's is more chronic. Not every case of Korsakoff is preceded by Wernicke's, however an individual with Korsakoff who continues drinking can have acute episodes of Wernicke's. The memory loss is the most significant feature of the condition with the majority of the other cognitive abilities unaffected. Korsakoff's differs from other types of dementia where the damage tends to be in the large area of the outer part of the brain (cortex) and a much wider range of abilities are affected (McCandless, 2009).

Parkinson's disease

Parkinson's disease is a degenerative disease of the nervous system associated with trembling of the arms and legs, stiffness and rigidity of the muscles and slowness of movement (bradykinesia). Approximately a third of those affected will go on to develop senile dementia. Parkinson's is caused by the progressive loss of dopaminergic neurones in the substantia nigra. As the cells die, symptoms develop as less dopamine is produced and transported to the striatum, the area of the brain that coordinates movement. The risk rises so that by the age of 80 more than two people per 100 of the population have developed some signs of the condition. Both sexes and all races appear to be equally affected. In a small minority of individuals Parkinson's may be inherited. These individuals usually develop the disease under the age of 50. Parkinson's is incurable but the symptoms can be controlled for many years. Treatment is primarily based on dopamine replacement using dopamine-enhancing drugs such as levodopa. This improves disability in most patients and reduces the risk of fatal complications. Surgical procedures have been used to reduce symptoms in some individuals. These procedures take place in the pallidum and the thalamus and involve lesioning (destroying cells in a target area by burning a hole), stimulation (electrically stimulating cells using a pacemaker) or transplantation (Schapira, 2010).

Traumatic brain injury

A traumatic brain injury (TBI) is any trauma that is nondegenerative and noncongenital. The injury is due to an external mechanical force and leads to permanent or temporary impairment of cognitive, physical and psychosocial functions with an associated diminished or altered state of consciousness. The injuries can range from a minor bump on the skull to serious brain injury. TBI are classified as either closed or open (penetrating) with the injuries divided into two subcategories: (1) primary injury, which occurs at the moment of trauma, and (2) secondary injury, which occurs immediately after trauma and produces effects that continue for an extended period of time that often causes more serious damage and harm than the primary injury (Zollman, 2011). Traumatic brain injury is associated with a variety of cognitive deficits (attention, memory and executive function) in later life and may lead to the development of dementia (Fleminger, Oliver, Lovestone, Rabe-Hesketh & Giora, 2003).

Primary injuries usually manifest as focal injuries (e.g. skull fractures, intracranial haematomas, lacerations, contusions, penetrating wounds), or they can be wide spread such as the case in diffuse axonal injury. Types of primary injuries include: skull fractures, auditory/vestibular dysfunction (impact force to the temporal area that leads to conductive or sensorineural hearing loss), intracranial haemorrhages, coup and contrecoup contusions (contusions that occur because of the creation of negative pressure when the skull returns to its normal shape with contrecoup located opposite the site of direct impact), concussions, diffuse axonal injury (extensive, generalized damage to the white matter of the brain caused by acceleration/deceleration produced by lateral motions of the head during the time of injury), and penetrating head injuries.

Secondary injury results as an indirect result of the primary and includes: ischemia (insufficient blood flow), autoneurotoxicity, reduction in glucose use, cerebral hypoxia, hypotension, cerebral oedema (swelling), hypercapnia (high carbon dioxide levels in the blood), meningitis and brain abscess. There are generally changes in the release of neurotransmitters, changes in the electrical activity, neurodegeneration as well as changes to the brain structures at the point of impact (Rutterford, 2011). There are a wide range of symptoms both physiological and psychological directly associated with the amount of damage. Table 14.3 classifies the variety of symptoms.

The prevalence of traumatic brain injury is not well documented, because most cases are not fatal, and individuals generally do not become hospitalized at the time of injury, therefore estimates are often based on existing disabilities. Wasserberg (2002) found that hospital Episode Statistics data for the 2000/2001 annual data set in the UK indicate that there were 112,978 admissions to hospitals in England with a primary diagnosis of head injury. The most common cause of minor head injuries was falls (22–43%) followed by assaults (30–50%). Road traffic accidents account for 25 percent and usually in the category of moderate-to-severe head injuries. It is believed that alcohol may be involved in up to 65 percent of all adult head injuries.

Frontotemporal neurocognitive disorder

Frontotemporal neurocognitive disorder also called frontotemporal dementia is a diverse group of uncommon progressive disorders that primarily affect the frontal and temporal lobes of the brain. In

Table 14.3 Traumatic brain injury symptoms based on severity

Mild/moderate	Severe
Confusion	Amnesia
Temporary memory loss	Paralysis
Temporary tinnitus	Emotional problems
Nausea	Epilepsy
Slurred speech	Slurred speech
Headache	Migraine
Depression	Permanent tinnitus
Fatigue	Confusion
Difficulty with balance	Inability to speak or form words
Mood swings	Permanent memory loss
Insomnia	Loss of coordination

frontotemporal dementia there is a selected degeneration of these two specific areas that produces personality changes, language difficulty and/or behavioural disturbances, although signs and symptoms can vary depending upon the portion of the brain affected and the amount of degeneration. Typically individuals with frontotemporal dementia present with deficits in semantic memory and executive ability. Frontotemporal dementia presents with different signs and symptoms than Alzheimer's disease with individuals developing behavioural and personality changes first and then memory difficulties last as well as generally occurring at younger ages, typically between the ages of 40 and 70. In Alzheimer's disease, individuals always have memory loss as the initial symptom and then develop behavioural and personality changes in the later stages and the disease begins between the ages of 65 and 85. In spite of these differences, frontotemporal dementia is often misdiagnosed as either a psychiatric problem or as Alzheimer's disease (Hodges, 2011).

Vascular neurocognitive disorder

This category was created to encompass the spectrum of impairment from mild vascular cognitive impairment to vascular dementia. This type of disorder is caused when impaired blood flow to areas of the brain is blocked and the neurons are deprived of food and oxygen. Cognitive impairment generally accompanies clinical syndromes associated with vascular disease of the brain such as stroke, but the precise frequency of vascular cognitive disorders is difficult to establish due to a vast number of other factors. For example, dementia has been documented in approximately one-third of elderly patients with stroke; however a subset of this group will also have Alzheimer's disease rather than a pure vascular dementia syndrome (Meyer, Rauch, Lechner & Loeb, 2002).

The diagnostic criteria for vascular dementia have continued to evolve and was originally modelled after Alzheimer's disease. However, early definitions of the disorder disproportionately emphasized deficits of new learning and memory rather than the pattern of motor slowing and executive deficits more typical of vascular dementia. The severity and specific types of brain damage on neuroimaging continue to be controversial and the required temporal link between the onset of cognitive changes and central nervous system changes restricts identification to the later stages. Vascular neurocognitive disorder is suspected after the individual's initial stroke and the individual develops a persistent and/or progressive cognitive deterioration. Symptoms are dependent upon the brain areas that have been affected and often impairment occurs gradually and there is a slow and steady decline. Vascular neurocognitive disorder presents with memory loss, confusion, difficulty concentrating, planning, impaired communication, reduction in the ability to carry out daily activities, and fatigue (Meyer, Rauch, Lechner & Loeb, 2002).

Amnestic disorders

This is a category of memory disorders. Memory is defined as a collection of distinct systems to either recall or utilize to perform a task. When utilizing memory the performance aspect is multiply determined and reflects the separate contributions of each of the following aspects of memory; memory supporting perceptual knowledge, working memory (also called short-term memory), memory supporting knowledge and memory for events. Each element of memory contributes to the completion of the task or recall.

Following injury or disease one or more of these elements can be damaged causing memory loss and impairment. The major structures involved in memory are the medial temporal lobe region specifically the hippocampal system.

Amnestic disorders have certain common elements but they do not form a homogeneous group in terms of their behavioural profiles. In fact amnesias can vary considerably in the severity of memory impairment, in the way in which the memory impairment appears or changes with time and whether they are accompanied by other cognitive deficits. The severity of memory impairment varies considerably among individuals (Seaman et al., 2006).

Causes of amnesia

Vascular accident e.g. stroke, closed head injury, Alzheimer's disease and other types of dementing disorders all produce varying degrees of amnesia. Memory impairment is frequently the earliest sign and the most telling deficit in the early stages. Despite the large differences in severity of amnesia among individuals, in all cases the amnesia has a profoundly adverse effect on their lives and affects all elements of well-being.

The most obvious difference among the amnesias is the presence or absence of cognitive deficits that are superimposed upon the amnesia. For example, the amnesia in Alzheimer's disease, although initially much like that seen in other cases of brain damage, gradually worsens and becomes complicated not only by additional memory deficits associated with damage to various regions but also by other cognitive deficits (e.g. agnosia, apraxia) (Baddeley, Kopelman & Wilson, 2004).

The additional deficits seen in Korsakoff's disease and Alzheimer's disease make the analysis of their memory impairments in relation to other instances of amnesia a considerable challenge and these additional deficits prove important in identifying other nervous structures that are being affected and that contribute to memory.

There are two components to amnesia: anterograde amnesia which is the impairment of memory for information acquired after the onset of amnesia and retrograde amnesia, which is the impairment of memory for information that was acquired normally prior to the onset of amnesia. This is why individuals with dementing illnesses can easily recall memories from the past but have a difficult time recalling recent history. It is not uncommon for individuals with Alzheimer's to be unable to identify grown children when they can recall photographs of their children when they were young (Parkin, 1999).

Anterograde amnesia selectively compromises long-term memory abilities while leaving working memory intact. Anterograde amnesia is global, affecting memory regardless of modality or material and it disrupts only a specific domain of long-term remembering, namely that of new facts and events. Anterograde amnesia spares the acquisition and expression of skilled performance, so although an individual may not be able to physically ride a bicycle they still have intact memories to allow them to remember how to do so. Finally, information that can be acquired in anterograde amnesia is inflexible, allowing it to only be expressed in limited contexts (Papanicolaou, 2006).

Retrograde amnesia is the impairment of memory for information that was acquired prior to the onset of amnesia. There are four features of retrograde amnesia that detail and explain important issues about the nature and organization of normal memory. First, retrograde amnesia differs for individuals over time; some last for decades and others for only several months or years. Second, most occurrences of retrograde amnesia affect recent memories more than remote/past memories. Third, retrograde amnesia in adulthood permanently affects all long-term memory with most of the information learned in early life is preserved. Finally skilled performance such as bicycle riding is spared (Papanicolaou, 2006).

Nearly all individuals with amnesia will have retrograde amnesia as a component of their impairment. The presence of retrograde amnesia provides us with important clues as to how memories are

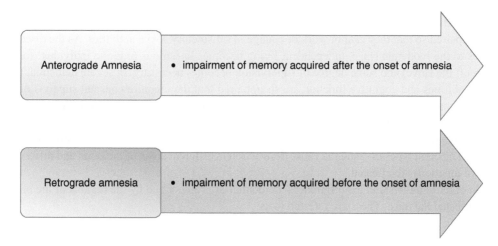

Figure 14.2   Types of amnesia

processed. From the initial acquiring of the memory to its eventual retrieval, it appears that amnesia exerts its effects from all levels. It may be that amnesia reflects problems either in the encoding of memories, maintenance or consolidation. Consolidation is a term referring to the process where short-term memories are transferred to long-term memory. If the problem begins with the encoding of memories then the information is not being fully processed by the structures of the brain and therefore not properly stored in a form that can be easily retrieved later. Alternatively, amnesia could be as a result of a failure in storage or maintenance and with time the information simply decays in spite of being properly encoded. Finally amnesia could also be a result of a failure in the retrieval process, in which case the information is being stored and preserved but cannot be accessed (Baddeley, Kopelman & Wilson, 2004).

An important aspect in the discrepancy between impaired and spared memory in amnesia seems to involve the way the memory is first acquired and whether it requires conscious recollection of the prior learning experiences. Those memories that require recollection of prior learning experiences appear to be more at risk than those memories that do not require conscious recollection.

Going back to our case study, Mr Zeidel's ability to drive a car appears to be intact while his memory for places appears to be eroding and his behavioural response is to become confused. His behavioural response is to endlessly continue driving in an attempt to recall familiar landmarks. Although his ability to read road signs remains intact his ability to recall specifically what the road signs indicate has been eroded from his memory (although certain signs will be retained such as stop signs etc.).

DEMENTIA

Dementia is a catch-all phrase that describes a debilitating syndrome involving a loss of cognitive functions, sometimes accompanied by personality changes, that interferes significantly with work or social activities. Dementias typically progress in stages – generally termed mild, moderate and severe, and eventually lead to death.

In mild dementias the person can live alone and can maintain adequate personal hygiene but they are impaired so that they cannot work or engage in satisfactory social activities. As the disease progress to the moderate stage, independent living becomes hazardous (e.g. the individual forgets to turn off the stove) and some degree of supervision becomes necessary. In severe dementia, the person's abilities and cognitive function are so impaired that they require constant supervision. They will be unable to provide a standard level of care for themselves and are often unable to take care of basic needs (Graham & Warner, 2009).

Although all dementias lead to the same depressing end, different varieties manifest in different ways. Different types of dementia cause destruction in different areas of the brain and different cognitive functions are affected.

In order to understand the differences, dementias are categorized by the regions of the brain that are affected the most. These are referred to as:

1   Those that affect the cortical regions specifically the cortex,
2   Those that affect the subcortical regions or those regions that are below the cortex and
3   Those that affect both and are referred to as mixed-variety dementias (Hughes, 2011).

Table 14.4 Stages of dementia

Mild	Moderate	Severe
Person is able to live independently	Independent living is hazardous and person requires a degree of supervision	Independent living is not possible
Engages in satisfactory social activities	Individual is unable to cope with social activities	Individual is incoherent or mute
Adequate personal hygiene	Personal hygiene is deteriorating	Unable to maintain minimal personal hygiene
Cognitive skills are impaired	Cognitive skills are significantly impaired	Cognitive skills are incapacitated

As a consequence of the dementias affecting different regions of the brain, the behavioural deficits that occur are also different in all three groups and are easily distinguishable. This difference provides a useful way of understanding brain–behaviour relationships and can provide families and caregivers an explanation of what is currently going on with the individual suffering from dementia as well as an idea of what problems they will have to face in the future as the dementia progresses (Buijssen, 2005).

It is important to remember that dementias also affect each individual in a slightly different way, and although there are three specific areas that are generally involved they do not always affect those regions exclusively. For example, even in subcortical dementias, some cortical damage is likely but we wouldn't classify this type of dementia as mixed variety. So the term subcortical dementia suggests that the major symptoms of the disease arise from damage in that region but other regions may also be affected.

The category of cortical dementias is generally the most identifiable because they display deficits that are easily recognizable such as aphasia, apraxia, agnosia, acalculia, spatial deficits and memory problems.

SPECIFIC TYPES OF DEMENTIAS

There are three types of dementias: cortical, subcortical and mixed-variety. The dementias that are considered cortical are: Alzheimer's disease, Pick's disease, and Creutzfeldt-Jakob disease. These three dementias generally have an insidious onset in which the first symptoms are difficulty remembering events, disorientation in familiar surroundings, problems finding the correct words to use or difficulty naming objects and changes in personality and mood. The cognitive decline thereafter is steady with the exception of CJD which is relatively rapid and progressive (Miller & Boeve, 2011).

The subcortical dementias do not result in specific cognitive deficits like the cortical dementias. Instead, they are more likely to manifest as changes in personality, slowness in the speed of processing cognitive tasks, lapses in attention and difficulties in goal-directed tasks or tasks that require construction. Motor dysfunction is a co-occurrence and there is some controversy as to whether the cognitive dysfunction occurs first or after the motor dysfunction. The diagnosis is relatively simple

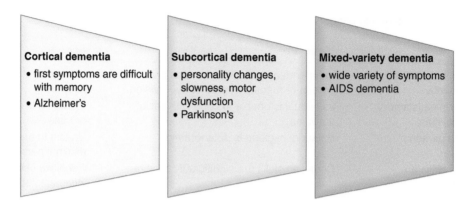

Figure 14.3   Types of dementia

as this group of dementias are distinguished by the combination of motor dysfunction. Specific examples are Huntington's disease and Parkinson's disease although many others fall into this category (Miller & Boeve, 2011).

Contrasting the two types of dementias, individuals with subcortical dementias will exhibit fewer difficulties on recognition tasks, and their deficits in memory will be relatively even across time periods. Individuals with cortical dementias tend to exhibit more difficulty with recently acquired information than with more distant information.

Mixed-variety dementias are disordered in such a way that both cortical and subcortical involvements seem to occur. In these cases, evidence of damage to both cortical and subcortical regions is apparent and they will exhibit a wide variety of personality changes, cognitive deficits and memory impairment. These dementias manifest in patterns that are midway between those observed in cortical and subcortical dementias. Examples of these types are vascular dementia and AIDS dementia (Burns & Winblad, 2006).

ALZHEIMER'S DISEASE

Alzheimer's disease was named after a neurologist who described a specific type of dementia. Alzheimer's disease has also been called senile dementia. This disorder is found worldwide and crosses over boundaries, gender and race.

Alzheimer's disease is characterized by a progressive decline in intellectual functioning. It begins as a loss of memory of recent events as well as personality changes that come in the form of mood disorders/depression. As it progresses to the intermediate stages it is marked with irritability, anxiety and continued deterioration of speech. Eventually the memory impairment progresses to the point that the individual is incapable of maintaining any type of conversation because both the context and prior information is lost. They are unable to answer simple questions such as where they are, where they live or what year is it. As the dementia continues its downhill progression they become disoriented, can easily become lost in what were once familiar surroundings and then finally in the latter stages lose their motor control and motor coordination. It is at this point when the individual enters into the terminal phase (Morris & Becker, 2004).

Accordingly, efforts to understand the neural basis of Alzheimer's amnesia have focused on the testing of Alzheimer patients who have yet to reach the advanced stages of the disorder. The memory deficits associated with predementia Alzheimer's disease are more general than those associated with medial temporal lobe damage, and Korsakoff's syndrome (Carlesimo & Oscar-Berman, 1992). In addition to large anterograde and retrograde deficits in tests of explicit memory, predementia Alzheimer patients often display deficits in short-term memory and in some types of implicit memory. Specifically implicit memory for verbal and perceptual is impaired but is intact for sensorimotor learning (Gabrieli, Corkin, Mickel & Growdon, 1993).

Alzheimer's disease is commonly an illness of aging although it does sometimes appear in individuals as young as 40. Prevalence statistics from the Alzheimer's research trust indicates that there are 820,000 people in the UK with dementia and that the cost to the UK economy will be £23 billion per year (Department of Health, 2011).

The consequences of this disease affect not just the individual sufferer but anyone who has any association with the individual. Alzheimer's disease results in a decline in many aspects of cognitive functioning and as stated previously does not simply involve memory loss but is generally accompanied by all of the following: aphasia, apraxia, agnosia, disturbance in executive function and personality changes. When the disease first manifests itself it is subtle and many simply dismiss the minor memory losses and moments of confusion to 'growing old'. It is not until the disease continues to progress that others begin to notice symptoms that go beyond simple aging. Often the individual is aware during the early stages that something is going terribly wrong, and will often attempt to hide the cognitive disruptions and memory loss. The continued decline eventually makes this impossible (Mulligan, Van der Linden & Juillerat, 2003).

Alzheimer's disease has been estimated to account for more than half of all cases of dementia observed in older persons and is considered to comprise two sub-syndromes. One is termed early onset Alzheimer's because it manifests itself before the age of 65. The other is the more widespread and is characterized by its onset after age 65. Early onset Alzheimer's is also dissimilar in that the deterioration is much more rapid (Morris & Becker, 2004).

At present there are no psychological or physiological tests that can definitively diagnose Alzheimer's disease in living individuals because the defining characteristics of the disease can only be determined by post-mortem examination. Generally when the memory loss is not explained by any other medical conditions and all other causes of dementia have been ruled out and the person's pattern of deterioration continues to be consistent with the disease, a diagnosis of Alzheimer's is given (Black, 2003).

It is only during autopsy when the specific neuroanatomical changes to the brain can be viewed that a definitive diagnosis is made. The two defining changes that occur in the brain are neurofibrillary tangles and amyloid plaques. Neurofibrillary tangles are threadlike tangles of protein in the neural cytoplasm and amyloid plaques are clumps of scar tissue composed of degenerating neurons, and an abnormal protein called amyloid. Individuals also suffer severe neuron loss across the nervous system with the pattern of neuronal loss greater in the temporal, frontal and parietal cortex (Black, 2003).

Amyloid plaques and neurofibrillary tangles can be observed in the brain of the average older individual without dementia and it is believed that these exist from damage sustained during the course of one's life. However the difference is that the person afflicted with Alzheimer's disease will have higher numbers and they will be in larger concentrations around the cortex and hippocampus. Again these changes are not uncommon in other types of diseases. For example large numbers of plaques are found in individuals with amyotrophic lateral sclerosis (ALS) which is a demyelinating disease (Waldemar & Burns, 2009).

The additional result of the tangles and amyloid deposits is further neuronal cell loss which can be seen on anatomical brain scans and images. The subcortical neuronal cell loss explains some of the difficulties individuals with Alzheimer's have. Typically these areas have high numbers of cholinergic input to the cortex and hippocampus. Low levels of acetylcholine have been linked to memory performance; thus, the large cell loss may explain the memory deficits associated with the disease (Davies, 1989).

Additionally individuals with Alzheimer's have reductions in the levels of enzymes that synthesize and break down acetylcholine as well as changes in the brain's ability to metabolize glucose. PET scans have shown marked reduction of metabolism in the posterior parietal cortex and some portions of the temporal lobe. Additionally a substantial decline in glucose utilization appears to precede the emergence of more severe cognitive impairment (Rosa-Neto & Leuzy, 2008).

Causes of Alzheimer's

Currently the aetiology of Alzheimer's disease is unknown although many theories exist about the possible causes. One theory proposes that the disease results from an autoimmune disorder in which the individual's own immune system turns against itself and destroys brain tissue similar to the way that multiple sclerosis victims' immune system destroys the myelin. Another theory is that there is a disruption in the blood–brain barrier that allows toxins into the brain. This disruption could be the result of an injury, a genetic flaw or childhood illness. A different theory proposes that a DNA deficiency causes inadequate transcription of messenger RNA resulting in inadequate production of proteins necessary for neuronal function. Another theory is that the amyloid plaques are a reaction to a virus that disrupts brain function years after the initial infection. Amyloid proteins are present in other parts of the body such as the blood vessels as well as the brain and as a result researchers have theorized that Alzheimer's disease may have a systemic nature. The last theory is that the productions of the amyloids occur in response to a chronic inflammation that affects the brain over time (Munoz & Feldman, 2000).

Research has mainly focused on the understanding of the overproduction of amyloids. Amyloid accumulation has been suggested as the causative agent in Alzheimer's disease leading to the other aspects of Alzheimer's pathology. However, other researchers feel that the amyloid accumulation may be a by-product of the real cause.

It is likely that there will never be one single causative factor for Alzheimer's disease, rather a number of genetic and environmental factors that combine to trigger off the disorder. The genetic contribution may simply provide the predisposition that provides the foundation for the disease to occur when all other environmental and social elements are in place and then the entire effect is aggravated by the aging process. Elements that could be activators for the genetic contribution could be: increased accumulation of environmental toxins, previous head injury or exposure to particular viruses. So although none of these by themselves can cause Alzheimer's they may increase the risk associated with developing it later in life.

The genetics of Alzheimer's

Studying the genetics of Alzheimer's has been difficult for a variety of reasons. First not all individuals who die from dementing illnesses have autopsies completed to make a definitive diagnosis. Second, individuals who are suspected of being carriers often die of natural causes before their symptoms become manifest.

Studies have shown that there is a major genetic component and that people with an Alzheimer's sufferer in their immediate family have a 50 percent chance of being stricken by the disease if they survive into their eighties and nineties (Breitner, 1990).

A gene called *ApoE* (apolipoprotein E) has been associated with Alzheimer's disease (Strittmatter and Roses, 1996). The most common forms of the gene are *ApoE2, ApoE3,* and *ApoE4.* Everyone has two copies of the gene, but people who have one or two copies of the *ApoE4* version are at much higher risk for Alzheimer's. How the different versions of the *ApoE* gene contribute to the development of senile plaques or neurofibrillary tangles has yet to be discovered.

The discovery that Alzheimer's disease has a genetic component has triggered a search for an Alzheimer's gene. Research has found that the early onset subtype of the disease appears to be linked to three mutations of the gene responsible for a larger amyloid precursor protein (Campion, Dumanchin, Hannequin, Dubois, Belliard, Puel, Thomas-Anterion, Michon, Martin, Charbonnier, Raux, Camuzat, Penett, Mesnage, Martinez, Clerget-Darpoux, Brice & Frebourg, 1999). Another intriguing element is that the defect found in Down's syndrome, chromosome 21, is also responsible for the production of amyloids which does cause many individuals with Down's syndrome to develop Alzheimer's disease in adulthood. In some family studies it has been found that the early-onset form of the disorder is linked to a mutation on chromosome 14 (Schellenberg, Bird, Wijsman, Orr, Anderson, Nemens, White, Bonnycastle, Weber & Alonso, 1992); and in some families, the more usual late-onset form of the disorder is linked to a mutation on chromosome 19 (Corder, Saunders, Strittmatter, Schmechel, Gaskell, Small, Roses, Haines & Pericak-Wance, 1993). Collectively, these results suggest that Alzheimer's disease is not a unitary disorder with a single genetic cause (Tanzi, 1991).

Head injuries

Various types of trauma to the head can cause injury to the brain. Head trauma can either be closed (where there is no intrusion into the skull) or open. It is not known how severe an injury must be in order for amyloids to form. Nicoll, Roberts & Graham (1996) found that the *ApoE4* gene magnified the amount of amyloids that formed in the brains of head injured individuals. This accumulation of amyloids was associated with increased morality following head injury and those individuals who survived the head trauma were at increased risk for developing Alzheimer's disease later in life.

Nicoll, Roberts & Graham (1996) also found that recovery from strokes caused by brain haemorrhages was influenced by *ApoE4* and reported that a higher proportion of individuals with the *ApoE4* version of the gene died of their strokes when compared to individuals who lacked that version of the gene.

Head injuries caused by boxing show similar effects. The severity of neurological syndromes in boxers increases in relation to the duration of their careers. In an exploratory study of 30 boxers it was found that those who had boxer's dementia or other brain damage tended to be the ones who had the *ApoE4* gene (Jordan, Relkin, Ravdin, Jacobs, Bennett & Gandy, 1992).

A further risk related to *ApoE4* is brain damage following open-heart surgery (Lelis, Krieger, Pereira, Schmidt, Carmona, Oliveira & Auler, 2006). Many patients who undergo bypass surgery complain that their minds are not as sharp afterwards; some recover from this condition, and some do not. Investigators gave 87 patients memory tests before and after open-heart surgery. Those who had the *ApoE4* gene were more likely to suffer memory impairments.

The importance of identifying people who are genetically susceptible to brain damage is that it allows researchers to explore how to prevent the *ApoE4* from forming amyloids, which could prevent or at least limit the amount of damage caused in later life. With the information it may be possible to find the pharmacological means to prevent the amyloids altogether.

Trace metals

Early studies with animals have identified neurofibrillary degeneration, similar to that in Alzheimer's disease, after the animals were given aluminum sales. Further research on Alzheimer's brains found 10–30 times the normal concentrations of aluminum. Research is ongoing and it is currently not known why aluminum accumulates or whether taking action to reduce the accumulation could be helpful (Adlard & Bush, 2006).

Blood flow

Originally, most dementing diseases were attributed to poor circulation and cardiovascular disease. More recently, studies have confirmed that there is a profound reduction in the amount of blood delivered to the brain and the amount of glucose extracted from the blood. PET students have allowed researchers to examine the metabolic mechanisms in Alzheimer's patients who are still living. They have found that in normal people, blood flow to the brain declines by over 20 percent between the ages of 30 and 60, but the brain compensates by more efficient oxygen uptake. In Alzheimer's there is an enhanced decline but no compensatory mechanisms. The greatest decreases in blood flow are found in those areas of the brain in which the most degenerative change is seen. What isn't known is whether the decline in blood flow and glucose use are causal or secondary to degenerative brain changes. As a result of this research there have been new pharmacological attempts to treat Alzheimer's involving stimulating brain blood flow but these attempts have been met with limited success (Khachaturian & Radebaugh, 1996).

Abnormal proteins

The three main pathological changes associated with Alzheimer's disease are plaques, neurofibrillary tangles, and granulovacuolar bodies. All three reflect the accumulation of protein that is not seen in normal brains. This has led to the suggestion that unusual proteins are being produced and are accumulating, thus disrupting normal protein production and use (Selkoe, 1994).

Neurotransmitter changes

The vast majority of research has focused on the findings that acetylcholine levels are reduced in Alzheimer's disease and this has led to the idea that changes in this transmitter are what cause the memory declines in individuals. The major problems with this direction is that first, there are marked reductions in many transmitter systems not just acetylcholine and second, the reductions in any one system fluctuate from individual to individual (Wasco & Tanzi, 1996). There are also multiple issues with estimating transmitter levels through the course of the disease. The brain is not easily accessible for samples so estimates must be taken from urine or blood samples and these are usually by-products of neurotransmitter metabolism. The other source is tissue obtained at autopsy and these samples then represent terminal levels of biochemical activity. A study conducted by Carlsson & Linquest (1962) showed that Alzheimer's patients showed greater reductions in two or more transmitters than the control group and that the neurotransmitter reductions, especially of acetylcholine and serotonin, may be relevant to cognitive declines.

Clinical symptoms and progress

The first sign of Alzheimer's disease is usually a mild deterioration of memory. Initially the person dismisses it but as the disease progresses the memory deterioration also progresses. Additionally there will be severe anterograde amnesia that is global and some elements of retrograde amnesia which become more pronounced as the disease progresses into the intermediate phases. The individual will also have difficulty with short-term memory which in turn makes it problematic for them to acquire new information. The symptoms continue to grow progressively more severe and diverse until a dementia develops that is so relentless that the patient is incapable of most activities (e.g. eating, speaking, recognizing a spouse and children, or even controlling the bladder). Toward the later stages of the disease, language problems such as aphasia usually become prominent. At this time, the patient's speech becomes sparse and empty of meaning (Gautheier et al., 2006).

In addition to compromising cognitive functioning, Alzheimer's disease causes personality changes. In terms of comparing their premorbid personality with their Alzheimer's they are generally more neurotic, vulnerable and anxious; less extroverted; more passive; less agreeable; less open to new ideas; and more depressed. Individuals with Alzheimer's disease generally do not exhibit odd or socially inappropriate behaviours which are more common in subcortical dementias. The personality changes are not correlated with the duration of the illness and generally begin to manifest relatively early in the disease. In some cases, the patients may exhibit psychiatric symptoms, for example, delusions, especially of persecution, especially during the later part of the illness. As a rule the more atypical an individual's personality before she or he is diagnosed with the disease, the more likely the person is to exhibit psychiatric symptoms such as depression and paranoid delusions (Lawlor, 1995).

Reisberg (1983) provides a detailed description of the stages of the disease and clinical symptoms. The disease is gradual and generally individuals with Alzheimer's spend several months to years in each of the stages.

Stage 1 Complaints of memory deficit are most frequently in the following areas:

a Forgetting where one has placed familiar objects;
b Forgetting names one formerly knew well;

c   Becoming lost when travelling to an unfamiliar location;
d   Co-workers become aware of the individual's relatively poor performance;
e   They may read a passage or a book and retain relatively little material;
f   Concentration deficit is evident on clinical testing.

Stage 2 – Denial begins to occur and mild to moderate anxiety is displayed. Denial is the dominant defence mechanism. The individual will display a flattening of affect and will withdrawal from challenging situations.

a   Decreased performance in demanding employment and social settings;
b   Decreased knowledge of current and recent events;
c   Decreased memory of personal history;
d   Concentration deficit on serial subtractions;
e   Decreased ability to travel, handle finances, etc.
f   Inability to perform complex tasks.

Stage 3 – The individual is slowly losing major cognitive function

a   Cannot function without some assistance;
b   Unable to recall a major relevant aspect of current life: e.g., address or telephone number; cannot recall names of close family members;
c   Cannot recall the name of schools which they attended;
d   Frequent disorientation to date, day, season, and place;
e   May occasionally forget the name of spouse;
f   Will be largely unaware of all recent events and experiences in their lives;
g   Retains some knowledge of their past lives but this is sketchy;
h   May have difficulty counting back or forward from and to 10;
i   Will require some assistance with activities of daily living, e.g. may become incontinent;
j   Can recall their own name and distinguish familiar from unfamiliar persons.

Stage 4

a   Personality and emotional changes occur;
b   These may include delusional behavior, obsessive symptoms, anxiety, or loss of purposeful behaviour;
c   All verbal abilities are lost. Frequently there is no speech at all – only grunting;
d   Incontinent of urine:
e   Requires assistance in toileting and feeding;
f   Loses basic psychomotor skill, e.g. ability to walk;
g   The brain appears to no longer be able to tell the body what to do.

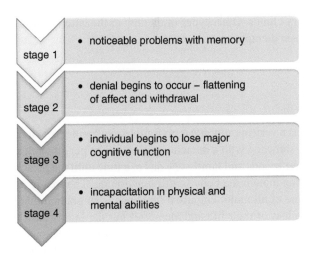

Figure 14.4   Stages of Alzheimer's

In the final stages of the disease, patients become susceptible to other disorders, such as infections, or pneumonia.

TREATMENT

The treatment for this category of disorders is to slow down the effects of the dementing illnesses whenever possible as there are no known cures and the disorders are terminal. Cholinesterase inhibitors are the key pharmacological treatment of choice for Alzheimer's disease. The cholinergic theory of memory has spawned numerous attempts to show that acetylcholine agonists can function as nootropics (memory-improving drugs). In spite of some positive results with laboratory animals (e.g. Meek, Smith, & Williams, 1989), the results in clinical studies with humans have not been as positive. The other types of treatment provided are for the symptoms of anxiety and depression.

Families may find it useful to have the individual tested within a 6-month interval to measure the approximate level of decline in terms of future planning and the projection for the degree of deterioration. Often families can find that the care required for someone in the last phases of Alzheimer's is difficult to manage and long-term planning can help assist families in setting up care facilities when they become necessary rather than reacting to an emergency. Individuals in these latter phases often do not recall family members, often take to wandering as they find their environment unfamiliar and are prone to accidents.

During the early phases of the disease the various talking therapies can be useful in helping the individual as well as their family adjust to the inevitable progression of the disease. Group activities and discussions aimed to stimulate the individual's mind can be useful as well as reminiscence therapy and memory clinics. Other types of therapy in the latter stages appear to be useful such as art therapy and music therapy.

FINALE

The long goodbye is a very appropriate term for those suffering from a dementing illness and those who are caring for someone with a dementing illness. The person with a dementing illness slowly slips away from their friends and family one day at a time until the person that they knew and loved no longer exists even though the body is still functioning. The steady progression of mental deterioration and decline of all major cognitive functions is so gradual that it leaves not only the sufferer mourning the loss of their life and memories but the family as well. Cognitive disorders do not have a happy ending. Perhaps at some point we will find the answers that will spare us from this disorder, but until then researchers will continue to search for the solutions. Sadly, our case study of Mr Zeidel did not end well. He was able to survive the horrors of a Nazi concentration camp only to revert backwards in time in his memories and relive them through his cognitive decline. Although he survived the camps the first time, in the end he did not survive them the second.

Summary

This chapter focuses on cognitive disorders that result in permanent damage to the brain. The section covered impaired consciousness and memory, orientation difficulties and attentional deficits. The chapter examined the biological basis of behaviour, the processes involved, genetic correlations, research and treatment strategies. Finally, it covered the psychosocial elements of these types of disorders and the stress placed on caregivers as well as society's role in providing the level of care necessary during the latter stages of many of the individuals afflicted by these disorders.

LEARNING TOOLS

Key terms

Acalculia – is acquired later in life due to a neurological disorder and refers to an inability to perform simple mathematical tasks such as adding, subtracting

Agnosia – the inability to recognize objects, shapes or sounds

Anterograde amnesia – the inability to create new memories after the event that caused the amnesia

Aphasia – refers to difficulty in producing or comprehending spoken or written language

Apraxia – the loss of the ability to carry out learned purposeful movements

Consolidation – the process where short-term memories are transferred to long-term memory

Cortex – the outer layer of the brain

Delirium – disturbance of consciousness and changes in cognition

Glia cells – non-neuronal cells that provide protection and support for the brain's neurons

Korsakoff's disease – a neurological disorder that is caused by the lack of vitamin B in the diet. It is usually acquired as a result of long-term alcohol abuse

Neurons – the cells of the brain that process and transmit information by electrical and chemical signalling via the synapses

Retrograde amnesia – the inability to recall events that occurred before the development of amnesia

Stimulus bound behaviour – an inability to shift attention from whatever is in the perceptual field

Subcortical – the brain structures that lie below the cortex

Study guide

1 Examine the current research in the treatment of Alzheimer's.
2 Examine the types of services that are available in your community. Are there specialist facilities? What type of help would be available to you if you had to care for a family member with dementia?
3 Research how music therapy is used with Alzheimer's patients.
4 Describe what the differences are between retrograde and antegrade amnesia.

Case study in focus

If Mr Zeidel was a relative, what treatment options would be available for him in your community? How would his past history interact with his cognitive disorder?

Personal development

Integrating all the information that you have learned in this chapter, explore the pros and cons of Terry Pratchett's ideology of a 'tribunal of mercy'. Would this be something that you would contemplate for yourself if you had been diagnosed with a progressive cognitive disorder?

Suggested reading

Hughes, J.C., Louw, S.J. & Sabat, S.R. (2006) *Dementia: Mind, meaning and the person*. Oxford: Oxford University Press.

Cayton, H., Graham, N. & Warner, J. (2002) *Dementia: Alzheimer's and other dementias: The 'at your fingertips' guide*. London: Class Publishing.

Overshott, R. & Burns, A. (2005) 'Treatment of dementia', *Journal of Neurology, Neurosurgery & Psychiatry*, 76: v53–v59.

References

Abbey, A. & McAuslan, P. (2004) A longitudinal examination of college men's perpetration of sexual assault. *Journal of Consulting and Clinical Psychology*, 72: 747–56.

Abbey, A., McAuslan, P. & Ross, L.T. (1998) Sexual assault perpetration by college men: The role of alcohol, misperception of sexual intent, and sexual beliefs and experiences. *Journal of Social and Clinical Psychology*, 17: 167–95.

Abrams, R. (2002) *Electroconvulsive Therapy*. New York: Oxford University Press.

Abrams, R. & Horowitz, S. (1996) Personality disorders after age 50: a meta-analysis. *Journal of Personality Disorders*, 10: 271–81.

Abramson, H.A. (1974) Respiratory disorders and marijuana use. *Journal of Asthma Research*, 11(3): 97.

Abramson, L.Y. (1982) Learned helplessness, depression, and the illusion of control. *Journal of Personality and Social Psychology*, 42(6): 114–26.

Abu-Akel, A. (1998) The study of cohesion in schizophrenia: Theory and application. *Issues in Applied Linguistics*, 9: 37–60.

Abu-Saad, K. & Fraser, D. (2010) Maternal nutrition and birth outcomes. *Epidemiological Review*, April, 32(1): 5–25.

Adamec, C. & Triggle, D.J. (2012) *Amphetamines and methamphetamine (Understanding drugs)*. New York: Chelsea House Publishers.

Adlard, P.A. & Bush, A.I. (2006) Metals and Alzheimer's disease. *Journal of Alzheimer's Disease*, 10: 145–63.

Adler, A. (1964) *The individual psychology of Alfred Adler*, ed. H.L. Ansbacher & R.R. Ansbacher. New York: Harper Torchbooks.

Adshead, G. & Jacob, C. (2008) *Personality Disorder: The definitive reader*. New York: Jessica Kingsley.

Afifi, T., Boman, J., Fleisher, W. & Sareen, J. (2009) The relationship between child abuse, parental divorce and lifetime mental disorders and suicidality in a nationally representative adult sample. *Child Abuse & Neglect*, 33: 139–47.

Ainsworth, M.D.S. (1985) Attachments beyond infancy. *American Psychologist*, 44: 709–16.

Airing, C.D. (1975) The Gheel experience: Eternal spirit of the chainless mind! *JAMA*, 230(7): 998–1001.

Akhtar, S. (1987) Schizoid personality disorder: A synthesis of developmental, dynamic and descriptive features. *American Journal of Psychotherapy*, 151: 499–518.

Akhtar, S. (1990) Paranoid personality disorder: A synthesis of developmental, dynamic and descriptive features. *American Journal of Psychotherapy*, 44: 5–25.

Akiskal, H.S. & McKinney, W.T. (1973) Depressive disorders: Towards a unified hypothesis. *Science*, 182: 20–29.

Akiskal, H.S. & McKinney, W.T. (1975) Overview of recent research in depression: Integration of ten conceptual models into a comprehensive frame. *Archives of General Psychiatry*, 32: 285–305.

Alajouanine, T.H. & Lhermitte, F. (1965) Acquired aphasia in children. *Brain*, 88: 653–62.

Alarcon, R. & Covi, L. (1973) Hysterical personality and depression: A pathogenetic view. *Comprehensive Psychiatry*, 14(2): 121–32.

Alexander, F.G. & Selesnick, S.T. (1966) *The History of Psychiatry*. New York: Harper and Row.

Alexander, J.C. & Smith, P. (2005) *The Cambridge companion to Durkheim*. New York: Cambridge University Press.

Alnaes, R. & Torgersen, S. (1988) The relationship between DSM-III symptom disorders (Axis I) and personality disorders (Axis II) in an outpatient population. *Acta Psychiatrica Scandinavia*, 78: 485–92.

Alpert, J., Uebelacker, A., McLean, A., Nierenberg, A., Pava, J., Worthington, J., Tedlow, J., Rosenbaum, J. & Fava, M. (1997) Social phobia, avoidant personality disorder and atypical depression: co-occurrence and clinical implications. *Psychological Medicine*, 27: 627–33.

Alzheimer's Disease International (2008) *The prevalence of dementia worldwide*. December 2008. Retrieved October 09, 2012. From http://www.alz.co.uk/adi/pdf/prevalence.pdf

Amato, P.R. (1999) Children of divorced parents as young adults. In E.M. Hetherington (ed.), *Coping with divorce, single parenting and remarriage*. Mahwah, NJ: Erlbaum, pp. 147–64.

Amato, P.R. (2000) Children and divorce in the 1990s: An update of the Amato and Keith (1991) meta-analysis. *Journal of Family Psychology*, 15: 355–70.

Albee, G.W. (1959) *Mental health manpower trends*. New York: Basic Books.

American Psychiatric Association. (1987) *Diagnostic and statistical manual of mental disorders* (3rd edn, revised). Washington, DC: Author.

American Psychiatric Association (2000) *Diagnostic and statistical manual of mental disorders* (4th edn). Washington, DC: Author.

American Psychiatric Association (2011) *Diagnostic and statistical manual of mental disorders* (4th edn, revised). Washington, DC: Author.

American Psychiatric Association (2012) *DSM-5 development*. Retrieved October 5, 2012. From http://www.dsm5.org/Pages/Default.aspx

Amstadter, A. (2008) Emotion regulation and anxiety disorders. *Journal of Anxiety Disorders*, 22: 211–21.

Anastasi, A. (1965) *Individual differences*. New York: Wiley.

Anderko, L., Braun, J. & Auinger, P. (2010) Contribution of tobacco smoke exposure to learning disabilities. *Journal of Obstetric, Gynecologic & Neonatal Nursing*, 39(1): 111–17.

Andersen, S.L. & Teicher, M.H. (2009) Delayed effects of early stress on hippocampal development. *Neuropsychopharmacology*, 29(11): 1988–993.

Anderson, I.M. & Reid, I. (2007) *Fundamentals of clinical psychopharmacology*. London: Cromwell Press.

Anderson, M. (2000) *The development of intelligence (Studies in developmental psychology)*. East Sussex: Psychology Press Ltd.

Andreasen, N.C. (1979) Affective flattening and the criteria for schizophrenia. *American Journal of Psychiatry*, 136: 944–7.

Andreasen, N.C. (1982a) *Negative symptoms in schizophrenia: definition and reliability*. Archives of General Psychiatry, 39: 784–8.

Andreasen, N.C. (1982b) Concepts, diagnosis and classification. In E.S. Paykel (ed.), *Handbook of affective disorders*. New York: Guilford Press, pp. 24–44.

Andreasen, N.C. (1984) *The Broken Brain: The biological revolution in psychiatry*. New York: Harper & Row.

Andreasen, N.C. (2001) Schizophrenia: the fundamental questions. *Brain Research Reviews*, 31(2–3): 106–12.

Andreasen, N.C. & Olsen, S. (1982) Negative versus positive schizophrenia: Definition and validation. *Archives of General Psychiatry*, 39: 789–94.

Andreasen, N.C., O'Leary, D.S., Flaum, M. & Nopoulous, P. (1997) Hypofrontality in schizophrenia: Distributed dysfunctional circuits in neuroleptic-naive patents. *Lancet*, 349: 1730–4.

Andreasen, N.C., Paradiso, S. & O'Leary, D.S. (1998) Cognitive dysmetria as an integrative theory of schizophrenia: A dysfunction in cortical – subcortical – cerebellar circuitry? *Schizophrenia Bulletin*, 24(2): 203–18.

Andrews, J.G. (1964) The nature of stuttering. *Med. J. Aust.*, 191: 919–24.

Antonello, S.J. (1996) *Social skill development: Practical strategies for adolescents and adults with developmental disabilities*. Needham Heights, MA: Allyn and Bacon.

Antony, M.M. & Barlow, D.H. (1998) Specific phobia. In V.E. Caballo (ed.) *Handbook of cognitive behavioural treatments for psychological disorders*. Exeter: Elsevier.

Antony, M.M. & Barlow, D.H. (2010) *Handbook of assessment and treatment planning for psychological disorders* (2nd edn). New York, NY: Guilford Press.

Arango, V., Huang, Y., Underwood, M.D. & Mann, J.J. (2002) Genetics of the serotonergic system in suicidal behaviour. *J. Psychiatry Res.*, 37: 375–86.

Argentero, P. & Setti, I. (2011) Engagement and vicarious traumatization in rescue workers. *International Archives of Occupational Environmental Health*, 84: 67–75.

Arnold, C. (2009) *Bedlam: London and its mad*. London: Pocket Books.

Aronfreed, J. & Paskal, V. (1970) The development of sympathetic behaviour in children: An experimental test of a two phase hypothesis. Reported in Aronfreed, J., The socialization of altruistic and sympathetic behaviour: some theoretical and experimental analyses. In J. Macaulay & L. Berkowitz (eds), *Altruism and helping behaviour*. New York: Academic Press.

Arrigo, B.A. & Shipley, S. (2001) The confusion over psychopathy (I): Historical considerations. *International Journal of Offender Therapy and Comparative Criminology*, 45: 325–44.

Ashton, C.H. (2001) Pharmacology and effects of cannabis: A brief review. *British Journal of Psychiatry*, 178: 101–6.

Ashton, H. (1987) *Brain systems, disorders and psychotropic drugs*. Oxford: Oxford University Press.

Astrom, R.L., Wadsworth, S.J., Olson, R.K., Willcutt, E.G. & DeFries, J.C. (2012) Genetic and environmental etiologies of reading difficulties: DeFries-Fulker analysis of reading performance data from twin pairs and their non-twin siblings. *Learn Individ Differences*, 22(3): 365–9.

Attwood, T. (2008) *The Complete Guide to Asperger's Syndrome*. London: Jessica Kingsley.

August, G.J., Stewart, M.A. & Tsai, L. (1981) The incidence of cognitive disabilities in the siblings of autistic children. *British Journal of Psychiatry*, 138: 416–22.

Austenfeld, J.L. (2004) Coping through emotional approach: A new look at emotion, coping and health-related outcomes. *Journal of Personality*, 72: 1335–64.

Avery, D.H., Eder, D.N., Bolte, M.A., Hellekson, C.J., Dunner, D.L., Vitiello, M.V. & Prinz, P.N. (2001) Dawn simulation and bright light in the treatment of SAD: a controlled study. *Biological Psychiatry*, Aug. 1, 50(3): 205–16.

Ayers, J., Templer, D.I. & Ruff, C.F. (1975) The MMPI in the differential diagnosis of organicity vs. schizophrenia: Empirical findings and a somewhat different perspective. *Journal of Clinical Psychology*, 31(4): 685–6.

Baddeley, A.D., Kopelman, M. & Wilson, B.A. (2004) *Memory disorders for clinicians*. Chichester: John Wiley & Sons.

Bagheri, M.M., Burd, L., Martsolf, J. & Klug, M.G. (2009). Fetal alcohol syndrome: Maternal and neonatal characteristics. *Journal of Perinatal Medicine*, 26(4): 263–9.

Bagwell, C.L., Newcomb, A.F. & Bukowski, W.M. (1998) Preadolescent friendship and peer rejection as predictors of adult adjustment. *Child Devlopment*, 69: 140–53.

Baird, K. & Kracen, A.C. (2006) Vicarious traumatization and secondary traumatic stress: A research synthesis. *Counseling Psychology Quarterly*, 19(2): 181–8.

Baker, H.F. & Ridley, R.M. (1996) *Prion diseases*. Totowa, NJ: Humana Press.

Baker, J. (2008) The role of psychogenic and psychosocial factos in the development of functional voice disorders. *International Journal of Speech-Language Pathology*, 10(4): 210–30.

Baker, L. & Cantwell, D.P. (1987) A prospective psychiatric follow-up of children with speech/language disorders. *Journal of the American Academy of Child and Adolescent Psychiatry*, 26: 546–53.

Baldessarini, R.J., Vazquez, G. & Tondo, L. (2011) Treatment of cyclothymic disorder: commentary. *Psychother Psychosom*, 80: 131–5.

Baldwin, D.S., Anderson, I.M., Nutt, D.J., et al. (2005) Evidence-based guidelines for the pharmacological treatment of anxiety disorders: Recommendations from the British Association for Psychopharmacology. *Journal of Psychopharmacology*, 19: 567–96.

Ball, J.S. & Links, P.S. (2009) Borderline personality disorder and childhood trauma: Evidence for a causal relationship. *Current Psychiatry Reports*, 11(1): 63–8.

Baltes, P.B. (1996) On the incomplete architecture of human ontogeny: Selection, optimization, and compensation as foundation of developmental theory. *American Psychologist*, 52: 366–80.

Ban, P. & Lewis, M. (1974) Mothers and fathers, girls and boys: Attachment behaviour in the one-year-old. *Merrill-Palmer Quarterly*, 20: 195–204.

Bandura, A. (1961). Psychotherapy as a learning process. *Psychological Bulletin*, 58: 143–59.

Bandura, A. (1976) New perspectives on violence. In V.C. Vaughan III & T.B. Brazelton (eds), *The family.* Chicago: Year Book Medical Publishers.

Bandura, A., Ross, D. & Ross, S.A. (1963) Imitation of film-mediated aggressive models. *Journal of Abnormal and Social Psychology,* 66: 3–11.

Bandura, A. & Walters, R.H. (1963) *Social learning and personality development.* New York: Holt, Rinehart, & Winston.

Barber, J.P. & Morse, J. (1994) Validation of the Wisconsin Personality Disorders inventory with the SCID-II and PDE. *J. Personal Discord,* 8: 307–19.

Barglow, P., Vaughn, B.E. & Molitor, N. (1987) Effects of maternal absence due to employment on the quality of infant–mother attachment in a low-risk sample. *Child Development,* 58(4): 945–54.

Barham, P. (1997) *Closing the asylum: The mental patient in modern society.* London: Penguin.

Barnes, G. (1995) Parents can help prevent teen alcohol, drug use. Support, monitoring key to prevention, study finds. Research in Brief [online]. Available: http//www.ria.org/summaries/rib/rib955.html.

Barnes, J., Anderson, L.A. & Phillipson, J.D. (2010) *Herbal medicines* (3rd edn). London: Sage.

Baroff, G.S. & Olley, J.G. (1999) *Mental Retardation: Nature, cause and management.* London: Brunner/Mazel.

Bartak, A., Spreeuwenberg, M.D., Andrea, H., Holleman, L., Rijnierse, P., Rossum, B.V., Hamers, E.F., Meerman, A.M., Aerts, J., Busschbach, J.J., Verheul, R., Stijnen, T. & Emmelkamp, P.M. (2010) Effectiveness of different modalities of psychotherapeutic treatment for patients with cluster C personality disorders: results of a large prospective multicentre study. *Psychother Psychosom,* 79(1): 20–30.

Bartlett, S.J. (2011) *Normality does not equal mental health: The need to look elsewhere for standards of good psychological health.* New York: Praeger.

Bateman, A. & Fonagy, P. (2009) Randomized controlled trial of out-patient mentalization based treatment versus structured clinical management for borderline personality disorder. *American Journal of Psychiatry,* 1666: 1355–64.

Bates, J.E. (1989) Application of temperament concepts. In G.A. Kohnstamm, J.E. Bates & M.K. Rothbart (eds), *Temperament in Childhood.* New York: John Wiley & Sons.

Baum, W.M. (1994) *Understanding behaviourism: Science, behaviour and culture.* New York: HarperCollins.

Bauwens, J. & Tosone, C. (2010) Professional posttraumatic growth after a shared traumatic experience: Manhattan clinicians' perspectives on post-9/11 practice. *Journal of Loss and Trauma,* 15(6): 489–517.

Bear, M.F., Connors, B.W. & Paradiso, M.A. (2006) *Neuroscience: Exploring the brain.* Baltimore, MD: Lippincott, Williams & Wilkins.

Beardslee, W.R., Versage, E.M. & Gladstone, T.R.G. (1998) Children of affectively ill parents: A review of the past 10 years. *Journal of the American Academy of Child and Adolescent Psychiatry,* 37(11): 1134–41.

Beauchemin, K.M. & Hays, P. (1996) Sunny hospital rooms expedite recovery from severe and refractory depressions. *Journal of Affective Disorders,* 40(1–2).

Beautrais, A.L., Joyce, P.R. & Mulder, R.T. (1999) Personality traits and cognitive styles as risk factors for serious suicide attempts among young people. *Suicide and Life-Threatening Behavior,* 29(1): 37–47.

Bebbington, P.E., Angremeyer, M., Azorin, J.M., Marwhaa, S., Marteau, F. & Toumi, M. (2009) Side-effects of antipsychotic medication and health-related quality of life in schizophrenia. *Acta Psychiatrica Scandinavica,* 119 (Supplement 438), 22–8.

Bechdolf, A., Thompson, A., Nelson, B., Cotton, S., Simmons, M.B., Amminger, G.P., Leicester, S., Francey, S.M., McNab, C., Krstev, H., Sidis, A., McGorry, P.D., & Yung, A.R. (2010) Experience of trauma and conversion to psychosis in an ultra-high-risk (prodromal) group, *Acta Psychiatr Scand.,* May, 121(5): 377–84.

Beck, A.T. (1990) *Cognitive therapy of an avoidant personality.* New York: Guilford Press.

Beck, A.T. (1991) Cognitive therapy: A 30-year retrospective. *American Psychology,* 46: 368–75.

Beck, J.S. (2011) *Cognitive behaviour therapy: Basics and beyond* (2nd edn). New York: NY: Guilford Press.

Beck, A.T. & Alford, B.A. (2008) *Depression: Causes and treatment.* Philadelphia, PA: University of Pennsylvania Press.

Beck, A.T., Brown, G., Berchick, R.J., Stewart, B.L. & Steer, R.A. (1990) Relationship between hopelessness and ultimate suicide: A replication with psychiatric outpatients. *American Journal of Psychiatry*, 147: 190–5.

Beck, A.T., Freeman, A. and Davis, D.D. (2007) *Cognitive therapy of personality disorders.* New York: Guilford Press.

Beck, A.T., Rush, A., Shaw, B. & Emery, G. (1979) *Cognitive therapy of depression.* New York: Guilford Press.

Beck, A.T., Ward, C.H., Mendelson, M., Mock, J.E. & Erbaugh, J. (1961) An inventory for measuring depression. *Archives of General Psychiatry*, 4: 561–71.

Becker, M.H. & Maiman, L.A. (1975) Sociobehavioral determinants of compliance with health and medical care recommendations. *Medical Care*, 13: 10–24.

Bedrosian, R.C. & Beck, A.T. (1980. Cognitive aspects of suicidal behaviour. *Suicide and Life-threatening Behavior*, 2: 87–96.

Beers, C. (1908) *A mind that found itself.* Garden City, NY: Doubleday.

Beigel, A. & Murphy, D.L. (1971) Assessing clinical characteristics of the manic state. *American Journal of Psychiatry*, 128: 688–94.

Beinart, H., Kennedy, P. & Llewelyn, S. (2009) *Clinical psychology in practice.* Oxford: Wiley-Blackwell.

Bejerot, N. (1970) *Addiction and society.* Springfield, IL: Thomas.

Belitsky, R. & McGlashan, T.H. (1993) The manifestations of schizophrenia in late life: A dearth of data. *Schizophrenia Bulletin*, 19(4): 683–5.

Bell, D.S. (1965) Comparison of amphetamine psychosis and schizophrenia. *British Journal of Psychiatry*, III: 701–7.

Bell, R.Q. (1968) A reinterpretation of the direction of effects in studies of socialization. *Psychological Review*, 75: 81–95.

Bell, R.R., Turner, S. & Rosen, L. (1975) A multivariate analysis of female extramarital coitus. *Journal of Marriage and the family*, 37: 375–84.

Bellack, A.S., Bennett, M.E. & Gearon, J.S. (2006) Development of a comprehensive measure to assess clinical issues in dual diagnosis patients: The substance use event survey for severe mental illness. *Addictive Behaviors*, Dec. 31(12): 2249–67.

Bellack, A.S., & Mueser, K.T. (1993) Psychosocial treatment for schizophrenia. *Schizophrenia Bulletin*, 19: 317–36.

Bellack, A.S., Turner, S.M., Hersen, M. & Luber, R.F. (1984) An examination of the efficacy of social skills training for chronic schizophrenic patients. *Hospital Community Psychiatry*, October, 35(10): 1023–8.

Bellman, M. (1966) Studies on encopresis. *Acta Paediatr Scand.* (suppl): 1.

Belsky, J. & Pluess, M. (2009) Beyond diathesis stress: Differential susceptibility to environmental influences. *Psychological Bulletin*, 135(6): 885–908.

Benjamin, R.A. (2003). The role of primary care professionals in nurturing healthy families and healthy communities. *Ethnicity and Disease*, 13(3 Suppl): 106–7.

Ben-Porat, A. & Itzhaky, H. (2009) Implications for treating family violence for the therapist: Secondary traumatisation, vicarious traumatisation and growth. *Journal of Family Violence*, 24: 507–14.

Benshoff, J.J. & Janikowski, T.P. (1999) *The rehabilitation model of substance abuse counselling.* Belmont, CA: Wadsworth.

Bentall, R.P. (1990) *Reconstructing schizophrenia.* London: Routledge.

Bentall, R.P. (1992) A proposal to classify happiness as a psychiatric disorder. *Journal of Medical Ethics,* 18: 94–8.

Bentall, R.P. (2003) *Madness explained: Psychosis and human nature.* Harmondsworth: Penguin.

Berbert, M. (2002) Creating conditions for good practice. Summary of national findings, Conference proceedings of Canadian Association of Social Workers Child Welfare Project. Ottawa: CASW.

Berenbaum, H. & Oltmanns, T.F. (1992) Medication effects: Conceptual and methodological issues in schizophrenia research. *Clinical Psychology Review*, 12: 345–61.

Berger, R. (1989) Female delinquency in the emancipation era: A review of the literature. *Sex Roles*, 21: 375–99.

Berk, L.E. (2008) *Child development* (8th edn). London: Allyn & Bacon.

Bernstein, A.S. (1987) Orienting response research in schizophrenia. *Schizophrenia Bulletin*, 13(4): 623–41.

Berrios, G.E. (1996) *The history of mental symptoms: Descriptive psychopathology since the nineteenth century.* London: Cambridge University Press.

Bewley, T. (2008) *Madness to mental illness: A history of the Royal College of Psychiatrists.* RCPsych Publications.

Bierer, J. & Elliott, D.M. (2003) Prevalence and psychological sequelae of self-reported childhood physical and sexual abuse in a general population sample of men and women. *Child Abuse & Neglect*, 27: 1205–22.

Billstedt, E., Gillberg, I.C. & Gillberg, C. (2011) Aspects of quality of life in adults diagnosed with autism in childhood: A population-based study. *Autism*, 15(1): 7–20.

Binks, C.A., Fenton, M., McCarthy, L., Lee, T., Adams, C.E. & Duggan, C. (2006) Psychological therapies for people with borderline personality disorder. *Cochrane Database Syst. Rev.*, 25(1).

Birch, S.H. & Ladd, G.W. (1996) Interpersonal relationships in the school environment and children's early school adjustment: The role of teachers and peers. In J. Jaana & K.R. Wentzel (eds), *Social motivation: Understanding children's school adjustment.* New York: Cambridge University Press, pp. 199–225.

Birmes, P.J., Carreras, D., Ducasse, J.L., Charlet, J.P., Warner, B.A. and Lauque, D. (2000) Peritraumatic dissociation, acute stress, and early posttraumatic stress disorder in victims of general crime. *Canadian Journal of Psychiatry*, 46: 649–51.

Black, D.L. (2003) Mechanisms of alternative pre-messenger RNA splicing. *Annual Review of Biochemistry*, 72: 291–336.

Black, D.W. & Boffeli, T.J. (1989) Simple schizophrenia: Past, present and future. *The American Journal of Psychiatry*, 146(10): 1267–1273.

Blackburn, I.M. & Davidson, K. (1995) *Cognitive therapy for depression and anxiety* (2nd edn). Oxford: Blackwell Science.

Blackburn, R. (1996) Replicated personality disorder clusters among mentally disordered offenders and their relation to dimensions of personality. *Journal of Personality Disorders*, 10: 68–81.

Blackburn, R. (1997) Psychopathy and personality disorder: implications of interpersonal theory. *Issues in Criminological and Legal Psychology*, 24: 18–23.

Blackwell, C.L. (1995) *Guide to enuresis: A guide to treatment of enuresis for professionals.* New York: Enuresis Resource and Information Centre.

Blackwood, D.H., Whalley, L.J., Christie, J.E., Blackburn, I.M., St. Clair, D.M. & McInnes, A. (1987) Changes in auditory P3 event related potentials in schizophrenia and depression. *British Journal of Psychiatry*, 150: 154–60.

Blais, M.A. (1997) Clinician ratings of the five-factor model of personality and the DSM-IV personality disorders. *Journal of Nervous and Mental Disease*, 185: 388–93.

Blatt, S.J. (2004). *Experiences of depression: Theoretical, clinical and research perspectives.* Washington, DC: American Psychological Association.

Blatt, S.J. (2010) *Experiences of depression: Theoretical, clinical and research perspectives.* Washington, DC: American Psychological Association.

Bleich, A., Brown, S.L. & Van Praag, H.M. (1991) *A serotonergic theory of schizophrenia, in the role of serotonin in psychiatric disorders,* ed. S.L. Brown and H.M. Van Praag. New York: Brunner/Mazel.

Bleier, R. (1984) *Science and gender.* Elmsfor, NY: Pergamon.

Blocker, M.L., Langleben, D.D., Urparel, K., Loughhead, J.W., Gur, R.C. & Sachser, N. (2009) Baby schema in infant faces induces cuteness perception and motivation for caretaking. *Ethology*, 115: 257–63.

Bloom, B.L., Asher, S.J. & White, S.W. (1978) Marital disruption as a stressor: A review and analysis. *Psychological Bulletin*, 85: 867–94.

Bober, T. & Regehr, C. (2005. Strategies for reducing secondary or vicarious trauma: Do they work? *Brief Treatment and Crisis Intervention*, 6(1).

Bobes, J., Gonzalez, M.P., Bascaran, M.T., Arango, C., Saiz, P.A. & Bousono, M. (2001) Quality of life and disability in patients with obsessive-compulsive disorder. *European Psychiatry*, 16: 239–45.

Bockoven, J.S. (1963) *Moral treatment in American psychiatry.* New York: Springer Publishing Co.

Boden, J.M., Fergusson, D.M. & Horwood, L.J. (2008) Cigarette smoking and suicidal behaviour: results from a 25 year longitudinal study. *Psychological Medicine*, 38: 433–9.

Boivin, M., Hymel, S. & Bukowski, W.M. (1995) The roles of social withdrawal, peer rejection and victimization by peers in predicting loneliness and depressed mood in childhood. *Development & Psychopathology*, 7: 765–85.

Bolte, S., Dziobek, I. & Poustka, F. (2009) Brief report: The level and nature of autistic intelligence revisited. *Journal of Autism and Developmental Disorders*, 39: 678–82.

Bonne, O., Brandes, D., Gilboa, A., Gomori, J.M., Shenton, M.E., Pitman, R.K. & Shalev, A.Y. (2001) Longitudinal MRI study of hippocampal volume in trauma survivors with PTSD. *American Journal of Psychiatry*, 158(8): 1248–51.

Bonnet, F., Irving, K., Terra, J.L., Nony P., Berthezene, F. & Moulin, P. (2005) Anxiety and depression are associated with unhealthy lifestyle in patients at risk of cardiovascular disease. *Atherosclerosis* 178(2): 339–44.

Boomsma, D.I., Busjahn, A. & Peltonen, L. (2002) Classical twin studies and beyond. *Nature Reviews: Genetics*, 3: 872–82.

Bornstein, R.F. (1997) Dependent personality disorder in the DSM-IV and beyond. *Clinical Psychology*, 4: 175–87.

Bornstein, R.F. (1993) The dependent personality: Developmental, social and clinical perspectives. *Psychological Bulletin*, 112: 3–23.

Bornstein, B.H. (1999) The ecological validity of jury simulations: Is the jury still out? *Law and Human Behavior*, 23: 75–91.

Bornstein, R.F. (2009) Assessment of personality. In D.C. Richard & S.K. Huprich (eds), *Clinical psychology: Assessement, treatment and research*. San Diego, CA: Elsevier, pp. 91–122.

Borthwick, D.W., Shahbazian, M., Krantz, Q.T., Dorin, J.R. & Randell, S.H. (2001) Evidence for stem-cell niches in the tracheal epithelium. *Am. J. Respir. Cell Mol. Biol.*, 24: 662–70.

Bowers, J.S. (2000) The modality specific and non-specific components of long-term priming are frequency sensitive. *Memory & Cognition*, 28(3): 406–414.

Boyce, P. (2011) Circadian rhythms and depression. *Aust Fam Physician*, 39: 307–10.

Bracken, B.A. & Keith, L.K. (2004) *Clinical assessment of behaviour professional manual*. Lutz, FL: Psychological Assessment Resources.

Braun, P., Kochonsky, G., Shapiro, R., Greenberg, S., Gudeman, J.E., Johnson, S. & Shore, M.F. (1991) Overview: Deinstitutionalization of psychiatric patients: A critical review of outcome studies. *American Journal of Psychiatry*, 138: 736–49.

Bray, I. & Gunnell, D. (2006) Suicide rates, life satisfaction and happiness as markers for population mental health. *Social Psychiatry and Psychiatric Epidemiology*, 41: 333–7.

Brazelton, T. B. (1969) *Infants and mothers: Differences in development*. New York: Dell.

Breggin, P. (2001) *The antidepressant fact book*. Cambridge, MA: Perseus Books.

Breitner, J.C. (1990) Life table methods and assessment of familial risk in Alzheimer's disease. *Arch Gen Psychiatry*, 47(4): 395–6.

Bremner, J.D., Innis, R.B., Ng, C.K., Stab, L., Duncan, J., Bronen, R., Zubal, G., Rich, D., Krystal, J.H., Dey, H., Soufer, R. & Charney, D.S. (1997) PET measurement of cerebral metabolic correlates of yohimbine administration in posttraumatic stress disorder. *Archives of General Psychiatry*, 54: 246–56.

Bremner, J.D., Vythilingam, M., Vermetten, E., Southwick, S.M., McGlashan, T., Nazeer, A., Khan, S., Vaccarino, L.V., Soufer, R., Garg, P., Ng, C.K., Staib, L.H., Duncan, J.S. & Charney, D.S. (2003) MRI and PET study of deficits in hippocampal structure and function in women with childhood sexual abuse and posttraumatic stress disorder (PTSD). *American Journal of Psychiatry*, 160: 924–32.

Brent, D.A. (1995) Risk factors for adolescent suicide and suicidal behavior: mental and substance abuse disorders, family environmental factors, and life stress. *Suicide and Life-threatening Behavior*, 25(1): 52–63.

Brent, D.A., Perper, J.A., Goldstein, C.E., Kolko, D.J., Allan, M.J., Allan, M.J. & Allman, C.J. (1988) Risk factors for adolescent suicide: A comparison of adolescent suicide victims with suicidal inpatients. *Archives of General Psychiatry*, 45: 581–8.

Breska, A., Moaz, K. & Ben-Shakhar, G. (2010) Interstimulus intervals for skin conductance response measurement. *Psychophysiology*, 48(4): 437–40.

Breslau, N., Davis, G.C. & Andreski, P. (1995) Risk factors for PTSD-related traumatic events: A prospective analysis. *American Journal of Psychiatry*, 152: 529–35.

Brew, B.J. (2007) HAD and the need for new trial design methodology. *AIDS*, 21(14): 1965–6.

Brewer, R.D. & Swahn, M.H. (2005) Binge drinking and violence. *JAMA* 294(5): 616–18.

Bride, B.E. (2004) Prevalence of secondary traumatic stress among social workers. *Social Work*, 52(1): 63–70.

Brieger, P. & Marneros, A. (1997) Dysthymia and cyclothymia: historical origins and contemporary development. *Journal of Affective Disorders*, 45(3): 117–126.

Bronfenbrenner, U. (1986) Ecology of the family as a context for human development: Research perspectives. *Developmental Psychology*, 22: 723–42.

Brooks, R. & Goldstein, S. (2004) *The power of resilience: Achieving balance, confidence and personal strength in your life*. Chicago: Contemporary Books.

Brown, B. (2009) *Understanding Twelve-step Programs: A quick reference guide*. New York: Dog Ear Publishing.

Brown, D.R. (2005) Neurodegeneration and oxidative stress: Prion disease results from loss of antioxidant defence. *Folia Neuropathologica*, 43(4): 229–43.

Brown, N.O. (1959) *Life against death: The psychoanalytic meaning of history*. Middletown, CT: Wesleyan University Press.

Brown, T.T. (1961) *The enigma of drug addiction*. London: Charles C Thomas Publishers.

Brown, E.S., Varghese, F.P. & McEwen, B.S. (2004) Association of depression with medical illness: Does cortisol play a role? *Biological Psychiatry*, 55(1): 1–9.

Brown, G.M., Seithikurippu, R., Pandi-Perumal, I.T. & Cardinali, D.P. (2010) In T. Partonen & S.R. Pandi-Perumal, *Seasonal affective disorder: Practice and research* (2nd edn). Oxford: Oxford University Press.

Brown, G.W. & Harris, T. (1978). Social origins of depression: A study of psychiatric disorder in women. London: Cambridge University Press.

Brown, M.A. & Munford, A.M. (1983) Life skills training for chronic schizophrenics. *Journal of Nervous and Mental Disease*, 171(8): 466–70.

Brunton, P.J. & Russell, J.A. (2008) The expectant brain: Adapting for motherhood. *Nat. Rev. Neurosci*, 9: 11–25.

Bryant, R.A. & Guthrie, R.M. (2007) Maladaptive self-appraisals before trauma exposure predict posttraumatic stress disorder. *Journal of Consulting and Clinical Psychology*, 75: 812–15.

Bryant, R.A. & Harvey, A.G. (1996) Initial posttraumatic stress responses following motor vehicle accidents. *Journal of Traumatic Stress*, 9: 223–34.

Bryant, R.A., Moulds, M.L., Guthrie, R.M., Dang, S.T., Mastrodomenico, J. and Nixon, R.D. (2009) A randomized controlled trial of exposure therapy and cognitive restructuring for posttraumatic stress disorder. *American Psychological Association*, 17(2): 113–31.

Bryson, S.E. (1997) Epidemiology of autism: Overview and issues outstanding. In D.J. Cohen & F.R. Volkmar (eds), *Handbook of autism and pervasive developmental disorders* (2nd edn). New York: Wiley & Sons.

Buchanan, N. & Coulson, H. (2012) *Phobias*. New York: Palgrave Macmillan.

Bugental, D.B., Blue, J. & Cruzcosa, M. (1989) Perceived control over caregiving outcomes: Implications for child abuse. *Developmental Psychology*, 25: 532–9.

Buijssen, H. (2005) *The simplicity of dementia: A guide for family and carers*. London: Jessica Kingsley.

Buitelaar, J.K., Hizink, A.C., Mulder, E.J., de Medina, P.G. & Visser, G.H. (2003) Prenatal stress and cognitive development and temperament in infants. *Neurobiological Aging*, 24(1): 53–60.

Burack, J.A. & Enns, J.T. (eds) (1997) *Attention, development and psychopathology*. New York: Guilford Press.

Bureau, M., Hirsh, E. & Vigevano, F. (2004) Epilepsy and videogames. *Epilepsia*, 45(1): 24–6.

Burns, A. & Winblad, B. (2006) *Severe dementia*. Chichester: Wiley & Sons.

Busfield, J. (2011) *Mental Illness*. Cambridge: Polity Press.

Buss, A.H. & Plomin, R.A. (1975) *A temperament theory of personality development*. New York: Wiley.

Butcher, J.N., Dahlstrom, W.G., Graham, J.R., Tellegen, A. & Kaemmer, B. (1989) *Minnesota Multiphasic Personality Inventory: MMPI-2: Manual for administration and scoring*. Minneapolis: University of Minnesota Press.

Butcher, J.N., Dahlstrom, W.G., Graham, J.R. & Tellegen, A. (2001) *MMPI-2: Manual for administration and scoring*. Minneapolis: University of Minnesota Press.

Butler, G. (1989) Issues in the application of cognitive and behavioural strategies to the treatment of social phobia. *Clinical Psychology Review*, 9: 91–106.

Button, T.M., Scourfield, J., Martin, N., Purcell, S. & McGuffin, P. (2005) Family dysfunction interacts with genes in the causation of antisocial symptoms. *Behavior Genetics*, 35(2): 115–20.

Byrne, M.E., Crowe, T.A. & Griffin, P.S. (1998) Pragmatic language behaviours of adults diagnosed with chronic schizophrenia. *Psychological Reports*, 83: 835–46.

Cadenhead, K.S., Swedlow, N.R., Shafer, K., Diaz, M. & Braff, D.L. (2000) Modulation of the startle response and startle laterality in relatives of schizophrenic patients and in subjects with schizotypal personality disorder: evidence of inhibitory deficits. *American Journal of Psychiatry*, 157: 1660–8.

Cadoret, R.J. & Winokur, G. (1975) X-linkage in manic-depressive illness. *Annual Review of Medicine*, 26: 21–5.

Calkins, S.D. (1994) Origins and outcomes of individual differences in emotional regulation. In N.A. Fox (ed.), *Emotion regulation: Behavioural and biological considerations, Monographs of the society for research in child development*, 59(2–3), Series 240. Chicago, IL: University of Chicago Press.

Calkins, S.D. & Bell, M.A. (2009) *Child development at the intersection of emotion and cognition (Human brain development)*. New York: American Psychologial Association.

Calvo, I.A., Gabrielli, N., Iglesias-Baena, I., Garcia-Santamarina, S., Hoe, K.L., Kim, D.U., Sanso, M., Zuin, A., Perez, P., Ayte, J. & Hidalgo, E. (2009) Genome-wide screen of genes required for caffeine tolerance in fission yeast. *PLoS ONE*, 4(8): e6619.

Campbell, M.L.C. & Morrison, A.P. (2007) The role of unhelpful appraisals and behaviours in vulnerability to psychotic-like phenomena. *Behavioural and Cognitive Psychotherapy*, 35: 555–67.

Campion, D., Dumanchin, C., Hannequin, B., Dubois, B., Belliard, S., Puel, M., Thomas-Anterion, C., Michon, A., Martin, C., Charbonnier, F., Raux, G., Camuzat, A., Penet, C., Mesnage, V., Martinez, M., Clerget-Darpoux, F., Brice, A. & Frebourg, T. (1999) Early-onset autosomal dominant Alzheimer disease: Prevalence, genetic heterogeneity, and mutation spectrum. *Am. J. Hum. Genet.* 65(3):664–70.

Canetto, S.S. & Sakinofsky, I. (1998) The gender paradox in suicide. *Suicide and Life-threatening Behaviour.* 28(1): 1–23.

Cann, P. & Dean, M. (2009) *Unequal ageing: The untold story of exclusion in old age*. Bristol: Policy Press.

Cannon, W.B. (1929) *Bodily changes in pain, hunger, fear and rage*. New York: Appleton.

Cannon, W.B. (1935). Stresses and strains of homeostatsis. *American Journal of Medical Science.* 189: 1–14.

Cantwell, D.P., Baker, L. & Matison, R. (1981) Prevalence, type and correlates of psychiatric disorder in 200 children with communication disorder. *Journal of Developmental and Behavioural Paediatrics,* 2: 131–6.

Caplan, A.L. (1992) Twenty years after. The legacy of the Tuskegee syphilis study. *Hastings Center Report*, 22(6): 29.

Cardno, A.G. & Gottesman, I.I. (2000) Twin studies of schizophrenia: From bow and arrow concordances to star wars mx and functional genomics. *Am. J. Med. Genet.* 97(1): 12–17.

Carlesimo, G.A. & Oscar-Berman, M. (1992) Memory deficits in Alzheimer's patients: a comprehensive review. *Neuropsychol Rev.* 3(2): 119–69.

Carlier, I.V., Lamberts, R.D. & Gersons, B.P. (1997) Risk factors for posttraumatic stress symptomatology in police officers: a prospective analysis. *Journal of Nervous and Mental Disease*, 185: 498–506.

Carlsson, A. (1988) The current status of the dopamine hypothesis of schizophrenia. *Neuropsychopharmacology,* 1: 179–86.

Carlsson, A. & Linquest, M. (1962) Effect of chlorpromazine or haloperidol on formation of methoxytyramine and normetanephrine in mouse brain. *Acta Pharmacol. Toxicol.*, 20: 140–4.

Carlsson, A., Persson, T., Roos, B.E. & Walinder, J. (1972) Potentiation of phenothiazines by methyltyrosine in treatment of chronic schizophrenia. *Journal of Neural Transmission*, 33: 83–90.

Carlsson, I. (1990) The creative personality. Hemispheric variation and sex differences in defence mechanisms related to creativity. Doctoral dissertation, Lund, Sweden.

Carlton, P.L. & Manowitz, P. (1984). Dopamine and schizophrenia: An analysis of the theory. *Neuroscience & Biobehavioral Reviews*, 8(1): 137–151.

Carr, A. & McNulty, M. (2006) *The handbook of adult clinical psychology: An evidence based practice approach.* New York: Routledge.

Carrion, J.L., Garcia-Orza, J. & Perez-Santamaria, F.J. (2001) Development of the inhibitory component of the executive functions in children and adolescents. *International Journa of Neuroscience*, 114: 1291–311.

Carver, C. & Gaines, J. (1987) Optimism, pessimism, and postpartum depression. *Cognitive Therapy and Research*, 11(4): 449–62.

Carver, C.S., Scheier, M.F. & Weintraub, J.K. (1989) Assessing coping strategies: A theoretically based approach. *Journal of Personality and Social Psychology*, 56(2): 267–83.

Caspar, F. (2003) Psychotherapy research and neurobiology: Challenge, chance, or enrichment? *Psychotherapy Research*, 13(1): 1–23.

Caskey, C.T., Pizzuti, A., Fu, Y.H., Fenwick, R.G. & Nelson, D.L. (1992) Triplet repeat mutations in human disease. *Science*, 256: 784–9.

Cassano, G.B., Dell'Osso, L., Frank, E., Miniati, M., Fagiolini, A., Shear, K., Pini, S. & Maser, J. (1999) The bipolar spectrum: A clinical reality in search of diagnostic criteria and an assessment methodology. *Journal of Affective Disorders*, 54(3): 319–28.

Castellanos, F.X., Elia, J., Kruesi, J.J.P., Gulotta, C.S., Mefford, I.N., Potter, W.Z., Ritchie, G.F. & Rapoport, J.L. (1994) Cerebrospinal fluid monoamine metabolites in boys with attention-deficit hyperactivity disorder. *Psychiatry Research*, 52: 305–16.

Cattell, R.B., Cattell, A.K. & Cattell, H.E.P. (1993) *Sixteen personality factor questionnaire* (5th edn). Champaign, IL: Institute for Personality and Ability Testing.

Cave, S. (2002) *Classification and diagnosis of psychological abnormality*. London: Routledge.

Ceccaldi, M., Joanette, Y., Tikhomirof, F., Macia, M., & Poncet, M. (1996) The effects of age-induced changes in communicative abilities on the type of aphasia. *Brain Lang.*, 54(1): 75–86.

Center, D.B. & Kemp, D.E. (2001) Antisocial behaviour in children and Eysenck's theory of personality: An evaluation. *International Journal of Disability, Development and Education* 49(4): 1465–346.

Cermak, S. & Groza, V. (1998) Sensory processing problems in post-institutionalized children: Implications for social work. *Child and Adolescent Social Work Journal*, 15: 5–37.

Chaffin, M., Kelleher, K. & Hollenberg, J. (1996) Onset of physical abuse and neglect: Psychiatric, substance abuse, and social risk factors from prospective community data. *Child Abuse & Neglect*, 20(3): 191–203.

Chapman, L.J. & Chapman, J.P. (1973) Problems in the measurement of cognitive deficit. *Psychology Bulletin*, 79: 380–5.

Chen, J. (1993) Dopaminergic mechanisms and brain reward. *Seminars in Neuroscience,* 5: 315–20.

Chen, Y.W. & Dilsaver, S.C. (1996) Lifetime rates of suicide attempts among subjects with bipolar and unipolar disorders relative to subjects with other axis I disorders. *Biological Psychiatry,* 39: 896–9.

Cheng, A.T., Chen, T.H.H., Chen, C.C. & Jenkins, R. (2000. Psychosocial and psychiatric risk factors for suicide: Case control psychological autopsy study. *British Journal of Psychiatry*, 177: 360–5.

Chiara, D.G. & Bassareo, V. (2006) Reward system and addiction: What dopamine does and doesn't do. *Current Opinion in Pharmacology*, 7(1): 69–76.

Chiarell, C., Welcome, S.E. & Leonard, C.M. (2012) Individual differences in reading skill and language lateralisation: a cluster analysis. *Laterality Asymmetries of Body, Brain and Cognition*, 17(2): 225–51.

Chiurazzi, P. & Oostra, B.A. (2006) *Expanding mutations/genetic anticipation*. eL.S.

Choca, J. & Van Denburg, E. (1996) *Manual for clinical psychology trainees*. New York: Brunner/Mazel.

Chrousos, G.P. (2000) Regulation and dysregulation of the hypothalamic-pituitary-adrenal axis: the corticotrophin releasing hormone perspective. *Endocrinol. Metab. Clinics*, 21: 833–58.

Cicchetti, D. (1984) The emergence of developmental psychpathology. *Child Development*, 55: 837–45.

Cicchetti, D. & Toth, S.L. (1994) Developmental psychopathology and disorders of affect. In D. Cicchetti & D.J. Cohen (eds.), *Developmental psychopathology* Vol. 2: *Risk, disorder, and adaptation*. New York: Wiley, pp. 369–420.

Cirulli, F., Berry, A. & Alleva. E. (2003) Early disruption of the mother–infant relationship: effects on brain plasticity and implications for psychopathology. *Neuroscience and Biobehavioral Reviews*, 27(1–2): 73–82.

Clark, D.M. (1986) A cognitive approach to panic. *Behaviour Research and Therapy*, 24: 461–70.

Clark, L.A. (1989) The anxiety and depressive disorders: Descriptive psychopathology and differential diagnosis. In P.C. Kendall & D. Watson (eds), *Anxiety and depression: Distinctive and overlapping features*. San Diego, CA: Academic Press.

Clark-Carter, D. (1997) *Doing quantitative psychological research: From design to report*. Hove: Psychology Press.

Clarkin, J.F., Fonagy, P. & Gabbard, G.O. (2010) *Psychodynamic psychotherapy for personality disorders: A clinical handbook*. Arlington,VA: American Psychiatric Publishing.

Clarkin, J.F., Levy, K.N., Lenzenweger, M.F. & Kernberg, O.F. (2007) Evaluating three treatments for borderline personality disorder: A multiwave study. *American Journal of Psychiatry*, 164: 922–8.

Clayton, P.J. (1981) The epidemiology of bipolar affective disorder. *Comprehensive Psychiatry*, 22: 31–43.

Clohessy, S. & Ehlers, A. (1999) PTSD symptoms, response to intrusive memories and coping in ambulance service workers. *British Journal of Clinical Psychology*, 38(3): 251–65.

Cloninger, C.R., Bohman, M., Sigvardsson, S. & Von Knorring, A.L. (1985) Psychopathology in adopted-out children of alcoholics: The Stockholm adoption study. In M. Galanter (ed.), *Recent Developments in Alcoholism*, 3: 37–51.

Cloward, R.A. & Ohlin, L. (1960) Delinquency and opportunity. In R. Cloward & L. Ohlin (eds), *Delinquency and opportunity*. London: the Free Press, 145–52.

Coccaro, E.F. & Siever, L.J. (2005) The neuropsychopharmacology of personality disorders. In F. Bloom & D. Kupfer (eds), *Psychopharmacology: The fourth generation of progress*. New York: Raven Press, pp. 567–1579.

Cohen, D., Paul, R. & Vokmar, F. (1987) Issues in classification of pervasive developmental disorders and associated conditions. In D.J. Cohen, A.M. Donnellan & R. Paul (eds), *Handbook of autism and pervasive developmental disorders*. New York: John Wiley & Sons, pp. 5–40.

Cohen, R.A. (1976) Manic-depressive illness. In A.M. Freman, J.I. Kaplan & B.J. Sadock (eds), *Comprehensive textbook of psychiatry* (2nd edn). Baltimore, MD: Williams & Wilkins.

Cohen, S. & Wills, T.A. (1985) Stress, social support and the buffering hypothesis. *Psychological Bulletin*, 98: 310–57.

Cohen, S., Tyrrell, D.A.J. & Smith, A.P. (1991) Psychological stress and susceptibility to the common cold. *New England Journal of Medicine*, 325: 606–12.

Cohn, A. (2006) *Constipation, withholding and your child: A family guide to soiling and wetting*. London: Jessica Kingsley.

Collins, S. & Long, A. (2003) Working with the psychological effects of trauma: Consequences for mental health-care workers – a literature review. *Journal of Psychiatric and Mental Health Nursing*, 10: 417–24.

Collins, W.A., Maccoby, E., Steinberg, L., Hetherington, E.M. & Bornstein, M. (2000) Contemporary research on parenting: The case for nature and nurture. *American Psychologist*, 55: 218–32.

Compton, A. (1972). A study of the psychoanalytic theory of anxiety. The development of Freud's theory of anxiety. *Journal of American Psychoanalytic Assn,* 20: 3–44.

Compton, W.M. & Volkow, N.D. (2005) Major increases in opioid analgesic abuse in the United States: Concerns and strategies. *Drug and Alcohol Dependence*, 81(2): 103–7.

Connolly, J.F. & Gruzelier, J.H. (1986) Persistent methodological problems with evoked potential augmenting-reducing. *International Journal of Psychophysiology*, 3: 299–306.

Connorton, E., Perry, M.J., Hemenway, D. & Miller, M. (2011) Relief workers and trauma-related mental illness. *Epidemiologic Reviews*. 34(1): 145–55.

Conwell, Y., Duberstein, P.R., Cox, C., Herrmann, J.H., Forbes, N.T. & Caine, E.D. (1996) Relationships of age and axis I diagnoses in victims of completed suicide: A psychological autopsy study. *Am. J. Psychiatry*, 153: 1001–8.

Conwell, Y. & Thompson, C. (2008) Suicidal behaviour in elders. *Psychiatr clin North Am.* 31(2): 333–56.

Cooksey, E.C. & Brown, P. (1998) Spinning on its axes: DSM and the social construction of psychiatric diagnosis. *International Journal of Health Services*, 28: 525–54.

Coombs, R.H. (2002) *Addiction counselling review: Preparing for comprehensive, certification and licensing.* New York: Taylor & Francis.

Cooper, C.L., & Dewe, P. (2004) *Stress: A brief history.* Oxford: Blackwell.

Cooper, D.N. & Krawczak, M. (1993) *Human gene mutation.* Oxford: BIOS Scientific publishers

Cooper, M., Todd, G. & Wells, A. (2008) *Treating bulimia nervosa and binge eating: An integrated metacognitive and cognitive therapy manual.* Abingdon: Routledge.

Cooper, M.J. (2003) *The psychology of bulimia nervosa: A cognitive perspective.* Oxford: Oxford University Press.

Cooper, P.J. (1995) *Bulimia nervosa and binge-eating: A guide to recovery.* London: Robinson.

Corcoran, C., Walker, E., Huot, R., Mittal, V., Tessner, K., Kestler, L. & Malaspina, D. (2003) The stress cascade and schizophrenia: Etiology and onset. *Schizophrenia Bulletin* 29(4): 671–92.

Corder, E.H., Saunders, A.M., Strittmatter, W.J., Schmechel, D.E., Gaskell, P.C., Small, G.W., Roses, A.D., Haines, J.L. and Pericak-Vance, M.A. (1993) Gene dose of apolipoprotein e type 4 allele and the risk of Alzheimer's disease in late onset families. *Science*, 261(5123): 921–3.

Corneil, W., Beaton, R., Murphy, S., Johnson, C. & Pike, K. (1999) Exposure to traumatic incidents and prevalence of posttraumatic stress symptomatology in urban fire fighters in two countries. *Journal of Occupational Health Psychology*, 4: 131–41.

Cornelius, J.R., Soloff, P.H., Perel, J.M. & Ulrich, R.F. (1990) Fluoxetine trial in borderline personality disorder. *Psychopharmacology Bulletin*, 26: 151–4.

Corr, P.J. (2008) *The reinforcement sensitivity theory of personality.* Cambridge: Cambridge University Press.

Corrigan, P.W. & Watson, A.C. (2002) The paradox of self-stigma and mental illness. *Clinical Psychology.* 9(1): 35–53.

Corruble, E., Ginestet, D. & Guelfi, J.D. (1996) Comorbidity of personality disorders and unipolar major depression: A review. *Journal of Affective Disorders* 37(2–3): 157–70.

Coryell, W. (1981) Obsessive compulsive disorders and primary unipolar depression: Comparisons of background family history, course and mortality. *Journal of Nervous and Mental Diseases*, 169: 220–4.

Cosgrove, G.R. & Rauch, S.L. (2003) Stereotactic cingulotomy. *Neurosurg. Clin. N. Am.*, 14(2): 225–35.

Cottrell, B. (2003) *Parent abuse: The abuse of parents by their teenage children.* Canada: Family Violence Prevention Unit.

Courtwright, D.T. (1997) Morality, religion and drug use. In A.M. Brandt & P. Rozin (eds), *Morality and health.* New York: Routledge, pp. 231–50.

Covington, M., He, C., Brown, C., Naci, L., McClain, J., Fjordbak, B., Semple, J. & Brown, J. (2005) Schizophrenia and the structure of language: The linguist's view. *Schizophrenia Research*, 77: 85–98.

Cowan, N. (1988) Evolving conceptions of memory storage, selective attention and their mutual constraints within the human information processing system. *Psychological Bulletin*, 104: 163–91.

Cox, B.J., Mota, N., Clara, I. & Asmundson, G.J.G. (2007) The symptom structure of posttraumatic stress disorder in the national comorbidity replication survey. *Journal of Anxiety disorders*, 22: 1523–8.

Cox, D.W., Ghahramanlou-Holloway, M., Szeto, E.H., Greene, F.N., Engel, C., Wynn, G.H., Bradley, J. & Grammer, G. (2011) Gender differences on documented trauma histories. Inpatients admitted to a military psychiatric unit for suicide-related thoughts or behaviours. *Journal of Nervous Mental Disorders*, 199(3): 183–90.

Cox, J.L., Holden, J.M. & Sagovsky, R. (1987) Detection of postnatal depression. Development of the 10-item Edinburgh postnatal depression Scale. *British Journal of Psychiatry*, 150: 782–6.

Cox, S.M. & Ludwig, A. M. (1979) Neurological soft signs and psychopathology: I. Findings in schizophrenia. *Journal of Nervous and Mental Disease*, 167: 161–5.

Crabbe, J.C., Harris, R.A. & Koob, G.F. (2011) Preclinical studies of alcohol binge drinking. *Annals of the New York Academy of Sciences*, 1216: 24–40.

Craib, I. (1997) *Classical social theory.* New York: Oxford University Press.

Craig, W.M., Henderson, K. & Murphy, J.G. (2000) Prospective teachers' attitudes toward bullying and victimization. *School Psychology International*, 21: 5–21.

Cramer, V., Torgerson, S. & Kringlen, E. (2003) Personality disorders and quality of life. A population study. *Comprehensive Psychiatry*, 47: 178–84.

Craske, M.G. & Barlow, D.H. (1993) Panic disorder and agoraphobia. In D.H. Barlow (ed.), *Clinical handbook of psychological disorders* (2nd edn). New York: Guilford Press.

Crider, A. (2008) Personality and electrodermal response lability: An interpretation. *Applied Psychophysiology and Biofeedback*, 33: 141–8.

Cross, S.E., Bacon, P.L. & Morris, M.L. (2000) The relational-interdependent self-construal and relationships. *Journal of Personality and Social Psychology*, 78: 791–808.

Crothers, L.M. & Levinson, E.M. (2004) Assessment of bullying: A review of methods and instruments. *Journal of Counselling & Development*, 82: 496–503.

Crowe, R.R., Noyes, R., Jr., Pauls, D.L. & Slymen, D. (1983) A family study of panic disorder. *Archives of General Psychiatry*, 40: 1065–9.

Csoti, M. (2001) *School phobia, panic attacks and anxiety in children*. London: Jessica Kingsley.

Cuijpers, P., Van Straten, A., Warmerdam, L. & Smits, N. (2008) Characteristics of effective psychological treatments of depression: A meta-regression analysis. *Psychotherapy Research*, 18(2): 225–36.

Culbertson, F.M. (1997) Depression and gender. *American Psychologist*, 52(1): 25–31.

Cullen, K. (2011) *Introducing child psychology: A practical guide*. New York: Icon Books.

Cummings, M. (2010) *Human heredity: Principles and issues*. Belmont, CA: Brooks/Cole.

Cunningham, M. (2003) Impact of trauma work on social work clinicians: Empirical findings. *Social Work*, 48(4): 451–9.

Currier, T.A., Etchegaray, M.A., Haight, J.L., Galaburda, A.M. & Rosen, G.D. (2010) The effects of embryonic knockdown of the candidate dyslexia susceptibility gene homologue DYX1C1 on the distribution of gabaergic neurons in the cerebral cortex. *Neuroscience*, 172: 535–46.

Cutting, J. & Murphy, D. (1987) Schizophrenic thought disorder. *British Journal of Psychiatry*, 152: 310–19.

Dainer, K.B., Klorman, R., Salzman, L.F., Hess, D.W., Davidson, P.W. & Michael, R.L. (1981). Learning-disordered children's evoked potentials during sustained attention. *Journal of Abnormal Child Psychology*, 9: 79–94.

Damasio, A.R. (1998) The somatic marker hypothesis and the possible functions of prefrontal cortex. In A.C. Roberts, T.W. Robbins & L. Weiskrantz (eds), *The prefrontal cortex*. New York: Oxford University Press. pp. 36–50.

Damasio, H., Grabowski, T., Frank, R., Galaburda, A.M. & Damasio, A.R. (1994) The return of Phineas Gage: Clues about the brain from the skull of a famous patient. *Science*. 264:1102–5.

Daniels, D. & Jenkins, P. (2010) *Therapy with children: Children's rights, confidentiality and the law*. London: Sage.

Darcy, A.M., Doyle, A.C., Lock, J., Peebles, R., Doyle, P. & Grange, D.L. (2011) The eating disorders examination in adolescent males with anorexia nervosa: How does it compare to adolescent females? *International Journal of Eating Disorders*, 45(1): 110–14.

Daruna, J. (2004) *Introduction to Psychoneuroimmunology*. New York: Academic Press.

Darwin, C. (1965) *The expression of the emotions in man and animals*. London: The University of Chicago Press.

Davenport, Y., Zahn-Waxler, C., Adland, M. & Mayfield, A. (1984) Early child-rearing practices in families with a manic-depressive parent. *American Journal of Psychiatry*. 141: 657–68.

Davies, D.C. (1989) *Alzheimer's disease: Towards an understanding of the aetiology and pathogenesis*. New York: Libbey.

Davies, R.W. & Morris, B.J. (2006) *Molecular biology of the neuron*. Oxford: Oxford University Press.

Davis, J.M. (1974). A two factor theory of schizophrenia, *Journal of Psychiatric Research*, 11: 25–9.

Davis, M. (1992) The role of the amygdala in fear and anxiety. *Annual Review of Neuroscience*, 15: 353–375.

Dawson, M.E., Nuechterlein, K.H., Schell, A.M., Gitlin, M. & Ventura, J. (1994) Autonomic abnormalities in schizophrenia: State or trait indicators? *Archives of General Psychiatry*, 51: 813–24.

Deakin, J.F.W. (ed.) (1986) *The biology of depression*. London: Gaskell.

Deater-Deckard, K. (2001) Annotation: Recent research examining the role of peer relationships in the development of psychopathology. *Journal of Child Psychol Psychiatry*, 42(5): 565–579.

Decety, J., Michalska, K.J. Akitsuki, Y. & Lahey, B.B. (2009) Atypical empathic responses in adolescents with aggressive conduct disorder: A functional MRI investigation. *Biological Psychology*, 80: 203–11.

Deckel, A.W., Hesselbrock, V. & Bauer, L. (1996) Antisocial personality disorder, childhood delinquency and frontal brain functioning: EEG and neuropsychological findings. *Journal of Clinical Psychology*, 52(6): 639–50.

Deep-Soboslay, A., Hyde, T.M., Callicott, J.P., Lener, M.S., Verchinski, B.A., Apud, J.A., Weinberger, D.R. & Elvevag, B. (2010) Handedness, heritability, neurocognition and brain asymmetry in schizophrenia. *Brain*, 133(10): 3113–22.

DeFries, J. & Fulker, D. (1985) Multiple regression analysis of twin data. *Behavior Genetics*, 15(5): 467–73.

DeFries, J. & Fulker, D. (1988). Multiple regression analysis of twin data: Etiology of deviant scores versus individual differences. *Acta Genet. Med. Gemellol.*, 37: 205–16.

DeFries, J., McClearn, G. & Plomin, P.M. (1989) *Behavioral genetics*. New York: Worth Publishers.

Degenhardt, L. & Hall, W. (2010). The health and psychological effects of ecstasy (MDMA) use. National Drug and Alcohol Research centre. University of New South Wales, Sydney. NDARC Monograph no. 62.

Delatte, R., Cao, H., Meltzer-Brody, S. and Menard, M.K. (2009) Universal screening for postpartum depression: An inquiry into provider attitudes and practice. *Am. J. Obstet. Gynecol.*.200: 63–4.

De Lint, J. & Schmidt, W. (1971) Consumption averages of alcoholism prevalence: A brief review of epidemiological investigations. *British Journal of Addiction*, 66: 97–107.

Del Ben, K., Scott, J., Chen, Y. & Fortson, B. (2006) Prevalence of posttraumatic stress disorder symptoms in firefighters. *Work & Stress*, 20: 37–48.

DeLong, G.R. (1993). Effects of nutrition on brain development in humans. *American Journal of Clinical Nutrition*, 57: 286S–290S.

DeMyer, M.K., Hingtgen, J.N. & Jackson, R.K. (1981) Infantile autism reviewed: A decade of research. *Schizophrenia Bulletin*, 7: 388–451.

Denes, A., Thornton, P., Rothwell, N.J. & Allan, S.M. (2010) Inflammation and brain injury: Acute cerebral ischaemia, peripheral and central inflammation. *Brain Behav. Immun.*, 24(5): 708–23.

Department of Health (2011) *Department of Health: National Health Service Landscape Review*. London: National Audit Office.

Depue, R.A. & Morrone-Stupinsky, J. (1999) Neurobiology of the structure of personality: Dopamine, facilitation of incentive motivation, and extraversion. *Behavioral and Brain Sciences*, 22: 491–569.

Depue, R.A., Slater, J.F., Wolfstetter-Kausch, H., Klein, D., Goplerud, E. & Farr, D. (1981) A behavioural paradigm for identifying persons at risk for bipolar depressive disorder: A conceptual framework and five validation studies. *Journal of Abnormal Psychology*, 90: 381–437.

Detre, T., Himmelhoch, J., Swartzburg, M., Anderson, C.M., Byck, R. & Kupfer, D.J. (1972) Hypersomnia and manic-depressive disease. *American Journal of Psychiatry*, 10: 123–5.

Di Chiara, G., Bassareo, V., Fenu, S., De Luca, M.A., Spina, L., Cadoni, C., Acquas, E., Carboni, E., Valentini, V. & Lecca, D. (2004) Dopamine and drug addiction: the nucleus accumbens shell connection. *Neuropharmacology*, 47(1): 227–41.

Diehl, J.J. & Paul, R. (2012) Acoustic differences in the imitation of prosodic patterns in children with autism spectrum disorders. *Research in Autism Spectrum Disorders*, 6(1): 123–34.

Diguarde, K.I. (2009) *Binge drinking research progress*. New York: Nova Science Publishers Inc.

Dijker, A.J.M. & Koomen, W. (2007) *Stigmatization, tolerance and repair: An integrative psychological analysis of responses to deviance*. Cambridge: Cambridge University Press.

Dimberg, U. (1990) Facial electromyography and emotional reactions. *Psychophysiology*, 27: 481–94.

Dixon, L.B., Dickerson F. and Bellack, A.S. (2010) The 2009 shizophrenia PORT psychosocial treatment recommendations and summary statements. *Schizophrenia Bulletin*, 36: 48–70.

Dobson, K.S. & Block, L. (1988) Historical and philosophical bases of the cognitive-behavioral therapies. In K.S. Dobson (ed.), *Handbook of cognitive behaviour therapies*. New York: Guilford Press.

Dodge, K. (1993) The future of research on conduct disorder. *Development and Psychopathology*, 5: 311–20.

Doherty, E. (1973) Labeling effects in psychiatric hospitalization: A study of diverging patterns of inpatient self-labeling processes. *Archives of General Psychiatry,* 32(5): 562–8.

Donaldson, C. (1998) Detminants of carer stress in Alzheimer's disease. *International Journal of Geriatric Psychiatry,* 13(4): 248–56.

Donaldson, M. (1986) *Children's minds.* London: HarperCollins Publishers.

Donenberg, G. & Baker, B.L. (1993) The impact of young children with externalizing behaviours on their families. *Journal of Abnormal Child Psychology,* 21: 179–98.

Dorman, J. (1995) The history of psychosurgery. *TeXMed* 91(7): 54–61.

Downey, G. & Coyne, J.C. (1990) Children of depressed parents: An integrative review. *Psychological Bulletin,* 108: 50–76.

Drabick, D.A.G. & Kendall, P.C. (2010). Developmental psychopathology and the diagnosis of mental health problems among youth. *Clinical Psychologist,* 17(4): 272–80.

Draguns, J.G. (1995) Cultural influences upon psychopathology: Clinical and practical implications. In A. Bergman & J. Fish (eds), Special issue: Multicultural influences on mental illness, *Journal of Social Distress and the Homeless,* 4: 89–114.

Draguns, J.G. (1997) Abnormal behaviour patterns across cultures: Implications for counselling and psychotherapy. *International Journal of Intercultural Relations,* 21: 213–48.

Drake, R.E., Bond, G.R. & Essock, S.M. (2009) Implementing evidence-based practices for people with schizophrenia. *Schizophrenia Bulletin,* 35(4): 704–13.

Dretzke, J., Frew, E., Davenport, C., Barlow, J., Stewart-Brown, S., Sandercock, J., Bayliss, S., Raftery, J., Hyde, C. & Taylor, R. (2005) The effectiveness and cost-effectiveness of parent training/education programmes for the treatment of conduct disorder, including oppositional defiant disorder in children. NIHR Health Technology Assessment programme: Executive summaries.

Dugas, M.J. & Robichaud, M. (2007) *Cognitive-behavioral treatment for generalized anxiety disorder: From science to practice.* New York: Routledge.

Dunn A.J. & Berridge, C.W. (1990) Physiological and behavioural responses to corticotrophin-releasing factor administration: Is CRF a mediator of anxiety or stress response? *Brain ResearchReviews,* 15: 71–100.

Dunn, E. C., Wewiorski, N.J. & Rogers, E.S. (2008) The meaning and importance of employment to people in recovery from serious mental illness: Results of a qualitative study. *Psychiatric Rehabilitation Journal,* 32: 59–62.

Dunn, J. & Kendrick, C. (1980) The arrival of a sibling: Changes in patterns of interaction between mother and first-born child. *Journal of Child Psychology and Psychiatry,* 21: 119–32.

Durkheim, E. (1957) *Suicide.* New York: Free Press.

Dwyer, D. (2002) *Glucose metabolism in the brain.* New York: Elsevier Science.

Eaves, L.J., Silberg, J.L., Meyer, J.M., Maes, H.H., Simonoff, E., Pickles, A., Rutter, M., Neale, M.C., Reynolds, C.A., Erikson, M.T., Heath, A.C., Loeber, R., Truett, K.R. & Hewitt, J.K. (1997) Genetics and developmental psychopathology: 2. The main effects of genes and environment on behavioural problems in the Virginia twin study of adolescent behavioural development. *Journal of Child Psychology and Psychiatry,* 38: 965–80.

Eccles, J.S., & Midgley, C. (1989). Stage-environment fit: Developmentally appropriate classrooms for young adolescents. In C. Ames & R. Ames (eds.), *Research on motivation in education: Vol. 3. Goals and cognitions.* New York: Academic Press, pp.139–186.

Eggebeen, D.J. & Knoester, C. (2001) Does fatherhood matter for men? *Journal of Marriage and the Family,* 63: 381–93.

Eghigian, G. (2010) *From madness to mental health: Psychiatric disorder and its treatment in western civilization,* Piscatawy, NJ: Rutgers University Press.

Ehlers, A. & Clark, D.M. (2000) A cognitive model of posttraumatic stress disorder. *Behaviour Research and Therapy* 38: 319–345.

Ehlers, A., Margraf, J., Roth, W.T., Taylor, C.G. & Birbaumer, N. (1988) Anxiety induced by false heart rate feedback in patients with panic disorder. *Behaviour Research and Therapy,* 26: 1–11.

Ehlers, A., Mayou, R.A. & Bryant, B. (1998) Psychological predictors of chronic post-traumatic stress disorders after motor vehicle accidents. *Journal of Abnormal Psychology*, 107: 508–19.

Eisler, R. (1988) *The chalice and the blade*. New York: HarperCollins.

Elliott, A. (2002) *Psychoanalytic theory: An introduction*. New York: Duke University Press.

Ellis, T.E. & Ratliff, K.G. (1983) Cognitive characteristics of suicidal and nonsuicidal psychiatric inpatients. *Cognitive Therapy and Research*, 10: 625–34.

Elnakib, A., Casanova, M., Gimelfarb, G., Switala, A. & El-Baz, A. (2012) Dyslexia diagnostics by 3D shape analysis of the corpus callosum. *IEEE Trans Inf technol Biomed*, 16(4): 700–8.

Emerson, E., Dickson, K., Gone, R. & Hatton, C. (2012) *Clinical psychology and people with intellectual disabilities*. Chichester: John Wiley & Sons.

Emery, R.E. (1982) Interparental conflict and the children of discord and divorce. *Psychological Bulletin*, 92: 310–30.

Emmons, T.D. & Webb, W.W. (1974) Subjective correlates of emotional responsivity and stimulation seeking in psychopaths, normals and acting-out neurotics. *Journal of Consulting and Clinical Psychology*, 42: 620–5.

Empson, J. & Nabuzoka, D. (2003) *Atypical child development in context*. New York: Palgrave.

Engels, F. (1983) *The origin of the family, private property and the state*. London: Penguin Books.

Epstein, M. H. (1999) The development and validation of a scale to assess the emotional and behavioural strengths of children and adolescents. *Remedial and Special Education*, 20(5):258–262.

Erdelyan, M. (2009) *Methadone Maintenance treatment: A community planning guide*. London: Centre for Addiction and Mental Health.

Erikson, E.H. (1995) *Childhood and society*. London: Vintage/Random House.

Erikss, T., Agerbo, E., Mortensen, B. & Westergaard-Nielsen, N. (2010) Unemployment and mental disorders. *International Journal of Mental Health* 39(2): 56–73.

Erlenmeyer-Kimling, L., Squires-Wheeler, E., Adamo, U.H., Bassett, A.S., Cornblatt, B.A., Kestenbaum, C.J., Rock, D., Roberts, S.A. & Gottesman, I.I. (1995) The New York high-risk project: Psychoses and cluster A personality disorders in offspring of schizophrenic parents at 23 years of follow-up. *Archives of General Psychiatry*, 52: 857–65.

Erwin, E. (2002) *The Freud encyclopedia: Theory, therapy and culture*. New York: Routledge.

Ettinger, R.H. (2011) *Psychopharmacology*. New York: Pearson Education.

European Centre for Disease Prevention and Control (2009) *Annual threat report*. Stockholm: ECDC

Eysenck, H. (1967) *The biological basis of personality*. New Jersey: Transaction Publisher.

Eysenck, H. (1987) The definition of personality disorders and the criteria appropriate for their description. *Journal of Personality Disorders*, I: 211–19.

Fairburn, C.G. & Beglin, S.J. (1990) Studies of the epidemiology of bulimia nervosa. *American Journal of Psychiatry*, 147: 401–8.

Falloon, I.R.H. & Liberman, R.P. (1983) Interactions between drug and psychosocial therapy in schizophrenia. *Schizophrenia Bulletin*, 9: 543–54.

Fancher, R.E. (1987) Henry Goddard and the Kallkak family photographs: Conscious skulduggery or Whig history. *American Psychologist*, 42: 585–90.

Fanciullacci, C., Allessandri, M. & Fanciullacci, M. (1998) The relationship between stress and migraine. *Functional Neurology*, 13(3): 215–23.

Fantegrossi, W.E., Murnane, A.C. & Reissig, C.J. (2008) The behavioural pharmacology of hallucinogens. *Biochemical Pharmacology*, 75(1): 17–33.

Farber, I.J. (1977) Manic-depressive psychoses. *NY State Journal of Medicine*, 77(12): 1904–5.

Farrar, M. (2002). Social movements and the struggle over race. In T. Malcolm & G. Taylor (2004) *Democracy and participation – popular protest and new social movements*. London: Merlin Press.

Farrington, D.P. (1991) Longitudinal research strategies: Advantages, problems and prospects. *J. Am. Acad. Child Adolesc. Psychiatry*, 30(3): 369–74.

Fatemi, S.H., Folsom, T.D., Reuitiman, T.J. & Thuras, P.D. (2009) Expression of GABA(B) receptors is altered in brains of subjects with autism. *Cerebellum*, 8(1): 64–9.

Faulkner, D., Littleton, K. & Woodhead, M. (1998) *Learning relationships in the classroom (child development in families, schools and society)*. New York: Routledge.

Fay, D. & Mermelstein, R. (1982) Language in infantile autism. In S. Rosenberg (ed.), *Handbook of applied psycholinguistics*. Hillsdale, NJ: Erlbaum, pp. 393–428.

Fay, W.H. & Schuler, A.L. (1980) *Emerging language in autistic children*. Baltimore, MD: University Park Press.

Foucault, M. (2006) *History of madness*. London: Routledge.

Feeny, N.C., Zoellner, L.A., Fitzgibbons, L.A. & Foa, E.B. (2000) Exploring the roles of emotional numbing depression and dissociation in PTSD. *Journal of Traumatic Stress* 13(3): 489–98.

Feigelman, S., Dubowitz, H., Lane, W., Prescott, L. Meyer, W., Tracy, J.K. & Kim, J. (2009) Screening for harsh punishment in a pediatric primary care clinic. *Child Abuse and Neglect*, 33(5): 269–77.

Feinstein, J.S., Adolphs, R., Damasio, A. & Tranel, D. (2011) The human amygdala and the induction and experience of fear. *Current Biology*, 21(1): 34–38.

Felsenfeld, S. & Plomin, R. (1997) Epidemiological and offspring analyses of developmental speech disorders using data from the Colorado Adoption Project. *Journal of Speech, Language and Hearing Research*, 40: 778–91.

Fenichel, O. (1999) *The psychoanalytic theory of neurosis*. New York: Taylor & Francis.

Fenichel, R.R. (1996) Drug-induced hepatotoxicity. *New England Journal of Medicine*, 334(13): 864.

Fernandez, S.V. (2010) Estrogen, alcohol consumption and breast cancer. *Alcoholism: Clinical and Experimental Research*, 35(3): 389–91.

Ferreira, V.M. & Sherman, A.M. (2007) The relationship of optimism, pain and social support to well-being in older adults with osteoarthritis. *Aging Ment Health*, 11(1): 89–98.

Fieve, R.R. (1975) Lithium prophylaxis in affective disorders. *NY State Journal of Medicine*, 75(8): 1219–21.

Figley, C.R. (ed.) (1983). *Trauma and its wake*. New York: Brunner/Mazel, pp. 53–69.

Firth, C.D. (1987) The positive and negative symptoms of schizophrenia reflect impairments in the perception and initiation of action. *Psychological Medicine*, 17: 631–48.

Firth, L. (2011) *Euthanasia and assisted suicide*. Cambridge: Independence Educational Publishers.

Fishman, D., Faulds, D., Jeffery, R., Mohamed-Ali, V., Yudkin, J.S., Humphries, S. & Woo, P. (1998) The effect of novel polymorphisms in the interleukin-6 (IL-6) gene on IL-6 transcription and plasma IL-6 levels and an association with systemic Onset juvenile chronic arthritis. *Journal of Clinical Investigation*, 102(7): 1369–76.

Fite, P.J., Colder, C.R., Lochman, J.E. & Wells, K.C. (2008) The relation between childhood proactive and reactive aggression and substance use initiation. *Journal of Abnormal Child Psychology*, 36(2): 261–71.

Fitzgerald, M.J.T., Gruener, G. & Mtui, E. (2011) *Clinical neuroanatomy and neuroscience*. New York: Elsevier.

Flanagan, B., Goldiamond, I. & Azrin, N. (1958) Operant stuttering: The control of stuttering behaviour through response-contingent consequences. *Journal of the Explanatory Analysis of Behav*, 1(2): 173–7.

Flanagan, J.C. (1978) A research approach to improving our quality of life. *American Psychologist*, 33: 138–47.

Fleminger, S., Oliver, D.L., Lovestone, S., Rabe-Hesketh, S. & Giora, A. (2003) Head injury as a risk factor for Alzheimer's disease: The evidence 10 years on; a partial replication. *Journal of Neurological Neurosurgical Psychiatry*, 74: 857–62.

Flynn, C.P. (1999) Exploring the link between corporal punishment and children's cruelty to animals. *Journal of Marriage and the Family*, 61: 971–81.

Foa, E.B. and Kozak, M.J. (1986) Emotional processing of fear: Exposure to corrective information. *Psychological Bulletin*, 99: 20–35.

Folstein, S.E. & Piven, J. (1991) Etiology of autism: Genetic influences. *Pediatrics*, 87(5): 767–73.

Fonagy, P. & Target, M. (2002) Early intervention and the development of self-regulation. *Psychoanalytic Inquiry*, 22: 307–35.

Foong, J., Maier, M., Clark, C.A., Barker, G.J., Miller, D.H. & Ron, M.A. (2000) Neuropathological abnormalities of the corpus callosum in schizophrenics: A diffusion tensor imaging study. *Journal of Neurology, Neurosurgery and Psychiatry*, 68(2): 242–4.

Fossati, P., Hevenor, S.J., Graham, S.J., Grady, C., Keightley, M.L., Craik, F. & Mayberg, H. (2003) In search of the emotional self: An MRI study using positive and negative emotional words. *American Journal of Psychiatry*, 160: 1938–45.

Foucault, M. (2006) *Madness and civilization*. London: Vintage Books.

Fournier, J.C., DeRubeis, R.J., Shelton, R.C., Gallop, R., Amsterdam, J.D. & Hollon, S.D. (2008) Antidepressant medications v. cognitive therapy in people with depression with or without personality disorder. *British Journal of Psychiatry*, 192: 124–9.

Fox, R. (1978) Abuse of benzodiazepines. *Lancet*, Sep 23, 2(8091): 681–2.

Frances, A.J. (1986) The classification of personality disorders: An overview of problems and solutions. *Annual Review of Psychiatry*, 5: 240–57.

Frances, A., First, M.B. & Pincus, H.A. (1995) *DSM-IV guidebook*. Washington, DC: American Psychiatric Press, Inc.

Frackowiak, R.S.J. (2004) *Human brain function*. California: Elsevier.

Freedy, J.R., Shaw, D.L., Jarrell, M.P. & Masters, C.R. (1992) Towards an understanding of the psychological impact of natural disasters: An application of the conservation of resources stress model. *Journal of Traumatic Stress* 5(3): 441–54.

Freeman, D., Bentall, R. & Garety, P. (2008) *Persecutory delusions: Assessment, theory and treatment*. New York: Oxford University Press.

Freidman, E.S. & Anderson, I.M. (2010) *Managing depression in clinical practice*. London: Springer.

Freud, S. (1936) *Beyond the pleasure principle*. New York: Bantam.

Freudenreich, O. (2007) *Psychotic disorders: PA: A practical guide*. Baltimore, MD: Lippincott, Williams & Wilkins.

Fricchione, G. (2004) Generalized anxiety disorder. *New England Journal of Medicine*, 351: 675–82.

Frick, P.J., Lahey, B.B., Loeber, R., Van Horn, Y., Christ, M.A.G., Hart, E.A., Tannenbaum, L. & Hanson, K. (1992) Oppositional defiant disorder and conduct disorder: A meta-analytic review of factor analyses and cross-validation in a clinic sample. *Clinical Psychology Review*, 13: 319–40.

Friedman, J.H. (2009) Fatigue in Parkinson's disease patients. *Current Treatment Options in Neurology*, 11(3): 186–90.

Frith, C.D. (1987) The positive and negative symptoms of schizophrenia reflect impairments in the perception and initiation of action. *Psychological Medicine*, 17(3): 631–48.

Frith, U. (1992) *Autism and Asperger syndrome*. Cambridge: Cambridge University Press.

Frodi, A.M. & Lamb, M.E. (1980) Child abusers' responses to infant smiles and cries. *Child Development*, 51: 238–41.

Fujii, D. & Ahmed, I (2007) *The spectrum of psychotic disorders: Neurobiology, ethiology and pathogenesis*. London: Cambridge University Press.

Fulker, D.W. (1979) Some implications of biometrical genetical analysis for psychological research. In J.R. Royce & L.P. Mos (eds), *Theoretical advances in behaviour genetics*. Alphen aan den Rijn, Netherlands: Sijthoff Noordhoff International, pp. 337–87.

Fulton, A.M., Murphy, K.R. & Anderson, S.L. (1993) Increasing adolescent mothers' knowledge of child development: An intervention program. *Adolescence*, 26(101): 73–81.

Gabrieli, J.D.E., Corkin, S., Mickel, S.F. & Growdon, J.H. (1993) Intact acquisition and long-term retention of mirror-tracing skill in Alzheimer's disease and in global amnesia. *Behavioral neuroscience*, 107(6): 899–910.

Gaddini, E. & Limentani, A. (1992) *A psychoanalytic theory of infantile experience: Conceptual and clinical reflection*. New York: Routledge.

Galaburda, A.M. (1993) Neuroanatomic basis of developmental dyslexia. *Neurol Clin*, 11(1): 161–73.

Galaburda, A.M. & Kemper, T.L. (1979) Cytoarchitectonic abnormalities in developmental dyslexia: A case study. *Annals of Neurology*, 6(2): 94–100.

Gao, Y. & Raine, A. (2009) P3 event-related potential impairments in antisocial and psychopathic individuals: a meta-analysis. *Biological Psychology*, 82: 199–210.

Garber, K.B., Visootsak, J. & Warren, S.T. (2008) Fragile X syndrome. *European Journal of Human Genetics*, 16(6): 666–72.

Gardner, A. & Davies, T. (2009) *Human genetics* (2nd edn). Banbury: Scion Publishing.

Gardner, R.J.M. & Sutherland, G.R. (2003) *Chromosome abnormalities and genetic counselling.* New York: Oxford University Press.

Gardner, R.J.M., Sutherland, G.R. & Shaffer, L.G. (2011) *Chromosome abnormalities and genetic counselling.* New York: Oxford University Press.

Garfinkel, P.E. & Garner, D.M. (1982) *Anorexia nervosa: A multidimensional perspective.* New York: Bruner-Mazel.

Garmezy, N. (1985) The NIMH-Israeli high-risk study: Commendation, comments and cautions. *Schizophrenia Bulletin*, 11: 349–53.

Garyfallos, G., Adamopoulou, A., Karastergiou, A., Voikli, M., Ikonomidis, N., Donias, S., Giouzepas, J. & Dimitriou, E. (1999) Somatoform disorders: Comorbidity with other DSM-III psychiatric diagnoses in Greece. *Comprehensive Psychiatry*, 40(4): 299–307.

Geary, D.C. (2010) Mathematical learning disabilities. *Advances in Child Development and Behavior*, 39: 45–77.

Gedo, J.E. (1988) *The mind in disorder: Psychoanalytic models of pathology.* London: Routledge.

Geller, E.S. (1995) Integrating behaviourism and humanism for environmental protection. *Journal of Social Issues*, 51: 179–95.

Gerson, R., Davidson, L., Booty, A., McGlashan, T., Malespina, D., Pincus, H.A. & Corcoran, C. (2009) Families' experience with seeking treatment for recent onset psychosis. *Psychiatric Services*, 60(6): 812–16.

Giampaolo, P., Caldirola, D., Arancio, C. & Bellodi, L. (1997) Panic attacks: A twin study. *Psychiatry Research*, 66: 69–71.

Gilger, J.W., Pennington, B.F. & DeFries, J.C. (1991) Risk for reading disabilities as a function of parental history in three samples of familes. *Reading and Writing*, 3: 205–17.

Gillberg, C., Svennerholm, L. & Hamilton-Hellberg, C. (1983) Childhood psychosis and monoamine metabolites in spinal fluid. *Journal of Autism and Developmental Disorders*, 4: 383–96.

Glider, P., Midyett, S.J., Mills-Novoa, B., Johannessen, K. & Collins, C. (2001) Challenging the collegiate right of passage: A campus-wide social marketing media campaign to reduce binge drinking. *Journal of Drug Education*, 31: 207–20.

Giordano, S. (2007) *Understanding eating disorders: Conceptual and ethical issues in the treatment of anorexia and bulimia nervosa.* Oxford: Oxford University Press.

Gjerdingen, D.K. & Yawn, B.P. (2007) Postpartum depression screening: Importance, methods, barriers and recommendations for practice. *Journal of the American Board of Family Medicine*, 20(3): 280–8.

Glennen, S. & Masters, G. (2002) Typical and atypical language development in infants and toddlers adopted from Eastern Europe. *American Journal of Speech-Language Pathology*, 11: 417–33.

Glocker, M.L., Langleben, D.D., Ruparel, K., Loughead, J.W., Gur, R.C. & Sachser, N. (2009). Baby schema in infant faces induces cuteness perception and motivation for caretaking in adults. *Ethology*, 115(3): 257–63.

Goddard, H.H. (1913) *The Kallikak family a study in the heredity of feeble-mindedness.* New York: BiblioLife, LLC.

Goldberg, D. & Huxley, P. (1991) *Common mental disorders.* London: Routledge.

Goldberg, D.P. (1968) A one-year survey of the prevalence of psychiatric illness in patients with disease of the small intestine. *Gut*, 9(6): 725.

Goldberg, D.P. (1972) *The detection of psychiatric illness by questionnaire.* London: Oxford University Press.

Goldberg, J., Harrow, M. & Grossman, L. (1995) Recurrent affective syndromes in bipolar and unipolar affective mood disorders at follow-up. *British Journal of Psychiatry*, 166: 382–5.

Goldman, H.H., Skodol, A.E. & Lave, T.R. (1992) Revising axis V for DSM-IV: A review of measures of social functioning. *American Journal of Psychiatry*, 149: 1148–56.

Goldman-Rakic, P.S. (1994) Working memory dysfunction in schizophrenia. *Journal of Neuropsychiatry and Clinical Neurosciences*, 6(4): 348–57.

Goldsmith, H.H. & Rothbart, J.K. (1991) Contemporary instruments for assessing early temperament by questionnaires and in the laboratory. In J. Strelau & A. Angleitner (eds), *Explorations in temperament: International perspectives on theory and measurements.* New York: Plenum Press, pp. 249–72.

Golier, J.A., Yehuda, R., Bierer, L.M., Mitropoulou, M.A., New, A.S., Schmeidler, J., Silverman, J.M. & Siever, L.J. (2003) The relationship of borderline personality disorder to posttraumatic stress disorder and traumatic events. *American Journal of Psychiatry*, 160: 2018–24.

Gooding, D.C., Tallent, K.A. & Matts, C.W. (2007) Rates of avoidant, schizotypal, schizoid and paranoid personality disorders in psychometric high-risk groups at five year follow-up. *Schizophrenia Research*, 94(1–3): 373–4.

Goodman, R. & Stevenson, J. (1989) A twin study of hyperactivity–II. The aetiological role of genes, family relationships and perinatal adversity. *Journal of Child Psychological Psychiatry*, 30(5): 691–709.

Goodwin, D.W. (1979) Alcoholism and heredity. *Archives of General Psychiatry*, 36, 57–61.

Goodwin, F.K. & Jamison, K.R. (2007) *Manic-depressive illness: Bipolar disorders and recurrent depression* (2nd edn). New York: Oxford University Press.

Goodwin, F.K. & Post, R.M. (1975) Studies of amine in affective illness and in schizophrenics: A comparative analysis. In D.X. Freedman (ed.), *The biology of the major psychoses*. New York: Raven Press, pp. 247–58.

Gorsuch, R.L. & Butler, M.C. (1976) Initial drug abuse: A review of predisposing social-psychological factors. *Psychological Bulletin*, 83: 120–37.

Gottesman, I.I. & Shields, J. (1982) *Schizophrenia: The epigenetic puzzle*. New York: Cambridge University Press.

Goulding, M.R. (2004) Inappropriate medication prescribing for elderly ambulatory care patients. *Archives of Internal Medicine*, 164(3): 305–12.

Gournay, K. (2010) Setting clinical standards for care in schizophrenia. *Nursing Times*, 92(7): 36–7.

Gower, P.L. (2005) *New research on the psychology of fear*. New York: Nova Science Publishers.

Grabe, S., Ward, L.M. & Hyde, J.S. (2008) The role of the media in body image concerns among women: A meta-analysis of experimental and correlational studies. *Psychological Bulletin*, 134(3): 460–76.

Graham, N. & Warner, J. (2009) *Alzheimer's Disease & other dementias (understanding)*. London: British Medical Association.

Grant, B.F., Hasin, D.S., Stinson, F.S., Dawson, D.A., Chou, S.P., Ruan, W.J. & Pickering, R.P. (2004) Prevalence, correlates, and disability of personality disorders in the United States: Results from the national epidemiologic survey on alcohol and related conditions. *Journal of Clinical Psychiatry*, 65(7): 948–58.

Gray, R., Wykes, T., Edmonds, M., Morven, L. & Gournay, K. (2004) Effect of medication management training package for nurses on clinical outcomes for patients with schizophrenia: Cluster randomised controlled trial. *British Journal of Psychiatry*, 185: 157–62.

Green, R.C., Roberts, J.S., Cupples, L.A., Relkin, N.R., Whitehouse, P.J., Brown, T., Eckert, S.L., Butson, M., Sadovnick, A.D., Quaid, K.A., Chen, C., Cook-Deegan, R. & Farrer, L.A. (2009) Disclosure of APOE genotype for risk of Alzheimer's disease. *New England Journal of Medicine*, 361(3): 245–54.

Greenberg, M.T. & Kusche, C.A. (1991) Emotional regulation, self-control and psychopathology: The role of relationships in early childhood. In D. Cicchetti & S.L. Toth (eds), *Internalizing and externalizing expressions of dysfunction*: Rochester Symposium on Developmental psychopathology, Vol. 2. New York: Cambridge University Press, pp. 21–55.

Greenblatt, G. (1996) *A history of neurosurgery*. Washington, DC: American Association of Neurological Surgeons.

Greene, J. (1991) *Introduction to psychology: Methodology handbook – correlational research designs*. London: Open University Worldwide.

Grieco, R. & Edwards, L. (2010) *The other depression: Bipolar disorder*. New York: Routledge.

Griskevicius, V., Goldstein, N.J., Mortensen, C.R., Sundie, J.M., Cialdini, R.B. & Kenrick, D.T. (2009) Fear and loving in Las Vegas: Evolution, emotion and persuasion. *Journal of Market Research*, 46(3): 384–95.

Grodniczuk, J.S. & Piper, W.E. (2001) Day treatment for personality disorders: A review of research findings. *Harvard Review of Psychiatry*, 9: 105–17.

Gross, J.J. (1997) Antecedent and response focused emotion regulation: Divergent consequences for experience, expression and physiology. *Journal of Personality and Social Psychology*, 74(1): 224–37.

Grossman, S.P. (1973) *Essentials of physiological psychology*. New York: Wiley.

Groth-Manat, G. (2003) *Handbook of psychological assessment*. New York: Wiley.

Gruenberg, E.M. (1967) The social breakdown syndrome-some origins. *American Journal of Psychiatry*, 123: 1481–9.

Gruenberg, E.M. (1973) Progress in psychiatric epidemiology. *Psychiatric Quarterly*, 47(1): 1–11.

Guerri, C., Bazinet, A. & Riley, E.P. (2009) Foetal alcohol spectrum disorders and alterations in brain and behaviour. *Alcohol and Alcoholism*, 44(2): 108–14.

Guidubaldi, J. & Perry, J.D. (1985) Divorce and mental health sequelae for children: A two-year follow up of a nationwide sample. *Journal of the American Academy of Child Psychiatry*, 24: 531–7.

Gilbert, D.G. (1995) *Smoking: Individual differences, psychopathology and emotion*. Washington, DC: Taylor & Francis.

Guitar, B. (2005) *Stuttering: An integrated approach to its nature and treatment*. Baltimore, MD: Williams & Wilkins.

Gunderson, J.G. (2007) Building structure for the borderline construct. *Acta Psychiatrica Scandinavica*, 89: 12–18.

Gunderson, J.G. & Links, P.S. (2008) Borderline personality disorder: A clinical guide (2nd edn). Arlington, VA: American Psychiatric Publishing Inc.

Gur, R.E., Kohler, C.G., Ragland, J.D., Siegel, S.J., Lesko, K., Bilker, W.B. & Gur, R.C. (2006) Flat affect in schizophrenia: Relation to emotion processing and neurocognitve measures. *Schizophrenia Bulletin*, 32: 279–87.

Gurvits, T.V., Shenton, M.E., Hokama, H., Ohta, H., Lasko, N.B., Gilbertson, M.W., Orr, S.P., Kikinis, R., Jolesz, F.A., McCarley, R.W. & Pitman, R.K. (1996) Magnetic resonance imaging study of hippocampal volume in chronic, combat-related posttraumatic stress disorder. *Biological Psychiatry*, 40: 1091–9.

Guterman, S.S. (1970) *The Machiavellians: A social psychological study of moral character and organizational milieu*. Lincoln, NE: University of Nebraska Press.

Haapasalo, J. (1990) Sensation seeking and Eysenck's personality dimensions in an offender sample. *Personality and Individual Differences*, 11(1): 81–4.

Hagglof, B., Andren, O., Bergstrom, E., Marklund, L. & Wendelius, M. (1997) Self-esteem before and after treatment in children with nocturnal enuresis and urinary incontinence. *Scandinavian Journal of Neurology and Nephrology*, 183: 79–82.

Hall, G.C. (1996) *Theory-based assessment, treatment and prevention of sexual aggression*. New York: Oxford University Press.

Hall, W. & Solowij, N. (2009) Adverse effects of cannabis. *Lancet*, 14: 352(9140): 1611–16.

Hamilton, M. (1959) The assessment of anxiety states by rating. *British Journal of Medical Psychology*, 1: 50–5.

Hamilton, M. (1960) A rating scale for depression. *Journal of Neurological and Neurosurgical Psychiatry*, 23: 56–61.

Hammerness, P., Basch, E., Ulbricht, C., Barrette, E.P., Foppa, I., Basch, S., Bent, S., Boon, H. & Ernst, E. (2003) St. John's wort: A systematic review of adverse effects and drug interactions for the consultation psychiatrist. *Psychosomatics*, 44: 271–82.

Hansen, K. & Bebbington, P. (2005) Patient compliance in schizophrenia: Subjective side effects have greater impact than severity of illness. *Schizophrenia Bulletin*, 31: 223–4.

Haque, N., Sobhani, M.E. & Ahmed, A. (2011) *Neuro-endocrine basis of immune modulation in response to stress and relaxation*. Saarbrucken: VDM Publishers.

Hare, R.D. (1999) Psychopathy as a risk factor for violence. *Psychiatric Quarterly*, 70(3): 181–97.

Hare-Mustin, R.T. (1983) A feminist approach to family therapy. *Family Process*, 17: 181–94.

Harlow, H. & Harlow, M. (1967) The young monkeys. *Psychology Today*, 1(5): 40–7.

Harlow, H.F. (1962) Social deprivation in monkeys. *Scientific American*, 207(5): 136–46.

Harris, P.L. (1989) *Children and emotion*. Oxford: Blackwell.

Harrison, R.I. & Westwood, M.J. (2009) Preventing vicarious traumatisation of mental health therapists: Identifying protective practises. *Psychotherapy Theory, Research, Practice Training*, 46(2): 203–19.

Hart, S.N. & Brassard, M.R. (1987) A major threat to children's mental health: Psychological maltreatment. *American Psychologist*, 42(2): 160–5.

Haslam, C. & Mallon, K. (2003) A preliminary investigation of post-traumatic stress among firefighters. *Work & Stress*, 17: 277–85.

Haslam, R.H.A., Dalby, J.T., Johns, R.D. & Rademaker, A.W. (1981) Cerebral asymmetry in developmental dyslexia. *Archives of Neurology*, 38: 679–82.

Hawkins, J.D., Catalano, R.F. & Miller, J.Y. (1992) Risk and protective factors for alcohol and other drug problems in adolescence and early adulthood: Implications for substance abuse prevention. *Psychological Bulletin*, 112(1): 64–105.

Haworth, J. (1995) *Psychological research: Innovative methods and strategies*. London: Routledge.

Haynes, J.C., Farrell, M., Singleton, N., Meltzer, H., Araya, R., Lewis, G. & Wiles, N.J. (2005) Alcohol consumption as a risk factor for anxiety and depression: Results from the longitudinal follow-up of the National Psychiatric Morbidity survey. *British Journal of Psychiatry*, 187: 544–51.

Heatherton, T.F., Hebl, M.R., Hull, J.G. & Kleck, R.E. (2003) *The social psychology of stigma*. New York: Guilford Press.

Hegde, M.V. & Saraph, A.A. (2011) Unstable genes unstable mind: Beyond the central dogma of molecular biology. *Medical Hypotheses*, 77(2): 165–70.

Heim, C., Mletzko, T., Pursell, D., Musselman, D.L. & Nemeroff, C.B. (2008) The dexamethasone/corticotrophin releasing factor test in men with major depression: Role of childhood trauma. *Biological Psychiatry*, 63: 398–405.

Heim, S., Grande, M., Meffert, E., Eickhoff, S.B., Schreiber, H., Kukolja, J., Shah, N.J., Huber, W. & Amunts, K. (2010) Cogntive levels of performance account for hemispheric lateralisation effects in dyslexic and normally reading children. *Neuroimage*, 53(4): 1346–58.

Heller, W., Etienne, M.A. & Miller, G.A. (1995) Patterns of perceptual asymmetry in depression and anxiety: Implications for neuropsychological models of emotion and psychopathology. *Journal of Abnormal Psychology*, 104: 327–33.

Helzer, J.E. & Hudziak, J.J. (2002) *Defining psychopathology in the 21st century: DSM-V and beyond*. Washington, DC: American Psychiatric Pub.

Hemovich, V. & Crano, W.D. (2009) Family structure and adolescent drug use: An exploration of single-parent families. *Substance Use and Misuse*, 44(14): 2099–113.

Hemphill, J.F. & Hart, S.D. (2002) Motivating the unmotivated: Psychopathy, treatment and change. In M. McMurran (ed.), *Motivating offenders to change*. Chichester: Wiley.

Hemphill, J.F., Hart, S.D. & Hare, R.D. (1990) Psychopathy and substance use. *Journal of Personality Disorders*, 8: 139–70.

Henderson, N.D. (1982) Human behaviour genetics. *Annual Review of Psychology*, 33: 403–440.

Hendron, J.A. & Taylor, B. (2012) The unseen cost: A discussion of the secondary traumatisation experience of the clergy. *Pastoral Psychology*, 61(2): 221–31.

Henig, R.M. (2001) *The monk in the garden: The lost and found genius of Gregor Mendel, the father of genetics*. USA: First Mariner Books.

Henn, D. & DeEugenio, D. (2006) *Barbiturates (Drugs: The straight facts)*. London: Chelsea House Publishers.

Henning, S., Herpertz, S. & Houben, I. (2008) Personality disorders: Conceptual issues and responsibility. *Psychiatry and Clinical Neurosciences*, 1: 5–17.

Herbert, R. (2007) Dealing with heterogeneity in clinical trials. *Journal of Manual and Manipulative Therapy*, 12(1): 1–2.

Hernana, S., Iturra, P., Solari, A., Villarroe, J., Jerez, S., Jimenez, M., Galleguillos, F., Leonor, M. & Bustamante, L. (2010) Fluoxetine response in impulsive-aggressive behaviour and serotonin transporter polymorphism in personality disorder. *Psychiatric Genetics,* 20(1): 25–30.

Hetherington, E.M. (1973) Girls without fathers. *Psychology Today*, 6: 47–52.

Hettema, J.M., Neale, M.C. & Kendler, K.S. (2001) A review and meta-analysis of the genetic epidemiology of anxiety disorders. *The American Journal of Psychiatry*, 158(10): 1568–78.

Hewitt, J. & Gabata, M. (2011) *Huntington's Disease*. New York: CreateSpace.

Hidalgo, R.B., Tupler, L.A. & Davidson, J.R.T. (2007) An effect size analysis of pharmacologic treatments for generalised anxiety disorder. *Journal of Psychopharmacology*, 21: 864–72.

Hierholzer, R. & Liberman, R. (1986) Successful living: A social skills and problem solving group for the chronic mentally ill. *Hospital Community Psychiatry*, 37: 913–18.

Himani, A., Tandon, O.P. & Bhatia, M.S. (1999) A study of P300-event related evoked potential in the patients of major depression. *Indian Journal of Physiological Pharmacology*, 43(3): 367–72.

Hjalmas, K., Bower, W., Coin, P., Chiozza, L.M., Von Gontard, A., Han, S.W., Husman, D.A., Kawauchi, A., Lackgre, G., Lottman, H., Mark, S., Rittig, S., Robson, L., Vande Walle, J. & Yeung, C.K. (2004) Nocturnal enuresis: An international evidence based management strategy. *The Journal of Urology*, 171(6): 2545–61.

Hodge, S.M., Makris, N., Kennedy, D.N., Caviness, V.S., Howard, J., McGrath, L., Steele, S., Frazier, J.A., Tager-Flusberg, H. & Harris, G.J. (2010) Cerebellum, language, and cognition in autism and specific language impairment. *J. Autism Dev Disord,* 40(3): 300–16.

Hodges, J. (2011) Alzheimer's disease and other dementias. In D.A. Warrell, T.M. Cox & J.D. Firth (eds), *Oxford Textbook of Medicine*. Oxford: Oxford University Press.

Hoff, L.A. & Morgan, B.D. (2010) *Psychiatric and mental health essentials in primary care*. New York: Routledge.

Hoffman, L.W. (1977) Changes in family roles, socialization, and sex differences. *American Psycholoigst*, 42: 644–57.

Hoffman, M. (1971) Identification and conscience development. *Child Development*, 42: 1071–82.

Hofmann, S.G. (2008) Acceptance and commitment therapy: New wave or morita therapy? *Clinical Psychology: Science and Practice*, 15(4): 280–5.

Hofmann, S.G., & Tompson, M.C. (eds) (2002) *Treating chronic and severe mental disorders: A handbook of empirically supported interventions*. New York: Routledge.

Hogarty, G.E. (1984) Depot neuroleptics: The relevance of psychosocial factor states perspective. *Journal of Clinical Psychiatry*, 45(5 pt 2): 36–42.

Holder, A. (2005) *Anna Freud, Melanie Klein and the psychoanalysis of children and adolescents*. New York: Karnac Books.

Holdwick, D.J., Hilsenroth, M.J., Castlebury, F.D. & Blais, M.A. (1998) Identifying the unique and common characteristics among the DSM-IV antisocial, borderline and narcissistic personality disorder. *Comprehensive Psychiatry*, 39: 277–86.

Hollander, E., Novotny, S., Hanratty, M., Yaffe, R., DeCaria, C.M., Aronowitz, B.R. & Mosovich, S. (2003) Oxytocin infusion reduces repetitive behaviours in adults with autistic and Asperger's disorders. *Neuropsychopharmacology*, 28: 193–8.

Holm, J.E. & Lamberty, K. (1997) The stress response in headache sufferers: Physiological and psychological reactivity. *Headache*, 37(4): 221–7.

Holmes, R.M. & Holmes, S.T. (2005) *Suicide: Theory, practice and investigation*. London: Sage Publications.

Holmes, S.E., Slaughter, J.R. & Kashani, J. (2001) Risk factors in childhood that lead to the development of conduct disorder and antisocial personality disorder. *Child Psychiatry and Human Development*, 31(3): 183–93.

Homan, K.J., Mellon, M.W., Houlihan, D. & Katusic, M.Z. (2011) Brief report: Childhood disintegrative disorder: a brief examination of eight case studies. *Journal of Autism Developmental Disorder*, 41(4): 497–504.

Horner, M.S. (1970) Femininity and successful achievement: A basic inconsistency. In J.M. Bardwick, E. Douvan, M.S. Horner & D. Gutmann (eds), *Feminine personality and conflict*. Belmount: Brooks/Cole Publishing Company.

Horwitz, A.V. (2004) *Creating mental illness*. Chicago: University of Chicago Press.

Howe, C. (2010) *Peer groups and children's development*. Oxford: Wiley-Blackwell.

Houle, M.M. (2000) *Tranquilizer, barbiturate and downer drug dangers*. Springfield, NJ: Enslow.

Howland, R.H. & Thase, M.E. (1993) A comprehensive review of cyclothymic disorder. *Journal of Nervous and Mental Disease*, 181(8): 485–93.

Huang, Y.F., Kuo, H.S., Lew-Ting, C.Y., Tian, F., Yang, C.H. & Tsai, T.I. (2011) Mortality among a cohort of drug users after their release from prison: An evaluation of the effectiveness of a harm reduction program in Taiwan. *Addiction*, 106: 1437–45.

Hughes, J.C. (2011) *Thinking through dementia*. Oxford: Oxford University Press.

Human Genome Program, U.S. Department of Energy (2008) *Genomics and its impact on science and society: A 2008 Primer*. U.S. Department of Energy, Office of Science, available online: http://www.ornl.gov/sci/techresources/Human_Genome/publicat/primer2001/primer11.pdf

Humphreys, J., Lee, K.A., Neylan, T.C. & Marmar, C. R. (2001) Psychological and physical distress of sheltered battered women. *Health Care for Women International*, 22 (4): 401–14.

Hutchings, S., Comins, J. & Offiler, J. (1997) *The social skills handbook: Practical activities for social communication*. New York: Speechmark Publishing Ltd.

Hyman, S.E., Malenka, R.C. & Nestler, E.J. (2006) Neural mechanisms of addiction: The role of reward-related learning and memory. *Annual Review of Neuroscience*, 29: 565–98.

Hynd, G.S., Marshall, R. & Gonzalez, J. (1991) Learning disabilities and presumed central nervous system dysfunction. *Learning Disability Quarterly*, 14: 283–96.

Hynd, G.S., Marshall, R. & Semrud-Clikeman, M. (1992) Developmental dyslexia, neurolinguistic theory and deviations in brain morphology. *Reading and Writing: An Interdisciplinary Journal*, 3: 345–62.

Illeris, K. (2008) *Contemporary theories of learning*. New York: Routledge.

Irons, G. (2009). Finding little Albert: A Journey to John B. Watson's infant Laboratory. *American Psychologist*, 64(7): 605–14.

Ishikawa, S.S. & Raine, A. (2002) Prefrontal deficits and antisocial behaviour: A causal model. In B.B. Lahey, T.E. Moffitt & A. Caspi (eds), *Causes of conduct disorder and juvenile delinquency*. New York: Guilford, pp. 277–304.

Isohanni, M., Oja, H., Moilanen, I. & Koiranen, M. (1994) Teenage alcohol drinking and non-standard family background. *Social Science and Medicine*, 38(11): 1565–74.

Israel, M. & Hay, I. (2006) *Research ethics for social scientists*. London: Sage.

Issenman, R.M., Filmer, R.B. & Gorski, P.A. (1999) A review of bowel and bladder control development in children: How gastrointestinal and urologic conditions relate to problems in toilet training. *Pediatrics*, 103(6): 1346–52.

Ivarsson, T., Broberg, A.G., Arvidsson, T. & Gillberg, C. (2005) Bullying in adolescence: Psychiatric problems in victims and bullies as measured by the youth self report and the depression of self-rating scale. *Nord Journal of Psychiatry*, 5: 365–73.

Iversen, T. (2008) Psychogenic obesity in children. *Acta Paediatrica*, 42(1): 8–19.

Ivnik, R.J. (1977) Overstatement of differences. *American Psychologist*, 33: 766–7.

Jackson, P.L., Brunet, E., Meltzoff, A.N. & Decety, J. (2004). Empathy examined through the neural mechanisms involved in imagining how I feel versus how you feel pain. *Neuropsychologia*, 44: 752–61.

Janowsky, D.S. & Risch, C. (1979) Amphetamine psychosis and psychotic symptoms. *Psychopharmacology*, 65: 73–7.

Jansen, A.S., Nguyen, X.V., Karpitskiy, V., Mettenleiter, T.C. & Loewy, A.D., (1995) Central command neurons of the sympathetic nervous system: Basis of the fight-or-flight response. *Science*, 270: 644–6.

Jansen, B.H., Hu, L. & Boutros, N.N. (2010) Auditory evoked potential variability in healthy and schizophrenia. *Clinical Neurophysiology*, 121(8): 1233–9.

Jansz, J. & Van Drunen, P. (eds) (2004) *A social history of psychology*. Oxford: Blackwell.

Jarvis, P., Holford, J. & Griffin, C. (2003) *The theory and practice of learning*. New York: Psychology Press.

Jasper, H.H. (1995) A historical perspective. The rise and fall of prefrontal lobotomy. *Advances in Neurology*, 66: 97–114.

Jenkins, P. (ed.) (2002) *Ethics in practice series: Legal issues in counselling and psychotherapy*. London: Sage Publications.

Jenkins, R., Bebbington, P.E., Brugha T., Farrell, M., Gill, B. and Lewis, G. (2000) The national psychiatric morbidity surveys of Great Britain – strategy and methods. *Psychological Medicine*, 27: 765–74.

Jimenez, S.S., Niles, B.L. & Park, C.L. (2010) A mindfulness model of affect regulation and depressive symptoms: Positive emotions, mood regulation expectancies and self-acceptance as regulatory mechanisms. *Personality and Individual Differences*, 49(6): 645–50.

Jiong, L., Johansen, C., Hansen, D. & Olsen, J. (2002) Cancer incidence in parents who lost a child. *Cancer*. 95(10): 2237–42.

Johnson, D.E. (2000) Medical and developmental sequelae of early childhood institutionalization in eastern European countries. In C.A. Nelson (ed.), *The effects of early adversity in neurobehavioral development.* Mahwah, NJ: C.A. Nelson, pp. 113–62.

Johnson, M.R. & Lydiard, R.B. (1995) Persoanlity disorders in social phobia. *Psychiatric Annals*, 25(9): 554–63.

Johnstone, T., Somerville, L.H., Alexander, A.L., Oakes, T.R., Davidson, R.J., Kalin, N.H. & Whalen, P.J. (2005) Stability of amygdale BOLD response to fearful faces over multiple scan sessions. *Neuroimage*, 25: 1112–23.

Joiner, T., Wingate, L., Gencoz, T. & Gencoz, F. (2005) Stress generation in depression: Three studies on its resilience, possible mechanism and symptom specificity. *Journal of Social & Clinical Psychology*, 24: 236–53.

Jones, C. & Hill, D. (2003) *Forms of ethical thinking in therapeutic practice.* London: Open University Press.

Jones, J.C. & Barlow, D.H. (1990). The etiology of post-traumatic stress disorder. *Clinical Psychology Review*, 10: 299–328.

Jones, P.B., Rantakallio, P., Hartikainen, A.L., Isohanni, M. & Sipila, P. (1998) Schizophrenia as a long-term outcome of pregnancy, delivery and perinatal complications: A 28 year follow-up of the 1966 north Finland general population birth cohort. *American Journal of Psychiatry*, 155(3): 355–64.

Jordan, B.D., Relkin, N.R., Ravdin, L.D., Jacobs, A.R., Bennett, A. & Gandy, S. (1992) Apolipoprotein E 4 associated with chronic traumatic brain injury in boxing. *JAMA* 278(2): 136–40.

Jordan, J.V. (1991) Empathy, mutuality, and therapeutic change: Clinical implications of a relational model. In J.V. Jordan, A.G. Kaplan, J.B.Miller, I.P. Stiver & J.L. Surrey (eds), *Women's growth in connection: Writings from the stone center.* New York: Guilford, pp. 283–9.

Jordan, K. (2010) Vicarious trauma: Something military and civilian therapists should know about when working with veterans. *Journal of Family Psychology*, 21(4): 225–37.

Jorm, A.F. & Jolley, D. (1998) The incidence of dementia: A meta-analysis. *Neurology*, 51(3): 728–33.

Joseph, H. & Quattrochi, R. (1997) *The neurobiology of cocaine addiction: From bench to bedside (Journal of addictive diseases series).* Binghamton, NY: Haworth Medical Press.

Joseph, J. (2004) *The gene illusion: Genetic research in psychiatry and psychology under the microscope.* Ross-on-Wye, Herefordshire: PCCS Books.

Joseph, J. (2006) *The missing gene: Psychiatry, heredity and the fruitless search for genes.* New York: Algora.

Joyce, P.R., McKenzie, J.M., Carter, J.D., Rae, A.M., Luty, S.E., Frampton, C.M. & Mulder, R.T. (2003) Temperament, character and personality disorders as predictors of response to interpersonal psychotherapy and cognitive-behavioural therapy for depression. *British Journal of Psychiatry*, 190: 503–8.

Juurlink, D.N., Hermann, N., Szalai, J.P., Kopp, A. & Redelmeier, D.A. (2004) Medical illness and the risk of suicide in the elderly. *Archives of Internal Medicine*, 164(11): 1179–84.

Kagan, J., Snidman, N., Arcus, D. & Reznick, J.S. (1994) *Galen's prophecy: Temperament in human-nature.* New York: Basic Books.

Kalant, H. (2010) Drug classification: Science, politics, both or neither? *Addiction*, 7: 1146–9.

Kalus, O. & Bernstein, D.P. (1995) Schizoid personality disorder. In W.J. Liversley (ed.), *The DSM-IV personality disorders.* New York: Guilford, pp. 58–70.

Kamphaus, R.W. & Reynolds, C.R. (2007) *BASC-2 Behavioral and emotional screening system manual.* Circle Pines, MN: Pearson.

Kanner, L. (1943) Autistic disturbances of affective content. *Nervous Child*, 2: 217–40.

Kantor, M. (2008) *Understanding paranoia: A guide for professionals, families, and sufferers.* Westport, CT: Praeger.

Kapardis, A. (2002) *Psychology and law: A critical introduction.* New York: Cambridge University Press.

Kapatzia, A. & Sygkollitou, E. (2008) Cyberbullying in middle and high schools: Prevalence, gender and age differences. Unpublished manuscript based on MSc thesis of A. Kapatzia, University of Thessaloniki, Greece.

Kaplan, P. (1991) *A child's odyssey.* St. Paul, MN: West Publishing Company.

Kasanin, J.S. (1944) *Language and thought in schizophrenia.* London: University of California Press.

Katz, R. (1997) Buffering children from marital conflict and dissolution. *Journal of Clinical Child Psychology*, 26(2): 157–71.

Katzung, B.G., Masters, S.B. & Trevor, A.J. (2009) *Basic and clinical pharmacology*. New York: McGraw-Hill.

Kazdin, A.E. (1993) Adolescent mental health: Prevention and treatment programs. *American Psychologist*, 48: 127–41.

Kazdin, A.E. (1995) Treatment manuals in clinical practice: Introduction to the series. *Clinical Psychology*, 5: 361–2.

Kazdin, A.E. (2010) *Single-case research designs: Methods for clinical and applied settings* (2nd edn). New York: Oxford University Press.

Keating, D.P. (2010) *Nature and nurture in early child development*. New York: Cambridge University Press.

Keefe, R.S., Silva, S.G., Perkins, D.O. & Lieberman, J.A. (1999) The effects of atypical antipsychotic drugs on neurocognitive impairment in schizophrenia: A review and meta-analysis. *Schizophrenia Bulletin*, 25(2): 201–22.

Kellerman, H. (2012) *Personality: How it forms*. New York: American Mental Health Foundation.

Kelsey, J.E., Nemeroff, C.B. & Newport, D.J. (2006) *Principles of psychopharmacology for mental health professionals*. New York: J. Wiley & Sons.

Kendall, P.C. & Ingram, R.E. (1987) Anxiety: Cognitive factors and the anxiety disorders. *Cognitive Therapy and Research*, 11(5): 521–2.

Kendler, K.S. (1985) Diagnostic approaches to schizotypal personality disorder. A historical perspective. *Schizophrenia Bulletin*, 11: 538–53.

Kendler, K.S. & Gruenberg, A.M. (1984) An independent analysis of the Danish adoption study of schizophrenia: VI. The relationship between psychiatric disorders as defined by DSM-III in the relatives and adoptees. *Archives of General Psychiatry*, 41: 555–64.

Kent, D. (2003) *History of psychology*. New York: McGraw-Hill.

Kern, J.K., Trivedi, M.H., Garver, E.R., Grannemann, B.D., Andrews, A.A. & Savla, J.S. (2009) The pattern of sensory processing abnormalities in autism. *Autism*, 10(5): 480–94.

Kernberg, O. (1980) *Boundaries and structures in love relations, in internal world and external reality*. New York, Jason Aronson.

Kernberg, O. (1993). *Aggression in personality disorders and perversions*. New Haven, CT: Yale University Press.

Kernberg, O.F. (1975) *Borderline conditions and pathological narcissism*. New York: Jason Aronson.

Keshavan, M.S. (2004) High risk studies, brain development and schizophrenia. In M. S. Keshavan, J.L. Kennedy & R.M. Murray (eds), *Neurodevelopment and schizophrenia*. London: Cambridge University Press.

Keshavan, M.S., Diwadkar, V.A., Harenski, K., Rosenberg, D.R., Sweeney, J.A. & Pettegrew, J.W. (2002) Abnormalities of the corpus callosum in first episode, treatment naive schizophrenia. *Journal of Neurology, Neurosurgery and Psychiatry*, 72: 757–60.

Ketelaars, M.P., Hermans, S.I.A., Cuperus, J., Jansonius, K. & Verhoeven, L. (2011) Semantic abilities in children with pragmatic language impairment: The case of picture naming skills. *Journal of Speech, Language and Hearing Research*, 54: 87–98.

Kety, S.S., Rosenthal, D., Wender, P.H. & Schulsinger, F. (1968) The types and prevalence of mental illness in the biological and adoptive families of adopted schizophrenics. In D. Rosenthal & S. S. Key (eds), *The transmission of schizophrenia*. Elmsford, NY: Pergamon.

Kevkovitz, Y., Tedeschini, E. & Papakostas, G.I. (2011) Efficacy of antidepressants for dysthymia: A meta-analysis of placebo-controlled randomized trials. *Journal of Clinical Psychiatry*, 72(4): 509–14.

Khachaturian, Z.S. & Radebaugh, T.S. (eds) (1996) *Alzheimer's disease: Cause(s), diagnosis, treatment and care*. Boca Raton, FL: CRC Press, Inc.

Kiecolt-Glaser, J.K., Newton, T., Cacioppo, J.T., et al. (1996) Marital conflict and endocrine function: Are men really more physiologically affected than women? *Journal of Consulting and Clinical Psychology*, 64: 324–32.

Kim, H.S. (2008) Culture and the cognitive and neuroendocrine responses to speech. *Journal of Personality and Social Psychology*, 94: 32–47.

Kim, Y.S., Koh, Y.J. & Leventhal, B.L. (2001) Prevalence of school bullying in Korean middle school students. *Arch Pediatr Adolesc Med*, 158(8): 737–41.

King, M. & Bearman, P. (2009) Diagnostic change and the increased prevalence of autism. *International Journal of Epidemiology*, 38(5): 1224–34.

Kingdon, D., Turkington, D. & John, C. (1994) Cognitive behaviour therapy of schizophrenia: The amenability of delusions and hallucinations to reasoning. *British Journal of Psychiatry*, 164: 581–7.

Kirk, S.A. & Kirk, W.D. (1971) *Psycholinguistic learning disabilities: Diagnosis and remediation*. Urbana: University of Illinois Press.

Klein, D.N., Depue, R.A. & Slater, J.F. (1986) Cyclothymia in the adolescent offspring of parents with bipolar affective disorder. *Journal of Abnormal Psychology*, 94: 115–27.

Klein, W.M.P. (2003) Self-prescriptive, perceived and actual attention to comparative risk information. *Psychology and Health*, 18: 625–43.

Klin, A. (1992) Young autistic children's listening preferences in regard to speech: A possible characterization of the symptom of social withdrawal. *Journal of Autism and Developmental Disorders*, 21: 29–42.

Klin, A., Carter, A. & Sparrow, S.S (1997) Psychological assessment of children with autism. In D.J. Cohen & F.R. Volkmar (eds), *Handbook of autism and pervasive developmental disorders* (2nd edn). New York: Wiley.

Klomek, A.B., Marrocco, F., Kleinman, M., Schonfeld, I.S. & Gould, M.S. (2007) Bullying, depression, and suicidality in adolescents. *J Am Acad Child Adolesc Psychiatry*, 46(1): 40–9.

Klug, W.S., Cummings, M.R., Spencer, C.A. & Palladino, M.A. (2009) *Essentials of genetics* (7th edn). New York: Pearson.

Knapp, S. J. (2011) *APA Handbook of ethics in psychology*. Washington, DC: American Psychological Association.

Knight, S.J.L. & Schmid, M. (2010) *Genetics of mental retardation: An overview encompassing learning disability and intellectual disability* (Monographs in human genetics). New York: S. Karger AG.

Knoester, C. & Eggebeen, D.J. (2006) The effects of the transition to parenthood and subsequent children on men's well-being and social participation. *Journal of Family Issues*, 27: 1532–60.

Kobasa, S.C. (1979) Stressful life events, personality and health: An enquiry into hardiness. *Journal of Personality and Social Psychology*, 37(1): 1–11.

Kohlberg, L. (1981) *Essays on moral development. The philosophy of moral development,* Vol. 1. San Francisco: Harper & Row.

Kohn, M.L. (1976) The interaction of social class and other factors in the etiology of schizophrenia. *The American Journal of Psychiatry*, 133(2): 177–80.

Kokaia, Z. & Lindvall, O. (2003) Neurogenesis after ischaemic brain insults. *Current Opinion in Neurobiology*, 13(1): 127–32.

Kokkinidis, L. & Anisman, H. (1980) Amphetamine models of paranoid schizophrenia: An overview and elaboration of animal experimentation. *Psychological Bulletin*, 88: 551.

Kokkinos, C.M. & Panayiotou, G. (2004) Predicting bullying and victimization among early adolescents: Associations with disruptive behaviour disorders. *Aggressive Behavior*, 30(6): 520–33.

Kolb, D.A. (1984) *Experiential learning: Experience as the source of learning and development*. New Jersey: Prentice-Hall.

Konopka, G. (1966) *The adolescent girl in conflict*. New Jersey: Prentice-Hall.

Konrad, A. & Winterer, G. (2008) Disturbed structural connectivity in schizophrenia – primary factor in pathology or epiphenomenon? *Schizophrenia Bulletin*, 34(1): 72–92.

Koob, G.F. & Moal, M.L. (2008) Neurobiological mechanisms for opponent motivational processes in addiction. *Philosophical Transactions of the Royal Society. B*, 363(1507): 3113–23.

Koocher, G.P. (2007) Twenty-first century ethical challenges for psychology. *American Psychology*, 62(5): 375–84.

Koocher, G.P. & Keith-Spiegel, P. (2008) *Ethics in psychology: Professional standards and cases* (2nd edn). New York: Oxford University Press.

Kornetsky, C. & Esposito, R.U. (1979) Euphorigenic drugs: Effects on the reward pathways of the brain. *Federation Proceedings*, 38: 2473–6.

Kousik, S.M., Graves, S.M., Napier, T.C., Zhao, C. & Carvey, P.M. (2011) Methamphetamine-induced vascular changes lead to striatal hypoxia and dopamine reduction. *Neuroreport*, 7(22): 923–8.

Kovas, Y. & Plomin, R. (2008) Learning abilities and disabilities: Generalist genes, specialist environments. *Current Directions in Psychological Science*, 16(5): 284–8.

Kraemer, H.C., Stice, E., Kazdin, A., Offord, D. & Kupfer, D. (2001) How do risk factors work together? Mediators, moderators and independent overlapping and proxy risk factors. *The American Journal of Psychiatry*, 158(6): 848–56.

Kraepelin, E. (1921) *Textbook of psychiatry* (8th edn). New York: Macmillan.

Kraepelin, E. (2010) *Dementia praecox and paraphrenia*. Reproduction of the original published in 1923. Delhi: Nabu Press.

Krampe, H. & Ehrenreich, H. (2010) Supervised disulfiram as adjunct to psychotherapy in alcoholism treatment. *Current Pharmaceutical Design*, 16(19): 2076–90.

Krashen, S.D. (1993) *The power of reading: Insights from the research*. Englewood, CO: Libraries Unlimited.

Kratochvil, C.J., Newcorn, J.H., Arnold, L.E., Duesenberg, D., Emslie, G.J. and Quintana, H. (2002) Atomoxetine alone or combined with fluoxetine for treating ADHD with comorbid depressive or anxiety symptoms. *Journal of the American Academy of Child and Adolescent Psychiatry*, 44(9): 915–24.

Kraus, N. (2012) Atypical brain oscillations: A biological basis for dyslexia? *Trends in Cognitive Sciences*, 16(1): 12–13.

Krishna, K., Taneja, S. & Gokhale, U. (2011) *Neuropsychiatric manifestations in HIV positive individuals*. New York: Lap Lambert Academic Publishing.

Krug, E.G., Kresnow, M., Peddicord, J.P., Kahlberg, L.L., Powell, K.E., Crosby, A.E. & Annest, J.L. (1998) Suicide after natural disasters. *New England Journal of Medicine*, 338(6): 373–8.

Kubzansky, L.D., Sparrow, D., Vokonas, P. & Kawachi, I. (2001). Is the glass half empty or half full? A prospective study of optimism and coronary heart disease in the normative aging study. *Psychosomatic Medicine*, 63(6): 910–16.

Kucharski, A. (1984) On being sick and famous. *Political Psychology*, 5: 69–81.

Kuhar, M. (2011) *The addicted brain: Why we abuse drugs, alcohol and nicotine*. New Jersey: FT Press.

Kutchins, H. & Kirk, S.A. (2003) *Making us crazy: DSM: The psychiatric bible and the creation of mental disorders*. New York: Free Press.

Kvikstad, A. & Vatten, L.J. (1998) Risk and prognosis of cancer in middle-aged women who have experienced the death of a child, *International Journal of Cancer*, 67(2): 165–9.

Lachar, D. & Gruber, C.P. (1993) Development of the personality inventory for youth: A self-report companion to the personality inventory for children. *Journal of Personality Assessment*, 61: 81–98.

Lader, M.H. (1983) Anxiety and depression. In A. Gale & J.A. Edwards (eds), *Handbook of biological psychiatry: Part II. Brain mechanisms and abnormal behavior – psychophysiology*. New York: Academic Press, pp. 225–47.

Lam, D., Watkins, E., Hayward, P., Bright, J., Wright, K., Kerr, N., Perr-Davis, G. & Sham, P.A. (2006) A randomized controlled study of cognitive therapy of relapse prevention for bipolar affective disorder: outcome of the first year. *Archives of General Psychiatry*, 60: 145–52.

Lambert, C.E. & Lambert, V.A. (1999) Psychological hardiness: State of the science. *Holistic Nursing Practice*, 13(3): 11–19.

Lane, H. (1976) *The wild boy of Aveyron*. New York: Harvard University Press.

Lanzkowsky, P. (1959) Investigation into the aetiology and treatment of pica. *Archives of Disease in Childhood*, 34(174): 140–8.

Larner, A.J. (2008) Monogenic Mendelian disorders in general neurological practice. *International Journal of Clinical Practice*, 62: 744–6.

Laruelle, M., Abi-Dargham, A., Gil, R., Kegeles, L. & Innis, R. (1999) Increased dopamine transmission in schizophrenia: Relationship to illness phases. *Biological Psychiatry*, 46: 56–72.

Lauer, R.H. & Lauer, J.C. (1994) *Marriage and family: The quest for intimacy*. Madison: Brown & Benchmark.

Lauriello, J. & Pallanti, S. (2012) *Clinical manual for treatment of schizophrenia*. Washington, DC: American Psychiatric Publishing.

Lavoe, M., Thorne, H.C., Jones, K.A.Y.H., Peters, S.P., Archer, S.N. & Dijk, D.J. (2009) Daily and seasonal variation in the spectral composition of light exposure in humans. *Chronobiol International*, 26(5): 854–66.

Lawlor, B.A. (1995) *Behavioral complications in Alzheimer's disease*. Washington, DC: American Psychiatric Press.

Lawrence, D.M. (2009) *Huntington's Disease*. London: Chelsea House.

Lazarus, R.S. & Folkman, S. (1984) *Stress, appraisal and coping*. New York: Springer.

Leahy, R.L., Holland, S.J.F. & McGinn, L.K. (2011) *Treatment plans and interventions for depression and anxiety disorders*. New York: Guilford Press.

Lees, R. & Stark, C. (2005) *The treatment of stuttering in the young school-aged child*. New York: Whurr.

Leichsenring, R. & Leibing, E. (2003) The effectiveness of psychodynamic therapy and cognitive behaviour therapy in the treatment of personality disorders: A meta-analysis. *American Journal of Psychiatry*, 160: 1223–32.

Lelis, R.G., Krieger, J.E., Pereira, A.C., Schmidt, A.P., Carmona, M.J., Oliveira, S.A. & Auler, J.O. (2006) Apolipoprotein E4 genotype increases the risk of postoperative cognitive dysfunction in patients undergoing coronary artery bypass graft surgery. *Journal of Cardiovascular Surgery*, 47(4): 451–6.

Lenzenweger, M.F. (2010) *Schizotypy and schizophrenia: The view from experimental psychopathology*. New York: Guilford Press.

Lenzenweger, M.F. & Willett, J.B. (2009) Does change in temperament predict change in schizoid personality disorder? A methodological framework and illustration from the longitudinal study of personality disorders. *Development & Psychopathology*, 21: 1211–31.

Leonard, B.E. (2003) Brain injury and mental retardation: Psychopharmacology and neuropsychiatry. *Human Psychopharmacology: Clinical and Experimental*, 18(2): 151.

Leonard, B.E. (2007) Psychopathology of depression. *Drugs Today*, 43(10): 705–16.

Leonard, H. & Wen, X. (2002) The epidemiology of mental retardation: Challenges and opportunities in the new millennium. *Mental Retardation and Developmental Disabilities Research Reviews*, 8: 117–34.

Leong, F.T.L & Austin, J.T. (2005) *The psychology research handbook: A guide for graduate students and research assistants*. London: Sage.

Leonhard, K., Beckmann, H. & Cahn, C.H. (1999) *Classification of endogenous psychoses and their differentiated etiology*. New York: Springer.

Lerner, J. (2000) *Learning disabilities*. New York: McGraw Hill.

Lerner, R.M. (1993) *Early adolescence: Perspectives on research, policy and intervention*. New York: Lawrence Erlbaum Associates.

Leucht, S., Corves C., Arbter, D., Engel, R.R., Li, D. & Davis, J.M. (2009) Second-generation versus first-generation antipsychotic drugs for schizophrenia: A meta-analysis. *Lancet*, 373(9657): 31–41.

Levav, I., Kohn, R., Iscovich, J., et al. (2000) Cancer incidence and survival following bereavement. *American Journal of Public Health*, 90:1601–7.

Levine, M.D. (1975) Children with encopresis: A descriptive analysis. *Pediatrics*, 56: 412–16.

Levine, M.P. & Smolak, L. (1992) Toward a model of the developmental psychopathology of eating disorders: The example of early adolescence. In J.H. Crowther, D.L. Tennenbaum, S.E. Hobfoll & M.A.P. Stephens (eds), *The etiology of bulimia nervosa: The individual and familial context*. Washington, DC: Hemisphere.

Levitan, I.B. & Kaczmarek, L.K. (2001) *The neuron: cell and molecular biology* (3rd edn). New York: Oxford University Press.

Levy, R.M., Bredesen, D.E. & Rosenblum, M.L. (1985) Neurological manifestations of the acquired immunodeficiency syndrome (AIDS): Experience at UCSF and review of the literature. *Journal of Neurosurgery*. 62(4): 475–95.

Levy, R.M., Bredesen, D.E. & Rosenblum, M.L. (1988) Opportunistic central nervous system pathology in patients with AIDS. *Ann Neurol*. 23(Suppl): S7–12.

Lewinsohn, P.M., Seeley, J. & Klein, D. (2006) Bipolar disorders during adolescence. *Acta Psychiatrica Scandinavica*, 108: 47–50.

Lewis, A.J., Gould, E., Habib, C. & King, R. (2010) *Integrative assessment in clinical psychology.* London: Australian Academic Press.

Lewis, B. (2006) *Moving beyond Prozac, DSM and the new psychiatry: The birth of postpsychiatry.* Ann Arbor: University of Michigan Press.

Lewis-Fernandez, R. & Kleinman, A. (1993) Culture, personality and psychopathology. *Journal of Abnormal Psychology,* 103: 67–71.

Lewy, A.J., Sack, R.L. & Singer, C.M. (1985) Immediate and delayed effects of bright light on human melatonin production: Shifting 'dawn' and 'dusk' shifts the dim light melatonin onset. *Ann NY Acad Science.* 453: 253–9.

Liabo, K. & Richardson, J. (2007) *Conduct disorder and offending behaviour in young people: Findings from research.* London: Jessica Kingsley.

Lichtman, A.H. & Martin, B.R. (2009) Understanding the pharmacology and physiology of cannabis dependence. In R. Roffman & R.S. Stephens, *Cannabis dependence: Its nature, consequences and treatment.* New York: Cambridge University Press.

Licinio, J. & Wong, M. (2005) *Biology of depression: From novel insights to therapeutic strategies.* New York: Wiley.

Lickey, M.E. & Gordon, B. (1991) *Medicine and mental illness.* New York: W.H. Freeman.

Lieberman, J.A., Stroup, T.S., McEvoy, J.P., Swartz, M.S., Rosenheck, R.A., Perkins, D.O., Keefe, R.S., Davis, S.M., Davis, C.E., Lebowitz, B.D., Severe, J. & Hsiao, J.K. (2005) Effectiveness of antipsychotic drugs in patients with chronic schizophrenia. *New England Journal of Medicine,* 353(12): 1209–23.

Lieberman, M.D. (2009) The brain's braking system (and how to use your words to tap into it). *Neuroleadership,* 2: 9–14.

Liebowitz, M.R. (1987) Social phobia. *Modern Problems of Pharmacopsychiatry,* 22: 141–73.

Lijffijt, M., Cox, B., Acas, M.D., Lane, S.D., Moeller, F.G. & Swann, A.C. (2012) Differential relationships of impulsivity or antisocial symptoms on P50, N100 or P200 auditory sensory gating in controls and antisocial personality disorder. *Journal of Psychiatric Research,* 46(6): 743–50.

Linde, K., Berner, M., Egger, M. & Mulrow, C. (1996) St. John's wort for depression – an overview and meta-analysis of randomised clinical trials. *BMJ,* 313: 253–8.

Linden, M., Habib, T. & Radojevic, V. (1996) A controlled study of the effects of neurofeedback on cognition and behaviour of children with attention deficit disorders and learning disabilities. *Biofeedback and Self-Regulation,* 21: 35–50.

Lindesay, J., Rockwood, K., & Rolfson, D. (2002) The epidemiology of delirium. In J. Lindesay, K. Rockwood & A. Macdonald, *Delirium in old age.* Oxford: Oxford University Press, pp. 27–51.

Lindon, J. (2010) *Understanding child development: Linking theory and practice.* New York: Oxford University Press.

Linehan, M.M. (1993) *Cognitive-behavioral treatment of borderline personality disorder.* New York: Guilford Press.

Link, B., Struening, E., Neese-Todd, S., Asmussen, S. & Phelan, J. (2001) The consequences of stigma for the self-esteem of people with mental illnesses. *Psychiatric Services,* 52(12): 1621–6.

Link, B.G. & Phelan, J. (1995) Social conditions as fundamental causes of disease. *Journal of Health and Social Behavior,* Spec. no: 80–94.

Livesley, W.J. & Jang, K.L. (2008) The behavioural genetics of personality disorder. *Annual Review of Clinical Psychology,* 4: 247–74.

Livingston, J.D. & Boyd, J.E. (2010) Correlates and consequences of internalized stigma for people living with mental illness: A systematic review and meta-analysis. *Social Science and Medicine,* 71(12): 2150–61.

Lobbestael, J. & Arntz, A. (2010) Emotional, cognitive and physiological correlates of abuse-related stress in borderline and antisocial personality disorder. *Behaviour Research and Therapy,* 48: 116–24.

Locke, R. (1992) Gender and practical skill performance in science. *Journal of Research in Science Teaching,* 29(3): 227–41.

Lockyer, L. & Rutter, M. (1969) A five to fifteen year follow-up study of infantile psychosis: III. Psychological aspects. *British Journal of Psychiatry,* 115: 865–82.

Loeber, R., Burke, J.D., Lahey, B.B., Winters, A. & Zera, M. (2000) Oppositional defiant and conduct disorder: A review of the past 10 years, Part I. *Journal of the American Academy of Child and Adolescent Psychiatry,* 39: 1468–84.

Loewenthal, D. (2011) *Post-existentialism and the psychological therapies: Towards a therapy without foundations*. London: Karnac

Logsdon, R.G., McCurry, S.M. & Teri, L. (2009) Making physical activity accessible to older adults with memory loss: The RALLI study. *The Gerontologist*, 49(Suppl 1): S3–S11.

Lopez, S.R. & Guarnaccia, P.J. (2000) Cultural psychopathology: Uncovering the social world of mental illness. *Annual Review of Psychology*, 51: 571–98.

Loranger, A.W., Sartorius, N., Andreoli, A., Berger, P., Buicheim, P., Channabasavanna, S.M., Coid, B., Dahl, A., Diekstra, R.G.W., Ferguson, B., Jacobsberg, L.B., Mombour, W., Pull, C., Ono, Y. & Regier, D.A. (1994) The international personality disorder examination. *Archives of General Psychiatry*, 51, 215–24.

Lord, C. & Schopler, E. (1987) Neurobiological implications of sex differences in autism. In E. Schopler & G.B. Mesibov (eds), *Neurobiological issues in autism. Current issues in autism*. New York: Plenum Press.

Lotter, V. (1978) Childhood autism in Africa. *Journal of Child Psychology and Psychiatry*, 19(3): 231–44.

Lou, W., Ni, Z., Dyer, K., Tweardy, D.J. & Gao, A.C. (2000) Interleukin-6 induces prostate cancer cell growth accompanied by activation of stat3 signaling pathway. *Prostate*, 42: 239–442.

Luckasson, R., Schalock, R.L, Spitalnik, D.M. & Spreat, S. (2002) *Mental retardation: Definition, classification and systems of support*. Washington, DC: American Association on Mental Retardation.

Lurie, S., Gawinski, B., Pierce, D. & Rousseau, S.J. (2006) Seasonal affective disorder. *American Family Physician*, 74(9): 1521–4.

Lutz, J. (2005) *Learning and memory* (2nd edn). Long Grove, IL: Waveland.

Luukinen, H., Koski, K., Kivela, S.L. & Paippala, P. (1996) Social status, life changes, housing conditions, health, functional abilities and life-style as risk factors for recurrent falls among the home-dwelling elderly. *Public Health*, 110(2): 115–18.

Lybeck-Brown, J.C. (2003) Vicarious traumatisation of psychotherapists: Implications for theory, training and practice. *Dissertation Abstracts International*: *Section B: The Sciences & Engineering*, 63(9–B).

Lykken, D.T. (1955) *The antisocial personalities*. Hillsdale, NJ: Erlbaum.

Lynch, M. & Cicchetti, D. (1997). Children's relationships with adults and peers: An examination of elementary and junior high school students. *Journal of School Psychology*, 35: 81–99.

Lysaker, P.H. & Davis, L.W. (2004) Social function in schizophrenia and schizoaffective disorder: Associations with personality, symptoms and neurocognition. *Health and Quality of Life Outcomes*, 2: 15.

Mace, F.C. & Knight, D. (1986) Functional analysis and treatment of severe pica. *Journal of Applied Behaviour Analysis*, 19(4): 411–16.

MacLachlan, M. & Smyth, C.A. (eds) (2004) *Binge drinking and youth culture: Reasons, ramifications and remedies*. Dublin: Liffey Press.

Macintyre, P. & Schug, S. (2007) *Acute pain management: A practical guide*. Philadelphia, PA: Elsevier.

MacMahon, E. (2006) Measles in the United Kingdom: Can we eradicate it by 2010? *BMJ*, 333: 890.

Maffei, C., Fossati, A., Lingiardi, V., Madeddu, F., Borellini, X. & Petrachi, M. (1995) Personality maladjustment, defences and psychopathological symptoms in nonclinical subjects. *Journal of Personality Disorders*, 9: 330–45.

Magee, W.J., Eaton, W.W., Witchen, H., McGonagle, K.A. & Kessler, R.C. (1996) Agoraphobia, simple phobia and social phobia in the National Comorbidity Survey. *Archives of General Psychiatry*, 53: 159–68.

Magner, L.N. (2002) *A history of the life sciences*. New York: Marcel Dekker.

Maher, B.A. (1974) Delusional thinking and perceptual disorder. *Journal of Individual Psychology*, 30: 98–113.

Maier, S.F., Watkins, L.R., & Fleshner, M. (1994) Psychoneuroimmunology: The interface between behaviour, brain and immunity. *American. Psychology*, 49(12), 1004–17.

Maier, W., Lichtermann, D., Klingler, T., Heun, R. & Hallmayer, J. (1992) Prevalences of personality disorders (DSM-III-R) in the community. *Journal of Personality Disorders* 6: 187–96.

Malson, H. (1997) Women under erasure: Anorexic bodies in postmodern context. *Journal of Community & Applied Social Psychology*, 9: 137–53.

Mandelstam, M. (2010) *Community care practice and the law*. London: Jessica Kingsley.

Mann, D.M., South, P.W., Snowden, J.S. & Neary, D. (1993) Dementia of frontal lobe type: Neuropathology and immunohistochemistry. *Journal of Neurology, Neurosurgery and Psychiatry*, 56(6): 605–14.

Manschreck, T.C., Maher, B.A., Rucklos, M.E. & Vereen, D.R. (1982) Disturbed voluntary motor activity in schizophrenic disorder. *Psychological Medicine*, 12: 73–84.

Manzato, E., Mazzullo, M., Gualandi, M., Zanetti, T. & Scanelli, G. (2009) Anorexia nervosa: from purgative behaviour to nephropathy. A case report. *Cases Journal*, 13(2): 46.

Marcus, S.M. (2009) Depression during pregnancy: Rates, risks and consequences – mother risk update. *Canadian Journal of Clinical Pharmacology*, 16(1): 15–22.

Maren, S. (2001) Neurobiology of Pavlovian fear conditioning. *Annual Review of Neuroscience*, 24: 897–931.

Marks, I.M. (1970) The classification of phobic disorders. *British Journal of Psychiatry*, 116: 377–86.

Marks, I.M. (1987) Behavioral aspects of panic disorder. *American Journal of Psychiatry*, 144, 1160–5.

Marneros, A. & Goodwin, F. (eds) (2005) *Bipolar disorders: Mixed states, rapid cycling and atypical forms.* New York: Cambridge University Press.

Marsella, A.J. & Kameoka, V.A. (1989) Ethnocultural issues in the assessment of psychopathology. In S. Wetzler (ed.), *Measuring mental illness: Psychometric assessment for clinicians.* The clinical practice series, No. 8, Washington, DC: American Psychiatric Press, pp. 231–56.

Marsh, D.T. Lefley, H.P., Evans-Rhodes, D., Ansell, V.I., Doerzbacher, B.M., La Barbara, L. & Paluzzi, J.E. (1996) The family experience of mental illness: Evidence for resilience. *Psychiatric Rehabilitation Journal*, 20(2): 3–12.

Marston, D. & Tindal, G. (1995) Performance monitoring. In A. Thomas & J. Grimes (eds), *Best practices in school psychology-III.* Washington, DC: The National Association of School Psychologists.

Martell, C.R., Dimidjian, S. & Herman-Dunn, R. (2010) *Behavioral activation for depression: A clinician's guide.* New York: Guilford Press.

Masliah, E., Mallory, M., Hansen, L., Alford, M., Albright, T., DeTeresa, R., Terry R., Baudier, J. & Saitoh, T. (1991) Patterns of aberrant sprouting in Alzheimer's disease. *Neuron*, 6(5): 729–39.

Maslow, A. (1946). Security and breast feeding. *Journal of Abnormal and Social Psychology*, 46: 83–85.

Maslow, A. (1973) *Dominance, self-esteem, self-actualization: Germinal papers of A.H. Maslow.* New York: Brooks/Cole.

Masten, A. & Coatsworth, J.D. (1998).The development of competence in favourable and unfavourable environments: Lessons from research on successful children. *American Psychologist*, 53: 205–20.

Masterson, J. (1999) *The narcissistic and borderline disorders: An integrated developmental approach.* New York: Brunner-Routledge.

Mathurin, P. & Deltenre, P. (2008) Effect of binge drinking on the liver: An alarming public health issue? *Gut*, 58: 613–17.

Matson, J.L. & Mahan, S. (2009) Current status of research on childhood disintegrative disorder. *Research in Autism Spectrum Disorders*, 3(4): 861–867.

Matson, J.L. & Sturmey, P. (2011) *International handbook of autism and pervasive developmental disorders.* New York: Springer.

Matthys, W., Lochman, J.E. & Lochman, J.E. (2009) *Oppositional defiant disorder and conduct disorder in childhood.* London: John Wiley & Sons.

Mattia, J.I. & Zimmerman, M. (2001) Epidemiology. In W.J. Livesley (ed.), *Handbook of personality disorders.* New York: Guilford Press.

Maurer, D.W. & Vogel, V.H. (1973) *Narcotics and narcotic addiction.* New York: Thomas.

Mauri, M., Sarno, N., Rossi, V.M., Armani, A., Zambotto, S., Cassano, G.B. & Akiskal, H.S. (1992) Personality disorders associated with generalized anxiety, panic and recurrent depressive disorders. *Journal of Personality Disorders*, 6(2): 162–7.

Mawer, S. (2006) *Gregor Mendel: Planting the seeds of genetics.* New York: Harry N. Abrams, Inc.

Maxfield, L. & Hyer, L. (2002) The relationship between efficacy and methodology in studies investigating EMDR treatment of PTSD. *Journal of Clinical Psychology*, 58: 23–41.

Maziade, M., Caron, C., Cote, R., Boutin, P., & Thiverge, J. (1990). Extreme temperament and diagnosis: A study in a psychiatric sample of consecutive children. *Archives of General Psychiatry*, 47: 477–84.

McAllister, F. (1995) *Marital breakdown and the health of the nation* (2nd edn). London: One plus One.

McAuliffe, W.E., Rohman, M., Santangelo, S., Feldman, B., Magnuson, E., Sobol, A. & Weissman, J. (1986) Psychoactive drug use among practicing physicians and medical students. *New England Journal of Medicine*, 315: 805–10.

McCabe, M. & Ricciardelli, L. (2011) Body image and body change techniques among young adolescent boys. *European Eating Disorders Review*, 9: 335–47.

McCabe, M.S., Fowler, R.C., Cadoret, R.J. & Winokur, G. (1971) Familial differences in schizophrenia with good and poor prognosis. *Psychological Medicine*, 1: 326–32.

McCall, R.B. (1981) Nature–nurture and the two realms of development: A proposed integration with respect to mental development. *Child Development*, 52: 1–12.

McCandless, D.W. (2009) *Thiamine deficiency and associated clinical disorders*. London: Springer.

McCann, L. & Peralmann, L.A. (1990) Vicarious traumatisation: A framework for understanding the psychological effects of working with victims. *Journal of Traumatic Stress*, 3(1): 131–49.

McClung, C.A. (2007) Role for the clock gene in bipolar disorder. *Cold Spring Harbor Symp on Quantitative Biology*, 72: 637–44.

McCord, W. & McCord, J. (1961) A familial correlates of aggression in non-delinquent male children. *Journal of Abnormal Social Psychology*, 62: 461–4.

McCord, W. & McCord, J. (1963) *The psychopath: An essay on the criminal mind*. Princeton, NJ: Van Nostrand.

McCrae, R.R., Costa, P.T., Ostendorf, F., Angleitner, A., Hrebickova, M., Avia, M., Sanz, J., Sanchez-Bernardos, M.L., Kusdil, M., Woodfield, R., Saunders, P. & Smith, P.B. (2000) Nature over nurture: Temperament, personality, and life span development. *Journal of Personality and Social Psychology*, 78(1):173–86.

McElroy, S.L., Phillips, K.A. & Keck, P.E. (1994) Obsessive compulsive spectrum disorder. *Journal of Clinical Psychiatry*, 55: 33–53.

McEwen, B.S. (2000) The neurobiology of stress: From serendipity to clinical relevance. *Brain Research*, 886: 172–89.

McFarlane, A.C. (1989) The aetiology of post-traumatic morbidity: Predisposing, precipitating and perpetuating factors. *British Journal of Psychiatry*, 154: 221–8.

McFarlane, A.C. (1998) The prevalence and longitudinal course of PTSD. Implications for the neurobiological models of PTSD. *Annals of the New York Academy of Sciences*, 821: 10–23.

McFarlane, A.C. & Atchison, M. (1997) The acute stress response following motor vehicle accidents and its relation to PTSD. *Annals of the New York Academy of Sciences*, 821: 437–41.

McFarlane, W.R. (2011) *Psychoeducational multifamily groups for families with persons with severe mental illness*. Hoboken, NJ: John Wiley & Sons.

McGoldrick, M., Pearce, J.K. & Giordano, J. (eds) (1982) *Ethnicity and family therapy*. New York: Guilford Press.

McGuffin, P., Owen, M.J. & Farmer, A.E. (1995) Genetic basis of schizophrenia. *Lancet*, 346(8976): 678–82.

McGuffin, P., Rijsdijk, F., Andrew, M., Sham, P., Katz, R. & Cardno, A. (2003) The heritability of bipolar affective disorder and the genetic relationship to unipolar depression. *Archives of General Psychiatry*, 60(5): 497–502.

McGuinness, D. & Pribram, K. (1980) The neuropsychology of attention: Emotional and motivational controls. In M.C. Wittrock, (ed.), *The brain and psychology*. New York: Academic Press, pp. 95–139.

McLeod, J. (2003) *An introduction to counselling*. New York: McGraw-Hill House.

McMurran, M. (1994) *The psychology of addiction*. London: Taylor & Francis.

McWilliams, N. (2011) *Psychoanalytic diagnosis: Understanding personality structure in the clinical process* (2nd edn). New York: Guilford Press.

McWilliams, S.A. & Tuttle, R.J. (1973) Long-term psychological effects of LSD. *Psychological Bulletin*, 79(6): 341–51.

Means, R., Richards, S. & Smith, R. (2008) *Community care, policy and practice* (4th edn). Basingstoke: Palgrave Macmillan.

Measham, F. & Brain, K. (2005) Binge drinking British alcohol policy and the new culture of intoxication. *Crime Media Culture*, 1(3): 262–83.

Mednick, S.A. & Schulsinger, F. (1967) The children of schizophrenics: Serious difficulties in current research methodologies which suggest the use of the high-risk group method. In J. Ramano (ed.), *Origins of schizophrenia*. Amsterdam: Excerpta Medica, pp. 179–200.

Mednick, S.A. & Schulsinger, F. (1968) Some premorbid characteristics related to breakdown in children with schizophrenic mothers. In D. Rosenthal & S. Kety (eds), *The transmission of schizophrenia*. New York: Pergamon Press.

Mednick, S.A., Vka, J.V., Gabrielli, W.F. & Itil, T.M. (1981) EEG as a predictor of antisocial behaviour. *Criminology*, 19(2): 219–30.

Meehl, P.E. (1990) Toward an integrated theory of schizotaxia, schizotypy, schizophrenia. *Journal of Personality Disorders,* 4(1): 1–99.

Meek, W.H., Smith, R.A. & Williams, C.L. (1989) Organizational changes in cholinergic activity and enhanced visuospatial memory as a function of choline administered prenatally or postnatally or both. *Behavioral Neuroscience.* 103(6): 1234–41.

Meggitt, C. (2006) *A child development: An illustrated guide* (2nd edn). Oxford: Heinemann.

Meichenbaum, D. (1972) Cognitive modification of test anxious college students. *Journal of Consulting and Clinical Psychology*, 39: 370–80.

Meichenbaum, D. (1973) Therapist manual for cognitive behaviour modification. Unpublished manuscript, University of Waterloo, Ontario, Canada.

Meichenbaum, D. (1977) *Cognitive-behavior modification: An integrative approach*. New York: Plenum.

Meichenbaum, D. & Cameron, R. (1973) Training schizophrenics to talk to themselves: A means of developing attentional controls. *Behavior Therapy*, 4: 515–34.

Meichenbaum, D. & Deffenbacher, J.L. (1988) Stress inoculation training. *Counselling Psychologist*, 16: 69–90.

Meichenbaum, D. & Turk, D. (1976) The cognitive-behavioural management of anxiety, anger and pain. In P.O. Davidson (ed.), *The behavioural management of anxiety, depression and pain*. New York: Brunner/Mazel.

Meichenbaum, D., Turk, D., & Burstein, S. (1975) The nature of coping with stress. In I.G. Sarsons & C.D. Spielburger (eds), *Stress and anxiety* (Vol II). New York: Wiley.

Meltzer, H.Y. & Stahl, S.M. (1976) The dopamine hypothesis of schizophrenia: A review. *Schizophrenia Bulletin*, 2(1): 19–76.

Meltzer, H., Gill, B., Hinds, K., & Petticrew, M. (2000) *OPCS surveys of psychiatric Britain, report 4: the prevalence of psychiatric morbidity among adults living in institutions*. London, HMSO.

Meltzer-Brody, S. (2011) New insights into perinatal depression: pathogenesis and treatment during pregnancy and postpartum. *Dialogues Clin Neuroscience*, 13(1): 89–100.

Meltzer-Brody, S. & Thorp, J. (2011) The contribution of psychiatric illness on perinatal outcomes. *BJOG*, 118: 1283–4.

Mendelson, B. (1974) The origin of the doctrine of victimology. In L. Drapkin & E. Viano (eds), *Victimology*. Lanham, MD: Lexington Books.

Menyuk, P. (1978) Linguistic problems in children with developmental dysphasia. In M. Wyke (ed.), *Developmental dysphasia*. London: Academic Press, pp. 135–8.

Mercer, C.D. (1991). Students with learning disabilities. New York: Macmillan.

Merikangas, K. & Weissman, M. (1986) Epidemiology of DSM-III Axis II personality disorders. In A. Frances & R. Hales (eds), *Psychiatry update*. Washington, DC: American Psychiatric Press.

Merikangas, K.R. (1990) The genetic epidemiology of alcoholism. *Psychological Medicine*, 20: 11–22.

Merikangas, K.R., Akiskal, H.S., Angst, J., Greenberg, P.E., Hirschfeld, R.M., Petukhova, M. & Kessler, R.C. (2007) Lifetime and 12-month prevalence of bipolar spectrum disorder in the National Comorbidity Survey replication. *Archives of General Psychiatry*, 64(5): 543–52.

Merikangas, K.R., He, J.P., Burstein, S.A., Swanson, S. & Avenevoli, D. (2010) Lifetime prevalence of mental disorders in U.S. adolescents: Results from the national comorbidity survey replication adolescent supplement (NCS-A). *Journal of the American Academy of Child & Adolescent Psychiatry* 49(10): 980–9.

Mersch, P.P.A., Middendorp, H.M. and Bouhuys, A.L. (1999) Seasonal affective disorder and latitude: A review of the literature. *Journal of Affective Disorders*, 53: 35–48.

Metzner, C. & Kraus, L. (2008) The impact of alcopops on adolescent drinking: a literature review. *Alcohol and Alcoholism*, 43(2): 230–9.

Meyer, J., Rauch, G., Lechner, H. & Loeb, C. (eds) (2002) *Vascular dementia*. New York: Futura Publishing Company.

Meyer, J.S. & Quenzer, L.F. (2004) *Psychopharmacology: Drugs, the brain and behavior*. Sunderland, MA: Sinauer Associates.

Meyerhoff, D.J., Blumenfeld, R., Truran, D., Lingren, J., Flenniken, D., Cardenas, V., Chao, L.L., Rothlind, J., Studholme, C. & Weiner, M.W. (2004) Effects of heavy drinking, binge drinking and family history of alcoholism on regional brain metabolites. *Alcoholism – Clinical and Experimental Research*, 28(4): 650–61.

Miller, A.L. (1998) St. John's wort (hypericum perforatum): Clinical effects on depression and other conditions. *Alternative medicine review: A journal of clinical therapeutic*, 3(1): 18–26.

Miller, B.L. & Boeve, B.F. (2011) *The behavioural neurology of dementia*. Cambridge: Cambridge University Press.

Miller, G.E. & Prinz, R.J. (1990) Enhancement of social learning family interventions for childhood conduct disorder. *Psychological Bulletin*, 108: 291–307.

Miller, J.W., Naimi, T. & Brewer, R.D. (2007) Is the binge-drinking glass half full or half empty: In reply. *Pediatrics*, 119(6): 1035–6.

Miller, M.W. (2003) Personality and the etiology and expression of PTSD: A three-factor model perspective. *Clinical Psychology: Science and Practice*, 10: 373–93.

Millman, J. (1978) Strategies for constructing criterion-refereced assessment instruments. Paper presented at the conference of large scale assessment, Denver, 1978.

Millon, T. (1981) *Disorders of personality: DSM-III: axis II*. New York: John Wiley and Sons.

Millon, T. (2004) *Masters of the Mind: Exploring the Story of Mental Illness from Ancient Times to the New Millennium*. Hoboken, NJ: John Wiley.

Millon, T. & Davis, R.D. (1996) *Disorders of personality: DSM-IV and beyond* (2nd edn). New York: Wiley.

Millon, T. & Davis, R.D. (1996) An evolutionary theory of personality disorders. In J.F. Clarkin & M.F. Lenzenweger (eds), *Major theories of personality disorder*. New York: Guilford, pp. 221–346.

Millon, T., Millon, C.M., Meagher, S., Grossman, S. & Ramnath, R. (2004) *Personality disorders in modern life*. New York: John Wiley and Sons.

Millon, T., Millon, C., Davis, R. & Grossman, S. (1997) *MCMI-III: manual*. Minneapolis, MN: NCS Pearson.

Milroy, C.M. (2011) Ecstasy associated deaths: What is a fatal concentration? Analysis of a case series. *Forensic Science, Medicine and Pathology*, 7(3): 248–52.

Mirin, S.M., Weiss, R.D., Griffin, M.L. & Michael, J.L. (1991) Psychopathology in drug abusers and their families. *Comprehensive Psychiatry*, 32: 36–51.

Mischel, W. & Liebert, R.M. (1966) Effects of discrepancies between observed and imposed reward criteria on their acquisition and transmission. *Journal of Personality and Social Psychology*, 3: 45–53.

Mitchell, A.J., Vaze, A. & Rao, S. (2009) Clinical diagnosis of depression in primary care: A metal-analysis. *Lancet* 374(9690): 609–19.

Mittal, V.A., Kalus, O., Bernstein, D. & Siever, L.J. (2007) Schizoid personality disorder. In W. O'Donohue, K. Fowler & S. Lilienfeld (eds), *Personality disorders: Toward the DSM-V*. Thousand Oaks, CA: Sage, pp. 63–79.

Mitty, E. & Flores, S. (2008) Suicide in late life. *Geriatric Nursing*, 29(3): 160–5.

Moch, S. (2011) Dysthmia: More than 'minor' depression. *SA Pharmaceutical Journal*, 78(3): 38–43.

Moerk, E.L. (1973) Like father like son: Imprisonment of fathers and the psychological adjustment of sons. *Journal of Youth and Adolescence*, 2(4): 303–12.

Moffatt, K., McConnachie, A., Ross, S. & Morrison, J. (2004) First year medical student stress and coping in a problem-based learning medical curriculum. *Medical Education*, 38: 482–91.

Moffitt, T.E. (1993) The neuropsychology of conduct disorder. *Development and Psychopathology,* 5: 135–51.

Mohr, D.C., Ho, J., Duffecy, J., Baron, K.G., Lehman, K.A., Jin, L. & Reifler, D. (2008) Perceived barriers to psychological treatments and their relationship to depression. *Journal of Clinical Psychology*, 66(4): 394–409.

Mol, S.E., Bus, A.G. & de Jong, M.T. (2012) Interactive book reading in early education: A tool to stimulate print knowledge as well as oral language. *Review of Educational Research*, 79(2): 979–1007.

Mook, D. (2001) *Psychological research: The ideas behind the methods*. New York: Norton.

Morgan, D.L. & Morgan, R.K. (2008) Single-participant research design: Bringing science to managed care. *American Psychologist*, 56: 119–27.

Morgan, S. (1988) Diagnostic assessment of autism: A review of objective scales. *Journal of Psychoeducational Assessment*, 6: 130–51.

Morgenstern, J. & Longabough, R. (2000) Cognitive-behavioral treatment for alcohol dependence: A review of evidence for its hypothesized mechanisms of action. *Addiction*. 95(10): 1475–90.

Morison, S.J., Ames, E.W. & Chisholm, K. (1995) The development of children adopted from Romanian orphanages. *Merrill-Palmer Quarterly*, 41: 411–30.

Morizot, J. & Le Blanc, M. (2005) Searching for a developmental typology of personality and its relations to antisocial behaviour: A longitudinal study of a representative sample of men. *Journal of Personality*, 73(1): 139–82.

Morris, R.G. & Becker, J.T. (2004) A cognitive neuropsychology of Alzheimer's disease. In R. Morris and J. Becker (eds), *Cognitive neuropsychology of Alzheimer's disease*. New York: Oxford University Press.

Morris, R.J. & Kratochwill, T.R. (1982) *Practice of child therapy* (2nd edn). New York: Longman Higher Education.

Morrison, P.J. (2010) Accurate prevalence and uptake of testing for Huntington's disease. *The Lancet Neurology*, 9(12): 1147.

Moussavi, S. (2007) Depression, chronic diseases and decrements in health: Results from the world health surveys. *Lancet*, 370: 851–8.

Moyer, R. & Sadee, W. (2011) *Functional genetics and psychiatric disorders*. New York: Lambert Academic Publishing.

Mueser, K.T. & Jeste, D.V. (2011) *Clinical handbook of schizophrenia*. New York: Guilford Press.

Mueser, K.T. & Y Fox, L. (2002) A family intervention program for dual disorders. *Community Mental Health Journal*, 38: 253–70.

Muir, W.J. & McKechanie, A.G. (2009) Can epigenetics help in the discovery of therapeutics for psychiatric disorders, especially schizophrenia? *Expert Opinion on Drug Discovery*, 4(6): 621–7.

Mulligan, R., Van Der Linden, M. & Juillerat, A. (2003) *The clinical management of early Alzheimer's disease: A handbook*. New York: Lawrence Erlbaum.

Munoz, D.G. & Feldman, H. (2000) Causes of Alzheimer's disease. *SMAJ*, 162: 65–72.

Muris, P. (2009) Fear and courage in children: Two sides of the same coin? *Journal of Child and Family Studies*, 18(4): 486–90.

Murphy, D. & Cutting, J. (1990) Prosodic comprehension and expression in schizophrenia. *Journal of Neurology, Neurosurgery and Psychiatry*, 53: 727–30.

Murray, H.A. (1943) *Thematic apperception test*. Cambridge, MA: Harvard University Press.

Myers, I.B., McCaulley, M.H., Quenk, N.L. & Hammer, A.L. (1998) *MBTI manual: A guide to the development and use of the Myers-Briggs Type Indicator*. Mountain View, CA: CPP, Inc.

Nadig, A. & Shaw, H. (2011) Acoustic and perceptual measurement of expressive prosody in high-functioning autism: Increased pitch range and what it means to listeners. *Journal of Autism Developmental Disorder*, 42(4): 499–511.

Naidu, S., Murphy, M., Moser, H.W. & Rett, J.M. (2005) Rett syndrome – natural history in 70 cases. *American Journal of Medical Genetics*, 25(1): 61–72.

Nansel, T.R., Craig, W. & Overpeck, M.D. (2004) Health behaviour in school-aged children bullying analysis working group. Cross-national consistency in the relationship between bullying behaviours and psychosocial adjustment. *Archives of Pediatric and Adolescent Medicine*, 158: 730–6.

Navia, B.A., Jordan, B.D. & Price, R.W. (1986) The AIDS dementia complex: I, Clinical features. *Annals of Neurology*, 19: 517–24.

Navia, B.A. & Rostasy, K. (2005) The AIDS dementia complex: Clinical and basic neuroscience with implications for novel molecular therapies. *Neurotox Rex*, 8: 3–24.

Neal, M.J. (2009) *Medical pharmacology at a glance.* Oxford: Wiley-Blackwell.

Neal, M.J. (2012) *Medical pharmacology at a glance.* Oxford: Wiley-Blackwell.

Neaum, S. (2010) *Child development for early childhood studies.* Glasgow: Learning Matters Ltd.

Nelson, W.M., Finch, A.J. & Hart, K.J. (2006) *Conduct disorders: A practitioner's guide to comparative treatments.* New York: Springer.

Nestadt, G., Riddle, M.A., Grados, M.A., Greenberg, B.D., Fyer, A.J., McCracken, J.T., Rauch, S.L., Murphy, D.L., Rasmussen, S.A., Cullen B., Pinto, A., Knowles, J.A., Piacentini, J., Pauls, D.L., Bienvenu, O.J., Wang Y., Liang, K.Y., Samuels, J.F. & Roche, K.B. (2009) Obsessive-compulsive disorder: Subclassification based on co-morbidity. *Psychological Medicine*, 39(9): 1491–501.

Nestadt, G., Romanoski, A.J., Chahal, R., Merchant, A., Folstein, M.F., Gruenberg, E.M. & McHugh, P.R. (1990) An epidemiological study of histrionic personality disorder. *Psychological Medicine*, 20(2): 413–22.

Nestoros, J.N., Ban T.A. & Lehmann, H.E. (1977) Transmethylation hypothesis of schizophrenia: Methionine and nicotinic acid. *International Pharmacopsychiatry*,12(4): 215–46.

Nettle, D. (2009) Beyond nature versus culture: Cultural variation as an evolved characteristic. *Journal of the Royal Anthropological Institute,* 15(2): 223–40.

New, A.S., Hazlett, E., Buchsbaum, M.S., Goodman, M., Reynolds, D., Mitropoulous, V., et al. (2004) Blunted prefrontal cortical 18-fluorodeoxyglucose positron emission tomography response to meta-chlorophenylpiperazine in impulsive aggression. *Archives of General Psychiatry*, 59: 621–9.

NHS (2009) *IAS Factsheet – impact of alcohol on NHS.* Retrieved from http://www.ias.org.uk/resources/factsheets/nhs.pdf.

Nicoll, J.A., Roberts, G.W. & Graham, D.I. (1996) Apolipoprotein E epsilon 4 allele is associated with deposition of amyloid beta-protein following head injury. *Nature Medicine*, 1: 135–7.

Nichols, D.E. (2004) Hallucinogens. *Pharmacology & Therapeutics*, 101(2): 131–81.

Nicholls, J.G., Fuchs, P.A., Martin, A.R. & Wallace, B.G. (2001) *From neuron to brain: Cellular approach to the function of the nervous system* (4th edn). Sunderland, MA: Sinauer Associates Inc.

Nittrouer, S., Shune, S. & Lowenstein, J.H. (2011) What is the deficit in phonological processing deficits: auditory sensitivity, masking or category formation? *Journal of Experimental Child Psychology*, 108(4): 762–85.

Nocjar, C. & Panksepp, J. (2002) Chronic intermittent amphetamine pretreatment enhances future appetitive behaviour for drug, food and sexual-reward: interaction with environmental variables. *Behavioural Brain Research*, 128: 189–203.

Nose, M., Cipriani, A., Biancosino, B., Grassi, L. & Barbui, C. (2006) Efficacy of pharmacotherapy against core traits of borderline personality disorder: Meta-analysis of randomized controlled trials. *International Clinical Psychopharmacology*, 21(6): 345–53.

Noshpitz, J.D. (1991) Disturbances in early adolescent development. In S.I. Greenspan & G.H. Pollock (eds), *The course of life. Vol. IV Adolescence.* Madison, WI: International Universities Press.

Novaco, R.W. (1975) *Anger control: The development and evaluation of an experimental treatment.* Lexington, MA: Heath.

Noyes, R., Clarkson, C., Cowe, R.R., Yates, W.R. & McChesney, C.M. (1987) A family study of generalized anxiety disorder. *American Journal of Psychiatry*, 144: 1019–24.

Nunez, P.L. & Srinivasan, R. (2006) *Electric fields of the brain: The neurophysics of EEG.* New York: Oxford University Press.

Nunnally, B.K. & Krull, I.S. (2003) *Prions and mad cow disease.* New York: Marcel Dekker.

Nussinovitch, M., Gur, E., Nussinovitch, N., Kaminer, K., Volovitz, B. & Nussinovitch, U. (2012) Medically treated anorexia nervosa is associated with normal P wave parameters. *Psychiatry Research*, Mar 13.

Oates, J. & Grayson, A. (2004) *Cognitive and language development in children* (2nd edn). Oxford: Wiley-Blackwell.

Office for National Statistics (2011) *Regional trends online tables, 10: Population and migration.* Jun 8, 2011. Retrieved from Office for National statistics research website. http://www.ons.gov.uk/ons/datasets-and-tables/index.html?pageSize=50&sortBy=none&sortDirection=none&newquery=elderly+population+projections

Oldham, J.M., Skodol, A.E., Kellman, H., Hyler, H.D. & Steven, E. (1995) Comorbidity of axis I and axis II disorders. *American Journal of Psychiatry*, 152(4): 571–8.

Olds, J. & Milner, P. (1954) Positive reinforcement produced by electrical stimulation of the septal area and other regions of rat brain. *Journal of Comparative and Physiological Psychology*, 47: 419–27.

Olek, M.J., Hohol, M.J. & Weiner, H.L. (2004) Methotrexate in the treatment of multiple sclerosis. *Annals of Neurology*. 39(5): 684.

Olfson, M., Mojtabai, R., Sampson, N.A., Hwang, I., Druss, B., Wang, P.S., Wells, K.B., Pincus, H.A. & Kessler, R.C. (2009) Dropout from outpatient mental health care in the United States. *Psychiatric Services*, 60: 898–907.

Ollendick, T.H. & March, J.S. (2004) *Phobic and anxiety disorders in children and adolescents: A clinician's guide to effective psychosocial and pharmacological interventions.* New York: Oxford University Press.

Olsson, A., Nearing, K.I. & Phelps, E.A., (2007) Learning fears by observing others: The neural systems of social fear transmission. *Social Cognitive and Affective Neuroscience*, 2: 3–11.

Onslow, M. (2003) From laboratory to living room: The origins and development of the Lidcombe Program. In M. Onslow, A. Packman & E. Harrison (eds), *The Lidcombe Program of Early Stuttering Intervention: A Clinician's Guide.* Austin, TX: Pro-ed.

Ormerod, P. & Wiltshire, G. (2009) Binge drinking in the UK: A social network phenomenon. *Mind and Society: Cognitive Studies in Economics and Social Sciences*, 8(2): 135–52.

Orris, J.B. (1967) Visual monitoring performance in the subgroups of male delinquents. *Journal of Abnormal Psychology*, 74: 227–9.

O'Shea, B. & Fagan, J. (2012) Lysergic acid diethylamide. *The Irish Medical Journal*, 94(7): 217.

Osmond, H. & Smithies, J. (1952) Schizophrenia: A new approach. *Journal of Mental Science*, 98: 309–15.

Osterweis, M., Solomon, F. & Green, M. (eds) (1985) *Bereavement: Reactions, consequences and care.* Washington, DC: National Academy Press.

Ouimette, P.C., Crosby, F. & Moos, R.H. (1997) Twelve-step and cognitive-behavioral treatment for substance abuse: A comparison of treatment effectiveness. *Journal of Consulting and Clinical Psychology*, 65(2): 230–40.

Owens, D.G.C., Johnstone, E.C. & Frith, C.D. (1982) *Archives of General Psychiatry*, 39: 452–61.

Oxenstierna, G., Bergstrand, G., Bjerkenstedt, L., Sedvall, G. & Wik, G. (1984) Evidence of disturbed CSF circulation and brain atrophy in cases of schizophrenic psychosis. *British Journal of Psychiatry*, 144: 654–61.

Palkovitz, R. (1987) Consistency and stability in the family microsystem environment. In D.L. Peters & S. Kontos (eds), *Annual advances in applied developmental psychology*, Vol. 2. New York: Ablex, pp. 40–67.

Palkovitz, R. (2002) *Provisional balances: The dynamics of involved fathering and men's adult development.* Hillsdale, NJ: Erlbaum.

Palmer, F. & Barnes, L. (2001) *Values and ethics in the practice of psychotherapy and counselling.* London: Open University Press.

Papanicolaou, A.C. (2006) *The amnesias: A clinical textbook of memory disorders.* Oxford: Oxford University Press.

Pardridge, W.M. (2006) Molecular Trojan horses for blood-brain barrier drug delivery. *Current Opinion in Pharmacology*, 6: 494–500.

Parker, J. & Benson, M. (2004) Parent–adolescent relations and adolescent functioning: Self esteem, substance abuse, and delinquency. *Adolescence*, 39(155): 519–30.

Parker, J.G., Rubin, K.H., Erath, S.A., Wojslawowicz, J.C. & Buskirk, A.A. (2006) Peer relationships, child development and adjustment: A developmental psychopathology perspective. In D. Cicchetti & D.J. Cohen (eds), *Developmental Psychopathology* (2nd edn). New York: Wiley.

Partonen, T. & Lönnqvist, J. (2000) Bright light improves vitality and alleviates distress in healthy people. *Journal of Affective Disorders*, 57: 55–61.

Pates, R.M. & Gray, N. (2009) The development of a psychological theory of needle fixation. *Journal of Substance Use*, 14(5): 312–24.

Patterson, C.H. (1984) Empathy, warmth and genuineness in psychotherapy: A review of reviews. *Psychotherapy*, 21: 431–8.

Patterson, G.R. & Dishion, T.J. (1988) Multilevel family process models: Traits, interactions and relationships. In R. Hinde & J. Stevenson-Hinde (eds), *Relationships and families: Mutual influences.* Oxford: Clarendon Press, pp. 283–310.

Patton, M.Q. (2011) *Developmental Evaluation: Alying complexity concepts to enhance innovation and use.* New York: Guilford Press.

Patton, J.E., Adler, T.F., Karala, C.M. & Meece, J.L. (2011) Socialization of achievement attitudes and beliefs: Parental influences. *Child Development*, 53: 310–21.

Paul, R. (1995) *Language disorders from infancy through adolescence: Assessment and intervention.* St Louis, MO: Mosby.

Paykel, E.S. (1976) Classification of depressed patients: A cluster analysis derived grouping. *British Journal of Psychiatry*, 118: 275–88.

Paykel, E.S. (2008) Basic concepts of depression. *Dialogues in Clinical Neuroscience*, 10(3): 279–89.

Payne, J.M., Moharir, M.D., Webster, R. & North, K.N. (2010) Brain structure and function in neurofibromatosis type 1: Current concepts and future directions. *Journal of Neurology, Neurosurgery and Psychiatry*, 81(3): 304–9.

Pearlstein, T.B., Howard, M., Salisbury, A. & Zlotnick, C. (2009) Postpartum depression. *Am J Obstet Gynecol*, 200(4): 357–64.

Perez, J. & Torrubia, R. (1985) Sensation seeking and antisocial behaviour in a student sample. *Personality and Inidividual Differences*, 6(3): 401–3.

Pennebaker, J.W., Kiecolt-Glaser, J. & Glaser, R. (1988) Disclosure of traumas and immune function: Health implications for psychotherapy. *Journal of Consulting and Clinical Psychology*, 56: 239–45.

Pennington, B.F. (1995) Genetics of learning disabilities. *Journal of Child Neurology*, 1: 69–77.

Pennington, B.F. & Bishop, D.V. (2009) Relations among speech, language, and reading disorders. *Annual Review of Psychology*, 60: 283–306.

Pereira-Chioccola, V.L., Vidal, J.E. & Su, C. (2009) Toxoplasma gondii infection and cerebral toxoplasmosis in HIV infected patients. *Future Microbiology*, 4(10): 1363–79.

Perese, E. (1997) Unmet needs of persons with chronic mental illnesses: Relationship to their adaptation to community living. *Issues in Mental Health Nursing*, 18(1): 18–34.

Perris, C. & McGorry, P.D. (eds) (1998) *Cognitive psychotherapy of psychotic and personality disorders.* Chichester: John Wiley.

Perry, J.L. & Carroll, M.E. (2008) The role of impulsive behaviour in drug abuse. *Psychopharmacology*, 200(1): 1–26.

Pervin, L.A. & Cervone, D. (2010) *Personality: theory and research.* London: John Wiley & Sons.

Peterfreund, E. (1983) *The process of psychoanalytic therapy: models and strategies.* London: Routledge.

Peters, D. (2001) *Understanding the placebo effect in complementary medicine. Theory, practice and research.* London: Churchill Livingstone.

Petersen, T. & McBride, A. (2001) *Working with substance misusers: A guide to theory and practice.* London: Routledge.

Petrill, S.A., Hart, S.A., Harlaar, N.. Logan, J., Justice, L.M.. Schatschneider, C., Thompson, L., DeThorne, L.S. Deter-Deckard, K. & Cutting, L. (2010) Genetic and environmental influences on the growth of early reading skills. *Journal of Child Psychology and Psychiatry*, 51(6): 660–7.

Pfiffner, L.M., Mikami, A.Y., Huang-Pollack, C., Easterlin, B., Zalecki, C. & McBurnett, K. (2007) A randomized controlled trial of integrated home-school behavioural treatment for ADHD, predominatly inattentive type. *Journal for the American Academy of Child and Adolescent Psychiatry*, 46: 1041–50.

Pfohl, B. & Blum, N. (1991) Obsessive-compulsive personality disorders: A review of available data and recommendations for DSM-IV. *Journal of Personality Disorders*, 5, 363–75.

Phares, V. & Compas, B.E. (1992) The role of fathers in child and adolescent psychopathology: Make room for daddy. *Psychological Bulletin*, 111: 387–412.

Pharoah, F., Mari, J., Rathbone, J. & Wong, W. (2006) Family intervention for schizophrenia. *Cochrane Database syst rev.* 18(4): CD00008.

Phelan, J.C., Bromet, E.J. & Link, B.G. (1988) Psychiatric illness and family stigma. *Schizophrenia Bulletin*, 24: 115–26.

Piaget, J. & Inhelder, B. (1972) *The psychology of the child*. New York: Basic.

Pickens, R.W., Svikis, D.S., McGue, M., Lykken, D.T., Heston, L.L. & Clayton, P.J. (1991) Heterogeneity in the inheritance of alcoholism. A study of male and female twins. *Archives of General Psychiatry*, 48(1): 19–28.

Pike, K.M., Hilbert, A., Wilfley, D.E., Fairburn, C.G., Dohm, F.A., Walsh, B.T. & Striegel-Moore, R. (2008) Toward an understanding of risk factors for anorexia nervosa: A case-control study. *Psychological Medicine*, 38: 1443–53.

Piotrkowski, C. & Telesco, G. (2011) Officers in crisis: New York City police officers who assisted the families of victims of the World Trade Center terrorist attack. *Journal of Police Negotiations*, 11(1): 40–56.

Pjrek, E., Winkler, D., Staastny, J., Praschak-Rieder, N., Willeit, M., & Kasper, S. (2007). Escitalopram in seasonal affective disorder: results of an open trial. *Pharmacopsychiatry* 40(1): 20–4.

Plakun, E.M. (1987) Distinguishing narcissistic and borderline personality disorders using DSM-III criteria. *Comprehensive Psychiatry*, 28: 437–43.

Plakun, E.M. (1990) *New perspectives on narcissism*. Washington, DC: American Psychiatric Press.

Plant, M. & Plant, M. (2006) *Binge Britain: Alcohol and the national response*. Oxford: Oxford University Press.

Platt, J.J. (2000) *Cocaine addiction: Theory, research and treatment*. New York: Harvard University Press.

Plomin, R., DeFries, J.C. & Loehlin, J.C. (1977) Genotype – environment interaction and correlation in the analysis of human behvior. *Psychological Bulletin*, 84: 309–22.

Plomin, Y. & Kovas, R. (2005) Generalist genes and learning disabilities. *Psychological Bulletin*, 131: 592–617.

Poland, G.A. & Jacobson, R.M. (2011) The age-old struggle against the antivaccinationists. *New England Journal of Medicine*, 364: 97–9.

Pollak, J.M. (1979) Correlates of death anxiety: A review of empirical studies. *Omega*, 10: 97–121.

Ponnudurai, R. & Jayakar, J. (2010) Mode of transmission of schizophrenia. *Asian Journal of Psychiatry*, 3(2): 67–72.

Porter, R. (2002) *Madness: A brief history*. Oxford: Oxford University Press.

Post, R.M. (1992) Transduction of psychosocial stress into the neurobiology of recurrent affective disorder. *American Journal of Psychiatry*, 149(8): 999–1010.

Post, R.M., Fink, E., Carpenter, W.T., & Goodwin, F.K. (1975) Cerebrospinal fluid amine metabolites in acute schizophrenia. *Archives of General Psychiatry*, 32: 1063–9.

Powers, W.T. (2008) *Living control systems ILL: The fact of control*. New Canaan, CT: Benchmark Publications.

Powis, D.A. & Bunn, S.J. (eds) (1995) *Neurotransmitter release and its modulation: Biochemical mechanisms, physiological function and clinical relevance*. Cambridge: Cambridge University Press.

Prechtl, H.F.R. (1984) *Continuity of neural functions from pre-natal to postnatal life. Clinics in Developmental Medicine*, Vol. 94. Oxford: Blackwell Scientific Publications.

Pressman, J.D. (2002). *Last resort: Psychosurgery and the limits of medicine*. London: Cambridge University Press.

Prien, R.F., Caffrey, E.M. & Klett, C.J. (1973) Prophylactic efficacy of lithium carbonate in manic depressive illness: Report of the Veterans Administration and National Institute of Mental Health Collaborative Study Group. *Archives of General Psychiatry*, 28: 337–41.

Pritchard, D.J. & Korf, B.R (2007) *Medical genetics at a glance*. New York: Wiley & Sons.

Rabin, B.S. (1999) *Stress, immune function and health: The connection*. New York: Wiley-Liss & Sons.

Rachman, S. (1976) The passing of the two-stage theory of fear and avoidance: Fresh possibilities. *Behavior Research and Therapy*, 14: 125–34.

Raine, A. (1989) Evoked potential models of psychopathy: A critical evaluation. *Journal of Psychophysiology*, 3(1): 29–34.

Raine, A. (2008) Neural foundations to moral reasoning and antisocial behaviour. *Social, Cognitive and Affective Neuroscience*, 1: 203–13.

Rait, D.S. & Glick, I. D. (2008) Schizophrenia: A family psychoeducational approach. In C.B. Taylor, *How to practice evidence-based psychiatry: Basic principles and case studies*. Arlington, VA: American Psychiatric Publishing.

Ramklint, M., Von Knorring, A.L., Von Knorring, L. & Ekselius, L. (2003) Child and adolescent psychiatric disorders predicting adult personality disorder: A follow up study. *Nord Journal of Psychiatry*, 57(1): 23–8.

Rantakallio, P., Jones, P., Moring, J. & Von Wendt, L. (1997) Association between central nervous system infections during childhood and adult onset schizophrenia and other psychoses: A 28 year follow-up. *International Journal of Epidemiology*, 4: 837–43.

Rapaka, R.S. & Sadee, W. (2008) *Drug addiction: From basic research to therapy*. New York: Springer.

Rapee, R.M. (1997). Psychological factors influencing the affective response to biological challenge procedures in panic disorder. *Journal of Anxiety Disorders*, 9: 59–74.

Rasmussen, N. (2009) *On speed: The many lives of amphetamine*. New York: New York University Press.

Rassool, G.H. (2008) Drugs and behaviour. A sourcebook for the helping professionals. *Journal of Advanced Nursing*, 18(1): 159.

Rath, P.K. (2001) *Personaltiy: Issues in assessment and the projective inventory approach*. New Delhi: Concept.

Ray, S.L. & Vanstone, M. (2009) The impact of PTSD on veterans'family relationships: An interpretative phenomenological inquiry. *International Journal of Nursing Studies*, 46(6): 838–47.

Read, J., Bentall, R. & Mosher, L. (2004) *Models of madness: Psychological, social and biological approaches to schizophrenia*. New York: Brunner-Routledge.

Read, J., Mosher, L. & Bentall, R. (2007) *Models of madness*. New York: Brunner-Routledge.

Rehm, J., Gmel, G., Sempos, C.T. & Trevisan, M. (2003) Alcohol-related morbidity and mortality. *Alcohol Research and Health*, 27(1): 39–51.

Rehm, J., Room, R. & Monterior, M., et al. (2004) Alcohol. In M. Ezzati, A.D. Lopez, A. Rodgers & C.J.L. Murray (eds) *Comparative quantification of health risks: Global and regional burden of disease due to selected major risk factors*, Geneva: World Health Organization.

Rehm, L.P. & Rokke, P. (1988) Self management therapies. In K.S. Dobson (ed.), *Handbook of cognitive-behaivoral therapies*. New York: Guilford Press.

Reich, J. (2000) The relationship of social phobia to avoidant personality disorder: A proposal to reclassify avoidant personality disorder based on clinical empirical findings. *European Psychiatry*, 15(3): 151–9.

Reich, J., Yates, W. & Nduaguba, M. (1989) Prevalence of DSM-III personality disorders in the community. *Social Psychiatry and Psychiatric Epidemiology*, 24: 12–16.

Reigier, D.A., Narrow, W.E., Kuhl, E.A. & Kupfer, D.J. (2010) The conceptual development of DSM-V. *American Journal of Psychiatry*, 166: 645–55.

Reisberg, B. (1983) *A guide to Alzheimer's disease*. London: Free Press.

Ressler, K.J. & Nemeroff, C.B. (2000) Role of serotonergic and noradrenergic systems in the pathophysiology of depression and anxiety disorders. *Depression and Anxiety*, 12(S1): 2–19.

Rett, A. (1966) On an unusual brain atrophy syndrome in hyperammonemia in childhood. *Wiener Medizinischer Wochenschrift*, 116(37): 723–6.

Ribble, M.A. (1944) Infantile experience in relation to personality development. In J. McV. Hunt (ed.), *Personality and the behaviour disorders*. New York: Ronald Press, pp. 621–51.

Ricciardi, M., Valsavoia, R., Russo, M., Ferraro, L., Alloro, D., Messina, N., Dolce, A. & Barbera, D. (2011) The effects of different levels of exposure on persistence of stress disorders in rescue volunteers: The case of the ATR 72 air disaster in Palermo. *Giorn Ital Psicopat*, 17: 303–8.

Richter, J. & Brandstrom, S. (2009) Personality disorder diagnosis by means of the temperament and character inventory. *Comprehensive Psychiatry*, 50(4): 347–52.

Ricks, D.M. & Wing, L. (1975) Language, communication and the use of symbols in normal and autistic children. *Journal of Autism and Developmental Disorders*, 5(3): 191–221.

Rinne, T., de Kloet, E.R., Wouters, L., Goekoop, J.G., DeRijk, R.H. & Van den Brink, W. (2002) Hyperresponsiveness of hypothalamic-pituitary adrenal axis to combined dexamethasone/corticotrophin-releasing hormone challenge in female borderline personality disorder subjects with a history of sustained childhood abuse. *Biological Psychiatry*, 52(11): 1102–12.

Ritsner, M.S. (ed.) (2009) *The handbook of neuropsychiatric biomarkers, endophenotypes and genes.* Volume II: *Neuroanatomical and neuroimaging endophenotypes and biomarkers.* London: Springer.

Rivet, T.T. & Matson, J.L. (2010) Gender differences in core symptomatology in autism spectrum disorders across the lifespan. *Journal of Developmental and Physical Disabilities*, 23: 399–420.

Roberts, E. (1977) *The GABA system and schizophrenia. Neuroregulators and psychiatric disorders.* Oxford: Oxford University Press.

Robertson, M. & Walter, G. (2007) An overview of psychiatric ethics I: professional ethics and psychiatry. *Australasian Psychiatry*, 15(4): 201–6.

Robins, E. & Guze, S.B. (1972) Establishment of diagnostic validity in psychiatric illness: its application to schizophrenia. *American Journal of Psychiatry*, 38: 381–9.

Robins, L. (1966) *Defiant children grown up.* Baltimore, MD: Williams & Wilkins.

Robins, L.N. (1991) Conduct disorder. *Journal of Child Psychology and Psychiatry*, 32, 193–212.

Robins, L.N., Locke, B.Z. & Regier, D.A. (1991) An overview of psychiatric disorders in America. In L.N. Robins & D.A. Regier (eds), *Psychiatric disorders in America: The epidemiologic catchment area study.* New York: Free Press, pp. 328–66.

Robinson, D.J. (1999) *Field guide to personality disorders.* Port Huron, MI: Rapid Psychler Press.

Robinson, P.H. (2009) *Severe and enduring eating disorder.* London: John Wiley & Sons.

Robinson, T.E. & Berridge, T.E. (2002) Addiction. *Annual Review of Psychology*, 54: 25–53.

Rodgers, B. (1997) Pathways between parental divorce and adult depression. *Journal of Child Psychology and Psychiatry*, 35(7): 1289–308.

Rodin, M. & Price, J. (1995) Overcoming stigma. Credit for self-improvement or discredit for needing to improvement. *Personality and Social Psychology Bulletin*, 21: 172–81.

Roemer, L. & Orsillo, S.M. (2007) An open trial of an acceptance-based behaviour therapy for generalized anxiety disorder. *Behavior Therapy*, 38: 72–85.

Rogers, C.R. (1961) *On becoming a person: A therapist's view of psychotherapy.* New York: Houghton Mifflin.

Rogers, C.R. (1980) *A way of being.* New York: Houghton Mifflin.

Rolf, J., Masten, A., Cicchetti, D., Neuchterlein, K. & Weintraub, S. (1990) *Risk and protective factors in the development of psychopathology.* New York: Cambridge University Press.

Rolfes, S.R. & Debruyne, L.K. (1990) *Life span nutrition: Conception thorugh life.* St. Paul, MN: West Publishing Co.

Roll, J.M., Rawson, R.A., Ling, W. & Shoptaw, S. (eds) (2009) *Methamphetamine addiction: From basic science to treatment.* New York: Guilford Press.

Romero, E., Luengo, M.A. & Sobral, J. (2001) Personality and antisocial behaviour: Study of temperamental dimensions. *Personality and Individual Differences*, 31: 329–48.

Ronningstam, E. & Gunderson, J.G. (1991) Differentiating borderline personality disorder from narcissistic personality disorder. *Journal of Personality Disorders*, 5(3): 225–32.

Ronningstam, E.F. (2001) *Disorders of Narcissism: Diagnostic, clinical and empirical implications.* Northvale, NJ: Jason Aronson.

Rorschach, H. (1942) *Psychodiagnostic: Methodik und Ergebnisse eines wahrnehmungs-diagnostichen Experiments* (2nd edn). (P. Lemkau & B. Kronenberg, trans.) Berne and Berlin: Huber, 1932; republished New York: Grune & Stratton.

Rosa-Neto, P. & Leuzy, A. (2008) Molecular imaging of Alzheimer's disease using PET. *International Psychogeriatrics*, 20: 1–8.

Rosen, B., Katzoff, A., Carrillo, C. & Klein, D.F. (1976) Clinical effectiveness of short vs long psychiatric hopsitalizaiton. I. Inpatient results. *Archives of General Psychiatry*, 33: 1316–22.

Rosen, J.W. & Burchard, S.N. (1990) Community activities and social support networks: A social comparison of adults with and adults without mental retardation. *Education and Training in Mental Retardation*, 25: 193–204.

Rosenbaum, J.J. & Covino, J.M. (2005) Stress and resilience: Implications for depression and anxiety. *Medscape Psychiatry and Mental Health*, 10.

Rosenhan, D.L. (1973) On being sane in insane places. *Science*, 179: 250–8.

Rosenheck, R.A. (2012) Introduction to the special section: Toward social inclusion. *Psychiatric Services*, 63(5): 425–6.

Rosenthal, D. (1971) *Genetics of psychopathology*. New York: McGraw-Hill.

Rosenthal, S.H. & Klerman, G.L. (1967) Content and consistency in the endogenous depressive pattern. *British Journal of Psychiatry*, 112: 471–84.

Rosqvist, J. (2005) *Exposure treatments for anxiety disorders: A practitioner's guide to concepts, methods and evidence-based practice*. New York: Routledge.

Ross, E.A., Watson, M. & Goldberger, B. (2011) Bath salts intoxication. *New England Journal of Medicine*, 365: 967–8.

Ross, R.G. & Compagnon, N. (2001) Diagnosis and treatment of psychiatric disorders in children with a schizophrenic parent. *Schizophrenia Research*, 50: 123–31.

Roth, R.T. & Lerner, J. (1974) Sex-based discrimination in the mental institutionalization of women. *California Law Review*, 62(3): 789–815.

Rothbart, M.K. (1981) Measurement of temperament in infancy. *Child Development*, 52: 569–78.

Rotter, J.B. (1972) *Clinical psychology*. New York: Prentice-Hall.

Rourke, B.P., Fisk, J.L. & Strang, J.D. (1986) *Neuropsychologial assessment of children: A treatment-oriented approach*. New York: Guilford Press.

Roussotte, F., Soderberg, L. & Sowell, E. (2010) Structural, metabolic and functional brain abnormalities as a result of prenatal exposure to drugs of abuse: Evidence from neuroimaging. *Neuropsychological Review*, 20(4): 376–97.

Roy, M.A., Neale, M.C., Pedersen, N.L., Mathe, A.A. & Kendler, K.S. (1995) A twin study of generalized anxiety disorder and major depression. *Psychological Medicine*, 25: 1037–40.

Roy-Byrne, P.P., Davidson, K.W., Kessler, R.C., Asmundson, G.J., Goodwin, R.D., Kubzansky, L., Lydiard, R.B., Massie, M.J., Katon, W., Laden, S.K. & Stein, M.B. (2008) Anxiety disorders and comorbid medical illness. *General Hospital Psychiatry*, 30(3): 208–25.

Roysamb, E., Kendler, K.S., Tambs, K., Orstavik, R.E., Neale, M.C., Aggen, S.H., Torgersen, S. & Reichborn-Kjennerud, T. (2010) The joint structure of DSM-IV axis I and Axis II disorders. *Journal of Abnormal Psychology*, 120(1): 198–209.

Rubin, J., Provenzano, F. & Luria, Z. (1974) The eye of the beholder: Parents' views on sex of newborns. *American Journal of Orthopsychiatry*, 44: 512–19.

Rudgley, R. (1995) *Essential substances: A cultural history of intoxicants in society*. New York: Kodansha America, Inc.

Russ, E., Lonne, B. & Darlington, Y. (2009) Using resilience to reconceptualise child protection workforce capacity. *Australian Social Work: The Journal of the Association of social Workers*, 62(3): 324–38.

Russell, G.F.M. (1979) Bulimia nervosa: An ominous variant of anorexia nervosa. *Psychological Medicine*, 9: 429–48.

Rutter, D.R. (1985) Language in schizophrenia: The structure of monologues and conversations. *British Journal of Psychiatry*, 146: 399–404.

Rutter, M. (1987) Psychosocial resilience and protective mechanisms. *American Journal of Orthopsychiatry*, 51: 316–31.

Rutter, M. (1990) Nature, nurture, and psychopathology: A new look at an old topic. *Developmental Psychopathology*, 3: 125–36.

Rutter, M. (1994) Debate and argument: There are connections between brain and mind and it is important that Rett syndrome be classified somewhere. *Journal of Child Psychology and Psychiatry*, 35, 379–81.

Rutter, M. (2011) Response: Growing consensus on classification needs. *Journal of Child Psychology and Psychiatry*, 52(6): 673–5.

Rutter, M., Moffitt, T.E. & Caspi, A. (2006) Gene–enviornment interplay and psychopathology: multiple varieties but real effects. *Journal of Child Psychology and Psychiatry*, 47: 226–61.

Rutterford, N. (2011) *Predictors of long term outcome following traumatic brain injury*. New York: LAP LAMBERT Academic Publishing.

Rutther, M. (1990) Psychosocial resilience and protective mechanisms. In J. Rolf, A.S. Masten, D. Cicchetti, K.H. Nuechterlein & S. Weintraub (eds), *Risk and protective factors in the development of psychopathology*. Cambridge, UK: Cambridge University Press.

Ryder, A.G., Schuller, D.R. & Bagby, R.M. (2006) Depressive personality disorder and dysthymia: Evaluating symptom and syndrome overlap. *Journal of Affective Disorders*, 91: 217–27.

Sabo, B.M. (2006) Adverse psychosocial consequences: Compassion fatigue, burnout and vicarious traumatisation: Are nurses who provide palliative and haematological cancer care vulnerable? *Indian Journal of Palliative Care*, 14(1): 23–9.

Sachdev, P. (2003) Neuropsychiatry. *American Journal of Psychiatry*, 160(5): 1014–15.

Sanchez, M.M., Ladd, C.O. & Plotsky, P.M. (2001) Early adverse experience as a developmental risk factor for later psychophathology: Evidence from rodent and primate models. *Development & Psychopathology*, 13: 419–49.

Sandler, J., Holder, A., Dare, C. & Dreher, A.U. (1997) *Freud's models of the mind: An introduction*. London: H. Karnac.

Sandtrock, J. (1994) *Child development* (6th edn). Madison, WI: Brown & Benchmark.

Sanislow, C.A., Little, T.D., Ansell, E.B., Grilo, C.M., Daversa, M., Markowitz, J.C., Pinto, A., Shea, M.T., Yen, S., Skodol, A.E., Morey, L.C., Gunderson, J.G., Zanarini, M.C. and McGlashan, T.H. (2009) Ten year stability and latent structure of DSM-IV schizotypal, borderline, avoidant, and obsessive-compulsive disorders. *Journal of Abnormal Psychology*, 118: 507–19.

Santrock, J.W. & Warshak, R.A. (1979) Father custody and social development in boys and girls. *Journal of Social Issues*, 35: 112–25.

Sarafino, E. (1998) *Health Psychology: Biopsychosocial interactions*. New York: John Wiley & Sons.

Sarbin, T.R. & Mancuso, J.C. (1980) *Schizophrenia: Medical Diagnosis or Moral Verdict?* New York: Elsevier

Sato, T., Sakado, K., Uehara, T., Sato, K., Nishioka, K. & Kasahara, Y. (1997) Personality disorder diagnoses using DSM-III-R in a Japanese clinical sample with major depression. *Acta Psychiatrica Scandinavica*, 95(5): 451–3.

Schachter, S. (1966) The interaction of cognitive and physiological determinants of emotional state. In L. Berkowitz (ed.), *Advances in experimental social psychology*, Vol. 1. New York: Academic Press.

Schaefer, C.E. (ed.) (1993) *The therapeutic powers of play*. Northvale, NJ: Jason Aronson.

Schaffer, M., Jeglic, E.L. & Stanley, B. (2008) The relationship between suicidal behaviour, ideation and binge drinking among college students. *Archives of Suicide Research*, 12(2): 124–32.

Schaie, K.W., Willis, S.L. & Caskie, G.I.L. (2004) The Seattle longitudinal study: relationship between personality and cognition. *Neuropsychol Dev Cogn B. Aging Neuropsychol Cogn.*, 11(2-3): 304–24.

Schapira, A.H. (2010) Complex I: inhibitors, inhibition and neurodegeneration. *Experimental Neurology*, 224(2): 331–5.

Schatzberg, A.F., Cole, J.O. & DeBattista, C. (2010) *Manual of clinical psychopharmacology*. Washington, DC: American Psychiatric Publishing Inc.

Scheerenberger, R.C. (1983) *A history of mental retardation*. New York: P.H. Brookes Pub.

Scheff, T.J. (2009) *Being mentally ill: A sociological theory* (3rd edn). New Brunswick, NJ: Rutgers.

Scheier, M.F., Matthews, K.A., Owens, J.F., Magovern, G.J., Lefebvre, R.C., Abbott, R.A. & Carver, C.S. (1989) Dispositional optimism and recovery from coronary artery bypass surgery: The beneficial effects on physical and psychological well–being. *Journal of Personality and Social Psychology*, 57: 1024–40.

Schellenberg, G.D., Bird, T.D., Wijsman, E.M., Orr, H.T., Anderson, L., Nemens, E., White, J.A., Bonnycastle, L., Weber, J.L. and Alonso, M.E. (1992) Genetic linkage evidence for a familial Alzheimer's disease locus on chromosome 14. *Science*. 258(5082): 668–71.

Schildkraut, J.J. (1965) The catecholamine hypothesis of affective disorder: A review of supporting evidence. *American Journal of Psychiatry*, 122: 509–22.

Schminke, M. (2010) *Managerial ethics: Managing the psychology of morality*. New York: Routledge.

Schneider, K.J., Bugental, J.F.T. & Pierson, J.F. (2001) *The handbook of humanistic psychology: Leading edges in theory, research, and practice*. London: Sage.

Schneier, F.R., Spitzer, R.L., Gibbon, M., Fyer, A.J. & Liebowitz, M.R. (1991) The relationship of social phobia subtypes and avoidant personality disorder. *Comprehensive Psychiatry*, 32: 496–502.

Scholey, A.B., Owen, L., Gates, J., Rodgers, J., Buchanan, T., Ling J., Heffernan, T., Swan, P., Stough, C. & Parrott, A.C. (2011) Is MDMA present in hair samples consistent with reported ecstasy use? *Addiction*, 106(7): 1369–70.

Schopler, E. & Mesibov, E. (1984) *The effects of autism on the family.* New York: Plenum Press.

Schug, R.A., Raine, A. & Wilcox, R.R. (2007) Psychophysiological and behavioural characteristics of individuals with both antisocial personality disorder and schizophrenia-spectrum personality disorder. *British Journal of Psychiatry,* 191: 408–14.

Schur, E.A., Noonan, C., Buchwald, D., Goldberg, J. & Afari, N. (2009) A twin study of depression and migraine: Evidence for a shared genetic vulnerability. *Headache,* 49(10): 1493–502.

Schwartz, G.E., Fair, P.L., Salt, P., Mandel, M.R. & Klerman, G.L. (1976) Facial expression and imagery in depression: An electromyographic study. *Psychosomatic Medicine,* 38(5): 337–47.

Scott, J.E. & Dixon, L.B. (1995) Assertive community treatment and case management for schizophrenia. *Schizophrenia Bulletin,* 21: 657–68.

Scott, S., Spender, Q., Doolan, M., Jacobs, B. & Aspland, H. (2001) Multicentre controlled trail of parenting groups for child antisocial behaviour in clinical practice. *British Medical Journal,* 323(28): 1–5.

Scott-Jones, D. (1984) Family influences on cognitive development and school achievement. In E.W. Gordon (ed.), *Review of research in education,* Vol. 11. Washington, DC: American Educational Research Association, pp. 259–304.

Scourfield, A., Jackson, A. & Nelson, M. (2009) Spectrum of neurological disease in patients with discordant HIV-1 RNA levels in plasma and cerebrospinal fluid. *Journal of Infection,* 60(3): 251–2.

Scourfield, A., Waters, L. & Nelson, M. (2010) Spectrum of neurological disease in patients with discordant HIV-1 RNA levels in plasma and cerebrospinal fluid. *Journal of Infection* 60(3): 251–2.

Seaman, J., Schillerstrom, J., Carroll, D. & Brown, T.M. (2006) Impaired oxidative metabolism precipitates delirium: A study of 101 ICU patients. *Psychosomatics,* 47: 56–61.

Seamans, J.K. & Durstewitz, D. (2006) Beyond bistability: Biophysics and temporal dynamics of working memory. *Neuroscience,* 139(1): 119–33.

Seifer, R. (2000) Temperament and goodness of fit. Implications for developmental psychopathology. In A.J. Sameroff, M. Lewis & L.M. Miller (eds), *Handbook of developmental psychopathology* (2nd edn). New York: Kluwer Academic.

Seligman, M.E.P. (1975) *Helplessness.* San Francisco: Freeman.

Selikowitz, M. (2009) *ADHD.* Oxford: Oxford University Press.

Selkoe, D.J. (1994) Alzheimer's disease: A central role for amyloid. *Journal of Neuropathology and Experimental Neurology,* 53: 438–47.

Selye, H. (1955) *The stress of life.* New York: McGraw-Hill.

Selye, H. (1976) The stress of life (rev. edn). New York: McGraw-Hill.

Senn, M. (1975) Insights on the child development movement in the United States. *Monographs of the society for Research in Child Development* 40, 304 (Serial no. 161).

Sesardic, N. (2005) *Making sense of heritability.* Cambridge: Cambridge University Press.

Shaffer, J.T. (2011) A comparison of firefighters and police officers: The influence of gender and relationship status. *Adultspan Journal,* 9(1): 36–49.

Shagass, C., Roemer, R.A., Straumanis, J.J. & Josiassen, R.C. (1985) Combinations of evoked potential amplitude measurements in relation to psychiatric diagnosis. *Biological Psychiatry,* 20(7): 701–22.

Shalev, A., Peri, T., Canetti, L. & Schreiber, S. (1996) Predictors of PTSD in injured trauma survivors: A prospective study. *American Journal of Psychiatry,* 153: 219–25.

Shapiro, F. (2001) *Eye movement desensitization and reprocessing: Basic principles, protocols and procedures.* New York: Guilford Press.

Sharkey, B. (2006) *Fitness and health,* (6th edn). Champaign, IL: Human Kinetics.

Shaw, M. & Riley, D. (1989) *Parental supervision and juvenile delinquency. Home Office Research study 83.* London: HMSO.

Shaywitz, B., Fletcher, J., Holahan, J. & Saywitz, S. (1992) Discrepancy compared to low achievement definitions of reading disability: Results from the Connecticut Longitudinal Study. *Journal of Learning Disability,* 25: 639–48.

Shaywitz, S. (1998) Current concepts: dyslexia. *New England Journal of Medicine*, 338: 307–12.

Shaywitz, S., Shaywitz, B., Fulbright, R., Skudlarski, P., Mencl, W. & Constable, R. (1997) Functional disruption in the organization of the brain for reading in dyslexia. *Proceedings of the National Academy of Science of the United States of America*, 95: 2636–41.

Shedler, J., Beck, A., Fonagy, P., Gabbard, G.O., Gunderson, J., Kernberg, O., Michels, R. & Westen, D. (2010) Personality disorders in DSM-5. *American Journal of Psychiatry*, 167: 1026–8.

Shedler, J. & Westen, D. (2004) Dimensions of personality pathology: An alternative to the five factor model. *American Journal of Psychiatry*, 161: 1743–54.

Shelton, A.L., Christoff, K., Burrows, J.J., Pelisari, K.B. & Gabrieli, J.D.E. (2001) Brain activation during mental rotation: Individual differences. *Society for Neuroscience Abstracts*, 27: 456.

Shen, G.H.C., Alloy, L.B., Abramson, L.Y. & Grandin, L.G. (2008) Social rhythm regularity and the onset of affective episodes in bipolar spectrum individuals. *Bipolar Disorders*, 10: 520–9.

Shenton, M.E., Kikinis, R., Jolesz, F.A., Pollak, S.D., LeMay, M., Wible, C.G., Hokama, H., Martin, J., Metcalf, D. Coleman, M. & McCarley, M. (1992) Left temporal abnormalities in schizophrenia and thought disorder: A quantitative MRI study. *New England Journal of Medicine*, 327: 604–12.

Sher, K.J. (1994) Personality and disinhibitory psychopathology: Alcoholism and antisocial personality disorder. *Journal of Abnormal Psychology*, 103: 92–102.

Shimizu, M., Seery, M.D., Weisbuch, M. & Lupien, S.P. (2011) Trait social anxiety and physiological activation: Cardiovascular threat during social interaction. *Personality and Social Psychology Bulletin*, 37: 94–106.

Shneidman, R. (1994) Clues to suicide reconsidered. *Suicide and Life-Threatening Behavior*, 24: 395–7.

Short, A.B. & Schopler, E. (1988) Factors relating to age of onset in autism. *Journal of Autism and Developmental Disorders*, 18: 207–16.

Siebert, A. (1996) *The survivor personality*. New York: Berkeley/Perigee Books.

Silveira, J.M. & Seeman, M.V. (1995) Shared psychotic disorder: A critical review of the literature. *Canadian Journal of Psychiatry*, 40(7): 389–95.

Silver, A.A. & Hagin, R.A. (2002) *Disorders of learning in childhood* (2nd edn). New York: Wiley.

Silver, L.B. (1989) Learning disabilities. *Journal of the American Academy of Child and Adolescent Psychiatry*, 28(3): 309–13.

Silverman, J. (1968). Perceptual control of stimulus intensity in paranoid and non-paranoid schizophrenia. *Journal of Nervous and Mental Diseases*, 139: 545–9.

Simpson, C. (1997) *Methadone*. New York: Rosen Publishing Group.

Singleton, N., Bumpstead, R., O'Brien, M., Lee, A. & Meltzer, H. (2001) *Psychiatric morbidity among adults living in private households, 2000*. Her Majesty's Stationery Office (HMSO): London.

Sinha, R. (2008) Chronic stress, drug use and vulnerability to addiction. *Annals of the New York Academy of Sciences*, 1141: 105–30.

Skinner, M.D. & Aubin, H.J. (2010) Craving's place in addiction theory: Contributions of the major models. *Neuroscience and Biobehavioral Reviews*, 34: 606–23.

Sklar, L.S. & Anisman, H. (1981).Stress and cancer. *Psychological Bulletin*, 89: 369–406.

Skodol, A.E., Gunderson, J.G., McGlashan, T.H., Dyck, I.R., Stout, R.L., Bender, D.S., Grilo, C.M., Shea, M.T., Zanarini, M.C., Morey, L.C., Sanislow, C.A. & Oldham, J.M. (2002) Functional impairment in patients with schizotypal, borderline, avoidant or obsessive-compulsive personality disorder. *American Journal of Psychiatry*, 159(2): 276–83.

Skodol, A.E., Gunderson, J.G., Pfohl, B., Widiger, T.A., Livesley, W.J. & Siever, L.J. (2002) The borderline diagnosis I: psychopathology, comorbidity, and personality structure. *Biological Psychiatry*, 51: 936–50.

Skrundz, M., Bolten, M., Nast, I., Hellhammer, D.H. & Meinlschmidt, G. (2011) Plasma oxytocin concentration during pregnancy is associated with development of postpartum depression. *Neuropsychopharmacology*, 36(9): 1886–93.

Slavny, P.R. & McHugh, P.R. (1975) The hysterical personality. A controlled study. *Archives of General Psychiatry*, 30(3): 325–9.

Sloan, D.M., Bradley, M.M., Dimoulas, E. & Lang, P.J. (2002) Looking at facial expressions: Dysphoria and facial EMG. *Biological Psychology*, 60: 79–90.

Smith, P.K., Cowie, H. & Blades, M. (2001) *Understanding children's development*. London: Blackwell

Smoller, J.W. & Finn, C.T. (2003) Family, twin and adoption studies of bipolar disorder. *American Journal of Medical Genetics*, Seminars in Medical Genetics 123: 48–58.

Smoller, J.W., Sheidley, B.R. & Tsuang, M.T. (2008) *Psychiatric genetics: Applications in clinical practice*. New York: American Psychiatric Publishing.

Smythies, J.R. (1963) *Schizophrenia, chemistry, metabolism and treatment*. Springfield: Thomas.

Snell, R.S. (2009) *Clinical neuroanatomy*, (7th edn). Baltimore, MD: Wolters Kluwer.

Snyder, C.R (2000) *Handbook of hope: Theory, measures and applications*. San Diego, CA: Academic Press.

Snyder, S.H. (1973) Amphetamine psychosis: A 'model' schizophrenia mediated by catecholamines. *American Journal of Psychiatry*, 130: 61–7.

Soloff, P.H., Meltzer, C.C., Becker, C., Greer, P.J., Kelly, T.M. & Constantine, D. (2003) Impulsivity and prefrontal hypometabolism in borderline personality disorder. *Psychiatry Research*, 123: 153–63.

Soloff, P.H., Meltzer, C.C., Greer, P.J., Constantine, D. & Kelly, T.M. (2000) A fenfluramine activated FDG-PET study of borderline personality disorder. *Biological Psychiatry*, 47: 540–7.

Solowij, N. & Battisti, R. (2008) The chronic effects of cannabis on memory in humans: A review. *Current Drug Abuse Reviews*, 1: 81–98.

Song, S.Y. & Swearer, S.M. (2002) An ecological analysis of school bullying: Understanding school climate. Paper presented at the annual meeting of the National Association of School Psychologists., Chicago.

Souza, V.B., Muir, W. J., Walker, M.T., Glabus, M.F., Roxborough, H.M, Sharp, C.W., Duncan, J.R. & Blackwood, D.H. (1995) Auditory P300 event-related potentials and neuropsychological performance in schizophrenia and bipolar affective disorder. *Biological Psychiatry*, 37: 300–10.

Speilberger, C. (1979) Preliminary manual for the State-Trait Personality Inventory (STPI). Unpublished manuscript, University of South Florida, Tampa.

Spielberger, C. (1996) State-trait anger expression inventory: Professional manual. Odessa, FL: Psychological Assessment Resources.

Sperry, L. (2003) *Handbook of diagnosis and treatment of DSM-IV-TR. Personality disorders* (2nd edn). Philadelphia, PA: Brunner-Routledge.

Spohn, H.E. & Paterson, T. (1979) Recent studies of psychophysiology in schizophrenia. *Schizophrenia Bulletin*, 5: 581–611.

Sroufe, L.A. (1985) Attachment classification from the perspective of infant caregiver relationships and infant temperament. *Child Development*, 56: 1–14.

Stack, S. (2003) Media coverage as a risk factor in suicide. *Journal of Epidemiology and Community Health*, 57(4): 238–40.

Starcevic, V., Berle, D., Fenech, P., Milicevic, D., Lamplugh, C. & Hannan, A. (2009) Distinctiveness of perceived health in panic disorder and relation to panic disorder severity. *Cognitive Therapy and Research*, 33: 323–33.

Steele, C.M. (1997) A threat in the air: How stereotypes shape intellectual identity and performance. *American Psychologist*, 52: 613–29.

Steiger, A. & Kimura, M. (2010) Wake and sleep EEG provide biomarkers in depression. *Journal of Psychiatric Research*, 44(4): 242–52.

Stein, D.J. & Ludik, J. (1998) Neural networks and psychopathology: An introduction In D. Stein and J. Ludick (eds), *Neural networks and psychpathology*. Cambridge: Cambridge University Press, pp. 3–13.

Stein, J.F. & Fowler, M.S. (1993) Unstable binocular control in children with specific reading retardation. *Journal of Research in Reading*, 16: 30–45.

Stein, M.B., Jang, K.L., Taylor, S., Vernon, P.A. & Livesley, W.J. (2002) Genetic and environmental influences on trauma exposure and posttraumatic stress disorder symptoms: A twin study. *American Journal of Psychiatry*, 159(10): 1675–81.

Steinhousen, H.C., Gundelfinger, R. & Metzke, C. (2009) Prevalence of self-reported seasonal affective disorders and the validity of the seasonal pattern assessment questionnaire in young adults findings from a Swiss community study. *Journal of Affective Disorders*, 115(3): 347–54.

Stephenson, P. & Smith, D. (1989) Bullying in the junior school. In D.P. Tattum & D.A. Lane (eds), *Bullying in schools*. Stoke-on-Trent: Trentham Books, pp. 45–57.

Stevens, A. (2001) *Jung: A very short introduction*. London: Oxford Press.

Stewart, J., de Wit, H. & Eikelboom, R. (1984) Role of unconditioned and conditioned drug effects in the self-administration of opiates and stimulants. *Psychological Research*, 91: 251–68.

Stopes, M. (1918) *Married love*. London: Fifield and Co.

Stout, C.E. (2004) Global initiatives. *American Psychologist*, 59: 844–53.

Stringaris, A., Maughan, B. & Goodman, R. (2010) What's in a disruptive disorder? Temperamental antecedents of oppositional defiant disorder: Findings from the Avon longitudinal study. *Journal of the American Academy of Child and Adolescent Psychiatry*, 49(5): 474–83.

Strittmatter, W.J. & Roses, A.D. (1996) Apolipoprotein E and Alzheimer's disease. *Annual Review of Neuroscience*, 19: 53–77.

Straus, M. (1999) The controversy over domestic violence by women: A methodological, theoretical and sociology of science analysis. In X. Arriaga & S. Oskamp. *Violence in intimate relationships*. Thousand Oaks, CA: Sage.

Strupp, H.H. & Hadley, S.M. (1977) A tripartite model for mental health and therapeutic outcomes with special reference to negative effects of psychotherapy. *American Psychologist*, 32: 187–96.

Sturtevant, A.H. (2001) *A history of genetics*. New York: Harper & Row.

Stuart-Hamilton, I. (2006) *The psychology of ageing: An introduction* (4th edn). London: Jessica Kingsley.

Sullivan, P.F., Kendler, K.S. & Neale, M.C. (2003) Schizophrenia as a complex trait: evidence from a meta-analysis of twin studies. *Archives of General Psychiatry*, 60: 1187–92.

Sullivan, P.F., Neale, M.C. & Kendler, K.S. (2000) Genetic epidemiology of major depression: Review and meta-analysis. *American Journal of Psychiatry*, 157(10): 1552–62.

Suveg, C., Southam-Gerow, M.A., Goodman, K.L. & Kendall, P.C. (2007) The role of emotion theory and research in child therapy development. *Clinical Psychology: Science and Practice*, 14: 358–71.

Swain, P. (2005) *Anorexia nervosa and bulimia nervosa: New research*. New York: Nova Science Publishers.

Swanson, H.L. & Hoskyn, M. (1998) A synthesis of experimental intervention literature for students with learning disabilities: A meta-analysis of treatment outcomes. *Review of Educational Research*, 68: 271–321.

Swartz, M.S., Blazer, D.G., George, L.K. & Winfield, I. (1990) Estimating the prevalence of borderline personality disorder in the community. *Journal of Personality Disorders*, 4: 257–72.

Sweet, J., Rozensky, R. & Tovian, S. (eds) (1991) *Handbook of clinical psychology in medical settings*. New York: Plenum Press.

Swerdlow, N.R. (2010) *Behavioral neurobiology of schizophrenia and its treatment*. London: Springer.

Swift-Scanlan, T., Coughlin, J.M., Lan, T., Potash, J.B., Ingersoll, R.G., Depaulo, R., Ross, C.A. & McInnis, M.G. (2005) Characterization of CTB/CAG repeats on chromosome 18: A study of bipolar disorder. *Psychiatric Genetics*, 15(2): 91–9.

Szasz, T.S. (1960) The myth of mental illness. *American Psychologist*, 15(2): 113–18.

Szasz, T.S. (2004) *Words to the Wise: A Medical-Philosophical Dictionary*. New Brunswick, NJ: Transaction Publishers.

Szmalec, A., Loncke, M., Page, M.P.A. & Duyck, W. (2011) Order or disorder? Impaired Hebb learning in dyslexia. *Journal of Experimental Psychology: Learning, Memory and Cognition*, 37(5): 1270–9.

Szmigin, I., Griffin, C., Mistral, W., Bengry-Howell, A., Weale, L. & Hackley, C. (2007) Re-framing binge drinking as calculated hedonism: Empirical evidence from the UK. *International Journal of Drug Policy*, 19(5): 359–66.

Tafa, M. & Baiocco, R. (2009) Addictive behaviour and family functioning during adolescence. *The American Journal of Family Therapy*, 37: 388–95.

Tai, S. & Turking, D. (2009) The evolution of cognitive behaviour therapy for schizophrenia: current practice and recent developments. *Schizophrenia Bulletin*, 35(5): 865–73.

Tanzi, R.E. (1991). Gene mutations in inherited amyloidopathies of the nervous system. *American Journal of Human Genetics*, 49(3): 507–10.

Taylor, L., Farone, S.V. and Tsuang, M.T. (2003) Family, twin and adoption studies of bipolar disease. *Current Psychiatry Reports*, 4: 130–3.

Taylor, R.M. & Morrison, L.P. (2002) *Taylor-Johnson Temperament analysis Manual*. Thousand Oaks, CA: Psychological Publications, Inc.

Taylor, S. (1982) *Durkheim and the study of suicide*. New York: St Martin's Press.

Taylor, S. (2009) *Clinician's guide to PTSD*. London: Guilford Publications.

Tecce, J.J. (1972) Contingent negative variation (CNB). In E. Niedermeyer & F. Lopes da Silva (eds), *Electroencephalography: Basic principles, clinical application and related fields* (2nd edn). Baltimore, MD: Urban & Schwarzenberg, pp. 657–79.

Teerikangas, O.M., Aronen, E.T., Martin, R.P. & Huttunen, M.O. (1998) Effects of infant temperament and early intervention on the psychiatric symptoms of adolescents. *Journal of American Child and Adolescent Psychiatry*, 37(10): 1070–6.

Temple, E., Deutsch, G.K, Poldrack, R.A., Miller, S.L., Tallal, P., Merzenich, M.M. & Gabrieli, J.D. (2003) Neural deficits in children with dyslexia ameliorated by behavioral remediation: Evidence from functional MRI. *Proceedings of the National Academy of Science USA*, 100(5): 2860–5.

Temte, J.L. & Greist, J. (1992) *Antipsychotic medications and schizophrenia: A guide*. New York: Dean Foundation.

Terestman, N. (1980) Mood quality and intensity in nursery school children as predictors of behaviour disorder. *American Journal of Orthopsychiatry*, 50(1): 125–38.

Terman, J.S., Terman, M., Lo, E.S. & Cooper, T.B. (2000) Circadian time of morning light administration and therapeutic response in winter depression. *Archives of General Psychiatry*, 58: 69–75.

Terrell, C. & Passenger, T. (2006) *ADHD, autism, dyslexia and dyspraxia*. New York: Family Doctor Publications Ltd.

Thackray, H.M. & Tifft, C. (2001) Fetal Alcohol Syndrome. *Pediatrics in Review*, 22(2): 47–55.

Theoharides, T.C., Donelan, J., Kandere-Grzybowska, K. & Konstantinidou, A. (2005) The role of mast cells in migraine pathophysiology. *Brain Research Review*, 49: 65–76.

Thomas, A. & Chess, S. (1977) *Temperament and development*. New York: Brunner/Mazel.

Thomas, D. & Chess, S. (1984) Genesis and evolution of behaviour disorder: From infancy to early life. *American Journal of Psychiatry*, 140: 1–9.

Thomas, D. & Woods, H. (2003) *Working with people with learning disabilities*. London: Jessica Kingsley.

Thomas, D., Chess, S. & Birch, H.G. (1977) The origin of personality. *Scientific American*, 223(2): 102–9.

Thrash, B., Karuppagounder, S.S., Uthayathas, S., Suppiramaniam, V. & Dhanasekaran, M. (2010) Neurotoxic effects of methamphetamine. *Neurochemical Research*, 35(1): 171–9.

Thylstrup, B. & Hesse, M. (2009) Ambivalence construct in schizoid personality disorder. *American Journal of Psychotherapy*, 63(2): 147–67.

Tiffany, S.T., Friedman, L., Greenfield, S.F., Hasin, D.S. & Jackson, R. (2011) Beyond drug use: A systematic consideration of other outcomes in evaluations of treatments for substance use disorders. *Addiction*, 107(4): 709–18.

Tillfors, M. & Ekselius, L. (2009) Social phobia and avoidant personality disorder: Are they separate diagnostic entites or do they reflect a spectrum of social anxiety? *Israel Journal of Psychiatry and Related Sciences*, 46(1): 25–33.

Tobin, S.S. & Kulys, R. (1981) The family in the institutionalization of the elderly. *Journal of Social Issues*, 37(3): 145–57.

Tohen, M., Vieta, E., Calbrese, J., Ketter, T.A., Sachs, G., Bowden, C., Mitchell, Centorrino, F., Risser, R., Baker, R.W., Evans, A.R., Beymer, K, Dube, S., Tollefson, G. D. & Breier, A. (2003) Efficacy of olanzapine and olanzapine-fluoxetine combination in the treatment of bipolar 1 depression. *Arch Gen Psychiatry*, 50(11): 1079–88.

Torgersen, S. (1983) Genetic factors in anxiety disorders. *Archives of General Psychiatry*, 40: 1085–9.

Torgersen, S. (1992) Genetics. In A.S. Bellack & M. Hersen (eds), *Psychopathology in adulthood*. Needham Heights, MA: Allyn and Bacon.

Torgersen, S., Kringlen, E. & Cramer, V. (2001) The prevalence of personality disorder in a community sample. *Archives of General Psychiatry*, 58: 590–6.

Torgersen, S., Lygren, S., Skre, I., Onstad, S., Edvardsen, J., Tambs, K. & Kringlen, E. (2000) A twin study of personality disorders. *Comprehensive Psychiatry*, 41(6): 416–25.

Torrey, E.F. (1998) *Out of the shadows: Confronting America's mental illness crisis*. New York: Wiley & Sons.

Tribe, R. & Morrissey, J. (2004) *Handbook of professional and ethical practice for psychologists, counsellors and psychotherapists*. New York: Brunner-Routledge.

Trippany, R., Kress, W. & Wilcoxon, A. (2004) Preventing vicarious trauma: What counsellors should know when working with trauma survivors. *Journal of Counseling and Development*, 82: 31–7.

Tsigos, C. & Chousos, G.P. (1996) Differential diagnosis and management of Cushing's syndrome. *Annual Review of Medicine*, 47: 443–61.

Tsuang, M., Bucher, K. & Fleming, J. (1982) Testing the monogenic theory of schizophrenia: An application of segregation methods of analysis to blind family study data. *British Journal of Psychiatry*, 140: 595–9.

Tsuang, M., Woolson, R., Winokur, G. & Crowe, D. (1981) Stability of psychiatric diagnosis: Schizophrenia and affective disorder followed-up over a 30–40 year period. *Archives of General Psychiatry*, 38: 535–9.

Turetsky, B.I., Bilker, W.B., Siegel, S.J., Kohler, C.G. & Gur, R.E. (2009) Profile of auditory information-processing deficits in schizophrenia. *Psychiatry Research*, 165(1–2): 27–37.

Turillazzi, E., Riezzo, I., Neri, M., Bello, S. & Fineschi, V. (2010) MDMA toxicity and pathological consequences: A review about experimental data and autopsy findings. *Current Pharmaceutical Biotechnology*, 11(5): 500–9.

Turk, D.C. & Wilson, H.D. (2010) Fear of pain as a prognostic factor in chronic pain: Conceptual models, assessment, and treatment implications. *Current Pain and Headache Reports*, 14(2): 88–95.

Turkat, I.D. (1990) *The personality disorder: A psychological approach to clinical management*. New York: Pergamon Press.

Turkington, D., Sensky, T., Scott, J., Barnes, T.R.E., Nur, U., Siddle, R., Hammond, K., Samarasekera, N. & Kingdon, D. (2008) A randomized controlled trial of cognitive-behavior therapy for persistent symptoms in schizophrenia: A five-year follow up. *Schizophrenia Research*, 98: 1–7.

Turley, B., Bates, G.W., Edwards, J. & Jackson, H.J. (1992) MCMI-II personality disorders in recent-onset bipolar disorders. *Journal of Clinical Psychology*, 48(3): 320–9.

Tyrer, P. & Steinberg, D. (2005) *Models for mental disorder: Conceptual models in psychiatry*. Chichester: Wiley.

Tyrrell, D.A.J., Parry, R.P., Crow, T.J., Johnstone, E. & Ferrier, I.N. (1979) Possible virus in schizophrenia and some neurological disorders. *Lancet*, 1: 839–41.

Tyson, P. (1993) The analyst's experience in the psychoanalytic situation: a continuum between objective and subjective reality. *Psychoanalytical Inquiry*, 13: 296–309.

Uhl, G.R. (1998) Hypothesis: The role of dopaminergic transporters in selective vulnerability of cells in Parkinson's disease. *Annals of Neurology*, 43(5): 555–60.

Ullman, S.E. (1995) Adult trauma survivors and post-traumatic stress sequelae: An analysis of reexperiencing, avoidance, and arousal criteria. *Journal of Traumatic Stress*, 8(1): 179–88.

Vaccaro, J.V. & Roberts, L. (1992) Teaching social and coping skills. In M. Birchwood & N. Tarrier (eds), *Innovations in the psychological management of schizophrenia*. Chichester: Wiley, pp. 103–14.

Vallar, G., Burani, C. & Arduino, L.S. (2010) Neglect dyslexia: A review of the neuropsychological literature. *Experimental Brain Research*, 206(2): 219–35.

Van Riper, C. (1982) *The nature of stuttering* (2nd edn). Englewood Cliffs, NJ: Prentice-Hall.

Van Walsum, K.L. (2004) Nos malades: Three examples of Christian influences in care for the insane in pre-revolutionary France and Belgium. *Journal of Psychology and Christianity*, 23(3): 219–33.

Vandivort, D.S. & Locke, B.Z. (1979) Suicide ideation: Its relation to depression, suicide and suicide attempt. *Suicide and Life-Threatening Behavior*, 9(4): 205–18.

Vellenga, B.A. & Christensen, J. (1994) Persistent and severely mentally ill clients' perceptions of their metnal illness. *Issues in Mental Health Nursing*, 15(4): 359–71.

Vellutino, F.R. (1979) *Dyslexia: Theory and research*. Cambridge, MA: MIT Press.

Vellutino, F.R., Fletcher, J.M., Snowling, M.J. & Scanlon, D.M. (2004) Specific reading disability (dyslexia): what have we learned in the past four decades? *Journal of Child Psychiatry*, 45(1): 2–40.

Venables, P.H. (1978) Psychophysiology and psychometrics. *Psychophysiology*, 15: 302–15.

Verkhratsky, A. (2007) Calcium and cell death. *Sub-cellular Biochemistry*, 45: 465–80.

Verkhratsky, A. & Butt, A. (2007) *Glial neurobiology*. Chichester: John Wiley & Sons.

Vickers, J.C., Dickson, T.C., Adlard, P.A., Saunders, H.L., King, C.E & McCormack, G. (1997) The cause of neuronal degeneration in Alzheimer's disease. *Progress in Neurobiology*, 60: 139–65.

Victor, C.R. (2010) Where now for social care in England? *BMJ*, April 21: 340.

Virk, J., Li, J., Vestergaard, M., Oleb, C., Lu, M. & Olsen, J. (2010) Early life disease programming during the pre-conception and prenatal period: Making the link between stressful life events and type-1 diabetes. *PLoS ONE*, 5(7): 11523.

Vitaro, F., Brendgen, M. & Tremblay, R.E. (2002) Reactively and proactively aggressive children: antecedent and subsequent characteristics. *Journal of Child Psychology and Psychiatry*, 43(4): 495–505.

Voeller, K.K.S (1991) Toward a neurobiologic nosology of attention deficit hyperactivity disorder. *Journal of Clinical Neurology*, 6: 2–8.

Volkmar, F.R. (1992) Childhood disintegrative disorder: Issues for DSM-IV. *Journal of Autism and Developmental Disorders*, 22: 625–42.

Volkmar, F.R., Cohen, D.J., Bregman, J.D., Hooks, M.Y. & Stevenson, J.M. (1989) An examination of social typologies in autism. *Journal of the American Academy of Child and Adolescent Psychiatry*, 28: 82–6.

Volkmar, F.R. & Nelson, D.S. (1990) Seizure disorders in autism. *Journal of the American Academy of Child and Adolescent Psychiatry*, 29: 127–9.

Volkmar, F.R., Paul, R., Klin, A. & Cohen, D.J. (2005) *Handbook of autism and pervasive developmental disorders, assessment, interventions and policy*, Vol. 2. Hoboken, NJ: John Wiley & Sons.

Volkow, N.D. & Fowler, J.S. (2000) Addiction a disease of compulsion and drive: Involvement of the orbitofrontal cortex. *Cerebral Cortex*, 10:,318–25.

Voracek, M. & Loibl, L.M. (2007) Genetics of suicide: A systematic review of twin studies. *Wiener Klinische Wochenschrift*, 119: 463–75.

Waern, M., Rubenowitz, E. & Wilhelmson, K. (2000) Predictors of suicide in the old elderly. *Gerontology*, 49: 328–34.

Wahl, O.F. (1995) *Media madness: Public images of mental distress*. New Brunswick, NJ: Rutgers University Press.

Walcott, T.A. (2007) *Drug and alcohol abuse research focus*. New York: Nova Science Publishers Inc.

Waldemar, G. & Burns, A. (2009) *Alzheimer's disease*. London: Oxford University Press.

Waldheter, E.J., Penn, D.L., Perkins, D.O., Mueser, K.T., Owens, L.W. & Cook, E. (2008) The graduated recovery intervention program for first episode psychosis: Treatment development and preliminary data. *Community Mental Health Journal*, 44: 443–55.

Wallace, C.J. & Liberman, R.P. (1985) Social skills training for patients with schizophrenia: A controlled clinical trial. *Psychiatry Research*, 15(3): 239–247.

Walters, G.D. (2002) The heritability of alcohol abuse and dependence: A meta-analysis of behaviour genetic research. *American Journal of Drug and Alcohol Abuse*, 28: 557–84.

Wang, L.J. & Sobie, E.A. (2008) Mathematical model of the neonatal mouse ventricular action potential. *American Journal of Physiology: Heart and Circulatory Physiology*, 294(6): 2565–75.

Ward, D. (2006) *Stuttering and cluttering: Frameworks for understanding and treatment*. New York: Psychology Press.

Wasco, S.M. & Campbell, R. (2002) Emotional reactions of rape victim advocates: A multiple case study of anger and fear. *Psychology of Women Quarterly*, 26: 120–30.

Wasco, W. & Tanzi, R.E. (1996) Etiological clues from gene defects causing early onset familial Alzheimer's disease. In W. Wasco and R.E. Tanzi, *Molecular mechanisms of dementia*. New Jersey: Humana Press.

Washton, A. (1991) *Cocaine addiction: Treatment, recovery and relapse prevention*. New York: W.W. Norton & Co.

Wasserberg, J. (2002) Treating head injuries. *BMJ*. 325(7362): 454–5.

Watson, J.B., & Rayner, R. (1920) Conditioned emotional responses. *Journal of Experimental Psychology*, 3: 1–14.

Watts, F.N., Powell, G.E. & Austin, S.V. (1973) The modification of abnormal beliefs. *British Journal of Medical Psychology*, 46: 359–63.

Webb, D. (2010) *Thinking about suicide: Contemplating and comprehending the urge to die.* Hereforshire: PCCS.

Wechsler, H., Davenport, A., Dowdall, G.W., Moeykens, B. & Castillo, S. (2012) Health and behavioural consequences of binge drinking in college: a national survey of students at 140 campuses. *JAMA*, 272: 1572–7.

Wechsler, H. & Nelson, T.F. (2001) Binge drinking and the American college student: What's five drinks? *Psychology of Addictive Behaviours*, 15(4): 287–91.

Weegmann, M. & Cohen, R.I. (2002) *The psychodynamics of addiction.* London: Whurr.

Weinberger, N.M. (2004) Specific long-term memory traces in primary auditory cortex. *Nature Reviews Neuroscience*, 5: 279–90.

Weinstein, N., Brown, K.W. & Ryan, R.M. (2009) A multi-method examination of the effects of mindfulness on stress attribution, coping and emotional well-being. *Journal of Research in Personality*, 43: 374–85.

Weisheit, R. & White, W.L. (2009) *Methamphetamine: Its history, pharmacology and treatment.* Center City, MN: Hazelden.

Weissenborn, R. & Duka, T. (2003) Acute alcohol effects on cognitive function in social drinkers: Their relationship to drinking habits. *Psychopharmacology*, 165(3): 306–12.

Wentz, E., Gillberg, I.C., Anckarsater, H., Gillberg, C. & Rastam, M. (2009) Reproduction and offspring status 18 years after teenage-onset anorexia nervosa: A controlled community based study. *International Journal of Eating Disorders*, 42(6): 483–91.

Werth, J.L., Jr. & Holdwick, D.J. (2000) A primer on rational suicide and other forms of hastened death. *The Counselling Psychologist*, 28: 511–39.

West, R. (2006) Addiction, ethics and public policy. *Addiction*, 92(9): 1061–70.

Wetzel, J.W. (1984) *Clinical handbook of depression.* New York: Psychology Press.

Weyrauch, K.F., Roy-Byrne, P., Katon, W. & Wilson, L. (2001) Stressful life events and impulsiveness in failed suicide. *Suicide and Life-Threatening Behaviour*, 31: 311–19.

Whalley, L.J. (2002) Brain ageing and dementia: what makes the difference. *The British Journal of Psychiatry*, 8: 369–71.

Whitacre, J.D., Luper, H.L. & Pollio, H.R. (1970) General language deficits in children with articulation problems. *Language and Speech*, 13: 231–9.

White, A.M. & Swartzwelder, H.S. (2005) Age-related effects of alcohol on memory and memory-related brain function in adolescents and adults. *Recent Developments in Alcoholism*, 17: 161–76.

White, H.R. & Jackson, K. (2006) Social and psychological influences on emerging adult drinking behaviour. *Alcohol Research & Health*, 28: 182–90.

White, N.M. & Hiroi, N. (1993) Amphetamine conditioned cue preference and the neurobiology of drug seeking. *Seminars in Neuroscience*, 5: 329–36.

Whitfield, M.L., Sherlock, G., Saldanha, A.J., Murray, J.I., Ball, C.A., Alexander, K.E., Matese, J.C., Perou, C.M., Hurt, M.M., Brown, P.O. & Botstein, D. (2000) Identification of genes periodically expressed in the human cell cycle and their expression in tumors. *Molecular Biology of the Cell*, 13(6): 1977–2000.

Whitney, E.N. & Hamilton, E.M.N. (1987) *Understanding nutrition* (4th edn). New York: West Publishing.

Wichers, M.C. & Maes, M. (2004) The role of indoleamine 2.3-dioxygenase (IDO) in the pathophysiology of interferon-alpha-induced depression. *Journal of Psychiatry and Neuroscience*, 29: 11–17.

Widiger, T.A. & Mullins-Sweatt, S.N. (2008) *Personality disorders in psychiatry* (3rd edn), Vol. 2, ed. A. Tasman, J. Kay, J.A. Lieberman, M.B. First and M. Maj. New York: Wiley & Sons.

Widiger, T.A. & Sanderson, C.J. (1997) Toward a dimensional model of personality disorders. In W.J. Livesley (ed.), *The DSM-IV personality disorders.* New York: Guilford Press, pp. 433–58.

Wiggins, O.P. & Schwartz, M.A. (2005) Richard Zaner's phenomenology of the clinical encounter. *Theoretical Medicine*, 26: 73–87.

Williams, A.M., Helm, H.M. & Clemens, E.V. (2012) The effect of childhood trauma, personal wellness, supervisory working alliance, and organizational factors on vicarious traumatisation. *Journal of Mental Health Counselling*, April 2012.

Williams, K.D., Forgas, J.P. & Von Hippel, W. (2005) *The social outcast: Ostracism, social exclusion, rejection and bullying.* New York: Psychology Press.

Willis, A.I., Herve, H. & Yuille, J. (2007) *The psychopath: Theory, research and practice.* Mahwah, NJ: Lawrence Erlbaum Associates.

Wilmshurst, L. (2008) *Abnormal child psychology: A developmental perspective.* New York: Routledge.

Wilson, M. (1993) DSM-III and the transformation of American psychiatry: A history. *American Journal of Psychiatry*, 150: 399–410.

Wilson, R.S., Evans, D.A., Bienias, J.L., Mendes de Leon, C.F., Schneider, J.A. & Bennett, D.A. (2003) Proneness to psychological distress is associated with risk of Alzheimer's disease. *Neurology*, 61(11): 1479–85.

Winstok, Z. (2011) The paradigmatic cleavage on gender differences in partner violence perpetration and victimization. *Aggression and Violent Behavior*, 16(4): 303–11.

Winger, G., Woods, J.H. & Hofmann, F.G. (2004) *A handbook on drug and alcohol abuse.* New York: Oxford University Press.

Winnicott, D.W. (1960) *The theory of parent–infant relationship in the maturational processes and the facilitating environment.* London: Karnac, pp.140–52.

Wise, R.A. (1996) Addictive drugs and brain stimulation reward. *Annual Review of Neuroscience*, 19: 319–40.

Wise, R., Chollet, F., Hadar, U., Fiston, K., Hoffner, E. & Frackowiak, R. (1992) Distribution of cortical neural networks involved in word comprehension and word retrieval. *Brain*, 114: 1803–17.

Witt, S.D. (1997) Parental influence on children's socialization to gender roles. *Adolescence*, 32: 253–9.

Wolf, W.E. & Mosnaim, A.D. (eds) (1990) *Post traumatic stress disorder: Biological mechanisms and clinical aspects.* Washington, DC: American Psychiatric Press.

Wolff, S. & Chick, J. (1980) Schizoid personality in childhood: A controlled follow-up study. *Psychological Medicine*, 10: 85–100.

Wolpe, J. (1961) The systematic desensitization treatment of neurosis. *Journal of Nervous Mental Disorders*, 132: 189–203.

Wolpe, J. & Rachman, S. (1960) Psychoanalytic evidence: A critique based on Freud's case of little Hans. *Journal of Nervous Mental Disease*, 131: 135–45.

Wong, E.H.F., Snowman, A.M., Leeb-Lundberg, L.M. F. & Olsen, R.W. (1984) Barbiturates allosterically inhibit GABA antagonist and benzodiazepine inverse agonist binding. *European Journal of Pharmacology*, 102(2): 205–12.

Wood, C. (1997) *Yardsticks: Children in the classroom ages 4–14: A resource for parents and teachers.* Greenfield, MA: Northeast Foundation for Children.

World Health Organization. (1993) *The ICD-10 classification of mental and behavioural disorders: Diagnostic criteria for research.* Geneva: WHO.

World Health Organization (2002) *World Health Statistics Annual 2001–01.* Geneva: WHO.

Wu, J. & Lingyu, H. (2009) Evaluation on effect of comprehensive rehabilitation exercises to improve the social adaptation ability for patients with chronic schizophrenia. *Chinese Nursing Research*, 29.

Wynbrandt, J. & Ludman, M.D. (2008) *The encyclopaedia of genetic disorders and birth defects.* New York: Facts on File.

Xue, L., Farrugia, G., Miller, S.M., Ferris, C.D., Snyder, S.H. & Szurszewski, J.H. (2000) Carbon monoxide and nitric oxide as coneurotransmitters in the enteric nervous system: Evidence from genomic deletion of biosynthetic enzymes. *Proceedings of the Nationall Academy of Sciences*, USA, 97: 1851–5.

Yamada, H., Cirrito, J.R., Steward, F.R., Jiang, H., Bin, M.B., Holmes, B.B., Binder, L.I., Mandelkow, E., Diamond, M.I., Lee, V.M. & Holtzman, D.M. (2011) In vivo microdialysis reveals age-dependent decrease of brain interstitial fluid tau levels in P301S human tau transgenic mice. *The Journal of Neuroscience*, 31(37): 13110–17.

Yatham, L.N. & Maj, M. (2010) *Bipolar disorder: Clinical and neurobiological foundations.* New York: Wiley.

Yildiz, S., Uzun, G., Uz, O., Ipcioglu, O.M., Kardesoglu, E. & Ozcan, O. (2008) N-terminal pro-B-type natriuretic peptide levels increases after hyperbaric oxygen therapy in diabetic patients. *Clinical and Investigative Medicine*, 31(5): 231–5.

Yoon, J.S. (2004) Predicting teacher interventions in bullying situations. *Education and Treatment of Children*, 27: 37–45.

Yoshida, H. (2007) ER stress and diseases. *FEBS Journal*, 274(3): 630–58.

Yoshimasu, K., Barbaresi, W.J., Colligan, R.C., Killian, J.M., Voigt, R.G., Weaver, A.L. & Katusic, S.K. (2010) Gender, attention-deficit/hyperactivity disorder and reading disability in a population-based birth cohort. *Pediatrics*, 126(4): 788–95.

Young, S.L. (2011) *Craving earth: Understanding pica: The urge to eat clay, starch, ice and chalk*. New York: Columbia University Press.

Yu, K., Cheung, C., Leung, M., Li, Q., Chua, S. & McAlonan, G. (2010) Are bipolar disorder and schizophrenia neuroanatomically distinct? An anatomical likelihood meta-analysis. *Frontiers in Human Neuroscience*, 4: 189.

Yudkin, J.S., Kumari, M., Humphries, S.E. & Mohamed-Ali, V. (2000) Inflammation, obesity, stress and coronary heart disease: Is interleukin-6 the link? *Atherosclerosis*, 148: 209–14.

Zahn-Waxler, C., Hollenbeck, B. & Radke-Yarrow, M. (1984) The origins of empathy and altruism. In M.W. Fox & L.D. Mickley (eds), *Advances in animal welfare science*. Washington, DC: Humane Society of the United States.

Zanarini, M.C. & Frankenburg, F.R. (1997) Pathways to the development of borderline personality disorder. *Journal of Personality Disorders*, 11(1): 93–104.

Zanarini, M.C., Young, L., Frankenburg, F.R., Hennen, J., Reich, D.B., Marino, M. & Vujanovic, A.A. (2002) Severity of reported childhood sexual abuse and its relationship to severity of borderline psychopathology and psychosocial impairment. *Journal of Nervous and Mental Disease*, 190: 381–7.

Zander, M., Hutton, A. & King, L. (2010) Coping and resilience factors in pediatric oncology nurses. *Journal of Pediatric Oncology Nursing*, 27(2): 94–108.

Ziebell, J.M. & Morganti-Kossmann, M.C. (2010) Involvement of pro and anti-inflammatory cytokines and chemokines in the pathophysiology of traumatic brain injury. *Neurotherapeutics*, 7(1): 22–30.

Ziegler, L., Segal-Ruder, Y., Coppola, G., Reis, A., Geshwind, D., Fainzilber, M. & Goldstein, R.S. (2010) A human neuron injury model for molecular studies of axonal regeneration. *Experimental Neurology*, 223(1): 119–27.

Zigler, E., Balla, D. & Hodapp, R. (1984) On the definition and classification of mental retardation. *American Journal of Mental Deficiency*, 89: 215–30.

Zimmerman, M. & Coryell, W. (1989) DSM-III personality disorder diagnoses in a nonpatient sample: Demographic correlates and comorbidity. *Archives of General Psychiatry*, 46: 682–9.

Zimmerman, M. & Mattia, J.I. (2001) The psychiatric diagnostic screening questionnaire: Development, reliability and validity. *Comprehensive Psychiatry*, 42: 175–89.

Zoccolillo, M., Pickles, A., Quinton, D. & Rutter, M. (1992).The outcome of conduct disorder: Implications for defining adult personality disorder and conduct disorder. *Psychological Medicine*, 22: 971–86.

Zollman, F.S. (2011) *Manual of traumatic brain injury management*. New York: Demos Medical.

Zuckerman, M. (1990) Some dubious premises in research and theory on racial differences: Scientific social and ethical issues. *American Psychologist*, 45: 1297–303.

Zuckerman, M. (2001) Adult temperament and its biological basis. In A. Eliasz & A. Angleitner (eds), *Advances in research on temperament*. Lengerich, Germany: Pabst Science, pp. 42–57.

Zung, W.W. (1965) A self-rating depression scale. *Archives of General Psychiatry*, 12: 63–70.

Author Index

Subject Index